Paradise Preserved

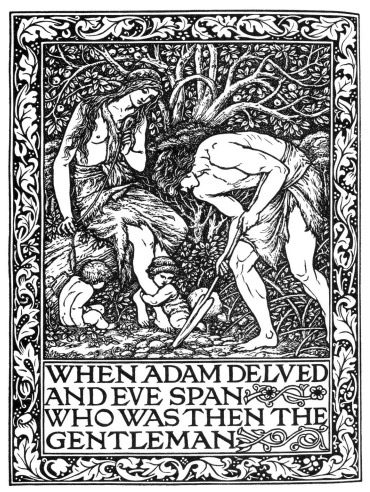

WHEN ADAM DELVED
AND EVE SPAN
WHO WAS THEN THE
GENTLEMAN

Burne-Jones, *Adam and Eve*

Paradise Preserved

Recreations of Eden in Eighteenth- and Nineteenth-Century England

MAX F. SCHULZ

University of Southern California

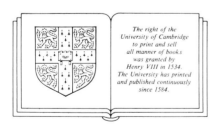

The right of the
University of Cambridge
to print and sell
all manner of books
was granted by
Henry VIII in 1534.
The University has printed
and published continuously
since 1584.

CAMBRIDGE UNIVERSITY PRESS

Cambridge
London   New York   New Rochelle
Melbourne   Sydney

Published by the Press Syndicate of the University of Cambridge
The Pitt Building, Trumpington Street, Cambridge CB2 1RP
32 East 57th Street, New York, NY 10022, USA
10 Stamford Road, Oakleigh, Melbourne 3166, Australia

© Cambridge University Press 1985

First published 1985

Printed in Great Britain at
the University Press, Cambridge

Library of Congress catalogue card number: 85-5959

British Library cataloguing in publication data
Schulz, Max F.
Paradise preserved: recreations of Eden
in eighteenth- and nineteenth-century England.
1. Paradise in art   2. Art, English – History
3. Paradise in literature   4. English poetry –
19th century – History and criticism
I. Title
704.9′48   N8234.PZ/
ISBN 0 521 30173 4

Contents

vi   *Contents*

Illustrations

Sources

Gift in memory of Dr. and Mrs. Hugo O. Pantzer by their children; no. 28 Henry
E. Huntington Library, San Marino, California; no. 30 Wadsworth Athenaeum,
Hartford, Connecticut, The Ella Gallup Sumner and Mary Catlin Sumner
Collection; no. 32 Fogg Art Museum, Harvard University, Bequest of Grenville
L. Winthrop; no. 33 Ashmolean Museum, Oxford; no. 34 Lord Sherfield (photo:
Royal Academy, London); nos. 35, 42 Birmingham Museums and Art Gallery;
nos. 36, 40 City of Manchester Art Galleries; no. 38 Delaware Art Museum,
Wilmington, Samuel and Mary R. Bancroft Memorial Collection; no. 41 Tyne
and Wear County Council Museums; nos. 50, 51, 52 Freer Gallery of Art,
Smithsonian Institution, Washington, D.C.; no. 53 National Gallery of Art,
Washington, D.C., Harris Whittemore Collection.

Preface

EDEN continues as a touchstone in the minds of Europeans and Americans for every kind of benign place, moment, and action – past, present, and future – testifying to the hold the myth retains on the human consciousness. A recent instance, almost naive in the unselfconscious reflex-like resort to its comforting inclusiveness as a metaphor, occurs in a Los Angeles Sunday newspaper review of an anthropological study arguing that humans inhabited California before the existence of the Bering ice bridge 12,000 years ago when Asians are presumed to have migrated east into North America. "Can it be," the reviewer asks, "that Southern California, land of eternal sun and seedbed of all those fruits and nuts, is the site of the Garden of Eden?" As a facetious refutation of the anthropologist's contention that native Americans moved west across the Bering bridge to people Euro-Asia in an earlier warm period lasting from 170,000 to 70,000 years ago, the reviewer queries: why would early man have "left California in the first place. It's one thing to be kicked out of the Garden of Eden but, even allowing for all those scheming snakes, what kind of man would abandon Eve and leave all those avocados and palm trees for Siberia?"[1]

So sounds the *vox populi* in the last quarter of a century which has watched political dreams of a new millennium turn nightmarish, and social institutions and intellectual systems falter and break down. Perhaps because of the failed promises of the twentieth century – because of the accelerating pain of history Mircea Eliade would phrase it – the present bears witness to a remarkable revival of born-again Christians. What this revivalist phenomenon may mean for the rest of the century is anyone's guess. The idea that one can construct facsimiles of lost Eden without waiting for the end of time, the *illud tempus*, has been firing secularized and historically emancipated imaginations insistently since the seventeenth century. These paradises are visible and explicable in varying degrees to an historical perspective; and it may be informative to look at the ways the English of the past two centuries have tried to mirror paradise in their gardens, art, literature, technology and engineering, and urban centers.

I am conscious of how philosophically suspect these days is any effort to perceive in events an historical pattern. It is a fashionable *mea culpa* for historians, philosophers, and scientists to admit that their models of reality are no less the products of the human mind's creative imagination than are the fictions of the novelist. "No matter," writes Fredric Jameson, "how genuinely temporal or historical in character" an author's original determinative choices of key factors, the sum of his insights add up to an abstraction, "an ideal cross section of the existential density of concrete history itself." Furthermore, "such a diachronic sequence" is necessarily dialectical, prone to "the reversal of limits, of the transformation from negative to positive and from positive to negative"; and in turn "an awareness of dialectical relationships involves or implies a diachronic framework as a necessary condition of their articulation."[2]

To accept one's historical perspectives as metaphoric systems is not to deny their substantive value. Rather, as a procedural tactic, it is to free one to make conscious decisions about the shapes these metaphoric models will take. I could have structured this study of eighteenth- and nineteenth-century England's continuing infatuation with paradise in more than one way: a dialectic between Eden defined as the pleasures of the primitive/natural world and Eden as the blessings of civilization,[3] an exhaustive survey of the meanings of a central trope such as the Blessed Virgin,[4] a theological debate over the changing sociology of the concept of paradise, an analysis of a literary genre such as the pastoral and georgic or of an art form such as landscape painting,[5] a review of scientific-religious cosmologies and comparative crypto-mythologies,[6] an examination of millenarian movements,[7] an intellectual history of the ideals of retirement and friendship, or any number of other alternatives.

Given the sweep of my critical net, which fishes for both symbolic models and actual instances of the earthly paradise, I have opted for an argument more representational than systematic. Without violating the chronology, I have limited myself to identifying and examining selected, historically important recreations of paradise rather than essaying a comprehensive survey of the development of an idea. Hence, one will not find here the kind of rigorously logical argument worked out in such great studies as Arthur A. Lovejoy's *The Great Chain of Being* (1936) and Ernst H. Gombrich's *Art and Illusion* (1960), nor the massive evidence accumulated in Nikolaus Pevsner's books on the architecture of England. True to Jameson's prognosis, however, that a diachronic sequence necessarily sorts itself into a dialectic, the images of paradise isolated successively from about 1710 to 1900 fall into a dialectical pattern identifying Eden first with gardens, then antithetically with urban enclaves, and finally in a kind of synthesis with aesthetic forms. While observing loosely the movement of this dialectic, my look at some earthly paradises of the eighteenth and nineteenth centuries, real and conceptual, has been guided in part by the visions of major writers and artists. If not they as articulators of their society's efforts to offset the discrepancy between the world we know and the one our spiritual needs tell us is possible, then who? Scientists, engineers, merchants? Accordingly, I have tried to be as sensitive to the ways gardeners, architects, and engineers have absorbed the recurrent paradigm of paradise into the work-a-day technological and economic stream of their experience as to the ways in which poets and painters have reduced traditional modes of Arcadian and Edenic, pagan-classical and

Christian thought to new rituals of reality. Together, they sum up literally and symbolically, I hope, the collective efforts since the eighteenth century of the English imagination to align – update, refashion, and represent – an unending spiritual ideal with a constantly changing reality.

I am less insouciant about another problem intrinsic to this study. The traditional methodology, critical tools, and historical frame of reference for the study of literature, art, and gardening is aesthetic. Contemporary comments by artists and observers are ordinarily couched in intellectual, critical, and psychological terms. As a consequence I found myself tracking the paradisal archetype, which is religious and mythic, through material not overtly religious or intentionally religious. A case in point is Sir Kenneth Clark's use of aesthetically defined categories to describe Samuel Palmer as a painter of *ideal* landscapes and Constable as the supreme painter of English *natural* landscapes.[8] Guided by a different set of signs, linking natural scenery and the paradigm of paradise, I have committed the heresy (or so the art historian might well charge) of treating Palmer and Constable, along with Thomas Bewick, as exponents of a common English joy in rural and village life and of the national pride in imagining that their rustic nooks of England were remnants of ancient Eden.

This hermeneutic indeterminacy is exacerbated by the intellectual shifts that have taken place since the seventeenth century in how we define our world. Northrop Frye has observed apropos of the metaphysics of both Newton and Darwin that "We have long since weathered the Newtonian crisis of separating mythological from natural space, and the Darwinian crisis of separating mythological from natural time."[9] It is during the period covered by this study that the Newtonian and Darwinian crises were impinging on the *locus* of the human consciousness, the mental horizon shifting from mythic and theological to historical and mathematical perceptions of space and time. The decline in authority during the nineteenth century of the Biblical record, accompanied by a decline of belief in an historical Fall, makes problematical to what extent the idea of paradise continues to be taken seriously and to what extent it becomes a convenient fiction for expressing the more generalized human nostalgia for what one recent critic has denominated the lost domain.[10] This naturalization of myth has forced me to use critical tools of inference and indirection – to practise an insinuating synecdoche of interpretation. Michelangelo's Doni Tondo rendering of Mary, Joseph, and Jesus (1501–05, Uffizi Gallery, Florence), for example, poses no difficulties of interpretation. It is what it purports to be, the portrait of a Tuscany couple and child offered as a Renaissance version of the Holy Family. But what are we to make of Ford Madox Brown's *Take Your Son, Sir!* (c. 1857, Tate Gallery) whose subject is prostitution and the fallen woman, or his *Last of England* (1855, City Museum and Art Gallery, Birmingham) which is a treatment of the immigration theme? The social realism of both these pictures surely also echoes, however covert or unaware Brown may have been about their typology, a medieval-Renaissance tradition, and leads us back to those early Holy Families.

Whether rightly or wrongly I have sought the figurations of Eden, Adam and

Eve, the Annunciation and the Blessed Virgin, the Holy Madonna and Child, and the Holy Family – all *topoi* associated with paradise known, lost, and regained – in the literature, art, gardens, and allied social, metaphoric, and historical spheres of eighteenth- and nineteenth-century English life. Precedent for such a procedure is not wanting. Much contemporary critical theory has formulated and illustrated the economy of examining the unity of an historical epoch by considering its modes of expression as part of a field of discourse which ordains the emergence of characteristic statements. By mediating the particular cultural, personal, scientific, and technological conditions affecting the complex negotiations with the world of English writers, artists, gardeners, and engineers, I hoped to make visible the submerged continuation of a religious *topos* into a secular age without vicious investment of it with unearned vigor, or contrariwise, reduction of it to a cliché and an abstraction.

One last observation. Theologically the concept of the *hortus conclusus*, or enclosed garden of paradise, along with the mystical dimensions of it fancied by medieval and Renaissance minds, is singular and conceptually ideal. I should have taken warning from that fact when I started hunting for it in every nook and shire of England. Yet, like Coleridge who kept hearing the tender undersong of love "in clamor's hour" ("Recollections of Love," 30), I have been beguiled by how ubiquitously the faith in a recoverable earthly paradise underlies and shapes our response to the world, despite its vehement secularization over the past three centuries and despite our possibly having long given up formal assent to the idea of an Eden lost at the beginning, and to be regained only at the end, of time.

Acknowledgements

I ENJOYED many kindnesses and courtesies, and incurred many debts, during the years this book was taking shape. The staff and lecturers of the Attingham School, particularly Helen Lowenthal, Helena Hayward, Sir George Trevelyan, and the late Sir Nikolaus Pevsner, the participants in the Attingham Summer seminar of 1977, and the enchanted owners who opened their homes and grounds to us – all contributed to my knowledge of eighteenth-century country houses and landscapes. Professors Walter B. Crawford, Donald J. Greene, John Halperin, and the late William Lankford saved me from blunders in early stages of writing; and the keen eyes and informed minds of Professors John Beer and R. S. Woof rescued the text from innumerable infelicities: solecisms, errors of fact, and lapses in style.

The Rockefeller Foundation provided me with seven weeks of uninterrupted leisure to write in the palatial setting of the Villa Serbelloni, during an extended residence in 1978 at their International Study and Conference Center in Bellagio, Italy, with a rare second stay of five weeks in 1982, this time as supernumerary to my wife. The National Endowment for the Humanities is my creditor for a Senior Research Grant in the summer of 1979, as is the University of Southern California for grants-in-aid of research and generous contributions of computer time over the years. In the latter instance, Professor Robert Dilligan, then chairman of the University Computer Committee, was an unfailing support system of one. Professor Irwin C. Lieb, Vice President and Dean of the College of Letters, Arts, and Sciences at the University of Southern California, underwrote in part the production and publication of this book with liberal allowances of freedom from the classroom and of insulation from printing costs.

Finally, every author should have the kind of wife and editor I was blessed with during the making of this book. My wife Muriel repeatedly rescued the text from the recesses of the computer where less proficient manipulators of the machine's arcane impulses had stranded it; and Andrew Brown assumed labors beyond his editorial responsibilities in his enthusiastic readiness to translate typescript into book. *Hic Caelum in Terra.*

Chapters 3 and 10 appeared earlier, in slightly longer form, in *Reading Coleridge: Approaches and Applications*, ed. Walter B. Crawford (1979) and in *Studies in Romanticism*, ed. David Wagenknecht (1980). I am grateful to the editors of those publications and to Cornell University Press for permission to include them here.

Introduction
The Continuing Mystique of Paradise

O happy and blessed Britain . . . Thy Gardens are like Paradise, thy Valleys like Eden, thy hills like Lebanon, thy Springs like Shiloh, thy Rivers like Jordan! Abundantly stor'd thou art with all the Blessings both of Heaven and Earth.

> Stephen Switzer, *Ichnographia Rustica: or, the Nobleman, Gentleman, and Gardener's Recreation* (1718)

MOST STANDARD STUDIES of the idea of an earthly paradise stop with the Renaissance,[1] as if with his entry into the modern period man the social planner, utilitarian, and technocrat put aside childish myths with the primitive stage of his juvenility. This position is put categorically by A. Bartlett Giamatti in a review of Joseph Duncan's fine study of *Milton's Earthly Paradise: A Historical Study of Eden* (1972):

The last chapter, "The Fading of Paradise," is the obligatory coda to such a book. All historians of paradise, whatever their perspective, have to face the fact that after 2,000 years their subject essentially disappears in the eighteenth century. It is never easy. Duncan does it manfully, and well, by showing how with Thomas Burnet's attempts to defend Scripture by reason in the 1680s and 1690s, the whole structure of a belief founded upon revelation and faith begins to crumble. The result, of course, was that "the mythic and miraculous almost disappeared." The study closes by looking at Pope's *Essay on Man.* Throughout the last chapter Duncan succeeds where previous writers on paradise have failed, for he manages never to sound as if he blamed the eighteenth century for what it had done to his lovely place.[2]

All one can answer to such a mythology of history is that such advocates of doomsday have read too much Swift and accepted too readily his dyspeptic rejection of a society bravely replanting and restructuring its world.[3] Neither interest in Eden, nor desire for return to it, ends of course with Milton's *Paradise Lost*; and I hazard the guess that Duncan would be among the first to agree, since he himself has called attention to the contemporary anthropological and psychological importance of paradise as a symbol of redemptive and pleasure principles. Mircea Eliade singles out "Nostalgia for Paradise" as one of the oldest and most constant of human longings. He defines this nostalgia as man's repeated attempt "to restore the paradisiac condition"; and in fact, as some specialized studies have noted, the apocalyptical recovery of "the state of freedom and beatitude before 'the Fall,'" through abolition of "the changes made in the very structure of the

I

Cosmos and in the human mode of being by that primordial disruption," was no less of consequence to the inhabitants of the eighteenth and early nineteenth centuries than to those of the Renaissance, Thomas Burnet notwithstanding.[4] Alexander Pope manages at the outset of his career to sum up with exactly the right note of Adamic despair and optimism the paradisal aspirations of his age. As Maynard Mack notes, *Windsor-Forest* (1704–13) begins "with an intimation of lost Eden":

> The Groves of *Eden*, vanish'd now so long,
> Live in Description, and look green in Song;   (7–8)

and ends with the glimpse "of a Paradise to be regained,"[5] one refulgent with the enlightenment faith in human engineering and human institutions to hasten Albion's "long-expected . . . Golden Days" when "each unmolested Swain / Shall tend the Flocks, or reap the bearded Grain" (355, 424, 369–70).

While the eighteenth-century mind still, by and large, accepted Genesis as a literal time-scale (the quaint Renaissance horologies of earthly history are still calculated through the century) its grasp of reality also now contended with more mundane theories of history. Jostling one another in ways not always neatly unified are two mind-sets. The archaic sensibility habitually and automatically read the landscape as a hieroglyph of divine order: it saw in a garden not the natural swellings and outlines of terrain but a "perfect microcosmic order of an ideal moral ecology";[6] and experienced in the mind's eye the agony and promise of Christ's salvation. Rather than delight in tracing the "mystical Mathematicks of the City of Heaven" in the history of gardens as had Sir Thomas Browne,[7] the modern sensibility put much of its faith in its own husbandry and horticultural theories, as had those savants John Evelyn and Abraham Cowley as early as the 1660s,[8] and some in the empirical study of nature as did members of the Royal Society. It was discovered in the course of the century that one could do a lot on one's own behalf toward improving the fallen ravaged earth, and that the beauty and peacefulness of a garden could communicate its Edenic qualities directly to the human associative experience without its having to be translated into emblematic terms. In short, the eschatology of the *hortus conclusus* shares its promise throughout the century with the immediacy and immanence of the landscape garden. The iconography of medieval and Renaissance gardens, walled and neatly divided into four equal plots with a fountain in the center, opens up in the poetic and picturesque phases of the landscape garden to become a series of composed scenes of forest and glade. As Pope's lines indicate, however, the new wedding of pastoral ideals and practical ends was no less pervaded by paradisal fantasizing than were the older religious goals.

Belief in paradise shifts ground in radical change of perspectives. Whereas the paradisal impulse of the Christian was once wholly and nostalgically Old Testament in its backward glance, and millenarian in its future prospects as set forth by the paradigm of the Blessed Virgin and the *hortus conclusus*, it now combines such archaic instincts with more historical and immediate motives calculated to realize paradisal bliss in the here and now, rather than in the there and then. Each human is literally, not just figuratively, a new Adam or Eve. "Parradice's only map," Marvell called Lord Fairfax's Appleton House in the 1650s. Marvell's habitual fallback upon emblematic and paradoxical language when envisioning the universal and the ideal yields ground in the next hundred years to the practical action, buttressed by garden manuals, of transforming conceit into actuality. The latter belief has Arthur Young in the second half of the eighteenth century riding country roads to test the earth and writing his books to advocate practical husbandry.

Anyone familiar with the books of the noted mythographer and philosopher of comparative religion, Mircea Eliade,[9] will recognize that I have been invoking his description of archaic and historical societies. In the former, man lives within a mythic network of divine archetypes whose extrahuman processes he repeats in his own activities, thus giving paradigmatic value to his life. For him there is no past and future, only an ever regenerative present in its repetition of celestial beginnings. In the latter, man lives in time, free to organize his present in ways calculated to affect his future. Such freedom releases him from the tyranny of conformity to archetypal patterns, but it conversely oppresses him with the burden of history and its terrors.

It is not to be assumed that the new historical and activist point of view suddenly and miraculously supplants the old ways of thought; rather, the two cosmologies, or modes of apprehension, exist side by side, often simultaneously in the same person, the old expectations continuing to guide the majority of people as always. But the balance between them is dynamic, with the historical and social steadily gaining momentum through the eighteenth and into the nineteenth century. This line of change culminates (if one is looking for neat milestones in time) with the Crystal Palace and Great Exhibition of 1851. Then, the metamorphosis of an idea recoils negatively on itself, and out of sterile disenchantment with the ability of either the archaic spiritual or the modern quantitative to command a felt assent, veers off into a re-affirmation of the perfect endless moment hopefully to be found in a work of art, in the still point of an aesthetic. Specifically, the Eden of Genesis, celebrated anew in the medieval and Renaissance enclosed garden of the Virgin Mary, receives renewal of meaning as a hieroglyph of divine order in the landscape gardens planted through the eighteenth century. The garden as holy metaphor and increasingly as fact is then seen to spread beyond its landscaped aristocratic boundaries and by the end of the century is democratically touted by the Romantics as including the entire terrain of earth. Nature's divine order is enclosed once again by the new technology of industry literally and symbolically in the Crystal Palace, a transformation that receives its most artful and restricted rationale in the 1880s in the form of a London dining room created by Whistler for a businessman.

The two hundred years described here work out their permutations of an unending human aspiration in terms of at least three historical stages and three configurations.

(1)   In the eighteenth century, particularly as conveyed by the *furor hortensis* of the age, paradise was a Whig ideal involving the creation of one's own Eden out of a country seat by filling in marshes, damming rivers, resloping hills, and planting trees. The new and old aristocracy alike, wearying of political solutions to life, retired to the country comfortable in the belief that they could reach the promised land by improving on nature; and even as they invoked their new historical prerogatives in improvement of their estates, they fell back on paradigmatic ways of viewing their handiwork. The fact that classical versions of paradise offered a less guilt-associated garden than the Eden of the Bible led them to erect classical temples to the memory of Eden. The temple-dotted landscape was for them a celestial center, *axis mundi*, whose perambulation repeated the practice of pilgrimage to a holy church or place, with the difference that their symbolic repetition of the ancient quest for divinity had value less as a ritual reversal of chaos (which it would have had for archaic man) than as a personal reclamation in time of the historically fragmented *mythos*. They strove to establish in their landscape gardens a finite instance of eternity between the poles of the atemporal beginning and end of things.

(2)   The Romantics impatiently leaped the ha-has surrounding their fore-bears's landscaped Edens in their eagerness to roam in a natural paradise of dell, rustic countryside, and unpopulated island. They struggled to redefine the world in organic terms as the scene of uninterrupted paradisal bliss; but they also continued to identify uneasily and contradictorily with the Christian model of life as a pilgrimage of the soul through a fixed and fallen world. When their idealistic aspirations were disappointed by the unmillenarian aftermath of the French Revolution, they turned inward, constructing an Eden out of equal parts of the materials of mythic imagination and of historical memory. But their intention of reabsorbing chaos into primordial unity was no longer an end in itself as it was for archaic man. The Romantics were instead concentrating on personal gesture, and were concerned with mythic resonances primarily as support of private needs. Hence, the duality of their perceptions often obscured their paradisal intentions, lending an ambivalence to their professed faith in an earthly Eden. Emotionally charged with a sacramental view of the universe, most of the major Romantics contended with an undercurrent of pessimism that sapped their expectations of realizing in this life a "calm circumference of bliss" (*Epipsychidion*, 550). The odds as Shelley privately gauged them here were long on any but extraordinary events, when the ordinary was what they were publicly betting on.

(3)   The Romantics had embraced an organic universe of process without knowing quite the full consequences of their embrace – although Coleridge in a drear moment in his old age, "This winter-time of my own Being," saw it clearly as "this bleak World of Mutabilities" (*CL*, VI, 532). The Victorians found the acceleration of mutagenesis, which had not been adequately foreseen, a drawback to the brave new world of science and technology. The rattling railway, expand-ing imperialism, engulfing geologic time, prolific industrialism – all left them scrambling to savor nature at diverse removes from actuality: in the secondhand

language of the Romantics, in the controlled environment of the greenhouse, and in the palace of art. As befits an increasingly industrialized and urbanized generation, the Victorians nostalgically acknowledged the ideal of a perfect order in fantasied towers, mythic islands, and enchanted cities, while conscientiously impelled contrariwise toward the utilitarian goal of the perfection of society through political, economic, and social planning.

Utopian, philanthropic, and socially conscious factory owners designed and built garden cities, bent on providing their workers with the most wholesome facsimiles of Eden that suburban planning and technological competence and social conscience could devise. Engineers linked one part of the garden island of England to another by way of canal, bridge, and railroad, at their best conscious that they were integrating park, hill, and river with steel and masonry into a new industrialized Xanadu, or Camelot. Painters not only memorialized the rural byways of a pastoral Britain, but also recorded the astringent wind, steam, and speed of an England that had become the factory of the world, rushing rich and poor alike into a material paradise that fulfills the Biblical promise of a land of milk and honey as prelude to permanent abode on the celestial plains.

But their unbridled expectation inevitably generated its reactionary disillusionment. The earthly paradise was often indistinguishable from an urban hell, and the Blessed Virgin of the *hortus conclusus* from the Venus Verticordia of the *hortus amoenus*. In the second half of the century the paradisal echo increasingly reverberated about a garden ruin – the vestige of a decay that visits its havoc on all organisms, human dreams and real gardens alike – causing its adherents to veer off into aestheticism in search of unvarying perfection. Where once Eden was the fecund domain of God available to all persons, it was now a plaything of artists, reserved for a coterie of initiates and reduced to such curvilinear biomorphs and mannered disdain for the natural as Whistler's Peacock Room.

When we reduce these historical stages to their underlying configurations, we end with three antitheses. The major one – a recurrent pattern of enclosure and openness – describes what amounts to the vortex-like halves of an inverted hour glass, starting at the still point and opening outward until boundaryless and all-inclusive, before narrowing back to another airless constricted space. Transversely crossing this movement are two sets of reactive figurations: a natural and external paradise altering into a metaphoric and internal one. It is not easy, individuals discovered, to keep so many conflicting intersections of historical time and atemporality, of reality and metaphor, from overlapping and cancelling one another. As the walled garden is breached and extended to encompass the wilderness, and corruption is unavoidably entangled with innocence, the Romantic poets, especially, turned in disillusion away from a suspect earthly Eden and its imperfectable mankind, internalizing paradise by metamorphosing it from a place into a state of mind. Such tormented changes in assumption inevitably left individuals caught in unresolved contradictions. Wordsworth's imagination, for example, pertinaciously clung to the view of Grasmere Vale as a remnant of Edenic real estate, even as he was poetically making it over into a landscape of the mind. Through all such eddies, doublings back on itself, and varying flow-rates of current, now Greenwich Mean Time and now Edenic time, however, English representations of nature as God's legacy, all that was left of the *axis mundi* besides human mythic memory of it, improved, naturalized, urbanized, and aestheti-cized earth through repeatedly different forms between 1710 and 1900, all in the name of paradise preserved.

PART I

Eighteenth-Century Landscape Garden Paradises

It puzzles much the sages' brains,
  Where Eden stood of yore;
Some place it in Arabia's plains,
  Some say it is no more.

But Cobham can these tales confute,
  As all the curious know;
For he hath prov'd, beyond dispute,
  That Paradise is Stow.
          Nathaniel Cotton, "On Lord Cobham's Garden" (1791)

The laws and customs of "this Earthly *Elysium*" are dictated by Reason, and regulated by social Love.
          J. Henrietta Pye, *A Short Account, of the Principal Seats and Gardens, in and about Richmond and Kew* (1760)

I

"Gardening Lords"

IN HIS unpublished Miltonic poem "The Country Seat" (late 1720s), the Scotsman Sir John Clerk of Penicuik (1676–1755) urged his contemporaries to choose

> a rural Life in Such a Field
> As EDEN's Garden best ressemble can
> Where first th' Almighty Power established Man.[1]

Clerk's enthusiasm for creating one's own paradisal prospect was shared by the aristocrats and gentry of his age, or at least by those who could afford to shift tons of earth in their pursuit of the elusive original bliss. Equally to the point, as Clerk's verses suggest, their *furor hortensis*, and their supreme achievement, the English landscape garden, had as a prototype the Biblical Eden and the tradition of paradise as a garden. Stephen Switzer (?1682–1745) was among the earliest of the professional gardeners to urge the new gardening principles, and, as the heir to at least a half century of garden manuals seldom failing to make the connection between lost Eden and gardening ("repairing the ruins of our first parents")[2] he used to stiffen the resolve of his aristocratic clients by assuring them in the same breath as he instructed them about the practical concerns of gardening that their endeavors were mandated by the creator and zealous guardian of Eden:

That the unhappy Lapse of our First Parents was the Occasion of that permanent Curse entailed on their Posterity . . . and that *Paradise* itself could no longer maintain its Glory and Splendour, than whilst it was under the immediate Care and Direction of Providence . . . It has been therefore the chief and laudable Undertakings of the Wise and Virtuous in all Ages, to endeavour at a Reparation of that Loss, by a studious and laborious Application towards the Redress of those Malignities contain'd within the scope of that dismal Imprecation, *Thorns and Thistles shall it bring forth*, and so to manure, cultivate, dress, and improve.[3]

The "Gardening Lords" (Pope's phrase)[4] of the Hanoverian era inhabited a spacious green world; and they were bent on making it more so. That their horticultural investments might earn them paradise as well as profit was a dividend they saw no reason to avoid or reject. Accordingly, the roll-call of

country houses rebuilt and of gardens redesigned – formal parterres of sixteenth-
and seventeenth-century taste ripped out and flower beds dug up to make way for
lawns and "natural" undulations of hill and meadow – reads like a *Who's Who* of
eighteenth-century historic Elysiums: Lord Cobham's Stowe, Matthew Prior's
Down Hall, Philip Southcote's Woburn Park ("Southcote's Paradise" Gray
called it), Pope's Twickenham, Ralph Allen's Prior Park, Lord Burlington's
Chiswick, Lord Lyttleton's Hagley, Lord Leicester's Holkham, Lord Carlisle's
Castle Howard, Lord Bathurst's Cirencester Park, William Shenstone's The
Leasowes, Robert and James Dormers' Rousham, Henry Hoare's Stourhead,
Lord Bingley's Bramham Park, Lord Egremont's Petworth, Edwin Lascelles'
Harewood, Henry Pelham's Esher Place, Lord Harcourt's Nuneham Courtenay,
John Aislabie's Studley Royal, the Duke of Newcastle's Claremont, the Duke of
Marlborough's Blenheim, the Earl of Pembroke's Wilton, the Duke of Grafton's
Euston, Thomas (father and son) Duncombe's Rievaulx and Duncombe terraces.
The list is endless.

Obviously, not every enthusiast for rural seclusion, or improver of his country
holdings, or planter of a garden in the eighteenth century saw himself as a latter-
day Adam reclaiming his birthright. The desultory comments and anecdotes on
gardening of Pope, Addison, Joseph Spence, Sir Thomas Whately, Philip
Southcote, William Shenstone, and Horace Walpole indicate that the *furor
hortensis* was fertilized no less, on occasion, by aesthetic dogmas and artistic taste
than by the Christian promise of redemption. *Ut pictura poesis* was heard on every
hand, as synod decrees, *miserere*, and the Book of Common Prayer had been
intoned in the previous century. Men like Lyttleton and Southcote, and the
latter's most successful imitator Shenstone, consciously followed artistic rules of
the picturesque and Augustan ideals of reflection and harmony more than the
spiritual echoes of an older time. Repeating Pope's first principle of gardening,
" 'Tis all painting," Southcote averred that "Perspective, prospect, distancing,
and attracting, comprehend all that part of painting in gardening."[5] "Garden-
scenes," Shenstone summarized, with his Leasowes and his neighbor Lyttleton's
Hagley no doubt in mind, "may perhaps be divided into the sublime, the
beautiful, and the melancholy or expressive."[6] Thus, it is no accident that Hagley
is associated with James Thomson's *The Seasons* or that The Leasowes is praised
by William Mason in his poem *The English Garden* (1772–81) as the place where
the painter's "enchanting art" is inspired,

> for Fancy here,
> With Nature's living colours, forms a scene
> Which RUISDALE best might rival.   (1, 165–68)

Scholars have tended to follow this strain of Pope and company's estimate of
their gardening interests, reading the "poetic garden"[7] of the 1720s and 30s as if it
were a three-dimensional poem. Inextricably fused with such harking after the
picturesque as a semantic form, however, can be discerned the by no means
discontinued habit of judging the natural world by religious and symbolical

frames of reference. While the rigor of allegorical thought which reduced a flower bed or a mountain top to hieroglyphs may have become outdated, the most passionate aesthetes would occasionally forget their artistic posture and reach for a religious analogy drawn from a persistent shared vocabulary, which retained much of Judeo-Christian iconography and paradigmatic assumptions. Thus, Pope in "To Bathurst" was able to praise the Man of Ross's betterment of his patrimony (which he "hung with woods," 253) as a remote analogue of the divine creation, and by implication see his lifelong act of civic and religious piety in a backwater Herefordshire parish as a reenactment of Adam and Eve's in better days and place before the Fall.[8]

As indicated by Pope's tribute to the Man of Ross, one of the most common of reference points was the idea of paradise. Mrs. Elizabeth Montagu, that litmus of bluestocking taste, comments about a visit to Mr. Archibald Bower in 1752: "I never saw any country more beautiful than about Chislehurst, where he lives. I cannot say much in praise of his habitation, which he terms his Paradise, but indeed to a mind as gay and cheerful as his, all places are a Paradise."[9] That Mrs. Montagu's sophisticated intelligence expresses some skepticism about this particular paradise confirms all the more the naturalness with which the age still reacted in traditional Christian terms. Equally to the point is the extent to which the paradisal *topos* often lay behind eighteenth-century gardening impetus. Mrs. Montagu herself was not wholly inoculated against Mr. Bower's propensity for seeing paradises in "all places". Here she is in August 1744 writing to the Duchess of Portland:

Stowe . . . is beyond description, it gives the best idea of Paradise that can be; even Milton's images and descriptions fall short of it, and indeed a Paradise it must be to every mind in a state of innocence.[10]

Like Mrs. Montagu, Pope often found a paradisal analogy irresistible when he contemplated his friends' gardens, especially if he had a hand in their design. Stowe prompted him in 1731 to exclaim, "if any thing under Paradise could set me beyond all Earthly Cogitations; Stowe might do it. It is much more beautiful this year than when I saw it before."[11]

Nor did it matter to denizens of the gardens that the design might be light years away in formal disposition of trees, walks, and seats from the natural groves and clearings of Eden, or that the design changed dramatically from the 1730s when William Kent was arbiter of taste to the 1770s when Capability Brown ruled England's grassy demesnes. For Eden existed in their minds as a mythological landscape which accommodated diverse places, situations, activities, and states of being no less than as a geographical territory to be developed here and now in present-day England. William Mason bore joyous witness to "A gleam of happiness primaeval . . . Ere vice defil'd, ere slavery sunk the world," in the gothic handiwork of the English "sons of CLAUDE" who like "Creation's king" were returning earth to its original condition (*The English Garden*, II, 204, 206; III, 323; II, 208) by planting it with trees once again. Clearly sentiment rather than

historical accuracy was the important thing, as in Edward Stephens's lines on
"Lord Bathurst's Park" at Cirencester:

> When first the beauteous *Eden* we survey,
> Unfolding shades a gravell'd walk display.[12]

The elegant touch of a "gravell'd" walk was an anachronism easily discounted by
garden denizens seeking the exquisite excitement of vicariously treading Adam
and Eve's ground.

How automatic it was for practical sensibilities to find Edens everywhere, never
mind that their conventional turns of thought had been schooled in classical
mythology and Horatian ideals, is exhibited by that tireless advocate of estate
building and planting the second Baronet of Penicuik, Sir John Clerk. In "The
Country Seat" he recalls "Antient Paradise" as if by rehearsed response when he
comes to describe an orchard, "of all Grounds . . . most ressembling" those
which witnessed mankind's worst lapse in judgment. The incongruous compulsion of Cobham to buy statues of Cain and Abel presumably for placement in the
Elysian Fields sector of his gardens is symptomatic similarly of the unexamined
urge to link a reverence for the classical past with a devotion to the Christian
heritage. Further complicating the ultimate intentions of the *furor hortensis* was a
newly awakened pagan awe before nature, which reached platitudinous proportions in the sacred rage elicited by a grotto, that "shrine for great Nature—Pope's
metaphysical Goddess,"[13] as one scholar has cheerfully termed it. To the laird of
Penicuik – to Pope, Cobham, Bathurst, Lyttleton, Shenstone, and the other
workers of a revolution in gardening in the first half of the eighteenth century –
nurtured on the classics as previous generations had been on the Bible, Parnassus
and Eden tended to merge. They found the haunt of the Muses indistinguishable
finally from the seat of our First Parents, the gardens of Alcinous and the Sabine
Farm situated where once was God's Mount.

Given the continuing widespread habit of citing Eden as the *locus classicus* of all
gardens, it is not surprising that the landscape garden, and its variants the
picturesque, the ideal, and the *ferme ornée* were justified throughout the century
by appeal to Milton, the great proponent of paradise in the previous century.
Joseph Spence advances the best insight on the subject, best because tentative and
unassertive in its claims and uncannily close in perception to what hindsight has
confirmed, when he comments that

Milton's paradise is chiefly like the new natural taste. Sir William Temple guessed at it, and
Addison has many strokes toward it in the *Spectators*. [The new style] began to be practised
a few years after the publication of the *Spectators*. (One cannot say how far any of our first
introducers of this taste might have been influenced, etc., but this is certain.)

(Spence, I, 421)

As if to confirm Spence's observation, peripatetic Sir John Clerk invoked Milton
on a trip south in 1734 when he visited Corby Castle, the Cumberland estate of
Thomas Howard. The house, he notes, overlooks the River Eden; and Howard
showed him "a passage in the 4th book of Milton's paradise [Lost] where he

describes the Garden of Eden which very near resembles the description one wou'd give of Corby Castle."[14] At mid-century Joseph Warton reaffirmed Spence's historical acumen, adding Pope to Milton as the two poets to whom Europe owes "this enchanting art of modern gardening."[15] And at the end of the century, in a letter of September 1794, Anna Seward, provoked by what she thought to be a dangerous radicalism in Payne Knight's analogy of picturesque landscaping to a political revolution, cites Milton's "description of the primeval garden" as an example of "the rational spirit of improvement," which she contends Lancelot Brown has realized in the present by "uniting the *utile* with the *dulce*" to render "Britain the Eden of Europe."[16]

In his *History of the Modern Taste in Gardening* (1771) Walpole deftly summarized half a century of crediting Milton with the principles "of the present style." In a bravura dismissal of the formal garden plans of the seventeenth century, Milton – Walpole hypothesizes – "judged that the mistaken and fantastic ornaments he had seen in gardens, were unworthy of the almighty hand that planted the delights of Paradise." God had placed Adam and Eve amidst acres of natural landscape enclosed by four rivers, where "every tree that was pleasant to the sight and good for food grew." "So minutely" do Milton's "ideas correspond with the present standard," Walpole concludes, quoting liberally from *Paradise Lost* to illustrate his point, who can doubt that modern gardening is but the execution of his imagined celestial design.[17]

So many witnesses attesting to Milton's presence in the eighteenth-century garden suggests that the belief, at least, was widespread that actual gardens had been laid out according to his poetic model. The scanty evidence of direct influence, however, reveals the Miltonic Eden to have been more a state of mind than a fact of gardening. That the age could reproduce the plan of paradise out of diverse rules of aesthetics, Roman principles of conduct, Horatian ideals of happy retirement, and Miltonic descriptions of Eden was possible because the era of the Georges was marvelously flexible in accommodating an outdated homogeneous world picture, even while revising that picture to fit new perceptions. For one thing, Milton had described an Eden patterned according to classical and Biblical learning in language which paid tribute to the horticultural geometry of the day and at the same time prophetically redesigned paradise as "a happy rural seat of various view." It was based on an assumption of perfection, which the garden theorists of the 1720s and 30s also prized, albeit of a different order. Milton's Adam and Eve must "dress / This Garden . . . Lop overgrown, or prune, or prop, or bind" daily its "wanton growth" (IX, 205–6, 210–11), for Nature tends to play "at will":

> Her Virgin Fancies, pouring forth more sweet,
> Wild above Rule or Art.
> (V, 295–97)

As propounded by the third Earl of Shaftesbury, Pope, and Addison,[18] the new aesthetic called for variety and informality of appearance; but its practitioners hypothesized that human faculties ("*the Forms which form*"), divine in origin, could come to the aid of the luxuriant forms of nature (*"the dead Forms"*) and hence help nature by due improvement to attain that perfection toward which its imminent force is always striving. " 'Tis thus the *improving* MIND, slightly surveying other Objects, and passing over Bodys, and the common Forms," Shaftesbury has Theocles asseverate in *The Moralists*, "ambitiously presses onward to Its *Source*, and views *the Original* of Form and Order," becoming in the process "artists in the Kind," improver of the external world as well as "self-improving Artist[s]."[19] And the ultimate "Perfection of *the* Universe" – that original natural "Magnificence beyond the formal Mockery of Princely Gardens"[20] – sought in their sylvicultural labors of improvement by what Christopher Hussey alludes to as the Pope-Bathurst-Cobham circle[21] was a replica of "the enchanting paths of paradise."[22]

The attentive husbandry of Adam and Eve, prescribed by Milton's Jehovah, established an example that the Whig lords emerging after the Glorious Revolution of 1688–89 could emulate with good Christian consciences, and at the same time materially improve their fortunes. Changing economic conditions and national considerations argued in favor of sweeping away along with the Stuart kings and absolute monarchy the grand formal gardens of the seventeenth century, which had been patterned after *le jardin français* of André Le Nôtre, the designer of the gardens at Versailles, to be replaced by natural plantings of trees and laying out of meadows. There was the need to replenish forests denuded during the interregnum of the Civil War and the Puritan regime. An added incentive for planting forests was its financial feasibility in future harvesting, and the need for economy under Queen Anne made such reclamation economically fashionable. Alexander Pope catches this materialistic turn of the age in his poem "To Richard Boyle, Earl of Burlington," when he praises the enlightened squire,

> Whose ample Lawns are not asham'd to feed
> The milky heifer and deserving steed;
> Whose rising Forests, not for pride or show,
> But future Buildings, future Navies grow:
> Let his plantations stretch from down to down,
> First shade a Country and then raise a Town. (185–90)

Not only was responsible stewardship reinforced by Milton's depiction of Adam and Eve at their daily chores and orisons, and by both patriotism and self-interest, but it also received stimulus, as had Milton, from idealistic role models of the classical past. "Happy the Man," Pope asserts in *Windsor-Forest* in an echo of the Horatian theme of the *beatus ille*, "who to these Shades retires . . . wandring thoughtful in the silent Wood" (235, 237, 249), and who

> looks on Heav'n with more than mortal Eyes,
> Bids his free Soul expatiate in the Skies,
> Amid her Kindred Stars familiar roam,
> Survey the Region, and confess her Home! (253–56)

If many who wrote about gardening in the eighteenth century had aesthetic principles and effects uppermost in mind – in the second half of the century when battle lines were drawn between Brownists, orientalists, and pictorialists, aesthetics provided the powder and shot fired on rival garden styles – most gardening enthusiasts also carried in the back of their heads the classical model of *beatus ille*, the happy man praised by Horace. This model of natural perfection, however, also had an Edenic underpinning, for the eighteenth-century gentleman could not acknowledge the harmonious scheme of nature without paying pious tribute to its benevolent Creator. In the artistic aspiration to realize the ideal landscape, the remembrance of the First Garden by way of the authority of Milton inevitably came to mind, giving (in Martin Price's words) a moral basis to garden theory.[23] Literary descriptions of Eden competed with depictions of the Roman Campagna and ancient traditions of moral order, as they had in Milton's conception of paradise. Less guilty feelings were associated with classical versions of paradise than with the Biblical one. The guardian serpent of the Hesperides countered the tempting serpent of Eden, offering Whig politicians a world of value imaged as a garden with which they might feel comfortable. They could retire from the never-ending strife of London political life to their country seats, there erecting classical temples to restore the appearance of "that Golden Age" which would make remembrance of Eden possible and "make those happy who on you depend," as the third Earl of Carlisle is eulogized in the poem *Castle Howard*[24] as having done for his progeny.

It is significant, in this regard, how often the practical impetus to recreate the ideal world, which lay behind much of this passionate building and planting, was conceived of as an Elysium linking the Christian paradise associated with the dawn of life and the classical paradise identified with the afterlife. An heroic handling of the theme occurs at Castle Howard, where John Hawksmoor's Mausoleum (begun 1728) dominates the landscape. Christopher Hussey termed it "the visual climax of the Elysium"[25] – that is, of the garden. The contour of the land and the siting of the architecture in the southeast end of the park pulls the visitor toward it as the culmination of a stroll from the house down a terraced Grass Walk to Vanbrugh's Temple of Four Winds (1726), then along a "River" past a "Roman Bridge" to the Mausoleum on its commanding hill site. The symbolism of this progression (three pyramids also dot the grounds) did not escape its designer. The poem *Castle Howard* stresses "the Limits of our Stay" on earth, and within a frame of reference to "the *Trojan* Prince" and his lineal descendants the Caesars, lauds the third Earl of Carlisle whose "Ashes" will repose in "This solemn Place" (the Mausoleum) from which his "gentle Shade" will "Ages hence" view the tranquil rural scene and the long "Line [of] a gen'rous Race." Stowe had a section of the gardens called Elysian Fields, with a River Styx meandering through; and The Leasowes, a Virgil's Grove (laid out in the 1740s), calculated to elicit feelings of elegiac gloom.[26] At Rousham a Vale of Venus with statues of Pan and Venus, as well as of Bacchus and Ceres in a nearby grove, played off its allegory of fertility against that of death represented by the Praeneste and its statue of the Dying Gladiator. As part of this interesting complex was constructed "Proserpine's Cave" which MacClary the gardener created out of plantings of "yew and other evergreens as dark and melancholy as it was possible to make it."[27] In a like manner a walk around "the sacred landscape" at Stourhead was conceived by Henry Hoare as an allegory of Aeneas' journey, with conscious allusions to the landscape of the underworld and Lake Avernus in *The Aeneid* (Bk. 6).[28] Not least of the allusions implied in this tour is possibly to Hoare's private bereavement (his young wife died in 1743), and his sublimation of it, like Aeneas' founding of a New Troy (Rome), in the creation of a new earthly paradise. Behind this repeated mix of nationalistic and self-aggrandizing allegorical trips through Hades rests the assumption that the earth could be made to conform to its original condition. These gardens communicate more than the traditional Christian message that in death one finds eternal life. They convey also the radical message that paradise is regainable on earth in historical time,[29] a belief increasing in fervor throughout the century to peak in the millennialism of the French Revolution.

Reinforcing the inclination of English gardening lords to hear paradisal overtones when surveying their estates was the proliferation of essays on Chinese gardens in the 1750s. Reputed to have exerted wide influence at that time on contemporary theories of gardening was Joseph Spence's translation of Father Jean-Denis Attiret's letter (from *Lettres édifiantes, écrites des mission* [1749]) published under the title *A Particular Account of the Emperor of China's Gardens near Pekin* in 1752. Chinese gardens had been vaguely and ethically associated with unspoiled nature and a superior kind of religious experience since at least Sir William Temple's dissertation *Upon the Gardens of Epicurus; or of Gardening, in the Year 1685*. Addison subsequently drew on Temple in his *Spectator* paper no. 414, of 25 June 1712, when he advocated the contrived wilderness of Chinese gardens as superior to the frozen artificiality of the French garden. Actually, the relationship of the Chinese garden to the English is less one of direct design than of parallel spiritual intentions. In 1772 when Goldsmith astonishes his visiting Mandarin (*The Citizen of the World*, or "Letters from a Chinese philosopher residing in London to his friends in the country") by introducing him to a *chinoiserie* summerhouse as a piece of "Chinese" architecture, an actual visitor from Peking would not have known what to make of the English landscape garden, nor have known how to associate "the flowing lawns and country spaces of the *jardin anglo-chinois* with China."[30] For the Chinese garden differs greatly from the English in its concentration of effects, in its tight spaces, its many buildings grouped together in courtyards, its intricate rockworks, its grotesque standing stones, and its lack of grassy distances. On the other hand, both national creations stand as profound symbols of the sum total of finite creation. The Chinese garden as a liminal zone looking at once to earthly and spiritual realms represents the abode of the Immortals with much less ambiguity than does the English garden; and its centuries-old tradition provided the English garden with a corroboration of precedence at least, and a vague model of sorts in the late 1700s. Intrinsic then to the Chinese garden in English minds was its divine symbolism, a spiritual dimension of *chinoiserie* which receives its climactic advocacy in Sir William Chambers's *Dissertation on Oriental Gardening* in 1772. Above its shrill polemics can be heard a justification for simulating yet another idea of timeless perfection in the effort to reconstitute the English countryside according to its original divine appearance.

In short, the religious thought residual in reference to eighteenth-century English gardens forms a complex matrix of associations. When we contemplate the *furor hortensis* within the context of the terms – sacramental labor and profitable farm management – Switzer uses to flatter and inspire his lordly clients, we find ourselves uneasily straddling incompatible worlds not unlike the interface Kenneth Clark perceived in Virgil's *Georgics* of a still viable degree of myth with an emergent social reality.[31] We all remember that Squire Allworthy's estate in *Tom Jones* (1749) is called Paradise Hall; and when Tom is expelled from home, Fielding comments, "The world, as Milton phrases it, lay all before him; and Jones, no more than Adam, had any man to whom he might resort for comfort or assistance" (Bk. VII, ch. 2). This is a famous instance of the extent to which the age, despite its flirtation with deism and its affairs with empiricism and moderation, resolutely stuck to its faith in gardens as the earthly sign, all that was left, of the benignity God once felt for his disobedient children. This faith is revealed even when the intent was practical and scientific, as in Samuel Collins's polemic on *Paradise Retriev'd: plainly and fully demonstrating . . . the method of managing and improving fruit-trees against walls, or in hedges . . . Together with a treatise on melons and cucumbers* (1717).[32]

Not least among Eden's accretion of features in its evolution from scriptural and classical times is the clear-cut differentiation drawn between paradise and the wilderness surrounding it. The American Hudson River painter Thomas Cole pictorially depicts this dichotomous world as starkly as any artist, in his *Expulsion from Eden* (c. 1827–28). The diminutive figures of Adam and Eve timidly venture out of Eden, all bright and verdurous, through a cleft of rock and across a ravine into a Salvatorial landscape of rock, fearsome darkness, and upheaved terrain. A painting by Jan Sieberechts of *The Gardens of Chatsworth, Derbyshire*, about 1690–1710 (Lord Sandys), delineates this paradisal geography in late seventeenth-century terms. The painting shows an Italian Renaissance palace surrounded on all four sides with rectilinear lawns, formally planted parterres, reflecting pools and fountains, all laid out on a flat plane and in scrupulously geometrical designs. Enclosing the whole is a massive wall separating this worldly *hortus conclusus* from the messy brutality of generative life in the foreground, where a bull copulates with a cow, a coach and six clatters over a rutted road, and horses, men and livestock mill about. In the middle distance sparsely settled land has been haphazardly cultivated into rough rectangles of farmland. Beyond loom the threatening Peak District hills. Here are depicted three kinds of nature: the earthly paradise contained within the walls of the garden enclosure, the uncouth rural existence surrounding it, and the uninhabited remainder of the fallen world, wild, tangled, and unkempt.

This is the prototype of Eden the eighteenth-century aristocrat inherited at the beginning of the century. As self-defined *beatus vir* he pursued a sylvicultural will-o-the-wisp that plowed under the mathematical cosmic model of the previous century. The broad axials bounded by walls yielded to circumferential walks and finally to trackless meadows, as the garden evolved from a contrived geometric paradise to an ideal landscape. Contributing paradoxically to that story of the gradual elimination of internal bounds, one area flowing into the adjoining and all suffused with the vernal force of the divine power, is the traditional association of paradise with a garden, which added its *imprimatur* to a religio-aesthetic movement bent on a merger of the three kinds of nature into a reconstituted paradise on earth.

Many replicate Edens dotted the eighteenth-century landscape. Of those planted from the 1720s to the 1790s only three need be singled out for a closer look. They are Stowe, Stourhead, and Hafod. Each incorporated into its design at once the persistent terrestrial–paradisal hope of its individual maker and the evolving aesthetical–horticultural ambitions of its historical period.

COBHAM'S STOWE: AN ELYSIUM AT QUARTER-CENTURY

"Paradise," Stephen Switzer observes in his preface to *Ichnographia Rustica: or, the Nobleman, Gentleman, and Gardener's Recreation*, "properly signifies *Gardens of Pleasure*"; and in the practice of gardening, in "that Eternal Honour . . . [which] carries with it . . . a Kind of Divine Revelation," the "Compact between God and Man . . . invalidated and broke" by Adam and Eve is renewed *de facto*, if not *de jure*, and "the Soul is elevated to unlimited Heights above, and modell'd and prepar'd for the sweet Reception and happy Enjoyment of Felicities, the durablest as well as happiest that Omniscience has created."[33] Nowhere in eighteenth-century England was there more sustained effort to prove the words of Switzer prophetic than at Stowe (Buckinghamshire). The landscaped grounds, lakes, groves, and serpentine streams of this garden were strategically embellished with temples, grottoes, statues, urns, and obelisks, as Rudolf Wittkower suggests, to reinforce the atmosphere of "carefully planned Elysiums" and to "stimulate a variety of literary associations." Those buildings "sacred to imaginary powers," according to a contemporary account, also raised a "pleasing [religious] enthusiasm in the mind," evoking inevitably sentiments of prelapsarian blessedness.[34]

At Stowe under the inspired eye of Richard Temple, first Viscount Cobham (1675–1749), the horticultural arithmetic of the previous age establishing geometrical patterns of hedge, walk, and tree as mathematical mirror of the divine world was slowly transformed into a Whig facsimile of Eden emphasizing the virtues of classical moderation and rural retirement. In its successive alterations, each bringing the garden into closer approximation to natural fields and informal groves, Stowe reflected evolving stages of taste through the middle decades of the century and simultaneously the changing structure of the garden as a paradigm of paradise.

The sensibilities of visitors were moved for more than half the century to avow their approval of the inspiriting transfigurations they witnessed taking place there. In the 1720s and 30s Alexander Pope annually delighted in the on-going metamorphosis of its "opening glades" joined to "willing woods," its varying of "shades from shades" ("Epistle to Burlington," 61–62). Gilbert West (1703–56), Cobham's nephew, rhymed the pleasures of a walk along the perimeters of the west gardens in 1732. "Of *Stowe's* Elyzian Scenes I sing," he promises in dedicatory lines to Pope, preparatory to extolling the views around Home Park.[35] Kent's masterpiece of sylvan peace to the east, the Elysian Fields, was possibly already in formation – it appears in Sara Bridgeman's 1739 plan – but West ignores it for the more eclectic "Elyzian Scenes" of Bridgeman's design to the west, where quincunx consorts with barnyard animals, and geometrical pools reflect the gloomy shade of evergreen groves. Classical architecture dominates every section of the garden and every page of the poem, taxing West's poetical ingenuity to find appropriate words of praise. Contrariwise, as a sign of the growing delight in a garden without didactic designs on one, Mrs. Elizabeth Montagu found difficulty in assimilating the clangor of lessons started up by the accumulation of temples and monuments which she thought already in 1744 disagreeably crowded the garden. Still, in spite of her disapproval of the parts, she thought the ensemble effect a paradise beyond description.[36] Cobham had been adding a heterogeneous assortment of structures "along the garden itinerary," as John Dixon Hunt remarks, "a Hermitage, which Kent introduced into one of his illustrations for Spenser, a Witch House, St Augustine's Cave, a Sleeping Parlour, and Dido's Cave."[37] In the little valley of the Elysian Fields cheek by jowl sat a Temple of Ancient Virtue, with statues of a Grecian lawgiver, general, poet, and philosopher, in dramatic confrontation with a temple of British Worthies, containing half-length busts in niches, on the opposite slope. As if the didacticism of that pretty scheme of associations did not fully tell the tale of history, the second Viscount Cobham punctuated the moral by placing a ruined Gothic Temple of Modern Virtue nearby, built by James Gibbs in the 1750s. When William Gilpin took his readers on a tour of the grounds in 1748 his youthful eye (he was twenty-four) reveled in the "Roman" vistas which had distracted Mrs. Montagu, while presciently admiring the newer taste for sylvan serenity. The running debate of Callophilus and Polypthon as they tour the grounds diplomatically puts the case for both viewpoints. Callophilus invokes Pope on nature's beauties being best regularized "under the Direction of *Art*," while Polypthon anticipates the taste of later decades by preferring the "elegant natural Views." Gilpin signals where his heart lies, however, when at the end he lets the debaters agree on the beauties of Kent's Elysian Fields. They leave by the Pavilion gate, with Polypthon assuring his friend that "he passed [through] with the greatest Reluctance, and went growling out of this delightful Garden, as the Devil is said to have done out of Paradise."[38]

By the 1750s the eastern half of the garden equaled the original western section in acreage, balancing sylvan informality with Attic associations not only in the

Elysian Fields but also in the Grecian Valley. The garden was on its way to becoming all of a piece. In the 1769 plan of J. C. Miller, the linear Bridgeman conception has visibly yielded to the pictorial composition of Kent and the "softening and Broadening"[39] process of Brown. The occasional mortal viewer might choose to laugh at the theatricality of the garden's ethical and paradisal pretensions: its classical temples, domes, statuary, and columns scattered about with a lavish hand, and its Elysian Fields contiguous to the banks of the River Styx. As early as 1740 the latter is objected to in Garrick's play *Lethe or Esop on the Shades*. But these are singular aberrations of minds with a farcical turn; to most sightseers the garden appeared to be an instance of God's having for once conceived and executed a scene of nature in perfect harmony with all its parts.

Christopher Hussey judiciously summarizes the achievement of seventy years of transformation at Stowe as the triumph of the Whig faith in disciplined freedom, its respect for natural qualities, its belief in the individual, and its hatred of tyranny. The groves created were distinctly those "of Attic land," the "purest truth / Of nature," to borrow James Thomson's description of the garden in a passage added to *The Seasons* in 1744 ("Autumn," 1054–57). The aim, as Hussey so aptly expresses it, was "to raise Nature to the human mind and by the same process raise the mind by exhibiting Nature's purest, i.e. ideal, truth, as a manlike God intended her to be before man's Fall degraded her with him. Regarded thus the creation of eighteenth-century landscapes, so far from mere indulgence, constituted an act of faith in the fundamental excellence of humanity and the perfectibility of Nature."[40] The "Roman" air of Stowe invited grave contemplation; and it was but a short step to take when dwelling on the symbolism of classical antiquity and its reminders of fame, virtue, and honor to reach considerations about the human pilgrimage through this world with its stress on the brevity and vanity of life. This is especially appropriate in such sections of Stowe as the Elysian Fields, where a Temple of Ancient Virtue inspired by the Temple of the Sibyl situated above the gorge at Tivoli invests its surroundings with the feelings of dread attached to a "sacred landscape" as well as arousing thoughts of public virtue.

Stowe represents the synthesis of efforts of three of the century's greatest landscape architects, touching with Bridgeman at one end the baroque conventions of the Grand Manner and with Brown at the other end the "untouched" rusticity of the Romantics, with Kent bridging the distance between the two in the taste for the pictorial. The impulse to create an ideal world of nature is strongly classical in this garden, which is limited in area and arranged with an eye for harmonious contrasts and repetitions, as is also Rousham (Oxfordshire) which preserves the concerted skills of Bridgeman and Kent at the height of their powers in the 1730s.[41] More idiosyncratic dispositions of nature included Castle Howard (Yorkshire), Studley Royal (Yorkshire), and Cirencester (Gloucestershire) whose owners – Lord Carlisle, John Aislabie, and Lord Bathurst – followed their own instincts in creating gardens conceptualized on a grand scale. The imagination of the 1720s and 1730s in general, however, was captivated by the circumscribed

Elysium – so Henrietta Pye characterized Twickenham, "this Earthly *Elesium*"[42]
– in which taste and ingenuity contrived unexpected scenes and pleasing variety,
but which was still comfortably comprehensible to the mind. Unsettling exposure
to the suggestive and the surprising demanded a compensatory retreat to the
security of the recognizable and the familiar. Pope's garden at Twickenham,
Kent's at Rousham, and Bridgeman's early efforts at Stowe enchanted visitors
because of their variegated effects, their blend of the predictable and the
unanticipated in scene after scene within a restricted area. The gardens at Stowe,
Lord Percival exclaims ecstatically in 1724,

> by reason of the good contrivance of the walks, seem three times as large as they are,
> contain but 28 acres yet took us up two hours [to tour]. . . . You think twenty times you
> have no more to see, and of a sudden find yourself in some new garden or vista as finished
> and adorned as that you left.[43]

As Jacques Rigaud depicts Stowe in 1734–36 in a series of drawings, commis-
sioned by Bridgeman and published by his wife Sarah in 1739 as *Views of Stowe*,[44]
nature perfected is a refined world of classical pavilions, temples, columns,
statutes, reflecting pools, terraces, open grassy courts, and gravel paths around
which in clock-wise fashion sociable ladies and gentlemen progress. Vistas across
a lake, down an alley of trees, or along a broad court occur, allowing the eye a
sense of space; but the vista seldom extends beyond the comfortable range of 20–
20 vision. The horizon is protectively screened by wall or hedge, rows of trees or
hills, which give boundary to the scenes. Alleys are not permitted to stretch to the
vanishing point; they terminate in statues and temples. The sublimity of
immeasurable space is inobtrusively but firmly kept at bay. One is not unaware of
the rough-hewn work-a-day world at large – the overgrown thicket and "woody
Theatre" of "Cedar, and Pine, and Fir, and branching Palm" (*PL*, IV, 141, 139),
with which Milton surrounds Eden. Plate 6 of Rigaud's scenes, "View from the
foot of the *Pyramid*" across Home Park, depicts on its "free *Lawn*" not the
"frisking Lambs" and "gadding Heifers" that Gilbert West liberally sprinkles
about in rhyme (at "play" and "[a]stray") but soberly grazing horses safely
separated by hedge and ha-ha revetment from the elegant throngs of people.

The scenes distinctly reflect their having been drawn by a Frenchman, albeit
muted to English taste in the monotony of the prospects, the earnestness of the
sightseers, the informality of the coming and going of coaches, greeting of guests,
and sober converse of strollers. While there is less animated gaiety than is to be
found in Watteau's *fêtes galantes*, and less bustle and show of crowds than is
depicted in Rigaud's 1730 scene of St. Cloud (France),[45] the affable world of
Stowe still belongs to a courtly life of social intercourse, as compared to the rustic
stillness and empty park drowsing in summer heat painted by Richard Wilson a
generation later in *Croome Court, Worcestershire* (1758, Birmingham Museum and
Art Gallery). At Croome Court we view a landscape characterized by solemnity,
even religious awe, before the miracle of nature. The grazing cows and deer, the
rustic group of three adults and a child sprawling in the foreground on the bank of

a stream – all bear silent informal witness to the scene. At Stowe the visitors still comport themselves in the style and with the refinement of manners that belong to Le Nôtre's grand concourses, bowing, doffing hats, and strolling sedately in silken gowns and brocaded coats. The circuit of the gardens is a "social hour" of "walk conducted o'er their loveliest spots,"[46] as befits a garden where the profusion and exuberance of Milton's Eden is pruned and regularized, where all is in good taste – an unruffled Whig Elysium.

HOARE'S STOURHEAD: AN ELYSIUM AT MID-CENTURY

By mid-century a taste for solitary meditation in unfrequented fields and forests was displacing the social exchange of impressions in public celebrated in Rigaud's drawings. As early as 1744 Joseph Warton in *The Enthusiast; or the Lover of Nature* had unabashedly rejected Stowe because its gardens, "deck'd with art's vain pomps," with "marble-mimic gods" and "attic fanes," cannot arouse in the viewer the raptures evoked by "forests brown, / . . . unfrequented meads, and pathless wilds" (2–9). Classical and gothic structures continue to decorate vistas but a subtle shift in focus was taking place. They share attention now with the free-standing trees among which they are situated. Alexander Pope's appeal in the "Epistle to Burlington" (1713) for "artful wildness to perplex the scene" (116) prosodically placed at least as much emphasis on *art* as on *wild*. In the horticulture of the second half of a century rushing towards the American and French Revolutions the stress is no longer moderately and evenly sustained. The pendulum is swinging from the artfully concealed boundaries, surprises, and pleasing confoundments Pope extolled ("Epistle to Burlington," 50–56) to the "boundless Green" (95) Capability Brown was to make almost a law of the land. The English landscape garden was on its way to becoming indistinguishable from the nature of the Romantic poets into which, A. Bartlett Giamatti remarks, "a man walked to find his better self and, hopefully, to become reconciled with it."[47]

One of the greatest gardens taking shape in the 1750s and 1760s was Stourhead (Wiltshire), the masterpiece of the banking family of Hoare. Since the three principal gardener-owners were separated by several generations in each instance, they span three centuries, making the growth of the garden a continuous index of evolving taste and garden styles, as well as of notions of what constituted the perfect setting for *beatus ille*.

Henry Hoare II (1705–85) determined the basic lines of the lake and surrounding hills, grotto, temples, and bridges that characterize the garden today, despite continued planting and extension for almost two hundred years. Advised by the architects Henry Flitcroft and Owen Campbell, protégés of Richard Boyle, third Earl of Burlington and close associate of William Kent, Henry Hoare conceived the garden as a classical (Claudian) landscape, masses of trees alternating dramatically with open areas, punctuated at strategic points with three picturesque views, all designed to be seen from a height: (1) from the terrace of the house a view across the lake of a fine Pantheon designed after one that recurs in

Claude's pictures, for instance *Coast View of Delos with Aeneas* (National Gallery, London) and *View of Delphi with a Procession* (Rome), of which there is a copy at Stourhead; (2) from the Pantheon a view across the lower end of the lake of the village of Stourton and a Palladian bridge presumably spanning a river flowing through the village but actually masking the end of the lake;[48] and (3) from a hill at the south end of the lake crowned by a Temple of Apollo, after one in Robert Wood's *Ruins of Balbec* (1757), a view of the north end of the lake spanned by a wooden bridge out of Palladio's *Dell'Architettura*, III. The effect sought was classical – an idealized landscape "ordered into sweetness and calm as the appropriate haunts of deities and favoured mortals."[49]

Interestingly, at about the time that Henry Hoare was starting to construct his lake garden along restrained elegiac lines invoking Aeneas and the classical Elysium, another man, Francis Tolson, was extolling in his old-fashioned emblematic book of devotions *Hermathenae* (?1740) a more rhapsodic, and vastly different kind of ancient and mystical, route back to "Eden's fatal Bow'rs" (Emblem xxiii, p. 69). And before he was done Henry Hoare revealed himself to be susceptible to similar urges of the spirit, simultaneously archaic and in the wind in his day. Stourhead was begun by him in the mid 1740s as an antidote to the grief felt at the death of his wife, which left him with three young children. The garden at first reflected the interests of the Burlington circle; but beginning about 1765 there was a pronounced turning away from the Palladian style toward the newer taste in Gothic wildness and Romantic solitude. Buildings added at this time include a rustic Hermitage (1771), and a "medieval" tower dedicated to King Alfred (completed 1772). The latter is situated in the farthest recesses of Six Wells Bottom in sylvan seclusion. Reflective of Henry Hoare's self-conscious fascination with the "eternality" of nature – the "ghostly language of the ancient earth" (*Prelude* [1805], II, 328) which Turner captures in the watercolor *At Stourhead* (British Museum) about 1800 – is his joke in a letter of 30 November 1771 to Henrietta, daughter of his son-in-law Charles Boyle, Lord Dungarvan, about the wood used in constructing the Hermitage and of his urge to "put in to be myself The Hermit."[50] Henry Hoare's allusion to the practice of hiring hermits to decorate grottos, follies, hermitages, and rustic huts has, of course, its contemporary side. Yet, the impulse behind his fanciful thought that a piece of oak, like a relic of the cross, might date back to "the Year of Our Lord 1000" and beyond to Antediluvian times, has for the moment, at least, little to do with his seeking still another instance of the picturesque connotative of philosophical retreat and the contemplative life. Like an undersong, his words give off faint echoes of a less sophisticated time when man and nature lived in harmony. Heard in the facetious manner is the longing to rediscover that moment in the history of mankind. Nor was the garden to be without its "haunts" of wilder imaginative aspect for making this possible. Hoare was busy planting trees in profuse abandon on the hills around the lake; and these sylvan plantations would eventually beckon the meditative wanderer to pensive solitude and occasional unrestrained acts of fancy.

The shift in emphasis from an Elysium of classical balance to an Arcadia of exuberent negligence, which occurred between the time of Bridgeman and of Brown, is vividly depicted in the series of sketches of Stourhead made by C. W. Bampfylde about 1770 and by the Swedish artist-gardener Fredrik Magnus Piper who visited England in 1779,[51] and in the watercolors done by F. Nicholson in 1813–14 – as compared to Rigaud's drawings of Stowe in 1734–36. Whereas the submission of nature to civilized refinement characterizes Rigaud's renderings of Stowe, the fecund promise of genesis animates Bampfylde's, Piper's and Nicholson's pictures. This effect pervades Bampfylde's panoramas, which disclose a Stourhead still in process of being planted. The hill top on which looms the Temple of Apollo has a line of trees outlining its crest; the rest of the slope down to the lake's edge is as yet unplanted. The lake looms immense in the sketches, exaggerated by the tiny scale of men and boats on it. Human presence is sparse and where visible, as with the temples, bridges, and the village of Stourton, is scaled down to the height of the trees and all but lost in their midst. It is a world of nature that is witness to creation. Nine years later in Piper's sketches, despite the landscape having filled more with trees, and the architecture given more prominence, the lake and hills present a pristine world of nature basking in the innocent days following creation.

We are contemporary here with the rage for the South Sea voyages of Captain Cook in the 1770s; with Sir Joshua Reynolds's display at the Royal Academy in 1776 of his full-length portrait of the young Polynesian Omai, who had been brought to England in 1774, depicted standing nobly against a background of palms clothed in his native robes, turban, and tattoo marks; and with John Webber's (1752–93) portrait of the Polynesian princess Poedooa, who was held as hostage on the S.S. *Resolution* for five days in November 1777, and is recorded by Webber, who accompanied Cook on his third expedition, "in her native tropical setting, a newly discovered Eve or Venus, nude to the waist with flowers adorning her hair and a frond-fan in her hand."[52] We are closer amidst the tree-topped hills of Stourhead, despite its Temples to Flora and Apollo and its Pantheon, to this solitary world of primitive man and "Nature's golden infancy"[53] than to the public concourses of Lord Cobham. Stourhead is a paradise vastly different in feel from the West Garden of Stowe designed in the 1720s by Bridgeman (although by the 1770s that garden too had evolved closer to its East Garden counterpart – and hence also to Stourhead).

Switzer had written in 1718 in *Ichnographia Rustica* that in the designing and planting of his country seat, "every Person makes to himself a Kind of a new Creation" (III, iii). Henry Hoare the creator of Stourhead took joy in his handiwork no less than the first Lord Cobham in Stowe, or than Jehovah in Eden. Nor did this divine feeling of creativity prevent him from wandering among the sylvan scenes at times like a new Adam, albeit an Adam often designedly tinged with the melancholy, if not the imperial destiny, of a later Aeneas. On Henry Hoare's tomb in the parish church at Stourhead is inscribed an epitaph attesting to

This far-fam'd Demi-Paradise he form'd:
And, happier still, here learn'd from Heaven to find
A sweeter Eden in a Bounteous Mind.
And priz'd them only as they lead to God.

The after-history of Stourhead's creation is of one family's attempt to find solace in its own perfectly ordered world of nature, consonant with the dynamic changing concept of what constitutes an earthly paradise. Richard Colt Hoare (1758–1838) was deeded the estate by his grandfather Henry in 1783, and he lived there from 1791 onwards. Almost immediately he began planting broad-leaved ornamental trees on the south, west, and east sides of the lake, to offset the unnatural combination, in his opinion, of his grandfather's planting of beech and fir, "Kent's favorite mixture."[54] Of equal importance in an indefinable way was also the urge of his social class to make a garden as appropriate to prelapsarian Eden as flawed *Homo sapiens* could devise and the organic natural world would allow. In the "pleasant soil" of Eden, Milton had written, God "caus'd to grow / All Trees of noblest kind for sight, smell, taste" (*Paradise Lost*, IV, 214, 216–17); and Pope as a follow-up had observed that "the Paradise of God's own planting" justified tree husbandry.[55] The eighteenth-century lordly planters heeded Milton's words and Pope's observation. The goal was a specimen of every kind of tree, "Variety without end" (*Paradise Lost*, VII, 542). Thus did avid sylvan "collecting" prompted by eighteenth-century archetypal (and aesthetic) preoccupations with "elegant variation"[56] merge with nineteenth-century scientific interest in domesticating exotic species, the most spectacular triumph of this sort being Joseph Paxton's success with the giant water lily *Victoria amazonica* in 1849. No doubt Britain's growth as an empire also whetted country squire's and nobleman's appetite alike for a garden reflective of that geopolitical fact. Trees imported from all parts of the world were domesticated in the arboretum at Stourhead. Its mixture of dark conifers and lighter hues of deciduous trees satisfied at once the religio-mythic urge for completeness[57] and the modern scientific aspiration for universality. The unalleviated shade cast by the dense boughs of cedars and cypresses also appealed to the developing taste for gothic gloom and for romantic wilderness. At the same time the evergreen nature of the trees, their eternal sameness as if immune to the seasons, symbolically suited the fancy of those who would replant their country seats into new Edens. One other decision of Colt Hoare's was to lay down a gravel path around the lake between 1792 and 1798, transforming the experience of the garden from a static viewing of three picturesque settings to a movable progress around the lake's margin, with recurrent glimpses of temples and tree-flecked hills. Thus over the decades without pretensions of divine infallibility and without pride of professional rectitude did the prosaic banking family of Hoare restore the old unfallen perfection to a piece of Wiltshire chalk where the southernmost edge of the county's escarpment drops onto the Dorset lowlands to where some three hundred yards west of the house the sudden fall of the land steeply to the valley meets the Stour River, and a spring known by Wiltshire locals as "Paradise coppice."[58]

JOHNES'S HAFOD: AN ELYSIUM AT THE TURN-OF-THE-CENTURY

Thomas Johnes (1748–1816), second cousin to Payne Knight and two years his senior, was one of a circle of young enthusiasts who shared with Payne Knight and Uvedale Price in the closing decades of the century delight in the "foaming stream" of mountain torrents, the "craggy summits," awful precipices, and wild ravines of "great Salvator's mountains" – all that in nature is a continuing visible sign of divine power and promise.[59] Knight and Price put their gardening beliefs into practice on their own estates Downtown and Foxley, which were well-known showplaces of the times; Johnes, however, was to realize most literally their holy writ of domesticating within one's garden paradise the sylvan fastnesses of the mountain sublime.[60]

Johnes's mother, Elizabeth, was the only child and heiress of Richard Knight of Croft Castle, Herefordshire. The Knights were a wealthy family of ironmasters who for three generations from the time of the Commonwealth had engaged in the iron trade at Coalbrookdale, Shropshire, and later at Wolverley, Worcestershire. Johnes's father, also named Thomas, hailed from Cardiganshire, where he owned lands which included the mountain property of Hafod. Through his parents the younger Johnes was thus heir to Croft Castle (which already boasted at least a four-hundred-year history at the time), extensive estates in Herefordshire, and vast tracts of land in West Wales.[61]

After a feckless youth, and a marriage which ended in the tragically early death of his wife two years later, Thomas Johnes in 1783 surprised everyone by going to live at Hafod, drawn irresistibly by the mountainous terrain, which he had visited for the first time only three years earlier. In 1784 he secretly married his first cousin Jane Johnes of Dolecothy, Carmarthenshire, and in 1786 laid the foundation stone of a new house at Hafod, destined to become famous in the last decade of the century as an elegant Gothic fantasy of pointed windows, stone tracery, pinnacles, and crenellations set in a valley amidst some of the wildest and most inaccessible mountains of West Wales.

In a watercolor painted by J. M. W. Turner in 1797 (Lady Lever Art Gallery) there appears an airy two-story stone structure with a towered center bay flanked on each side by a pair of pinnacles followed by broad-spaced double-mullioned gothic windows. The height is accentuated by a dome and by second-story windows, which soar almost half as high again as those of the first floor. For all its impressive size, the building gives off a fragile air of insubstantiality, as if its faint ecclesiastical splendor had materialized overnight and its hold on reality was commensurately tenuous. One-story wings of three bays each terminating in lofty towers (possibly planned by John Nash, later to be the architect of Brighton Pavilion) thrust out from each side of the central structure, imparting to its height a graceful horizontal movement as well as the suggestion of mysterious cloisters behind the walls. To the right of the entrance is attached an octagonal library of Moorish antecedents crowned with a dome and cupola, and decorated with pierced stone work and costly marbles. Turner frames this apparition of Merlin with rank arboreal growth rising out of the bottom edge of the picture, with some branches partly obscuring one wing of the building, as if to emphasize its wild Welsh setting. A "Foaming stream" courses in the foreground, separated from the house by a short stretch of lawn. Immediately behind the house rear the precipitous mountains of Cardiganshire, wreathed with low lying clouds. The painting is a marvelous composition in which the artist's attempt to reconcile the ambivalent vertical and horizontal thrusts of the house strains to maintain itself against a mightier vertical thrust of nature. Overall is invested a fairytale quality of make believe. At any moment one expects the magical palace to vanish from its rude surroundings in a peal of organ music.

In the 1780s Johnes consciously set out to create an Eden in an eight-square-mile area of this mountain fastness. The walled circumference, gardens, and house answered decidedly to his romantic image of paradise, disclosing that there were dim recesses in the late eighteenth-century mind which still answered to the "ghostly language of the ancient earth" (*Prelude* [1805], II, 328). Within this Welsh preserve seemingly untouched by the hand of man since Adam and Eve's fall from grace, he and his new wife determinedly led the "simple" life of shepherd-and-shepherdess then in vogue, not unsimilar to the make-believe of the Prince of Wales and Mrs. Fitzherbert who in these years were practicing like roles in Brighton where the Prince had leased the "superior farmhouse"[62] that would eventually metamorphose into the oriental pleasure palace of Brighton Pavilion. Unlike "Prinny" and his twice-widowed wife, the newly wed Johnes planned their mountain paradise according to the aesthetic principles of their cousin Payne Knight. The site of the house, a long narrow valley through which foamed the Ystwyth River, was eminently suited for a garden which capitalized on the natural beauties of the landscape.

The new enthusiasm of the times for mountain scenery and his closeness to the Knight–Price circle obviously affected Johnes's sense of earthly perfection. His inclination for the precipitate, the irregular, and above all for the "deep romantic chasm which slanted / Down the green hill athwart a cedarn cover" ("Kubla Khan," 12–13),[63] may have also been formed, in part, during his impressionable years growing up at Croft Castle. A short walk from the house to the northeast is a steep, narrow declivity known as Fish Pool Valley, which had probably been landscaped by the 1760s. Planted with mixed deciduous and evergreen trees, it presented an unruly variety of outlines, textures, and colors, which were reflected in the water of a chain of fish ponds along the floor of the chasm. A series of footpaths descended into the valley, weaving back and forth across a stream, to provide views of the ponds, quarry, and grotto. All in all it was an excellent early instance of the kind of picturesque scenery that Knight was to advocate in the 1790s. The end-of-the-century rage for the "sublime irregularities of nature" are succinctly summed up by the artist friend of Blake and cousin of the dramatist Richard Cumberland, the peripatetic George Cumberland, who ticks off its distinctive modes by way of comparison to other Welsh sights. Downtown Castle, Knight's own country seat, "has a delicious woody vale, most tastefully managed; Llangollen is brilliant; the banks of the Conway savagely grand; Barmouth romantically rural; the great Pistill Rhayder is horribly wild; Rhyder Wenol, gay, and gloriously irregular." Combining "the effects of all in one circle" are Hafod and its surrounding mountains.[64]

As Cumberland implies in this allusion to Hafod, Johnes's conception of paradise, while decidedly eclectic, could be called eighteenth-century Miltonic. He laid out miles of ornamental walks leading to natural waterfalls and grottoes. He stretched elegant bridges across ravines and streams to reach a perfect place for a seat or viewing station. To the chagrin of Payne Knight, who was to recommend in 1816 against purchase of the Elgin Marbles, Johnes also had a taste for marble statuary and scattered pieces by his sculptor friend Thomas Banks liberally over the grounds. His gift for the exotic revealed itself in the peacocks that preened themselves on the lawns. As the house and garden adornments indicated Johnes did not mind mixing architectural and historical styles. The remnants of planting of an earlier time were incorporated into the overall design, lending to the garden an air of the eternal in its union of past and present. Appropriately, given the paradisal intentions, he created a real Garden of Eden hidden away in the woods below the house at the end of a shady path near the river. One entered it through a stone portal carved with the figures of Adam and Eve in Coade's cement and dated 1793. It was a flower garden, incongruously following formal designs: "two acres of undulating lawns embroidered with flower-borders and sweet-smelling shrubs" set down in a glade at the foot of a steep, jagged mass of rock soaring several hundred feet above it (*P Paradise*, p. 95). It conformed exactly to what eighteenth-century imaginations nurtured on Milton and weaned on the picturesque conceived as the garden in which first man and woman disported. And George Cumberland, reaching for an analogue to Hafod and its neighborhood, drew on Milton's description of Eden in *Paradise Lost* to capture for his readers how the "steep wilderness" girdling the place suggested the "verdurous wall of Paradise," its "Insuperable highth of loftiest shade" ascending "Shade above shade" into "a woody Theatre" overlooking and enclosing a "rural mound."[65]

Like the good husbandman of classical times, praised by Virgil and Horace and revived by such scientifically motivated, practical-minded horticulturalists as Arthur Young, Johnes set out to turn the alternately boggy and flinty soil of Hafod into an ideal farm. For almost thirty years he never ceased planting trees, as if bent on covering the mountains surrounding Hafod to their peaks with leafy plantations. Between 1795 and 1801 alone he set out two million, sixty-five thousand trees, nearly half of them larches (*P Paradise*, p. 169). He urged the peasants in the vicinity to adopt new farming methods, and set them an example with his own innovations. On the milder slopes and along the river he grazed a large herd of cows. These costly ventures were financed by his selling off his other estates over the years as creditors pushed him for payment. First to go was Croft Castle, then Stanage Park, the old home of his Grandmother Knight, and finally his estates in Cardiganshire. So long as he could afford developing Hafod, where his heart was planted along with the trees and gardens, he remained sanguine, dubbing it the Happy Valley after the ideal abode in *Rasselas*, in celebration of the bucolic peace he enjoyed there.

Like that contemporaneous Welsh shrine to the ideals of friendship and rural retirement, the "Little Paradise" of Plas Newydd created by the famous ladies of Llangollen,[66] Hafod had become a showplace by 1800. A list of the guests, the curious and the serendipitous who visited or stumbled upon it between 1790 and 1810, reads like a *Who's Who* of end-of-the-century England. To name Edward Lord Chancellor Thurlow, Sir Joseph Banks, Samuel Rogers, Thomas Stothard, Francis Chantrey, James Edwards, Henry Fuseli, William Wyndham, Lord John Russell, Robert Fulke Greville, and George Cumberland, not to mention Payne Knight, and Uvedale Price who had built a house at Aberystwyth, can only suggest the wonder with which the intelligentsia of the day made the difficult pilgrimage across the mountains to enjoy for a brief sojourn the exquisite thrill of late eighteenth-century mock-prelapsarian serenity. Visitors are full of the wonders of the place and of the happiness of its inhabitants. Dr. James Anderson, a Scots authority on agriculture, who advised Johnes in his planting, writes Cumberland in 1804:

I have just seen our friend Mr. Johnes, and find him the same and as keen a farmer as ever. He is certainly blessed in possessing as good a disposition and as steady a flow of animal spirits as any human being ever possessed. He talks of Hafod as a paradise, and of his improvements with rapture, as if he had never met with a single disappointment in his life.

(*P Paradise*, p. 171)

Cumberland was so taken with Johnes's paradise that he published *An Attempt to Describe Hafod* (1796), which leads one on a painstaking tour of the gardens inch by inch and plant by plant. From 1800 onwards Johnes received numerous acknowledgements of his services to agriculture and afforestation. And as late as a visit in 1814 the librarian and antiquarian Thomas Dibdin refers to Hafod as Johnes's "paradise blooming in the wild" (*P Paradise*, p. 236). Perhaps the climactic appraisal of Hafod attesting to its far-flung paradigmatic fame belongs to Blake. In the poem *Jerusalem* Johnes is mythicized as "Hereford, ancient Guardian of Wales, whose hands / Builded the mountain palaces of Eden, stupendous works!"[67]

By 1814, however, misfortune had afflicted the house and the Johnes family, if not as yet the garden. In the early morning hours of 13 March 1807 the house burnt to the ground, leaving only the outer walls standing. Still "resolved to inhabit his Eden, although driven out by the flaming minister,"[68] Johnes set to work rebuilding Hafod again; but in the summer of 1811 his beloved daughter and only child Mariamne died at the age of twenty-seven after years of wasting illness, and five years later on 20 April 1816 the "Khan of Hafod" (*P Paradise*, p. 175) himself was dead. After Jane Johnes had buried her husband beside their daughter, she moved to a cottage in Devon where she died in 1833. Hafod was to stand shuttered and uninhabited for the next seventeen years while the gardens slowly went to seed. In 1925 John Summerson described the "Garden of Adam and Eve" as a "nightmare tangle of rhododendrons and fig-trees . . . the portals . . . collapsing and the future of the whole scene . . . dark."[69] The final curtain rang down on the remnants of Johnes's paradise in 1958 when the shell of the house was dynamited. The garden had by then reverted through neglect and lumbering interests to the craggy wilderness that had greeted the young Thomas Johnes when he first came riding up the valley to view his Welsh ancestral properties, and "spell-bound, vowed that here was Paradise" (*P Paradise*, p. 247).

So ended possibly the most single-minded pursuit of Eden in eighteenth-century England.

CAPABILITY BROWN'S LANDSCAPES:
TO "FRESH WOODS AND PASTURES NEW"

The practice of organizing the eighteenth-century garden as a rural paradise rests on the assumption that Edenic and fallen earthly abodes occupy overlapping, synchronous positions. This conflation of eschatological and human mystiques has had a long and varied history. Mircea Eliade argues that man once regularly participated in the mythical beginning of things by way of ritual repetition and the ideology of the eternal return. Western pagan and Christian practices were no exception. The movement of the soul mapped by such Neoplatonists as Plotinus and Porphyry established a pattern irresistible to subsequent generations of Western religious thinkers. Dante toiling round and round Mt. Purgatory in a microcosmic enactment of the *Commedia*'s spiral structure of possession, loss, and recovery as he ascends to paradise is only one of the more celebratory medieval variants on this pattern. Similarly, each worshipper could vicariously follow Jesus in his final hours by making a circuit of the stations of the cross situated around the walls of the church. With Western Europe's emergence from medieval apprehensions of reality to Renaissance modes of thought, church architecture also, after centuries of Gothic *frisson*, again began to emulate the human-centered organization of experience implicit, but not always observed, in ritual repetition. The Gothic church reflected spiritual obsessions not intrinsically circular. The forward movement from nave to altar reproduced symbolically the linear eschatology of the world running from Creation to Second Coming. Furthermore, the columns in nave and transept soaring from heavy piers at floor level upward in ever narrowing forms to the thin point of the spire provided a perfect architectural expression of the medieval desire to dematerialize earthly dross in the celebration of the etherialized heavenly spirit. The tension between the simultaneous upward and inward thrust of walls and columns, and their contrary gravitational pull downward and outward was structurally equivalent to the tension in medieval man between his spiritual and bodily impulses. The configuration of nave and transept resolved this tension. It reminded the worshipper of what was once Christ's supine and crucified state, and of each person's humble participation in the same Passion and Ascension through his voluntary renunciation of the joys of the body. The impulse of the Renaissance, moved by Platonic ideals, was to push man to the center of the cosmos. Encompassing in his anatomical parts the whole of the earthly and the heavenly, he was, in effect, a celestial center (to use Eliade's term) in his own right. The centralizing tendency of the baroque church is a reflection of this new, almost excessive, centripetal concentration of human perspective. The dome occupies a dominant central place over a square edifice. Nor does it take much visual imagination to see such a structure as another analogue to the human figure, this one accentuating the glorious ascendency of the head, as indicative of man's intellectual grasp of religious faith and of his assumption, erect and alive, of the central place in the scheme of things.[70]

The Pazzi Chapel, by Brunelleschi (?1377–1446), in S. Maria Croce (Florence) perfectly embodies the centripetal ideal. It is more than twice as wide as it is long – to be exact, two bays and four Corinthian pilasters wider – with the dome dominating the center of the area. The anthropomorphic effect is to emphasize the vibrant uprightness of the human figure. The usual rhythm of a long nave leading to the altar has been reversed in favor of the contrary, a wide shallow room lit by an overhead dome. In effect the rectangle of the nave has been turned ninety degrees, with the front wall articulated by windows, contrary to the usual clerestory fenestration along the sides of the nave. As a consequence light floods in on the worshipper standing in the middle of the room rather than on God and the altar, which here occupies a recess in the back wall, in partial gloom. On the walls Della Robbia medallions of the twelve Apostles and of the four Evangelists add a decorative punctuation to the man-centeredness of the architectural concept.

Blake was to compile bits and pieces of this visionary man-centered perspective into an extreme description of life as simultaneously a literal and a symbolic enactment of primordial origins. But already before him individuals in his century, following the lead of Milton, were finding that it represented no extreme exercise of mind to experience the eighteenth-century landscape garden as a new scene of human bliss. The Miltonic legacy, with its nostalgia for a divinely perfect abode, was part of the intellectual furniture of the century, revealed not only in the walks of Stowe and Stourhead but also in *Rasselas* (1759) and *Tom Jones* (1749). The first sums up the ambiguity of happiness: the discontent of the human spirit with its lot and yet its compulsive reiteration of the ideal life. We are told that Rasselas will return to Abyssinia (although it is not likely back to the Happy Valley)[71] aware that happiness is neither permanent nor to be taken for granted, still moved nevertheless by the need to seek a life of fulfillment that he knows is unobtainable. Ending on a less disillusioned note, Tom Jones, that exponent of eighteenth-century English values, confirms in his paradigmatic expulsion from home and eventual return to Squire Western's family seat and marriage to Sophia the human confidence that the original rightness of things can be reasserted however east of Eden the exile; and if Tom has not explicitly found paradise he certainly has reached a place contiguous to it – Squire Allworthy's Paradise Hall – where he grew up as a boy.

Corollary to the Miltonic inspired nostalgia for Eden was a penchant, refined almost to singularity, of searching out in the configurations of earth signs of the original garden. Are not Gilpin's indefatigable pilgrims, Callophilus and Polypthon, participants in effect in just such an age-old ritual during their journey to and tour of the varied scenes of Stowe? Complete even to seeing their peregrination, particularly their departure, as an analogue of the original drama enacted in Eden! The harmony of the place elicits from Polyphton the grudging admission that he imagines he has been readmitted for a short spell into Eden. As an analogue of his feelings, he uses Satan's words of admiration (*Paradise Lost*, IX, 103, 114), "in spite of Envy," for newly created earth:[72]

> Terrestrial Heaven——
> With what Delight could I have walk'd thee round.

On a more informal note, the sacred associations for Henry Hoare of the garden at Stourhead are invoked in a letter to his nephew Richard in January 1755: "I hear you have been at Stourd, without the dame, so fear you *saw undelighted all delight* [cf. *Paradise Lost*, IV, 286–324] tho' you trod the enchanting paths of paradise."[73] Thus did the first creator of this Wiltshire Elysium invoke Milton's winsome description of Adam and Eve, in a letter to the man who would marry his daughter and become the father, losing the wife in the process, of the second great developer of the gardens.

How deeply engrained was this habit of mind is illustrated by its persistence not only in contemporary contemplations of Stowe and of Stourhead but also in the calculations – at once economically and religiously oriented – of their privileged gardeners. A Whig aristocrat like Richard Temple, Lord Cobham (1675–1749), was from all accounts a tough, hard-bitten professional soldier and practical politician. Still, his resignation from the Walpole government in 1733 over a matter of moral principle, and his subsequent political exile, coincides with his increased gardening interests at Stowe. In this regard, Vanbrugh's pyramid built in the northwest corner of the gardens in 1724–26, with its inscribed lines celebrating Horatian retirement, was strikingly prescient. The West Garden, completed by the early 1730s, reflects nothing personally unusual to set it apart from other gardens of the time, other than Bridgeman's transitional design which copes brilliantly with a difficult site and with the legacy of unorganized arrangements of predecessors. But the last fifteen years of Cobham's life, coincident with his retirement from government into political opposition, saw a radical evolution of garden design in the new East Garden, where the Elysian Fields and Grecian Valley were being planted; and their layout was determined, it is believed, as much by the genius of Cobham as by the professional architects he employed. His concentrated development of the family acres may not have represented a conscious alternative to the painful existential state of being a discarded part of history-in-the-making. The fact, though, is that Cobham thereafter pursued a dual life at Stowe, combining the Roman ideals of civic virtue, personal honor, and rural retirement with the immediate concerns of fame and party politics. Christopher Hussey wittily encapsulates Cobham in these latter years of his career as a man busy cultivating, besides his garden, that dissident faction of Whigs known as the Boy Patriots or Cobham's Cubs, who sided with the Prince of Wales in the squabbles with the King and Prime Minister.[74] And all these feverish long and short-term goals are given complex symbolic form in the laying out of the Elysian Fields, where are adroitly sited Kent's Temples of Ancient Virtue (copied from the Temple of Vesta at Tivoli) and Modern Virtue (a sham ruin) and his Shrine of British Worthies.[75]

Not just the Cobham enclave of Pelhams, Grenvilles, and Lyttletons, but the Tory circle linked with Pope (Bathurst, Burlington, and Joseph Spence), as well as an assortment of poets, gentry, and aristocrats – Philip Southcote, William Shenstone, Sir John Clerk, second Baronet of Penicuik, the Hoare banking family, and Lord Carlisle at Castle Howard – all managed to juggle prudent estate management and hard-headed involvement in worldly financial and political affairs, with a gardening mania that exulted in the analogue to Adam's and Eve's matinal labors of lopping, pruning, propping, and binding the "wanton growth" of nature (*Paradise Lost*, IX, 210–11). Thus were their lives interiorized, in harmony at once with mythic and temporal processes. The placid rhythm of eternity implied in the *furor hortensis* is exalted in the lines on "Castle Howard" (*c.* 1733) that praise within a Christian frame of reference Lord Carlisle's labors, even as "Time gently glides away," to improve his lands for his progeny – in short, which praise on both ritualistic and practical planes his responsible husbandry of the talents God vouchsafed him. By thus placing the exorbitant cost of estate development within a noble, and even transcendent, set of referents individuals like Lord Carlisle and Viscount Cobham who bridge the seventeenth and eighteenth centuries eased the anxiety of decisions that were otherwise part of the indefinite directionless flow of events. This view of one's place in history of course short cuts the Christian eschatological purview of the world as running from Creation to the Second Coming, by comfortingly realizing that end symbolically in an historical moment otherwise without cosmogonal significance.

The mind that could entertain at once such incompatible ideas lived simultaneously in theological and historical frames of reference. It could see the garden under its stewardship as a new Eden, while holding firmly onto the commonsensical reservation that the landscaped park was only metaphorically Eden *redivivus*. Its capacity for political and religious compromise, for maintaining contradictory beliefs in unresolved tension, gave it a high tolerance for living with multi-purpose situations. Not Pope and Johnson, and their generations, but Coleridge, Wordsworth, Shelley, and kindred souls sought a transcendent historically all-purpose explanation for the mystery of life!

One should not underestimate the degree to which the eighteenth-century mind could juggle supernatural and scientific credulity in the marvelous. That paragon of knowledge Dr. Erasmus Darwin (1731–1802), in his meteorological speculations about winds in Note XXXIII to *The Botanic Garden* (1789–91), can advance the theory that

Though the immediate cause of the destruction or reproduction of great masses of air at certain times, when the wind changes from north to south or from south to north can not yet be ascertained; yet as there appears greater difficulty in accounting for this change of wind for any other known causes, we may still suspect that there exists in the arctic and antarctic circles a BEAR or DRAGON yet unknown to philosophers, which at times suddenly drinks up, and as suddenly at other times vomits out one-fifteenth part of the atmosphere: and hope that this or some future age will learn how to govern and domesticate a monster which might be rendered of such important service to mankind.

At the same time, one should not dismiss the possible change in habit of thought signaled by the contradictory assertiveness and tentativeness of Dr. Darwin's words. One cannot be sure whether he is devising an explanation he means his readers to take literally or symbolically, or both at once. This practice of blurring, and confusing, fact and symbol is particularly noticeable in the late eighteenth-century mind-sets of the first generation of Romantic poets Blake, Coleridge, and Wordsworth, as they strove to make divine sense out of a world rapidly undergoing quantification.

The same duality of attitude in coping with the earthly experience informs a poem like Goldsmith's "The Deserted Village." Complicating the texture of its statement is the poem's uncertain incorporation of a frame of garden reference being pioneered by Capability Brown in the second half of the century.

That the poem resonates with more than socio-cultural nostalgia – that inherent in Goldsmith's estimation of late eighteenth-century rural England is a Christian Edenic *mythos* – is indicated by the allusion of the poetic narrator, as he makes his round of the village, to its "lovely bowers of innocence and ease" (5). Embedded in his words is a matrix of Christian other-worldly expectations that the poem never adequately articulates, although the impulse to do so is there. When the narrator comments early in the poem,

> I still had hopes, my long vexations past,
> Here to return – and die at home at last, (97–98)

he has in mind more than a simple homecoming. In his return to his native village to die, after a lifetime of "wanderings round the world of care" (85), he is also realizing his heavenly home, for the village is an *axis mundi*, mythically a latter-day repetition of original paradise. The idea of this ultimate earthly destination is semantically residual in the diction and emerges in full ironic force when the lines are read with the changing paradisal configuration of the eighteenth-century garden in mind.

The irony lies in the narrator's failure to recognize the gamut of his pessimism. If Goldsmith had been fully conscious of the symbolic resonances of his poetic references he would have seen that "the park's extended bounds" (277) not only doomed the village but translated its self-contained cycle of customs and pastimes into a diffused form unconducive to the patterns of mythic repetition on which the village life had been predicated. For the change in perspective, realized by the forced removal of the village and consequent extension of the prospect visible from the manor house, reflects a change in perception taking place in the 1760s and 1770s.[76]

This shift in visual vocabulary was being explored as early as the 1730s and 1740s at Claremont, Chiswick, and Rousham, especially, and above all at Stowe where much of the east gardens and specifically the Elysian Fields had already been laid out, probably by William Kent, and the Grecian Valley by Capability Brown. Brown had left his position as head gardener at Stowe about 1750 to strike out on his own, quickly establishing himself as the dominant landscape architect in England in the second half of the century.[77] Whether he was responsible for the change in visual expectations, or was an expression of it, is one of those cultural mysteries always baffling scholars; more certain is that the undirected visual experience of his broad reaches of park inevitably diluted the radial route's ritual language of repetition. At Blenheim – as also at Heveningham (Suffolk), Holkham (Norfolk), Longleat (Wiltshire), Temple Newsam (Yorkshire), Petworth (Sussex), Weston Park (Shropshire), and a host of other places – Brown went beyond the modest desire of Thomas Howard at Corby Castle, who wished for a limited three-dimensional Eden in which he could stroll, like Adam and Eve of yore, in the cool of the day. With a visual vocabulary purged of picturesque and emblematical contrivances – of columns and temples dedicated to heathen deities and heroes – he transformed the precipitous but small scale of England's "hills and valleys" and unpretentious "pleasant pastures" into vast landscapes sublime.[78] He elongated the expanses of lawn and reaches of water, extended the curves of hill and belts and clumps of trees, until the Edenic grove had become a celestial plain. In the slow maturation of the trees that he planted by the thousands for future generations are incorporated temporal measures that, like his opening of space, function on a scale unconfined to human rhythms. In an unanticipated way, which must have caused smiles in the sanctums of heaven, Brown's efforts to satisfy the desires of his clients to transform their country grounds into earthly paradises led to conceptions of such impersonal scale and in such quiet hues of green unalleviated by other color that human intimacy was banished.

An added irony for our reading of "The Deserted Village" is that a likely candidate for the identification of Auburn is Nuneham Courtenay, Oxfordshire, which was removed by the first Earl Harcourt to a new site in approximately 1761–64 to improve the view from his house.[79] The newer diffused visual vocabulary thus initiated by the first earl was completed by the second, who brought in Brown to do it; and the resultant grounds were eventually celebrated by the poet William Whitehead under the title "The Late Improvements" (1787). It is the historical view of man as reflected in the new landscape that Goldsmith is ostensibly condemning in his objection to the demise of the ancient village; yet Goldsmith has contaminated the point of view of the poem with this historical perspective. "The Deserted Village" is hesitant to commit itself unreservedly to the symbolic recitation that is its professed frame of reference. Instead it digresses into economic and social denunciation of the wealthy, in short, assumes the historical perspective of the object of its criticism. "The Deserted Village" is an early instance of the gathering gloom felt more on the pulse than articulated in the mind that was to envelop the nineteenth century in a darkening night of disappointment and lowered expectations. In a sense the eulogist of the deserted village is more pessimistic than the elegist who had sung his age's epitaph some twenty-five years earlier in the country churchyard. Goldsmith's poem laments not just the end of a village, and a time-honored way of life, but unintentionally also the cessation of a way of thinking, an archetypal habit of mind increasingly unfashionable to the autonomous, historically oriented mind. It is no wonder that the poem's rhetorical structure and point of view is indeterminate, at once a paradigmatic exercise, a public and ritualistic utterance of mythic disposition with a *dramatis persona* (dimly re-enacted in the sacred purlieus of the eighteenth-century garden); and an existential gesture, a personal and historical remembrance of a landscape with internalized topography (subtly subsumed in the undifferentiated Brownian landscape).[80] In effect, "The Deserted Village" straddles multiple means of coming to terms with experience: the first is hallowed by ritualistic practice it is reluctant to give up, and the second articulated by subjective needs it is timid about asserting. Goldsmith would have been easier of mind in the nineteenth century with its acceptance of expressive modes of statement, or better yet in our century, which recognizes that no one form of discourse is inevitable or necessary.[81]

The landscape garden of Kent and Burlington, of Cobham, and Hoare, and their circle of friends, at mid-century, was ordinarily a circumferenced Eden, its vistas and perspectives terminating with temples, rotundas, mausoleums, and architectural and sculptural reminders of divine virtues and human follies. It contained a complete and ordered world comprehended by the social interaction and associative turns of mind of its participants. The Brownian garden, on the other hand, at its sublimest swept unobstructed to the horizon, with the implication that the same scene continued beyond the belt of trees and the immediate ring of hills. Not only was the point of view unprescribed, but the perspective was visually incomplete. One does not expect to encounter Adam and Eve in these parks husbanding, pruning the "growing plants," and tending the flowers (*PL*, IV, 438). One wanders in them, but one is never quite on terms of intimacy with their green world. They do not offer the participative space that Rigaud depicted Stowe in 1734 as providing. Nor do they offer room for the Arcadian drama of human life that one finds invariably quickening the landscapes of Claude Lorrain and Nicolas Poussin. No snake can be imagined to inhabit Brown's landscape, as it does Poussin's *Landscape with a Man Killed by a Snake* (*c.* 1648, National Gallery, London). Kew Gardens, contrariwise, for all its acreage brings man into intimacy with the close eclectic order of its groves, flower beds, vistas, "sunny spots of greenery" ("Kubla Khan," II), and reaches of the Thames, making it a true *public* garden. Lawn parties want a wall, a grove of trees or clump of shrubbery, a house against which to define the human presence. Brown's imagination thrived on an austerer range of visual forms and hues, whose exposed plains offer little incentive for social pastimes, any more than do common fields. Deer, cows, and sheep still figure as part of the landscape, but people are diminished and isolated by the bald immensities of his parks. Brown has translated the latter-day Eden of nature-perfected into a pure paradisal abstraction.

One anonymous contemporary lauded Brown as the representative "great Artist," whose "barren tracts with every charm illumes, / At his command a new Creation blooms."[82] Using less inflated language, one can say that Brown helped sensitize the first generation of Romantics to the beauties of less structured scenery outside the garden and to the presence of the divine in the slope of field and in the hues of pasture and woods, as well as in the precipitous heights of mountain and depths of sky. Brown created landscapes from the outset of his career that move toward the Romantic ideal of a world which knows no distinction between the natural and the domesticated, the profane and the sublime. The ultimate Brownian enthusiast evolved into the Wordsworthian Romantic who cut across fields in spontaneous exploration of meadows and dells which were valued for their own intrinsic holiness. Thus was the *hortus conclusus* steadily extended until it consisted of the whole goodly universe, its Edenic identification scarcely distinguishable from the actual countryside.

For a brief fifty years the English garden functioned symbolically, and literally, as a paradise; but it was a *hortus conclusus* without Angel of Annunciation, Blessed Madonna, or immortal child. It is a new Eden in which are installed latter-day Adams and Eves in knee breeches and afternoon gown, who fear no divine exclusionary restrictions.

PART II

Romantic Paradisal Bowers, Valleys, and Islands

One good gift has the fatal apple given, –
Your *reason*: – let it not be overswayed
By tyrannous threats to force you into faith
'Gainst all external sense and inward feeling:
Think and endure, – and form an inner world
In your own bosom – where the outward fails;
So shall you nearer be the spiritual
Nature, and war triumphant with your own.
Byron, Cain, II (1821)

But there are wanderers o'er Eternity,
Whose bark drives on and on, and anchor'd ne'er shall be.
Byron, Childe Harold 3 (1816–17)

But foolish man foregoes his proper bliss,
Ev'n as his first progenitor, and quits,
Though placed in paradise, (for earth has still
Some traces of her youthful beauty left)
Substantial happiness for transient joy.
William Cowper, The Task, III (1785)

Paradise, and groves
Elysian, Fortunate Fields – like those of old
Sought in the Atlantic Main – why should they be
A history only of departed things,
Or a mere fiction of what never was?
For the discerning intellect of Man,
When wedded to this goodly universe
In love and holy passion, shall find these
A simple produce of the common day.
Wordsworth, Prospectus to The Recluse (1800)

He heard, borne on the wind, the articulate voice
Of God; and Angels to his sight appeared
Crowning the glorious hills of paradise;
Or through the groves gliding like morning mist
Enkindled by the sun. He sate – and talked
With winged Messengers; who daily brought
To his small island in the ethereal deep
Tidings of joy and love.
Wordsworth, The Excursion, IV (1814)

2

Blake and the Unending Dialectic of Earth and Eden

GARDENING had quickened the imaginations and energies of a small class of people, along with some poets and artists, for almost the whole of the eighteenth century. Landscape gardens, whose blissful acres were part of a newly sanctified and democratized earth, seemed to provide them with a halfway Eden. By the first decades of the nineteenth century the rage for improvement of country-house landscapes had become institutionalized enough to instigate the reaction of laughter. The obsession with do-it-yourself home-Edens now puzzled observers, and participants, as often as not – when it was not offending defenders of tradition and frequenters of nature alike. Crabbe speaks for the prosaic majority when he lets the wealthy landowner George in *Tales of the Hall* (1819) dare voice a profane counter-view to the lordly one of the previous hundred years.

> 'Brother,' said Richard, 'do I hear aright?
> Does the land truly give so much delight?'
> 'So says my bailiff: sometimes I have tried
> To catch the joy, but nature has denied;
> It will not be – the mind has had a store
> Laid up for life, and will admit no more:
> Worn out in trials, and about to die,
> In vain to these we for amusement fly;
> We farm, we garden, we our poor employ,
> And much command, though little we enjoy;
> . . .
> Man takes his body to a country seat,
> But minds, dear Richard, have their own retreat;
> Oft when the feet are pacing o'er the green
> The mind is gone where never grass was seen,
> And never thinks of hill, or vale, or plain,
> Till want of rest creates a sense of pain,
> That calls that wandering mind, and brings it home again.
>
> (IV, "Adventures of Richard," 92–101, 118–24)

Others besides Crabbe were having fun at the expense of the gardenists. Thomas Love Peacock savages Humphry Repton as Marmaduke Milestone in *Headlong Hall* (1816), as does Jane Austen in *Mansfield Park*, where she quizzes the disruption in the name of "improvement" of the estate, which is for her a symbol of moral order and social tradition to be preserved.[1]

The idea of nature and of the garden had undergone too many shifts in shape in a brief century to sustain conviction. Thomas Burnet's *Theory of the Earth* (1684–90) attributed nature's ruined and chaotic appearance to the Fall. In the second half of the seventeenth century Charles Cotton had written of the walled formal gardens of Chatsworth: "This is *Paradise*, which seated stands / In midst of *Deserts*, and of barren *Sands*."[2] As depicted in the engraving in Kip's *Views* Chatworth's cultivated and contained grounds contrast strikingly with the untidy natural world of the Peak country surrounding it. One hundred years later it is the surrounding country not the walled geometrical garden being hailed as paradise. Which introduced new problems, not least being the incompatibility of earth's mundane actuality with the spiritual metaphor the Romantic poets wished to make of it. Their linking of metaphors with images of the world, and then identifying those mental images with actuality – as in Coleridge's famous religiously tinged definition of the symbol in *The Statesman's Manual* (1816): "the translucence of the Eternal through and in the Temporal. It always partakes of the Reality which it renders intelligible; and while it enunciates the whole, abides itself as a living part in that Unity, of which it is representative" (*CC*, VI, 30) – left them mistaking their interiorized paradisal worlds for the exterior one they moved about in. Other less imaginatively agile individuals simply turned away from nature when the whole goodly earth failed to live up to expectations, to nourish states of awe, to comfort spiritually, and to sustain economically. They sought for representations of Eden in the unconventional panaceas and products of an increasingly industrialized world, or like brother George in *Tales of the Hall* turned back to an older time-tested Christian solace.

Preoccupying the times were problems which made a mockery of the retirement and *beatus ille* dreams of the past. Malthus's dire predictions about population seemed to render Arcadia beyond the reach of most. More to the immediate point, bread prices and protectionist Corn Laws as often as not were turning rural life into an obscenity. The problem called for statistics and Coleridge was urging his friend Tom Poole in 1800 to put his knowledge of costs, income, grain production, and rural suffering at the service of the nation – and not incidentally at the service of Coleridge who used the matter supplied by Poole to write a series of essays on scarcity, monopoly, and farmers for the *Morning Post*. Almost three decades later, in *Colloquies on the Progress and Prospects of Society* (1829), Southey was to question the nation's easy utilitarian optimism over the burgeoning Gross National Product, aiming at its unexamined trust in gross averages the indignation of a poet who saw no reason for national self-congratulation so long as individuals suffered from poverty and the level of living conditions continued to sink for so many. In short, the age was calling forth new sensibilities, nurtured contradictorily by revolutionary ardor and *fin de siècle* pessimism, democratic winds and humanitarian sympathies, industrial disruption and *Naturphilosophie*. The most ardent of the new generations turned their backs on aristocratic parks of unchanging paradise with their "skulking, sly haw-haw[s]" separating not only park from unimproved nature without but also the favored few from the vast ranks of society.[3]

Such a one is Blake. Bent on shocking the righteous – "The Elect" he satirically names them a few years later in *Milton* (7:1; E,99) – by identifying himself (and by analogy all men) with Jesus Christ, and in turn with the unfallen Adam, the thirty-three year old William Blake prophesies in 1790 at the beginning of *The Marriage of Heaven and Hell* (3; E,34):[4] "Now is the dominion of Edom, & the return of Adam into Paradise."

For all his revolutionary social outrage and his Londoner's fondness for rural fields Blake did not covet as his model of paradise the aristocratic gardens of the eighteenth century. Nor did he find attractive the prevalent sentiment of associating paradise with unspoiled nature, so succinctly stated by John Locke apropos of the new trans-Atlantic lands: "In the beginning all the world was America." Blake eventually equated England anagogically with Palestine, and London with Jerusalem, in the poem *Jerusalem*, but never was that equation meant with the same simple literalness that Locke's was. The only way Blake could entertain the idea of paradise was to strip it of its orthodox geographical limitations in favor of its human dimensions. Thus its physical whereabouts, whether city bound or country free, were irrelevant, since its existence, or non-existence, was determined by daily acts of cognizance. In Blakean terms, any person, depending on his perception of life, "builds a Heaven in Hells despair" or contrariwise "builds a Hell in Heavens despite" ("The Clod & the Pebble," E,19). The crucial factor is that paradise has no existence separate from the "moments & Minutes & Hours / And days & Months & Years & Ages & Periods" built by the sons of Los (*M*, 28:44–45; E,125). Hence, unlike the orthodox garden of Adam and Eve, Blake's paradise pervades all the days of one's life.

Arguing against what he believed was Joshua Reynolds's acceptance of sensation as the source of our knowledge, Blake internalizes human perception, using a garden image that slyly repudiates at the furthest reaches of his epistemological argument the fatal garden of Hebraic–Christian tradition:

Reynolds Thinks that Man Learns all that he Knows I say on the Contrary That Man Brings All that he has or Can have Into the World with him. Man is Born Like a Garden ready Planted & Sown. This World is too poor to produce one Seed.
(Annotations to Sir Joshua Reynolds, E,645–46)

Only thus is the human form divine equivalent to an ideal garden. With these sentiments Blake put the dying eighteenth and the aborning nineteenth centuries on notice that the idea of paradise would increasingly for the generations of the Romantics be staked out in the interior world of man even as its narrow Biblical boundaries were being resurveyed to encompass the firmament and the starry heavens of the universe.

The story he tells of mankind's fall into generation, and eventual rise into regeneration, is by now familiar to all but the most casual reader of the late prophecies – and the casual reader is an alien species seldom found wandering amidst the tangled thickets of their mythopoeic territory. In the Lambeth poems – *The Books of Urizen, Ahania*, and *Los, The Song of Los*, and *Europe* (*c.* 1794–95) – Blake concentrated on formulating a cosmic myth of creation and a history of mankind in time, which in part parodies Milton's *Paradise Lost*, by interpreting creation as a Fall from eternal intellectual and spiritual unity into corporeal disunity. It is basically a story of the Eternal Urizen's (reason) defection and usurpation of power from before time down to the present moment and of Los's (imagination) recurrent struggle to arrest the fragmentation, and to right the imbalances, brought on by Urizen's excesses. As my summary hints, these poems attempt to set forth a psychodrama of human error as much as a mythomachy of eternal misjudgment.

In the late prophecies – *The Four Zoas, Milton*, and *Jerusalem* (*c.* 1797–1818) – the human perspective becomes pronounced, as does also the prophetic effort to formulate a way man can break the iron cycles of history and return to his original paradisal unity. Albion, who stands for collective humanity, and when whole is the same as Jesus and the Divine Family of man, has lain in stony sleep for ages because the disaffected parts of his being have fallen into self-love and strife. This disunity Blake chooses for the most part to dramatize in metaphorical terms of sexual jealousy and domination. The principals in the seemingly endless round of treachery and betrayal are the Eternals Urizen, Urthona (imagination as embodied in the figure of Los), Luvah (emotion and energy), and Tharmas (bodily instincts and drives), and their myriad sons, daughters, and wives or female emanations. Albion's sleep, or "Eternal Death" (*J*, 4:2; E,145), is what we commonly know as life: mortal, sexually generative, and bound by the senses. The states of being it encompasses are called by various temporal and spatial names, the most frequent being Ulro and Generation. The "Eternal Life" to which Blake would awaken Albion, and all mankind, is contrariwise one of limitless imaginative expansion and multiple perspectives. The young Blake had hoped to find this Golden world in the guilt-free exercise of erotic energy, symbolized by Orc, and most unambiguously proclaimed in *America* (1793), *The Marriage of Heaven and Hell* (1790–93), and *Visions of the Daughters of Albion* (1793).[5] In terms of Blake's *mythos* of place, this sexual bliss, which includes conjugal affection and motherly love, becomes Beulah. The highest aspiration of the imaginative self, however, is located in the spiritual love of Eden, the gateway to eternal vision and the ultimate realization of gestalt wholeness of being.

Blake's is the most explicit and thoroughgoing effort of all the Romantics to devise a mythopoetics explaining how mortal and eternal life, and by extension all the "fallen" earth, not just a favored portion, are one and the same. Inwardness and centrality, love and self-annihilation, are key concepts in the reticulation of this Blakean paradise. The turbulent repetitiveness of the "story" in the prophetic books has dismayed readers for almost two centuries. It has become gradually apparent, however, that the eddying concentration on the "minute

particulars" of a moment, of a human relationship, or of an attitude, in the poems
central to the mature utterance of Blake's myth is intended to divert the reader's
attention away from the simple linear concern for what happens next. Blake's aim
was to draw the reader into the expanding center of each word, which becomes for
him "a World in a Grain of Sand" ("Auguries of Innocence," E,481).[6] The same
intent applies for each design, which serves the subsidiary function of further
impeding the progression of the reader down the printed page. And in our
exploration of the dimensions of the representative Eternals we are forced to
traverse the infinite recesses of our inner selves. Fiercely iconoclastic, Blake was
bent on dismissing eighteenth-century cartography of time and place, the
mechanized space of Lockian psychology, which encloses man within his own
body, "till he sees all things thro' narrow chinks of his cavern" (*MHH*, 14; E,39)
and "the Aerial Void" (*M*, 35:52; E,135) of Newtonian physics, "if space it may
be calld," which loses man in a "tedious . . . void boundless" (*MHH*, 19, 17;
E,40–41). Blake deplored both as indefinite and abstract, and insisted on
substituting true globes with forever expansive, forever inclusive centers.[7] There
the "Expanding Eyes of Man behold the depths of wondrous worlds" (*FZ*,
138:25; E,391) dating back to the infinite spaces of First Man. There, in "the
Auricular Nerves of Human life," is found the ancient and ever new "Earth of
Eden" (*FZ*, 4:1–2; E,297).

Forms of containment were anathema to Blake, the enclosed circle and arching
cover generally representing repression and confinement. One thinks of *The
Ancient of Days* (1794), the frontispiece to *Europe*, with its great rendering of
Urizen's heroic but futile effort to put boundaries on the cosmos with a puny pair
of compasses. Leaning out of the blood red ball of the sun to probe the dark chaos
(to his mind) of the universe, he is the archetype of our imprisoned minds, slaves
to misconceptions of time and space and to conformity of thought and action. On
the human and scientific levels, Blake makes the same statement in his color print
of *Newton* (1795), which depicts that savant at the bottom of the sea of time and
space, bent over like Urizen in rapt concentration on the lines he is drawing with a
compass. Here, Newton is portrayed as one of those "Sons of Los" who gives "to
airy nothing a name and a habitation / Delightful! with bounds to the Infinite"
(*M*, 28:3–4; E,124).

Hence in Blake's cosmology the circumscribed point and the expansive center
carry variant meanings. A human center can be either closed or open. Fallen
nature is a closed center, best symbolized by Satan, whose "Great Selfhood" has
"a white Dot" at its center, "from which branches out / A Circle in continual
gyrations" to become "a Heart" (*J*, 29:17–20; E,173). As a parody of Locke's
mathematical reduction of eternity to remembered duration,[8] Satan's selfish heart
is a bounded circle of white – of undefined nothingness. As happened with tragic
irony to Urizen in *The Book of Urizen*, Satan in the effort to restrict his selfhood to
perceptible bounds has realized the opposite: indefiniteness. Just as Locke in
conceiving of eternity as an "immensity" of segments of duration (1, 278–79) can
only end with unlimited segments that will never add up to eternity, so Satan as

errant man is using the wrong means. One can no more base the quantitative knowledge of infinity and eternity on sensation and memory (I, 293) than one can define a circumference by retracting it to an exquisite center of white.

The "human form divine" becomes an open center of continuous expansion through the activity of the imagination. In contrast to the fallen form's white dot Blake develops the image of the red globule of blood as the basis of eternity and infinity. "Every Time less than a pulsation of the artery / Is equal in its period & value to Six Thousand Years," he writes,

> For in this Period the Poets Work is Done: and all the Great
> Events of Time start forth & are concievd in such a Period
> Within a Moment: a Pulsation of the Artery.
>
> (*M*, 28:62–63, 29:1–3; E,126)

In the intervals between moments of measured time, the particular and the eternal can mingle, because these intervals can only be perceived by the imagination. With such moments of expanding vision can Los build eternity in time. Infinity is similarly constructed out of perceived space:

> And every Space that a Man views around his dwelling-place:
> Standing on his own roof, or in his garden on a mount
> Of twenty-five cubits in height, such space is his Universe;
> And on its verge the Sun rises & Sets . . .
> . . .
> The Microscope knows not of this nor the Telescope. they alter
> The ratio of the Spectators Organs but leave Objects untouchd
> For every Space larger than a red Globule of Mans blood.
> Is visionary: and is created by the Hammer of Los
> And every Space smaller than a Globule of Mans blood. open
> Into Eternity of which this vegetable Earth is but a shadow:
> The red Globule is the unwearied Sun by Los created . . .
>
> (*M*, 29:5–8, 17–23; E,126)

It has been argued that Blake's epistemology represents in the instance of the globule of blood, a reaction to Locke's materialism, which cannot conceive of the infinite other than in observed measurable terms. "Blood, to the naked eye, appears all red," Locke had written, "but by a good microscope . . . shows only some few globules of red . . . and how these red globules would appear, if glasses could be found that could yet magnify them a thousand . . . times more, is uncertain."[9] For Blake, individuals are potential centers of timelessness and depthlessness, because they comprise not only globules of blood but also the interstices between, which resist the telescope but not the visionary. "I . . . feel a World within / Opening its gates" (*FZ*, VIIa, 86:7–8; E,354) Los the artist furiously informs the unloving Spectre of Enitharmon, and apropos of this interior world, Blake wrote in *Jerusalem*, "there is no Limit of Expansion! there is no Limit of Translucence. / In the bosom of Man . . . from eternity to eternity" (42:35–36; E,187). In the human body only the imagination can develop "bounds to the Infinite putting off the Indefinite / Into most holy forms of Thought" (*M*,

28:4–5; E,124). Space as we conventionally define it, enclosed by walls, bounded by the horizon, or measured by motion, is replaced with an expansive world of individual perspective, a depthless cosmic circle, viewed coinstantaneously from multiple vantage points within the immediate world of our senses and without the inherited world of our cultural assumptions.

The activity of the imagination, with its creation of eye opening art, and its acknowledgement of the viewer's uniqueness, offers each human a route to infinite and eternal forms of delight. Love, with its corollary virtues of self-annihilation and forgiveness, makes available an additional route. Thus, in *Milton*, Ololon who is Milton's six-fold emanation as the composite of his three wives and three daughters abandons her aloof virginal being amidst the Divine Family to unite in self-annihilation with Milton, who with a like selflessness has left his immortal abode to enter "Eternal Death" once again. Their mutually redemptive actions insure Milton's casting off his objective rationalizing self, correcting the errors he had perpetuated in his poems, especially the negating injustice done to Satan, and with that apocalyptic deed releasing mankind from mental and spiritual bondage. Similarly, in *Jerusalem*, only when Los has a change of heart watching "Every Minute Particular" of Albion harden into a darkened and closed center (cf. 19:25–39; 45:2–38; E,163,192) and in pity forgives Albion's willfulness does he begin to reverse Albion's contraction and, as with Jesus's love, break "thro' the Central Zones of Death & Hell" to open up to view "Eternity in Time & Space" (75:21–22; E,229).

The point to keep in mind is that self-annihilation represents an alternative to the hated doctrine of atonement. In demanding of every individual the exercise of selfless love, the principle of self-annihilation brings the sacred hierarchy of the Christian mystery within the grasp of every person. It reduces holy exclusivity to the scale of humanity. This is the gift the Blakean (not the Christian) Jesus presents to the selfhood of Albion at the end of *Jerusalem*, as prelude to Albion's following suit and thereby casting off his selfhood, reuniting his sundered parts Urizen, Urthona, Luvah, and Tharmas, and rejoining his "lovely Emanation" Jerusalem in apocalyptic return to a joyous "Eternal Day" in Paradise (96–97; E,253–54).

Blake does not leave us in doubt as to the means by which humans may reclaim paradise. Nor does he equivocate on where we are to find this paradise. With great inventiveness, in a variety of forms, Blake sets forth his vision that the full cycle of existence, including the higher paradisal joy, is not to be found in translation from a lower to an upper world, nor in transference from a temporal to an eternal abode; rather it is located within the readily accessible and continuously expansive parameters of one's globuled body and one's unfettered imagination. "Awake! . . . expand! / I am in you and you in me, mutual love divine" (*J*, 4:6–7; E,145), Jesus is heard exhorting an obdurate and suspicious Albion in the opening lines of *Jerusalem*. If Albion would learn this simple lesson, the most succinct of Christian teachings, then "Fibres of love from man to man" (as opposed to the vegetative imprisoning fibres of the Polypus) would unite all parts of "Albion's pleasant land" (4:8; E,145). Paradise can thus originate wherever a person chances to be at any given moment. In place and time, the Blakean "Golden Age," as Hazard Adams has noted, "is no more a past period than it is a future period. It is simply the timeless reality."[10]

So Blake depicts it in the watercolor *The River of Life* (*c.* 1800–05, Tate Gallery), as a joyous, yet strangely disjunctive, confluence of mythical and mortal life. Permanence and transience both paradoxically characterize the scene: a river flows through a settlement of houses, which are not quite human habitations, as its inhabitants are not quite mortal, but look rather like stock other-worldly figures who might have just stepped forth from either the Hesperides, Heaven, or a suburban Arcadia. An adult (presumably Jesus) and two children float down river toward a sun haloed by angels and loving couples. An angel glides above the mortals, while on both sides of them additional angels pipe away like shepherds strayed out of pastoral Sicily. Along the shore individuals stroll before their houses. One plucks fruit from a tree. A complex mood of serenity and exaltation, and state of becoming and being, pervade the scene.

As one might deduce from the incongruencies of the scene in *The River of Life* Blake found it easier to describe the route back to paradise than to envision paradise itself out of the *disjecta membra* of his reading and his observations of an erring humanity. Indeed, throughout his productive life his eyes looked more steadily on the mundane world than on its renovated millennial counterpart. Almost from first to last the din of gynecological warfare, the vertiginous vortex of history, and the outcries of a self-victimizing society fill his pages verbally and pictorially – a Satanic Polypus of life that crowds out the peaceful paradisal dawns infrequently glimpsed through its tangled growth.[11] *Jerusalem* may open and close with illustrations (the three-piece sequence of Frontispiece, Title page, and Plate 4; and the concluding Plates 97, 99, and 100) offering the reader hope of an optimistic conclusion to earthly woes; but the predominant motif, as Erdman suggests, is "Albion's fall and entrapment."[12] Blake promises us Jerusalem the city of paradise but mostly shows us a baleful garden of experience. Interesting in this regard is Blake's early metamorphosis of the rose garden and Blessed Virgin of the *hortus conclusus* into a church cemetery where "Priests in black gowns" walk their rounds "binding with briars, my joys & desires" ("The Garden of Love," 11–12; E,26). And the Blake *Concordance* shows that *night* is alluded to much more often than *day*, and *death* figures as one of Blake's most frequently used words, often in the sense of what we know as everyday life.

Blake's preoccupation with paradise obsessively encompasses the *agon* of the fallen, those who cannot, or will not, change their ways. This peculiarity of perspective sets up again and again an ambiguity which readers have found difficult to decipher. An instance is the question of whether *Albion rose* is celebrating liberation or exhibiting error.[13] Another is *The Book of Thel*, which has elicited diametrically opposed interpretations argued with equal plausibility. It has been proposed that the poem is primarily (1) about being born, (2) about

1   Blake, *The River of Life*

growing up, and (3) about dying, with Thel's flight (in Mitchell's words) read as
"either a satire on Thel's adolescent inability to come to terms with life or a
panegyric on her good sense in fleeing this rough world for a realm of spirituality."[14] When one gets to the late prophecies such ambiguities multiply. Plate 25
of *Jerusalem* shows Albion with three women (Tirzah, Vala, and Rahab, his
daughters, become equally his mothers Tirzah, Vala, and Rahab and the three
Fates) either contributing to his demise or comforting him back to life. We can
read the picture both ways, Mitchell confesses: "as a . . . giving and sustaining [of]
life as well as a taking [of] it away."[15] Similarly, the great Plate 42 of *Milton*, which
depicts a man and woman lying in partial embrace on a rock, with an eagle
hovering overhead, has been interpreted as both a sexual aftermath and a spiritual
prelude. Erdman suggests that the two people are lovers lapsed into post-coital
tristesse, which "may also imply a reluctance to respond to the Last Trumpet's call

49

2   Blake, *Milton*, plate 42

to mortal things, rise from the 'Couch of dread repose' (44:32–33), and 'go forth
to the Great Harvest & Vintage' (50:1) in which nations and sexes . . . are
consumed to arise as One in Jesus (49:10–21)." Susan Fox, contrariwise, sees
them as Albion and Jerusalem (Adam and Eve; any fallen man and woman)
awakening to a reunion of contraries in eternity where male–female relationships
are sexually de-emphasized.[16]

Blake's grasp of reality is necessarily based on a dialectic between temporal and
eternal. His intention is usually to demonstrate, as in *The Marriage of Heaven and
Hell*, their equivalence, but the palpable reality of the fallen world had a way of
insinuating itself into his envisionment of a spiritual world. As a result the paradise
on earth that Blake claims is there awaiting all mortals as their birthright turns out
to be, with the exception of the expanded imaginative perception of the holy
oneness of things, remarkably like the mundane world already so familiar to us. It
essentially embraces quotidian life raised to a psychic wholeness of self and to a
loving union with one's sexual contrary. Thus, while Ololon's descent from Eden
to merge with "Milton's shadow as a Dove upon the stormy Sea" and become a
"Moony Ark" in the culminating action of *Milton* (42:6–7; E,142) partakes of
mythic dimensions, Catherine Blake's comparable gesture of self-annihilation
occurs at a historical moment in time and place on earth. She steps out of her
cottage, though "sick with fatigue" (36:32; E,136), into the Felpham garden to
stand in loving relation beside William as his "sweet Shadow of Delight" (42:28;
E,142).

In the gestalt wholeness implied by this simple event – in a previous action
Milton had entered William's left foot – Blake marshals the resources of his
language to resonate (in Susan Fox's words) with "apocalyptic significance." The
scene presents she adds in explanation, "a vision that comprehends not only their
familiar manifestations in time, but also their eternal reality." Standing as one in
the garden, Catherine and William are not only "the incarnation of Milton and
Ololon" but "also the inspired imagination united with its product, Los and
Enitharmon rising together over England."[17] What Blake wrote was:

> Immediately the Lark mounted with a loud trill from Felphams Vale
> And the Wild Thyme from Wimbledons green & impurpled Hills
> And Los & Enitharmon rose over the Hills of Surrey
> Their clouds roll over London with a south wind, soft Oothoon
> Pants in the Vales of Lambeth weeping oer her Human Harvest
> Los listens to the Cry of the Poor Man: his Cloud
> Over London in volume terrific, low bended in anger.
>
> Rintrah & Palamabron view the Human Harvest beneath
> Their Wine-presses & Barns stand open; the Ovens are prepar'd
> The Waggons ready: terrific Lions & Tygers sport & play
> All Animals upon the Earth, are prepard in all their strength
> To go forth to the Great Harvest & Vintage of the Nations
>
> (42:29–39; 43:1; E,142–43)

According to Fox the lines herald "The end of time"[18] and the coming of eternity.

Yet, in plain terms, the reference to Los and Enitharmon simply represents Blake's announcement, not without its forlorn prophetic hope, that he is returning "After . . . three years slumber on the banks of the Ocean" (*J*, 3; E,143) to resume in London his life of arduous intellectual warfare against the closed hearts and minds of his fellow citizens and the repressive institutions of his society. And, in fact, if we discount its mythological machinery the language describing the apocalypse alludes to an ordinary early nineteenth-century suburban backyard and Sussex countryside. "Almost literal" are Susan Fox's words. "We stand in a rural garden, where a lark is no angel nor a flower a mighty demon, where a storm is a natural event however threatening, where even presses and barns and ovens and wagons are part of the landscape."[19]

For a moment's "pulsation of the artery" in the garden at Felpham Blake experienced eternity – but only for "A moment," and then his "Soul returnd into its mortal state / To Resurrection & Judgment in the Vegetable Body" (42:26–27; E,142). As a consequence, the "Great Harvest & Vintage" stands only poised to begin. There is no millennium as yet, only Blake's imaginative premonition, to date, that England awaits a renovation of time. With ready wit Erdman comments, "the word 'Finis' on Plate 50 marks the end of the poem, not of Time."[20] The regenerated nude Milton of Plates 1 and 16, after having plunged through the fires of self-annihilating wrath (Plate 1) and come out on the sunny side of night (Plate 16), continues to stride toward the expectant unclothed Ololon of Plate 50, without reaching her in this poem.

Eden (or Eternity, or Paradise), according to S. Foster Damon, "partakes of Eternity, but . . . also partakes of this world."[21] Without seeming to be aware that she is making essentially the same point, a puzzled Susan Fox describes the Eden of *Milton* as "a highly ambiguous state." It incorporates error and truth, imagination and dogma. Hostility and anger are not absent from it; nor is it wholly free of measured time. And it is vulnerable to damage and corruption.[22] Blake's Eden is necessarily so because it geographically and physically consists of the temporal world and all its limited strife prone forms; but it also conceptually and potentially is the eternal world realizable by a shift in perspective. The universe does not change, our view of it changes – although in such perceptual alteration is radically implied an alteration of form and substance as well.

If Eden appears in *Milton* indecipherable at times from the fallen world it is because that poem is Blake's most personal expression of his constant struggle to inhabit Eden while constrained to live in eighteenth-century England. In its narrative Blake most valiantly strives to contain at once both temporal and eternal states of existence. It is difficult to convey an inner-directed paradise in terms of everyday pursuits, when the visible evidence all about one is that society pursues as usual its profane way. Blake may in his own imagination bridge the dialectical gap between Eden and the generative world, and as an artist may show the "[Dear] Reader"[23] how he too can manage the imaginative perception; but as an *honest* artist he cannot claim the millennium as yet when readers in Wimbledon and Lambeth can look out their windows and observe the same old streets, and the same wrongs and injustices, still there.

Blake–Los, the eternal artist, is forced to work with the substances of a humanity forever lapsing into error. The artistic knitting together of mankind's fallen parts – the "ongoing interpenetration of eternity and time" as promised in the concluding lines of *Jerusalem* (99:1–4; E,256)[24] – is a never-ending task. The consciousness of eternity in time depends not on a one-time born-again experience but on repeated self-annihilation, since the stereotypes of thought are constantly reasserting themselves. *Jerusalem* culminates a forty-year struggle of Blake to spell out in the illuminated pages of his prophecies how Fourfold Man can free himself of the spectres of "the Tree of Good & Evil," the "cruel heel" of thought control, the "Desolation" of poverty, and the wars of nations (98:47–53; E,256); and how in as many "beautiful Paradises" as there are people they may converse

> together in Visionary forms dramatic which bright
> Redounded from their Tongues in thunderous majesty, in Visions
> In new Expanses, creating exemplars of Memory and of Intellect
> Creating Space, Creating Time according to the wonders Divine
> Of Human Imagination. (98:25, 28–32; E,255)

In *Milton* Blake restricted his hopes to the rededication of his and Catherine's labors to bring about "the Great Harvest & Vintage of the Nations" (*M*, 43:1; E,143). When he moved on to *Jerusalem* the millennium he envisioned at its conclusion is as positive a prediction as he ever permitted himself to contemplate about the large arenas of society and of nations. But it is not a reality he pictures there, only a "vision" of what he knew was possible if man would break free of the shackles of selfhood and, like Albion, discover within himself "the Humanity Divine" (*J*, 96:37; E,253). With artistic integrity Blake tags the imagined gathering together of Albion's scattered and divisive parts, and his reunion with the awakened Jerusalem, modestly as "the Vision of Albion" (97:5; E,254).

More than one commentator has remarked upon the difficulty of locating the climax of *Jerusalem* – the turning point when Albion is motivated to awake from his stony death-sleep. Mitchell's effort to determine the moment of peripeteia left him with the sum total of Minute Particulars of error set forth by all the episodes in the poem, forcing him to conclude that "By all the measures of cause and effect" *Jerusalem* could have ended with the opening confrontation of Christ and Albion as Antichrist, or it "could have gone on indefinitely like *Tristram Shandy*."[25] In a sense, then, as Mitchell is at pains to prove, the poem is a compendium of the fallen world into which the reader can enter at will. And Blake concludes it after one hundred plates because, in part, he is an artist in search of a symbolic ordering of reality, and because, in part, he is a prophet who has allowed himself the luxury of willing an apocalyptic triumph of the Divine Vision, and its sublimations of time in the consciousness of eternity.

Even here, though, Blake's final statement – the illustrated Plate 100 – retreats to the realistic recognition that Los's hammer and anvil, and Enitharmon's loom, must never cease the redemptive shaping and weaving of time and space. In the service of this Sisyphean task, Los is pictured on the left hurrying toward the open "Night of Death" (97:3; E,254), carrying the globed sun of illumination on his shoulder like a hod and casting light onto the serpent temple at his feet. On the right Enitharmon similarly is busy drawing from a spindle thread which drapes down from a moon ark to a second serpent temple reaching out from the Druidic circle of trilithons in the center, which is Golgonooza the eternal city of art representative of the dialectical union of the profane and the divine that is always abuilding in time and space.[26]

Given the Biblical signification of Eden as a garden, and given Blake's use of Eden as a symbol of mankind's achievement of psychic and sexual harmony, it is inevitable that he at times identifies a garden with the human body. His analogy of man to a garden, in the margin of his copy of Reynolds's *Discourses*, comes to mind. "Every Generated Body in its inward form," he asserts elsewhere, "Is a garden of delight & a building of magnificence" (*M*, 26:31–32; E,122). Although

3   Blake, *Jerusalem*, plate 100

the Hebraic–Christian myth of the Garden of Eden does not accord with his version of the Fall, Blake is sufficiently a man of his time that he continues to respond to the strong connotations still associated with a garden. Although paradise is no longer for him entirely a place of physical dimensions, a garden sticks in his London bred imagination as a powerful metaphor for the expansive center of every person's life. When Los's sons befriend Albion's children, they "provide houses & gardens." In the next line Blake transforms this literal beneficence into a metaphor for the benefactor and beneficiary alike:

> And every Human Vegetated Form in its inward recesses
> Is a house of Ple[as]antness & a garden of delight. (*J*, 73:49–51; E,227)

With even stronger paradisal overtones, Mary is said to emanate "into gardens & palaces upon / Euphrates" (*J*, 61:30–31; E,210) when released from psychological bondage by Joseph's overcoming his doubts of her fidelity.

During the years of rejection following his return to London from Felpham, however, despair often filled his days and nights, making it difficult for him to keep the divine vision. His was a "Wisdom . . . sold in the desolate market where none come to buy" (*FZ*, 35:14; E,318); and he had to learn to accept this neglect. He strove to make the bleak London streets of his everyday life correspondent to an inner visionary world of experience. But for the ordinary prosaic person organic energy in its promethean aspiration is not limitless. Human faculties are quickly gagged by circular reduction, and forced into repetitions of a nonparadisal order. Such defines the symbolic action of "The Mental Traveller," where the vortex of human history is ever subject to the entropic cycle of nature, and the repetitive assumptions of science and religion. Blake makes this point over and over from *Songs of Innocence and of Experience* to *Jerusalem*. The human form divine contains within itself a garden whose "trees bring forth sweet Extacy"; but without constant self-annihilating vision, the trees "shed [their] fruit" ("The Mental Traveller," 89, 100) before it can be harvested.

In *The Four Zoas* Blake optimistically sets Los to the "Wonders of labour" of building Golgonooza, until its domes are energetically piled "pillars high":

> terrific in the nether heavens for beneath
> Was opend new heavens & a new Earth beneath & within
> Threefold within the brain within the heart within the loins.
>
> (87:6–10; E,354)

The sensibility directing these words retains its optimism, despite the recognition that Los continues to be "Filled with doubts in self accusation" when he beholds "the fruit / Of Urizens Mysterious tree" (*FZ*, 87:14–15; E,354). When Blake adapted this material to Book 1 of *Jerusalem*, however, his view of human nature had darkened. He had become ruefully aware of the limitations of Beulah, and of the human sensorium. Los's efforts to raise Golgonooza are now a "terrible eternal labour!" (12:24; E,154), to which he must exhort Albion's sons: "Go on, builders in hope: tho Jerusalem wanders far away, / Without the gate of Los: among the dark Satanic wheels" (12:43–44; E,154).

Given Blake's London residency for most of the years of his life, it is not surprising, yet still prescient of him, as the climactic regeneration of the children of Albion approaches in *Jerusalem*, that Blake thought of the garden metaphor in tandem with the important architectural symbols of house, palace, and city; for Golgonooza the holy City of Art, which gives way to Eden the Heavenly City of Love, will reappear in the mid-nineteenth century, not without its own historically engendered trilithons, as a desperate aesthetic substitute for the no longer imaginable Arcadia in an increasingly industrialized and urbanized age. Blake foreshadows these changes when he replaces the pastoral metaphor of husbandman and wine press in *The Four Zoas* with the urban metaphor of builder and brick kilns in *Jerusalem*. He had turned away in 1803 from Felpham's Vale after three years of troubled sojourn in "the sweetest spot on Earth," where "Heaven [had] open[ed] . . . on all sides of golden Gates,"[27] to live and work again in "Babylon on Euphrates," amidst the smoke and din of London's "furnaces of affliction" (*M*, 38:20; E,138), there to follow his destiny, and increasingly the destiny of the century, to weave "bowers of delight on the current of infant Thames" (*J*, 83:50; E,239) by ever building and rebuilding the walls and roots of Jerusalem's city out of the materials of art. At Blake's death "the Universal Brotherhood of Eden" (*FZ*, 3:5; E,297) was no closer to realization than it had been in 1790 when he had announced in *The Marriage of Heaven and Hell* its imminence. Yet, his city-bred temperament and his election to live out his life in London is readily prefigurative of the symbolic centrality of the city as paradise and the fact that the interior paradise must be fashioned among, if not out of, the factories and faceless rows of houses of England, or abandoned at last as a lost dream of man.

3

Coleridge and the Enchantments of Earthly Paradise

To solve both private and public problems, Coleridge characteristically fell back upon the "purus Metaphysicus." Like the other Romantic poets, however, he was constrained at times to adopt strategies for confronting reality that were multiform, drawing indiscriminately on psychology, myth, theology, as well as metaphysics. Always, though, the object of Coleridge's concern was spiritual and aesthetic, the wedding of man's soul, as well as of his mind, to "this goodly universe / In love and holy passion" (to use the apt words of Wordsworth in the closing lines of *Home at Grasmere*, MS. D, 806–07, 810–11), and the giving of artistic form to "the spousal verse / Of this great consummation" through the reduction of "multitude to unity" and "succession to an instant" (*Biographia Literaria*, ch. 15).

One of the most insistent forms this myth of integration took in the Romantic period was a harking back to paradise, to a time when man lived in a golden age of harmony with himself, his fellow man, and God. Coleridge was a sophisticated heir of a tradition stretching in English back to the Renaissance and in Latin and Greek back almost to the beginnings of western culture. And in that tradition the earthly paradise is identified with a *genius loci* where man and nature occupied a magic, expressive space, and formed a whole mythically associated with a garden.[1] For Coleridge, as two hundred years earlier for Shakespeare, England's "valleys, fair as Eden's bowers" ("Ode to the Departing Year," 123), provided this secluded and enclosed holy place, "this other Eden, demi-paradise" (*Richard II*, II, i). In part, Coleridge's awe for his "Mother Isle" has its patriotic side, with his country in a war of survival against a rapacious France. His praise of the sanctified island, in "Fears in Solitude" (1798), originates in such sentiments:

> O native Britain! O my Mother Isle!
> How shouldst thou prove aught else but dear and holy
> To me, who from thy lakes and mountain-hills,
> Thy clouds, thy quiet dales, thy rocks and seas,
> Have drunk in all my intellectual life,
> All sweet sensations, all ennobling thoughts,
> All adoration of the God in nature,
> All lovely and all honourable things,
> Whatever makes this mortal spirit feel
> The joy and greatness of its future being?

57

> There lives nor form nor feeling in my soul
> Unborrowed from my country! O divine
> And beauteous island! thou hast been my sole
> And most magnificent temple, in the which
> I walk with awe, and sing my stately songs,
> Loving the God that made me!   (182–97)

At other times his soul, dilating with paradisal fervor, soared abroad, escaping England's shores. When he gazed on a sunset over the ocean, all seemed

> Less gross than bodily; and of such hues
> As veil the Almighty Spirit, when yet he makes
> Spirits perceive his presence.   ("This Lime-tree Bower," 41–43)

And there in the empyrean sublime his soul momentarily took up its paradisal abode.

Toward the conclusion of her monumental two-volume history of the theme of the Happy Man in seventeenth- and eighteenth-century English poetry, Maren-Sofie Røstvig summarizes the transformations that had occurred to the classical conception of golden groves and the Christian conception of Eden, and to the concomitant dimensions of space and place. By the end of the first quarter of the eighteenth century, she says, space had

become the new *hortus conclusus* of the meditating Christian. What had begun in the seventeenth century as a belief in a small, charmed circle inside a world pervaded by death and corruption, was carried over into the eighteenth century as an ever widening sphere of perfection. After the seventeenth-century garden came the open landscape of the early eighteenth century, and, hard upon the heels of this event, the whole terrestrial scene and, finally, space itself. By 1728 the belief had triumphed that *all* was perfect, and the process of extending the limits of the landscape of retirement could go no further. The magic grove of the Hortulan Saint had become an 'undistinguish'd void' penetrated by a 'universal smile.'[2]

The traditional view of paradise as a garden enclave had restricted Eden historically to moments at the beginning and end of time and geographically to a narrow plot of ground. Residual in Romantic definitions of the space–time continuum was the notion of an extended Eden, which not only included the whole earth, but incorporated the cosmos, and which was realizable in the here and now. "The earth is all before me" (*Prelude*, I, 15), Wordsworth exults in a reversal of Milton's view of Adam and Eve's exile from Eden. Not the wilderness as it struck first man but an all-encompassing paradise, so the terrestrial world stretching away to the horizon appeared to Wordsworth's eyes:

> Beauty – a living Presence of the earth,
> Surpassing the most fair ideal Forms
> Which Craft of delicate Spirits hath composed
> From earth's materials – waits upon my steps,
> . . . Paradise, and groves
> Elysian, Fortunate Fields . . . why should they be
> A history only of departed things,
> Or a mere fiction of what never was?

For the discerning intellect of Man . . . shall find these
A simple produce of the common day.

(*Home at Grasmere*, MS. D, 795–808)

The extended Eden, both terrestrially and cosmically, was a millennial possibility that Coleridge sought both poetically and philosophically. Yet, by neither route was he able to realize unalloyed paradisal bliss. Despite his Romantic proclivity to identify "a new Earth and new Heaven" ("Dejection," 69) with the spirit genius lurking in every "green and silent spot, amid the hills" ("Fears in Solitude," 1) and in every "roaring dell, o'erwooded, narrow, deep" ("This Lime-tree Bower," 10), Coleridge like Milton's Satan looked longingly on the verdant terrestrial scene of Eden but hesitated to enter and claim it as his birthright. As for the larger world beyond the firmament, despite his intellectual ache "to behold and know something *great* – something *one & indivisible*," he could not entirely rid his mind of the suspicion that, in a sense, in his internalizing of paradise, he was counterfeiting infinity.[3] Then there was, he knew, the insuperable logistics of internalizing in ideal form the messy world external to one. Coleridge was logician enough to recognize the arbitrariness of conceptualizing a landscape of the senses as paradisal, although in his Highgate years (1816–34) as his thoughts revolved ever more exclusively about religious matters and the welfare of his own soul, he was content to entertain such solipsistic comforts rather than face a reality imperfect and disjunctive. Whether Coleridge's reservations as regards paradise are also characteristic of his contemporaries is problematical. What is evident, though, is that as the age "progressed" wearily into the first decades of the nineteenth century faced with the Napoleonic juggernaut year after year, the advent of leafy paradise in the public consciousness retreated back into the myths of the past. From our perspective in time, his personal hesitancies seem to prefigure the public disillusionment of the Victorians, looking out on the brick wastes of their cities. Paradise was no longer attainable simply by stepping into some rural bower or by imagining a poetical (read symbolic and personal) version of it.

In the last quarter of the century, then, at least some heirs to the legacy of cosmic perfection and of cosmic voyages such as that on which Akenside takes the reader in *The Pleasures of Imagination* found the bequest from their ancestors less than an enrichment of their lives. One problem was that the "universal smile" permeating space added up to less a plenum than a spiritual vacuum. It can be said with some accuracy that the first generation of Romantics expended much intellectual energy in extricating the mind from their embryo existential situation – in re-uniting lived duration with eternity, *locus mundus* with infinity, and time with space. "If I do not greatly delude myself," the irrepressible Coleridge not yet thirty informs Tom Poole in a letter of 16 March 1801,

I have not only completely extricated the notions of Time and Space; but have overthrown the doctrine of Association, as taught by Hartley, and with it all the irreligious metaphysics of modern Infidels – especially, the doctrine of Necessity. This I have *done*; but I trust, that I am about to do more – namely, that I shall be able to evolve all the five senses, that is, to deduce them from *one sense*, & to state their growth, & the causes of their difference – & in this evolvement to solve the process of Life & Consciousness.   (*CL*, ii, 706)

This follows by one month a February letter in which he had proudly cited his being in deep philosophic pursuit of the subject: "Change of Ministry interests *me* not – I turn at times half reluctantly from Leibnitz or Kant even to read a smoking new newspaper" (*CL*, ii, 676).

That was 1801. Interestingly, back in 1797–98 Coleridge had enjoyed for a brief year or so "by way of his poetry" leaps of imagination which freed him from those isolated instants of sensation without discernible connectives, instants to which the psychology of his day otherwise condemned him. And one of his insights in those years is the ultimate derivation of all diversity of phenomena, all exponential forms, including such comprehensive categories as time and space, from an elemental and active Power self-divisible into perceptible contrary forces. It would be another fifteen years before he could begin to define this philosophy of nature in formal terms; but "Frost at Midnight" contains an early poetic expression of his intuitions of a dynamic (as opposed to empirical/associationist) resolution of "the process of Life & Consciousness."

At the start of the poem, Coleridge is vexed by the calm, "its strange / And extreme silentness" (9–10). In a real sense, physically as well as mentally, he is isolated from the other inhabitants of his house and from the "numberless goings-on of life" (12) in the village and beyond. Confined not only by the four walls of his room but also by the limited horizon of his irritable thoughts, he remains imaginatively blind and deaf (in "this hush of nature," 17) to the invisible creative operation of the frost. By the end of the poem, in the famous and oft-quoted final stanza, his understanding has expanded to comprehend that the imperceptible processes of the "secret ministry of frost" (72), of the gentle breathings of his child Hartley, and of the meditation of his mind are parts of the same single creative process of life, participants in the original divine act that continues inexhaustibly. He arrives at this insight by connecting his lonely boyhood at Christ's Hospital, where "pent 'mid cloisters dim, / [He] saw nought lovely but the sky and stars" (52–53), to the far different childhood he envisions for Hartley who shall "wander like a breeze / By lakes and sandy shores, beneath the crags / Of ancient mountain, and beneath the clouds" (54–56). With these spatial and temporal projections of his memorial and prophetic imagination, Coleridge breaks out of his sterile confinement-to-isolated-moments, the "vacancies / And momentary pauses" of his thought (46–47), in which he finds himself trapped at the beginning of the poem; and breaking out he communes not only with an observable world of nature, of summer and winter, icicles, owls, and apple trees, but also with the "numberless goings-on of life" by which these objects come into being, as well as with past and future through the conjoinment of generations. In the interface of two childhoods in Coleridge (his own and his son's), two kinds of time interlock: the poet's ruminative sense of human time, past and future, comes into synchrony with eternal time, without loss – indeed with extension – of grounding in the spatial boundaries of two places and two persons. It is a unity comprehending all seasons, all generations, and all distances between heaven and earth, both mental and actual, that is realized in the final lines of the poem when Coleridge imagines Hartley's future in language descriptive of the present winter scene outside his cottage. Its multi-faceted polar configurations of inner–outer, past–future, time–space, summer–winter, creative–created, light–sound receive concentrated expression in the image of the formative icicle "Quietly shining to the quiet Moon" (74).

Synesthetic fusion of light and sound is one of Coleridge's most persistent conceptual forms for conveying his vision of "the one Life within us and abroad." References to this union appear everywhere in his writings, in his intimate notebook efforts to come to terms with his life as well as in his attempts to formulate a philosophy of nature. The disjunction of light and sound established the figurative polarities of his psychic life in such poems as "Dejection: An Ode" (1802) and "To William Wordsworth" (1807); and the fusion of their properties symbolized his refusal to accept a relativistic knowledge tied to sense data, such as the description of the universe provided by science.

That Coleridge was responsive, however, to the imperatives of the new empirical models of reality is discernible even at subliminal levels of his thought. He was painfully aware of how one's susceptibility to events keeps forcing one to break out of a fixed perspective on things to a relative view that takes into account the possibility that when we change any unit in a complex of parts we create a new set of relationships. The use of multiple perspectives to the events of the wondrous voyage related in "The Ancient Mariner" – the Wedding Guest's, the old mariner's, the marginal glossist's, and finally the minstrel narrator's – is an aesthetic acknowledgement by Coleridge of an existential situation of which he is philosophically only half conscious. A similar multiplicity of view-point is intrinsic to the historical and visionary versions of Xanadu presented in "Kubla Khan." But Coleridge refused to give his whole-hearted philosophical allegiance to this limited and relativistic sensory world. All his life he struggled to formulate an absolute and holistic version of reality. He does not deny the Newtonian universe, he impatiently dismisses it for mistaking material effects for ontological explanations, in short, for not getting at the means by which the universe operates. Between the great years of bardic vision (1796–98) and the equally great years of metaphysical conception (1815–19), Coleridge reaches for a metascientific world in which clock time and paced-off space of the phenomenal scene yield to a plenum of elemental creative energies that find their primal and ideal source in God.[4] His preoccupation with the problem is revealed in a remarkable series of moon-and-skyscapes he records in his notebooks in the autumn and winter of 1803.

One of the most illuminating is recorded on "Wednesday Morning, 20 minutes past 2 o'clock. November 2nd. 1803."[5]

The Voice of the Greta, and the Cock-crowing: the Voice seems to grow, like a Flower on or about the water beyond the Bridge, while the Cock crowing is nowhere particular, it is at any place I imagine & do not distinctly see. A most remarkable Sky! The Moon, now waned to a perfect Ostrich's Egg, hangs over our House almost – only so much beyond it, garden-ward that I can see it, holding my Head out of the smaller Study window. The Sky is covered with whitish, & with dingy *Cloudage*, thin dingiest Scud close under the moon & one side of it moving, all else moveless: but there are two great Banks of Blue Sky— the one stretching over our House, — away toward Castlerigg, & this is speckled & blotched with white Cloud – the other hangs over the road . . . this is unspeckled, all blue – 3 Stars in it / more in the former Break – all unmoving. The water leaden white, even as the grey gleam of Water is in latest Twilight. – Now while I have been writing this & gazing between whiles (it is 40 M. past Two) the Break over the road is swallowed up, & the Stars gone, the Break over the House is narrowed into a rude Circle, & on the edge of its circumference one very bright Star – see! already the white mass thinning at its edge *fights* with its Brilliance – see! It has bedimmed it – & now it is gone – & the Moon is gone. The Cock-crowing too has ceased. The Greta sounds on, for ever. But I hear only the Ticking of my Watch, in the Pen-place of my Writing Desk, & the far lower note of the noise of the Fire – perpetual, yet seeming uncertain / it is the low voice of quiet change, of Destruction doing its work by little & little. (*CN*, I, 1635)

Coleridge is clearly intrigued here by the polarities of motion–stasis, light–dark, and sound–silence exhibited in nature – by what at first appears to be an anomaly of "cloudage" moving in a sky otherwise dominated by motionlessness, an observation which is disputed even as he watches by two breaks of blue sky closing. Equally fascinating to Coleridge is the luminescent tug-of-war between the dingy white scud of cloud, echoed in the leaden white of the river, and the brilliant light of moon and stars. And even as he is concentrating on these spatial phenomena, there sounds persistently on the periphery of his consciousness the constant ("for ever") voice of the river in conjunction with the localized and temporal crow of the cock, and as undersong of both (but unobserved) the persistent ticking of his watch. For a few brief moments of total absorption in the scene, Coleridge experiences the synchronization of eternal and chronometrical times. But as the stars fade behind the cloud and the moon disappears behind the house, the cock-crowing also ceases, leaving him aware for the first time since his vigil began of the noise of the fire in the grate, "the low voice of quiet . . . Destruction doing its work by little & little."

Several of Coleridge's observations here foreshadow his subsequent development of a dynamic philosophy of nature. Empirically, he remarks that the constant alterations of light in the sky have aural analogues in the terrestrial notes of change; hypothetically, he ascertains a vital union of light and sound, which is paradoxically revealed in the measurable motion of heavenly objects in space and in the recordable passage of earthly intervals of time. (The parallel of leaden-white color in river and cloud, while not contradictory of subsequent theorizing, does not prove to be a fruitful observation.) Equal in significance to his linking of the separate sounds of watch, cock, and fire to the chiaroscuro of moon and stars is his effort to isolate not only a permanence of form and essence in the skyscape but also to discern a continuous process in the natural landscape. He longs to discern a causal succession leading from observation of earthly and meteorological fact to apprehension of cosmic design and its divine intentions. A dozen years later, in the conclusion (ch. 24) to *Biographia Literaria*, he will write an explicit confession of his hope that in temporal events he can glimpse intimations of eternity:

The sense of Before and After becomes both intelligible and intellectual when, and *only* when, we contemplate the succession in the relations of Cause and Effect, which like the two poles of the magnet manifest the being and unity of the one power by relative opposites, and give, as it were, a substratum of permanence, of identity, and therefore of reality, to the shadowy flux of Time. It is Eternity revealing itself in the phenomena of Time: and the perception and acknowledgement of the proportionality and appropriateness of the Present to the Past, prove to the afflicted Soul, that it has not yet been deprived of the sight of God.   (*BL*, II, 234)

In 1803, Coleridge has an intimation that the voice of the Greta, as opposed to the ticking of his watch, has provided him with just such a nexus between mundane and ideal worlds.

Almost twenty years after the icicle and moon lines of "Frost at Midnight" his conceptualization of such light and sound concatenations are given their most memorable poetic phrasing in the 1816–17 addition to "The Eolian Harp":[6]

> O! the one Life within us and abroad,
> Which meets all motion and becomes its soul,
> A light in sound, a sound-like power in light,
> Rhythm in all thought, and joyance everywhere –
> Methinks, it should have been impossible
> Not to love all things in a world so fill'd;
> Where the breeze warbles, and the mute still air
> Is Music slumbering on her instrument.   (26–33)

The "one Life" lines, written at a time when Coleridge had just completed the *Biographia Literaria*, are an instance of his successful transmutation of philosophical thought into poetic expression; for embedded in the lines is a well defined religio-scientific world picture, in which the divine act of creation through the interpenetration and synthesis of the primary powers of light and gravity continuously generates and gives rise to all properties of matter, all forms and degrees, of the phenomenal world. In a brilliant exegesis of the "one Life" passage, M. H. Abrams[7] shows that the conception of life propounded there derives from Jacob Boehme's *The Aurora*, Friedrich Schelling's *Naturphilosophie*, and Humphry Davy's chemical–electrical theories – all of which Coleridge had managed by 1816–17 to integrate into a metaphysical confirmation of his brave claims made in 1801 to Poole of having extricated the notions of time and space from Hartleian determinism.

In any formulation of the basic premises of Coleridge's intellectual system, however, one must go beyond the poetic density of "The Eolian Harp" and the metaphysical shorthand of *Biographia Literaria*. As with such earlier cosmological speculators as Johann Kepler (1571–1630) and Henry More (1614–87), Coleridge in his eclectic search after truth about the universe is intent on assimilating a metaphysical–theological paradigm to a quantitative–scientific universe, on fitting a Christian schema to the cosmic model of his day. Each man offered a metaphysic based on historically earlier speculations, but carefully accommodated

to new scientific data; and each plumbed for a mathematical harmony underlying, and in causal relationship to, the world of the senses. The problem for
these men, as likewise for Ralph Cudworth (1617–88), Isaac Barrow (1630–
77), and Descartes (1596–1650), was where to locate God and how to define
spirit in relation to matter. While stopping short of complete identification of God
with space, More repeatedly, albeit uneasily, looks upon space as an immense and
omnipresent potentiality of the divine essence, if not actually identical with God's
presence.

Like More, Coleridge sees the terrestrial world as a spatially defined
materialization of the "Unitrine omnipresence" of God.[8] That is, he sees space as
a metaphysical independent entity, the ground of an infinite God whose existence
beyond the world involves space. Uneasily aware like another Cambridge
Platonist, Isaac Barrow, that God's "continued life before the creation of things in
motion involved time,"[9] Coleridge does not rule time out of his considerations;
but he has a tendency to associate it with the particular and the phenomenal (it is
what he feels on his pulse), while reserving the ideal and transcendent to space. By
mid-1818, in notebook and letters, Coleridge was pushing toward conceptualization of a Deity whose "Unitrine" essence is more than actuality and yet in whose
omnipresent powers originates the forces of light and gravitation that are the
source of the phenomenal world. In this seamless triadic development from the
ineluctable to the mundane, paradise logically follows as an ever-present possibility of the earth we tread and the space we occupy. Thus, space rather than time
occupies the most important place in Coleridge's theogony. Still, their exact
relationship worried him and he was forever trying to fix it in various typically
Coleridgean formulations of contraries and triads. In one such formulation, time
is seen to be concomitant with the willed act of the individual, and space with that
of the Divine Will which is the ground of all acts. In this counterpoise of a
personalized time into a transcendent space, Coleridge chose to emphasize the
Logos, the substance of the word, in God's command, "Let there be Light" –
hence the space through which the light was suffused – rather than the act of
utterance, as had Jacob Boehme, when sound, hence time, would be primary.

Coleridge's ontological concern with the relative functions of time and space is
everywhere evident in his attempts to formulate a philosophy of nature which, in
Abrams's words, "is a sustained evangel."[10] With almost breathless inclusiveness
he pushes beyond Kant's regulative disposition of the categories, identifying
gravitation and light as "the symbola generalissima of all physical Science." By
making them "common measures each of the other," he deduces from them "the
Genesis of Length, Breadth, and Depth, and any number of related triplicities:
attraction–repulsion–extension, magnetism–electricity–galvanism." From these
equations it is only a step to the experiments of Sir Humphry Davy (1778–1829)
and further analogies in confirmation of the ladder of creation "per descensum"
from the divine Unitrine presence to the lowest material form. Hence also
Coleridge's admiration for Davy, the one contemporary chemist who, he believed,
was most likely to prove the "mutual penetration & intus-susception" of physical
and divine energies in "the natura rerum – i.e. the birth of things" (*CL*, IV, 760–

61) – until disappointment in Davy's acceptance of Dalton's atomic theory separated them philosophically.

Coleridge was trying to restate an older quantitative definition of time–space in new organic terms, and to link the divine nature of eternity–infinity to the transitory earth. At times, in his profound effort to reduce the facts of empirical observation and the facts of mind to the one "visible organismus of the whole *silent* or *elementary* life of nature,"[11] as in *The Theory of Life* (c. 1816) and in his Royal Society lecture of 1825 "On the *Prometheus* of Aeschylus," he resorted to a geometric shorthand that can appear unworthy of his thoughts. Yet, when he engaged in a game of correspondences, as he often did in the last twenty years of his life, he had serious ends in sight. The movement of mind from the natural scene to the symbolized universe in Appendix C of *The Statesman's Manual* (1816) is yet another of the many instances of his constant desire to realize a world of values sustained by a world of phenomena. Through his study window he sees the sun shine on the landscape. In the communion of sun and vegetation, "each in its own cast" and "all as co-existing in the unity of a higher form, the Crown and Completion of the Earthly, and the Mediator of a new and heavenly series," he conjectures, is to be found "the record and chronicle of her [Nature's] ministerial acts, and inchase[d] the vast unfolded volume of the earth with the hieroglyphics of her history."[12] By way of such contemplation of the spiritual oneness of the universe did Coleridge entertain hopes of locating and surveying the earthly paradise, a demi-paradise he might know cognitively and convert into his own through the intellectual experience of his system-making.

There was, unfortunately for Coleridge, however, a dark underside to his willed philosophy of belief in the once infinite, now quantified, distances of the heavens, which he desperately strove to respiritualize, an underside of self-misgiving that was always castrating his imaginative desire to bring "the whole soul of man into activity" (*BL*, ch. 14). If Coleridge could give lodging in his mind and in his *Logosophical* theory to the far reaches of space, he was unable in a lifetime of effort to accord its "Phantoms of sublimity" (*CN*, I, 791) the same warm hospitality in his heart and in his poetical practice. On the pulses of his sensibility space was less a reassuring plenum and repository of divine extension than an infinite unbounded landscape, "Barren and soundless as the measuring sands" ("Limbo," 16). It is negation, the "darkness, and blackness, and . . . empty space," which Cain yearns for as surcease from this life ("The Wanderings of Cain," 40–41). It is the terrifying emptiness of the "wide wide sea" ("The Ancient Mariner," 233), according to the gloss, that led the guilt-ridden solitary figure of the Ancient Mariner to project onto the moon and stars a sociable yearning for his "own natural home." Similarly, in "Constancy to an Ideal Object" when Coleridge imagines a cottage inhabited by himself alone, unshared, he thinks of

> a becalmèd bark,
> Whose Helmsman on an ocean waste and wide
> Sits mute and pale his mouldering helm beside.   (22–24)

Recoiling from the limbo of lonely space, Coleridge sought solace in the domestic grove of "This Lime-tree Bower," the backyard of "The Nightingale," or the cottage doorway of "The Eolian Harp"; so he oscillated fretfully between expansive desire to encompass all and fearful recoil from "Vacancy and formlessness,"[13] between sallying forth in the loving comfort of "a goodly company" ("The Ancient Mariner," 604) and enclosing himself within the secure walls of Xanadu. His neurotic sensitivity to the unbounded was even afflicted at times by the multiplicity of "goings-on" in the world, as in "Frost at Midnight," leaving him unaccountably disquieted in the security of his cottage. Only when multeity was reconciled into unity did Coleridge's disquiet resolve into contemplative serenity.

Perhaps it was his *horror vacui* as much as anything else which drove him at times to crowd words at the beginning and end of books and in the margins of pages already comfortingly printed and which contradictorily left him at other times paralyzed before a blank sheet of paper. Almost up to his death his poetry bears testament to his psychological terror of vacancy, whether of cosmic dimension or of personal inner intensity. Like a sleepless astronomer searching the barren night skies for signs of planetary life, Coleridge probed his feelings of emptiness. "I sate alone," he begins "The Garden of Boccaccio" (1828), "Cow'r'd o'er my own vacancy! / And . . . watch'd the dull continuous ache, / Which, all else slumb'ring, seem'd alone to wake" (4, 8–10). In "Love's Apparition and Evanishment" (1833) he likens his "vacant mood" and the "sickly calm" of his heart to a "ruin'd well" beside which "a lone Arab, old and blind" sits and vainly plumbs for some "human sound." His fear was of an emotional limbo from which his normally teeming mind shrunk.

The adjectives he applied to space again and again reveal his dread of emptiness. In that strange poem "Limbo" (1811) the "horror of blank Naught-at-all" (33) is equated with the oxymorons of "Lank Space" (15) and "weary Space / Fettered from flight, with night-mare sense of fleeing" (12–13). One is claustrophobic in its dimensionlessness and the other paralytic in its directionless motion.[14] The terror expressed here is of imprisonment in a cosmic vacuum of sorts, of sequestration in "a spirit-jail secure" (32) of uninterrupted nothingness stretching to infinity on all sides.

His *horror vacui* recoils from the immeasurable, from an endless extension that in effect may as well be nowhere. In a notebook entry of 1814 he despairs because "Angels, Devils, Saints, Blessed Spirits, with none or indefinite Forms," open up to him "the Enormous and the Immeasurable . . . fearful Depths" instead of "resolving of all into finite Beauty, as the balance of the whole and the component parts, and the union of the opposite qualities of Distinctness and Comprehension in the mid point of Clearness." Faced with this yawning incorporeality, this absence of reticulated parts, Coleridge finds that the ethereal vagueness of spirits instills in him a "boundless yearning" that is a "negation of Life" instead of a "Serene Complacency or cheerful Pleasure" (*CN*, III, 4213). The location of objects in space was necessary to define not only his sense of self but also of time. "I remember," he writes in the 1820s in one of his notebooks, when first I saw the connection between Time, and the being resisted; Space and non-resistance – or unresisted Action – that if no object met, stopped, or opposed itself to my sight, ear, touch, or sensitive power, tho' it were but my own pulse rising up against my own thumb, I could have no sense of Time; & but for these, or the repetition of these in the reproductive Memory or Imagination, should have no Time . . . For in truth, Time and Self are in a certain sense one and the same thing: since only by meeting with, so as to be resisted by, *Another*, does the Soul become a *Self*. What is Self-consciousness but to know myself at the same moment that I know another, and to know myself by means of knowing another, and vice-versa, an other by means of & at the moment of knowing my Self. Self and others are as necessarily interdependent as Right and Left, North and South.[15]

Hence Coleridge's imagination desperately fixed on objects, landmarks, anchorings that steady and orient the mind in defining the self in relation to the outside world. Moon, stars, and clouds in the otherwise blank sky accordingly drew his attention throughout his life. Skyscapes fill his notebooks and punctuate intense moments in his poems. They concentrate the Ancient Mariner's consciousness. The inability to orient oneself by their sight becomes in "Limbo" a haunting image of "growthless, dull Privation" (35):

> An Old Man with a steady look sublime,
> That stops his earthly task to watch the skies;
> But he is blind – a Statue hath such eyes; —
> Yet having moonward turn'd his face by chance,
> Gazes the orb with moon-like countenance,
> With scant white hairs, with foretop bald and high,
> He gazes still, – his eyeless face all eyes; —
> As 'twere an organ full of silent sight,
> His whole face seemeth to rejoice in light!
> Lip touching lip, all moveless, bust and limb –
> He seems to gaze at that which seems to gaze on him!   (20–30)

The lines seemingly convey the gestalt of man and nature, in contrast to the definitiveless circumambience of limbo.

> No such sweet sights doth Limbo den immure,
> Wall'd round, and made a spirit-jail secure,
> By the mere horror of blank Naught-at-all,
> Whose circumambiance doth these ghosts enthral.   (31–34)

But the sight of man defined in time by the otherness of the moon's light is contaminated by the disquieting circumstances of the situation. Inadvertently, and contrary to Coleridge's explicit intentions, the image offers yet another instance of limbo, man reduced to lifeless statue in a stance of intense yearning for nexus by way of light with a celestial body it can neither see nor feel nor measure.

Clearly, for Coleridge the divine plenum had not turned out as perfect as the *beatus vir* of 1728 had believed when he extended the *hortus conclusus* to embrace first the open landscape and then "the whole terrestrial scene."[16] It is significant that Coleridge characterized limbo as the opposite of place, "Not a Place, / Yet name it so" (11–12). For assuagement of the *horror vacui* instilled by the "undistinguish'd void" that had become the *hortus conclusus*, Coleridge turned back to the *locus amoenus*; but the lime-tree bower, the sunny dell, the earthly garden presented him with literary and ethical problems, which compromised his resolve to create and his capacity to take pleasure in an English version of "Eden's bowers" where "Dwelt the first husband and his sinless mate" ("The Improvisatore," 51–52). Moral scruples replaced ontological and metaphysical anxieties, inhibiting his contentment in a private and aesthetic solution to the desire for "The peacefull'st cot" – "a home, an English home, and thee" in some corner of the country ("Constancy to an Ideal Object," 18, 20).

The *locus amoenus* was no more free of ambivalences and hesitancies for Coleridge than was for him the identification of the endless reaches of the heavens with the *hortus conclusus*. By the time of the Renaissance it had acquired sinister connotations. Whereas the Greeks had kept the Blessed Isles distinct from the bewitched island of Circe, the late medieval and Renaissance man pictured the garden as both the place of ultimate redemption and of destructive temptation. If it was the Garden of Adonis, it was also the Bower of Bliss. The earthly paradise was easily transformed into an enchanted garden whenever the tree of life was ignored for the tree of knowledge, the sacred spring abandoned for a Narcissan fountain, agape jilted for eros. A. Bartlett Giamatti characterizes the enchanted garden as a "beautiful-seeming earthly paradise, which in reality is a dangerous and deceptive place where man's will is softened, his moral fibre unraveled, and his soul ensnared. It is the garden where insidious luxury and sensual love overcome duty and true devotion."[17]

Coleridge's verse celebrations of the secluded bower and enclosed garden are tinged more often than not with the ambivalence of this literary heritage, which he complicates with his personal self-doubts. The results are poems that exhibit mixed feelings of elation and of guilt, either repudiating themselves or oscillating between contrary impulses. "The Eolian Harp" (1795) fits the first definition, "Reflections on Having Left a Place of Retirement" (1796) the second.

Critics have made much of Coleridge's unexpected recantation at the end of "The Eolian Harp" of what he characterizes as a momentary succumbing to speculation about false principles. Two schools of thought have developed about this critical problem. There are those who take for granted that he is denying in the last verse paragraph less the whole of the preceding part of the poem than the immediately preceding paragraph, in which he broaches the "vain Philosophy" that "all animated nature" may respond like "organic Harps" to "one intellectual breeze, / At once the Soul of each, and God of all" (44–48). And there are those who consider the poem to be lacking in thematic unity, because nothing in earlier lines prepares us for the ending.[18]

In their concentration on Coleridge's metaphysical "maunderings," the critics have neglected his equally whole-hearted submission to luxuriant feeling when he likens the eolian harp to a coy maid:

> How by the desultory breeze caress'd,
> Like some coy maid half yielding to her lover,

It pours such sweet upbraiding, as must needs
Tempt to repeat the wrong! And now, its strings
Boldlier swept, the long sequacious notes
Over delicious surges sink and rise,
Such a soft floating witchery of sound
As twilight Elfins make, when they at eve
Voyage on gentle gales from Fairy-Land,
Where Melodies round honey-dropping flowers,
Footless and wild, like birds of Paradise,
Nor pause, nor perch, hovering on untam'd wing!   (14–25)

It is possible that mixed with his remorse felt for momentarily giving way to pantheistic "shapings of the unregenerate mind" (55) is his shamed recoil from the sensual fantasies that animate the first half of the poem (the second verse paragraph), which would explain his abashed return at the end of his poetic fantasizing to the real presence of the woman beside him. If so, Coleridge would have us believe then that Sara is admonishing him on two scores. As a "Meek Daughter in the Family of Christ" (53), she mildly reproves his heretical divagations; and as a "heart-honour'd Maid" (64) she recalls him also from his erotic daydreams.

Although the final version of the poem seems to emphasize the metaphysical theme, it is significant that an early draft (MS. R., 1797) devoted more space to the sybaritic topic. In an extension of the analogy of harp and "coy maid," the seductive harmonies of the lute conjure up a further image of voluptuous lotus land:

Music such as erst
Round rosy bowers (so Legendaries tell)
To sleeping Maids came floating witchingly
By wand'ring West winds stoln from Faery land.

In the final version the allusion to luxuriant bowers of "sleeping Maids," where one softly sinks into bewitched repose, was excised in favor of neutral reference to "twilight Elfins" voyaging "on gentle gales from Faery-Land." One should not forget, in this context, that the "white-flower'd Jasmin" (4) and the myrtle (Venus's flower), which grow unpruned in licentious profusion about the cottage, are ambiguously associated with both paradisal Innocence (cf. also *CL*, VI, 678) and earthly Eros ("Meet emblems they of Innocence and Love," 5). Similarly, "the star of eve" is linked by Coleridge to wisdom (7–8); yet we also know it as the planet Venus, on which point Coleridge is suspiciously reticent. In short, just as Coleridge ostensibly turns away in the final lines from the "idle flitting phantasies" (40) of atheistical "vain Philosophy," so he had previously shied away through revisions from the attractiveness of the Bower of Bliss.

Thus does Coleridge ambivalently cope with a subject whose sere flowers reach back to Renaissance poetry and whose roots extend even farther into antiquity, a subject that can yet touch the nerve ends of a foster child of the French Revolution, an idealistic young man with a turn for ratiocination and apocalyptic dreams neurotically facing an undesired marriage. He may momentarily have succumbed to pre-marital desires, which he quickly rejected as unworthy of his betrothed's better nature. If so, such desires were self-generated. As their subsequent connubial history suggests, Sara Fricker was no Acrasia tempting Samuel into sensual, and hence moral, corruption. If he was enticed into marriage, the tempter was more Southey than Sara, assisted by Coleridge's own overwrought moral sensibility, both men believing that Coleridge had "compromised" Sara with his courtship promises. We have equal difficulty in visualizing intellectually timid Sara and her "governessy" Christianity (Humphry House's witty label) as a poetic emblem of Mary, whom Christian tradition placed in the garden as a Second Eve to confirm the promise of man's return to Eden. In this poem of complex antecedents the tradition of *locus amoenus* and of *hortus conclusus* lurk in the background; the ubiquitous scent of "honey-dropping flowers" and the melodies of "birds of Paradise" (here submerged in the image of the lute and its "delicious surges" of sound sinking and rising) hint alike at Hesperidean and Miltonic presences. Yet we cannot categorize the poem as one or the other, no more than we can identify it unequivocally as a nuptial poem, or a pastoral poem, or a meditative–descriptive poem, or a millenarian poem. In "The Eolian Harp," the paradisal subtheme of blissful retirement and the teleological theme of pantheism are kept as chastely separate as Coleridge's subtle verbal powers and his not altogether consciously controlled psyche could manage.

In "Reflections," written in the following year, but commemorating the same place, Coleridge more unequivocally identifies his theme with the Edenic tradition of paradise won for a brief spell and then lost indefinitely.[19] Unlike his unhappy ancestors Adam and Eve, who were expelled from Eden, he and his bride choose to leave their "Blesséd Place," a "green and woody . . . Valley of Seclusion" (17, 7–9), because he guiltily rejects its "selfish luxury". But not unmixed in the voluntary decision is the religious recognition stemming from the Fall that conjugal serenity may translate fearfully into sexual enchantment. Rather than "dream away the entrusted hours / On rose-leaf beds, pampering the coward heart / With feelings all too delicate for use" (46–48), he re-enters the world of work on behalf of his fellow men,

> I therefore go, and join head, heart, and hand,
> Active and firm, to fight the bloodless fight
> Of Science, Freedom, and the Truth in Christ.   (60–62)

Coleridge has been goaded into this action by his puritanical conscience reacting to the "slothful loves and dainty sympathies" (59) of the garden bower. From atop the "stony Mount" overlooking his cottage, he has had a vision of God's omnipresence. The reminder of Eden, and the reason for its loss, dashes his enjoyment of the Valley of Seclusion. Spread before his sight mountain, sheep, clouds, fields, river, landscaped parks, woods, cottages, and city spires stretch to the channel with its islands, sailboats, coasts, and "shoreless Ocean." "It seem'd like Omnipresence!" Coleridge exclaims,

> God, methought,
> Had Built him there a Temple: the whole World
> Seem'd *imag'd* in its vast circumference.   (27–40)

But the attractiveness of the scene for Coleridge echoes a hilltop prospect glimpsed by Jesus, in *Paradise Regained* (II, 285–97), of what appears to be a new Golden Age but proves to be the false setting for Satan's banquet temptation (II, 338–65). Because of the discrepancy of his "Blest hour!" (42) in comparison to the fate of his "brother man" (53), he cannot rid himself of suspicion that he is being tried, like Jesus, with temptations destructive of his peace.

The ambivalence of Coleridge's attitude toward his secluded dell is revealed in the successive titles of the poem, "Reflections on Entering into Active Life" and "Reflections on Having Left a Place of Retirement"; in his return at the end of the poem to nostalgic recollection of his "dear Cot" with its jasmin, myrtles, and roses; and in his millenarian prayer that all men might share in such bliss through the Second Coming's restitution of Eden on earth: "Speed it, O Father! Let thy Kingdom come!" (71).

It is interesting in this context to recognize how second nature is millenarian language to the age. Anthony John Harding, paraphrasing John Passmore's distinction between two kinds of expectations of a perfected society, writes that the millennialist "looks to Christ's Second Coming as the condition of such a society's coming into being, whereas for Augustine and his followers the City of God is a historical reality, the glory of which is that it represents and foreshadows on earth the true Eternal City." In his late political thinking, Harding adds, Coleridge "is close to the spirit of Augustinianism."[20] In the mid-1790s, although his language at times sounds millenarian, and he numbered then among his philosophical–theological enthusiasms the Christian millenarians Joseph Priestley and Ralph Cudworth, only in a playfully fanciful way can Coleridge, even in his cautiously militant Watchman guise, be considered a millenarian himself. It is just as likely that the prayer concluding "Reflections" is his indirect way of asserting that no remedy can come to England without a change in its present government, a conviction which the two bills introduced in the Commons and the Lords in November 1795 on seditious meetings and treasonable practices made dangerous to express openly and categorically.

Coleridge's complex response to the ethical question of retirement versus active do-goodism has literary and cultural sides to it as well as personal and political. In the second quarter of the eighteenth century, as Røstvig demonstrates, the *beatus vir* aspired to the ideal of moral benevolence and public virtues, a radical departure from the practice of the classical figure, who historically had retired to a rural backwater for self-centered reasons. Self-imposed exile was justified now by its assumption of duty to one's fellow men, "so as to share with them that feeling of joyous benevolence with which nature had inspired him in his solitary moments."[21] For the Romantics a life of solitary communion with nature for selfish reasons once again held irresistible attraction, but the convention of moral benevolence and public virtues that had animated the *beatus vir* the previous fifty years still exerted its influence. One hears the two voices in Wordsworth, in the visionary raptures prompted by nature (his spots of time) and in the "still sad music of humanity" infiltrating his consciousness at such moments. The social contradictions inherent in the dichotomy are given comic expression when Coleridge reverses the pattern of private benefit leading to public benevolence by inviting the beneficiary, in the form of a hard-worked ass ("I hail thee Brother"), into "the Dell / Of Peace and mild Equality to dwell" ("To a Young Ass" [1794], 26–28).

A tension between paradisal seclusion and work-a-day world informs "The Eolian Harp" and "Reflections." The garden becomes the setting for an inner struggle between succumbing to sensual ease and pursuing the arduous Christian way. Pleasure is "a Sorceress," Coleridge asserts in a notebook entry of 1803, who pitches "her Tent on enchanted ground." She is a *fata Morgana* "born of Delusion." "Happiness can be built on Virtue only," he concludes, "must of necessity [have] Truth for its foundation" (*CN*, I, 1375).

In two other of the Conversation poems – "This Lime-tree Bower" and "Frost at Midnight" – the situation of the poet is contrived to let him minimize the risk of aspiring to full direct participation in the joy of "A new Earth and new Heaven" ("Dejection," 69). That happiness (or illusion of happiness) is awarded to others. Charles Lamb and Hartley Coleridge are blessed with seeing and hearing "the lovely shapes and sounds intelligible / Of that eternal language" of the "great universal Teacher" ("Frost at Midnight," 59–60, 63), while Coleridge faintheartedly occupies the borderland of paradise, imprisoned in a lime-tree bower or isolated in his midnight study, condemned as if for some crime like the Ancient Mariner's to dwell apart from the pious company of men and the holy presence of nature. And when, as recorded in "Reflections," he finds himself partaking of the bliss of earthly paradise, his conscience is constrained to expel from it the Adam in him.

The ambiguity of Coleridge's response to Eden *redivivus* as recorded in the Conversation poems contains a variety of intellectual forces, which he is striving not always successfully to assimilate into poetic unity.

First, there is the thrust of his age to realize paradise in actual form. The Romantics continued to hope like their fathers and grandfathers that it was possible to institutionalize paradise on earth in their own time, principally either by political fiat or by rural retreat. But Romantic expectations were compromised by at least two cultural shifts. Eighteenth-century landscape gardeners worked, and thought, in terms of restricted and controllable plots of earth; the Romantics had all of nature and the whole world of mankind to accommodate to the ideal. Cobham and Hoare could self-indulgently invest their gardens with a theological symbolism appropriate to their sense of well-being; but Coleridge and Wordsworth had to assert against much evidence to the contrary that nature – all this goodly earth – was liberating, perfecting, and inspiriting. They had to contend with the counter forces of a nation at war, in the throes of industrial and agricultural dislocation, and under alternately mad and capricious rule, all working to mitigate, to qualify, and to deny their millennial optimism. For a brief while, Coleridge placed all his hopes in Pantisocracy, his short-lived bubble of illusion about emigrating to America to found a communal paradise with like-minded individuals. Once the bloom of political and social optimism had wilted for him he turned to nature, within whose actual horizons he hoped to find spiritual dimensions commensurate with the original Eden. For the bulk of his fellow inhabitants on earth, however, that prospect remained a distant paradise of poetic, and visual, metaphors. The discrepancy of status between the privileged few sequestered in their shared paradise and the excluded commonalty, of the elect and the many, plagued the poetic consciences of Coleridge and Wordsworth, with which they struggled all their lives without finding a satisfactory solution.

Second, there is the eighteenth- and nineteenth-century emphasis on utility, which enlisted in its philosophical wake sundry varieties of do-good societies, socially conscious forms of muscular Christianity, and institutions based on the pleasure–pain stimulus. Although private happiness was held to be a natural goal and a public aim, the theorists of utility were not sympathetic in practice with what they considered to be the self-indulgence of solitary nature worship or of exclusive utopian communities.

Third, there is the Miltonic literary tradition, which describes paradise in a mixture of classical and Christian terms, emphasizing its appearance as an idyllic but divinely disciplined garden. Contrariwise, as a warning to the incautious Christian who would seize on the garden bower as proof of his election to grace, there is the counter tradition of the garden as enchanted rather than holy, a place insidiously seductive in its sensual luxury and ultimately destructive of man's moral will.

Fourth, there are Coleridge's feelings of unworthiness, of having misused his talents and consequently of having lost the chance to enter celestial Jerusalem except by the grace of God's divine intervention.

The contradictions produced by Coleridge's ambivalence before what he presumed to be earthly paradise are evident. He extolled nature but restricted it to quiet dells and leafy enclosures. He revered the natural virtues of earth's vast and varied prospects but retreated from them to the controlled responses of his mind. It is interesting in the context of the contending influences on Coleridge's thought that while his evocations of garden enclosures ordinarily echo Edenic harmonies, intermingled with them are also heard the overtones of sensuality. If sex was not inimical to the Miltonic prelapsarian paradise, still it inevitably carried connotations of shame, guilt, and imperfection into the postlapsarian garden. Latent always in Coleridge's mind is the worry that such joy is not conducive to man's future welfare. "The Eolian Harp" and "Reflections," even though ostensibly one anticipates and the other recalls his honeymoon idyll, contain consciously contrived earthly paradises which he is constrained to repudiate wholly or in part. Another, "Fears in Solitude," describes "A green and silent dell" (1, 228) in which he luxuriantly lapses into "half sleep" and "dreams of better worlds" (26), until, lulled "by nature's quietness / And solitary musings," his "heart / Is softened, and made worthy to indulge / Love" (229–32). Although the frame of reference of his emotion here is social and political, a humanitarian protest against war and human exploitation, the words that creep into his statement – softening heart, indulgent love, enervated half sleep, world of dreams – have residual meanings critical of the senses and even sinister in connotation when read in the context of his fears of the enchanted garden. Hence, it is not surprising to learn that he is obliged to depart the green and "low dell" after having succumbed a few hours to self-indulgent desires of surcease from the active struggle against wickedness. Two later poems – "A Day-dream" (*c.* 1802) and "Recollections of Love" (*c.* 1807) – associate his love of Sara Hutchinson with the green peaceful-ness of woodland bower. In each instance the beloved appears as a phantom in a daydream:

> You stood before me like a thought,
> A dream remembered in a dream.   ("Recollections," 21–22)

The censoring mind of the poet will not have any more corporeal presence in the garden than might be made by the "brooding warmth" that lies heavily on his breast and adds to the "depth of [his] tranquil bliss" ("A Day-dream," 21–22). The ardor inherent in the situation is transferred to the "woodland wild Recess," the "sweet bed of heath" swelling up, then sinking with "faint caress," as if the beloved were there ("Recollections," 1–5). Two poems written toward the end of his life – "The Garden of Boccaccio" (1828) and "Love's Apparition and Evanishment" (1833) – indicate that Coleridge continued to equate the garden bower with erotic enchantment, tremulous warmth of feeling in the region of the heart, dreamy indolence and (in "Love's Apparition," 9–16) "vacant mood," "sickly calm," and "idle brain," all attesting to the difficulty encountered by the soul's power to draw sustenance from the "secret ministry" ("Frost at Midnight") of nature, or to take comfort in the sacred void of space.

The psychological breaching of the garden enclosure by the sensual heart of Coleridge's desires had both its cultural antecedents and its worldly correlatives. The walled garden as allegorical of the regenerated soul protected from the wilderness outside by wall and from the sun of divine justice inside by trees had a long literary tradition, as Stanley Stewart shows in *The Enclosed Garden.*[22] Milton's Eden was walled against the wilderness and further protected by a forest of trees and by the steep sides of the mountain whose top it occupied. Sixteenth- and seventeenth-century gardens are shown in prints and paintings, like Jan Sieberechts's depiction of *The Gardens of Chatsworth* (*c.* 1710, Lord Sandys),[23] to be similarly walled against the uncouth countryside very much like moated and bastioned castles built to withstand siege.

An interesting example of this conventional separation of the "ideal enclave" from the threatening energies of the untamed and unchaste world is presented in Bellini's painting *Sacred Allegory* (*c.* 1488, Uffizi Gallery, Florence). The fore-ground contains a geometrically perfect square paved in a pattern of alternating colors of diamond-shaped marble and surrounded by a balustrade. The severely aesthetic scene is enlivened by a tree in a pot placed at the mathematical center, its trunk clasped by a child. Standing and sitting on the periphery are St. Paul, St. Joseph, St. Sebastian, Job, and the Virgin flanked by two saints, all (with the exception of St. Paul) either "sunk in contemplative melancholia . . . as if they found it inexhaustibily satisfying," or gazing in rapt attention on the child. The scene, as John H. Armstrong further notes, "is now thought to be a landscape-fantasy organized around the idea of paradise; and the design of the enclosure in the foreground is based on the traditional paradise-garden."[24] Contrasted to the foreground scene of Christian piety and ordered harmony, and separated by a body of water, is a landscape of rocky coast and hills, a shepherd sitting in a cave surrounded with his sheep, a centaur pacing the shore, a man descending rough-hewn steps to the water's edge, and a village with people and animals standing about – all this stretching from middle to far distance. Armstrong finds in the landscape "an unmistakable Hesperidean atmosphere"; and if he is right, then the painting presents us with two balanced versions of the "ideal enclave," the pagan and the Christian, the fearsome world of nature reduced imaginatively by the one to a golden age and the other to an emergent world picture reassuring in its mathematical regularity. But for the mood of mid-day torpor, however, the scene contains few details specifically Hesperidean – and there is that disturbingly intrusive figure of the centaur. Except for the tone of " 'touching Chastity' which marks all Bellini's incursions into material which even borders on the profane,"[25]

4 Bellini, *Sacred Allegory*

the two scenes are more contrastive than complementary, the foreground paradisal tableau representing the Renaissance ideal of an ordered and harmonious world, the middle distance depicting the fallen world of nature, rough, irregular, and only partly tamed by the agencies of society and religion. How else explain the figures of boys holding apples shaken down from a tree by another in the center middle ground? Is not the picture reminding us at once of the circumstances surrounding the Fall and of the reversal of that act through Christ's birth? A confirmation of this reading appears in Bellini's *The Blood of the Redeemer* (1460–65, National Gallery, London) where there occurs an identical contrast between a similar geometrically ordered world in the foreground, identified with Christ's redemptive promise of the eventual return of paradise, and a natural world in the middle ground that is uncultivated, barren, and wild.

By Coleridge's day the latter had become the necessary transition to the natural sublime, by way of the evolving nature and garden aesthetic of the eighteenth century; but given Coleridge's metaphysical hesitancies it is not surprising to find in "Kubla Khan" a mixed bag of garden styles: an old-fashioned prospect "girdled" by "walls and towers," with formal gardens and park of "forests ancient as the hills," intermixed with the new taste for "sinuous rills" and "deep romantic chasm." The poem ostensibly celebrates in Xanadu that combination of divine order and profane disorder that Bellini in Renaissance Venice had followed as horticultural and architectural ideal. With one important difference in degree. Of supreme focus in the Khan's paradisal grounds, and granted a position of commanding assertion, is an architectural fantasy given over to pleasure, which in Bellini's and even in the Whig aristocrat's worlds played a discreet and self-effacing secondary role to the greater imperative of moral didacticism. Charles I. Patterson, Jr., has called our attention to the essential divergence of Coleridge's aesthetic from that of Milton and the Old Testament poets. At the center of the Khan's landscape garden stands a pleasure dome, while at the center of Eden (in *medio paradisi* in the Vulgate) stood the Tree of Life and the Tree of Knowledge of Good and Evil. The two trees exercise man's faculty for moral choice; the dome caters to his taste for the sensuous.[26] This shift of emphasis in Romantic aesthetics, while clinging to a spiritual base through its link with the divine expression of nature, did not displace an older Christian code of moral accountability. The two claimed equal allegiance in the minds of many Romantics and, in the instance of Coleridge, posed contradictory impulses which show up in his poetic paeans to paradise.

Like the earthly garden of Biblical tradition, the rural Arcadia of Virgilian song, and the lake country reality of Wordsworthian visionary experience, Xanadu is infiltrated with insidious temptations and grievous disorders. In the mirrored reflection of its artistic order is imaged the disruptive impulses of the enchanted garden of Renaissance poems and the blind forces of nature. If Xanadu has its serene glades, sunny hills, sacred river, and "gardens bright with sinuous rills," it also has its dark underside of sexual energy,

that deep romantic chasm which slanted
Down the green hill athwart a cedarn cover!
A savage place! as holy and enchanted
As e'er beneath a waning moon was haunted
By woman wailing for her demon-lover!   (12–16)

The wailing woman takes her place as the latest in the lineage of enchantresses that stretches from Circe and Eve to Alcina and Acrasia. Beneath the appearance of aesthetic harmony in the garden lurks a threat to the spiritual health of man. The pleasurable indolence of the place masks a savagery native to its cyclic rhythms of violent birth, sunny life, and icy death. Coleridge along with Byron and Shelley knew, as the eighteenth-century builders of landscape gardens could afford to ignore, that the free run of paradise (witness the fates of Adam and Eve, and Satan) risks a compensatory retribution.

In a poem with the dense poetic texture of "Kubla Khan" there is, of course, a confluence of the personal, literary, and mythological. So much has already been written about the parallels between Coleridge's description of Xanadu and literary references to paradise, with special emphasis on Milton's description of Eden in *Paradise Lost*, that there is no need to repeat them here.[27] Most recently, E. S. Shaffer has extended the frame of reference of Xanadu to include the accumulated lore of the history of Eden, specifically the oriental versions of paradise that contributed their tributary streams of pre and postlapsarian and pre and postdiluvian times to the syncretic geography of Eden. In her eyes, "Kubla Khan" is the single most successful English Romantic expression of the new mythological syncretism, the new historicity of myth which guided the comparative mythologists of the late eighteenth century to treat the Christian story of human origins as one of the world-wide primitive myths, all telling the same truth under different guises. In "Kubla Khan" "all of Asia is present in one spot" (p. 165), a landscape "combining still-remembered paradise, wilderness, enclosed city, and cultivated court . . . City and country, rural yet populous, idyllic yet threatening, holy yet secular, sacred yet fallen, court and cot – it is tempting to see the stereotypes of the eighteenth century merging into those that will dominate the nineteenth. Just for this moment, in this exotic setting, they exist simultaneously, and express a permanent condition of man."[28]

Besides the earthly paradise-enchanted garden design is an important paradise–Hades (or heaven–hell) configuration, examined by Maud Bodkin in *Archetypal Patterns in Poetry* as long ago as 1934. In a closely reasoned discussion which includes studies of analogues not only in "Kubla Khan" and *Paradise Lost* but also in *The Earthly Paradise* of William Morris, in the *Aeneid* of Virgil, and in the *Commedia* of Dante, Bodkin defines an archetypal rebirth pattern in which the soul moves from "the agony of hell, symbolized by blind darkness and cavern depths" to a vision of "the heavenly heights." "The image of the watered garden and the mountain height show some persistent affinity with the desire and imaginative enjoyment of supreme well-being, or divine bliss, while the cavern depth appears as the objectification of an imaginative fear."[29] The aspiration is to leave behind temporal bafflement and pain *en route* to a plane of eternal illumination.

As regards "Kubla Khan," one controversial tradition would have it that Coleridge followed the negative route of poppy fumes to this goal. If Alethea Hayter is right in her description of polar wastes, Northern lights, endless extensions of time and space, boundless plains and seas as characteristic of opium dreams,[30] then Coleridge's sensitivity to the reaches of the sky and his lifelong effort to fit the heavenly spaces into a teleological frame of reference is a startling instance of the massive coadunating power of his mind. In this instance, it struggled to give moral and metaphysical validity to the fragments of his drug-induced thoughts within the context of a Newtonian–Christian world picture. Reality resides in the act of unifying contraries, he was fond of asserting. What greater act of reconciliation than the incorporation of opium visions of chilly, lighted vaults of space, here confined to "Caverns measureless to man," into the historical earthly garden, as an eighteenth-century extension of God's gift to man of the *hortus conclusus*!

Equally embedded in the literary–biographical undersong of the poem is the tradition of the divine guide. Dante is led by Beatrice in his ascent to paradise. Coleridge is helped in his "imaginative experience of transition from personal desire to ideal aspiration" by his vision of "an Abyssinian maid," a persona for the female inspiration who assumes the role of divine guide in his poetry.

The person who most often filled this role after 1800 was Sara Hutchinson.[31] But the intensity of Coleridge's unrequited passion for her, exacerbated by his domestic situation, made him a treacherous pilgrim and her an untrustworthy divine guide. Her physical form kept materializing in his paradisal bower, deflecting his aspirant eyes to profane earth. As in "Kubla Khan," Coleridge was never quite able to separate his vision of the Abyssinian maid from that of the woman wailing for her demon-lover. In "The Picture" (1802), he ironically records a failed resolution to curb his longing. Coleridge's thinly disguised narrator–lover pushes deep into a "tangle wild of bush and brake" (14) to flee female enchantments, in search of "the spirit of unconscious life" (20) untouched by emotional agitation. In the "silent shade" of an oak tree he congratulates himself on being "safe and sacred from the step of man" (52–53), that is, woman, specifically his beloved: "these are no groves / Where Love dare loiter" (27–28). As the rest of the poem makes clear, Coleridge is scourging his paradise of the corporeal presence of his "Love" the better to inhabit it with her "form divine" (75). This idealized vision is intended to accompany him on his pilgrimage; but by the end of the poem the lure of the real woman has led him to forsake his hilly sacred grove for the pastoral vale where she lives.

After 1802 Coleridge's intellectual compulsion to free his earthly paradise of traditional temptation by idealizing Sara Hutchinson became psychologically urgent as he sought a resolution to his hopeless love for her. In a curious fragment possibly written at the time of his departure for Malta in 1804 he purifies away all Sara Hutchinson's earthly dross (see *CN*, II, 2055n):

All look and likeness caught from earth
All accident of kin and birth,
Had pass'd away. There was no trace
Of aught on that illumined face,
Uprais'd beneath the rifted stone
But of one spirit all her own; –
She, she herself, and only she,
Shone through her body visibly.   ("Phantom," 1–8)

The need to dematerialize his passions leads him to identify the "pure Love of a good man to a good woman" (*CN*, II, 2540) with his knowledge of the good, the true, and the beautiful.

The best, the truly lovely, in each & all is God. Therefore the truly Beloved is the symbol of God to whomever it is truly beloved by! – but it may become perfect & maintained lovely by the function of the two / The Lover worships in his Beloved that final consummation of itself which is produced in his own soul by the action of the Soul of the Beloved upon it, and that final perfection of the Soul of the Beloved, which is in part the consequence of the reaction of his (so ammeliorated & regenerated) Soul upon the Soul of his Beloved / till each contemplates the Soul of the other as involving his own, both in its givings and its receivings, and thus still keeping alive its *outness*, its *self-oblivion* united with *Self-warmth*, & still approximates to God!   (*CN*, II, 2540)

By such contemplation, Coleridge hopes, he will win surcease from "reckless Despair" (*CN*, II, 3148) and maybe even achieve a modicum of "divine Joy" (*CN*, 3092) with its glimpse of the heavenly plains.

If the twin images of "the high garden-land, sunlit, watered, blossoming, of the earthly Paradise, and . . . The heavenly heights beyond, infinitely remote, radiant, and commanding an infinitely far-ranging prospect" – with attainment in that order of progression – are for Coleridge "a recurring phase and permanent element of lived experience"[32] and human expectance, it is equally a fact of the felt experience and the examined life that no man is fully armored against the haunting danger of a reverse movement from Heaven to Hell. The earliest myths contain the story of the fall of the rebel angels into hell and of the expulsion of our first parents from Eden. Coleridge is not unmindful of the obverse of human desires and divine promise. In "Kubla Khan" one "progresses" not upward but downward into "the caverns measureless to man." The sacred river Alph rises from a deep chasm to flow for a brief space through the high gardenland only to sink "in tumult to a lifeless ocean."

The emotional pattern of Coleridge's life confirmed the profane archetype, contra the heavenly one, as an ever-present threat to his aspirations. From childhood he had been accustomed to the possibility that he was undeserving of happiness. Last born and the Benjamin of his father, he had been the object of his older brothers' jealousy. At nine he had been "orphaned" by his father's death, wrenched from the security of a large family and the familiarity of the market town of Ottery St. Mary and "exiled" to the hellish competitiveness of Christ's Hospital and the alien din of London. Whether he suffered guilt feelings for his father's death is conjectural.[33] But that he believed his mother had abandoned him is evident in his subsequent alienation from her and his repeated references to surrogate mothers. Marriage to Sara Fricker culminated in unhappy separation from wife and children rather than in domestic bliss. Love for Sara Hutchinson and William and Dorothy Wordsworth caused more pain than joy over the years.

Is it any wonder that the history of "Kubla Khan" is one of ambiguity: the absence of explicit mention of it, the belated publication, the aborted ending! Coleridge's inclusion of the daemonic damsel in Xanadu is consistent with his ambivalence toward the garden's promise of supine refreshment of soul and with his flight from the earthly paradises celebrated in "The Eolian Harp" and "Reflections." In the only surviving autograph of the poem, the Crewe manuscript,[34] Coleridge had assigned the name Amora to the holy mountain referred to by the Abyssinian maid in her song. It is intriguing, given the submerged pun on love in the word that he changed it to Abora, which is identified in scriptural and literary commentary as one of the rivers of Eden.[35] The Abyssinian maid and her "symphony and song" of Mount Abora are further distanced by Coleridge to "A vision once I saw." And like the feat of Merlin fifty years later in Tennyson's *Idylls of the King*, Coleridge prefers to build his pleasure dome of song ("in air") rather than of mortar and stone. Psychologically, the shift from the opening laudatory description of Xanadu and the Khan's architectural achievement to the concluding celebration of the powers of the poetic imagination conforms to the pattern of emotion and imagery Maud Bodkin found in her study of Western literature. It also conforms to the tendency of the first generation of English Romantic poets to reject the earthly paradise, in the very instance of espousing it, for the more reassuring phantoms of their mind. Coleridge longed to enjoy the supreme well-being of his paradisal vision, but he shrank in dread from a bliss that might prove to be sin temptingly disguised. In this sense the caves of ice objectify his fear of Xanadu as a potential Bower of Bliss; and his transformation of it in the last section of the poem into a "symphony and song" is his way of retaining the "experience of fascination" while alleviating the "pain of fear . . . in the relief of expression."[36] The figments of the imagination pose less threat and are easier to control than the stench of the senses, whose imperatives assail one's will and lay siege to one's days.

The natural earth in all its widespread formations represented for Coleridge an organic paradisal whole. Unfortunately, his ability to enjoy the earthly Eden he wished literally to witness in this life on all sides of him and the heavenly paradise he allegorically saw himself as a Grey-haired Passenger[37] progressing toward in holy pilgrimage was compromised by doubt and disquiet. The misfocused overlap of the two paradises are hardly conducive to confidence in their being one and the same. Moreover, the Sunday stroller from Bristol ("Reflections") and the visitor from Porlock ("Kubla Khan") were always showing up in one or another Clevedon, or Xanadu, idyll as a reminder of an outside world that did not match the paradisal template. Coleridge was caught in an irresolvable contradiction. He took comfort in the earthly garden he and all humans presumably inhabited yet distrusted its virtuous appearances and feared to stay there; he longed to be of it yet kept fleeing from it to the security of the mind and soul.

Less understood is how the simultaneous feelings of desire and dread Coleridge had for paradise also affected his philosophical – ontological and theological – insights. Creation was an unending re-creative activity for him. That is the assumption behind his famous definition of the imagination in the *Biographia Literaria*, where he posits that the divine creation is an eternal re-creation. Human perception is a continuous repetition of this divine re-creation in the mind of each person, while the poetic imagination is an echo of perception, whose observed objects "it dissolves, diffuses, dissipates, in order to recreate" (*BL*, ch. 13).[38] Thus, Coleridge could pursue the idea of renewable permanence, his metaphysics propounding a continuing apprehensible world, but his emotional misgivings would not permit him to entertain the idea of an eternally preserved paradise.

The same reticence, interestingly, had muted the report of his participation in Humphry Davy's experiments with nitrous oxide, or "laughing gas," in 1799 and 1800, and inhibited his conjectures about the infinite bliss of its mind-expanding power.[39] In fairness to this account of Coleridge's hesitance before paradise it is worth mentioning, as a footnote to the intellectual history of the changing idea of paradise, that the first giddy possibilities fantasized about Davy's discovery of nitrous oxide did not include recovery of Eden. Accounts of the "adventurous philosophers" (Mrs. Beddoes called them that in a letter of May 1799), who cooperated with Davy at Thomas Beddoes's Pneumatic Institute in Bristol in experiments in breathing the gas, exulted over the ecstasy of sensation but did not take the obvious step of identifying this "unmingled pleasure" (so Coleridge described it) with a new inner spatial dimension of paradise. It was not until the second half of the nineteenth century that "the latent religious aspect of the nitrous oxide experience" was admitted by users and analysts;[40] and it is not until William James disclosed its consciousness-altering effects definitively in *The Varieties of Religious Experience* (1902) that the English-speaking world faced up to the mystical potentialities of "a genuine metaphysical revelation" – a converge[nce] of a kind of insight" or "reconciliation" – in such anaesthetics.[41]

Evil had a real and palpable existence for Coleridge; and he saw himself as a man sentenced to a tautological oscillation from unrequited yearning for joy – sensuous and spiritual – to cowardly shrinking from its antithesis. Nor did the pleasure–pain psychology of his day disabuse him of the meretricity of his body's – and soul's – experience. Out of the depth of his complex response to these twin reflexes, he jeers at Hume's "one *Moment*," the simplistic reduction of his "whole being" to "an aggregate of successive single emotions" (*CN*, II, 2370). "I have never loved Evil for its own sake," he exclaims on Sunday, 23 December 1804, "no! nor ever sought pleasure for its own sake, but only as the means of escaping from pains that coiled round my mental powers, as a serpent around the body & wings of an Eagle! My sole sensuality was *not* to be in pain!" (*CN*, II, 2368). Two weeks later he reviews his life, ticking off decisive actions – his hesitant courtship of Mary Evans, his marriage to Sara Fricker, his quarrel with Southey – as being always motivated negatively by dread rather than positively by hope. He wishes to yield himself up to joy; but an inner moral imperative maintains hard-core resistance to the world of the senses. "I write melancholy, always melancholy," he jots in his notebook in 1803; "You will suspect that it is the fault of my natural Temper. Alas! no. – This is the great Occasion that my Nature is made for Joy – impelling me to Joyance – & I never, never can yield to it. – I am a genuine *Tantalus*" (*CN*, I, 1609). In 1808 he acknowledges a symbiotic relationship in his person of love, pain, joy, and the spiritual state of his being:

Love unutterable fills my whole Spirit, so that every fibre of my Heart, nay, of my whole frame seems to tremble under its perpetual touch and sweet pressure, like the string of a Lute – with a sense of vibratory Pain distinct from all other sensations, a Pain that seems to shiver and tremble on the threshold of some Joy, that cannot be entered into while I am embodied.   (*CN*, III, 3370)

The ground here of his moral inhibition was his fear of the earthly body's desires.

At the opposite end of the moral spectrum was recognition of how attractive to him was withdrawal from the world. He longed at moments to give himself up to what John Armstrong calls "that seductive torpor" of the paradisal ideal, to float like the Indian Vishnu "along an infinite ocean cradled in the flower of the Lotos, & wake once in a million years for a few minutes – just to know that I was going to sleep a million years more" (*CL*, I, 350). At one remove Xanadu filled Coleridge with dread. That *"New Paradise"* – as "Perdita" Robinson called it in her poem to Coleridge – was for him, he concluded in bleak self-judgment, as for most fallen sons of Adam, the abode of the temptress Indolence and the sorceress Pleasure.[42] Outside the regular course of life, isolated, rarefied, and exclusive, it might be a fool's paradise, where a "dream of great internal activity" might lull him into sterility of spirit and imagination and "outward inefficience." "I found in my Books and my own meditations," he laments in 1809, "a sort of high-walled Garden, which excluded the very sound of the World without. But the Voice within could not be thrust out – the sense of Duty unperformed, and the pain of Self-dissatisfaction, aided and enforced by the sad and anxious looks of Southey, and Wordsworth, and some few others most beloved by me and most worthy of my regard and affections" (*CL*, III, 216). Not "sunny spots of greenery" ("Kubla Khan") but desolation ("The Wanderings of Cain"), ocean desert ("The Ancient Mariner"), flinty soil ("Ode to the Departing Year"), "dark-brown gardens" and wintry winds ("Dejection: An Ode"), and a dry well ("Love's Apparition and Evanishment") await the eager soul that would enter the sacred garden enclosure of the self and by that action risk shutting itself off from life and the regenerative sense of duty fulfilled.

Given his pre-nineteenth-century sense of social activism and piety, and his personal guilt over his sloth, failed promise, and sensual addiction to drink and drugs, there is little wonder that Coleridge uneasily feared that every flowery bower was in reality an enchanted garden.

4
Wordsworth and the *Axis Mundi* of Grasmere

AS A YOUNG MAN during the *fin de siècle* of the eighteenth century Coleridge briefly preached the millenarian idealism of the time, which, as he advanced into the new century, he compounded with conventional Christian pessimism felt about this world and about his own all-too human personal shortcomings. Wordsworth provides us with yet another touchstone for the Romantic dilemma concerning the recovery of Eden. His enthusiasm for the perfectability of man was initially bound up with the French Revolution, as it was for Blake and Coleridge. "Bliss was it in that dawn to be alive, / But to be young was very heaven!" (*Prel*, x, 693–94) – so Wordsworth understood the presumptions of his age, and the workings of his own mind, if *The Prelude* is any guide to them. When the French solution to society's ills failed to live up to promises, Wordsworth's passionate faith in human and earthly goodness was realigned in a general philosophical sense with nature and in a specifically personal way with his boyhood in the Lake Country and with his decision in 1799 to locate permanently in Grasmere Vale. That piece of real estate, however, and Wordsworth's subsequent poetic effort to define it as a remnant of Eden, proved to be of a different order than the French Revolution so far as its actual bearing on the daily affairs of society. Besides the illogic of a relatively inaccessible part of England standing as representative of the rest of the country, the tendency of Wordsworth's mind to finesse the obvious limitations of place by dwelling on it as a supreme fiction of his sensibility served only to co-opt Grasmere as a symbol of paradise.

Wordsworth's tale of his first glimpse of Grasmere "While . . . yet a Schoolboy"[1] has been known at least since the posthumous publication of *Home at Grasmere* in 1888. In that poem he tells of the impression that the vale made on him as he looked down on its "huge Concave" (*HatG*, 42) from the height of Loughrigg Terrace on the southern rim of the lake. "What happy fortune were it here to live!" he claims to have sighed to himself:

> And if I thought of dying, if a thought
> Of mortal separation could come in
> With paradise before me, here to die.   (9–12)

Strange sentiments for a boy to be murmuring, but prescient, for at the age of twenty-nine, after years of wandering far from the Lake Country he returned to Grasmere, settling into Dove Cottage with Dorothy, his intention that

> here
> Should be my home, this Valley be my World.   (42–43)

That was December 1799. As much in joyous response to spring following a cold winter, as a start at fulfilling his (and Coleridge's) grandiose intentions of writing an omnibus poem, entitled *The Recluse; or Views of Nature, Man, and Society*, which would sum up the spiritual and intellectual odyssey of mankind,[2] Wordsworth began writing *Home at Grasmere* in early 1800.

The poem was earmarked at the time to answer to Wordsworth's immediate poetic expectations and to fulfill in part his long-range ambitions. It was tagged as the first book of the first part of the three-part *Recluse*. As such it was intended to demonstrate Wordsworth's powers as a philosophical poet. It was to be a down payment in earnest of the great poem he still meant to write, and a confident affirmation of the question Wordsworth had asked himself in Goslar, Germany, the previous winter:

> Was it for this
> That one, the fairest of all rivers, loved
> To blend his murmurs with my Nurse's song,
> And from his alder shades, and rocky falls,
> And from his fords and shallows, sent a voice
> That flowed along my dreams?
>
>   (1798–99 Two-Part *Prelude*, 1–6)

In Goslar, cut off from intercourse with Coleridge other than by letter, isolated from the citizenry in a foreign town, with the Harz Mountains a daily presence, Wordsworth's memories had harked back to the years when he was growing up in the Lake Country. Goaded into self-questioning about his poetic vocation, he had been fired to search the experiences of his childhood and youth for signs of his being a chosen person. The immediate result had been most of what would come to be called the great spots of time – the incidents of boat-stealing, trap and nest robbing, ice skating, and lake drowning, the "There was a boy" lines, the episodes of the gibbet and woman with a pitcher, and the holiday wait for horses. Back in England in May 1799, he and Dorothy moved in with the Hutchinsons at Sockburn, Durham. There he began in October crafting these patches of poetry into a continuous poem, which became in December when finished the 1798–99 Two-Part *Prelude*.

When he began *Home at Grasmere* several months after finishing the Two-Part *Prelude*, however, he continued to shy away from the philosophical directions Coleridge intended for *The Recluse* into the more congenial personal channels of celebrating his return to Grasmere, and of analyzing the state of his mind. Even with his digression into autobiography Wordsworth found the poem hard going, its materials recalcitrant to shaping. He struggled to finish it, as best we can conjecture, until at least 1806. Significantly, in this regard, *Home at Grasmere* represents a failed effort of Wordsworth to convert observed phenomena into mythic symbols, chief among these being the conversion of Grasmere into a latter-day paradise *redivivus*.

Home at Grasmere is a tardy rearguard paean of joy at the advent of the millennium. The poem is among the last of a group of poems of the 1790s – which include Coleridge's "Religious Musings" and Blake's *America* and *Europe* – heralding, in response to the political events of the time, a new thousand years of goodness. These poems are part of a larger seventeenth- and eighteenth-century intellectual-poetic tradition which identified joy with prelapsarian innocence. Crucial alike to Coleridge's "Dejection: An Ode" and Edward Young's *Night Thoughts* (1742–45; especially Nights IV, VI, & VIII), the concept is given epigrammatic finality in Young's poem "Resignation":

> Joy is our Eden still possess'd:
> Be gone ignoble grief!
> 'Tis joy makes gods, and men exalts.

The "sweet sounds and harmonies" ("Tintern Abbey," 142) of nature provide the main vehicle by which joy returns the soul to the Edenic state, solemnly invoked in *Home at Grasmere* in "the spousal verse" of man and nature Wordsworth dedicates himself in the apocalyptic conclusion to singing for humanity's sake:

> I feel sweet passions traversing my Soul
> Like Music; unto these, where'er I may,
> I would give utterance in numerous verse.   (*HatG*, 961–63)

Thus does Wordsworth enlist a world view already rendered old-fashioned by scientific empiricism and sensationalist psychology, a notion of world harmony linking divine and mundane spheres in a "Hope for this earth and hope beyond the grave . . . Of joy in widest commonalty spread" (*HatG*, 965, 968).[3] As a late poem, however, in a centuries-old tradition, *Home at Grasmere* shows weariness and doubt, misgiving and self-questioning. Like a gloomy understrain in the poem is heard the nagging disquiet of Wordsworth about Grasmere's living up to his claim for it as "a perfect place" (*HatG*, 22).[4] Qualifying his hosannas to the Vale, although seldom allowed overtly to surface in words, is an unasked question: when he looks at the Vale and thinks he sees "paradise before me" (*HatG*, 12) is he deluded by his desires and its beauty into transfiguring an ordinary village and valley into a chimerical *axis mundi*, and in doing so, rashly arrogating to himself the original sin of Adam's acting independently and in defiance of God's edict? The disaffection at the heart of *Home at Grasmere* indicates that Blake's capacity to internalize paradise as a human property common to all regardless of where one dwells was not as readily shared by Wordsworth, or, as we shall see, by others of the first and second generations of English Romantics.

Wordsworth's unease is revealed fleetingly and indirectly in subtle ways that temper the anticipatory mood which originally moved Wordsworth into song. The submerged doubt appears even at the outset when Wordsworth allows an unwanted echo of unresisted temptation and loss of paradise momentarily to filter into his consciousness. He recalls his boyhood feelings upon his first sight of Grasmere Vale. It was "All that luxurious nature could desire, / But tempting to the Spirit" (23–24). The undercurrent fear of giving way to sin embedded in these lines – comparable to the recoil from ravishment of a tree in "Nutting," lines initially written in Goslar as one of his memories of early preparatory years, but which he excluded from *The Prelude* – is firmly covered up by Wordsworth with the substitution for "tempting" of "stirring" (MS.D), which tersely establishes an alternative oxymoron between stillness of body and excitement of spirit. But Wordsworth's censoring mind had its work cut out for it, since his misgivings about Grasmere kept permeating his words of thanksgiving. There is, for example, the trope of imprisonment contradicting his expression of joy at the unrestricted movement of all "winged creatures" associated with the Vale. The birds are "Lords / Without restraint of all which they behold"; yet their liberty is restricted to "the bounds of this huge Concave" (32–42). There is repeatedly expressed an insecurity of possession. "'Tis mine for life: dear Vale" (52), Wordsworth exults in 1800; yet his shaky sense of ownership, buttressed by memory (personal, historical, and mythic) of dispossession, prompts him by 1812–16 to qualify his certainty to "'tis mine, perchance for life, dear Vale" (MS.D) and to quibble over verbal mood (shifting from MS.B "here / Should be my home" to MS.D "here / Must be my Home," 42–43). There are the tortured, heavily deleted and revised lines (MS.B, 55–98) that simultaneously glory in "unappropriated bliss," ownership, and "gain" won by "an act / Of reason that exultingly aspires," while disclosing apprehensive and irresolute intentions, along with fears of the act being "deemed / A condescension or a weak indulgence / To a sick fancy." The residual fear here of the consequences of filching from heaven itself the forbidden garden of ease sounds a falsetto voice in the mercantile language, in the confusion of the heavenly Lord with an earthly lord of a country estate, and in the assertive pugnaciousness of "What I have gained, / Shall gain, must gain." No wonder Wordsworth wisely added a propitiatory "thanks to God / For what hath been bestowed" (102–03), and in revision for MS.D wisely deleted most of the unstable exaltation.

In effect, Wordsworth alternates in *Home at Grasmere* between self-congratulatory exaltation in his good fortune and fearful suspicion of his insecure hold on it. He likens himself to Adam:

> What Being, therefore, since the birth of Man
> Had ever more abundant cause to speak
> Thanks.   (117–19)

But he cannot forget what happened to Adam – and can happen to him, the most recent avatar of First Man and recipient of God's bounty. As so often with human beings when caught in such shaky circumstances, Wordsworth overcompensates by asserting his hold on paradise as irrevocable.

> The boon is absolute; surpassing grace
> To me hath been vouchsafed; among the bowers
> Of blissful Eden this was neither given
> Nor could be given – possession of the good
> Which had been sighed for, ancient thought fulfilled,
> And dear Imaginations realized
> Up to their highest measure, yea, and more.   (122–28)

The frantic multiple reference of "this" (124) to "boon . . . absolute," "surpassing grace," "possession of the good" and / or of "blissful Eden" sounds a deep-seated uncertainty, however, which spurs Wordsworth to call on the tutelary spirits of the place to confirm and support his tenancy:

> Embrace me then, ye Hills, and close me in;
> Now in the clear and open day I feel
> Your guardianship; I take it to my heart;
> 'Tis like the solemn shelter of the night.   (129–32)

Wordsworth has had proof in his own life that parental security cannot be taken for granted, and that foster parents come in handy at times. A deep suspicion that the divine parentage of human beings is insufficient claim on God the Father, and that God might withdraw his support, prompts Wordsworth to back up that lineage (after all it is stained by disobedience from Adam onward) with a protective secondary line-up of adopted guardians, the hills which nurtured him as a boy. To ensure that his claim to the Vale is legitimate, and that he is worthy of his inheritance, Wordsworth also casts himself in the role of a pilgrim who has earned his way to this holy "Centre" – "A termination and a last retreat" (166–67) – through humble faith and perseverance. The hardships of the move into Dove Cottage, especially the journey in a winter month to Grasmere, is transformed into an archetypal trial of the soul. The Biblical tone of the language is pronounced.

> Bleak season was it, turbulent and bleak,
> When hitherward we journeyed, and on foot.   (218–19)

The journey is seen as a time of testing. "The naked trees, / The icy brooks" – the whole "Stern . . . face of nature" – questions the pair of travelers: "Whence come ye? To what End . . . through my dark domain?" (227–33). Yet, when their way into the promised land proves ultimately unimpeded, and they reach "that hallowed spot" to which their steps "were tending" (250–51), the occasion proves less than one of unalloyed joy, is mysteriously mixed with sadness.

Given this record of Wordsworth's inhibited misgivings about fashioning his return to Grasmere into a sign that mankind was about to resume its paradisal birthright, it is not surprising to find that he temporarily abandoned *Home at Grasmere* probably by the summer–fall of 1800 when he became busy preparing the second edition of *Lyrical Ballads*. In 1802 and the first half of 1803 he concentrated on "small Poems," much to the disgust of Coleridge who wished Wordsworth to get "on with the Recluse exclusively";[5] but instead Wordsworth was drawn again to explore and expand the story of his awakening imagination, as if seeking confirmation anew that Grasmere was a chosen place and he its chosen prophet. During the first three months of 1804 he was hard at work expanding *The Prelude* into a five-book poem. In March 1804 he decided to extend it further. Sustained writing over the next fifteen months (to June 1805) resulted in the thirteen-book *Prelude* of 1805. *Home at Grasmere* is meant to follow at each stage of *The Prelude* as the hard-won fruits of the personal history related there, and to affirm triumphantly the message of the "Glad Preamble" (*Prel*, I, 1–54) and of "the spousal verse" (*HatG*, 959–1048), both of which Wordsworth may have written in an outpour of optimism as early as January 1800.[6] Among its litanies of divine beneficence, the latter proclaims the new revelation that "Paradise and groves / Elysian, fortunate islands, fields like those of old / In the deep ocean" are "the growth of common day" to "minds . . . wedded to this outward frame of things / In love" (996–1001). In a desperate piece of jobbery, Wordsworth uses this assertion of the "great consummation" of "the individual Mind . . . to the external world" (1004–08) to bring *Home at Grasmere* to an unearned completion of sorts sometime in 1806.

Three doubts eat away (not always silently) at the millenarian heart of *Home at Grasmere*: at its claims that Grasmere is an earthly Eden, that its "Inmates" are "not unworthy of their home" (858), and that Wordsworth is a chosen spokesman for these prophetic announcements. Notwithstanding, Wordsworth manages to pray bravely that his verse may, "as a Light hung up in heaven" like a new star of Bethlehem, "chear / Mankind in times to come" (1033–34). In his mind, however, the issue seems not to have been so easily settled; and in 1808 he essayed again the task of establishing Grasmere Vale as a symbolic representation of earthly paradise, and of demonstrating the individual imaginative growth recorded in *The Prelude*, with a new start at *The Recluse*.

The consequences this time around, in "The Tuft of Primroses," reached disaster proportions. With *Home at Grasmere* Wordsworth had struggled after six years to a resounding conclusion reflecting more the mood of 1800 with which he began the poem than the crippling doubts revealed at its core. "The Tuft of Primroses" jerks from topic to topic before stopping on an uncompleted sentence. Their subsequent fates fit the genesis and aborted parturitions of each. *Home at Grasmere* limped into print in 1888, while "The Tuft of Primroses" remained buried among Wordsworth papers until 1949 when it appeared modestly as Appendix C to an edition of *The Excursion*.[7]

A crucial difference between *Home at Grasmere* and "The Tuft of Primroses" is that the latter elegiacally admits that process rules the Vale no less than the rest of earth. In *Home at Grasmere* Wordsworth had designated the specific locality of Grasmere to be an *axis mundi*, "A blended holiness of earth and sky" (163), a "Centre,"

> A Whole without dependence or defect,
> Made for itself and happy in itself,
> Perfect Contentment, Unity entire.   (167–70)

Unhappily, this "timeless" paradise has withstood the diurnal turn of earth poorly. And "The Tuft of Primroses" records melancholy change more than it substantiates continuity and permanence. After a brief thanksgiving for finding the flower, "the voice / Of a surpassing joyance" (55–56), imperishable still on the lonely and otherwise barren mountain crag, Wordsworth rehearses the affecting destruction and death which has visited – or always resided – in the Vale. An "aerial grove" (98) of trees once gracing its center, linking like "a second Heaven"[8] with the heavenly skies, is now reduced to "here and there a straggling Tree . . . left / To mourn . . . To pine and wither for its fellows gone" (102–04). Worse even are the deaths which have decimated several generations of a venerable family, and left desolate their dwelling and gardens.

Bent on treating this or that beloved patch of England as representative of Edenic Earth, the English Romantic poets had in disillusion to come to terms with the frailties of human nature. Wordsworth was as unyieldingly honest in this regard as any of them. He stumbles repeatedly against the stubborn facts of mundane existence in his striving to look on Grasmere at once as an identifiable locality and as a divinely favored spot. When, in *Home at Grasmere*, he tries to claim natural goodness for the "dwellers in this holy place" (366), he incriminates himself in self-validating circularity of thought. The dalesmen of Grasmere *ipso facto* "Must needs themselves be hallowed" because of where they dwell. Wordsworth is moved to this self-betrayal of reasoning by having unworthily (to his mind) conjectured that a pair of swans on Grasmere lake may have been shot by a dalesman. And he follows up his self-confounding testament of faith in the Vale and its inhabitants with the curious confession that some are "Debased" and not "untainted" (423–29), and with three tales about the local shepherds exemplary of infidelity, woe, hardship, unending labor, and loneliness – alleviated by love, endurance, kindliness, and joy. His hesitant view of the human lot, here imperfectly muted and quasi-Ecclesiasticus, is given less inhibited voice in "The Tuft of Primroses." The utterance of mountains and streams "pleads, beseeches, and implores" mankind to "nobler purposes" (251–58).

> In vain: the deafness of the world is here
> Even here, and all too many of the haunts
> Which Fancy most delights in, and the best
> And dearest resting-places of the heart
> Vanish beneath an unrelenting doom.   (259–63)

Despite such recurrent misgivings, Wordsworth had turned toward the end of *Home at Grasmere* to envision the society residing in Grasmere as an example to the rest of the world of a "true community,"

> One Household under God for high and low,
> One family and one mansion; to themselves
> Appropriate and divided from the world.   (822–24)

By a strange constriction of the Vale's "many into one incorporate" (820), these "Inmates not unworthy of their home, / Dwellers of the Dwelling" (858–59), metamorphose into the single Wordsworth family and Dove Cottage. The disquiet of Wordsworth's mind, however, resonates in the double negative of "not unworthy." Nor does the retreat to one "beautiful and quiet home" (863) turn out to be as complete in itself as at first claimed. The legerdemain of a return symbolically to the original pair in Eden by a series of reductions, first from the world at large to the community of Grasmere, then to William and Dorothy in Dove Cottage, is unaccountably reversed when the desired Edenic twosome is reached. At once it is determined that the household is to be "enriched . . . with [one] Stranger" after another. Since to William and Dorothy their seafaring brother John, also Coleridge, and "Sisters of our hearts," the three Hutchinson sisters (869), are not "Strangers," they have to represent less fortunate inhabitants of fallen earth who must be accounted for as occasional partakers of the fortunate pair's bliss. Thus is the divine plenitude of the original brother and sister adulterated? or augmented? person by person from the unhallowed world without into an ever extended family. The intention of the verses here is ambivalent. Less uncertain is the occupants' fear that their hold on the new Eden is as tenuous as the First Couple's, a fear that is conveyed by the clamorous insistence of the imperative and conditional tenses. They *must* "be, with God's will, a happy band" (874) and William *must*, "if . . . divinely taught . . . speak . . . Of what in man is human or divine" (907–09).[9]

The problems posed by *Home at Grasmere* are addressed again in "The Tuft of Primroses." There Wordsworth retreats further from identifying "the aetherial frame" with "this deep vale, its earthly counterpart" (*HatG*, 852–53). Turning away from both the Vale and its counterpart Dove Cottage, Wordsworth reduces the embrace of Grasmere's hills to the annual recurrence of a fragile flower and translates the symbol of the single family and its precarious abode into the narrow dedication of a religious community, the mountain hermitage of St. Basil and "solemn haven" (513) of the Chartreuse. In point of poetic fact the "Power and a protection for the mind" (*HatG*, 458) that Wordsworth from early on in his eulogy of the Vale argues to be one of its symbolic values does not appear to have worked effectively on his behalf. Even his determined will to believe in the natural perfection and purity of Grasmere and in his power to perceive and to "impart it[s]" (901) promise of peace to others – asserted with such heroic resolution at the end of *Home at Grasmere* (875–958) – dwindles in "The Tuft of Primroses" to an echo of itself in the desperate resort to the "embodied dream" (540) of a monastic order. The "majestic, self-sufficing world" of Grasmere, "This all in all of Nature" (*HatG*, 204–05), proves incapable of sustaining the weight of meaning attributed to it.

As more than one critic has remarked, Wordsworth's failure to finish *The Recluse* is explained, in part, by his inability in *Home at Grasmere* and in "The Tuft of Primroses" to make of Grasmere Vale a functional symbol. At the heart of that failure is the improbable dream of finding in Grasmere's natural virtues an inviolate Eden figurative of enjoyment by the "widest commonalty spread" (*HatG*, 968). As if a sign, a recognition, of this fact is the Wordsworths' household transfer in May 1808 from Dove Cottage to Allan Bank, a newly-erected large house across the valley, which William and Dorothy had excoriated, when it was being built, as "a temple of abomination" despoiling "the sweet paradise of Grasmere."[10] But that repugnance yielded of necessity three years later to the practical needs of a growing family, for Wordsworth who had married in 1802 now required more rooms than Dove Cottage afforded. The move was the first step in his withdrawal from Grasmere Vale, which he completed in 1813, relocating for the rest of his life at Rydal Mount on the road to Ambleside, only two miles from Grasmere but a world apart from it as reflected in the social make-up of the two villages and in the psychological perspective of the youthful poet become the ponderous Distributor of Stamps for Westmorland. Thus was Wordsworth's millenarian imagination as regards Grasmere, schooled in the heady hopes of the 1790s, further compromised by matrimonial and parental responsibilities, not to mention the other realities of the age and of his personal life. These were the decades of Napoleonic and post-Napoleonic power politics, and of industrial dislocations, wartime shortages, and economic inequities – all illustrative of obdurate human nature. Then there were the personal tragedies of the death by shipwreck of his brother John, and the disaffection of Coleridge.

In another personally far-reaching way Wordsworth had begun to withdraw from the extreme limitations of Grasmere Vale as paradise at least as early as 1804 when he set to work seriously to write the five-book, and hot on its heels the thirteen-book, *Prelude*, which explicitly re-invents the circumstances in his life as an interior journey of the mind leading him not just to Dove Cottage, Grasmere, but to *Home at Grasmere* and *The Prelude*, and their classification of his return as of one to a private landscape of the mind as much as to a happy valley visited once in boyhood. Already, in the late valedictory lines of *Home at Grasmere* Wordsworth is maneuvering to redefine paradise, relocating Grasmere, where he had initially expected to find it, in his mind – and by extension in the human mind – as a metaphor for inner contentment he glories now in discovering to be his.[11] Unfortunately, by this instinctive tactic – and the sidestep by which Wordsworth anoints himself poet spokesman of the Vale, however private and removed from the rest of the world he finds himself, reveals that Wordsworth is only half-conscious of his feint – Wordsworth identifies his sense of the poet's condition with his sense of the human condition. For that reason, Wordsworth continues to hold in loose solution the geographical and the mental ideas of paradise, not clearly recognizing their incompatibility.

The question of paradise, its presence and place in our lives – whether it is actually accessible

> in the very world which is the world
> Of all of us, the place in which, in the end,
> We find our happiness, or not at all   (*Prel*, x, 726–28)[12]

or apprehensible by mortals only in an internalized form as a witness of God's grace working in one preparatory for the real thing in afterlife – embodied a complex conundrum at the heart of Wordsworth's conception of himself as a poet. There was his deep-seated urge toward a personal poetry that separated him, as special and unique, from society. At the same time the role of poet retained for him its time-honored public function as seer, teacher, and herald. His oscillations from private to public utterances vividly document his uncertainty. There are his successive ever longer versions of "The Poem to Coleridge" (*The Prelude*) concerning the growth and history of his own mind, which was known to his intimate circle of friends and family but never published in his lifetime. Opposed to it, and interspersed between its successive texts, stand the stuttered segments of *The Recluse – Home at Grasmere*, "The Tuft of Primroses," and *The Excursion* – whose unfinished state haunted Wordsworth for almost fifty years. Yet, there was movement if not progression, as Wordsworth aged, pursued his earthly pilgrimage, and followed his poetic destiny.

The doggedness of his continued expansion of *The Prelude* between 1800 and 1805, and his revisions in 1816/19 and in the 1830s, paradoxically reveal the contrary socially responsible direction his poetry would take in the second half of his life. The France books of *The Prelude* (IX–X) read suspiciously like a determined second effort of Wordsworth (counting the temporarily blocked *Home at Grasmere* as the first) to give vocal expression to the millenarian expectations which had animated him and his generation in the 1790s. But the utterance eludes poetic conviction in *Home at Grasmere*; and it remains stylistically half-digested in *The Prelude*. The France books are made up mostly of flat pell-mell narration. Exceptions with "a strain / More animated" (x, 636–37) are the "Bliss was it in that dawn" (x, 693–728) and the Robespierre (x, 441–567) passages. At other times the narration becomes drily argumentative, faithfully mirroring Wordsworth's state of mind at the time:

> now believing,
> Now disbelieving, endlessly perplex'd
> With impulse, motive, right and wrong, the ground
> Of moral obligation – what the rule,
> And what the sanction . . . demanding *proof*,
> And seeking it in everything. (x, 893–98)

Consequently, these books stand apart from the sublime elevation of the ordinary, of Books I and II, and of so much of the rest of the poem.

Wordsworth's replacement of Dove Cottage in *Home at Grasmere* with the monastery in "The Tuft of Primroses" is not capricious. If the glorified self-image of a sublime recluse was to figure for his fellow beings as an emblem of their birthright, he had to find a way of uniting his isolate self with the vast bulk of society, for whom Grasmere Vale was an impractical solution to the banishment from Eden. The combination of paradisal seclusion and holy chastisement embedded in the monastery image answered to the needs of both his imagination and his poetic creed. But Wordsworth needed more than a metaphor to resolve the duality of purpose inhibiting his completion of *Home at Grasmere* and "The Tuft of Primroses." A larger shift in conception of the poet was called for.

Illuminating the hesitancies of mind with which Wordsworth contended from roughly 1800 onward, and feints in the art of survival he practiced in his poetry, is a sequence of three sonnets – "Seclusion," "Continued," and "Reproof" – from *Ecclesiastical Sonnets* (Part I, XXI–XXIII), first published as *Ecclesiastical Sketches* in 1822, but added to and republished repeatedly to almost the end of Wordsworth's life. When juxtaposed to *Home at Grasmere* and *The Prelude*, these three sonnets place in complex relationship a series of human alternatives – the "war-worn Chieftain" and the "Sublime Recluse," Wordsworth and "venerable Bede," the indolent Romantic poet and the active Christian votary – correspondent to the kind of poet he was trying to be, and to the language and form his poetry was to become. Eventually settled by the weight of time and acceptance, and the accumulation of poems, these questions surfaced from at least his first formal try at *The Recluse* in the recalcitrant lines of *Home at Grasmere* and remained disquietingly present until well into the 1820s.

Wordsworth had exulted with Miltonic bravado in the Glad Preamble to *The Prelude*, begun probably 18 November 1799,[13] that the world lay before him (I, 15) as he walked toward Grasmere for another look at the house where he would shortly begin a new life. His Adamic voice yearned, he tells us,

> towards some philosophic Song
> Of Truth that cherishes our daily life;
> With meditations passionate from deep
> Recesses in man's heart, immortal verse
> Thoughtfully fitted to the Orphean lyre. (I, 230–34)

But his imagination "Turn[ed] recreant" (I, 260) to such "awful burthen," prompting him to "Take refuge" in the comforting thought that "mellower years will bring a riper mind / And clearer insight" (I, 235–38). The direction his truancy then took is the familiar Wordsworthian one toward solitude, of straying "about / Voluptuously through fields and rural walks . . . given up / To vacant musing" (I, 252–55), which in *The Prelude* and *Home at Grasmere* Wordsworth is at great pains to translate as prophetic truths of "The human Soul of universal earth, / Dreaming on things to come" (*HatG*, MS.D, 837–38),

> Of the individual Mind that keeps her own
> Inviolate retirement, subject there
> To Conscience only, and the law supreme
> Of that Intelligence which governs all.
> (*HatG*, MS.D, 772–75)

In the three *Ecclesiastical Sonnets*, the terms of the Wordsworthian sojourn on "This dawning earth" (*Prel*, V, 538) receive considerable redirection.[14] Whereas Wordsworth's imagination had fruitfully taken refuge in voluptuous solitary communion with the natural and enclosed world of Grasmere Vale, "The war-worn Chieftain quits the world" for the "cloistered privacy" of Monks, "not to dwell / In soft repose" but to do active penitence in his cell "At morn, and eve, and midnight's silent hour" for his soul's salvation ("Seclusion," 4–9). As if measuring the dimensions that such a change in frame of reference has for his value system, Wordsworth follows up the conventional Christian sentiments of "Seclusion" with a playful reiteration, in "Continued," of the Romantic ethos of *The Prelude* and *Home at Grasmere*:

> Methinks that to some vacant hermitage
> *My* feet would rather turn – to some dry nook
> Scooped out of living rock, and near a brook
> Hurled down a mountain-cove from stage to stage,
> Yet tempering, for my sight, its bustling rage
> In the soft heaven of a translucent pool;
> Thence creeping under sylvan arches cool,
> Fit haunt of shapes whose glorious equipage
> Would elevate my dreams. A beechen bowl,
> A maple dish, my furniture should be;
> Crisp, yellow leaves my bed; the hooting owl
> My night-watch: nor should e'er the crested fowl
> From thorp or vill his matins sound for me,
> Tired of the world and all its industry.

While superficially linking nature and monasticism, "Continued," in fact, ridicules the Romantic retirement theme, and indirectly dismisses the creed, intoned in the late passages of *Home at Grasmere*, which aspired to attach a symbolic value to Wordsworth's happy solitude there. The mocking lines of "Continued" transform Grasmere Vale, by silent implication, into a "vacant hermitage." The evidence rests in the third sonnet, which shatters with a "Reproof" Wordsworth's fancied reversion, in "Continued," to a recluse of the old Romantic dispensation. The two sonnets contrast the Wordsworthian Solitary to Bede. The result is a moral redefinition of the "voluptuous indolence" which Wordsworth had described, without undue guilt, in the opening lines of *The Prelude*. In "Continued" Wordsworth imagines himself a "Sublime Recluse" again, who half-satirically, half-nostalgically, fashions his furniture out of nature's resources, a "beechen bowl" and a "maple dish," leaves for a bed, and hooting owl for a night-watch, and who sees "soft heaven" in "a translucent pool." The ironic negation implied in the extravagance of sentiment, and, however obliquely, in the veiled identification of the Romantic self as a latter-day Narcissus, is explicitly confirmed by the contrary "Perpetual industry" of Bede beside "a wild coast" where "billows beat." The terms of "cloistered privacy" have been carried to a communal completion unknown to either the penitential Chieftain or the Romantic Solitary. When their songs of self-interest are placed beside the "toil stupendous" with which Bede put his learning at the disposal of church and humankind, the rich duality of reference of "Sublime Recluse" is fully realized. Idle Romantic solitude has been transmogrified into the Victorian work ethic and its parade of communal virtues.

Wordsworth's repeated use of "recreant" in reference to these diverse actions also alerts us to his unease with the heroics of his Adamic persona. In *The Prelude* his distress at the imagination's recreant retreat (I, 260) from its "holy services"

(1, 63) is balanced by his gay insouciance to be free to "stray about / . . . through fields and rural walks, / And ask no record of the hours" (1, 252–54). In *Ecclesiastical Sonnets*, "recreant soul," appearing appropriately only in "Reproof" the last of the three sonnets, describes each of the three types depicted: the Chieftain who has betrayed his military oath of duty, the Romantic Solitary who turns away from his sacred commitment to other than the self, and Bede whose fidelity to the spiritual needs of church and community places in relief their dereliction by defining the reverse sense of the term.

The reproof is pointed, however much it takes place dialectically between sonnets and between a poetic persona and the imagined "Shade" of an historical figure. In *Ecclesiastical Sonnets* Wordsworth hit upon the solution that had evaded him in *Home at Grasmere*. Not in personal prophecy but in church history; not in the promisory "I" but in the realized institution; not in the natural self but in authorized and lived tradition; not in private worship, but in public offering Wordsworth found the means of mirroring his youthful sense that "the actual world of our familiar days" (*Prel*, XII, 362) gives "sight / Of a new world" (*Prel*, XII, 370–71) – that

> Not favour'd spots alone, but the whole earth,
> The beauty wore of promise, that which sets,
> To take an image which was felt, no doubt,
> Among the bowers of Paradise itself,
> The budding rose above the rose fullblown.
>
> (*Prel*, X, 702–06)

Once devised, it is no wonder he kept adding sonnets to the original 1822 *Ecclesiastical Sketches*, publishing successive revised and expanded editions from 1822 to 1845.

This is not to say that the *Ecclesiastical Sonnets* sounds Wordsworth's triumphant vision of the earth in "Infinity's embrace" (*ES*, Part 3, XLV). Their public voice oversees a retreat from his ungoverned glory in "the walks of homely life" (*Prel*, XII, 265) that reigns unruly in *Home at Grasmere* and ultimately escapes his governance. At the same time, the voice contrives an affirmation of the sacred nature of our "native turf" (*ES*, Part 3, XLI) historically consonant with the church and the providential responsibility to humanity of the recluse Bede. Poem by poem the *Ecclesiastical Sonnets* reaches, not unlike the Gothic architecture whose "daring art" (*ES*, Part 3, XLV) Wordsworth lauds, toward exaltation of "the eternal City – built / For the perfected Spirit of the just!" ("Conclusion," *ES*, Part 3, XLVII). The conventional Christian piety at the conclusion of *Ecclesiastical Sonnets* is the price Wordsworth paid for finding a way to translate his private internalized paradise into an assured public catechism answering to the spiritual hopes and needs of his audience as much as to his own wants.

The faith in an earth "nowhere unembellished by some trace / Of that first Paradise whence man was driven" (*Prel*. [1850], III, 111–12) persists to the end of his life in a secure nook of Wordsworth's mind as a relic of the idyllic promises of his and Dorothy's coming to Grasmere in 1800. But again and again Wordsworth hesitates over its reality when couched solely in terms of his personal experience. His after-thought is to qualify his initial intuition, is to resort to negative phrasing, as in "Nowhere unembellished," and to water down original assertions in revision.[15] Even in that dawn of hope in the winter of 1799–1800 when he and Dorothy settled into Dove Cottage the Edenic dream had had an air of unattainable nostalgia about it – "that perfect age / How dear to think of"[16] – that prefigures its sinking into forgetfulness with the light of common day. After *Home at Grasmere* and "The Tuft of Primroses" Wordsworth did not attempt again a full poetic transformation of "this stained world"[17] into the limpid prelapsarian one. Instead, he sublimated his interior voice to the test and discipline of history, and submitted realization of the millennium to the test and promise of the historical church. He put his poetic voice to the communal service of his fellows, institutionalizing its vision of imminence. By this means he gained a language for earthly bliss that *Home at Grasmere* had lacked, even as, paradoxically, he lost its felt advent.

5
Byron's and Shelley's Hesperian Islands

THE EARTH Coleridge and Wordsworth looked out upon, especially in the Lake Country, still held fast to its timeless agrarian pursuits and pastoral mood, making it possible for them to mistake their interiorization of paradise as a facsimile of the outer countryside. Byron's and Shelley's post-Napoleonic world was fast changing into the urban and industrial environment that is so familiar to the inhabitants of the twentieth century. Wordsworth could congratulate himself at the beginning of the new century on his return to Grasmere Vale and the paradise of his boyhood years, and Coleridge could quietly move north to share it even though five years earlier he had banished himself from the seductive sylvan (and honeymoon) bower of Clevedon, Somersetshire, in response to the socially-conscious imperative that he not callously enjoy his private millennium when the public still hungrily awaited the scripturally announced one – or at least that is the way he reconstructed his actions in the poem "Reflections on Having Left a Place of Retirement" (1796). Byron and Shelley, contrariwise, looked out on a world marred among other things by the dandyism of the Regency and post-Waterloo years, the massacre at Manchester, and the accumulating stain of smoke and steam in the sky – all of which seemed to forebode a distant cataclysmic event, and were read by some as portent of apocalypse. Byron with his abiding sense of lost bliss read the signs as further evidence of the passing of the earthly paradise; and Childe Harold, that "wandering outlaw of his own dark mind" (3, iii), became for the post-Napoleonic generations representative of the eternal Cain each saw as his mortal fate. Shelley with his intermittent glimpses of "some unseen Power" that "Floats though unseen amongst us" ("Hymn to Intellectual Beauty," 1–2) claimed the signs of the times as harbingers of a restored perfection; and he was forever urging his fellow sufferers to hasten toward it, although his public trumpet call of hope grew muted as the years advanced.

Philosophically and temperamentally poles apart the two friends nevertheless are like the opposing sides of a coin in their hopes and fears for mankind. Both claimed human faculties rather than divine fiat as the source of authority and power, but Byron in gloomy defiance and Shelley in ecstatic assertion. Both affirmed love, "passion's golden purity" and "The fountains of our deepest life" (*Epipsychidion*, 571, 570), as the spiritual basis of paradise, and the alembic which could render earth into a new Eden, but Byron despairingly allows its alchemy

97

only retrospective and transient force while Shelley irrepressibly anticipates its future and permanent reign. Both acknowledged the force of nature and the pilgrimage of man through an enslaved world, but Byron fixates on flawed human nature and the endless inconclusiveness of its reach for perfection whereas Shelley dwells on ideal nature and its generative power to transform the real into absolute terms.

Their personal lives intertwined, first in 1816 when they met in Switzerland and sailed around Lake Leman together, and regularly after 1818 when their mutual exile from England prompted each off and on to seek consolation in the other's company. Although *Childe Harold 3* stands as a reminder of Shelley's impact on Byron in the early days of their friendship, Byron's sardonic disillusionment more likely functioned in their day-to-day relations as a counter weight to Shelley's incorrigible idealism than the reverse, which Shelley confirms in *Julian and Maddalo* (1818–19). Furthermore, as domestic tragedy and worldly malice irremediably touched his last years, Shelley found it ever more difficult to muster beyond irregular inspired moments his belief in the durability of the earthly paradise; and first-hand attachments such as those which sustained Constable's and Palmer's faiths in the Stour and Shoreham valleys had not been part of his transient life. The lengthening elegiac shadow of life slowly qualified Shelley's early confidence in the mind's capacity to triumph over a sordid world that is the multitude's daily experience. If he could still end *Prometheus Unbound* (1818–19) with the ringing faith that through love, gentleness, virtue, wisdom, and endurance mankind can "defy Power which seems Omnipotent," and "reassume / An empire o'er the disentangled Doom," in Hope creating "From its own wreck the thing it contemplates" (IV, 568–74), he also was ready to credit mutability and evil and flawed human nature, "The oppressor and the oppressed" multitudes alike (*Peter Bell the Third* [1819], III, 253), as formidable antagonists to achievement of these goals. In less politically contentious mood he willingly admitted that

> The sweetest flowers are ever frail and rare,
>   And love and freedom blossom but to wither;
> And good and ill like vines entangled are,
>   So that their grapes may oft be plucked together.
>
> ("Marenghi," X, 47–50)

Despite the incompatibility of their temperaments, Byron and Shelley found bridges and connectives across the gap in their outlooks, sunny moments streaking across Byron's nighttime landscape, and shadows pocketing Shelley's Golden Age with gloom. And the suffused golden nimbus of orthodoxy with which a Constable and a Palmer might bless their vales remained repugnant to both to the end.

In one respect the several generations of Romantics shared a *topos* – enveloping, encircling, centering – for the contour of paradise. They were all seekers of the symmetrical, or spiritual, moment outside time, when one felt the self a living part of the surrounding natural whole. This moment includes Blake's human form divine – in its fallen guise the body of Albion as an island – an internalized and individualized center with its own circumference available to each person regardless of place or time; Coleridge's and Wordsworth's tree-shaded bowers, sylvan *genii locorum* scattered through the Quantock hills and Westmorland fells; Palmer's and Constable's durable river valleys; Keats's cool spirit-haunted grottoes and caves; and Byron's and Shelley's (and after them Tennyson's and Arnold's) island Elysiums far from shipping lanes and "the tattered pall of time" ("Lines written among the Euganean Hills," 172), sunny axes of divine favor, where human love enjoys more than human intensity. Whatever the form it represents a center of sacred energy in an otherwise profane mutable world. For such "wanderers o'er Eternity" as Byron and Shelley, "Whose bark drives on and on, and anchor'd ne'er shall be" (*Childe 3*, lxx), the appeal metaphorically and actually of fixed abode and blessed prospects was irresistible. Surrounded by the debris of civilization, sated on the crass social indulgences of England and the dissipated moral grandeur of Italy, these two dissident members of the British aristocracy who had fled the oppressive hypocritical gaiety of "Regency" London to move restlessly amidst the indifferent decay of Venice, Pisa, Naples, and Ravenna, let thoughts of some wandering isle of the antipodes, a natural enclave at the farthest remove from civilization, push their imaginations to the outermost limits that mythology and modern travel allowed them to conceive.

Lord Byron (1788–1824) was born too late to believe with the faith of a Thomas Johnes in the heterogeneous consolation that characterizes Hafod. How rag-tag and indecorous Byron would have considered its complication of perfection out of cultural odds and ends, aesthetic shreds-and-patches, and politico-economic jobbery is conveyed to us by his description of Norman Abbey, that stale Edenic county seat of Amundevilles in Canto 13 of *Don Juan*. Its model his childhood home of Newstead Abbey, the poetic reconstruction displays the mixed feelings of its author's "grand impression" (lxvii) of its "Sad, but serene . . . grey ruin" (lxiv) and his ironic distaste for what he calls its not "quite lawful marriage of the Arts" (lxvii). At one level the lines record a disgraced aristocrat's elegy in exile of a lionized period in his life when he observed like others of his social class the long weekend ritual of the country seat, elevated by the eighteenth-century money-and-power cliques into a new-model preservation of paradise. The conventionality of the poetic diction, the artificiality of the inverted syntax, and the worn neo-classical movement of the balanced phrases disclose, however, the worldly-wise poet-narrator's present scepticism about this particular form of Eden. In the park herds of "dappled foresters" "quaff" from a brook which "murmured like a bird" (lvi). There is a river whose "liquid bed" in places runs so turgidly ("which its soften'd way did take") that its "flood" like the inverted syntax of its description appears almost to reverse its flow (lvii). In another part of the forest it "dash'd" into a "steep cascade," before sinking into a "rivulet" whose "windings" proceed "now gleaming, and now hiding," "now clear, now blue . . . as the skies their shadows threw" (lviii). The florid language parodies the mannerisms

of the picturesque tradition and the affectations of Byron's poetic contemporaries; and the passage contrasts sharply with the Horatian "plain style" of
the poem.[1] As if to cap this dismissal of a hackneyed Eden, whose Gothic decay
and pastoral peace the vogue in the previous century had left tacky and shopworn,
the presumed earthly paradise is here further polluted by the corrupt weekend
company who flock from the city to sample its elevating atmosphere.

Aside from Milton and Blake, no English poet probably was more obsessed
with the myth of the Fall and of man's eternal damnation than Byron.[2] In Don
Alfonso standing supplicatingly before the seductive Donna Julia, Byron gives us
an emblem of all humankind through history who have stood "like Adam
lingering near his garden, / With useless penitence perplex'd and haunted" (*DJ 1*,
clxxx). It is appropriate then that the idea of paradise – and its loss – held his
imagination in thralldom, and that Eden figures ubiquitously in his poems as a
metaphoric yardstick for measuring the extent to which the world has fallen away
from this ideal. All about him Byron saw tantalizing vestiges of paradisal glory in
the "magic waste" (*Childe 2*, xciii) of the earthly abode: in remembered childhood
innocence, in the ardent human heart, in rapturous first love, in fiercely sustained
freedom, in noble scenery, in time-consecrated Greece, in Parnassus, and in
supportive art and poetry.

Robert Gleckner makes the acute observation that Byron was plagued less "by
the idea of original sin, of man's inherited damnation," than by "a world that
renders man's propensity to good (however small) nugatory and sentences him to
eternal exile, alone."[3] "From our birth," Byron complained, "the faculty divine /
Is chain'd and tortured – cabin'd, cribb'd, confined" (*Childe 4*, cxxvii). Byron's
gaze is finally, then, less on the Fall and banishment from Eden, which becomes a
metaphor for loss, than on "the consequences of the Fall,"[4] on an earthly
pilgrimage fraught with disappointment, endlessly enticing one to the portals of
Eden only to find there that the gates remain eternally shut. Thus is man seen as
an eternal wanderer; and so Byron defined himself literally, and paradigmatically
– "I . . . a northern wanderer, weep for thee" – in "Ode to Venice" (5). From
Childe Harold to Don Juan, through the literary guises of the Giaour, Corsair,
Cain, and Manfred, man is portrayed as doomed to exile equally by outer
circumstances and by inner defects – as much by social virtues of generosity,
loyalty, and honesty as by personal vices of malice, duplicity, and fear. Jerome J.
McGann, following Herbert Marcuse, has refocused Gleckner's observation,
stigmatizing this recurrent existential lesson as a "second" fall that is an
unnecessary product of "superfluous" evil and of the disintegration of civil order
into barbarous violence.[5] According to McGann, Byron translated the myths of
Original Sin against God and Paradise Lost into transgressions against society and
the consequent loss of civilization. The second fall thus becomes the product of
socio-political outrage rather than of moral-spiritual sin. McGann's surmise is
attractive because it places Byron within the coming Victorian intellectual
tradition that associated paradise with civilization. The fault with this neat
confinement of earthly paradise to civil order, unfortunately, is that Byron was

too embued with the Romantic attitudes of his generation to exclude the corruption of human nature from his prognoses about the spiritual health of the body politic. Byron was finally no less ambivalent about the positive value of civilization than he was about the sacramental order of nature and the human propensity to good. Indeed, an act of violence against the community, which McGann characterizes as a second fall, is viewed by Byron when perpetrated by an individual such as Castlereagh, to have been motivated as likely by an inner moral weakness as by a political power struggle.

Byron's jaundiced view of mainland civilization allowed him to entertain occasional positive feelings for islands as antipodean nurseries of heroic companies of people. Associated in his mind with a mythological golden age, an heroic Hellenic past, and a sunny Mediterranean sea, they are "blessed isles" over which "every season smiles / Benignant" (*The Giaour*, 7–8). They loomed in his mind as places to escape from the conformist pressures of society, places to which one fled in imagination, undaunted by "the roar / Of breakers" (*DJ 10*, iv), because they were isolated from the demoralizing lures of civilization. Such islands figure for Byron as symbols of universal desire, rectifying however momentarily the primal sentence of humans to unrequited longing for perfect happiness. In this respect they held for him the appeal they have historically had for men staring up at the stars traveling through boundless space and more prosaically for seafarers "leaving land far out of sight" to venture out on "The Ocean of Eternity" (*DJ 10*, iv). They are places of safety and refuge in the "deep wide sea of misery" ("Lines written among the Euganean Hills," 2).

But not for long! Inevitably, the corrupt world invades the farthest atoll, or the archipelago succumbs to internal flaws. As instances sprinkled through his verse indicate, Byron looked on islands as tentative havens at best. The island stronghold of the Corsair – "more than doubtful Paradise . . . of earthly hope" (III, vi, 1406–07) – fails to survive the change in fortunes of its Adamic landlord. Venice – greatest of "These Edens of the eastern wave" (*The Giaour* 15) – now "Sinks, like a sea-weed, into whence she rose!" (*Childe 4*, xiii). Evoked as "Eve of the land which still is paradise!" (xlvi) in *Beppo* Byron sardonically admits as one might of a woman once loved whose beauty has inevitably succumbed to the ravages of time, that Venice is now a land less of "mirth and innocence" than of "milk and water" (lxxx). And the Cycladic island on which Don Juan and Haidee, "Nature's bride" (2, ccii), walk "hand in hand" (2, clxxxiv) along the beach like the world's first parents, and first lovers, remains their earthly paradise only until Haidee's freebooter father Lambro, a "sea-solicitor" of sorts (3, xxvi), returns to mete out the rough justice of a father and a property owner outraged by the illegal filching of what is his.

In mythology, islands have been fearsome places as readily as havens of safety. Quite literally they often posed a threat to life in the moment when refuge beckoned most enticingly at the line where sea and rock met. At psychological and symbolic levels of apprehension, while marking them as sacred centers of life, as omphalos offering a superior, unchanging, and desirable existence, tradition has recognized that islands harbored the negative aspect of the life force as well, the anti-mother archetype, a witch, a siren, who can undo the positive energies of earth, making them dark places of the unknown, of mystery and disaster. Thus have islands been identified equally with the earthly paradise and with its inversion, the enchanted garden, where all is illusion, artificiality, and sterility. If the western isles of the "Age of Gold" (*DJ* 6, lv) lie in the farthest reaches of the earth's waters, fearsome islands dot the sea closer to home, the haunts of Circe, Calypso, and the sirens ever posing a threat to mariners, as Odysseus and his sailors learn to their horror, where love turns men into beasts, desire holds them captives, and enervation enslaves them.

That Byron was not unaware of this negative side to the earthly paradise is apparent in the ambivalent details he uses repeatedly to describe Juan and Haidee's love. Haidee is at once nurturing mother to Juan (she – that is, her maid Zoe – cooks him appetizing meals) and vampire dependent on his life for her own (her mouth "seem'd almost prying into his for breath," 2, cxiii). At another time he lies beneath her gaze "Hush'd as a babe upon its mother's breast" (2, cxlviii); while like Death itself (so she is described in Canto 2, cxvii) she bends over him in his sleep "with hush'd lips, that drank his scarce-drawn breath" (2, cxliii).

Like other terrestrial promises of Eden, island Elysiums meet with Byron's usual skepticism; and he can resort to them for an image of illusion, and false hope, with easy suavity when it suits his poetic needs, as in a deleted stanza of *Childe Harold 2*:

> Frown not upon me, churlish Priest! that I
>   Look not for Life, where life may never be,
>   I am no sneerer at thy phantasy—
>   Thou pitiest me, alas! I envy thee,
>   Thou bold Discoverer in an unknown sea
>   Of happy isles and happier tenants there—
>   I ask thee not to prove a Sadduccee;
>   Still dream of Paradise thou know'st not where,
> Which if it be thy sins will never let thee share.[6]

One comes upon *The Island* then with surprise. The last long poem and dramatic tale Byron wrote before he left Italy for Greece in the summer of 1823 and his death the following April, it appears to represent a complete volte-face. Thus has the poem been wonderingly read by most (when read and dealt with seriously at all). In the "miraculous" preservation of the Highlander Torquil from the pursuing English sailors sent to apprehend the Bounty mutineers, in his resurrection from the undersea cave to live happily ever after with Neuha on the island of Toobonai, and in the rebirth metaphor and the enduring paradise motif underscored by these events – Byron is held to have yielded to his dream that the damned human race could mitigate through love the divine edict of the Fall.[7]

So to read *The Island* we must accept first that Byron reversed himself on attitudes he had clung to for almost a lifetime, second that he uncharacteristically identified Eden with primitive peoples and manners, and third that he regressed stylistically to the outlook and form of the early oriental narratives, with Fletcher Christian an inward-brooding guilt-ridden Byronic hero *redivivus*. It would be easier to entertain such surprising inconsistencies and atavisms if we knew how much Byron was familiar with the primitivist theorizing of his contemporaries and with the literature of the early South Pacific explorations of Wallis, Cook, Bougainville, and others. We know, however, little more than what Byron himself cites in a headnote to the poem as his sources. And that tantalizing allusion to "The foundation of the following story . . . [being] found partly in Lieutenant Bligh's 'Narrative of the Mutiny and Seizure of the Bounty, in the South Seas, in 1789'; and partly in 'Mariner's Account of the Tonga Islands'" is of little help. So far as can be determined Byron was unfamiliar with the actual details of the Bounty hearing and courtmartial of the captured mutinous sailors; and he seems not to have learned of the discovery of Pitcairn Island and the subsequent fate of Fletcher Christian.[8]

One cannot ignore the possibility that the romantic and relatively uncertain aftermath of the Bounty mutiny, and the unknown nature of that part of the world, leaving him free to invent what he pleased, appealed as much to Byron as anything in the skimpy facts that were known. Equally important to a poet who took pride in his sales was that the subject still had popular appeal. For all the extensive literature which had heralded in the last quarter of the eighteenth century the newly discovered paradises of the South Seas, the information tended to be forbiddingly technical or suspiciously impressionistic. The conflicting claims for life on the islands were especially contradictory. The initial tendency had been to make much of the idyllic life of the islanders. Bougainville had called Tahiti "the new Cytherea," and Joseph Banks had deplored the inadvertent killing of a Tahitian, saying, "If we quarrelled with those Indians, we should not agree with angels."[9] With surprising rapidity, however, this initial euphoria brought on by the discovery supposedly of the closest known earthly approximation to Eden gave way to more realistic perceptions. There were shortcomings in this paradise. All the early explorers reported as a minor irritant the propensity to theft of the natives, and to the fragility of their existences. They noted also that the angelic natives were unable to resist European vices; and the final disenchantment was to learn that the natives often lived violent and brutish lives. In 1791 the surgeon on H.M.S. *Pandora* observed that the ravages of venereal disease were already afflicting the Tahitians; and in 1796 the London Missionary Society sent four missionaries to that by now sorely tested island to rehabilitate its paradisal state by civilized Christian means.

A similar mixed view of the blessings of civilization and of the chimera of primitive Edens informs *The Island*. Byron generally refuses to pretend that innocent nature can survive intact the passionate embrace of civilization. When he meditates on Neuha's and Torquil's love, he gloomily predicts that the South Seas Eve will learn from Europe's fallen son "Passion's desolating joy" (II, 112), which is "powerful over every heart, but most / O'er those who know not how it may be lost" (II, 113–14), and in that knowledge will lose her island paradise.

Some hundred lines later, yielding to Romantic illusions, however, Byron blandly ignores his augury to assert, apropos of the return of the mutineers to Tahiti, that "The New World stretched its dusk hand to the Old,"

> Tamed each rude wanderer to the sympathies
> Of those who were more happy, if less wise,
> Did more than Europe's discipline had done,
> And civilised Civilisation's son!   (II, 239, 268–71)

Never mind the decree of God and the inherent moral defect of man, Byron momentarily lets himself fantasize, the island paradises of the South Seas need not succumb to the vices of European culture. They will bask endlessly in the sun of their insular innocence. Yet, Byron's reservations about human happiness and earthly prospects more often than not compromise his optimistic sentiments. Ambiguity colors his effort to cast the Bounty mutiny in a cosmic scheme of consequences. He attributes the mutiny to its seamen's languishing, like latter-day Odysseans, for return to "the happy shores without a law" (I, 209) where "summer years and summer women smile" (I, 28), thus making Eden its own subversive inciter to vice and crime – and agent of its own destruction.

Uneasy compromises with conviction pervade the poem's self-contradictory truce with illusion. Only by reducing Neuha and Torquil – both grown adults – to "children of the isles" (II, 274) and Toobonai to an as "yet infant world" (IV, 420), by blurring Torquil to a half-savage (II, 304) and like Neuha "nourish'd amidst nature's" mountainous wilds (II, 276), and by pretending that no third and fourth ships will follow the first and second to Toobonai to disrupt Neuha and Torquil's "happy days" (IV, 419), can Byron assume for his narrative purposes that Torquil will hold onto his "Paradise . . . breathing in the sigh / Of Nature's child in Nature's ecstasy" (III, 199–200) beyond the first blissful gush of love. Even by thus simplifying his mature judgment about man's chances of attaining in a "sea-green isle" a second "guilt-won Paradise" (III, 39), Byron cannot give himself up unreservedly and unimaginatively to the dream. He readily constructs a bitter end for Fletcher Christian and the other mutineers:

> Proscribed even in their second country, they
> Were lost; in vain the World before them lay.   (III, 43–44)

Byron echoes here Milton's oft-quoted bitter-sweet summation of Adam and Eve's departure from Eden, which more than one Romantic poet had used contrariwise to express his joyous faith in this world as a sacred and unfallen extension of Eden, equivalent and perhaps even superior to it. Byron had so invoked the lines in "Epistle to Augusta" (1816) to describe his hope that in nature he would find reason for living. Such philosophic hope he denies the mutineers. The subtitle of the poem is "Or Christian and His Comrades." As its title promises, *The Island* devotes as much space to their crime and punishment, as to the recreation of a South Sea island Eden. The level of regard Byron held for the latter sections of the poem is conveyed in a letter of 25 January 1823 to Leigh

Hunt. In a sneering reference to "the most *pamby* portions of the Toobonai Islanders," he wagered that they will nevertheless "be the most agreeable to the enlightened Public."[10]

In calling the paradisal descriptions of Toobonai the "pamby portions," Byron was passing judgment on more than their poetic value, however much the quality of the verse was included in his strictures, and it is surprisingly uneven for a poet at the height of his powers. After a strong start narrating the events of the mutiny, the verse deteriorates into grammatical and syntactical confusion in Canto 2, especially in the opening sections which attempt to establish the idyllic setting of Toobonai. In giving us an example of the songs of Toobonai, as a way of defining the paradisal scene, Byron relied heavily on prose translations of Tonga Island songs. Byron's impatience with the sentiments is evident, and reflects his disbelief that man can imaginatively, let alone literally, ever know paradise again. Byron's interest lies elsewhere in the poem: in the narrative of the mutiny, in the guilty defiance of Fletcher Christian, in the buffoonery of Ben Bunting, in the chase and fight with the mutineers, in the tensions consequent on the meeting of civilized and savage cultures (Old and New Worlds), and in the nature of a savage paradise.

The mixed content of *The Island* makes as probable as any other Robert D. Hume's conjecture that the poem is not so much a throwback as a new departure – a sort of romance *Don Juan*.[11] Remaining constant, which ever, is Byron's lifelong effort to make sense out of human knowledge – but divine denial to mankind – of paradise. The South Sea island of Toobonai and the seraglio of the Sultan in *Don Juan* represent extreme shifts in Byron's lexicon for testing the feasibility of unalloyed love in paradisal seclusion – one a world of uncorrupted nature at the farthest reaches of the then-known shipping lanes, the other a world of corrupt society in the innermost recesses of a megalomanical court, Neuha and Dudu as "Child[ren] of Nature" (*DJ* 6, lx) and Torquil and Juan born of Adam and fated to repeat the error of their illustrious primal ancestor. The parallel – and one can multiply it with other instances – questions the viability of the Toobonai Eden as adamantly, however indirectly, as does the model for them all, the island idyll of Juan and Haidee. We can read its pattern of events as an epitome of Byron's ambivalent view of human expectations *vis-à-vis* lost paradise. A pilgrim, one of civilization's outcasts, on "The Ocean of Eternity" (*DJ* 10, iv) washes up on an island in the antipodes. There – "Where all is Eden, or a wilderness" (*DJ* 4, liv) depending on whether one is in love or not – he meets one of "Nature's bride[s]" (*DJ* 2, ccii). Isolated from corrupt, and corrupting, society, the earth "to their young eyes" (*DJ* 2, cciv) returns to its Edenic "early days" (*DJ* 2, clxxxvi) and they to masquerading as its once "so young, and . . . so innocent" children (*DJ* 2, clxxii, 4, xv). Inevitably though their "earth[ly] Paradise" (*DJ* 2, cciv) yields to the decadence of civilization and to the greed of human nature. The return of Haidee's father to find his hard-won wealth being consumed by daughter, lover, and retainers merely completes their "fall" from "happy . . . Indulgence of their innocent desires" (*DJ* 3, xiii) to sophisticatedly laying wanton waste to the world's store of food, drink, and sex. Thus, "to the awe-struck world" are "Elysium's gates" forever being "unlock'd" (*Childe 1*, xviii), and as inexorably closed, "with heart-aches ever new" afflicting. "The immedicable soul" (*Childe 4*, cxxvi).

To get a daily position of Byron and Shelley in their voyages across "The Ocean of Eternity," and to fix each one's daily latitude and longitude in relation to the other, calls for more sensitive navigational aids than is available to modern criticism. And if the relatively steady position of Byron in relation to paradise is not always easy to measure, the audacious tacking of Shelley toward its wandering isle demands much finer instruments of critical delicacy. Aboard Shelley's intellectually freighted vessel Eden appears to be at once a more symbolic and a more literal destination than it was for the common–sensical Byron who was inclined to use paradise as a trope, a directional device for orienting himself, a star to steer by, rather than a haven to sail toward. Shelley was a daring, at times rash, sailor who unhesitatingly steered according to sketchy and imprecise charts whose notations on the "fairy isles" (*Epipsychidion*, 193) had them in some instances scattered accidentally and unpredictably about the uncharted deeps, and again in others as "foamless isles" pinpointed in unvarying positions of unchanging clime.

The nature of the voyage at the close of *Epipsychidion* (1821) has caused much critical controversy. In imagination Shelley sails in a "bark" with "Emilia" Viviani, his "heart's sister" (415), toward "a far Eden of the purple East" (417) where under the eternally "blue heavens" (544) they will live forever as "one / Spirit within two frames" (573–74). The question of whether the union of their two hearts in "love's rare Universe" (589) is sexually of body or spiritually of soul, or both sequentially and simultaneously, alerts us to the broader question of Shelley's poetic intentions. Even in the *hortus conclusus* God entered Mary to conceive Christ as guarantor of eternal life to her garden. And man in all the glorious immortality of his soul now substitutes for God. Or so Shelley would have us believe. And the nature of the paradisal island on which this imagined consummation takes place partakes of the same dualities. Shelley conceives of it as at once a secluded member of the Sporades in the Aegean Sea and an Hesperian isle of "green and golden immortality" (469). It contains "thick woods where sylvan forms abide: / And many a fountain, rivulet, and pond" (435–36), which might be found in an English landscape garden. At the same time it shimmers in Shelley's imagination as an ideal, immaterial "isle 'twixt Heaven, Air, Earth, and Sea" (457), on which no flesh-and-blood feet walk except in "antenatal dream" (456) or in annihilating immortality (586–87). As such it is "An atom of th' Eternal" (479) as bright and elusive "as that wandering Eden Lucifer" (459) – Venus in her guise as morning star and ethereal refuge of unfallen Eden – which makes the voyage to this island paradise finally then a voyage to a "far goal beyond the limits of the known world . . . a voyage of the spirit, a return to the source."[12]

A similar set of disparate relationships inform the "flowering islands" scattered about "the waters of wide Agony" (66–67) of "Lines written among the Euganean Hills" (1818). The "green isle" (1) of the poem includes the "mountains

Euganean" (70) into which the poet has fled for a few hours from his personal distress and amidst which he sits penning his poetic paean, the "cities fair" dotting the "waveless plain of Lombardy" (91–93), the many islanded city of Venice, a single day in the poet's life, and a metaphoric place of escape for the human mariner navigating "the deep wide sea of Misery" (2). Thus the "green isle" for the poet is a physical refuge. It also as certainly represents for him a mental–spiritual realm transfigured into that ultimate human haven a "healing Paradise" (355) which lies beyond mutable "passion, pain, and guilt" (345) in a "clime divine and calm" (358) – a paradise ironically still attached to earth by its link in Shelley's memory with the serene garden landscape of a "dell 'mid lawny hills" (346).

These island Elysiums are images for the unobtainable. Like Mont Blanc, the Cloud, the Skylark, and Emilia herself, they are part of the material world and yet divinations as well of a reality beyond human apprehension. They invariably converge in Shelley's mind with the primitivist Christian myth of Eden, implicit in the final words of "Lines written among the Euganean Hills" which presage (somewhat desperately since the prediction has for vehicle the verb "must be" [335], the hypothesis "even now, perhaps" [338], and the unstated comparison to "then") that "the earth [will] grow young again" (373).

That the idea of an island Elysium held out to Shelley both actual and symbolic promise of a personal refuge from the "polluting multitude" ("Lines written among the Euganean Hills," 355) and its illiberal influences is signified by the way he grasps at the idea in a letter to Mary Shelley six months after writing *Epipsychidion*. Visiting Byron at Ravenna in August 1821, where he was drawn into helping solve the question of where Byron and his mistress the Countess Guiccioli might live, Shelley writes to Mary of his weariness with his fellow man:

My greatest content would be utterly to desert all human society. I would retire with you & our child to a solitary island in the sea, would build a boat, & shut upon my retreat the floodgates of the world.

Three years before in "Lines written among the Euganean Hills" he had still permitted to sift upward into his consciousness, despite his despondency, the idealistic hope that the "healing Paradise" (355) of a "flowering isle" might subdue the rage of the multitude and cause the spirit of every individual enticed there to "repent its envy vain" (372). In the letter to Mary he has second thoughts:

If I dared trust my imagination it would tell me that there were two or three chosen companions beside yourself whom I should desire. – But to this I would not listen. – Where two or three are gathered together the devil is among them, and good far more than evil impulses – love far more than hatred – has been to me, except as you have been its object, the source of all sort[s] of mischief.[13]

The public accessibility to healing sanctuaries has narrowed to private exclusivity in answer to pressing personal needs, but the mythopoeic value of islands continues constant.

In her fine analysis of "Lines written among the Euganean Hills," Judith Chernaik makes an observation about that poem's structure which unintentionally squints at the larger incongruity endemic to Shelley's poetic recreation of a politico-social paradise.

The poem moves from images of change as accidental and unpredictable (the occasional green isle) or as meaningless (the succession of "Day and night, and night and day,") to images of change as the rhythm of life itself, a ripening in harmony from morning to noon to evening.[14]

To the incongruity of the anti-clerical Shelley invoking traditional Edenic symbolism is conjoined his imposition of the cycle of the seasons onto the eternality of paradise. The latter introduces a perennial metaphysical quandary intrinsic to the paradox posed by a mutable natural world *vis-à-vis* an immutable spiritual world. Nor has the quandary been helped by the Biblical location of paradise within a garden enclosure, which needlessly intertwines the earthly and the heavenly. Nor have commentators from the medieval syllogists to the eighteenth- and nineteenth-century Vulcanists and Neptuneans adequately resolved the resultant contradictions.

An explicit instance in Shelley's poetry is "The Sensitive Plant" (1820), which not surprisingly has baffled readers bent on a coherent reading of the poem.[15] The sensitive plant, a variety of *Mimosa pudica*, is an annual growing among the perennials. The garden is an "undefiled Paradise" (I, 58) paradoxically subject to the "gusty winds" of autumn (III, 38) and the frost and "frozen air" (III, 104) of winter. And just as the mimosa succumbs to the change in seasons, so the "Eve in this Eden" (II, 2), the Lady who tends the garden, suffers the capricious fate of dying "ere the first leaf looked brown" (II, 60). And her demise leaves the garden untended, and deteriorating into a tangled, "monstrous undergrowth," "cold and foul," of "decaying dea[th]" (III, 59, 17, 64). Finally, whereas the perennials revive "from their ruined charnels" (III, 117) with the coming of a new spring, the sensitive plant and its ministrant of love remain forever inanimate parts of the "cold, oppressive and dank" earth (III, 11).

Shelley's "explanation" for the disturbing chain of events in this mythopoeic fable is to question the archetypal pattern itself, by casting into doubt the poem's version of events, which as poet he chose to give. In the Conclusion he muses ingenuously:

> Whether the Sensitive-plant, or that
> Which within its boughs like a spirit sat
> Ere its outward form had known decay,
> Now felt this change, – I cannot say.

> Whether that Lady's gentle mind,
> No longer with the form combined
> Which scattered love – as stars do light,
> Found sadness, where it left delight,

I dare not guess

. . .

It is a modest creed, and yet
Pleasant if one considers it,
To own that death itself must be,
Like all the rest, – a mockery.

That garden sweet, that lady fair
And all sweet shapes and odours there
In truth have never past away –
'Tis we, 'tis ours, are changed – not they.

For love, and beauty, and delight
There is no death nor change: their might
Exceeds our organs – which endure
No light – being themselves obscure.

As a gloss on these lines, Donald Reiman dryly comments, "The statement of the conclusion is simply that, since we know *our organs* (of sensation, reasoning, etc.) to be *obscure* (dark, dim), the sequence of events related in parts First, Second, and Third may not be the true picture. Because he knows human perceptions to be fallible, the poet can still hold his *modest creed*, even after relating the apparent death of the Lady and the destruction of the beautiful garden."[16]

In his distrust of ecclesiastical institutions, and of the doctrines they formulate, Shelley is forced into exorbitant reliance on the mind's sweet reasonableness and the heart's steadfast love. Man was given speech, Asia exclaims in an appropriately long speech to Demogorgon in which she reviews the up-and-down destiny of mankind to date; "and speech created thought," she adds, "Which is the measure of the Universe." Shelley would like to have believed that those two tools (speech and thought), plus the "majesty of love" (*Prometheus Unbound*, II, iv, 72–73, 42), were sufficient to insure a new earthly paradise; but Byron and Shelley lived in a religious age, which demanded more divinely authorized powers. Despite the throne being occupied by a superannuated *beau idéal*, whose spendthrift aesthetic sensibility scandalized, yet set, in part, the tone of the age, a more authentic sign of the times was Coleridge agonizing over ways of reconciling traditional religion with myth and the new Higher Criticism. To advance belief in an island Elysium without the subsoil of the Christian Eden is to force a fallback to less defined archetypes, and inevitably to drift cognitively into metaphor, or what is worse for a poet, into silence. "The deep truth is imageless," Shelley has Demogorgon answer Asia when she asks about the ultimate source of power. Other than that unsatisfactory profundity, Demogorgon can only saturninely pile up words, "Fate, Time, Occasion, Chance and Change" (*Prometheus Unbound*, II, iv, 116, 119). As in this instance, Shelley repeatedly stubbed his toe against the profound opaqueness of eternity. In the absence of faith in the benevolent Providence of a personal Christian God Shelley is compelled to substitute his poetic language as mediator between mortality and immortality, between the mutable and the immutable, and between the material and the immaterial – a linguistic act of faith more demanding than that asked by Jehovah. Shelley never adequately solved the intellectual problem; and a consequence is the relativism resorted to in the "Conclusion" to "The Sensitive Plant." At other times his poetic assertion of hope translates into an act of will, as in "Lines written among the Euganean Hills," where he contends that "Many a green isle *needs must be* / In the deep wide sea of Misery" (1-2, my italics). If it were otherwise, life would be unbearable.

One of the surprising resonances encountered in a poetry dedicated to instituting heaven on earth is its contrary susceptibility to the attractive nuances of death. Judith Chernaik phrases it neatly when she notes that Shelley repeatedly "expresses a delight in life and the beauty of living things so intensely felt that it impels him to believe in immortality. Yet he feels an equally certain and intense apprehension of death, mutability, imperfection, as the condition of life. There is not much distance in Shelley's poetry between his affirmation of hope and his pessimism, nor does he ever try to resolve the problem of God and immortality."[17] The world darkened visibly for Shelley in the latter part of his life, as the years tempered and matured his youthful idealism. With his domestic and marital relationship to Mary in frigid stasis, and with political tyranny seemingly impregnable – his faith in humankind and his optimistic linking of nature's cyclic rebirth to the moral and political rehabilitation of nations appeared ever more quixotic. Instead of seeing change beginning anew in spring, he was increasingly prone to see it forever ending on a wintry note. "Withered leaves" were less a herald of quickening "new birth" ("Ode to the West Wind," 64) than a memorial to endless death.

Although Byron and Shelley started out by laying claim to different islands in the paradisal archipelago, they end closer in spirit than one would have supposed possible, given their antithetical religious natures. Each poet attributed extravagant importance to love as one of the few "constants" still within the purlieu of human experience that had not wholly ended with the loss of original paradise, even though in the experience of love, as with Juan and Julia, the first Fall is unavoidably re-enacted. If Shelley's expectation of "unawakened Earth['s]" restitution ("Ode to the West Wind," 68) through love to its original youthful goodness becomes increasingly tentative, Byron's cynicism about love as an escape from the encroachments of society acquires nuances of ambiguity impossible to sort out satisfactorily, partly because incomplete as in the final cantos of *Don Juan* and partly because genuinely dualistic as in *The Island*.

For both poets Hesperian islands belong finally more to mythography than to geography. Apropos of his disenchantment with sexual love – its inevitable detumescence and consequent disorder (that which "bears within its breast the very germ / Of Change" [*DJ 14*, xciv]) – and its link with the lost "terrestrial Paradise," Byron wrote: "I went seeking it – God knows where – did I find it?— Umph!—Now & then – for a minute or two."[18] Shelley, seeking the same will-o-the-wisp in a rarefied metaphysical realm, was repeatedly forced to draw back

from the "intense inane" (*Prometheus Unbound*, III, iv, 204), which he found to be
– short of death – beyond human ken. Despite his unqualified embrace of
"passion's golden purity" (571) in the ecstatic conclusion to *Epipsychidion*, when
his and Amelia's souls would melt, "transfigured" into one, "ever still / Burning,
yet ever inconsumable" (578–79), he only fancies the eternality of their union.
The very words used to conceive such transcendence carry with them sufficient
dross to keep the flight of imagination earth-bound and within the realm of
limited human capabilities. It is no wonder then that Shelley exclaims "Woe is
me!" – following the *O Altitudo* of "one life, one death, / One Heaven, one Hell,
one immortality, / And one annihilation" (585–87). At one level of his mind his
question, "What Adonais is, why fear we to become?" (459) taps a doubt that
gives the query in *Adonais* (1821) as much a real as rhetorical flourish, for it is
based on a "sustaining Love . . . blindly wove / By man and beast and earth and
air and sea," which may burn "bright or dim" (481–84), may likewise burn
"through the inmost veil of Heaven" (493), or simply consume one's "cold
mortality" (486) leaving nothing. There is a realistic strain in Shelley which draws
him back from unqualified assent to his most extreme poetic assertions of locating
the Eternal in the "mossy earth" and which makes him hesitate to follow word
with deed when he places it in the "sphered skies" (491). Such hard-won
reservations bring him into sneaking sympathy with Byron's pessimism about
finding and colonizing that "unreach'd Paradise" (*Childe 4*, cxxii) every person
catches glimpses of silhouetted in the fleeting sunshine of earthly love.

Two generations of Romantic poets witnessed, for all the apparent millenary
portents, a period of steadily reduced expectations. The earthly paradise seemed a
more distant event in 1830 than in 1795, as growing up during the American and
French Revolutions is succeeded by coming of age during the Napoleonic
outrages. Faith in a "new world of man" (*Prometheus Unbound*, IV, 157) had
waned markedly from Blake's hard-won reconstitution of Jerusalem out of the
quotidian, through the self-congratulations of Wordsworth and self-recrimin-
ations of Coleridge, to the Calvinism of Byron and the antinomies of Shelley.
One must turn to the visual artists to find the old hope still tenderly nursed, alive
and intact.

6

Bewick's, Constable's, and Palmer's *Locus Paradisus*

IN EIGHTEENTH-CENTURY BRITAIN the pastoral strain combines in a peculiarly English way both the idylls and the bucolics of Virgil. The leisurely life of a golden age and the work-a-day world of the present flourish together as a single ideal in paintings and poems alike. The fusion conveys an enigmatic tone to George Lambert's depictions of harvesting in *Extensive Landscape with Four Gentlemen on a Hillside* (1733, Yale Center for British Art) and *Hilly Landscape with a Cornfield* (1733, Tate Gallery), and, unfortunately, a prosaic falsetto to John Dyer's eulogy of sheep growing and the woolen trade in *The Fleece* (1757). In the poems of Blake, Coleridge, and Wordsworth one hears intermittently the minor key of this Virgilian counterpoint darkening the major motif of humanity's, and nature's, divinity.

The intrinsic duality of an order that partakes at once of the real and the otherworldly is assimilated at its best in the work of three artists – Thomas Bewick (1753–1828), John Constable (1776–1837), and Samuel Palmer (1805–81) – whose productive lives span the fifty-year period stretching roughly from 1785 to 1835, which links the landscape gardening of the eighteenth century to the industrial manufacturing of the nineteenth. Little evidence of the millenarianism that fired the 1790s is visible in their work. Each was, however, in his way, staunchly moralistic and religiously conservative, with Palmer sharing the earlier Romantics' transcendental fervor for nature. Through the circumstances of birth, and choice, each is identified with a specific locality of England. This each celebrates with such undeviating intensity – the daily round of village life, the ancient rural ways – that the unchanging English country world they record reads like a palimpsest of the original pastoral and agrarian existence Adam and Eve and their descendants succeeded to after the expulsion from Eden.

Bewick was a bluff northerner and common-sensical child of the eighteenth century. Like a graphics-oriented Theophrastes, he catalogues in his small woodcuts persistent country types and preoccupations, hunting and fishing, and all the barnyard drama of a communal golden age. At the opposite end of the continuum Palmer prefigures fervid Victorian piety, alleviated in his case by a gift for self-deprecatory irony. A South Londoner who grew up looking out on the Dulwich hills toward the hop fields, meadows, orchards, and downs of Kent and Surrey, he bears witness, with visionary eccentricity in the best of his paintings and sepia drawings, to the promise those hills gave that "the country beyond them is Paradise."[1] The center is occupied by Constable. Hailing from East Anglia and living most of his adult years in London, he gives us a balanced portrait of rural occupations, natural scenery, and ordinary joys.

The years of these men's most inspired recreations of a paradisal rural England were anything but serene and uneventful. Two wars with the American colonies were fought. The French Revolution filled three decades with the hysterical din of invasion fears, mob-rule paranoia, Pitt–Fox parliamentary crises, the Twin Acts and other repressive political measures, and the Napoleonic Wars. George III lapsed in and out of madness, and his son and heir apparent in and out of solvency, marriage, and disreputable companionships. The rates – and the growing numbers of the impoverished – nagged at everyone's consciences, and pocketbooks. Malthus stirred up darker depths of the human soul than most cared to look at. Nor did things quiet down after Bonaparte was sent to St. Helena. The plight of the rural laborer grew ever worse, and he ever more violent. Rick burning lit up the nights of the southern shires. Workers broke the machines that were rendering them redundant. Riots and conspiracies flourished: the Peterloo massacre, the Cato Street Conspiracy. Queen Caroline suffered her scandal. Religious fanaticism and controversy grew ever louder. Joanna Southcott redefined God's sex. Edward Irving enthralled the intellectuals and upper classes of London. Holy Land Pilgrims prepared to go to Jerusalem to greet the Millennium. More practically the Acts of 1828 and 1829 lightened the burden of dissenters and Catholics but exercised the concern of Anglicans. Whole classes of people seemed to be agitating for reform, climaxing in the great experiment of the Reform Act of 1832. It is against this background of national alarm and unrest that Bewick, Constable, and Palmer strove each to relive the "good old days" in his own imagination and to remind other English of them, by associating the common joys of rural activity and the personal fulfillment of village life with prelapsarian wholeness of heart. Each sought, with sophisticated artistry, to establish separate rustic nooks of England as representative of the bountiful sum of human knowledge.

For Bewick, master of the woodcut, it was the rolling country and modest villages of Northumberland along the Tyne River to the west of Newcastle. In his *Memoir* (written in old age from 1822 to 1827 and not published until 1862 by his daughter) he tells how as a young engraver seeking his fortune in London, he quit a promising future there after less than a year to return home to "The Country of my old friends" where "the manners of the people of that day – the scenery of Tyne side, seemed altogether to form a paradise for me & I longed to see it again."[2] And in the vicinity of Newcastle-on-Tyne he lived most of the rest of his life, an active champion of the natural riches of the region – protective of its streams teeming with salmon and of its fields with game. Of a practical Christian, if sometimes morbid, turn of mind, he deplored the game and fishery laws which secured this god-given bounty for the sport of the rich, and inevitably set the classes against each other. His was a Christian dream of a land whose fruits were commensurately shared by all (cf. *Memoir*, pp. 170–78). Conscious of living in a changing environment, where the "filth from Manufactories . . . many tons in a year, [was] washed off the uncleaned streets of large towns *only* by heavey showers of rain" (*Memoir*, p. 174), he clung to the belief that an estimable world could be reconstituted by people of sober industry and good will. The ultimate simplicity of his faith is epitomized by his exhortation to "the Ladies of the British Isles . . . to become florists." Not only would the exercise out of doors "enliven or exhilerate their spirits," but the horticultural activity would make the earth once again a garden.

To see this ought to be the wish of every sensible man – for what would this world be without their help to alleviate its burdens – it would appear a barren waste – it could no longer be a wide spread garden of Eden nor an earthly paradise within the reach of our enjoyments. (*Memoir*, pp. 164–65)

Such ingenious pieties should not obscure the mischievous wit, Rabelaisian earthiness, and genial tolerance of human folly animating Bewick's vision of a late eighteenth-century earthly paradise. The limitations of man's capacity for refined action is seldom absent from Bewick's observation of his world. He rarely pretended that he was offering us other than a backwater society with rough manners. In exquisite minuscule vignettes, which he introduced as tailpieces to such works as *A General History of Quadrupeds* (1790) and *A History of British Birds*, Vol. I, *Land Birds* (1797), and Vol. II, *Water Birds* (1804), he lovingly records the daily round of village life: boys tormenting a dog with a can tied to his tail, holiday inebriants straddling tombstones in the local graveyard as if riding to hounds, a bumpkin relieving himself against the stone ruin of a wall, a frantic mother observing at a distance her toddler daughter pulling the tail of a draft horse, a boy fighting off an angry intimidating goose, piglets recoiling in alarm before a ruffled pheasant, a drunken clod peering befuddled at two moons in the night sky, a man traversing a stream by way of the overhanging bough of a tree, and a man burdened with fire wood trudging along a road.[3]

Bewick's world for all its remoteness from the mills of the Midlands and the commerce of London was visibly in transition like the rest of England from an agricultural eighteenth century to an industrial nineteenth century. Nowhere is his quizzical observation of this change, with its encroachments on the Tyneside landscape, presented with more delicately balanced response than in the vignettes on the title pages of *British Land Birds* and *British Water Birds*. In the latter, five boys engage in the timeless sport of sailing boats in a quiet backwater of the Tyne, while overhead in the middle distance drifts smoke from a colliery across the Northumbrian hills toward the lantern-towered cathedral of Newcastle. In the former, a tilted tombstone and a raven on a scraggly shrub bear foreground witness to a river clogged with barges and to a hilly horizon of windmills over which the smoke from a colliery is blowing. Bewick's late Georgian propensity to see life exuberantly yet realistically and steadily is crisply caught in the ironic illusion of the vignette (*British Birds*, 1, 175) in which he boldly superimposes his thumb print, roughly actual size, on a pastoral landscape about one inch wide of a thatched cottage and a horseman. With this inspired self-conscious assertion of the artist's control over his imagined world, he calls attention to the smallness and fragility of the pastoral idyll at the end of the eighteenth century, whose reality seems to depend so precariously for its preservation on the omnipotence of a thumb print.[4]

Less Rabelaisian, and less relieved by a sense of humor, Constable persisted throughout an adulthood lived mostly among urban scenes to invest with sacramental value his memories of growing up in East Bergholt and his annual renewals of knowledge at first-hand of this quiet spot whose daily and seasonal rhythms had changed little since Elizabethan times. Although he painted many scenes of the meadows, Bishop's grounds, and river surrounding Salisbury Cathedral, of the horizontal perspectives of Hampstead Heath, and of the flat sweeps of beach and sea at Brighton and Weymouth, his imaginative life continued firmly attached to the unemphatic features of the Suffolk countryside of the Stour Valley, with its river and canals wandering through a narrow vale of drowsing meadows and farm fields, diverted by a myriad of locks, past Flatford Mill and the village of Dedham to the sea.

There is a description written in 1816 by Humphry Repton of a stereotypical landscape, "which may rather be called tame and beautiful, than romantic or picturesque," that suggests the taste of the time.

It consists of a river quietly winding through a valley; a tower on the summit of a wooded promontory, and a cottage at the foot of the hill; a distant village spire, and more distant hills, mark the course of the valley: to all this is added a foreground, consisting of two large trees to the left, and three small ones to the right.[5]

Repton could just as easily have been summarizing here the contents of a

5   Bewick, from *British Water Birds*

Constable painting. Uncannily attuned to the taste of the first decades of the nineteenth century, Repton inadvertently pinpoints for us the probability that Constable expresses in his Stour Valley pictures prevalent expectations as much as Claudian conventions. In his depictions of Dedham Vale, in addition to the constant prospect of river and village, Constable fashions a turn of the century version of the Virgilian middle state,[6] man engaged in the timeless occupations of boat building, ferrying, canal tending, flour milling, fishing, reaping, hunting, and farming. The difficult task Constable set for himself was to convey this agrarian world in realistic terms, yet charged with the Adamic overtones of his childhood memories of the area.

One does not have to look at many of Constable's portrayals of the Stour Valley – for example, the two pictures of *Dedham Vale* done twenty-six years apart, the first in 1802 (Victoria and Albert Museum) and the second in 1828 (National Gallery of Scotland, Edinburgh) – with trees, river, and perspective guiding our eyes toward the tower of Dedham church rising above the horizon in the distance, to realize that one is looking at an English image of paradise. This is not to say that Constable's fidelity to the observed scene is not everywhere adhered to, particularly in each picture's faithful observation of the season.[7] The 1802 landscape drowses in the full glow and hush of summer, the sky blank of clouds, the river firmly confined within its banks, the verdure dense and profuse. In the valley all is still and listless. The only motion is that of a hot wind blowing through the tops of the trees right foreground. The 1828 landscape (exhibited at the Royal Academy that April and painted in the preceding months), is crowded with rain-laden clouds. The river swollen and overflowing its banks in the foreground reappears

6   Bewick, from *British Land Birds*

in the middle distance from behind Stratford St. Mary bridge to spread seemingly across the whole valley in a fertile renewal of the plain, as the white gleam on the waves is picked up and repeated by the chill morning hoar frost atop the meadows. In the foreground the trees lash and strain in the wind. Without denying the temporality of the world depicted here, in fact honestly acknowledging the processes of growth and change, Constable lets us glimpse from a vantage point above ground level a vision of a fruitful plain that quickens our literary and pictorial remembrances of paradise. Guiding our response to the scene is the masterful contrast of the wild growth on the heights in the foreground to the smooth undulating lines of the cultivated valley.

Like Wordsworth, Constable eschewed many of the artistic conventions and cultural *topoi* that provide a common ground for artist and audience, in favor of looking steadily at the object and forcing it by the very intensity of his contemplation to give up its meaning. The detail in the background of his pictures is treated with the same concentration as the features in the foreground. With the aid of magnification one can see the figure of a farm worker striding across a field at the far right of *Flatford Mill* (1817, Tate Gallery), saw slung across his shoulders, red sash tied around his loose tunic; and one can count the cows grazing on the far side of a line of trees toward which the man is heading. Similarly, in the middle distance of *Hampstead Heath* (*c.* 1820, Fitzwilliam Museum, Cambridge) the staid figures strolling at alderman's pace, the children playing and digging, the sheep grazing, the animal lovers and Sunday idlers drifting about the heath are caught uncannily by deft touches of color and strokes of brush. Rarely does Constable fail to reward study of the minute details of his backgrounds. Often barely perceptible to the naked eye, a micro-drama of country life goes on among the trees and meadows that give boundary to his world. It pays even to enlarge sections of the foreground (for example the right hand side of *The Hay Wain* [1821, National Gallery], where a man in black hat and red neckerchief steps out of the reeds on the river bank into a rowboat) to see the intense care with which Constable renders the tilt of stem, droop of leaf, arrest of body, and decay of river pilings and fence rails. His is the religious knowledge that the parameters of our experience are first established by the milestones of the everyday world.

In contrast to Crabbe's and Clare's less than idyllic record of country life, "The poor laborious natives of the place," "the stinted meal," and the pain of village life (*The Village*, I, 42, 169; II, 2), the busy figures in Constable's pictures partake anonymously and innocently in the happy routine of rural ease. In part this is due to historical circumstances. Enclosure in East Anglia added to the arable acreage farmed and hence increased the need for farm laborers. Elsewhere, as in the Midlands to the west, where Clare wrestled with a shrinking market for his labors, enclosure tended to retire farmland to pasture, reducing the demand for farm workers. In part it is due also to Constable's fixation on the remembered happy Valley of his boyhood and youth, when "the bloomy flush of life" ("Deserted Village," 128) still shed the "chearful influence" of its charms on all

7   Constable, *Dedham Vale* (1828)

rural toils (32–34), and, as a young Rasselas, the son of a prosperous miller and member of the local gentry, he followed the leisurely summer pursuits of a schoolboy rather than the backbreaking labor from sunup to sundown of a farm worker. Constable may recreate an agrarian world that blinks too readily at the horrors of rural life and the plight of the rural laborer during war years of chronic high bread prices. Raymond Williams's socialist reading of English literary history would have it so. Deplorable in his eyes is the captive subservience of pastoral art to eulogy of a Golden Age that did not even exist in the ostensible models, the idylls of Hesiod, Theocritus, and Virgil.[8] Yet, it does rain in Constable country, and people do work there. In comparison to pastoral landscapes both before and after, Constable's are a model of probity, retaining the pastoral mood without the sentimentality or slick idealization of Francis Wheatley, without the nostalgic evocation of the seventeenth-century Italian *campagna* of Richard Wilson, without the sweet otherworldly fantasy of Samuel Palmer, without the private arrangement of shape, line, and color of Gainsborough, and without the abstracted dream world of Alexander Cozens.

Despite his nostalgia, exacerbated by prolonged sojourn in London, Constable resisted the easy deployment of his landscapes according to academic definitions of the genre, bent instead on what Karl Kroeber has called a "'demythologizing' of landscape."[9] How rigorously Constable dispenses with Christian iconography as well while yet imprinting on his world its recall of paradise is immediately discernible when we compare the *Dedham Vale* paintings with two great pictures of a century earlier, Watteau's two versions of *Embarkation for Cythera* (1717–18, Louvre, Paris; and Schloss Carlottenburg, Berlin). Unabashedly using the language of classical symbolism, Watteau drapes pilgrims' capes on his otherwise fashionably dressed lords and ladies of the court of Louis XIV, fills the air with cupids, and places a statue of Cythera conspicuously in a grove dedicated to love. Closer to Constable's own time is the marvellous reconstitution of paradise in the paintings and drawings of Samuel Palmer executed from about 1825 to 1835. A picture like *In a Shoreham Garden* (c. 1829, Victoria and Albert Museum), however, for all its ecstatic depiction of the garden at (first) dawn, is unable to eliminate the negative implications of loss residual in the *topoi* of the Edenic story: the apple tree center foreground, a single woman (Eve?), and vegetables coiled like snakes around poles.

Similarly, one of Palmer's associates at Shoreham, Edward Calvert, ever more pagan than Christian in his art, yet feels compelled to load his evocations of earthly paradise with reminders of man's fall from grace. In *The Ploughman* (1827, Victoria and Albert Museum), a heavy-thighed Blakean male strides sturdily behind a wooden plough and team of horses – an insistent reminder of man's sentence to earn his daily bread by the sweat of his brow. Behind him a serpent, coiled around a tree, is transfixed by an angel, and in the background the three Graces dance. At the end of the ploughed furrows stands a Christlike shepherd and his flock awaiting the sweaty pilgrim with the promise of a new Eden. The paradisal enclave can never again be the unalloyed perfection it was before the Fall. Nostalgically, Calvert reminds us of that irrevocable fact again in his watercolor evocation of an uncomplex medieval world in *The Primitive City* (1822, British Museum). Against a background of pastoral occupations – sheep-herding and transporting produce to town – an Eve-like nymph, larger than life in proportion to the background figures, dreamily walks through a small orchard, reaching absent-mindedly behind her to pick forbidden fruit yet again from one of the trees.

To depict a *locus paradisus* in the realistic terms of one's own time, as Constable attempted, is to grapple with the disjunctive, intransigent reality of objects undergoing growth and decay. One cannot overstate the extraordinary intensity of Constable's response to the fleeting moment, nor his compulsion to fix that moment, to give it permanence, as part of an unchanging rural scene. "The world is wide," he remarks, "no two days are alike, nor even two hours; neither were there ever two leaves of a tree alike since the creation of the world; and the genuine productions of art, like those of nature, are all distinct from each other."[10] In a letter to his closest friend, the Rev. J. Fisher, Constable rehearses his love for "the sound of water escaping from Mill dams. . . . Old rotten Banks, slimy posts, and

8   Watteau, *Embarkation for Cythera*

brickwork." "I love such things," he avers.[11] And it is significant to know how Flatford lock appears in paintings of the 1820s in various stages of disrepair and decay, contrary to the almost certain upkeep of the actual lock by his brother Abram who operated the family mill nearby.[12]

Constable's problem, at whose solution he toiled with undaunted courage unique among his artist contemporaries, was to find ways to arrest the signs of mutability by fixing them in an unending moment – usually that seemingly interminable pause of diurnal motion at high noon – of suspended animation, the instant transcendentalized by focus of our sight on a church tower and eternalized by the formal composition of hills, trees, sky, and plain. His pictorial world is bent on capturing a sense of mythic continuity, even though not explicitly depicted, which connects the prelapsarian world with a postlapsarian age of Virgilian rural activity. It is important then that the agricultural pursuits appear timeless, part of the unchanging rhythms of a self-contained world. Consequently, in the Constable picture the effect is of an arrest of motion, the genre scene saying: this is what these men have been doing for centuries and will continue to do. Constable labored to make the structural components of his painting support this goal.

Painted at the height of his powers, *The Cornfield* (1826, National Gallery, London) exhibits all the technical artifices and philosophical strategies Constable commanded to achieve a pictorial harmony affirming the essential oneness of the temporal and eternal worlds, in which the mundane routines of human existence imperceptibly become the unchanging order of a rural scene. Karl Kroeber has written perceptively about the picture's symbolic handling of time, specifically the progression from the boy drinking at a pool in the foreground, to the hunter passing by in the middle distance, to the farm laborers working in the corn field, and finally to the church tower crowning the background – a "progression from youth to the hope of life beyond death within the context of nature."[13] Juxtaposed to this human rhythm of growth, decay, and rebirth, is a comparable rhythm in the natural world: an old and broken tree is balanced against others in full leaf, and a worn plow lies abandoned outside the ripening field of grain.

But Constable is not content with a simple spatial-qua-temporal structuring of his late summer country scene. For all his painterly fondness for the surfaces and textures of things, and preoccupation with the transit of time, he paints within a classical–Christian frame of reference that recognizes the existence of a more idyllic, perfect world than this fallen version of it. In this respect his presentations of the gentle Suffolk countryside are equivalents of Blake's reference to England's "green & pleasant bowers" (*J*, 77:12; E,231) and of Coleridge's eulogy of his "mother Isle," its "valleys, fair as Eden's bowers" ("Ode to the Departing Year," VII, 122–23). Constable characteristically organizes his material to recall through both spatial and temporal means the Christian promise of life everlasting. Adroitly using the shadows thrown by the trees in the foreground as a funnel to the sun-flooded field of grain glimpsed through an opening of the leaves, he draws our attention deep into the painting beyond the immediately visible. The structural line directs our eye up the path past the boy, his dog, and small flock of sheep, across a footbridge, through an open gate, out of the deep shadows and into the hot noonday stillness of the field of grain, where all the light in the picture is centered as if at the end of the dark tunnel of earthly existence. This marshalling of chiaroscuro in the service of thematic statement represents a dramatic improvement over the thematically irrelevant exercises in shadow and sunlight Constable attempted in such early paintings as *Golden Constable's Flower Garden* (1815, Ipswich Borough Council) and *Malvern Hall* (1809, Tate Gallery). If the field of grain is not a conscious reminder of Eden, in contrast to the shaded rusticity of the country lane – since grain is a product of fallen man's labor, rather than part of the natural growth of paradise – it at least gives off low-keyed echoes of the Biblical promise of God's beneficence, as also do the configuration of the sheep in the lane and the silhouette of the church tower on the horizon. And if not explicitly Edenic, the scene yet offers a representation of an agrarian golden age that myth places some time between God's creation of earth and our present toilsome situation.

Graham Reynolds has pointed to this middle ground of the pastoral world by way of noting a different set of configurations in the Constable landscape. In most of the Stour scenes, "Almost every natural object or group of objects seen by

9   Calvert, *The Ploughman*

Constable . . . was the direct product of man's intervention with Nature. The trees cut back . . . the division of the land, its hedges, fences, and lanes, even the course of the river, were under his control."[14] Karl Kroeber, in a commentary on Reynolds's observation, both corroborates and qualifies what "can be regarded as industrialized rural landscapes."

The point need not be exaggerated, but in *The Leaping Horse*, for example, our attention is drawn to the dam blocking the stream, the boat making use of the wind to navigate, and the

10   Palmer, *In a Shoreham Garden*

man riding – in sum, to human control. Constable, to be sure, is no enthusiast for technological industrialization; riding, sailing, milling are cooperations with the natural, not subjugations of it. Constable's affinities are to the farmer, not the industrial entrepreneur.[15]

Even more pertinent than his affinities to the farmer for understanding Constable's art are the deeply religious parameters of his vision. And pertinent here is the Christian design of life as a pilgrimage of the soul through a temporal world towards its eternal home in God's heavenly city. In this respect, it is striking how many of Constable's mature landscapes of the Stour Valley involve journeying, whether bargemen struggling to move the bulky hulk of a flat boat, a wayfarer toiling along a canal path, an ubiquitous river winding toward the haven of Dedham and its omnipresent church tower and beyond it to the estuary of Harwich Water. Meyer H. Abrams[16] has shown how natural it was for the Romantic artist to use the trope of life-as-a-circular-return-from-exile as a paradigm of the human odyssey. It was a time of revolution and war, of political uncertainty, and of intellectual anxiety. An organically open-ended cosmos yawned, its infinite and eternal space an intimidating contrast to the familiar confines of the earthly paradise. The consequence was a longing for the consummation of one's earthly quest by return to one's origins; and the Stour Valley seemed to answer this religious need, quietly persistent in the minds of those familiar with its rural byways. When Gainsborough essayed a *View of Dedham* (*c.* 1768–70, Museum of Art, Philadelphia) he observed the scene with an uncanny prefigurative recognition of what the eyes of Constable were to behold. There are the familiar tree-shaded foreground, the sunlit wheat field in the middle distance, and the tower of Dedham church behind it, plus a vagrant with pilgrim's staff seated in rest on the ground, while a horseman and a man with his dog wind their way toward Dedham (and the church?). Wordsworth relates in *The Prelude* how he started life in the Lake Country, was separated from it in his youth, and toiled for years on the road back to "the chosen Vale." His thought when as an errant boy he first caught sight of Grasmere Vale – "Within the bounds of this huge Concave; here/ Should be my home, this Valley be my World" – provides a verbal analogue to Constable's painting:

> 'What happy fortune were it here to live!
> And if I thought of dying, if a thought
> Of mortal separation could come in
> With paradise before me, here to die.'
> (*Home at Grasmere*, Ms.B. 42–43, 9–12)

In *The Cornfield* one glimpses the field of grain radiant in the light of a sunny noon through the rustic gloom of a lane down which one must trudge past weathered broken gate, blasted tree, and straggling bushes to reach the promised land of plenitude, which becomes an extension of the lane leading the traveler in a long curve to a church tower awaiting him at the end of the pilgrimage. The Heavenly City of God (or the dome and towers of its earthly symbol the church)

11   Constable, *The Cornfield*

enthroned on a hill in the background is a commonplace of late medieval and Renaissance paintings. In Vittore Carpaccio's fresco of *St. George Slaying the Dragon* (*c.* 1507, Scuola San Giorgio Degli Schiavoni) just such a domed church crowns a steep and rocky hill behind St. George, interpreted as a promise of man's eventual redemption from sin and death by Christ's sacrifice and grace. And so the tower of Dedham church concentrates in its form some of the same iconography of *aera sub gratia*. In this context the shepherd boy's slaking his thirst at the pool and his driving his sheep down the lane acquire symbolic meaning in addition to the naturalistic explanation.

Constable country as we know it in the pictures is the mythopoeic product of a mind restructuring its experiences to fit a rural ideal. His paintings of the gentle downs of Suffolk are replicas partly of the Stour Valley, partly of an inner landscape that sustained his imagination during his years of exile in London. In short, the landscape identifiable as Constable country is one of his own devising out of a limited number of recurring details; it does not accord exactly with the real place, even allowing for the changes of 150 years. In his repetition of a few familiar objects: the house of Willy Mott, a laborer's cart being filled or emptied, the lock at Flatford Mill, barges on the river, and meadows flanking it, with browsing cows and trees, Constable reveals, as contrasted to Turner's polymath memory, an inelastic but obsessively intense visual imagination. When one visits the Dedham–East Bergholt area one experiences a shock of recognition without being able to identify any view exactly as it appears in the paintings. Constable knew each part of the vale, its meadows, its trees outlining the hills and fields, its ubiquitous church towers, its fence railings and canal locks, its boatmen, and its river flowing to the channel estuary; and he saw it whole in his mind's eye, even while shifting details about to create new pictorial entities.

A striking instance is his placement of Dedham and Langham church towers so that in picture after picture one or the other is discovered as a familiar object on the horizon, where the eye comes finally to rest – as in the 1802 and 1828 versions of *Dedham Vale*, in the two variations of *A Boat Passing a Lock* (exhibited 1824, Trustees of the Walter Morrison Pictures Settlement; and 1826, Royal Academy of Arts), in *The Cornfield*, in *View on the Stour near Dedham* (exhibited 1822, Henry L. Huntington Library, San Marino, Calif.), in *The Leaping Horse* (exhibited 1825, Royal Academy of Arts, London), in the two versions of *The Glebe Farm* (exhibited 1827 and *c.* 1831, Tate Gallery), and in other depictions of the river, locks, and meadows, such as the variant treatments of *Dedham from Langham* (*c.* 1812, Tate Gallery and Ashmolean Museum, Oxford) – all of which situate in the middle distance the crenellated square presence of one of these towers. In these varied scenes the bell tower appears to be located in some shifting central part of the valley, most strikingly near the mouth of the Stour River where it winds through marsh flats before flowing into the North Sea yet seemingly visible in whatever direction one looks. The fact, of course, is that both Dedham and Langham churches stand some miles upstream of that *locus terminus*. Faithful to the appearance in these pictures of a church tower, though, is the omnipresence of churches in the valley. If one observes the vale from the hills fringing it, say in the vicinity of Dedham, which lies on the south side about midway on an east–west axis, one can see a church and its tower or steeple in whatever direction, whether up, down, or across the valley. The ubiquitous presence of Dedham and Langham towers in his depictions of the vale may, of course, function as an eye-catcher, a painterly equivalent of the follies, or mock architectural structures placed by garden architects on the tops of hills to concentrate our view of the prospect; and, again, it may point to a part of Constable's memory that is cleansed of irrelevant details and concentrated on ultimate matters.

That Constable's art grips our imaginations as the real thing is a testimony to his honest eye. For all the Virgilian idyll of depicting man in harmony with his physical circumstances the scenes are touched with the unsentimental recognition that perfection does not last even on this happy portion of earth. The latter view uncontestably darkened with age. Cases in point are the transformation of Flatford lock in the 1820s, when Constable allows it to fall into a state of disrepair which, Leslie Parris wittily observes, Constable's brother Abram, "responsible for the upkeep of the actual lock, would never have permitted";[17] the gradual metamorphosis of Willy Lott's house "into the sinister, rambling place seen in the 1835 'Valley Farm'"; and the recurrent dramatic weather besieging Salisbury and Brighton in the pictures of the late 1820s and early 1830s. But with what quiet understatement is the point ordinarily made! – in the record of the changing seasons, the weathering of fence rails, the successions of generations of man, and the blighting of trees. The usual low-keyed optimism maintained without blinking away the reality of change and loss is dramatized by the contrastive pessimism of Watteau's compulsion to paint a second, reverse pilgrimage depicting lovers reluctantly departing from the isle of Cythera to return to a harsh unloving inharmonious world, and by the obsessive allusions of Palmer and Calvert to apple tree and serpent. That Constable as he grew older reacted with increasing ambivalence to the Romantic model of flux is undeniable. One need only look at a late picture like the full-size sketch for *Hadleigh Castle* (c. 1828–29, Tate Gallery) and the final painting (exhibited 1829, Mr. and Mrs. Paul Mellon) where the focus is initially at least, on the enduring castle tower. Silhouetted against a sky rent with storm, the ruin catches the light of the heavens as it thrusts upwards against the destructive forces of time and the elements. For all the seeming heroics of the tower, the painting does not deny that the walls are a shell of their former grandeur. An empty monument to a violent past, it is ultimately superseded in our eyes and those of the artist by the unobtrusive figures of shepherd and sheep who prevail against inclement weather and the years alike on the slope below its crumbling stones.

With greater visionary intensity than Bewick and Constable, Samuel Palmer depicted the English countryside as a portion of "Temporal Creation" that was like a "veil of heaven, through which her divine features are dimly smiling."[18] "Considering Dulwich as the gate into the world of vision," he wrote in an 1824 sketchbook from a painter's point of view with the technical problems in mind, "one must try behind the hills to bring up a mystic glimmer like that which lights our dreams. And those same hills (hard task) should give us promise that the country beyond them is Paradise."[19] He accordingly retired for about seven years (roughly 1826/27 to 1834/35) in his youth to the Kentish village of Shoreham, where from time to time with such other fellow "Ancients" as Edward Calvert (1799–1883), George Richmond (1809–96), and Francis Oliver Finch (1802–62),[20] and with Blake's wood-engravings for Dr. Robert John Thornton's *Pastorals of Virgil* (1821) in mind, he tried to locate that pastoral dream "of little dells, and nooks, and corners of Paradise."[21] Most of Palmer's paintings and brush and pen drawings in sepia that we still prize were done at this time. If we translate Calvert's habitual pantheism – and its Platonic or "Phrygian" language – into Christian references, his words for the landscapes of Finch will do equally well for those of Palmer in these years:

When Finch transcends to the valleys, dear to his tastes are the garden and the grove, sacred places, bowers votive to peace, and to friendship, seats and walks, where what is noble in converse with men and with Gods, may be safe from disturbance. . . . The Genius of his choice insists on an extended Mythic sense and on conditions of eternal law . . . a people uninterrupted in a life of thought, mid waters and shadowy recesses of grove; where, robed in peace and in presence of Athene, they mark her virgin gravity, and meditate the depths of her principles.[22]

As if cast under a spell the valley and hilly environs of Shoreham radiate in Palmer's pictures with magical flowering trees and resound with the pipes of shepherds. Nor, for Palmer (Geoffrey Grigson makes the important point), was a shepherd merely pastoral, or Virgilian, any more than he was for Blake. "Palmer's shepherds are the shepherds of *Pilgrim's Progress*, shepherds in the Delectable Mountains, with their gardens, and orchards, and vineyards, and streams – the mountains from which the Celestial City was visible."[23] In keeping with the supernal freight of his shepherd–pilgrims, uncanny light pervades their earthly abode, like a message from on high, as in *The Bright Cloud* (1833–34, Tate Gallery) where the leaves of the trees glow brightly in answer to the heavenly blossom of the cloud's effulgence, while on a grassy slope a woman pipes to a recumbent man and his sheep.

In a humble, but determined mood of self-dedication shortly before retiring to Shoreham he wrote in his notebook sometime between November 1822 and June 1824 to "Lay up, silently and patiently" materials for painting mighty themes on Christ's life. In the meantime, he reminded himself that "smaller subjects of separate glories of Heaven might be tried – hymns sung among the hills of Paradise at eventide."[24] And "eventide" in the Shoreham vale, paradoxically, was for him the time of day when he could best "bound upwards; pierce the clouds; and look over the doors of bliss."[25] Daringly faithful to his sense of the rustic theater he would make symbolic of the holy universe, he transforms the traditional sun-drenched Eden into twilight and star and moonscape settings. In contrast to Constable's visions of a rural Eden at high noon, Palmer's give us paradise at sunrise and sunset and during the watches of the night.

In one of his poems that has survived, "Twilight Time" (1825), Palmer captures in words the "trembling light" which "Glimmers behind the little hills and corn, / Lingering as loth to part" (1–3):

> sweet visionary gleam
> That softly lookest through the rising dew;
>   Till all like silver bright;
>   The Faithful Witness, pure, & white,
>   Shall look o'er yonder grassy hill,
>   At this village, safe, and still.
>
> . . .
>   Methinks the lingring, dying ray
>   Of twilight time, doth seem more fair,
>   And lights the soul up more than day,
>   When wide-spread, sultry sunshines are.   (7–12, 22–25)

A Hilly Scene (1826, Tate Gallery) presents a similarly bewitched nighttime ruralscape in which a high field of grain is overshadowed by a gothic church spire. Behind the village, but because of flattened perspective seeming to rise out of it, is a multi-leveled hill on which cows who might better be asleep in the barn graze under a crescent moon. The picture resonates with an unearthly atmosphere "Where pain and vice full seldom come" ("The Shepherd's Home," 8).[26]

Deeply religious in a religiously turbulent period, Palmer found in nature a harmony and unity he sorely missed elsewhere. Out of a misguided attempt to reassure his mentor John Linnell that he was studying diligently at painting by taking likenesses of nature, he writes on 21 December 1828 in mounting rapture about nature's supratopographical system.

Every where curious, articulate, perfect, and inimitable of structure, like her own entomology, Nature does yet leave a space for the soul to climb above her steepest summits: as, in her own dominion she swells from the herring to leviathan; from the hodmandod to the elephant, so, divine Art piles mountains on her hills, and continents upon those mountains.

However, creation sometimes pours into the spiritual eye the radiance of Heaven: the green mountains that glimmer in a summer gloaming from the dusky yet bloomy East; the moon, opening her golden eye, or walking in brightness among innumerable islands of light, not only thrill the optic nerve, but shed a mild, a grateful[,] an unearthly lustre into the inmost spirits, and seem the interchanging twilight of that peaceful country, where there is no sorrow and no night.[27]

Linnell would certainly have connected this outpouring of words disapprovingly with Palmer's pictures. But Palmer's spirituality had a scrupulosity too refined for Linnell's hard-headed percipiency to penetrate. Palmer did not expect for a second to find paradise on earth; he was too orthodox an Anglican for that. Yet in contemplation of how "Terrestrial Spring showers blossoms and odours in profusion," which seem to "'Breathe on earth the air of Paradise,' " he can entertain momentarily the belief, he exclaims incautiously in the same letter to Linnell, that "indeed sometimes, when the spirits are in Heav'n, earth itself, as in emulation, blooms again into Eden"[28] – sentiments not calculated to assuage the suspicions of Linnell's pre-Victorian practical turn-of-mind about Palmer's enthusiasm.

We should not forget – as Linnell very much wished to – that Palmer was one of the last of the second generation of Romantics, and, like a Wordsworth and a Coleridge, could still stand in unqualified visionary awe before nature. He read there a language rendering visible the divine, reassured in this practice by such Christian writers of the seventeenth century as Milton, Isaac Barrow, and John Fletcher, whom he was in the habit of reading.[29] The narrow valley of Shoreham became for him a rural Delphi of sacred centers, each of the trees, hills, dells, cornfields, and villages occupying a luminous space radiating energy outward from its own center. There is no other way of characterizing the explosive fecundity and "conflagration of colour"[30] captured by such paintings as *The Magic Apple Tree* (1830, Fitzwilliam Museum), *In a Shoreham Garden* (c. 1829, Victoria and Albert Museum), *Pear Tree in a Walled Garden* (c. 1829, privately owned), *An Ancient Barn* (c. 1829, privately owned), and *Pastoral with Horse-chestnut* (c. 1829, Ashmolean Museum); or the "ripeness to the core" (Keats, "To Autumn," 6) instinctive in so many of the sepia drawings of 1825: *A Rustic Scene, Valley with a Bright Cloud, Early Morning, Late Twilight,* and *The Valley Thick with Corn* (all in the Ashmolean Museum).

The procreative mystery of the earth is adumbrated in picture after picture. In the December 1828 letter to Linnell, Palmer had declared of "the thousand repetitions of little forms, which are part of its own generic perfection," that "Nature, with mild, reposing breadths of lawn and hill, shadowy glades and meadows, is sprinkled and showered with a thousand pretty eyes and buds and spires and blossoms, gemm'd with dew, and is clad in living green."[31] The rounded hills and hidden dells of Kent, and later of Devonshire, redolent of female forms, entranced Palmer as gateways to a mysterious sacred place of origin.[32] Processions of rustics and cattle, shepherds with their sheep, and rural workers of various sorts wind through a defile past golden clearings where reapers are at work toward a declivity in which a haven of houses beckons: *A Pastoral Scene* (1835, Ashmolean Museum), *The White Cloud* (c. 1833/34, privately owned), and *The Bright Cloud* (?1834, privately owned). In others a road leads to the village over which looms the sharp gothic spire of a church, thrusting upward through dense foliage like a giant phallus: *A Country Road Leading towards a Church* (1830, privately owned) and *Evening: A Church among Trees* (c. 1830, Tate Gallery). In *Scene at Underriver* (c. 1833/34, privately owned) three figures led by a fourth on horseback are about to enter a narrow lane between towering fields of hops and golden corn toward a cliff swathed, and all but hidden, by an almost tropical growth of autumnal colored trees, bushes, and underbrush.

One must keep in mind, when contemplating the implosive sexual energy animating these visions of a fecund moonlit Eden, that between 1825 and 1835

12   Palmer, *A Hilly Scene*

Palmer was a deeply religious bachelor in his twenties, lonely and shy, living for months at a time in Shoreham without companionship other than his beloved nurse's and his bookish father's. Surrounded by an astonishing annual outburst of fecundity, his responsive ardent nature achieved release in the contemplation of an environment in which the systolic pulsation of ever-renewable life surges in unison with the divine will. The postRegency–preVictorian religious attitudes that contributed to Palmer's visionary world were modified by his friendships – Blake's idiosyncratic Christianity, Calvert's paganism, Linnell's dogmatic iconoclasm, and his mother's family's Baptist creed – and by his own personal traits of antique serenity and puritan severity. He led an aggressively ascetic existence at Shoreham, and carried on a lofty portentously religious correspondence with his friend Richmond, before lapsing in later years into gentle

13   Palmer, *The Harvest Moon*

14   Palmer, *Coming from Evening Church*

passive resistance to a world more crassly interested in improving outwardly than in growing inwardly.

These disparities are successfully sublimated in the Edenic vision of a worshipful community of people conceptualized in *Coming from Evening Church* (1830, Tate Gallery). Stern church elders with their wives and children stream out of church and up a lane; yet, like antediluvian patriarchs who have lost their way in the postlapsarian world, they move entranced, intent on an inward vision. Behind them pointed gothic roofs of houses and church strain upward to form with steeple and trees a canopy of leaves through which floats a full autumn moon. The goodly company of worshippers seems to have strayed out of our sinful world, caught in the earthly grip of temporal and spatial limitations, and now sleepwalks through a rural scene where time stands still and space is two-dimensional, upon which a full moon forever shines in an eternal translucent night.

By the early thirties Palmer was losing the joyous naiveté of vision that had graced Kentish rural byways with nooks of Eden, as if obedient to Linnell's directive that he become a marketable Victorian landscapist – which to Linnell's disgust never happened. He married Linnell's daughter in 1837 nevertheless and honeymooned for two years in Italy. The sun-saturated classicism of its great Renaissance paintings had an indelible conventionalizing impact on his moon-and-shade drenched sensibility. In old age, however, Palmer returned to the bucolic visions of Shoreham days in a small group of etchings and mezzotints whose eclectic jumble of landscapes and of human activities under night skies presents a world at once familiar in its work-a-day scenes and strange in its archaism, a world of his own device through which he steps with wondering eyes. In *The Bellman* (1879) and *The Lonely Tower* (1879), illustrations of Milton's "Il Penseroso", and in *Opening the Fold* (1880), etched for his *English Version of the Eclogues of Virgil* (1883), he wonderingly recalls a mental landscape that breathes simultaneously the air of Italian mountains and the Roman campagna, the vibrancy of Kentish hills and cottages, and the archaism of sheepfold, piping shepherds, and rooks rising in the sky over distant habitations.[33] Both early and late the best have the perverse child's outlook of the individual who has decided against all dictates of commonsense to abide awhile in a make-believe Eden however jerry-built by the pressures of reality and twisted from the original bias by the forces of social change.

The labors of Constable to find timeless landscape equivalents for the daily routines and familiar scenes of the Stour Valley, and the failure of Palmer to sustain his vision of Kent as a corner of paradise, bear mute witness to the confusion about rural England. Were its pockets of solace pastoral reminders of paradise or archaic backwaters overlooked by a developing technological civilization? Signs of the times are John Martin's (1789–1854) illustrations to Milton's great poem, which supplied him in the 1820s with some of his most congenial subjects, although it is significant in his pictorializations of *Paradise Lost* that he found Hell a more inspirational theme than Eden.[34] The mezzotint *Pandemonium* depicts an "Egyptian–Babylonian" palace rising tier on tier of columned levels out of an immense plain of flames, teeming with fallen angels addressed by Satan from a high rock. The picture epitomizes the duality of Martin's imagination. One of the beneficiaries of Milton's poetic legacy he was stirred enough by his witness of a civilization coming into being to conceptualize Milton's pastoral work in architectural forms and in urban settings. The tiered arches of the bridges and aqueducts of his day supplied Martin with a marvelous road over which Satan traverses Chaos (in *Bridge over Chaos*). The same form provided him with a cavern of over-arching trees under which Adam and Eve quake as they hear the admonitory voice of God after their act of disobedience (in *Adam Hearing the Voice of the Almighty*). The tree-lined aisles of seventeenth-century gardens have metamorphosed into expressions of nineteenth-century engineering might, nightmarish transformations of such arches as portrayed in *Chirk Aqueduct* (1804) painted by John Sell Cotman (1782–1842) and as incorporated into the bridges being designed by Telford, Brunel, and others.

It is as if in what might justifiably be termed Martin's pre-Victorian imagination the trees and meadows, valleys and hills, of the Kent–Brownian garden and of the Romantic landscape have been reorganized to show the underlying

15 Palmer, *Opening the Fold*

mechanistic basis of all natural forms. The urban experience in its splendor of stones, pavements, teeming multitudes, and soaring heights has superseded the pastoral memory with its tender of natural solitude and chthonic wild-wood notes. When Martin thought of paradise his imagination leaped forward to the eventual Heavenly City of God, not backward to the original Garden of Eden. His gigantic late paintings *The Last Judgment* (1853, Tate Gallery) and *The Plains of Heaven* (1853, Tate Gallery) direct our eyes to the heavenly city shimmering in blinding divine light on the horizon as the goal of every man after an arduous trudge across a wild Salvatorean terrain. Martin's imagination fed on histrionics. The urban colossi of the Biblical past merged in his mind with the London and manufacturing centers of his day. He painted *Belshazzar's Feast* in 1820–21 as a massive courtyard setting with Belshazzar on a balcony high above the populace, and *The Fall of Nineveh* in 1829, its columns and walls receding *ad infinitum*. They were for him the index of paradise – and of hell – not the verdant groves of Eden, which he depicted as a frightening mottle of deep shadows and glaring sunlight alternating in a trackless wilderness, where mordant trees and bushes droop nightmarishly, and the fountain Eve bathes in oozes Stygian inkiness.

Palmer and Constable may be the last English landscapists to look on rural contours as sacred ground. They clung to the myth of an agrarian paradise at the cost of public derision and neglect. Palmer managed nevertheless only intermittently to hold his vision intact. Compounded of sterner stuff, Constable's imagination when necessary prevailed against the artistic conventions of his day, forging a new vocabulary to give his memories expression. Theirs was the gift of continuing to see the agricultural scene as it had appeared to the "wond'ring Eyes" (*Paradise Lost*, VIII, 257) of Adam in those first dawns before social commentary and labor rights had cast a pall over it. Then "enlight'n'd Earth['s] . . . happy Light" spread over "Hills and Dales . . . Rivers, Woods, and Plains" (*Paradise Lost*, VIII, 274, 285, 275) as Adam set forth at God's instructions "To Till" His consecrated acreage, "and of the Fruit to eat" (320). Even the toiling bargemen and occasional strolling hunter (as in *The Cornfield*) fail to mitigate the serenity of this rural world; they are absorbed into the setting, a natural part of its processes of never ending growth and decay. And this valley paradise is light moons away in time and place, although a few hundred miles and twenty years or more apart, from the half-wild Eden Emily Brontë will fashion for Heathcliff and Catherine Earnshaw to roam in. The cottage sentiment which was to sweep the increasingly city-bound early and mid-Victorian society reflects an ambiguity of attitude never properly sorted out by those most attracted to it; and it led naturally to the enshrinement of Hardy's Wessex as a flawed Eden, where an old-fashioned pastoralism is forced to accommodate a new irony of cosmic indifference.[35] Only in the isolated cases of Graham Sutherland (1903–79) and Paul Nash (1889–1946) has English landscape painting since approached to any extent the unclouded faith with which Palmer and Constable looked on country roads, ploughed fields, and pasture lands, each in his own distinct way, one ecstatically eccentric, the other modestly low-keyed, as hieroglyphs of divine order.

7

Crabbe's and Clare's Enclosured Vales

BEWICK AND CONSTABLE were graced with optimistic imaginations, at once visionary and practical. They offered what seemed to be a tough-minded purchase on a Christian–classical ideal, forward looking in its reification of the new philosophy of cosmic change, while still retaining the reassuring timelessness of the rural round. George Crabbe (1754–1832) and John Clare (1793–1864), country bred, East Anglian, and backward looking, fashioned a bleaker version of the paradisal ideal, as dimly retained in its postlapsarian correlative of village and agricultural life. Religiously conservative, they lamented Eden's removal from the landscape, recalling the original loss paradoxically in the record of banishment fated to be felt anew by every son and daughter of Adam and Eve. Fallen and flawed human nature tempered the world of Crabbe; and unstable land and farming conditions darkened the mind of Clare. Theirs was an overt expression of lapsarian gloom, heard as a counterpoint to the millenarian hosannas of fellow Romantics, and characterized the age as genuinely as the fireworks of rejoicing which sporadically lit up the sky between the 1780s and the 1830s. As much as Coleridge and Wordsworth, who evolved from youthful ardor to senior citizen sententiousness, Crabbe and Clare signaled the degree to which the period from the 1780s to the 1820s as middleman negotiated the difficult transfer from exuberant Georgian self-election to inhibited Victorian self-questioning.

Crabbe took Christian comfort in the belief that his bleak disclosures of village life's oppressiveness and "Nature's niggard hand" were the truthful underside to a pastoral tradition fostered by centuries of poets. He tirelessly sounded in *The Village* (1783) and later in *The Parish Register* (1807), *The Borough* (1810), *Tales* (1812), and *Tales of the Hall* (1817) an early warning alarm that the bucolic England honored in poems for two hundred years, if it ever existed outside the pages of poets, was sorely beleaguered now by all too evident realities of mechanization, overpopulation, unequally distributed wealth – and the ever present fact of fallen human nature.

Actually, Crabbe's was not the only voice of despondency heard, just one of the bluntest. Raymond Williams has surveyed the modulation that took place in the second half of the eighteenth century from celebratory poems addressed to happy tenants of country houses to elegiac poems expressing loss and regret over the changes occurring to the landscape.[1] The energetic Edenic goal of the "Gardening Lords" of the eighteenth century was thus a fitting analogue – and climax – to the country house poems of the seventeenth century. But the retrospective melancholy and humble simplicity celebrated by a Goldsmith also reflects a new plebian outlook beset with a growing unease that was to modulate into Crabbe's anti-pastoral stridency, Jane Austen's ironic scrutiny of country house life, and Cobbett's energetic social and economic warnings about the plight of rural England.

It was an age (1785–1825) that mixed Methodistic enthusiasm and Paleyan rationalism. Millenarian prognoses, cult saviors, and revival of occult and unorthodox knowledge[2] jostled with moral legalisms, game-shooting parsons, and the interiorization of imagination. Crabbe instinctively gravitated toward the second group.[3] As a latitudinarian minister of the Church of England, beneficiary of the patron system, and holder of plural benefices, he seems to have accepted without much crisis of conscience the unsentimental practical Georgian world in which he had been born. Underlying his worldly success, however, lay the bedrock of his having grown up in the fishing village of Aldeburgh in the bleak lowlands, "burning sand" and "sterile soil" (*The Village*, I, 65, 72), of Suffolk, where the human relations of the rough fisherfolk and laborers minus the protective manners of polite society were visible with Wordsworthian intensity to an observant boy. He was struck by the recurrence of human types and tragedies; and like his great Puritan poetic predecessor, he found absorbing the moral drama of man's continued repetition of his original blunder. The fall from grace – paradise lost and its psychological consequences for humankind, not paradise regained – has his unabated attention. As if to underline this preoccupation Crabbe wrote a poem of reminiscence, "Infancy" (1816; published in 1834), in which he relates a river excursion he took as a child. It was a joyous sunny sail until some drunken men and a rain storm turned the voyage into a frightening experience. What had begun as a taste of "paradise without taint of sin" (83–84), became a confirmation of "the general doom" (*The Borough*, "Amusements," IX, 180) assigned all humankind. This was "a portentous experience for the child Crabbe," Robert L. Chamberlain contends.[4] It contained a truth, Crabbe came to believe, that every individual must learn: "th' imagined paradise" of infant and youthful minds must inevitably give way before the disillusioning reality of age.

> Enchantment bows to Wisdom's serious plan,
> And Pain and Prudence make and mar the man.
>
> (*The Library*, 593–94)

In one of his finest controlled poems, "The Natural Death of Love" (*Tales of the Hall*, XIV) Crabbe explores the compensatory satisfactions of this knowledge. He has his married couple face up to the truth that the magic charm of their love, which once led each to fantasize of the other that "Not the Arabian sweets so fragrant were, / Nor Eden's self, if aught with Eden might compare" (180–81), has vanished before the onslaught of "th' awakening strife and care, / That we as, tired and toiling men, must share" (229–30). The poem is Crabbe's "Intimations Ode," and the mature marital wisdom he allows his lovers to win is correlative to the sober light of common day Wordsworth soberly assigns his heaven-born child.

The vast bulk of Crabbe's poetry contains surprisingly few references to paradise. And those few ordinarily remind us of our punishment as earth dwellers, doomed to wrest our livelihood from its flinty surface. The opening lines of *The Village* (1783) are justly famed for their outraged protest at the unequal distribution of the earth and at the failure of poets to look honestly at this fact. The unforgettable picture he paints of farm laborers "beneath the dog-star's raging heat, / When the knees tremble and the temples beat" (I, 144–45), derives its moral intensity, however, as much from an oblique religious rectitude as from its explicit social indignation. The knowledge of guilt as well as of famine informs the lines. Besides the fact of the bad land, and the concentration of the wealth in a few hands, there is the irrevocable fate of mankind, however they may complain, to spend their days in "fruitless toil and labour in vain" (I, 133–34). In the end, the low and the great,

> poor, blind, bewilder'd, erring race;
> Who, a short time in varied fortune past,
> Die, and are equal in the dust at last.   (*The Village*, II, 98–100)

After *The Village* Crabbe fell silent, not publishing again, with the trivial exception of *The Newspaper* (1785), until 1807, when *The Parish Register* appeared. With this poem Crabbe mutes his outrage over the lot of the poor, and concentrates his attention on the inexhaustible universe of human virtues and vices, strengths and frailties,

> How pass'd the youthful, how the old their days;
> Who sank in sloth, and who aspired to praise;
> Their tempers, manners, morals, customs, arts,
> What parts they had, and how they 'mploy'd their parts;
> By what elated, soothed, seduced, depress'd,   (I, 9–13)

a subject from which he rarely digressed in the thousands of lines he was still to write. Nor does he often let himself forget, *pace* pastoral and paradisal, that

> Since vice the world subdued and waters drown'd,
> Auburn and Eden can no more be found.
>   (*The Parish Register*, "Baptism," I, 25–26)

In most of Crabbe's subsequent poetry the underlying view prevails that Eden is unattainable in our temporal abode. His tales are homilies on how the inflexible laws of sinful human nature and of unforgiving political economy insure this irrevocable fact. Thus does religious dogma and agrarian industrialism provide Crabbe with a conservative context for a poetic universe in which redemption plays a bit part. At the end of "The Boat Race" (*Posthumous Tales*, XVIII) he offers conventional Christian solace:

'It is the Heavenly will':
And in that will our duty bids us rest,
For all that Heaven ordains is good, is best;
We sin and suffer – this alone we know,
Grief is our portion, is our part below;
But we shall rise, that world of bliss to see,
Where sin and suffering never more shall be.   (302–08)

Not until the end of the world will full moral redemption come to man and woman when they will once again know paradise.

The life, labors, poetry, and agonies of Clare add a real-life gloss to the imaginative creations of Wordsworth and Crabbe. Almost like a footnote to their different reconstructions of the human pilgrimage through Regency England, the flawed record of Clare's life and poetry closes out a time when in Wordsworth's case poets could still believe in the natural world as an unfallen place coeval with Eden, and in Crabbe's case still believe in the indivisibility and universality of place and person. The connected tales of *The Parish Register* and *The Borough* at the beginning of the nineteenth century exhibit a touch of independent genius that Crabbe's contemporaries to their credit generously recognized. They could not gauge the degree to which Crabbe's narrative practices anticipated the great practitioners of the Victorian novel, but they had no trouble recognizing his comfortable summation of the generalizing tendencies and humanitarian impulses of the eighteenth-century mind. To conceive a poem of the length, complexity, and originality of *The Prelude*, however, is a major accomplishment at any time. That Wordsworth managed the feat at the beginning of the nineteenth century, in rural England, combining quite disparate modes of perception, makes it a remarkable achievement. If the psychology of his day provided him with the ground for conceiving the growth of his imagination as a linear process, the pattern in the poem of constant return to one's starting place in the diurnal round of existence, along with a circular sense of space and of a fixed center, harked back to a structuring of reality rendered old-fashioned by the changing appearance of the English countryside (more accelerated in the midland and southern shires in Wordsworth's lifetime than in the Lake Country) by way of enclosure and industrialization.

The medieval plan of open-field farming surrounded a village with fields, some tilled, some fallow, some reserved for grazing, usually on a rotating three to four year cycle, worked communally by the inhabitants. Roads and paths led to the outermost parts and places of the fields, but seldom beyond or out of the parish. One's sense of space was accordingly identified with a place whose boundaries were circumscribed, fixed, and complete. One's daily movements were essentially circular, out into the surrounding fields and back to one's house, a reassuring measure of life engrained on the rural mind by centuries of work habit and domestic arrangement.

With the enclosure of land a totally different orientation of space was forced on the consciousness. Each farmer's holdings were consolidated into a contiguous the unified grant of land. Roughly rectangular in shape, the contours and peculiarities of the terrain permitting, the reconstituted farms were strung along roads newly laid down or redefined through the parish, straightened and extended to connect with other towns. The orientation was clearly linear; the direction of movement was out of the village in a straight line toward the next village. The impetus in the round of activities was delocalized.

What effect this change in spatial orientation could have on an individual's assumptions and expectations is illustrated in the rustic's traumatic sense of geographical and ideational dislocation suffered by Clare. In his *Autobiography* Clare refers to his Northamptonshire village of Helpston as encompassing his whole world. According to Eric Robinson and Geoffrey Summerfield, and John Barrell as well, when Clare traveled from it his sense of place ("Sense of Helpston," Barrell prefers to call it),[5] which was equivalent to his sense of reality and of identity, caused him to experience feelings of alienation and exile. Clare tells of a walk he took when a child across Emmonsailes Heath in search of "the world's end." Although soon lost, he "eagerly wanderd on" unafflicted by fears. Thus he "rambled along the furze the whole day," he writes,

till I got out of my knowledge when the very wild flowers seemd to forget me & I imagind they were the inhabitants of new countrys the very sun seemd to be a new one & shining in a different quarter of the sky.[6]

"Out of my knowledge" – a striking phrase – was common enough in Clare's day for regional disorientation as a result of being in a place one does not know; but the phrase clearly carries a deeper layer of meaning to Clare, for whom being in unfamiliar country geographically corresponded to a radical disorientation epistemologically. He was literally out of his knowledge of all things, not just spatially but also cognitively.

Exile of humankind from their true home in paradise has always furnished poets with a metaphor for alienation. So Milton imagined the state of mind of Adam and Eve when "with wandring steps and slow" they "took their solitarie way" (*Paradise Lost*, XII, 648–49) out of Eden into the world. So Keats imagined his sojourn on earth far from heaven's bourne when he paralleled it to "the sad heart of Ruth . . . sick for home," standing "in tears amid the alien corn" ("Ode to a Nightingale," 66–67). And so Clare imagined his and his family's move in 1823 to the village of Northborough four miles from Helpston, his poems – especially one of the best, "The Flitting" – recording in paradisal terminology the drabness that the landscape had suddenly assumed.

To find a move of four miles so disconcerting is difficult for us to conceive of in the century of the automobile and the supersonic airplane. Equally incomprehensible to the twentieth-century urban dweller is the pathos of Clare's lament for the transformation of his native Helpston under an act of enclosure between 1809 and 1820.[7] For Clare, attached from childhood to particular trees, stream, fields, and to the *genius loci* of specific places, the effacement of familiar haunts by enclosure left him sorely disoriented. It aroused in him a profound sense of loss, which he often articulates by analogy to the loss of paradise. In "Emmonsales Heath" he contrasts the pristine "maiden soil" of the heath to the newly created farm lands. On the heath "wild weed blossoms waken blythe / That ploughshares never wrong."

> Creations steps ones wandering meets
> Untouched by those of man
> Things seem the same in such retreats
> As when the world began.

With such words of wonderment Clare articulates for generations of mute peasants the appeal of a few square yards of earth. And in a poem like "The Mores" he gives voice to the poignant feelings of generation after generation in the eighteenth and nineteenth centuries who find themselves one day barred from fields they have tramped all their lives. Clare bitterly assails the fences, "mangled garbs," that meet fences "in owners little bounds / Of field and meadow large as garden grounds / In little parcels," where once

> Far spread the moorey ground a level scene
> Bespread with rush and one eternal green
> That never felt the rage of blundering plough
> Through centurys wreathed springs blossoms on its brow
> Still meeting plains that stretched them far away
> In uncheckt shadows of green brown and grey
> Unbounded freedom ruled the wandering scene
> Nor fence of ownership crept in between
> To hide the prospect of the following eye
> Its only bondage was the circling sky
> One mighty flat undwarfed by bush and tree
> Spread its faint shadow of immensity
> And lost itself which seemed to eke its bounds
> In the blue mist the orisons edge surrounds.   (1–14)

Now all "Is faded . . . vanished . . . with commons wild and gay / As poets visions of lifes early day" (17, 39–40). "Enclosure came" and the land was leveled, as he memorably laments in "Remembrances," "by the never weary plough."

There remains a question as to whether the tragedy of Clare's life – his sense of a fair world now vanished – was due to the enclosing of fields he roamed in as a boy or to his growing into manhood with its inevitable closing in of boundaries. According to Robinson and Summerfield, the countryside about Helpston – "every single tree . . . and every single blade of grass" – in Clare's memory was "a special act of the Creator" and participated "in the freshness before the Fall." It "was not only the map of Clare's boyhood" and "part of a rural landscape cruelly altered by enclosure"; it was even more significantly "Clare's Paradise, his Garden of Eden." Clare identifies the fields of his boyhood before enclosure with "the landscape of Eden before the Fall" and populates it with his boyhood love, Mary Joyce, who figures as "Eve to Clare's Adam."[8]

No, objects Barrell. No such pattern of imagery is consciously and consistently invoked in the poetry. The imagery of Eden "seems to be applied to the landscape of Helpston indifferently whether it is still open or enclosed"; and in the poem "Helpstone" itself lines about Eden that refer to Clare's childhood "are followed by a passage in which Clare prays that he may in his old age return to Helpstone and die there." Ironically enough, Barrell observes, these lines – "And, as reward for all my troubles past, / Find one hope true – to die at home at last!" (155–56)

– are borrowed directly from Goldsmith's

> I still had hopes, my long vexations past,
> Here to return – and die at home at last;
> (*The Deserted Village*, 95–6)

but whereas Goldsmith's hope cannot now be fulfilled, Clare has not been so thoroughly expelled from his Eden that he cannot look forward to a comfortable old age there. I think we have to conclude that Clare was, at this stage, simply unable to organise his response to the enclosure or to Helpston; and that there is no scheme of imagery that will help him out of his confusions, of the difficulty he finds in distinguishing between his own meaning and that of the poets he is imitating.[9]

Again, somewhat later, Barrell comments, "it's hard to grasp quite what Clare's nostalgia is for: whether it is for a vision of Helpston which has inevitably left him as he has grown older, or for a Helpston which has undergone the concrete change of being enclosed."[10]

I have quoted the exchange between Robinson / Summerfield and Barrell at length because it addresses a problem recurrent to this study, the difficulty of assaying the degree to which metaphor and plangent phrase can be read as glimpses into the archetypal recesses of the mind's storehouse, and can be interpreted as an attempt by that individual, and by his society, to come to terms with an imperfect world that resists replication of the archetype. No doubt Robinson and Summerfield exaggerate when they reify Clare's metaphoric recreation of Helpston as Eden (confusingly complete with an Eve named Mary). In this regard though, it is striking that in his asylum years Clare persisted in fantasizing that he was married to Mary, thus recreating the Eden of his youth out of the demented needs of his old age. Barrell no less errs when he inflates their estimates for polemical purposes. The irony is that his blunt literalism blocks his recognition that Clare's lines are as hopeless in the context of his life despite their seeming contrary assertion as are the narrator's in "The Deserted Village" from whom Clare borrowed both cheerless perception and ironically positive language.

The fact is that Clare laments both growing-up and enclosure equally and indiscriminately as root causes of his loss of paradise. In his *Autobiography* he can pinpoint his angst in Edenic terms of innocence and experience: "Ah what a paradise begins with life & what a wilderness the knowledge of the world discloses. Surely the Garden of Eden was nothing more than our first parents entrance upon life & the loss of it their knowledge of the world." And then a few pages later, without any grasp of being contradictory or confusing, he can blame his profound sense of unease on enclosure: "I lovd the lonely nooks in the fields & woods & my favourite spots had lasting places in my memory that bough that when a schoolboy screened my head before enclosure destroyed them."[11] Nor was Clare's nostalgia for the happy rural order of his childhood (presumably the 1790s), which hé remembers as paradisal, and whose disappearance he blames at times on the pitiless redistribution of once commonly held tracts of land, all that unique with him. The time escalator of nostalgia, as Raymond Williams strikingly calls it, moves each generation backward in memory to recover the "good old days" of an immediate past, bringing us inevitably to Eden, that ultimate "well-remembered garden again."[12] The progress of agrarian capitalism at the end of the eighteenth and into the nineteenth centuries exacerbated this perennial sense of the disruption of rural routines and habits of mind. The plain tragedy of Clare's world is that it would not stay constant. It failed to remain an intimately loved place, circumscribed enough to know in every detail, static, and unvarying as an Eden. Instead, the familiar face of things altered under the improving social and economic status of the farmer as contrasted to that of the landless laborer. The ruthless plough and shovel of enclosure

> like a buonaparte let not a thing remain
> It levelled every bush and tree and levelled every hill
> And hung the moles for traitors – though the brook is running still
> It runs a naked stream cold and chill.
>
> ("Remembrances," 67–70)

At the same time the comfortable security of place altered under the transforming gaze of his growth from carefree boy, when time seemed to stand still, into careworn man in whom baffled dismay before change harvested disillusioned anger.

> O I never thought that joys would run away from boys
> Or that boys should change their minds and forsake mid-summer joys
> But alack I never dreamed that the world had other toys
> To petrify first feelings like the fable into stone
> Till I found the pleasure past and a winter come at last
> Then the fields were sudden bare and the sky got over cast
> And boy hoods pleasing haunts like a blossom in the blast
> Was shrivelled to a withered weed and trampled down and done
> Till vanished was the morning spring and set the summer sun
> And winter fought her battle strife and won.
>
> ("Remembrances," 51–60)

William Cobbett (1763–1835), more than a generation older than Clare, writing at roughly the same time recalls in *Rural Rides* (1830) and in his *Autobiography* the vanished world of the 1770s in words that reverberate with the pointed association of its once timeless ways with the idyll of paradise. Cobbett tirelessly traveled the back lanes and byways of southern shires, looking for remnants of the Old England that existed when he was a boy. What he found as often as not instead was a land still struggling to recover from agricultural reforms accelerated by twenty years of war. Rather than a contented yeoman tenantry living in harmony with landowners like paradisal enclaves left over after the expulsion from Eden, he saw fields devastated by feckless and ruthless husbandry alike ("the people at Westminster . . . know how to turn paradise itself into hell"), disenfranchised workers laboring at make-work on roads, and the newly rich (stock-jobbers Cobbett invariably assumes) barricaded behind fences, freshly planted hedgerows, and signs warning off poachers like the one he passed outside Canterbury: "*Paradise Place. Spring guns and steel traps are set here.*"[13]

As with Cobbett's, the plain tragedy of Clare's world is that, like so many of his redundant fellow farm laborers, who were denied a livelihood, Clare found himself not only deprived of his social reality but, worse yet, dispossessed of his comforting sense of belonging to a fixed place. Poverty forced him to move elsewhere. Madness imprisoned him. Whether Clare's nostalgia is prompted by a *cri de coeur* for the innocence of childhood or by outrage at enclosure, there is no question that he recalls Helpston with more than poetic convention as a paradise now lost:

> Oh, happy Eden of those golden years
> Which memory cherishes, and use endears.
>
> ("Helpstone," 141–42)

He had learned all too well the fate Crabbe assigned each person. With age comes the fading of celestial brightness and the onset of common day, and disillusionment. Clare's difficulty in adapting childhood's "Enchantment" to the lowered expectations of adulthood's prudential ways and "Wisdom's serious plan" may have expressed the personal side of the man, but the existential dolor that he articulated sounds the universal cry of mankind down through the centuries and, as well, the historically immediate alienation of the dispossessed rural laboring class living through the agricultural revolution in the early decades of the nineteenth century.

The attachment of Clare's imagination to a single place (Helpston) and to a dominant pattern of experience (Eden once known and loved, now lost) restricts it to circling endlessly a mile or two of terrain and to recurring obsessively to a geographically identified set of objects. John Barrell has demonstrated brilliantly and at length how Clare's poetry is bent on capturing the multiplicity of details, and the particularity of each, that comprises this landscape, a manifold of details that is hard won at the expense of composition and order. The Clare poem underplays syntactical connection, allowing the "continuum of successive impressions" to appear as if it were "one complex manifold of simultaneous impressions."[14] A descriptive poem like "Emmonsails Heath in Winter" where all the images are syntactically of equal weight is comparable to the diffuse landscape of Constable where every detail is equally important. In both the focus is less on one thing than on all things at once. Hence, despite the linear, temporal necessities of the poetic line, Clare's verse seeks a sense of enclosed space in its efforts to encompass everything in a given place in one glance.

In addition to the syntactical transformation of a linear statement into an enclosed spatial component is the tendency of Clare's poetic statements to eddy around a few observations. He repeats images, obsessively returning to already mentioned objects and activities. As Barrell observes, the last words of "Emmonsails Heath in Winter" are "and start again." Although the primary reference of the words is to the flight of a flock of birds, the phrase also "directs our attention back, too, to the start of the poem, so that the images in the poem become like beads on a necklace: they cannot change places with each other, but can be told in a circle in such a way that we lose the sense of beginning and end, and so of one sort of order."[15]

The persistence of Clare's concentration on a still moment in time, in an almost Blakean effort to perceive there the timeless, is apparent when "Emmonsails Heath in Winter" is read with comparable lines by Crabbe in mind, for example, a description of the grounds surrounding "The Ancient Mansion" (*Posthumous Tales*, x). Conscious of poetic predecessors stretching back from Pope and Thomson to Horace and Virgil, Crabbe organizes his generalized observations into a chronological progression that follows the natural cycle of the year. A litany of flowers, fruits, and grains, and agricultural activities identify each successive season: spring blossoms into summer, which yields its bounty to autumn, before coming to rest in winter. This cyclical reassurance of the "eternal" does not seem to have moved Clare's hard peasant mind to quite the easy acceptance it did his fellow Romantics.

The thrust of Clare's imagination is centripetal; but experience has also made it despairing. In the opening lines of the first stanza of "Signs of Winter," he flirts with the idea of collapse of the center of his world:

> Tis winter plain the images around
> Protentious tells us of the closing year
> Short grows the stupid day the moping fowl
> Go roost at noon – upon the mossy barn
> The thatcher hangs and lays the frequent yaum
> Nudged close to stop the rain that drizzling falls
> With scarce one interval of sunny sky
> For weeks still leeking on that sulky gloom
> Muggy and close a doubt twixt night and day
> The sparrow rarely chirps the thresher pale
> Twanks with sharp measured raps the weary frail
> Thump after thump right tiresome to the ear
> The hedger lonesome brustles at his toil
> And shepherds trudge the fields without a song.   (1–14)

Here, "the closing year" becomes symptomatic of the ever narrowing circle of time and space, of noon as the meeting place of day and night, and of light and dark, the constant rain reinforcing the collapse of day and night into perpetual dusk. Only the shrewd reservation of his rustic's sensibility holds the world together in its familiar cyclical form. Localized through dialect, which grants nothing unobserved, he in effect stays change by the concentration of his language on familiar and routine activities until the seasonal cycle can right things and bring all back to normal again. And true to his peasant's ability to take comfort in rural activities, Clare reassembles the circumscribed whole of his world in stanza 2, by observing the antic life of the barnyard, mostly playful reiterations of closure ("The cat runs races with her tail").

Barrell associates the characteristic circular movement of Clare's imagination with the visual and ambulatory nature of an archaic open-field environment. At an even deeper level of human consciousness, a circular, enclosed idea of space and time is intrinsic to the paradisal ideal. Clare never wanted the innocent natural world of Helpston to change. He dreamed lifelong for a land, as he sings in the Asylum poem "The Maid o' the West," "that knoweth no decay." He delighted in reminding himself, and drew comfort from the reminder, that a poet's love of nature is "like Heaven's love," and in the security of that blessedness, "Like the calm of heaven," nature's "gifts . . . spread far and wide," her flowers "her very scriptures upon earth" ("Poets Love Nature"). But nature, society, and people, he learned to his sorrow, are organisms that grow into new forms, alter appearances, and eventually decay.

Economic interests born of the Industrial Revolution were invading and disrupting the unvarying occupations of the rural year, rendering archaic the bucolic existence honored in georgic and pastoral poetry. The attenuation, if not demise, of these poetic forms, coinciding with the new commercial instincts revolutionizing agriculture, was far advanced by the time Clare published his first books *Poems Descriptive of Rural Life and Scenery* (1820) and *The Village Minstrel* (1821).[16] Their definition of rural routine as a way of life was losing out to farming's new identification as a negotiable business venture. In holding forlornly to antiquated habits of mind Clare was manifestly more old fashioned than Wordsworth, his senior by twenty years. More vulnerable than the Westmorland sage's, less armed by irony against contrary viewpoints, Clare's poetry employs a perspective – the heart's desire – that harks back to golden ages and to Edens of the human spirit. It recognizes the social and economic transformations of the agricultural revolution, the surface changes wrought to the landscape and to remembered landmarks; but it comes to terms with these transformations by juxtaposing them to nostalgic memories of a timeless childhood and to a mythic moment of paradise enshrined in literary convention. Increasingly in the post-Northborough and Asylum poems written in the 1830s and 40s his only recourse was to deny the changes by imagining a nonlocal universal nature, as in "Poets Love Nature." In these poems the formal structure of thought reinforces the conception of a perfect invariable nature, an abstract world that can substitute for and approximate to the Edenic neighborhood of his boyhood memories.

Typical is the internal order of "The Peasant Poet," written after 1842:

He loved the brook's soft sound
　　The swallow swimming by
He loved the daisy covered ground
　　The cloud bedappled sky
To him the dismal storm appeared
　　The very voice of God
And when the Evening rock was reared
　　Stood Moses with his rod
And every thing his eyes surveyed
　　The insects i' the brake
Were creatures God Almighty made
　　He loved them for his sake
A silent man in lifes affairs
　　A thinker from a Boy
A Peasant in his daily cares—
　　The Poet in his joy.　　　　　　　　　　(1–16)

In each two line segment the movement of thought is from below to above, from earth to sky, from mundane to spiritual, and from spatial to conceptual. Brook is transvalued by swallow, ground by sky, storm by the voice of God, rock by Moses, insects by creatures of God. The effect, as in the pre-1832 poems, is a manifold of simultaneous impressions, with at least one significant difference, the impressions no longer enumerate a beloved locale of Helpston but envision a "bright land" ("The Maid o' the West") that makes up part of a permanent earth–sky totality. The internal relationship of the couplets is architectonic and conceptual rather than syntactic; and in their contrastive progression Clare is absorbing the natural world and the flotsam of his life into an all-inclusive abstraction. Each image is perceived as a step negotiated in the perilous path of the soul leading from the simple external continuums of nature to the final complex temporal–spatial contrasts of silent man-thinking boy and careworn peasant-joyous poet. In all the contraries the poem is working to confirm the transformation of earthly dross into ethereal permanence. It is significant in reference to the poem's vulnerability and frankness that the abab rhyme pattern leaves each initial couplet of contraries uncompleted (comparable to the endless enumeration of images to be found in the pre-Northborough poems) and dependent on the intellectual observation in the next two lines for a conclusion. Thus, two progressions characterize the developing statement of the poem. Every first couplet starts a structural component that is secured only by the conclusion of the quatrain in which it occurs. At the same time, each four-line segment builds toward the final couplet of the poem and its assertion of the inviolate sensibility, or inner space, of the poet, the only Eden penniless demented Clare can command that encompasses all.

　　The same handling of form describes the late poem "A Vision," even to stanzaic organization and to advancement of thought from wry acceptance of the transience of earthly existence to welcome apprehension of a substitute poetic immortality. With uncanny similarity "Remembrances" also repeats the thematic pattern and rhyme sequences of "The Peasant Poet." A world of local landmarks bountiful and personally known is opposed to a leveled and plowed terrain familiar only because of its ubiquitous similarity with others. This time, though, Clare has supplemented his sense of spatial dislocation with temporal equations – spring–winter, boy–man, past–present – along with the by now familiar universalizing pattern of the spatial contraries. In the intensity of his effort to remember the details of a boyhood and of a rural scene forever altered from what they once were, he desperately includes in the manifold of impressions the present prospect as well as the distant memory. The sense of circular space includes a sense of circular time, as the poet tries to imagine the past experience, and that way give it the kind of permanence a "spot of time" had for Wordsworth.

Two contrary impulses pull at Clare, and at a poem like "Remembrances." There is the need to remain true to his situation and there is the need to keep alive against all appearances to the contrary the hope that this blighted earth can be transmuted back to the paradise that once was. More often than not his clinging to the reality of his situation, adumbrated by the stanzaic form, becomes less psychologically imperative than his need to believe in its reversibility. Against the force of this desire Clare frequently finds it difficult to maintain the cognitive distinctions between an idyllic *then* and a rueful *now* stipulated by the tripartite organization of the stanza and of the rhyme pattern:

> O words are poor reciepts for what time hath stole away
> The ancient pulpit trees and the play
> When for school oer little field with its brook and wooden brig
> Where I swaggered like a man though I was not half so big
> While I held my little plough though twas but a willow twig
> And drove my team along made of nothing but a name
> 'Gee hep' and 'hoit' and 'woi' – O I never call to mind
> Those pleasant names of places but I leave a sigh behind
> While I see the little mouldiwarps hang sweeing to the wind
> On the only aged willow that in all the field remains
> And nature hides her face while theyre sweeing in their chains
> And in a silent murmuring complains.
>
>   ("Remembrances," 29–40)

Clare struggles to keep separate the two sets of experiences and the two time periods, but they keep blurring at the edges. He cannot help seeing the "aged willow" still as it was when he played plowboy in the "little field" that now farm land surrounds. Similarly, in stanza 6, he minimizes the stark alteration of the countryside through enclosure, defining it as a shift in outlook produced by a boy's loss of summer haunts upon the onslaught of winter. For a moment, in this stanza, past and present are clapped into one, as the lines appear to describe a change of seasons that occurred one year in his childhood.

Clare's substitution of an earth–heaven progression in so many of his late poems for the child–adult antithesis we have just been looking at is indicative of his desperation, and the extremity of the accommodation forced on him and a lot of other farm laborers by the non-idyllic condition of early nineteenth-century rural life. To realize a world, now reduced to memory, of "quiet woods and gravel springs"

> Where little pebbles wear as smooth
> As hermits beads by gentle floods
> Whose noises doth my spirits sooth
> And warms them into singing moods
>
> ("The Flitting," 92–96)

he had to revert to an even older mythic pattern of return to a spiritual starting place, the rondure of a life time that brings man home again to his heavenly abode.

> Fancy spreads Edens wheresoe'er they be;
> The world breaks on them like an opening flower,
> Green joys and cloudless skies are all they see;
> The hour of childhood is a rose's hour. . . .
>
> ("Joys of Childhood," stanza 3)

In his lonely exile the Eden myth – paradise known once but lost now forever – provided him with an entranced link with the past, and is a testimony to the emotive hold the myth still had on the mind of the rural Englishman. Which was, however, both a strength and a liability for Clare the poet. It provided him with an authentic vocabulary for organizing his inchoate feelings, less studied than that borrowed from Goldsmith, Shenstone, Thomson, Collins, Langhorne, and other eighteenth-century poets of sentiment; but it also established the boundaries of his thought, restricting his imagination to a limited range of experience that he was unable, or reluctant, to break out of. The backward spiraling movement of Clare's felt response is touched on by Raymond Williams, when he observes that the poet's efforts to retrieve his lost sense of childhood happiness is "developed into a whole convention, in which not only innocence and security but peace and plenty have been imprinted, indelibly, first on a particular landscape, and then, in a powerful extension, on a particular period of the rural past, which is now connected with a lost identity, lost relations and lost certainties." Clare's "most crucial recognition," beyond which he had nowhere to go, finally, was that the original dispossession is, as it has always been, of paradise.[17] In "The Flitting" one can see Clare frantically drawing a correspondence between the blasted impermanent earth of his native Northamptonshire and the original pastoral perfection of the prelapsarian world:

> pasture molehills used to lie
> And talk to me of sunny days
> And then the glad sheep resting bye
> All still in ruminating praise
> Of summer and the pleasant place
> And every week and blossom too
> Was looking upward in my face
> With friendship welcome 'how do ye do'
> All tennants of an ancient place
> And heirs of noble heritage
> Coeval they with adams race

And blest with more substantial age
For when the world first saw the sun
These little flowers beheld him too
And when his love for earth begun
They were the first his smiles to woo

. . .

And still they bloom as in the day
They first crowned wilderness and rock
When abel haply crowned with may
The firstlings of his little flock
And Eve might from the matted thorn
To deck her lone and lovely brow
Reach that same rose that heedless scorn
Misnames as the dog rosey now   (121–36; 145–52)

John Clare was born in 1793 and died in 1864; John Martin the painter of
horrendous scenes of nature and the illustrator of Milton was born in 1789 and
died in 1854. Both are transitional figures, born when the Romantic sense of
security in benevolent nature prevailed, but living on as productive artists into the
era of Victorian acclimatization with urban industrialized life. Both clung
vehemently to the familiar scene and when, because of the evolving temper of the
times, it escaped them, they created it out of whatever resources were at hand. As
one critic notes, the novelty of Martin's designs for *Paradise Lost* "lies in his being
the first artist to create a sense of place, to conjure up the appearance of Hell,
Paradise, and Pandemonium."[18] Clare's attachment to what was essentially a
medieval sense of order, his inability to find solace in a nature unassociated with
one familiar place, his dislocation in a world rapidly urbanizing and industrializ-
ing makes him an interesting precursor of the generation of Tennyson, Browning,
and Arnold. Their difficulty was in experiencing nature directly. Access to it was
often possible for them only by way of the mediation of Romantic poetic
language. If they were disinherited by historical circumstances from utilizing a
mode of organizing human experience, which had been viable for centuries until
the immediate past, they were as yet not entirely comfortable with, and often
similarly cut off from, their new urban environment even when they tried to
define it in terms of the substitute Eden of the Heavenly City of God.

PART III

Victorian Heavenly Cities and Blessed Damozels

'Twould come but to a trifling price
To make it quite a paradise;
I cannot bear those nasty rails,
Those ugly broken mouldy pales:
Suppose, my dear, instead of these
We build a railing, all Chinese,
Although one hates to be exposed:
'Tis dismal to be thus enclosed;
One hardly any object sees –
I wish you'd fell those odious trees.
. . .
Our house, beholders would adore,
Was then a level lawn before,
Nothing its view to incommode,
But quite laid open to the road;
While ev'ry trav'ler in amaze,
Should on our little mansion gaze,
And pointing to the choice retreat,
Cry, that's Sir Thrifty's country seat.

Robert Lloyd, "The Cit's Country Box" (1757)

Were we required to characterise this age of ours by any single epithet, we should be tempted to call it, not an Heroical, Devotional, Philosophical, or Moral Age, but, above all others, the Mechanical Age. It is the Age of Machinery, in every outward and inward sense of that word.

Thomas Carlyle, *Signs of the Times* (1828–34)

The country blooms – a garden, and a grave.

Oliver Goldsmith, "The Deserted Village" (1770)

I recall to myself the old fame of London, its sublime position in the world, its interesting society, till I feel an impatient enthusiasm, which makes quite a child of me again. Think only, dear Anna, to hear the very hum of that immense place, to see from afar its dense cloud of smoke! These things, little and ordinary as they would be to many, would, I know, under particular circumstances, fill my eyes with tears and bring my heart into my throat till I could not say a word. But then to stand on Tower Hill, in Westminster Abbey, upon some old famous bridge . . . or even to have before one's eyes some old grey wall in Eastcheap or the Jewry . . . will be to me a realisation of many a vision and speculation.

Mary Howitt (1829)

Books can instruct, and books can amuse, and books can exalt and purify; beauty of face and beauty of form will come with bought pictures and statues, and for the government of a household hired menials will suffice; but fondness and hate, daring hope, lively fear, the lust for glory, and the scorn of base deeds, sweet charity, faithfulness, pride, and chief over all, the impetuous will, lending might and power to feeling – these are the rib of the man, and from these, deep-veiled in the mystery of her very loveliness, his true companion sprang. A being thus ardent will often go wrong in her strenuous course – will often alarm – sometimes provoke – will now and then work mischief, and even perhaps grievous harm, but she will be our own Eve after all – the sweet-speaking tempter, whom Heaven created to be the joy and the trouble of this "pleasing anxious" existence.
A. W. Kinglake, "The Rights of Women," *The Quarterly Review* (December 1844–March 1845)

8

From Natural Landscape to Controlled Environment

LONDON: *Rus in Urbe*

AT THE SAME TIME as the Romantics were working out their philosophy of nature, which in theory extended the nobleman's paradisal enclosure to include the whole earth as a divine garden but which in practice tended to localize the site and to internalize the ideal, a new class of men, mechanical geniuses and corporate entrepreneurs, Captains of Industry Carlyle was to call them, were building roads, canals, and bridges, perfecting the technology, expanding the manufactures, and pursuing the land developments that would correct the hardships of travel and improve the quality of life. In 1759 the first canal was dug, in 1779–80 the first iron bridge installed, in 1830 the first railway laid, and in 1851 the iron and glass Crystal Palace erected.

The changes to the face of England implied in these events, which roughly encompass 100 years, evoked ambivalent responses. Hailed as symbiotic metamorphoses of natural forces into industrial might, they were alternately deplored, romanticized, misunderstood, metonymized, and intellectualized. Assumptions about nature and man were inevitably affected. There was a subtle alteration of the old doctrine of natural plenitude to accommodate the new principle of mercantilistic abundance. The long awaited life of plenty was believed yet again to be near at hand. In anticipation of this new world the mechanical was often mistaken for the natural, garden suburbs for the country, public pleasure gardens for private Edens, and mean streets of columnared row houses for the Attic spirit of Vitruvius, Palladio, and Inigo Jones.[1] The confusion – and the debate – over the two versions of reality and two ways of life exercised the British throughout the nineteenth century, since the spirit of the one marking the culmination of eighteenth-century theories of nature and society never entirely vanished, as the manic energy of the other foreshadowing the creation of a nineteenth-century urban civilization gave visible evidence of its dynamic presence wherever one turned.

A case in point is the ambivalence that attended the transformations of London – its inexorable expansion north, south, and west, its accommodation of the railway, and its introduction of garden suburbs – with the accompanying raised expectations of its inhabitants. In 1804 the French architect Claude-Nicolas Ledoux (1736–1806) published a book in which he presented his designs for an ideal city whose neighborhoods, dedicated to peace and happiness, would be planted with gardens rivaling Eden.[2] The book encapsulates the dream of the century: a society living harmoniously in an urban environment of natural rightness, with streets harking back to the prototype of leafy lanes between trees, and of buildings whose columns are reminders of the Edenic forest. London never quite realized this dream. Its West End squares, and parks, its garden suburbs, and its pleasure gardens are attempts to "excite pastoral ideas in the mind," *rus in urbe*,[3] just as the railways pickaxing, tunneling, and lurching through the city in the 1860s especially,[4] and the Thames dock system devouring land and river frontage with such developments as the St. Katharine basin to the east of Tower Hill are contrary evidences of the mercantile and industrial drive to give different form to the dream.

Private land development in the West End, uncoordinated and without overall plan, had been going on for two hundred years, ever since the fourth Earl of Bedford had received a license in 1630 to build the Covent Garden Piazza as a speculative venture on land lying east and west of his house and garden. Throughout the next two centuries speculative building northward and ever westward was pursued in fits and starts through civil war, interregnum, restoration, and Whig establishment. In haphazard fashion were laid out the great squares and surrounding streets that give the present West End its distinctive Georgian appearance. Lincoln's Inn Fields, Bloomsbury Square, Bedford Square, St. James Square, Essex Street, Red Lion Square, Hanover Square, Berkeley Square, the streets behind Burlington House, Grosvenor Square, Cavendish Square, and in the old Marylebone fields, Portman Square, north to St. John's Wood and south to Belgravia. These squares usually retained a touch of greenery; but the basic conception in all the feverish estate development remained unabashedly urban: tall narrow houses with contiguous walls placed in long narrow lots, with a garden or courtyard at the back. Controversy over how London might best be expanded, however, was never entirely silent, especially in the second century of this phenomenal growth. Should classical and Palladian ideals be followed? Or should a "country-in-town" be sought? The author of *Critical Observations* (1771), possibly James Stuart, jeered at the "preposterous idea" of "a garden in a street." The "awkward imitation of the country" by the West End Squares, he fulminated, was doomed to failure. The fenced sheep walks in Cavendish Square, Hanover Square, and Red Lion Square create the contrary "idea of a butcher's pen" and "air of a cow-yard." The "smoke and bustle of the town" inevitably makes its presence felt, he contended, reducing such "rural ideas" to an absurdity. It would be far better to acknowledge the urban environment and strive to enhance it with appropriate embellishments as was being done at Bath.[5]

While titled holders of estates were developing their London holdings into "mock parks" the inner-city dwellers were expanding outward into the surrounding countryside. As early as Queen Anne's reign there was a counter stream of the wealthy classes to the villages encircling London. Merchants, doctors, lawyers, master tradesmen, and their "City famil[ies], mewed up in a brick court all the week, would trek out on a summer Saturday to a tea-garden or else to their own private pleasure-garden with neat cottage." Inevitably, many contrived to stay. This migration in search of a happier abode took several forms. Neighboring villages like Hampstead offered country sites for individual houses or terraces. At the same time the roads issuing from the city northward to Islington and southward through Lambeth to Kennington and Camberwell opened up tempting and conveniently accessible building sites. In the undeveloped lands between city and villages, just as today along the routes of new freeways, developers created tracts of instant communities, such as Camden Town, Somers Town, and Pentonville to the north. The names of many of these "instant suburbs" betray the irrepressible hopes of their inhabitants. They include not just modest claims for the rural character of the place, as in Grove, Ivy, Belmont, Prospect, Willow, Oak, or Woodbine, but also expressions of deeper human instincts as in Pleasant, Eden, Paradise, and Elysium.[6]

The dreams of "instant paradise" driving many of the city-pent into the suburbs received theoretical and professional support from the urban landscape architect J. C. Loudon (1783–1843), the man who brought plane trees to the London squares and streets, substituting their annually renewable green leaves for the soot blackened evergreens that had contributed to the gloomy appearance of the city. Bent on instructing newly affluent commercial and industrial classes in the selection of their first house beyond the confines of the inner city, he set out to prove in *The Suburban Gardener, and Villa Companion* (1838) "that a suburban residence, with a very small portion of land attached, will contain all that is essential to happiness, [as] in the garden, park, and demesne of the most extensive country residence."[7]

There were at least three identifiable moves to the suburbs in the second half of the nineteenth century. The first came in the 1840s, and may have been as much a cause as a result of Loudon's proselytizing. As Walter L. Creese notes, the population of London rose by one-fifth during that decade, with the expanding middle classes bent on finding for themselves a better life – still popularly identified with "the Romantic wish to flee into woodland alleys and places of nestling green."[8] A second expansion of suburbs occurred from 1877 to 1887, and a third from 1897 to 1899.

Not everyone was enthralled with the prospects of pastures and glades going under the rapacious axes and saws of builders. Just as large sections of America look with incredulous shock on the sprawl of Los Angeles, so, many mid-Victorians found the scramble for a residential plot of ground unseemly. In a contemporary novel a character exclaims:

in the environs of London . . . from Paddington to Putney, what vagaries in brick and mortar – what barbarisms in Portland stone! – In all directions, for ten miles round the capital – villas – villas – villas! A villa is one of the first indications of prosperity on the part of the professional man. Thriving merchants – popular actors – popular dentists – popular lawyers – popular all sorts of things, are sure to have their Tusculum, their *rus in urbe*, their Eden, their 'appiness 'ouse![9]

Contrary to the implication conveyed by such a display of outrage at the ubiquitous villa – that Londoners were everywhere moving into private dwellings in park-like environments – London remained relatively poor in garden suburbs. Among the most famous are East and West Park Villages (1824–25) laid out by John Nash on the east side of Regent's Park; Bedford Park (1875–81) designed by R. Norman Shaw, remembered by Yeats who lived there when a boy as a story-book place, and satirized by G. K. Chesterton as Saffron Park in *The Man Who Was Thursday* (1908); and Hampstead Garden Suburb in (1905–08). In general, though, the garden suburb was taken up, often with more zest than taste, by dwellers in the midland and northern parts of the country. Examples are Edensor (1838–42), built by Joseph Paxton for the Duke of Devonshire on his Chatsworth Estate, and Birkenhead Park (1843–47) near Liverpool also by Paxton; the Hanover Square and Zoological Gardens (1836–38) near Manchester; Saltaire (1850s), built by Titus Salt for his mill workers near Bradford, Yorkshire; and Akroydon model village (1861–63) near Halifax, founded by Edward Akroyd for his factory workers and families in the pious interests of "house and home attachment."[10]

London never adequately solved its problem of depressing miles of brick and stucco faced streets. The best it managed was a partial integration of Regency London's West End parks, Georgian squares, and thoroughfares. The person who figures principally in the redesign of the West End is John Nash (1752–1835). He remains shadowy and enigmatic, although the impulse behind his city planning is clear enough: the need for the transfiguring order of architectural solidity as a counter weight to the shadowiness of his private life and early career and to the insecurity of a long service under an unpopular and scapegrace monarch during the uncertain years of the Regency. His plan was a daring social gesture in its importation of country panoramas into borough precincts on a city-wide scale. Equally daring is the historical imagination which imposed the eighteenth-century country house and its Edenic environs onto the London square, crescent, and gridiron, although one should not forget in this context that Nash had been in partnership in the 1790s with the landscape gardener Humphry Repton, and had been associated as a country-house architect with the building of Hafod. No less admirable are the pertinacity and brilliant architectural improvisation displayed during the more than twenty years that it took him to execute his grand design, when he was forced at every step to reconcile divergent opinions prompted by economic timidity and by state policy.

To measure the originality of his achievement, one has only to place it in the context of earliest instances of town planning. The most successful – and according to John Summerson one of the first – previous to Nash's Regent's Park project was the terrace complex in Bath of Queen Square, Gay Street, the Circus, and the Royal Crescent by the John Woods, senior and junior, from 1729 to

1769.[11] One can say with only minimal exaggeration that all subsequent town planning in England, until Nash, figures as so many footnotes to the inspired extemporizations of the Woods, especially their adaptation of the Roman Colosseum to rows of townhouses. And the architectural character of Nash's Regent's Park terraces and of Regent Street owes much to the Woods of Bath. The difference, however, is equally significant. The Bath group of buildings – and the copies it spawned – concentrates on an architectural unity of structure and street. It is unselfconsciously urban. It was part of Nash's genius to integrate with this seventy-five year tradition of town planning the concurrent English love for country retirement.

Nash's original plan (1811–12) envisioned Carlton House as a southern boundary, with Regent Street as a "Royal Mile" leading to Regent's Park (to be developed out of old Marylebone Park that had reverted to the Crown in 1811) in which were to be situated many charming villas, a double circus, a serpentine lake, woody groves, and a picturesque canal. Around the margins were to rise stately terraces, and in the south-east corner a marketing and working-class quarter. It was a noble piece of town planning, intent on providing the aristocracy with a picturesque urban version of the alluring groves and elegant architecture of their beloved country estates.

Almost from the start Nash had to improvise compromises, modifications, and cutbacks in the original conception. Most of the villas in Regent's Park were disallowed by the Treasury, the canal was relegated to the northern boundaries of the Park, the great double circus was discontinued after the bankruptcy of its lessee. Eight villas were eventually built, half a circus, Park Crescent (*c.* 1812–22), and the extravagant terraces beginning with Cornwall Terrace in 1821 and ending with the "sheer architectural frolic" of Cumberland Terrace in 1826–27. To the northeast arose East and West Park Villages (begun 1824), romantic cottage villages, all "trees, water, fanciful gables and balconies," which were the prototype for housing estates in England, "no two houses alike," until the Second World War.[12] Not the least of Nash's brilliant improvisations involved the twists and turns of Regent Street, the exquisitely adjusted design of houses along its many blocks, and its calculated placement separating the garden estates of the West End from the untidy warrens of Soho. His attention to existent contours, and sensitivity to excessive disturbance of established streets and neighborhoods, distinguishes the Regent Street project from most urban plans – although Nash was not always immune to the typical destructive virus of city planning, as his unexecuted proposal for linking the Trafalgar Square area and Covent Garden indicated. And even with his care in siting Regent Street, more than 700 houses had to be demolished. This demolition is a minor blot, however, when seen in the context of the task Nash had undertaken. With Regent's Park and Regent Street he exhibited a social and architectural conscience that contrasts strikingly, for example, to the ruthlessness of Georges-Eugene Haussmann, who some twenty years later supported by the imperial mandate of Napoleon III blasted a network of arterial boulevards through centuries-old neighborhoods to create the sweeping vistas of modern Paris. And in keeping with his callous disregard of the city dwellers for whom his modernization was intended, Haussmann's imagination remained urban focused, unlike Nash's, which was forever recalling the English countryside even when designing his great terraces and Palladian fantasias along Regent Street.

In 1821 the Prince Regent was crowned George IV. He soon after abandoned his *pied-à-terre* Carlton House for the newly converted (begun 1825) Buckingham Palace. Carlton House, which had provided a rationale for the southern end of Regent Street, was pulled down to make way for a building scheme. That gave Nash the opportunity to counterbalance Regent's Park on the north by a redesigned and planted St. James's Park (1827) on the south, and the curving picturesque surprises of the Regent's Park Terraces at the northern end by the colossal linear blocks of the two Carlton House Terraces (1827–32) and Carlton Gardens (1827–28) at the southern end. These terraces with their classical fantasies of Corinthian and Ionic colonnades, triumphal arches, and commanding pediments framed against the green tracery of Regent's and St. James's Parks offered the Regency and post-Napoleonic aristocracy a sophisticated facsimile of country house and country environs.

As for the lower and middle classes, they could still ramble on Sundays into the fields and pastures to the north and west of the city, or seek out the many eighteenth-century pleasure gardens scattered about the environs of London. The latter often offered, however, a sorry version of fallen paradise, for they had passed their period of widest social acceptance and were undergoing fluctuations of fortune, often changing from weekend spa to afternoon tea garden to night-time amusement center for discreet assignations to public tavern, and in at least one instance to Methodist tabernacle, and often back again to a place where families innocently congregated to drink curative waters.

The London pleasure gardens date back to the jolly days of Charles II and the more sedate years of Queen Anne.[13] Their heyday, however, was from 1750 to 1775, when for a generation or so before the American and Napoleonic wars closed in the horizons of England and hobbled its means of pleasure, Londoners could escape the teeming city into its still pastoral suburbs where they might partake in the rage for tea drinking and pretend for a few carefree hours that they were Colin Clouts and fair Rosalind, if not Adam and Eve. These gardens were a commercial version, often in narrow congested compass of three acres, of the private landscape gardens of the aristocracy. They formed an irregular belt around the city of Mahometan Paradises (so Addison's Mr. Spectator apostrophized Vauxhall Gardens, not uncritically, in the spring of 1712, in *The Spectator*, No. 383), as close in as Sadler's Wells and as distant as the Spaniards in Hampstead. Here the royal Princes of the House of Hanover and Fleet Street seamstresses, gallants and apprentices, bankers and pickpockets, aldermen, merchants, swells of every rank and ladies of good position rubbed elbows, sipped tea, drank chalybeate water, ate syllabub, listened to concerts, danced and promenaded in the ubiquitous Long Room, strolled the graveled garden paths, and watched fireworks. For a few hours they could forget the din and dirt of the city in a ceaseless *fête-champêtre*, no less exciting because commercial and staged. Shabby by daylight the gardens under the magic of a thousand lights became an artificial Eden – so Dickens alluded to the ballroom of the Greenwich Fair (*Sketches by Boz*, 1836). And so Farmer Colin a hundred years earlier had described Vauxhall Gardens to his wife after a trip to town in 1741:

> Oh, Mary! soft in feature,
>   I've been at dear Vauxhall;
> No paradise is sweeter,
>   Not that they Eden call.
>
> Methought, when first I entered,
>   Such splendours round me shone,
> Into a world I ventured,
>   Where rose another sun:
>
> While music, never cloying,
>   As skylarks sweet, I hear:
> The sounds I'm still enjoying,
>   They'll always soothe my ear.

It is worth keeping in mind when trying to imagine the gaiety of those who drank the unpalatable mineral waters and lingered over the attenuated teas and gluttonous cakes of these wells that most streets of the city were too noisy and crowded and country roads too often muddy for pleasant promenading or extended sojourning. Nor should be minimized the compulsion (and delight) of the English to seek the out-of-doors on a sunny day, to stroll under trees and listen to nightingales (as Pepys more than once records), to eat and drink in the midst of nature, after chafing indoors through a cold and wet winter. It is no wonder that a three-acre garden with a gravel walk and a row of lime trees could give a taste of leafy paradise to a Londoner's Saturday or Sunday excursion into the country. In their colorful displays as at the Spaniards where the walks were ornamented with over forty quaint designs such as the signs of the Zodiac, the Tower of London, the pathway of the planets, and the pyramids of Egypt, these gardens often fostered such an association in their combination of things earthly and celestial. Properly speaking, most, however, partook less of the Edenic than of popularly defined notions of a fallen Moorish warrior's Elysium. The Oxford Street Pantheon was dubbed "Baalbec in all its glory" by that ubiquitous observer of the social scene Horace Walpole, who, of course, was being witty at the expense of the commercial nature of such pleasure-seeking places. In them, public fantasy took precedence over private contemplation of the more serious sort induced by the emblematic and aristocratic gardens with which Walpole was also familiar. The pleasure garden represented for most classes an easily accessible escape from humdrum reality. Ranelagh thus appears to Miss Lydia Melford in Smollett's *Humphry Clinker* (1771) as "the inchanted palace of a genie"[14] adorned with the most exquisite performances of painting, carving, and gilding, enlightened with a thousand golden lamps, that emulate the noon-day sun; crowded with the great, the rich, the gay, the happy, and the fair; glittering with cloth of gold and silver, lace, embroidery, and precious stones. While these exulting sons and daughters of felicity tread this round of pleasure, or regale in different parties, and separate lodges, with fine imperial tea and other delicious refreshments, their ears are entertained with the most ravishing delights of musick, both instrumental and vocal. (Vol. 1, Letter of 31 May)

In his pioneering study of eighteenth-century London pleasure gardens, Warwick Wroth (1858–1911) surveyed those to be found in six geographical areas surrounding London. There were the sites closest in to the City, grouped to the north in Clerkenwell and in what is today part of Central London. Farther west, centering on Marylebone Gardens, was another cluster of places located in what is present-day Regent's Park and environs. To the north in Islington's and Pancras fields, along Penton Street, and in the villages of Highbury, Kentish Town, and farthest afield in Hampstead were situated additional pleasant rendezvous. To the southwest in Chelsea was a popular group of gardens, the most famous being Ranelagh. Across the river in south London, gardens were scattered through Lambeth to as far east as Rotherhithe, with the perennial favorite and long-lived Vauxhall (1661–1859) commanding attention above all others.

Wroth discerns in this "herbacious border" of gardens surrounding London three kinds of pleasure resorts: (1) the great gardens – Cuper's, Marylebone, Ranelagh, and Vauxhall – owing their popularity with all classes to evening concerts, dancing, masquerades, fireworks, and facilities for eating, drinking, and promenading; (2) the spas, wells, and mineral springs such as Pancras Wells, Bagnigge Wells, Sadler's Wells, and Islington Spa, which catered to the vogue for morning and afternoon drinking of curative waters; and (3) tea gardens, generally small and unpretending but blessed with rural charm, where working class families could gather on a Sunday for games of skittles and bowls, and gregarious bouts of tea drinking in bowers and alcoves.

The character of the gardens could be dynamic, tonish and in vogue under one owner, deteriorating into rowdy and disreputable haunts under another pro-prietor. Thus, the Dog and Duck in St. George's Fields, which had enjoyed considerable repute in the 1750s and 60s for its mineral waters, is lampooned as a place of dissolute habits in Garrick's Prologue to *The Maid of the Oaks* acted at Drury Lane in 1775:

> St. George's Fields, with taste and fashion struck,
> Display Arcadia at the Dog and Duck,
> And Drury misses here in tawdry pride,
> Are there "Pastoras" by the fountain side;
> To frowsy bowers they reel through midnight damps,
> With Fauns half drunk, and Dryads breaking lamps.

A refrain equally pronounced, which runs through Wroth's account, is the gradual succumbing of the gardens to the encroachments of the city. Marylebone and Cuper's were gone before the end of the eighteenth century. Ranelagh survived until 1803, Vauxhall until 1859. Not without ironic rue, Wroth notes that at the time of his writing, three churches occupied the sites of Vauxhall, Belsize House, and the Spa Fields Pantheon, "none of them in their day examples of austere morality," that the extended terminus of the Midland Railway had obliterated Pancras Wells, and that Waterloo Road had severed Cuper's Gardens.

Finch's Grotto, after having been a burial ground and a workhouse, is now the headquarters of our London Fire Brigade. . . . The Three Hats is a bank; Dobney's Bowling Green, a small court; the Temple of Apollo, an engineer's factory, and the sign of the Dog and Duck is built into the walls of Bedlam.

Throughout his history is heard the melancholy sound of developers' hammers and saws. In 1775 White Conduit House and Gardens, "Standing on rising ground, and environed by pleasant country lanes and pastures . . . commanded towards the north fine views of Hampstead and Highgate"; but by 1833 "brickfields and rows of houses had destroyed its rural aspect." As late as 1841 Copenhagen House, a favorite Sunday tea garden with the middle classes, still afforded a view over hay fields to Highgate; but the builders were making their way up from the south, and about 1852 the Corporation of London purchased Copenhagen House, grounds, and adjacent fields – about seventy-five acres – and swept away the old tavern and tea gardens to make way for construction of the Metropolitan Cattle Market.[15]

George Cruikshank (1792–1878) has caught the feverish building spirit of the time in an 1829 cartoon "London going out of Town, or The March of Bricks and Mortar." In the left background sits London, its skyline dominated by the dome

16   Cruikshank, *London going out of Town*

London going out of Town. — or — The March of Bricks & Mortar.

of St. Paul's under a pall of smoke from innumerable chimney pots; in the right background basks a serene country scene. But not for long! Marching out from the city are phalanx after phalanx of brick houses, flanked by armies of hod carriers, navvies, and carpenters. With invincible industry they are uprooting the hayfields, knocking over rail fences, and filling in ponds. From kilns spew endless streams of bricks, raining down like missiles on retreating haystacks and routed sheep and cows. The trees still standing bend before the fury of the building assault. It is a battle scene of devastation, the old rural ways of English life under siege. In alarmed disarray, the rustic contingents can only advise each other, with stiff-upper-lipped puns, to "go farther afield for we are *losing ground* here" to the "Barbarians, who threaten to encase and destroy us in all *manor* of ways."

Thus did the city inexorably encroach upon and supersede the pleasure gardens still within walking distance for Londoners in the eighteenth and early nineteenth centuries, where for a few shillings they could know for an hour or two the sylvan fulfillment of their parents back to the first who trod England's fair and pleasant hills. By 1852 the chief Romantic witnesses to the world as an earthly paradise had absented themselves for some years from its felicity. Coleridge had been lying in Highgate Churchyard[16] for eighteen years, and Wordsworth had been dead for two years. The omnivorous appetite of London for land, and the spreading Coketowns and Black Country of the high Victorian period, most memorably recorded by Dickens, seemed at times to have inherited the earth. The increase in the number of cemeteries in London in these years is of dubious symbolic value; still it may be of some macabre interest to know that the golden age of cemetery lay-outs, from 1820 to 1850, intended to correct the inadequacy of the old parochial burial grounds with their inefficient crowded interments and gaseous after effects,[17] coincides with the demise of the pleasure gardens. New pleasurable (paradisal) ventures continued to open within the city into the second half of the nineteenth century. Cremorne (*c.* 1843–77) and the Sydenham Crystal Palace (1851–1936) are the most famous. But their existence in the long run was economically incompatible with the urban civilizing of Middlesex and Surrey.

Perhaps coincidentally with the demise of the eighteenth-century pleasure garden, perhaps not, is the compensatory counter flurry of construction of that sophisticated architectural version of the social garden scene and quintessential urban locus of leisure activity, the London club. Between 1810 and 1850 at least a dozen grand edifices were erected, mostly in Pall Mall.[18] A more visible echo of the rural purlieus that once surrounded London is the public park, a sterile vestige of the belief in *ut Albion paradisus*, its domesticated rose gardens, "heath," lawns, "arboretums," and playing fields exhibiting a precarious equilibrium of the meaningful past with a volatile present. From the perspective of London (and as the nineteenth century advanced a perspective increasingly equivalent to that of England's) the aristocratic paradises of the eighteenth century, the parks, wildernesses, gardens, and lakes of Stowe, Blenheim, Petworth, and Stourhead seemed to have yielded up their Edenic prerogatives to the bourgeois reaches of Regent's, Hyde, and St. James's Parks smartly faced by endless rows of houses.

There is a woodcut executed by Thomas Bewick for Volume 2 (*Water Birds* [1804], p. 107) of his *History of British Birds*, which captures the duality of perspective that beset inhabitants of Regency England. A scene along the Tyne River, it depicts in the middle ground a factory or, more likely, colliery commanding a bluff, and in the farther distance on the opposite shore a provincial mansion house. At first glance the two structures, representative of conflicting social and economic realms, appear to be in simple juxtaposition. A closer look, however, discloses that the industrial structure not only looms larger – and more important – because of its proximity to the foreground, but that it is belching a dense column of smoke spreading over the river, the house, and the whole of the Tyne valley. Two elderly men stand silent in the foreground beside a beached barge on a spit of land, staring at the scene containing within its borders the apparitions of past and future.

In its depiction of provincial serenity the woodcut hauntingly reminds us of a rural ideal; in its prescient observation of industrial clutter it foretells the transformation to come. The psychology of an imagination which could comprehensively and dispassionately entertain these disparate items is impressive; and our admiration is heightened when we learn that Bewick was no foe of progress. He recalls in his memoir having engraved "the plan of the projected Canal from Newcastle to Carlisle for Ra. Dodd the Engineer – & plans of the Estates & views of the Mansion house of a few Gentlemen, who opposed the line of [the] Canal on the north side of the Tyne, as projected by Mr. Chapman the Engineer" and that

the whole *scheme* of this great, *this important national as well as local undertaking*, was baffled & set aside – and most men of disurnment were of opinion that the coal owners *below Bridge* were the cause of it – The canal, as projected by Mr. Dodd, in 1795 would have certainly opened out a *territory* of coal, that might have affected their interest & it would appear, at

17   Bewick, View of the River Tyne

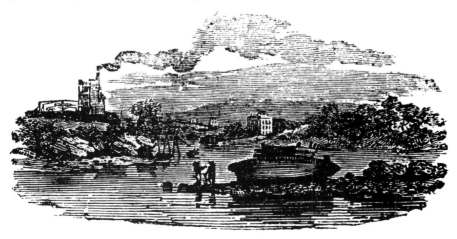

least, that they dreaded it & in this case as in almost every other case, private interest is & was found to over power public good.[19]

Bewick's woodcut characterizes in microcosm the bifurcated frame of mind of country dwellers and (to use one of Bewick's favorite terms) "borough mongers" alike, as they bore witness to England's headlong rush into the industrial age. It was almost as if a dogma had gotten abroad in the land promising that technology would offer material consolation, if not a panacea, for loss of the natural environment and the uncomplicated state of mind of an earlier paradise.

As seen through the lens of paradisal aspirations, the reaction throughout the nineteenth century to technology and industry as forces of change and indexes of achievement demonstrates that the messy partnership of tradition and innovation plagued more than one generation in the transition from the myth of eighteenth-century rural solitude to the myth of nineteenth-century urban bustle. Factories, bridges, railways, and above all, the Crystal Palace of 1851 – in short, the new industrial and urban complex – stand as visible self-images of high Victorian culture and as paradigms of how the organization of utility and value in commerce and industry as well as in the arts could ease the drudgery of the human lot, realize the ideal of plenty, and redeem one fortunate piece of earth. Still, not everyone's hunger for contentment was appeased by such iron and glass symbols of progress. There was no dearth of voices who recalled the charm of coaching days and the natural quiet of rural byways, and, like Dickens, who deplored the noise of machines, the greed of the new captains of industry, and the despoilment of the landscape.

THE TECHNOLOGICAL SUBLIME OF CANALS, BRIDGES, VIADUCTS, AND TURNER'S GREAT WESTERN LOCOMOTIVE

Except for London and the emergent industrial cities of the Midlands, England still retained its rural appearance and bucolic rhythm through the early decades of the nineteenth century, before the coming of the railway in 1830. It takes an exercise of historical imagination for minds accustomed to computer generations and aerospace shuttles to visualize England and its towns and villages as they were in those decades, relatively unchanged for hundreds of years, with the populace still dependent on the horse or on human legs for transportation. One need only look at the coaching prints of James Pollard[20] to realize that the England of Keats and Byron was the England yet of Fielding and Johnson, a country of coaches, slow communication, and restricted travel. Only as recently as 1750 to 1790 had the untended ravages of centuries been corrected in a spate of road building, following the uprising of 1745 and the march of the Stuart pretender Charles Edward's Highland army as far south as Derby, unopposed because absence of roads hampered concentration of a Hanoverian army. In the 1790s the postal service was reformed by John Palmer (1742–1818) and fleet mail coaches began their omnipotent daily trips down country, memorably described as they were during the Napoleonic years by De Quincey in *The English Mail-Coach* (1849).

The heyday of coaching was realized just before steam spelled its demise. Between 1810 and 1840 the industry employed 30,000 men and 150,000 horses, and managed 150 miles in a day (the first long-distance coach was the *Wonder*, one of Edward Sherman's, which made the jog from London to Shrewsbury in fifteen hours) and attained average speeds of eleven miles an hour on the London to Manchester run with the celebrated *Telegraph* coach. At Hounslow, the first stage out of London on the Bath and Exeter roads, over 2,500 horses were stabled for coaching and posting. The exploits of coachmen like Sam Hayward of the Birmingham to Shrewsbury stage were legendary, not unlike the driver De Quincey memorializes as the "venerable crocodile." They drove their four-in-hands through crowded streets and archways with only inches to spare, at breakneck speed, their skilled horsemanship, steel nerves, and steady hands all that staved off the crippling, or the death, of their passengers.[21]

Exploits equally audacious but of a different order were in the making at the same time. After Newton revealed God to be the Original Engineer, it was logical that His divinely inspired yet primordial model be succeeded in the next one hundred years by engineering marvels designed to correct the few irregularities left over from the initial divine labor. There was a theological, then, as well as scientific, bedrock to support the building of canals, bridges, viaducts, and aqueducts, and in the nineteenth century, railways and steamships.

The first great adventurer in the technological sublime was James Brindley (1716–72), who undertook in 1759 to build for Francis Egerton, third Duke of Bridgewater (a prefigurative name!) a canal from his coal mines in Worsley seven miles to the mills in Manchester. Convinced that canals are best maintained at one level, to avoid locks, Brindley started with an underground gallery at the depth of the coal strata and crossed the River Irwell at Manchester on an aqueduct forty feet high. A squat masonry structure of three arches it was long regarded as the eighth wonder of the world,[22] and people came great distances to see boats sailing on a bridge over other barges on the river below. But canal builders in the second half of the eighteenth century quickly aspired to more grandiose flights of engineering. Whereas mountains had intimidated and frustrated medieval man, eighteenth-century engineers contrived to float over them on a staircase of pools. A sublime instance was the "angel's flight" of the Bingley Great Lock on the Leeds and Liverpool Canal opened in 1777. The canal is lifted out of Airedale, on the Yorkshire side by a series of three double locks and four staircases of three locks each, in a stretch of sixteen miles, culminating with the Bingley flight of five locks in a staircase which rises sixty feet in less than 150 yards. Each of the five pools can take craft up to sixty-two feet long by fourteen feet wide. The stone walls on either side of the large weirs to each pool climb the steep hill like medieval battlements, awesome testaments to their builder's confidence and audacity.

Men like Josiah Wedgwood (1730–95), Thomas Bentley (1731–80), Matthew Boulton (1728–1809), and Francis Egerton, Duke of Bridgewater (1736–1803), all promoters of canal building, were bold businessmen as well as devout believers in England's technological mission. Their aim was direct access by water of their

18   John Sell Cotman, *Chirk Aqueduct*

manufacturing centers to the source of raw materials and to the markets for their products. Brindley died in 1772, before the completion of his master plan for a Grand Canal to connect the Trent River in the southeastern portion of the Midlands with the Mersey River in the northwestern end, but the work went on until 1777 when the two rivers were joined, linking the two coasts from the Irish to the North Sea. At the same time networks of canals were being dug in the Birmingham–Wolverhampton–Stafford districts and in the Leeds–Manchester–Liverpool areas. Paul Mantoux notes that

At the end of the eighteenth century merchandise of every kind, from all parts of the country, could be seen journeying up and down the main waterways, such as the Trent and Mersey Canal: salt from Cheshire, corn from East Anglia, pottery from Staffordshire, coal from Wigan and Newcastle, pig iron from the upper Severn, worked iron and copper from Wolverhampton and Birmingham. The most important item was coal. Everywhere branches from the main lines penetrated right to the heart of the mines.[23]

These canals were hastening the time when England could boast to the world that its technological supremacy had created a new kind of Eden, one of controlled environment and of industrial abundance.

The classical age of canals and aqueducts gave way to the new era of railways and viaducts in the next fifty years. Two engineers, in particular, are associated with this stage in the romance of English technology, Thomas Telford (1757–1834) and Isambard Kingdom Brunel (1806–59). Nineteenth-century artists depicted these aqueducts and viaducts as immense structures of masonry and iron, vaulting quiet country vales, their watercourses lifting high over trees and rooftops – as if in some uncanny way the Pax Romana again extended its sway over the island. Their message to the countryside was that England had inherited the grandeur that once was Rome's with the difference that whereas Rome's might was based in part at least on ephemeral military prowess, Pax Britannica rested solidly on industrial and technological know-how. So at least one minor poet, John Scott, imagined in his equivocal tribute to the New River aqueduct ("Our mercenary stream") in Hertfordshire:

> a work
> Of matchless skill, by those who ne'er had heard
> How, from Preneste's heights and Anio's banks,
> By Tivoli, to Rome's imperial walls,
> On marble arches came the limpid store.[24]

John Sell Cotman (1782–1842) catches some of the same awe of the time for these multi-arched monoliths in his often reproduced water color *Chirk Aqueduct* (1806–07, Victoria and Albert Museum).[25] He has painted with broad washes of color a fraction more than three spans of the structure crossing a small rural stream in hilly land. Details are minimized (neither humans nor animals are visible) in deference to a composition that emphasizes the commanding presence of the aqueduct looming over the still scene. An alien form introduced into the countryside, it already appears to have established its right to be part of the rural setting, its massive Romanesque arches like a series of proscenium frames

19   Brunel, The Royal Albert Bridge at Saltash

dramatizing, and in effect, verifying the natural backdrop of a rambling rail fence and full-leafed trees. Overhead soars the aqueduct, creating its own skyline. In the foreground the vaulted pillars are reflected in the stream they traverse, the watery image rooting them in the locality and elongating their height, already exaggerated by the perspective from below and downstream of them. In the pale English sunlight the tan masonry of the aqueduct blends with the similar tans of the ground on which the pillars stand; while the flow of the river analogically establishes that water courses overhead in the duct. The impression conveyed by the structure (built by Telford 1796–1801) is one of imperturbable industrial force conspiring with the persistent processes of nature to create a new order.

Bald formulations of the technological sublime, with unveiled assertions of power, abound in mid-nineteenth-century depictions of railway viaducts. Those built by Brunel and Telford, especially, captured artists' imaginations. The viaduct for the South Devon Railway over the Valley of the Erme, for example, stood 114 feet high; and one artist[26] has exaggerated its height by reducing the scale of the people strolling at the base of the double pillars to minute figures. Even the four-car train crossing overhead is diminished to toy size in comparison to the bulk and perpendicularity of the viaduct. The Royal Albert Bridge, also by Brunel, crosses the Tamar River at Saltash on giant masonry stancheons spanning the industrial and dock side sections of the city. Opened 1859, its roadbed runs, according to contemporary pictorial records, high above the river, factories, and houses. It appears to be airborn, above the smoke and crowded waterway, rendering everything below Lilliputian in scale. The sunlight itself is seemingly reduced to shining through the lower reaches of the piers. Whereas Chirk Aqueduct in a bold sortie claims the countryside as its own, in Cotman's painting, the Saltash Bridge in mid-nineteenth-century recordings remains arrogantly indifferent to the scene it overleaps. Thus dramatically telling were the changes during two generations in the structure of feeling toward the technological transformation of England!

Other marvels of the age were Telford's Pont Cysyllte Aqueduct, opened in 1805 across the River Dee at a maximum height of 127 feet on nineteen spans of fifty-three feet each; Brunel's Wharncliffe Viaduct, which was opened in 1837 across the Brent Valley near Hawell, sixty-five feet high on eight double-pillared arches of seventy-foot spans; and the Welwyn Viaduct, which was opened in 1850 and crossed peaceful fields of grain 100 feet high on forty arches of thirty-foot spans. Telford's masterpiece – the Pont Cysyllte Aqueduct – in size and in combination of stone piers and high-grade cast-iron troughs eleven feet ten inches wide for the barges was considered the supreme achievement of canal engineering. In contemporary artists' conceptions, these roadways in the sky stride across the peaceful English countryside on colossal stone piers, sun pouring through their circular arches, to proclaim the majesty redivivus of British industry, no longer the simple aqueducts of antiquity bringing water to thirsty cities but part of a complex network of canals and railroads distributing throughout the land the manufactured goods that will usher in a new golden age.

Their substantial forms allied to a capacity for echoing the past in their delivery of a future established their romance with the skies as more than an idle flirtation; it was a secure marriage of the sublime and the practical.

The first cast-iron bridge – the famous Iron Bridge which crosses the Severn River about a half mile downstream from Coalbrookdale, Shropshire – was built in 1779–80 by John Wilkinson and Abraham Darby III after a design by Thomas Farnolls Pritchard (1723–77), and officially opened on New Year's Day 1781. Its single arch of 100 feet at a height of forty-five feet spans the river on five slender main ribs. The openness of the vault, increased by radials acting as braces

20   Brunel, The Erme Valley Viaduct

between the main ribs and the road bed, give the bridge an airy grace that no stone arch could achieve. Contemporary accounts and engravings place the bridge in the kind of picturesque circumstances usually associated with Gilpin's tours of the Lake District. It is sited in "a winding glen between two immense hills . . . thickly covered with . . . the most beautiful sheets of hanging wood."[27] Depictions of the bridge tend to accentuate the steepness of these hillsides and the wildness of the rocky eminences flecked with trees and a few lonely houses, thus hallowing this auspicious instance of man's engineering skill with the benediction of a romantic natural setting not unlike the actual Gorge, yet exaggerated in comparison to the hills which line the Severn's banks at this spot.

It was seventeen years before the second iron bridge was built, in 1796, across the Wear River at Sunderland, with a span of 236 feet at a height of 108 feet, more than twice that of the Darby Bridge across the Severn, allowing full-rigged sea-going ships to sail under it. After that iron bridges began popping up all over England; and the imaginations of ironmasters and engineers knew no bounds, as tellingly punctuated by the elegant but impractical design by Telford in 1801 for replacing London Bridge with a shallow cast-iron span of 699 feet. With the use of iron, suspension bridges became possible; and in 1819–26 Telford hung a bridge across the Menai Straits, which successfully combined the airy lightness of the cables with the massive grandeur of the multiple arches of the masonry viaducts at each end of the span. It and Brunel's Clifton Suspension Bridge, a single 702 foot span hung across the River Avon at Bristol that was begun in 1836 but not completed until 1864, challenged numerous artists to capture pictorially the

21   The Iron Bridge

22   Telford, The Menai Bridge

impression these bridges gave to contemporaries of causeways consorting with cloud-banked skies, far above the dwarfed ships sailing under them.

The boundless optimism of early nineteenth-century engineering is nowhere more evident than in the Thames Tunnel between Rotherhithe and Wapping, built (1825–43) by the Brunels, father Sir Marc Isambard (1769–1849) and son Isambard Kingdom.[28] Despite repeated disasters, work stoppages, labor strikes, and irruptions of the river, the tunnel was pushed to completion in eighteen years. In an 1835 aquatint by J. Harris, after T. Bury, the modified three-quarter oval vault has an elegance one associates with the boulevards of Paris, its smooth walls and plaster moldings that mark the support arches flooded with light from periodic observation openings. Indeed, the tunnel recedes to a point so distant that the coast of France is as easily envisaged at the other end as merely the other side of the river. The gas lamplights and the casual strollers shown – a nurse and child, a well-dressed couple, and a family group in Sunday attire – do nothing to disabuse one of this fantasy. The implied power of the British mercantile system necessary to conceive of such a tunnel is here veiled in a suavity that masks rich paradisal–underworld associations. When seen alongside John Martin's *At the Brink of Hell*, an illustration for Milton's *Paradise Lost* (x, 312–18, 347–51)

173

showing the route Satan takes when he traverses chaos from Hell to the "outside bare / Of this round World" (x, 317–18), the two pictures show one instance of how the Christian myth of creation was absorbed by the technological sublime of the age, and Satan metamorphosed into a nineteenth-century Captain of Industry and builder of bridges. In the chiasmus that the two pictures complete, Brunel's tunnel takes us underground as a means of reaching a new Eden at its end, while Martin's vaulted road brings Satan up into the open air of a world about to fall. The engineer as earthly creator is posed in a naked display of his power in an 1858 photograph of Isambard Kingdom Brunel standing full length before the anchor chains of his steamship *Great Eastern*. The chain is strung up perpendicularly to make a solid backdrop of iron links each larger than a man's head. In front of them stands their maker, in top hat and cigar, his hands nonchalantly tucked into his trouser pockets. Self-esteem and confidence animate the figure. It is a portrait of the new Merlin of the times, the master of mechanics who can make iron ships float and iron bridges soar through space, a Victorian fakir who has substituted the dead weight of mammoth anchor chains for the customary hemp rope to stand on end at his command.

Canals and viaducts, and even bridges, still belong to the leisurely round of rural life of eighteenth-century England. They were an extension of industrial activity without embodying in themselves a clanking form of it. They could be assimilated into the peaceful countryside. The steam engine and the railway represented, however, a transformation of the agrarian world. Romantic and early Victorian artists viewed the alteration of their worlds with mingled appreciation and despair. *The Progress of Steam*, to use the title of a series of satirical prints in the late 1820s and early 30s, was not welcomed by everyone. Nostalgia for a golden rural age lingered on, making much more desolate the sense of devastation being caused by the industrial revolution. Arthur Young finds himself alternately fascinated and repelled by the "horrors art has spread" along the beautiful Coalbrookdale Gorge: "the noise of the forges, mills, etc. with all their vast machinery, the flames bursting from the furnaces with the burning of the coal and the smoak of the lime kilns, are altogether sublime, and would unite well with craggy and bare rocks, like St. Vincent's at Bristol."[29] A similar vein of sentiment animates Philip James de Loutherbourg's (1740–1812) painting *Iron Works at Coalbrookdale* (c. 1800), which catches anew a quarter of a century later the tone of ambivalence toward "trade's unfeeling train" in the age of iron and steam. In the narrow declivity of the Severn Valley straggle a group of belching stacks, lurid swirls of smoke rising to the low-hanging clouds. An unnatural glow from the foundries casts deep shadows on the ground and river. It is a scene of awesome, man-made desolation, to which the smoke and flames lend an air of hellish mystery. Loutherbourg is affected by the display of unleashed technological powers; but he is not quite ready to see these industrial artifices as objects of sublimity, although his baroque response to deep space and to "theatrical" contrasts is clearly moving in that direction.

To the social dislocation of agrarian capitalism that Raymond Williams chronicles[30] was added a technological metamorphosis of the countryside. There was widespread opposition, for example, to the railroads. Wordsworth expresses the hopes and misgivings the new modes of transportation aroused in the older generations in his 1833 sonnet "Steamboats, Viaducts, and Railways." "Howsoe'er" technology may "mar / The loveliness of Nature," he opines, it will never "prove a bar / To the Mind's gaining that prophetic sense / Of future change, that point of vision." A decade later Dickens captures the chaos the railroad created in its drive through cities, in his description in *Dombey and Son* (1846–48) of the devastation in the name of progress of Staggs's Gardens, "regarded by its population as a sacred grove."

The first shock of a great earthquake had, just at that period, rent the whole neighbourhood to its centre. Traces of its course were visible on every side. Houses were knocked down; streets broken through and stopped; deep pits and trenches dug in the ground; enormous heaps of earth and clay thrown up; buildings that were undermined and shaking, propped by great beams of wood. Here, a chaos of carts, overthrown and jumbled together, lay topsy-turvy at the bottom of a steep unnatural hill; there, confused treasures of iron soaked and rusted in something that had accidentally become a pond. Everywhere were bridges that led nowhere; thoroughfares that were wholly impassable; Babel towers of chimneys, wanting half their height; temporary wooden houses and enclosures, in the most unlikely situations; carcases of ragged tenements, and fragments of unfinished walls and arches, and piles of scaffolding, and wildernesses of bricks, and giant forms of cranes, and tripods straddling above nothing. There were a hundred thousand shapes and substances of incompleteness, wildly mingled out of their places, upside down, burrowing in the earth, aspiring in the air, mouldering in the water, and unintelligible as any dream. Hot springs and fiery eruptions, the usual attendants upon earthquakes, lent their contributions of confusion to the scene. Boiling water hissed and heaved within dilapidated walls; whence, also, the glare and roar of flames came issuing forth; and mounds of ashes blocked up rights of way, and wholly changed the law and custom of the neighbourhood.

In short, the yet unfinished and unopened Railroad was in progress; and, from the very core of all this dire disorder, trailed smoothly away, upon its mighty course of civilization and improvement. (I, 6)

The omnipotent demand of the railroad for right of way blithely split towns and disfigured ancient ways. Venerable Ludgate Hill itself was not spared the disfiguration of an iron trestle over which rattled trains that bisected the view of St. Paul's from the lower reaches of the street. As late as 1899 the Great Central Railway severed the Old Town of Leicester with a viaduct three-quarters of a mile long, effectively creating "two towns" where for centuries there had been one.

The locomotive, with its fierce blasts of hot air and its inexhaustible power, both terrified and exhilarated Dickens's generation. The railway station became a symbol of an age solemnly committed to self-improvement. Dickens looked through the open arch of Euston Station, with its "columns of gigantic girth," and saw "a vista to the railway world beyond" (*Dombey and Son*, I, 15). W. P. Frith feared that Paddington Station lacked picturesqueness, but he persevered to produce in *The Railway Station* (1862, Royal Holloway College) one of the century's most popular paeans to the age of travel by steam.[31] Carlyle could exult in the speed and inexorable motion of the train, as he did on his first railway ride in 1839,[32] and he could admit that the hum and clank and smoke and flames of the Birmingham iron works on the whole are "not without its attractions, as well as repulsions." But he could also, as in *Sartor Resartus* (1833–34) use the steam engine as a metaphor for all that is moribund: "To me the Universe was all void of Life, of Purpose, of Volition, even of Hostility: it was one huge, dead, immeasurable Steam-engine, rolling on, in its dead indifference, to grind me limb from limb" (Bk. II, Ch. 7, "The Everlasting NO"). More than he was possibly aware, Carlyle expresses the increasing tendency to confuse the organic and the mechanical, to treat the machine as if it were almost an inexorable supernatural force. The early Dickens similarly pays tribute to the train as a juggernaut, a fierce creature of destructive energy and whirlwind havoc. Memorable is Dombey's brooding ride:

Away, with a shriek, and a roar, and a rattle, from the town, burrowing among the dwellings of men and making the streets hum, flashing out into the meadows for a moment, mining in through the damp earth, booming on in darkness and heavy air, bursting out again into the sunny day so bright and wide; away, with a shriek, and a roar, and a rattle, through the fields, through the woods, through the corn, through the hay, through the chalk, through the mould, through the clay, through the rock . . .

Through the hollow, on the height, by the heath, by the orchard, by the park, by the garden, over the canal, across the river, where the sheep are feeding, where the mill is going, where the barge is floating, where the dead are lying, where the factory is smoking, where the stream is running, where the village clusters, where the great cathedral rises, where the bleak moor lies, and the wild breeze smooths or ruffles it at its inconstant will; away, with a shriek, and a roar, and a rattle, and no trace to leave behind but dust and vapour: like as in the track of the remorseless monster, Death!   (I, 20)

The painter who most completely assimilated the conflicting experiences of the transitional years 1810 to 1840 was J. M. W. Turner (1775–1851). Born in the same decade as Coleridge and Wordsworth, he died the year of the Crystal Palace and the Great Exhibition. In 1797 when they were learning to be poets, he was spending his nights at Dr. T. Munro's house in Adelphi Terrace, London, turning out with Thomas Girtin topographical watercolor sketches of the English countryside. Two of his greatest paintings – *The Fighting Téméraire, Tugged to Her Last Berth* (1838, National Gallery, London) and *Rain, Steam and Speed: The Great Western Railway* (1844, National Gallery, London) – explore the conflicting emotions that a person who came to maturity in a still bucolic time felt as he watched the world hurtle into the industrial age.

The Fighting Téméraire depicts a ghostly white man-of-war, her sails furled, a derelict marked for scrap, being towed to Deptford by a grimy steam-tug, a squatty fraction of her size. It is twilight, and their course is athwart a path of red cast on a glassy sea by the setting sun. Behind the tug can be seen two other ships in full sail, reminding us of the proud mastery of the waves that was the Téméraire's when she was at Trafalgar. Both are ghostly white, like the Téméraire, foreshadowing the end of the glorious era of sailing and the advent of the clanking age of steam. With arrogant indifference the tug churns toward us, its elongated black stack belching fire, cinders, and smoke which are blown toward the tall masts and empty spars of the Téméraire. The smoke stack for all its exaggerated length is puny and ugly beside the graceful height and bulky mass of the ninety-eight gunner; but there is no question that the diminutive tug has carried the day. The twilight belongs to the Téméraire, the dawn of the next day is the tug's; and the contrast is emphasized by distribution of the cool pallor of the moon over the sailing ships and of the warm orange-red glow of the sun over the tug. "From one angle," a biographer notes, "Turner exalts the triumph of the industrial world of steam-power over the handicraft world of the old ships. The work is permeated with a sense of historical change, of remorseless destruction and renewal."[33] The painting acknowledges unsentimentally the might of a new technology, without yielding up in any way the ancient knowledge that the advance of civilization and of efficiency is often won at the cost of nobility and beauty.

Rain, Steam and Speed makes the same statement with greater economy of means and complexity of reaction. Out of a swirling torrential world of mist and obscurity thunders a train toward us across a viaduct. Below on the river bank, barely discernible and as if out of another time, a man plows behind a pair of horses, several horsemen canter across a field, and a boat labors on the river. The composition of the two pictures is similar. There is the same diagonal movement from back to front, the same luminous integration of machine and nature, the same antithesis of past and future. In *The Fighting Téméraire* the primary drama is between the two elemental forces of sail and steam, of wind and heated water, as represented in the two kinds of ships, which also stand as emblems of successive historical periods. In *Rain, Steam and Speed* the harbinger of the new civilization overwhelms us with its presence. All else, the river, the plains on either side, the people and the land, all the figurative elements of the landscape, are reduced to almost abstract forms, by the swirling atmosphere of rain, mist, and steam. The train alone retains its massive black shape on the trestle as it rushes high above the minute barely distinguishable people and blurred volumes of land and water beneath. Turner's Great Western locomotive is unaffected by the harsh weather; its speed is constant, its momentum and direction unfaltering, its performance an unmistakable demonstration of the superiority of technology over nature.

Turner's paean to steam and mechanical power, however, is not without its sense of the rich ambiguities of progress. The locomotive, with its flaming fire box, appears to be rushing through the dim light gulping into its insatiable maw the vital sustenance of the day. As if to confirm its omnivorousness a frightened rabbit races down the track in front of it. One thematic statement certainly made by the painting is its premonition of a world in which the omnipotent machine will alter the natural world. The train appears to be emerging from the dim confines of an older bucolic era and speeding toward a brave new age of technology. At the same time one cannot fail to notice that the train, in its act of triumph, is immersed in the natural elements, its power defined as a portion of nature's energy. Unlike the intrusive pollution of the golden sea by the smoking tugboat in *The Fighting Téméraire* the broiling steam of the locomotive, reverting to its natural form in the process of propelling the train into a new age, is assimilated into the turbulent squall of wind and rain. Turner thus retains his sense of awe before the cosmic energy of nature in his acceptance, even exaltation, of the new native forms assumed by it, revealing his recognition that nature is still the underlying source of power in all things, albeit drafted into an equal partnership now with man-made machines.

He conveys the same vision in other paintings of about the same time. In *Snowstorm – Steamboat off a Harbour's Mouth Making Signals in Shallow Water and Going by the Lead* (1842, National Gallery, London) a steamer all but engulfed by spray and waves – it is almost literally one with the maelstrom of heaving ocean and wind-lashed snow – labors valiantly toward a rent of celestial blue sky in the center of the stormy vortex. Even more explicit is the merger of steam and natural elements in *Staffa: Fingal's Cave* (1832, Gavin Astor Collection). An ebony ship steams across a lurid sea toward a baleful sky and orange-red sun about to drop below the horizon. Its trail of smoke floats parallel to the surface of the water until finally absorbed into the bright cloud of mist at its stern. Thus at one with sky and waves, the engineered ark of a new Noah, the ship steers across empty swells of ocean toward the source of its watery world.

Although nature is tainted by the Fall for Turner, and made no less so by nineteenth-century translations of it into mechanical forms of force, *Rain, Steam and Speed* hangs on in the teeth of the inclement weather to a Romantic conception of a more innocent time. The Virgilian round of pastoral activities continues to transpire in sadly muted, and even eclipsed, fashion beneath the viaduct. Its participation in the cyclicity of life, which characterizes the natural paradise of earth, is an implicit reminder of an older way that has been passed over in favor of the urban center and its Eden of indiscriminate industrial abundance towards which the train hurtles. In a profound sense the Romantic side of Turner's sensibility has expanded to embrace a large many-faceted reality that includes steamships and trains. Although they do not appear to be as immediately dependent on the elements as sailing ships, the locomotive and the steam engine are actually efficient rearrangements of the basic principles of nature. And Turner's intuition is to treat them as such. Whereas about 1807, for a brief period, the serene scenes along the upper reaches of the Thames River – between Walton and Windsor – captivated his imagination, urban civilization increasingly vied with Arcadian simplicity for the attention of his artist's eye.

By mid-century, receptivity to the paradisal possibilities of the machine was not limited to engineers. Nor was it limited to the declamatory point of view of painters like Joseph Wright of Derby (1734–97) of an earlier generation, who celebrated science and industry, such as the forging of iron, in Carravagesque pictures full of dramatic contrasts of light and shadow. In his grasp of the organic essence of the machine and of its displacement of nature in the development of British civilization, Turner had grown far beyond the naive comprehension of

Wright's late eighteenth-century genre scenes. He saw the machine as a power in the garden, and perceived that many people, although he may not have entirely agreed with them, were ready to laud the machine as the final achievement leading to man's reclamation of a peaceful and contented life. At no time in the nineteenth century was this faith more evident than in the year of Turner's death, when England in a piety of mercantile ritual exhibited to the world its technological feats in the Crystal Palace and the Great Exhibition of the Industry of All Nations.

9
Paxton's Hyde Park Crystal Palace

IN THE TWO DECADES preceding mid-century, England throbbed with anticipatory ferment. The Tractarians and the Oxford Movement were striving Janus-like to resurrect tradition and dogma as a revitalized future. The Gothic Revival (which gathered momentum in the 1840s and 50s) was redefining the skyscape with silhouettes of the past. The search for the Nile was feverishly extending English presence under the sun. The Chartists were presaging that apocalypse was at hand. The agitation over political reform was expanding the "old boys'" club in Parliament to include an emergent manufacturing class and representatives from new factory towns. All promised the advent of a better society, but none sent forth vibrations more pervasively than the groundswell of technological innovations, which signaled to participants and onlookers alike that paradise regained was just around the corner in mid-Victorian England.

The engineering genius of Brindley, Telford, Stephenson, and Brunel was making England one nation (while helping to create Disraeli's two nations in another sense), by linking town to country, and one end of the land to the other. They and other practical minded visionaries – architects and speculators as well as engineers – blithely ignored the dire prophecies of the Malthusians. Their sights were set on insuring that the magic spires of Merlin took concrete shape, and thereby incidentally turning England into an urbanized demi-paradise.

Nothing in nineteenth-century England more aptly signals the advent of the historical mentality, and its alignment with urban industrialism, than the London World Fair of 1851, with its Crystal Palace and its up-to-date presentation of mankind's progress toward achievement of the perfect life. Even the prosaic Members of Parliament, for all their fiscal and political concerns about the price of corn and the level of parish rates, managed on this occasion to rise to an inspired vision of the city as a new kind of earthly paradise. Under the goading of Prince Albert and of the Prime Minister, Lord John Russell, they entertained the celestial sight of a glass and iron edifice rising in Hyde Park, which would simultaneously confirm their faith in an *urbus conclusus* and their confidence in being the chosen people. That the enterprise was calculated to popularize the notion that England was the best of all possible worlds and the financial center of the universe no doubt helped to shape their receptivity to this particular brand of business-as-usual Elysium. Better yet the entire venture was to be privately financed. They had only to approve the use of Hyde Park as a site. So, over the minority opposition of Colonel Charles de Laet Waldo Sibthorpe, ultra-Conservative M.P. for Lincoln, a Crystal Palace rose, shimmering and fair, in the greenery and sunlight of Hyde Park between Rotten Row and Kensington Gate. Construction was begun by the London firm of Fox and Henderson about 1 August 1850, with the enormous quantities of glass supplied by the Chance Brothers of Birmingham; and the Great Exhibition of the Industry of All Nations was officially declared open nine months later on 1 May 1851 by Queen Victoria and Prince Albert, who led a procession the length of the building, 1,848 feet from end to end.

The main structure, situated on an east–west axis, was composed of three receding tiers – what today is often called a "wedding-cake" design. In the center a transept bisected the otherwise straight line of the structure, lifting a graceful arch above the flat roofs of the nave and aisles. To neutralize, in part, at least, the criticism of Colonel Sibthorpe, the transept had been added to allow some mature elm trees on the site to remain standing inside the building.

Called a palace, it was much more suggestive of a cathedral, in keeping with the religious impulse behind Prince Albert's role in its inception. As Philip James Bailey sardonically proclaims in *The Age; A Colloquial Satire* (1858):

> Friend.
> Then came that great event, the Exhibition,
> When England dared the world to competition . . .
> But still, I hold, we were triumphant seen
> In iron, coal, and many a huge machine . . .
> Author.
> Peace-men had then their beatific vision;
> And Art-schools were to render earth Elysian.

The language describing its geometries of space – nave, aisles, transept – was drawn from church architecture. Stylistically, the Crystal Palace managed to use the modern materials of sheet glass and cast iron to evoke the classical and Gothic idioms of the past. The "rose windows" at the north and south ends of the transept, the rhythmic design of iron columns and glass bays terminating in rounded arches (echoing the inexorable march of pillars toward the altar of a Romanesque church), the effect of pointed Gothic arches created by the ridge-and-furrow roofs and the x-crossed trusses, and the vast soaring reaches of space – all combined to suggest a secular place of worship. Contemporaries delighted in comparing it to the other great cathedrals. The compilers of the *Art-Journal Illustrated Catalogue of the Crystal Palace Exhibition* (1851), for example, noted that the Crystal Palace was "about four times the size of St. Peter's, at Rome, and six times that of St. Paul's."[1] Above it, Thackeray assured his readers in a ballad on the opening day ceremonies, as befits such "fabric vast,"

> God's boundless Heaven is bending blue,
> God's peaceful sunlight's beaming through,
> And shines o'er all.
> ("May-Day Ode," 149–52)

The inauguration of the Great Exhibition corroborated the ecclesiastical atmosphere of the building. While the Royal Family sat on a dais in the transept, surrounded by ladies-in-waiting, statesmen, and military heroes, organ sounds were heard of the National Anthem, which "was taken up by 'a multitude of voices, like the sound of mighty waters.'"[2] The Archibishop of Canterbury offered a prayer, followed by the Hallelujah Chorus. Remarks of a more secular nature by Prince Albert and the Queen did not dispel the devotional air of the proceedings. Queen Victoria described the sight as "magical,"

> so vast, so glorious, so touching. One felt – as so many did whom I have since spoken to – filled with devotion, more so than by any service I have ever heard. The tremendous cheers, the joy expressed in every face, the immensity of the building, the mixture of palms, flowers, trees, statues, fountains, the organ (with 200 instruments and 600 voices, which sounded like nothing), and my beloved husband, the author of this "peace Festival," which united the industry of all nations of the earth – all this was moving indeed, and it was and is a day to live forever.[3]

The religiosity of the occasion, its high seriousness, for Queen Victoria is concentrated in her use of the word *industry*, with its pun on the Biblical injunction that man must earn his bread by the sweat of his brow, but also with the millennial hint that a new mechanized industry promised to make the old human labor unnecessary. As Thackeray remarked, "She breathe[d] amen to prayer and hymn" ("May-Day Ode"). *The Times* echoed the Queen in finding the proceedings replete with millennial overtones:

> There was yesterday witnessed a sight the like of which has never happened before and which in the nature of things can never be repeated. They who were so fortunate as to see it hardly knew what most to admire, or in what form to clothe the sense of wonder and even of mystery which struggled within them. The edifice, the treasures of art collected therein, the assemblage and the solemnity of the occasion, all conspired to suggest something even more than sense could scan, or imagination attain. There were many there who . . . had not seen anything to compare with this . . . Above them rose a glittering arch far more lofty and spacious than the vaults of even our noblest cathedrals . . . It was felt to be more than what was seen or what had been intended. Some saw in it the second and more glorious inauguration of their Sovereign; some a solemn dedication of art and its stores; some were most reminded of that day when all ages and climes shall be gathered round the Throne of their Maker.[4]

As if to confirm these intimations of divine election, the aeronaut Charles Spencer ascended in his balloon from Hyde Park to announce the official opening of the Exhibition. Less reverent in sentiment was *Punch* about "The Glass Store" (p. 195) and the Exhibition it housed. Much in the January to June 1851 issues of the magazine lampooned "the Paradise in Hyde Park" (p. 225), where "the whole of ADAM'S race collected together for the first time since they were scattered on the plain of Shinar" (p. 188).

So much for *Punch*'s hilarity, whose iconoclasm indirectly paid tribute to the near universal acclaim and quasi-hallowed mood generated by the event. Londoners proud of the mechanical and commercial supremacy of English exhibits and country folk hushed by the grandeur filed through the halls,

23 The Crystal Palace, Interior View of south transept

24   The Crystal Palace, Exterior View of south transept

6,039,205 altogether, in the summer of 1851. Exceptional was the Susan Flood whose remote Devonshire village and evangelical training had left her unprepared for the voluptuous bliss of the Hellenic statuary, causing her to "run amok," as remembered years later by Edmund Gosse in *Father and Son* (1907), and start to smash "the naked figures with the handle of her parasol" (ch. 11). Most visitors found the Crystal Palace less a "temple of Belial" than a cathedral raised, with its samples of riches and wonders, to commemorate the august future. "Temple of Peace," M. Digby Wyatt called it in his chapter on "The Construction of the Building" in the *Official Descriptive and Illustrative Catalogue*, and Disraeli termed it "that enchanted pile which the sagacious taste and the prescient philanthropy of an accomplished and enlightened Prince have raised for the glory of England."[5] Charles Kingsley preached a sermon four days after the opening in which he said that "it was like going into a sacred place." He expatiated on the progress of man and civilization that the Exhibition heralded: "If . . . those forefathers of ours could rise from their graves this day, they would be inclined to see in our hospitals, in our railroads, in the achievements of our physical science, confirmation of that old superstition of theirs, proofs of the kingdom of God, realizations of the gifts which Christ received for men, vaster than any of which they had dreamed."[6] With their unctuous air of pride in English industry and in the Protestant ethic, Kingsley's words recall his prophecy of several years earlier, in the novel *Yeast* (1848), of the imminence of a new era of bountiful plenty and of well-being. The protagonist Lancelot Smith says to his Roman Catholic cousin,

"when your party compare sneeringly Romish Sanctity, and English Civilization, I say, 'Take you the Sanctity, and give me the Civilization!' . . . give me the political economist, the sanitary reformer, the engineer; and take you saints and virgins, relics and miracles. The spinning jenny and the railroad, Cunard's liners and the electric telegraph, are to me, if not to you, signs that we are, on some points at least, in harmony with the universe; that there is a mighty spirit working among us, who cannot be your anarchic and destroying Devil, and therefore may be the Ordering and Creating God." (ch. 5)

Lancelot Smith's faith in the ordering and creating God – English practical genius – is uncannily verified, like a divine sign, Kingsley would have his fellow communicants believe, by the appearance a few years later of the Crystal Palace in nine miraculous months of gestation in Hyde Park.

After decades of hardship – the Napoleonic Wars, poor harvests and high costs of bread, climaxed by the Hungry Forties – the Crystal Palace and the Great Exhibition of 1851 reconfirmed English faith in the future of their country, in its destiny and greatness. The shining glass cathedral, enclosing 989,924 square feet of exhibition area, over 100,000 exhibits with more than 50 per cent of the exhibitors British, and full-sized trees rising to a lofty glass vault of roof through which could be seen celestial depths of blue, offered England at mid-century a symbol of its workaday realities and of its hidden dreams. It also doubled in function in its display of more than one Englishman's success story and fairy-tale achievement. None more so than that of the man who had drawn its plans.

It is "a greenhouse larger than ever greenhouse was built before," Ruskin wrote of the Crystal Palace;[7] and rightly so, for its designer was Joseph Paxton (1801–65), born in Milton Bryant, Bedfordshire, the son of a farmer but the spiritual heir to Bridgeman, Kent, Brown, Repton, and the other landscape visionaries of the previous hundred years. At the age of twenty-five he was appointed superintendent of the Duke of Devonshire's gardens at Chatsworth, and at the time of the construction of the Crystal Palace he was manager of the Duke's estates at Chatsworth, Chiswick, Hardwick, and Lismore. A restless, inventive man, he had branched out in his activities to include the design of industrial and public works, bridges, reservoirs, and gasworks, the building of country houses, and the development of urban communities. Horticulture remained, however, a key influence on his thought. He had erected a Great Conservatory at Chatsworth in 1836–41, and a lily house in 1848–50, whose construction of columns and hollow wooden beams (to function as gutters and drains) was reputedly patterned after the under leaf of the giant Guiana lily Victoria Regia, which he had domesticated. The Crystal Palace was a similar kind of building writ large.

As the conception of an individual who was both horticulturalist and man of business, the Crystal Palace summed up the paradisal impulses of 150 years. It incorporated at once the aspirations of the gardeners of the eighteenth century and of the industrialists of the nineteenth century. If not an actual conservatory its construction was such that it could have functioned as one. It light blue iron girders and glass walls, even with the handicap of canvas awnings on the roof to shield the inside from the sun, brought Hyde Park into functional relationship with the exhibits. The separation of inside and outside, of exhibits and setting, was further minimized by the plants growing inside the building: the Sibthorpe elms, a giant olive tree (planted to celebrate the Crystal Palace as a Temple of Peace), tropical foliage, palms, flowers, and splashing fountains, as Queen Victoria noted with awe. All this gave it the semblance of a giant greenhouse. Some Hyde Park sparrows were even fooled into taking sanctuary there from the March cold of 1851, by nesting in the elms before the roof was covered.[8]

In this garden setting were installed the exhibits of machinery, raw materials, textiles, foods and home furnishings, foreign displays, and fine arts. Here, the engineering prowess of England promised a new paradise of ease and comfort. A major theme of the Exhibition was the extent to which the raw materials of nature succumbed to "the ingenuity and skill of the nations of the earth."[9] Prince Albert's remarks at a banquet given by the Lord Mayor of London in support of the project are characteristic of the millenarian mood occasioned by the growth of technology and industry. "The Exhibition of 1851," he said, "would afford a true test of the point of development at which the whole of mankind had arrived in this great task, and a new starting point from which all nations would be able to direct their further exertions."[10] In keeping with this noble goal and with the general principle of harmony the official policy was one of international cooperation. Through the friendly rivalry of nations the human race would advance arm in arm toward a new millennium grounded on the manufactured exploitation of the riches of the earth.[11]

The Crystal Palace and the Great Exhibition it housed was very much a Victorian *hortus conclusus*, its zones frequented by an anointed Queen destined to embody the national ambition of old-fashioned Christian providence and modern industrial power and to be near canonized in her own time as the nation's blessed madonna. However much the four-fold division of space centering on a water fountain parodied the layout of ancient, medieval, and Renaissance paradises, the optimal climatic conditions of this garden enclosure were guaranteed by English technology rather than as in the past being dependent on God's meteorological goodwill. Human ingenuity had wedded the garden and the city, rural and urban environments, to create an improved Eden of modern taste and living comforts. Under the bright vault of the transept, as if planned from the start, stood symbols of the two forces of nature and technology. At one end Sibthorpe's elm trees towered toward the skylight. Opposite them loomed the Coalbrookdale iron gates, a monument of ornamental ironwork produced at the historic foundry on the Severn River where Abraham Darby in 1708 had made cast iron for the first time by smelting with coke instead of charcoal. Between the elms and the gates, at the sacred center of the Crystal Palace, where transept and nave intersected, stood Osler's Crystal Fountain – four tons of pure crystal glass soaring twenty-seven feet high – the *axis mundi* for all visitors, and in its union of glittering glass and sparkling water a microcosm of the united efforts of man and God to create a perfect earth, in England, as celebrated by the Exhibition.

Besides the official classifications of raw materials, machinery, manufactures, and fine arts, the exhibits included an exotic cornucopia of international displays. Visitors could wander up one side of the nave and down the other, poke into the side aisles, digress into the transepts, and ascend to the galleries, in a movable feast of sights and sounds, ever returning to Osler's Crystal Fountain, "the culminating point of view from every quarter of the building."[12] *The Art-Journal Catalogue* led its readers around the Crystal Palace on just such a tour of the Exhibition, not unsimilar to that Gilbert West and William Gilpin gave their eighteenth-century readers as a sample of the wonders of Stowe; it introduced sightseers first to the dazzling variety of things in the north and south transepts visible from the center, then guided them down one side and up the other of the western division of the nave, and across the transept for a circuit of the eastern nave, before taking them into the galleries. We could be back in an eighteenth-century garden on a circular tour of the environs, except for the difference that we are observing the manufactures of man instead of the landscape of God, in an iron and glass structure of aisles, courtyards, and galleries that is a monument to free enterprise and the factory system instead of in a park of serpentine lakes and hills that is a testament to Horatian and Biblical prototypes. It is the commercial pleasure garden of 1851 instead of the aristocratic pleasure garden of 1751 – but the aspiration to tread the paradisal enclosure again is no less fervent.

Any extended comparison of the Crystal Palace Exhibition to the landscape garden of the eighteenth century discloses equally profound differences, reflective of the changes in social and metaphysical assumptions about the world that the hundred years had witnessed. The Georgian acceptance of the theological doctrine of natural plenitude had succumbed to a Victorian commitment to the economic gospel of industrial abundance. And the Crystal Palace with its Great Exhibition evangelically trumpeted the advent of this New Eden according to the New Gospel. Its singular refinement over past conditions was the installation of a factory in the English countryside. The celestial parks of Stowe and Stourhead were to make way for the mill towns of Sheffield and Wolverhampton, sunshine cohabiting with smoke, Kent's, Gibbs's, and Flitcroft's temples replaced with the new style *axis mundi* of Darby's, Roebuck's and Wilkinson's foundries. Whereas a sense of hierarchical order in the world still prevailed in the eighteenth century, extending from the lowest organic life on earth upward to God and His angels at the top, with many occupying a favored position high in the scale of things, now the national goal, and notion of perfection, is a cornucopia of disparate items, very much like a modern department store. Organic holism has given way to bountiful, but mechanically assembled plenty.

Despite the assortment of exhibits into four major categories, the Great Exhibition remained fragmentary, a collection, or gathering, of the things of civilization, whose main unifying principle was the commercial motivation that had brought them all together under one roof. The visitor strolling about the Crystal Palace passed a kaleidoscope of objects, colors, and materials. Libidinous nude statues (Susan Flood's horrified witness to the contrary, the American sculptor Hiram Powers' *Greek Slave* was one of the most popular) jostled with home furnishings like the Spaniard Thomas De Megne's iron bedstead, agricultural machinery with iron cups and alarm clocks, Nasmyth's giant steam-hammer with an ornamental bronze street lamp, the Crampton Locomotive with a penknife of 1851 blades, furs and antlers of the Canadian frontier with ornamental furniture of the French Empire, Russian carpets with Spanish laces.

A sense of the rich hodgepodge of the Exhibition is conveyed by the circular tour of the Crystal Palace to which *The Art-Journal Catalogue* treated its readers. The travelogue is too long to quote in its entirety; but two sentences from the first paragraph and the whole of the third will give some idea of the unsorted sights anticipated by the Victorian sightseer:[13]

On entering the building, for the first time, the eye is completely dazzled by the rich variety of hues which burst upon it on every side; . . . Forming the centre, or nearly so, of the entire building, and dividing alike the transept and the nave, rises the gigantic fountain of Messrs. Osler, the culminating point of view from every quarter of the building; whilst at the northern end the eye is relieved by the verdure of tropical plants and the lofty and overshadowing branches of forest trees . . .

Crossing the Transept, and pursuing our course to the left, we enter the western division of the nave. We have here the Indian Court, Africa, Canada, the West Indies, the Cape of Good Hope, the Mediaeval Court, and the English Sculpture Court, including works of Gibson, Baily, Mac Dowell, Foley, Carew, Marshall, Behnes, Hogan, Bell, Jones, Stephens, Thornycroft, Watson, etc. To these succeed Birmingham, the great British Furniture Court, Sheffield, and its hardware, the woollen and mixed fabrics, shawls, flax, and linens, and printing and dyeing. The long avenue leading from the Mediaeval Court to the end of the building is devoted to general hardware, brass and iron-work of all kinds, locks, grates, etc.; whilst behind it, and parallel with it, but occupying three times its breadth, is the department for agricultural machines and implements. At the back of this division is the long narrow gallery occupied by the mineral products of England. Passing the small compartment of glass which runs transversely under the great organ gallery, across the nave, we have the cotton fabric and carriage courts, leather, furs, and hair, minerals and mineral manufactures, and machinery; including cotton and woollen power-looms in motion. The next is the largest compartment in the building, comprising machinery in motion, flax, silk, and lace, rope-making lathes, tools, and mills; minerals and mineral manufactures, furniture, marine engines, ceilings, hydraulic presses, steam hammers, fire engines, etc. Then follow paper and stationery; Jersey, Ceylon, and Malta, with the Fine Arts Court behind them; railway and steam machinery in motion; building contrivances, printing, and French machinery, occupying the whole of the last compartments on both sides the nave, as well as those which face the transept. Crossing to the left of the Crystal Fountain, we have Persia, Greece, Egypt, and Turkey, Spain, Portugal, Madeira and Italy, musical instruments, and chemicals; France, its tapestry, machinery, arms, and instruments, occupying two large courts; Belgium, her furniture, carpets, and machinery; Austria, with her gorgeous furniture courts, and machinery furniture; the Zollverein, with its octagon room, the most tastefully-arranged compartment in the building; North of Germany and Hanse Towns; Russia, with its malachite doors, vases and ornaments; and the United States, with its agricultural implements, raw materials, etc., occupying all that part of the nave which terminates with its organ, if we except a small gallery on the north-east side, devoted to English paper-hangings. From this extremity of the building, and from the organ gallery more especially, the finest *coup d'oeil* of the nave and its adjoining galleries may be obtained.

The new ethic of superabundance appears everywhere in mid-Victorian England, nowhere more ostentatiously than in the cluttered living rooms, domestic monuments to the abhorrence of a plain surface and to the revulsion from an unfilled space. The ideal is indiscriminately revealed both in those loose and baggy monsters the three-decker novels of the age and in the painstaking detail and even tonality of Pre-Raphaelite paintings. Copiousness characterizes the giant canvases of William Powell Frith (1819–1909), such as *The Derby Day* (1858, Tate Gallery) and *Life at the Seaside: Ramsgate Sands* (RA 1854, The Royal Family); the excesses of Sir Gilbert Scott's Albert Memorial (1872) in Kensington Gardens, and any number of facades of grand hotels, jails, court houses, and railway stations. Lewis Carroll catches the enthusiasm for the manifold in the madcap incongruities, simultaneities, and improvisations of the Queen of Heart's croquet game, where everyone plays at the same time and nothing remains stationary.

Something of this exuberance had even infiltrated the gardens at Chatsworth, not surprisingly, considering that Paxton, who caught up in his person the industry, copious activities, taste, guiding precepts, and ruling passions of the period, had been for most of twenty-five years its head gardener. While there is a definite circular route in the Chatsworth garden, starting from the north-east corner of the house and moving south down the Broad Walk, then east through the Azalea Dell, Ravine, and Pinetum, before turning north through the Arboretum past the Grotto Pond and the Great Cascade, where the walk turns west in a series of bends down the hill to the house again – seldom does one have visible evidence of this fact during one's circumambulation of the garden, as one

has in the West Garden at Stowe and at Stourhead. Rather, one is restricted
visually by ground formation and planting to a limited portion of an unusually
variegated garden at any one time. In a sense the garden offered repeatedly the
effect of superabundance, variation, and fragmentation, as similarly experienced
at the Crystal Palace Exhibition, but in natural rather than mechanical and
architectural terms. In the central areas of the garden – the Wellington Rock, the
Strid, the Robber's Stone, the Ring Pond, and Willow Tree Fountain – the effect
is one of exuberant prodigality. The Wellington Rock area – with its massive
boulders seemingly tumbled carelessly from the hands of a Titan among trees and
bushes clinging to a slope to provide a romantic series of arches, dens, and cliffs
among which Schiller's *Räuber* might have lurked – provides a perfect microcosm
of the whole. Gone are the vast lawns developed by Capability Brown for the
fourth Duke, which left the house sitting impressively in the midst of its stark
Peaks setting. As seen in the mid-century painting by Richard Wilson, to the west
and south-west the formal gardens of the first Duke have been swept away in favor
of grass running from the house to the relocated river. To the east the lawn
reaches up the hill to the Great Cascade, the rest of the steep incline covered by
trees. Under Paxton's nineteenth-century hand the lawn shrank to the slopes
below the cascade and to those ringing the Emperor Fountain and Canal Pond
south of the house. Aerial views of the garden today, virtually unchanged since
Paxton's time – with the exception of the pleached limes on the south-front lawn,
the serpentine beech hedge bordering the walk south from the Ring Pond, and the
formal box-hedge maze on the site of Paxton's Great Conservatory – show a rich
profusion of trees, boulders, walks, hedges, pools, fountains, and formal beds, all
seemingly the product of a teeming and energetic imagination, which has just
managed to keep in check the Victorian compulsion for clutter.

In the new ethic of superabundance, so splendidly exhibited under Paxton's
guiding hand at both the Crystal Palace and at Chatsworth, all things, pieces,
and parts acquire equal importance, because equally valuable commercially, or
aesthetically. Nowhere is this attitude more visible than in the fine art displays of
the 1851 Exhibition. The illustrated descriptive account of selected exhibits in
The Art-Journal Catalogue comments enthusiastically on the eclectic styles,
ornamentation, "gorged designs," and *trompe-l'oeil* of the objects. The populace
was fascinated with the imitation of one material by another, and with the
substitution of one object for another – with all the ambiguities intrinsic to the
border area ordinarily separating technology from design: with floral ornaments
created out of leather, with an inkstand designed in the form of fish and objects
connected with the sport of angling, with furniture constructed of papier-mâché
and gutta percha, and with phaetons adopting the shape of swans and nautilus
shells. The visitors doted on anachronistic decorations and styles and on novel
and tricky gadgetry: a cotton machine covered with scarab decorations, a
"gothick" engine, a pianoforte with sea dragons for legs designed to serve also as a
table when shut down, and a life-preserving portmanteau.[14] Here indeed was a
new kind of Eden! A cornucopia of manufactured goods to guarantee the good
life.

Not everyone was enthralled, however, with these marvels. William Morris, then a young man of seventeen, recalled these design eccentricities thirty years later in lectures on the arts and crafts as the "last resource of the decrepitude of art," and sneered at a *"raison d'être* of decorative art" which puts its skills to such puerile uses as to "make stone look like ironwork, or wood like silk, or pottery like stone" to serve viewers an excuse for some parlour guessing game of " 'How was it done?' "[15] Ruskin was equally unimpressed, as one might expect, by these "paltry arts of our fashionable luxury."[16] But theirs were minority dissents. The prevailing sentiment (as Ruskin admits) was pride in English mechanical know-how; and praise was heard everywhere for the industrial ingenuity which had triumphed so over nature.

Ornamentation, form; commerce, art; part, whole; copy, creation: such niceties of distinction were mixed willy-nilly in the zeal for production. Converts to the ethic of super-abundance could cheerfully multiply pieces with relaxed concern for order, sequence, arrangement. In comparison to Paxton's utilization of assembly-line methods and prefabrication of heterogeneous materials in the building of the Crystal Palace, Wedgwood's revolutionizing of the pottery industry in the second half of the eighteenth century belongs to another world in its continued regard for order and proportion, and above all in its preservation of the idiosyncrasies of the craftsman's skill. Wedgwood's potters still had to start the process by throwing a pot; but Paxton's glaziers, carpenters, and structural ironworkers put up posts, walls, and roofs in every direction seemingly without plan, their construction all over and at once, as the photographs and engravings of the event bear witness.

Dickens captures the passion of the age for mechanical assemblage, as contrasted to organic growth, with the dimly lit taxidermy shop and disjunctive, fragmented speech of Mr. Venus, in *Our Mutual Friend* (1864–65). The shop's mysterious recesses are "stuck so full of black shelves and brackets and nooks and corners," jammed with "a muddle of objects, vaguely resembling pieces of leather and dry stick," with what Mr. Venus in dead seriousness calls "Bones warious,"

'Skulls, warious. Preserved Indian baby. African ditto. Bottled preparations, warious. Everything within reach of your hand, in good preservation. The mouldy ones a-top. What's in those hampers over them again, I don't quite remember. Say, human warious. Cats. Articulated English baby. Dogs. Ducks. Glass eyes, warious. Mummied bird. Dried cuticle, warious. Oh dear me! That's the general panoramic view.'   (1, 7)

A perfect emblem of the art of assemblage, which the age put on a paying industrial basis, is the skeleton for an art school that Mr. Venus, "Articulator of human bones," has contrived out of his inventory, "One leg Belgian, one leg English, and the pickings of eight other people in it" (ch. 7).

How different are the paradigmatic repetitions performed in the Crystal Palace and in Mr. Venus's shop from those symbolized in the circuit walks of Stowe and Stourhead gardens. The eighteenth century still gave assent to an hierarchical order in the natural world descending from God through man to the lower beasts, in which each thing is clearly distinguished from all others. It is no accident that the century gave birth to Linnaeus (1707–78) and his taxonomy. This clarity about the identity of place and of person prevailed for most people at least until the 1780s and 90s when cracks in its smooth facade became too insistent for the discerning few to ignore. Gainsborough and Wordsworth, for example, not to mention Blake, show early signs of distress at dualities in a world where once singularity supposedly prevailed. With the acceptance of steam driven engines as a source of energy equivalent to the natural forces, ambiguities of form creep in as well. A "muddle of objects" or a manifold of parts replace categorical and holistic concepts of a whole. The Victorian mind happily substituted the train schedule for cosmic time and the railroad track for measurement of space, and admired W. P. Frith's crowded painting, *The Railway Station* (1862, Royal Holloway College, Univ. of London), with its anecdotal portrayal of a train platform, for what was taken to be the drama of life. The ultimate reduction of organic growth to mechanical assemblage came with the industrial ideal of interchangeable parts and mass assembly lines. And towards this goal the engineering and managerial genius of nineteenth-century England was rushing as fast as possible.[17] In the standardization of shapes and sizes and in the prefabrication of the building materials for the Crystal Palace, Paxton unerringly caught at mid-century the essence of the Victorian hope for a perfect world.

For some the euphoria of the Great Exhibition was short-lived. Fifteen years later Dickens, who was no believer in the New Jerusalem of products and finance, had divined, in *Our Mutual Friend*, the *reductio ad absurdum* of the industrial enterprise. He dramatizes it in his description of the Podsnaps' dinner plate, which was of "Hideous solidity . . . made to look as heavy as it could, and to take up as much room as possible."

Everything said boastfully, "Here you have as much of me in my ugliness as if I were only lead; but I am so many ounces of precious metal worth so much an ounce; – wouldn't you like to melt me down?" A corpulent straggling epergne, blotched all over as if it had broken out in an eruption rather than been ornamented, delivered this address from an unsightly silver platform in the centre of the table. Four silver wine-coolers, each furnished with four staring heads, each head obtrusively carrying a big silver ring in each of its ears, conveyed the sentiment up and down the table, and handed it on to the pot-bellied silver salt-cellars. All the big silver spoons and forks widened the mouths of the company expressly for the purpose of thrusting the sentiment down their throats with every morsel they ate. (I, 11)

At its worst the confusion of values produces the laminated pretense of the Lammles and the varnished simulation of the Veneerings; and the doubling of the table setting and dinner guests in the "great looking-glass above the sideboard" of the Veneerings' dining room (I, 2) lends to the scene the ultimate transference of reality into reflection, underscoring the falsity of this materialistic, get-rich-quick, manufacturing and merchandizing society.

Historical man had harnessed paradise to a new cycle of economic laws; but to Dickens's doubting eyes the England of his day revealed few signs of the Millennium. The opposite appeared closer to actuality, for Coketowns were spewing soot all over the Black Country and railways were slicing through towns and hamlets making of them twin towns and sister hamlets. Dickens's most memorable, and complete, symbol for the assemblage ideal, with its automatic decline from Palace to dung heap, are the three dust hills that rise out of Boffin's Bowers to tease greedy eyes in the neighborhood of Holloway. Repositories of rubbish collected in the city, they represented to his contemporaries the doctrine of abundance in its most ineffable form. Quite literally they are the junk yard of the dazzling goods put proudly on display in the Crystal Palace. Intrinsic to the industrial enterprise are the principles of production, depreciation, and consumption, which place value equally on the shiny new produce and on the discarded relic. And money is made out of both ends of the process: in the manufacturing of things and in the disposing of them when broken, worn, and obsolete. "Dirt is money," Dickens says. Which is his metaphoric way of calling attention to the breakdown of values when a cash-nexus replaces traditional regulatory systems and hierarchies of order. In a stunning conceit (I, 12) he equates paper currency with dust raised by spring gusts of wind in London, whirling about the streets blinding and choking its inhabitants with debris of their own making, which is contrasted, by implication, to the usual quickening of life under the benign influence of April wind and rain.

Dickens is attacking the money-getting of his age and the Crystal Palace was a shrine to that money getting: its glass walls were designed to reveal to the world that England was the foremost industrial nation in the world, the richest and most providential society in history. In Disraeli's, Kingsley's, and Victoria and Albert's eyes the Crystal Palace was confirmation of man's ability to create a heaven on earth. To Dickens's, Ruskin's and Morris's eyes its accumulation of manufactured goods presaged still more dust heaps. Thus, a skeptical mind could dismiss its gesture of a bountiful earth as reductive. The natural paradises of Capability Brown's "eternal undulating" landscapes (Knight, *The Landscape*, 1794) at Blenheim, Petworth, and Chatsworth, as well as of Coleridge's wooded recesses in the hills of Somerset and of Wordsworth's majestic heights in the fells of Cumberland and Westmorland, had dwindled to Paxton's captive elms and potted ferns on nineteen steel-and-glass enclosed acres of Hyde Park, which would in its turn deteriorate along with the other gilded objects of the Crystal Palace, to accumulate into Dickens's dust heaps. Landscape gardening had continued profitable, with some job retraining, as golden rubbish sifting and heaping.

In the 1850s, though, Dickens's analysis had not yet been heard. And by any architectural measurement, the Crystal Palace was a daring success, the culmination of a century of exploits in the technological sublime. Above all, it achieved an imaginative fusion of the garden and the city to re-affirm the possibilities of paradise on earth in terms of old ends and new means. It put nature under controlled conditions. In this perfect environment were displayed the amenities for ameliorating the harsh life that man had been heir to east of Eden for thousands of years. Without its being explicitly so denominated, the Crystal

Palace (removed to Sydenham, Kent, and officially reopened by Queen Victoria on 10 June 1854) epitomized England's world-wide hegemony in the second half of the century. Little strain of the literary imagination is needed to see the British Empire as embodying just such a geographical gathering of nations and peoples, accumulated and held glued together by Queen Victoria, the "grandmother of Europe." Like the Crystal Palace the Empire was an inspired assemblage, a political ideal imposed as a collage onto the globe itself, blessed and confirmed by the Diamond Jubilee.

For the rest of Victoria's reign the Winter Park and Garden of the Crystal Palace offered Londoners, the citizen beneficiaries of this assemblage ideal, a paradise-for-the-day. Its tarnished surfaces, however, betrayed its industrial and commercial origins; and as the decades advanced, it acquired more of the look of an amusement park. Its facilities in that direction were easily expanded and added to, since most of the statuary and architectural courts were copies, constructed of ersatz materials. Victorian tolerance for pretence and the eclectic was seemingly inexhaustible. With the passage of time its tawdriness, the incongruous setting and grouping of tropical palms and northern gothic, of Egyptian sarcophagi *vis-à-vis* Italian classical columns, became ever more apparent. Still, the Crystal Palace Winter Park housed, with the surrounding Garden, the limited substance of a "pipe dream" (so Dostoyevsky's Underground Man called it) that the brick-bound imagination of the masses could apprehend, and appreciate. For a brief few hours they could believe in the indestructibility of their dreams. In its fusion of nature and technology, in its presentation of the continuity of human history, and in its self-contained assurance that "God's in His Heaven" and "All's right with the world," the Sydenham Crystal Palace was as satisfactory an expression of mundane paradise as the high Victorian period could conceive.

IO

Turner's Fabled Atlantis: London, Venice, and Carthage as Paradisal Cityscape

THE FOG AND RAIN-CHILLED ENGLISH have flirted with sunny Italy since at least the sixteenth century; and in the nineteenth they felt particular tenderness for Florence and especially Venice. Thanks to Byron, Ruskin, and Turner – and at the end of the century, to Whistler – Venice looms in nineteenth-century English minds not only as a city of stone-encrusted palaces, of statues, of night fog and the interminable sound of the sea, but above all as a haven for "the paradisaical pinks, purples, yellows and greens"[1] of the Mediterranean sun creeping into crumbling courtyards and seeking out narrow canals lined by tall houses. Comfortably connected with these historical and urban facts, Venice also recalled to their minds Byron's bittersweet epitome of it as the ruins of a once noble paradise[2] and his mythic identification of it – "the greenest island of my imagination"[3] – with the Blessed Isles. As such Venice stirred the imaginations of English visitors as it had animated those of its builders and inhabitants. The image of the city as a reconstituted paradise is caught in the symbolism of the Fig-tree and Vine Angles of the Doge's Palace. In the corner joining the Piazzetta and Sea Facades, medieval stonecutters bore eternal witness to man's Fall; and in the corner joining the Sea and Rio Facades, to man's survival of the flood and resumption of the good life on earth. Adam and Eve, and Noah and his sons – representing the mythic progenitors of the city, itself "The master-mould of Nature's heavenly hand" (Byron, *Childe 4*, xxv) – have stood ever since facing the rain and the sun and the shifting waters of the Adriatic, as perpetual reminders to Venetians and visitors alike of the city's ghostly origins.

Just as the beached rocks of Tyre and the palaces of Venice were once "'as in Eden, the garden of God'" (thus Ruskin opens Volume I of *The Stones of Venice*), so the river reaches of London in their turn assume this hallowed identification with God's domains.[4] And just as Ruskin's history of the stones of Venice recapitulates this mythic tale of mankind, so does Turner's sun-and-sea drenched record of the past imperial powers Venice and Carthage, and by inference England whose heaven-granted fortunes are currently ascendant. Turner visited Venice in 1819, 1835, and 1840, for a total of about six weeks, sufficient for his quick study and astounding visual memory to recreate in London that watery urban world in all its sacred and profane moods again and again in the 1830s and 1840s, as seen from the bay and along its canals, like some fabled Atlantis risen from the ghostly depths to offer confirmation anew of the ceaseless City of God.

An analogous supernal touch characterizes his celebration of other cities painted between 1820 and 1845, in both the early manner of topographical and Italian picturesque and in the late manner of radiating light and color when concrete reality is dissolved in a sea of yellow, mauve, and turquoise. In a rendering of *Rome: St. Peter's from the Villa Barberini* (1819, Tate Gallery) the dome of St. Peter's sits in a halo of morning light, appropriately exalted as the temporal seat of God's reign, enthroned on its columns and flanked by a court of Vatican buildings and by the trains of Bernini's colonnade. Similarly, in *Lausanne: Sunset* (c. 1841, British Museum), Turner focuses our sight on three or four church spires and crenellated towers looming out of a swirling haze of burnt sienna and yellow, the rest of the city dissolved in vaporous glory. In the foreground is the silhouette of a round turreted structure reminiscent of the dressing tents of medieval jousters on the field of tourney, which completes the fantasy that one might be glimpsing Camelot on its hill at the moment when Merlin's magic has begun to fail him and Arthur's city to disappear into the chronicles of prehistory. *Zurich* (c. 1842, British Museum) presents a city seemingly emerging from the receding waters of the deluge, expectant in the glow of a new day, with all the inhabitants on rooftop and jetty come out to wonder. *Florence from San Miniato* (c. 1828, British Museum) dreams in the benign light of late afternoon: from the vantage point of the church of San Miniato al Monte on the hill above the Piazzale Michelangelo, one looks past a peasant *fête-champêtre* in the foreground, towards a panorama of the city, its red-tiled roofs, the river and its bridges, and, most striking of all, the elegant towers and dome of the Palazzo Vecchio, Giotto's Campanile, and the Duomo soaring above the cityscape like indices of God. *View of Orvieto* (1828, Tate Gallery) shows that city in the distance on its clifflike plateau thrusting above the Claudian plain, one undifferentiated cube of ocher like an antique monument to a divine past, rendered more sublime by its contrast to the mundane reds and browns of the foreground, with its prosaic scene of two women laundering clothes at a fountain. More than one English cathedral city is similarly framed by peaceful countryside or viewed through valleys in the distorting mist and rain like ecstatic hilltop towns of Italy, ghostly white cathedral towers asserting their spiritual presence against the black vortex of clouds and density of sky.

Venice, "throned on her hundred isles" (Byron, *Childe 4*, i), particularly, but the other cities as well, answered in Turner's visual experience to both a personally and culturally derived need to fix on the urban scene as a symbolic recurrence of "the land, which still is Paradise" (Byron, *Beppo*, xlvi). For centuries first the enclosed garden, and then in recent memory the whole "Spirit of Nature," its "forms / Perennial of the ancient hills" (*Prelude* [1805], VII, 735, 725–26), had confirmed the original human knowledge of earthly paradise and the imminent reclaim of its blissful precincts. In the nineteenth century the corollary myth of the community of souls in a city on a hill acquired new mythic force with the growth of an urban industrial society. Raymond Williams makes an interesting observation in *The Country and the City* (1973) about the change in attitude two hundred years ago toward the city: "As London grew, dramatically, in the eighteenth century, it was being intensely observed, as a new kind of landscape, a new kind of society" (ch. 14). Conventional ways of seeing the city as antithetical to the innocent country and as the source of economic and social blight inevitably underwent revision. The inexorable enlargement of this one English city demanded that it be dealt with as a microcosm of the nation at large. With a shock of recognition sophisticated observers observed that the city was not all evil, that it harbored the creature comforts of production and the civilized orders of society, that it was, in the opinion of Voltaire, the symbol of progress and enlightenment, superior to a golden pastoral age, which had not been virtuous so much as ignorant, because lacking in industry and urban pleasure.

The new fiction of the city as a center of moral value accompanied an increasing ambiguity of opinion about the ancient myth of the garden. By the end of the Regency, Londoners were looking on the enclosed garden of earlier centuries, as on nature generally, with distinctly troubled eyes. They still clung to that part of the Romantic legacy which held a leafy bower in awe as a place of "powers" and "presences" of soul-satisfying serenity; but its *genius loci* as often as not in their daily experience now was found to be in a city park, West End square, or sooty patch of backyard greenery enveloped by brick walls. As Andrew Griffith remarks, whereas for the Romantic poets nature surrounded the city, and egress meant escape to one's true self (one thinks of Wordsworth's exultant enfranchisement, "from yon City's walls set free" [1, 7], in the opening lines of *The Prelude*), for the Victorian Londoner the city invaded the fields, closing off escape routes except that inward to "the embowered selfhood."[5] The Celestial City of God was invoked, albeit more often inferentially than overtly, to ennoble the new city experience, just as attempts also continued at accommodation of the two worlds. Although little read by his contemporaries, Blake was an early unbiased witness to the complication of a paradise equally rural and urban, which received his most fervent endorsement in the millenarian conclusion to *Jerusalem*. Matthew Arnold tried to remain true to the Romantic creed, while not denying the realities of his own world and time. In "Lines Written in Kensington Gardens" he sought to recreate the magical ambience of a verdant world of natural piety within earshot of the "impious uproar" of Kensington High Street. Not without irony, and some pathos, Kensington Gardens surrounded by the din of London is pressed into substituting for a Lake Country retreat, as Arnold re-asserts the Wordsworthian credo of nature's palliative power. Tennyson's receptivity to the new grammar of feeling is reflected, contrariwise, in his effort to enshrine the city and its society as a reconstructed Camelot.

No one among his contemporaries who embraced both natural and human environments, and who looked with equal fascination on a past time and on the present moment, assimilated and combined in his art the divergent tendencies with greater tension and yet inclusiveness than Turner. His visual conception of the city as a paradigm of the earthly paradise is complex, and is interwoven with his equally complex idea of nature. He retained consistently held responses to both from early in his life to its end, and yet changed his positive emphasis away from nature towards the city as he lived beyond his Romantic youth into his Victorian old age. He could contemplate a rural scene with as much serenity, and at times with equal Edenic fervor, as Blake and Constable. He might have agreed with Samuel Palmer that one must try to paint the light behind the hills of Dulwich ("hard task") so as "to bring up a mystic glimmer" that would "give us promise that the country beyond them is Paradise."[6] Yet his compulsive examination of nature also generated contradictory feelings. Its titanic forces fascinated him, while the history of its cataclysmic destructiveness and the association of that destructiveness with the fall of mankind filled him with a cynical sense of the cheat of hope. Jack Lindsay assigns to Turner's mythological evocations and to his "intensification of natural harmonies in a more or less realistic scene" the brunt of "Turner's continual attempt to depict the earthly paradise." This account of Turner's faith in a nature "restlessly moving towards [a renewed] paradise"[7] discounts too facilely the painter's lifelong contemplation of the special equipoise of city and sea, of the man-made in harmony with the elements and the natural process of "movement, clash, dissolution, and re-integration,"[8] which characterizes the great maritime centers of the past and of the present.

Born in 1775, Turner had inherited a reverence for the Italian landscape painters of the seventeenth century and a Romantic esteem for the *campagna* as the handiwork of God; but he had also grown up in London and he shared the urban dweller's bittersweet romance with the mysterious alleys, brick piles, and water reaches of great lake, river, and seaport towns. It needs to be emphasized though that toward neither rural nor urban worlds, however tender and intimate his memory of them, did Turner often give wholly uncritical assent. An inner core of inviolate reservation marked his wry holding of the world at arm's length. The strange psychological fact about Turner, in its bluntest form, may be that his complicated artist's sensibility, which included no small degree of sadistic suspicion in its human makeup,[9] was incapable finally of giving unreserved allegiance to any thing except the colorful painted worlds of its own imaginative making. Which makes all the more representative of the age Turner's general observations that the city, especially in its guise as radiant expression of civilization and as symbol of the eternal City on a Hill, finally engaged the imagination and satisfied the need for order better than the equally established model of a pastoral world as earthly paradise.

The problem in setting forth this view is how to convey linearly what was existentially nonchronological. That is not to say that Turner's painterly style did not progress and evolve, rather that his command of his world, formed early and remaining stable, was remarkably manifold and heterogeneous throughout. His personal life, too, achieved analogous heterogeneity. There was his association with the Royal Academy. There were his relationships with his father and mother, his liaison with Sarah Danby, and his life with Mrs. Booth. Each was pursued independently of his career as a painter, without intrusion or interference from his other daily affairs. It was Turner's Draconian method of dealing with an unruly and hostile environment. There is something of the same urge to compartmentalization in his painting. Alternatively, successively, and simultaneously he painted topographical landscapes, visionary scenes, sea subjects, heroic historical events, watercolors and sketches for etchings and engravings. In one sense, though, his art reflects a coherent life-long effort: his single-minded creation through his painting of an ordered world. His pictures literally were his world. He held on to them tenaciously, selling them with reluctance, and afterward trying to buy them back. He looked on them as extensions of himself; and when he died 19 December 1851 he left to the nation a bequest of 100 finished paintings, 182 unfinished pictures, and 19,049 drawings and sketches in color and in pencil, with the condition that they be kept intact.[10] By means of their symbolism his pictures allowed him to organize his segmented world; to render a rational view of the political struggles of the Napoleonic era, of the mythopoeic imaginings of his age, and of the psychological traumas of his private life.[11] That he attempted to realize these goals of order principally as a painter of landscapes and sea scenes forced him to face directly the changes in perception of nature that European culture had been witnessing for a century or more. During the first five decades of the nineteenth century, with ever increasing insight, he described a physical world of sea and sky in a perpetual state of change and at times of cataclysmic flux. Against that volatile cosmic process Turner placed the relative continuity and fixedness of the city.

What prompted a painter of nature like Turner, whose Romantic eye had been nurtured on the serene landscapes of Claude and the stirring seascapes of Willem van de Velde the younger (1633–1707), Jacob van Ruysdael (1628/29–82) Claude-Joseph Vernet (1714–89), and Philip James de Loutherbourg (1740–1812),[12] and whose taste espoused the English–Claudian tradition of Richard Wilson (1714–82), to turn to cityscapes and increasingly in the second half of his life to depict the city as an integral, and often principal, part of a larger whole of natural process?

The question takes on even sharper pertinence when one places Turner's celebration of cities against the context of the taste of the time, since the subject of the ruins of empire – the sort of theme Byron was touting as early as 1812 in *Childe Harold's Pilgrimage* – was popular with painters and poets in the 1820s and 30s.[13] Besides John Martin, who did a series on cities at the moment of destruction – *The Fall of Babylon; Belshazzar's Feast; The Destruction of Pompeii and Herculaneum*; and *The Fall of Nineveh* – Edwin Atherstone wrote a poetic epic on *The Fall of Nineveh* (1828) and one on *The Last Days of Herculaneum*, Bulwer Lytton wrote *The Last Days of Pompeii* (1834), and Tennyson wrote the schoolboy poem *Armageddon* (c. 1824). A measure of the quirky independence of Turner's mind, as well as perhaps of its needs, is his capricious disregard of what his fellow artists were doing in his emphasizing instead the stability and longevity of cities. It is not that he was ignorant of the fall of urban empires – his paintings of Carthage are evidence to the contrary – just that he preferred to concentrate on their grandeur. Interestingly, he had painted catastrophes at the turn of the century, in such pictures as *The Fifth Plague of Egypt* (1800, Herron Art Museum, Indianapolis), *The Destruction of Sodom* (*c.* 1805, Tate Gallery), and *The Deluge* (1804–05, Tate Gallery). In these, according to Jack Lindsay, he had been seeking "to combine the images of the earthly paradise and the threat of disaster."[14] Indicative of Turner's radical blend of traditionalism and iconoclasm is that in his treatment of this theme he transferred the taste for catastrophic events to their natural occurrences and linked the antique tradition of the earthly paradise with the rise of cities and civilizations.

Given the influence on his art of Claude,[15] not to mention the general Classical–Christian tradition, it would not have been surprising if Turner had accepted the traditional view of the earthly paradise as a garden. As Turner was acutely aware, however, the original mythic paradise as well as classical and historical pastoral versions have been spoiled by human contention and sexual strife, and seemingly

25   Turner, *The Goddess of Discord choosing the Apple of Contention in the Garden of the Hesperides*

as a matter of course have shared in the discordancy of the Fall. *The Goddess of Discord Choosing the Apple of Contention in the Garden of the Hesperides* (1806, Tate Gallery) sums up one strand of his developing attitude. Against a background of broiling storm-tossed clouds and precipitous mountain cliffs, as if premonitory of the Fall, the transaction occurs which introduces contention into the Golden Age. On the nearest peak stretches the monstrous dragon of the Hesperides airing himself in the mountains instead of guarding the apples. The baleful link of discord with nature is suggested by Turner's painting the dragon as almost indistinguishable from the jagged setting "of which he has become almost a part."[16] The momentous act is depicted in the foreground on the banks of a stream flowing through a peaceful valley. Female inhabitants of the pastoral scene – some carrying water and others washing clothes, while a retinue of nymphs loll at ease under an apple tree – watch from both sides of the river in arrested curiosity, as Ate reaches forth her hand for the apple of contention. As with Eve's transgression over another apple, the earthly paradise itself will partake of the suffering and degradation of man.

Similar reminders of this chain of events occur in *The Fates and the Golden Bough* (1834, Tate Gallery) and in *The Bay of Baiae, with Apollo and the Sibyl* (1823, Tate Gallery). In the former even as the golden bough is raised triumphantly aloft and nymphs dance joyously, a cat trembles in the foreground before a snake, Turner's emblem of "terror, or temptation," according to Ruskin, "which is associated with the lovely landscapes" throughout Turner's life as a reminder of fallen nature.[17] In the latter picture a white rabbit crouches in a patch of sunlight, frozen by fear of a nearby snake. There is a less direct acknowledgement of fallen animal nature, along with an indirect allusion to the primal sin and its consequences, where we would least expect it in Turner's paintings, in the landscape of *The Lake, Petworth Park: Sunset, Fighting Bucks* (c. 1829, Petworth House, Sussex). In the eerie light of a russet sunset, deer, cows, sheep, and horses graze peacefully in the park before the lake. Flanked on the left by a clump of Lancelot Brown's chestnut trees and on the right by a tree-capped hill they comprise a segment of the Peaceful Kingdom of God in an Edenic vale. With one discordant exception. In the right foreground two white bucks struggle with locked horns, while a group of does placidly await the outcome. Although a cricket game in progress to the left under the clump of trees humorously minimizes the sting of the human correlative to the contest of the bucks, sexual rivalry assumes a real presence in an otherwise deceptively paradisal scene. A political and human version of such dissension is included in *Phryne Going to the Public Bath as Venus – Demosthenes Taunted by Aeschines* (1838, Tate Gallery). As in *The Bay of Baiae*, the human action takes place on a foreground hill in the deep shadow of several trees framing the picture. The explosive political situation between Demosthenes, exponent of Greek city-democracy, and Aeschines, advocate of Macedonian royal rule, develops as Phryne and her maidens file past in ironic commentary on the contentious men bringing disquiet to the countryside.

In an attempt to account for Turner's conceptualization of nature, Lindsay argues that "we cannot understand what [Turner] is saying unless we first grasp that he is making his judgements or criticisms inside the universe of Thomson and Akenside." This assignment of major influence on Turner's thought concentrates principally on Akenside's theory of life as "a quest for . . . self-fulfilment in terms of an organic relation between man and nature. . . . When everything is harmoniously developed, an idyllic relationship is born in which the earth becomes Hesperidean, a 'visionary landscape.'" The transformation of earthly life, according to Akenside, is brought about by the action of memory/imagination, which is attuned to the external beauties of nature:

> So the glad impulse of congenial pow'rs,
> Or of sweet sound, or fair-proportion'd form,
> The grace of motion, or the bloom of light,
> Thrills thro' imagination's tender frame,
> From nerve to nerve: all naked and alive
> They catch the spreading rays.
> (*The Pleasures of Imagination* [1754], I, 116–21)

As a result of the activation of the imagination the soul becomes responsive "to that harmonious movement from without":

> Then the inexpressive strain
> Diffuses its enchantment: fancy dreams
> Of sacred fountains and Elysian groves,
> And vales of bliss.
> (*The Pleasures of Imagination* [1754], I, 123–27)

Thus, the image of paradisal earth is the product of imaginative harmony and of actual experience. "We have here," Lindsay concludes, "the key to Turner's continual attempt to depict the earthly paradise, whether by mythological evocation or by an intensification of natural harmonies in a more or less realistic scene."[18]

This is a shrewd observation, and has the historical merit of placing Turner, Romantic born, in the eighteenth-century intellectual tradition of his years of coming of age. Even though he was aesthetically innovative in ways far in advance of the high Victorian era into which he lived, his reaction to events up to the middle of the nineteenth century continued to be culturally directed by habits of mind by then old-fashioned.

One qualification – and it is crucial – needs to be added to one that Lindsay advances about the instrumentation of Turner's thought. Lindsay concedes that Akenside did not set forth his "scheme in uncritical optimism." Political tyranny and social misconduct, according to Akenside, have in time distorted the imaginative activity of man and broken the continuity of the original harmony. Thomson presents a corrective version of life in the "Spring" section of *The Seasons* (1746). Man is portrayed as having once enjoyed "that concord of harmonious powers" (276) when "Nature too looked smiling on" (258) and "winds and waters flowed / In consonance" (270–71); but man's perverse "ever-changing views of good and ill" (298) subsequently altered it to an "endless storm" (300) of disaffected nature. Lindsay admits that Turner, too, while accepting "the truth of Akenside's picture of man's place in the universe and his need for integration, considered that the problem was far more complicated than had been allowed." Hence the fragmentary poem "The Fallacies of Hope" (as opposed to Akenside's *Pleasures of Imagination* and Campbell's *Pleasures of Hope*, "both of which exercised a crucial influence on Turner") in which during much of his adult life Turner "sought to express the contradictions and the complexities"[19] of his suspicions about hope's deception. In this poem – more the idea of a poem than an actual one so far as the evidence indicates – which he identified with the excerpts he attached to his pictures, Turner reveals a profound disillusionment underlying not only his psychic make-up but his philosophical outlook as well.

Even after accounting for this qualification there still is a problem not addressed by Lindsay, which besets his schematization of Turner's thought. It assumes the Christian cosmic myth – paradise known, lost, and regained – which is fine; but it also assumes Turner's belief in a progressive theory of history, in which the renewed earthly paradise will come about by way of the steady improvement of "nature . . . restlessly moving towards this paradise."[20]

Nothing about Turner's depiction of the earthly scene lends confidence to such a view. His conception of nature is dynamic, but not particularly progressive. At the outset he was drawn to titanic disturbances in nature, especially of the ocean. These he painted at the same time that he was depicting the English landscape, particularly views along the Thames River, "with a warmth and lyricism unprecedented in British painting."[21] He responded with imaginative energy to the mountainous terrains of Wales and the English Lake Country. The sublime discordancies of the latter, its capricious shifts of weather, and dizzying alternations of sunshine and rain, all reminded him of Genesis and of post-Genesis destruction. *Morning Amongst the Coniston Fells, Cumberland* (1798, Tate Gallery) economically captures Turner's antithetical response. The picture divides roughly in two. One half flows down into the dark. Could the waterfall be intended by Turner as a visual pun to carry the idea of the Fall? The other half records a sunrise with the awestruck wonder of first man. In the center appear a shepherd and shepherdess, presumably alluding to lines from *Paradise Lost* (attached to the picture when Turner exhibited it) in which Adam and Eve sing their morning orisons "Ye Mists and Exhalations" (v, 185). Thus does the picture recall at once what was mankind's birthright and is now its lamentable legacy.

Turner could rarely give his unqualified assent even to the most benign appearances of nature. His ambivalence about nature's potential, whether apocalyptic or obliterative, is illustrated by his treatment of Norham Castle, which he painted many times, beginning with a watercolor in 1798, and returning to it again in watercolor three times between 1820 and 1833, climaxing his obsession with the subject in the unfinished oil painting *Norham Castle, Sunrise* (c. 1835–40, Tate Gallery). It is unlikely that Turner's final laying-on of paint, as was his habit on varnishing days at the Royal Academy annual shows, would have altered the essentials of the scene. The broadly brushed undercoats reflect accurately the luminescence of the Turnerian world. The castle and mountain loom dimly in a misty middleground, while a cow drinking at the river's edge in the foreground has all but vanished in an impalpable blue haze.

The cow appears to stand in a Tweed River that has expanded indefinitely in the rarefied atmosphere, its flow enveloping its banks and all the earth to the castle, until it merges indefinably with the sky in one continuous infinite space. Hazlitt's rigid illusionary sense of reality and of the painter's responsibility prompted him, in trying to puzzle out Turner's intentions as early as 1816, to write,

The artist delights to go back to the first chaos of the world, or to that state of things when the waters were separated from the dry land, and light from darkness, but as yet no living thing nor tree bearing fruit was seen upon the face of the earth. All is "without form and void." Some one said of his landscapes that they were *pictures of nothing, and very like*.[22]

A recent critic reverses the implications of Hazlitt's perception by asking the question, "isn't it possible that he [Turner] saw the wraiths of landscape features as objects that were disappearing rather than emerging? They look like the victims of an inundation of light as inexorable as a deluge. There is at least the possibility that they are the records of an exultant brush with nothingness."[23] Lindsay completes this eschatological rehearsal of Genesis, and its aftermath, by refining Robert Melville's insight into a reaffirmation of life, of the Creation, and of the earthly idyll. "The Castle," he concludes, "is certainly coming up out of the deluge, reborn or purified as the earthly paradise."[24]

The differences of opinion over the final effect of the Turnerian subject and manner illustrated here – creation before or after? paradise lost or regained? ante or postdiluvian? – reflect the ambiguity of Turner's attitude toward nature and the idea of a paradisal earth. Ceaseless primal chaos contrasts with the static beauty of country and city dreaming in perpetual sunlight. The symbolic action of the deluge, as both an end and a new beginning, obsessed his imagination. As early as 1802 he criticized Nicolas Poussin's painting of *The Deluge* (1660–64, Louvre) for being too placid, the water rising imperceptibly and almost peacefully. In 1804–05, in youthful competition with Poussin, he painted his own version of *The Deluge* (Tate Gallery), which portrays a wild ocean storm of water, rain, and waves obliterating horizon and sky, and engulfing trees, rocky promontories, and land.[25] In less thematically explicit ways, in paintings dealing with other subjects, for example, *Snow Storm: Hannibal and His Army Crossing the Alps* (1812, Tate Gallery), there is often implicit in his orchestration of form and atmosphere the paradigmatic pattern of the engulfing flood and of the unstable earth.

Both real water and ethereal vapor bathed the *locus paradisus*, posing a constant threat to human hopes, at every stage of Turner's visual pilgrimage in the second half of his life, until the earth all but vanished under an inundation of light and color. In fact, Turner's tendency to portray the cataclysmic propensities of nature on a cosmic scale increased with age, becoming most pronounced in his late colorist style. One has only to name some of the most famous: *Slavers Throwing Overboard the Dead and Dying – Typhoon Coming On* (1840, Museum of Fine Arts, Boston), *Snow Storm – Steam-Boat off a Harbour's Mouth Making Signals in Shallow Water, and Going by the Lead* (1842, National Gallery), *Rain, Steam and Speed – The Great Western Railway*, and *Sunrise, with Sea Monsters* (c. 1845, Tate Gallery) – to notice how many are concentrated in the last decade of Turner's life. The dynamic and disruptive forces of nature are also associated by Turner in these years with the iron and steam products of the Industrial Revolution, which still aroused in Victorians ambivalent reactions. Two famous instances are the locomotive in *Rain, Steam and Speed* and the smoke belching tugboat in *The Fighting Téméraire, Tugged to Her Last Berth*.

Turner's conception of nature as an unpredictable field parallels his development of a painterly syntax which distinguishes his impressions of its elemental energies from his depictions of urban harmony and repose. In the early years of the century he carefully arranged his planes in horizontals, verticals, and diagonals, following the order, among others, of Richard Wilson, and perhaps of Nicolas Poussin, in such historical epics as *The Fifth Plague of Egypt* (1800, Herron Art Museum, Indianapolis) and *The Tenth Plague of Egypt* (1802, Tate Gallery).[26] In both, though, architecture interestingly occupies a central place, the lines of the buildings placed parallel to those of the hills, with light from the sky focused on the planes of the city while the hills lie shrouded in shadows. Single-point perspective, which underlies diagonal structuring, assumes a fixed and completed world. And it is significant that Turner habitually uses this composition in his depictions of Venice even in the 1840s. At the same time, from about 1812 onwards, beginning with *Hannibal and His Army Crossing the Alps*, Turner increasingly rejects the classical composition of diagonals and pyramids in favor of dynamic spirals and gyres to render the titanic energies of nature. Such late paintings as *Shade and Darkness – The Evening of the Deluge* (1843, Tate Gallery) and *Light and Colour – The Morning After the Deluge* (1843, Tate Gallery) are organized radically according to this plan, their vortexes of color and swirls of bubble pictographs presenting a universe in perpetual process of creation and of dissolution.

The circle, of course, can and has traditionally symbolized a perfect and complete universe. Eighteenth-century literature influential on Turner's thought is full of this use of the image. The Newtonian cosmos set the stage with its planets, its "mazy wheels," locked into their orbits. The Thomsonian universe followed a subsidiary form of this cosmic organization – as did those of the Romantic poets, especially Shelley and Keats – in adopting as a structural device the circular, closed system of the cycle of the seasons. And one hardly need be reminded of the metaphoric extension of the circumambient into religious conceptions of the soul's yearning for completion of its circular pilgrimage from temporal to eternal abodes. Similarly, the balanced stasis of the Virgilian pastoral scene perfectly suited the age's cosmic fixation. Coleridge, Wordsworth, and Constable all clung to a vision of the perfect life, reflective of their eighteenth-century commitment to a meaningful universe, in the teeth of their half-conscious acceptance of a contrary metaphysic of dynamic process. And Turner himself painted the self-contained worlds of country estates, like the placid rural scene of *Somer-Hill, near Tunbridge, the Seat of W. F. Woodgate, Esq.* (1811, National Gallery of Scotland) and *Roby Castle, The Seat of the Earl of Darlington* (1818, Walters Art Gallery, Baltimore), often by commission, until his first Italian tour.

Eventually, though, Turner, like his predecessors Fuseli and Piranesi, shied away from conventional treatments of space. His vision was more captivated by the cosmic sublime than by the Virgilian pastoral, which after all is limited to a measurable piece of real estate, while the sublime reaches to encompass the very place of God. Fuseli has his actors play out their drama against an undifferenti-ated background that lifts them off the terrestrial mundane and deposits them in a Stygian non-space. Piranesi in his *Carceri* series shows endless rooms, stairways, and ramps leading always to more of the same. The space enclosed is indefinable. Neither laterally nor perpendicularly can the limits be determined. Turner similarly seldom closes his vortexes of color. Whether waves or clouds, they curl and swirl in dramatic open forms always in process of expanding or contracting.

Not in a natural, or garden, setting nor in the continuing drama of nature but in classical cities, "Sun-girt" (Shelley, "Lines written among the Euganean Hills," 115) and set apart from the foreground human action, is where Turner sought the *locus paradisus*. Nor should we find his transference of attention from the kindly aspects of nature to the inexorable and destructive, and his shift in paradisal emphasis from enclosed garden to sea-girdled town, difficult to understand, since such changes in emphasis were reflective, in part at least, of the intellectual and cultural forces to which he was responsive during his lifetime. Turner was trained as a topographical artist to appreciate the beauty of the urban scene as part of the earthly setting. His earliest drawing dated with certainty is a copy of an engraving of a view of Oxford, signed "W. Turner, 1787." And in 1789 Turner *père* was hanging his then fourteen-year old son's drawings of London scenes in his barber shop. In the early 1790s when he and Thomas Girtin (1775–1802) were in the employ of Dr. Thomas Monro, copying watercolors by the landscapist John Robert Cozens (1752–99), Turner was also assiduously doing architectural views and church interiors in the topographical manner with great accuracy of detail. He showed eight watercolors at the Royal Academy Exhibition in April 1795, one hung in the "Antique Academy," and the other seven hung together, and as their titles indicate, mostly in the prevailing descriptive mode: *Marford Mill, West Entrance of Peterborough Cathedral, Transept of Tintern Abbey.*[27] As late as 1809, with the panoramic view of *London (from Greenwich)* (Tate Gallery), Turner still clung to topographical conventions. Somewhat timid of letting his vague depic-tion of the city of London on the distant horizon, its spreading rooftops a blur beyond the curve of the Thames, stand alone, as the announced subject, as he would have done in his late manner, he has interposed between the viewer and this "murky veil" (*Turner Poems*, p. 80) the architectural distraction of the Greenwich Royal Marine and Navy Buildings in the middle distance, which are delineated with careful detail. In the opinion of many, truth-to-nature was the primary *raison d'être* of the landscape artist. That assumption lies behind Ruskin's defence of the truth of Turner's skies and water in Volume I (1843) of *Modern Painters*, and behind Ruskin's own imaginatively limited but fastidiously delineated drawings of flora, sculpture, and architecture. At their best Turner's cityscapes fuse the two perspectives of fidelity to topological precision and compulsion to a more visionary view of the earthly abode into a moving witness of the primal human loss.

Furthermore, the depiction of antique civilizations held a high place in art in the second half of the eighteenth century. The archaeological studies of Giambattista Piranesi (1720–78), in particular, gave impetus to this taste in England. Piranesi's intoxication with the majestic grandeur of Rome's past and his highly subjective treatment of space[28] anticipates Turner's fascination with the festive beauty of Venice in decline and his audacious handling of form as an exploration of atmospheric effects. This future development is already visible in a watercolor of *Old London Bridge* (Tate Gallery) painted about 1797. The masonry of the bridge's irregular Norman arches and piers is lovingly limned, as are such vignettes of city life as a crowded hansom traversing the bridge, figures huddled in shadow or sunning themselves on the stone bases of the piers, and a towboat tied up at one. At the same time, the hard angularity of the usual architectural drawing is softened by light, which suffuses the sky, turns the oily swirls of the river into molten liquid, and glows through an arch of the bridge. The translucent atmosphere lessens the density of the stone bridge. Along with the river-level viewpoint and the irregular soaring of the bridge's arches the diffusion of light gives the bridge the effect of floating on the wooden pilings belted round its piers. Through the arches are visible the vaults of another bridge and both embankments of the river, the shadowy buildings of one side diaphanous and insubstantial, while those of the other side gleam white in the sunshine, rising from the water in tall and congested vivacity, windows etched by shadow and walls reflected in the shining water.

Here, at the outset of his career, Turner reveals a landscape of the mind, with its tensions and ambiguities, which will be mirrored some twenty years later in the Venice he discovers drowsing over past greatness in its Adriatic lagoon. Ruskin makes the explicit comparison in his essay "The Two Boyhoods" in the fifth volume of *Modern Painters*, in portraits of the boyhoods of Turner and Giorgione. To an artistic boy sensitive to historical precedents, who grew up within walking distance of the Thames "with its stranded barges and glidings of red sail, dearer to us than . . . Venetian lagoon,"[29] and who came of professional age in the years of England's triumphs over Napoleonic France, London must have seemed indestructible, a fit successor to Venice. There were guarded moments of optimism, particularly for a few years at the beginning of the new century, when Turner exulted in his native city, seeing its "spires pierce the doubtful air, / As gleams of hope amidst a world of care" (*Turner Poems*, p. 80). A muddy administrative center of government in rural eighteenth-century England, London had become in Turner's lifetime the financial and industrial capital of the Western world, its busy river crowded with sails, its teeming populace absorbed by "Commercial care and busy toils" (*Turner Poems*, p. 80). In the catalogue description of *London (from Greenwich)* he appended a poem expressing cautious admiration for commerce. Other lines he wrote about 1808 on the "Silver Thames" reveal a similar sentiment (*Turner Poems*, p. 99). Both Venice and London were maritime cities, Venice "Ocean's child" (Shelley, "Lines written among the Euganean Hills" 116), London river nurtured. One was a monument to mercantilistic imperialism in the past, the other in the present. Both were built on the bedrock of its citizenry's liberty. First one, then both, function in Turner's mind as indices of certainty and of continuity in a world of human instability and natural flux.

At the same time Turner's native gloom was in constant contention with his Victorian dream of an urban paradise. As late as 1840 he could enlist his cynicism about "fallacious Hope" in condemnation of the slave trade, attaching to the picture *Slavers Throwing Overboard the Dead and Dying – Typhoon Coming On* lines of verse which sneer at entrepreneurship and conclude with the question, "Where is thy market now?" (*Turner Poems*, p. 86). Although he was prone early on in his career to couple the earthly paradise with the rise of cities and civilizations, he recognized with innate skepticism that cities can disappoint one's expectations, for they suffer from moral flatulence and inner decay like the humans who build them. "Fallacious Hope beneath the moon's pale crescent shone, / Dido listened to Troy being lost and won" (*Turner Poems*, p. 88) are the lines he sardonically appended to *Aeneas Relating His Story to Dido* (1850, Tate Gallery), one of his last paintings before his death, reminding us not only of Troy's destruction, but also of the cruel disillusionment of Dido's hopes and of the eventual rise and fall of Rome. Melancholy suffused Turner when he contemplated the deflection from duty and honor of an urban populace, and the consequent destruction of a great center of cultural and national identity. *Dido Building Carthage; or the Rise of the Carthaginian Empire* (1815, National Gallery) and *The Decline of the Carthaginian Empire* (1817, Tate Gallery) show both sides of Turner's imaginative grasp of the meaning of the city.

The former depicts a city of busy galleys, of maritime bustle along the water banks, and of marble villas, rotundas, and temples in process of construction. Under a golden sky the multi-storied, columned buildings and hanging gardens climb the steep North African coastline from the water's edge. All is bathed in a Claudian rosy hue. The tone is still one of high endeavor. Optimistic effort characterizes the scene. No display of opulence as yet disfigures the city; rather, industry and energetic resolution mark its every precinct. Placed in the context of the other Aeneas–Dido studies, *Dido Building Carthage* is a poignant statement of Turner's psychological drive for security and of his substitution of a higher destiny in his art for the lesser personal satisfactions of wife and family.[30] He considered it one of his best and stipulated in his will that it be hung along with his *Sun Rising Through Vapour* (1807, National Gallery, London) between two Claudes, *Seaport, with the Embarkation of the Queen of Sheba* (1648, National Gallery), and *The Marriage of Isaac and Rebekah* (commonly known as "The Mill," 1648), because he believed they complemented each other. Here he portrays Dido when her private desires coincided with her public duty, before the diversion of her love to Aeneas and his desertion to follow his own national destiny had rendered delusive the hopes of the city and its queen.

In *The Decline of the Carthaginian Empire*, the arrogance of Hannibal and the voluptuous decadence of the populace have completed the reversal of fortunes initiated by Dido's infatuation. But there is no pleasure taken in the decline. Turner mourns the demise of a great city, which he depicts from the same vantage point as in the earlier painting. Carthage is shown at the height of its opulence. Marble stairs now cover the sand and rock leading down to the water. Barges filled with pleasure seekers rush aimlessly about the lagoon. Elaborately carved and decorated structures rise tier on tier up the terraced hillsides. Crowds of men and women recline in vacant indolence about the embankment and the balconies of the palaces. The apparent power and plenitude are everywhere illusory, as is

26 Turner, *Dido Building Carthage*

hinted at also by the swaths of flowers which litter the pavement, by the discarded objects of revelry and public festivals that slither and coil among the debris, and by the yellow light of a setting sun which gilds the buildings in ephemeral gold. A gloss on the state of Turner's mind is contained in the verses on the delusive smile of Hope, from "The Fallacies of Hope," which he attached to the picture when he sent it to the Royal Academy in 1817.

The extent to which Turner thought in terms of the city as providing man with a perfect locus of paradise regained is revealed in the attraction the theme of Dido and the rise and fall of the Carthaginian empire had for him, which he conceptualized symbolically in the vigorous growth and supine decadence of a city. The continuing appeal of the theme is illustrated by the four Carthaginian pictures he showed in the next to last year of his life in the 1850 summer exhibition of the Royal Academy: *Mercury Sent to Admonish Aeneas* (1850, Tate Gallery), *Aeneas Relating His Story to Dido* (1850, Tate Gallery), *The Visit to the Tomb* (1850, National Gallery), and *The Departure of the Fleet* (1850, National Gallery).

If not Carthage, that erstwhile "city of hope" and failed earthly paradise which had succumbed to the temptations of personal desire, then which of the great cities Turner pictured satisfied a paradisal definition of order? Rome lingered on in its imperial ruins overshadowed by the Vatican; and London risked following in the steps of Carthage, its struggle with France analogous to Carthage's with Rome.[31] In its pride of sea power and its arrogance of mercantile might London appeared to be tempting the fates that visit with decay and disorder societies which have lost the knack and the will to pursue a life of high endeavor and ascetic taste; and the burning of the Houses of Parliament in October 1834 (depicted in Turner's 1835 painting of the same name [Cleveland Museum of Art], in which the sky and river are filled with the reflections of hellish red flames of destruction) is seen by Turner as a warning to England of what could be its fate.

Of all the places Turner was drawn to paint, Venice best fulfilled his need for a symbolic place of order. It had a past whose glory was still visible, still relatively intact, offering pictorially an image capturable on canvas. It was not only a city but also a part of the sea, which had never failed to kindle Turner's imagination. Historically, although diminished from its Renaissance grandeur, even from its twilight splendor of the eighteenth century, and now under Austrian rule where once it was its own proud ruler, its towers could still be seen in "the amber-coloured ether" of its "orient" skies, the waters of its lagoon offering haven and comfort from the shifting uncertainty of the "deep wide sea of Misery," as Shelley gratefully acknowledged. Thus, if the earthly paradise was impossible in its guise as garden, because of the corruption of human nature and the resultant imperfection of the physical world (not to mention accumulating evidence making the myth of a once perfect world ever more fabulous), this jeweled city basking in Mediterranean sun promised better. Turner clung to that illusion in the face of the obvious fact that cities too were the reflection of human virtues and vices, as the disappointing histories of Carthage and Rome attested. When he wished, though, he could concentrate his eyes on the appearance of things, glorying in a world of surfaces, light and color, while playing down the human dimension.[32]

Among urban centers Venice most directly accommodates in its structure and rule the contrary flux of nature, the ceaseless motion and frequent cataclysms of wave, wind, and rain. Ocean and seaport are binary parts of a world of confusion and system. So Shelley apostrophized Venice, in "Lines written among the Euganean Hills," and so Turner painted it. What seemed eternal freshness, in the excitement of his first discovery of the city, is revealed in two watercolors executed in 1819. In *San Giorgio from the Dogana, Venice: Sunrise* (British Museum) and *Venice, from Giudecca Looking East: Sunrise* (British Museum) the city lies low on the horizon shimmering in the mist, its multitude of white walls, domes, towers and pillars a long line of colored light beckoning the traveler to unveil its mysteries. In other pictures of this period, the city bustles with inexhaustible life. When one penetrates the mist and travels its canals one encounters the barges and gondolas of a busy port city, as in the watercolor *Venice: The Rialto* (1820, Indianapolis Museum of Art).

To move from that watercolor to an oil painting of the same scene *Grand Canal, Venice* (1837, Henry E. Huntington Library and Art Gallery) done fifteen years later is to enter a different city entirely – and to discover that more than one Venice occupied Turner's mental landscape. The Venice of the 1830s recalls the grandeur of its past greatness, but now arrested and unvarying, fixed in the amber of a golden sunlight and in the steady blue of a Mediterranean sky. The palaces lining the Grand Canal lean rigidly against each other, their windows blank, not only in the Huntington painting, but also in pictures like *Grand Canal, Venice* (1835, New York Metropolitan Museum of Art) and *Venice: The Dogana of San Giorgio Maggiore* (c. 1834, National Gallery of Art, Washington, D.C.). The gondolas and boats hang suspended in the water. A stillness pervades the city despite throngs of people on the quays and of crowded boats in the canals.

It is instructive to compare the 1820–21 watercolor and the 1837 Huntington Library oil painting, since both had as their source a pencil sketch made on Turner's first trip in 1819. In the watercolor the canal is securely contained on both sides by receding lines of wealthy merchants' and nobles' houses extending to the Rialto in the near middle distance. It is a city solid and reassuring. In the oil painting the angle of vision has shifted toward the right bank, lifting its buildings uncomfortably high in a ragged skyline to the Rialto now in the far distance. The houses tower above the masses of people gathered on the quay and on the boats. The eye moves restlessly back and forth from the Grimani palazzo to the Rialto, and up and down the canal, lighting on the undifferentiated sea of people who stand about everywhere for no apparent reason.[33] The tense, unresolved atmosphere with its impending undisclosed expectancy is not unlike that of *The Decline of the Carthaginian Empire*.

Although the rippling skyline of a city, rather than the rolling hills and meadows of the earthly landscape, best engaged Turner's paradisal vision, the fact is that by the 1830s, whether painting countryside, sea, or city, he betrays a tension between prophetic affirmation and negation of the world. For all the seeming brave activity and the glowing color tonality in which it is painted, the Venice of the 1830s maintains a tenuous hold on reality. Absent are the solid stone spans of Old London Bridge, built to carry the stream of London traffic for centuries. With wry understatement Rothenstein and Butlin have commented that Turner's vision here differs "from the on-the-whole topographically accurate Canaletto"; rather, like Piranesi, Turner makes us feel, however inadvertently, the precariousness of civilization.[34] Thus ironically has Turner harbored in his mind's eye more than perhaps he would have wished to admit of the taste of the time for the subject of the ruin of empires.

Given Turner's sense of Venice as a museum piece, more real in the images left by past artists than the crumbling stone, slack water, and rusty boats beheld by the eye in the present, it is not accidental that he was drawn in the late 1830s to pay tribute to his great topographical predecessors. In *Bridge of Sighs, Ducal Palace and Custom House, Venice: Canaletti Painting* (RA 1833, Tate Gallery), Turner introduced into the cityscape the eighteenth-century painter who had limned it so well and so precisely. Since the more romantic perceptions of Guardi (1712–93) might have been more congenial to Turner's own, it is as if, for the moment, Turner tried to comprehend the city through the eyes of a less self-critical, less subjective age. In another painting *Juliet and her Nurse* (1836, Private Collection) he removed Juliet from Verona in a burst of whimsey and installed her in the more imperial and mythic place of Venice. There is a double focus haunting these attempts of the 1830s to capture the time-haunted city in essential and actual terms simultaneously, one merging uneasily into the other.

Still, Venice remains a real city, its long history of exposure to both west and east visible in its facade; and Turner is moved at times to portray it in carefree mood, as in *Venice – Noon*; *Venice – Sunset, A Fisher*; *Venice, Evening, going to the Ball* and *Morning, returning from the Ball, St. Martino* (all exhibited 1845, Tate Gallery); and at other times in its continuing life struggle with a watery world, as in *Storm at Sunset, Venice* (1835, Fitzwilliam Museum, Cambridge) and *Storm in the Piazza* (1835, National Gallery of Scotland).

The Venice painted in the 1840s, contrariwise, is an unreal city, a product more of Turner's transfiguring imagination than of his recording eye. In such pictures as *The Dogano, San Giorgio, Citella, from the Steps of the Europa*, entitled *The Giudecca* (1842, Tate Gallery) and *Venice: Maria della Salute* (1844, Tate Gallery) he concentrates as much on the reflections in the water as on the actual churches, houses, and boats. The object and its mirrored image blurred into one vaporous whole, the city appears to be absorbing the sea into the porous striations of its stone, becoming one in the slow accumulation of centuries with the sea it annually weds. In painting after painting from this decade – *The Grand Canal* (1840–45, Tate Gallery), *Procession of Boats with Distant Smoke, Venice* (c. 1845, Tate Gallery), *Venice – Maria della Salute* (1844, Tate Gallery), *Approach to Venice* (1844, National Gallery of Art, Washington, D.C.) – the city has all but vanished. Once awash in the morning light of Eden before it faded back among the ordinary days of man, it is now translated into a liquified light that is its final element.

27 Turner, *Venice: The Rialto*
28 Turner, *The Grand Canal, Venice*

It is a city celebratory of death as much as of life. The accent is on the end of the day, as in the watercolor *Sunset, Returning from Torcello* (c. 1835, British Museum). The city, a line of orange brown, has all but disappeared beneath the horizon. Only a few pilings and the bulk of a boat, like so much flotsam, disturb the slack turquoise waters. Such also is the symbolic import of *The Sun of Venice Going to Sea* (1843, Tate Gallery) with its puns embedded in the title. Freighted with a human cargo, *The Sun of Venice* sails past silent clusters of boats into an unknown and uncertain future. Behind it shimmers a mirage of the city, diffused in the reflected light of sky and sea, and rendered explicitly unreal by transfer as a reflection onto the sail of the ship. Lines from "Fallacies of Hope" printed in the catalogue of the Royal Academy when Turner exhibited the picture direct our attention to the painful irony of life:

> Fair shines the morn, and soft the zephyrs blow,
> Venezia's fisher spreads his painted sail so gay,
> Nor heeds the demon that in grim repose
> Expects his evening prey.[35]

Similarly, the Venice of *San Benedetto, looking towards Fusina* (exhibited 1843, Tate Gallery)[36] is a funereal city, despite the chromatically hot colors, the high

29   Turner, *San Benedetto, looking towards Fusina*

intensity yellows and blues Turner used with avidity in his late pictures. In the upper half of the canvas, a fiery twilight sky of liquid yellow swallows up the city in a sea of light spreading fan-like to a vanishing point on the horizon. In the lower half a brownish yellow lagoon reaches diagonally toward the same still point. On the water to the left, like barges with ghostly cargoes to be ferried across the River Styx, sit four shadowy gondolas freighted with people. They are preceded by the sable silhouette of a fifth gondola moving slowly outward in the center of the picture. In the year prior to Turner's visit to Venice in 1819, Shelley and Byron had likened the black painted gondolas of the city to a "funereal bark" (*Julian and Maddalo*, 88) and "a coffin clapt in a canoe" (*Beppo*, xix); and so Turner pictures them after some twenty years and two further visits. They are ships of hope turned like *The Sun of Venice* into Sunset Ships of doom. To the right more barges with their human cargoes await silently their turn to make the passage toward the obliterating light at the convergence of sea and sky. The mood of the scene is hushed, somber.

Turner's acclamation of the earthly paradise in its nineteenth-century avatar of the seaport has merged imperceptibly with its contrary *topos* of infernal permanence, to create an Atlantean world in which sea and sky, the city and its watery reflection, life and death, unite in a seamless continuum, where the final act of submersion, or evaporation, ends less in nothingness than in a Platonic "one" that knows no transience.[37]

II

Tennyson's Celestial Camelot

THE ROMANTICS had their visionary cities. The two most integral to a
millenarian notion of paradise renewed are Jerusalem – the earthly London in its
mythic and eternal form – that the husbandry of the sons and daughters of the
Eternal Man (Albion) foreshadows at the end of *Jerusalem* and its adjunct
Golgonooza, the city of art which Los builds in Book 2 of the poem as a place of
refuge until Jerusalem herself can be reclaimed. A prospect different in kind from
Blake's is Turner's golden cityscape, the bejeweled and vaporous Mediterranean
(and Italian) counterpart of his stolid English (and Dutchified) celebration of the
Thames riverside, the Fen country, and the mountains and lakes of Wales and
present-day Cumbria. Other Romantics captivated by "golden cities" of their
imagination were Wordsworth for whom London to his boyish fancy before he
saw it belonged with the fabulous metropolises of antiquity (cf. *Prelude*, VII, 81–
90), and Shelley for whom the city was one of the repositories of revolutionary and
regenerative power (the subtitle of his first version of *The Revolt of Islam* was
"The Revolution of the Golden City").

In all their eyes – whether lake country poet, Londoner, or down country
dweller – these mythic metropolises, "Gift of Imagination's holy power," merged
into an actual London dominated by "The huge majestic Temple of St. Paul."
"Pure, silent, solemn, beautiful,"[1] it "served as virtual synecdoche for the city"
to three centuries of English.[2] Its dome rose above the cityscape, and like a sacred
mountain pre-empted the place where heaven and earth were joined.

Despite such reverent symbolic resonances, the city occupied a distinctly
troubled and ambivalent place in the Romantics' view of reality. In their daily and
poetic lives it was either an image of the diseased mind or of the reclaimed soul,
either a Bedlamic superimposition on a serene landscape or the sky-bound
extension of an already divinized countryside. One thinks of Wordsworth's
(specifically the Solitary's) Augustinian city that rears its towers out of the vapors
and clouds of a sunny day, following an all-night storm, in *The Excursion*, a
"Fantastic pomp of structure without name, / In fleecy folds voluminous,
enwrapped" (II, 859–60). Qualifying his human awe before the vision of this
"mighty city" of Miltonic "Clouds, mists, streams, watery rocks and emerald
turf" is the Solitary's disquieting characterization of it as a "*wilderness* of

building" (*The Excursion*, II, 835, 853, 836, my italics). More explicit is the ambivalence of Coleridge and Keats toward their architectural fantasies, prescient of the complex attitude the Victorians were to develop toward their urbanized civilization. Coleridge's wariness of earthly paradise prompts him to concentrate its essence in the pleasure dome of Kubla Khan; and his profound unease with this "miracle of rare device" ("Kubla Khan," 34) leads him to question its permanence: to dream of its future destruction by war and to minimize the substantiality of its stones by re-erecting it out of song. Keats similarly constructs for the love union of Lycius and Lamia a marvelous palace whose "faery-roof" is supported by "A haunting music" ("Lamia," II, 122–23); and like all things reliant on magic it evaporates under the analytic stare of Apollonius and the hoarse skepticism of the vulgar "herd" (II, 150) in the noisy street. Nor did Turner's cityscapes of the 1840s escape entirely his profound grasp of the ephemerality of things. Disappearing under the erosion of light and time they are testimonies to the conviction that nothing is lasting, nothing has substantiality. There was also the Biblical-mythological identification of some cities as recipients of God's wrath for being centers of evil. A deep-seated religious revulsion toward urban centers was felt at a residual level of the Romantic consciousness. Having the unenviable claim of "most often cited" is the whorish Babylon. It provides Blake with the fallen counterpart to Jerusalem; and it is invoked by Byron when through Juan's eyes he looks at London ("mighty Babylon," *Don Juan II*, xxiii).

Still, cities – the community of humans and the architectural assemblage of forms that give them their actual and mythic importance – have always had their advocates; and in the early decades of the nineteenth century they were increasingly enlisted as an expression of the ideal civilized life, culminating in Ruskin's grand moral dialectic between Gothic structures and Renaissance facades. In the eyes of the aristocrats of the eighteenth century their great baroque, Palladian, and classical country houses offered symbolically more than an earthly domicile set in the grandly landscaped gardens through which they circuitously pursued their way back to lost paradise. Nineteenth-century merchants and captains of industry were to translate this rural idyll into ever more insistently architectural terms – and by implication into the earthly City of God.

Minaret-capped towers, dizzying pinnacles, and conical domes of a perfect, albeit somewhat exotic, medieval past exercised the imaginations of Victorians well into the second-half of the century. The proud roofline of Gilbert Scott's St. Pancras Hotel (1867–74) built alongside St. Pancras railway station (1862), all gables, chimneys, towers, and spires silhouetted against the sky, speaks boldly of amalgamating a half-remembered, half-documented, half-fantasied past with the industrial iron-and-steam age present. It is a solid sign of man's Godlike mastery of the physical world. Then there are the Houses of Parliament (1836–52) by Sir Charles Barry, with the aid of that supreme gothicist A. W. N. Pugin. Antiphonal to the rhythm of its columnared and fenestrated walls are its spires and pinnacled towers, bravely festooned with metal bunting and flags as at a medieval tournament.

The reason for all this exoticism is not easily explained. The medley of industrial and medieval can be attributed, in part, to an architectural philosophy of historical eclecticism; to an antipathy for the baroque because of its associations with Roman Catholicism and with political tyranny; and to a religious and socio-aesthetic revival of a taste for the Gothic. Such fabled structures also supplied a need of the age for symbols of spiritual order and of perfection. They represented the unexamined faith of engineers and architects, of businessmen and politicians, raised to a kind of iron-and-stone reality, that in the nineteenth-century industrial city of men could be realized the earthly City of God.

In his long career Alfred, Lord Tennyson (1809–92) shared with his fellow Victorians most of the aspirations and disillusions about the holy garden and the heavenly city which characterize the period. One of his earliest associations of the heavenly city with a real city occurs in his Chancellor's Prize-poem "Timbuctoo" (1829). The half-mythical, half-historical status of that fabled center, whose remains were an object of searches in the 1820s, epitomizes Tennyson's embodiment of the unattainable in the shape of legendary bricks and walls. The spires, rooftops, and towers that make up the Tennysonian city are neither exactly mundane nor spiritual. They lead a shadowy existence analogous to the nineteenth-century fate of Eden, whose mountain-top site, once extolled as historical fact by Milton, was now lumped with the mythical islands of the Hesperides and of the Lotos Eaters. For Tennyson neither the old garden nor the new city quite answered to a prescription for healing the ancient wound separating humans from the divine world. Arnold lamented that he and his confreres wandered between two worlds, one dead and the other not yet having struggled into existence. Tennyson extended the limited historical context of Arnold's reference to include a sense of cosmic exile from both the eternal and mortal worlds. So Sir Bedivere felt as he watched the funeral barge of King Arthur float away until it "Looked one black dot against the verge of dawn," and then turned to resume his daily round, a man rudely awaking to a bleak day without illusion, while he yet half continued to live amidst the ruined dream of Camelot and "the true old times" ("Morte d'Arthur" [1833–34], 271, 229).

No poem more unequivocally asserts this view than "The Lady of Shalott" (1832, 1842 much revised). With it, at the outset of his career, Tennyson offered his tribute as a young poet to Thomson's *Castle of Indolence* (1748), and thus, like Coleridge, De Quincey, Wordsworth, Keats, and a host of earlier eighteenth-century writers, accepted Thomson's recognition of the special state of mind in which poetic creation begins. The Lady of Shalott secreted away from the world on her island within the "Four gray walls, and four gray towers" (I, 15), of her castle represents Tennyson's extreme acceptance of the need for the inviolate imagination to pursue its integral mission in silence and isolation. There, the Lady "weaves by night and day / A magic web with colours gay" (II, 37–38), her only contact with outside life a mirror on which is reflected the ceaseless traffic up and down the highway and river. Only when she disrupts this routine, lured from the mirror by the flashing image of Sir Lancelot to look directly at him, is the magical perfection of her life destroyed. Exposure to the sunny beauty of flower, field, and city ironically brings on her heart a mortal chill and on her blood a thickening freeze.

We need not linger over the conventional reading of the poem: that it memorializes the onset of Tennyson's lifelong struggle to settle a personal and artistic dilemma about the role of the poet and the nature of the creative process. Nor need we struggle with the conundrum this dilemma points to. If isolation is a *sine qua non* for the development of art, then how is eventual sterility staved off? And if art is the product of an alienation which derives from the opposition of the creative imagination to society, then how can the poet periodically assume his public role without loss of that tension?[3]

Problematical is the degree to which the Lady of Shalott's tower retreat held for Tennyson traditional paradisal meanings. Medieval and Renaissance iconography equated the Blessed Virgin not only with the fruitful garden but also with the house of God often depicted within the garden enclosure. All three paradigms – especially as subsumed in Mary's person – symbolized God's dispensation of Grace by way of his Church. In this context, the lancet windows of a Gothic tower, when depicted, were emblematic of the illuminating light of the Christian faith. A careful distinction was made, however, between the soul with its prospect of eternal life and the body, which suffers the curse of time and was associated with the natural world outside the garden and church walls.[4] The Lady of Shalott's strategy for maintaining the pretense that this mortal gulf does not exist is to assimilate the "Shadows of the world" (II, 48) reflected in her mirror into the art of her loom. In this she is not unlike other tenuous spirits of the age, for example the hero of Sydney Dobell's poem *Balder* (1853), who took his cue from Byron's Manfred and lived above the earth-bound in an "old tower gloomy and ruinous" (I, i) the better to challenge the divine edict against humans setting themselves up as gods. In such retreats they alternately luxuriated in morbid self-analysis or elevated their "Trances of thought and mountings of the mind" (*Prelude*, I, 20) into the serene empyrean in vain search after visitations of eternity.

The claustrophobic constriction of the Lady of Shalott's life is aptly rendered by Holman Hunt's painting *The Lady of Shalott* (1882–1905, Wadsworth Athenaeum, Hartford, Conn.). The picture was begun as a sketch in 1850, and elaborated into an illustration for Moxon's edition of Tennyson's *Poems* (1857), before undergoing more than one translation into oil at the end of the century (there is another version, oil on panel, *c.* 1889–92, City Art Galleries, Manchester). Within the octagonal brass frame on which is stretched the web of her weaving, the Lady stands, literally encircled by her effort to translate the shadows of fallen earth into an autonomous spiritual form. It is not insignificant in this regard that the pictures (more precisely icons) on the wall of her tower room include (in the Moxon illustration) a Christ on the cross. In the Wadsworth

30   Holman Hunt, *The Lady of Shalott*

Athenaeum painting one oval picture depicts Hercules (typologically a prefiguration of Christ) and the other the Christ child. They represent surely Hunt's placement of the poem within a Christian frame of reference. The Lady's charmed encirclement by the ideal forms of her own creation extends to her being wrapped round by the skeins of her yarn in an iconographic merger of her person symbolically with the images taking shape on the loom. Her outer skirt is hiked up in swirls around her knees and her hair spreads out in waves like a massive halo. Placed inside the frame with her, as if her whole life transpired there, is a combination table with teapots and candelabra. Most of the woven part of the warp and weft is circular in shape as well, with balls of yarn dangling from the ends of the strings. Behind the Lady hangs a circular mirror in which can be glimpsed Sir Lancelot on his horse beyond shadowy Gothic arches.

This description in no way exhausts the details by which Hunt has reiterated the paradigmatic enclosed world of the Lady. In his pictorial interpretation of Tennyson's poem, Hunt pinpointed a basic difference of attitude between the early Romantics and his and Tennyson's contemporaries. Whereas both generations accepted the fact of an expanding universe, the Romantic's expectation of change remained optimistic, while the Victorian's turned pessimistic. Coleridge at times seems to seek in the paradisal bower a retreat from the cares and demands of the world of domestic and practical affairs; but even at its most exclusive, as in the walled garden of Xanadu, the enclosure is for him a comprehensive totality, containing softly contoured garden, mazy river, angular fathomless chasm, icy caverns, and pleasure dome in which is heard the mingled measure of fountain and cave, of indolence and savagery, harmony and disorder. Xanadu represents a vatic attempt to encompass the extremes of life rather than an aesthetic effort to filter out disagreeable parts through the exercise of art. In a heuristic sense, the circle symbolized for the Romantics less a fixed and restrictive whole than an organism growing into ever more inclusive unities. This ceaseless act is at the heart of Coleridge's effort to understand and to embrace the world of experience. In a moment of self-revelation in his notebooks, when describing his mode of conversation as an uninterrupted issue of sound from his mouth, he seizes wittily on the trope of expanding circular waves caused by an agitation of water: like the waves his thoughts

go on from circle to circle till I break against the shore of my Hearers patience, or have my Concentricals dashed to nothing by a Snore – that is my ordinary mishap.

(*CN*, II, 2372)

Contrariwise, Tennyson saw life as a "relentless series of cycles" alleviated only at those infrequent moments in time when an individual or people has the will to accept the divine imperative of God's providence. In fact, in the early 1830s Tennyson and the Apostles, a Cambridge group of moral aesthetes, had only disdain for the idea of inevitable progress. The rise and fall of civilizations argued rather, in their eyes, a recurrent pattern in which the collective spirit of a society as free agent worked the providential and putative divine will. History was accordingly an "organic growth arranging itself in epochs and repeating itself in cycles." So Schopenhauer had argued: "Throughout and everywhere the true symbol of nature is the circle because it is the schema or type of recurrence."[5] One emblematic sense of the circle for Romantics and Victorians was a vortex or a spiral, or, as in the instance just quoted from Coleridge, an ever-expanding wave. The allegiance of the Romantics to this paradigm of reality, however, was secured by its being benignly structured in the expectant form of expansion and growth. The famous description, in *Milton* (15:21–35; E,108–09), of the vortexes of perception epitomizes the key position the image had from Blake to Turner[5a] in the conceptualization of a material world opening into a spiritual one. To Tennyson and his generation – the sanguine evolutionary claims of *In Memoriam* (1850) notwithstanding – this circle of repetitive change, given the general skepticism, appeared just as likely to lead to constriction and decay. In his own memorial appraisal at mid-century, Arnold refers to his age as an "iron time / Of doubts, disputes, distractions, fears" ("Memorial Verses" [1850], 43–44), a distressing thought brought vividly home to him by the death of Wordsworth, the occasion of these verses. In 1852, Arnold notes in some additional elegaic verses that Wordsworth had grown "old in an age he condemned / . . . looked on the rushing decay / Of the times which had sheltered his youth," and

> Felt the dissolving throes
> Of a social order he loved.
>
> ("Youth of Nature," 28–32)

Eventually, Tennyson was to explore the resultant structure of feeling in *Idylls of the King*, a poem whose completed sequence Jerome H. Buckley has called "the most trenchant and best sustained treatment of social decline in Victorian poetry."[6] In *Idylls* he was to acknowledge the bleak historical likelihood that the civic enclosure as symbolized by the brotherhood of knights seated at the Table Round was unable to hold against the external forces of disintegration or against the internal resistance to discipline, because of the counter debilitating process of material ease that is the by-product of civilization. Worse, modulation of the sacred trust of the knights into an hysterical quest for a glimpse of the Holy Grail accelerated the process of entropy. The dispersal of the knights in this mad cause is inspired by a vision of Sir Percivale's sister, who binds Sir Galahad to the same "deathless passion" ("The Holy Grail," 163) with a plait of her hair wound about him as a sword belt. He in turn infects Sir Percivale and the rest. By the time Tennyson finished the *Idylls* he had come to realize that the civic enclosure was as readily pervaded by dread as imbued with spiritual promise.

But before Tennyson arrived at that public acknowledgement of the seemingly pointless ebb and flow of human activity and of the instability of institutions and the unreliability of people, he tested the earthly City of God as conceived ideally by the artistic imagination and as teased into possibility by industrial and technological magic. From the tension of a static and bounded paradise in antithesis to an evolving organic earth, which the Romantics resolved by redefining paradise as equivalent to and indistinguishable from the natural world, he resolutely placed the ideal environs of the "tower-encircled" (Thomson, "Autumn," 114) palace of art in opposition to nature with its Darwinian terrors and in opposition to the busy urban work-a-day with its utilitarian practicalities. For, as Hunt's painting of *The Lady of Shalott* illustrates, there was a way to escape the depressing imprisonment of cyclical history. That was to deny the dizzying cycles of change with the fixed and complete system of art. Arnold imagines Goethe in despair at "Europe's dying hour" as saying, "The end is everywhere, / Art still has truth, take refuge there" ("Memorial Verses," 27–28). Hesitantly endorsed by Tennyson and his contemporaries, the idea gained in attraction as the century wore on, receiving finally a kind of artistic benediction in the paintings of Whistler and in the aesthetics of Pater.

That the impracticalities of this restrictive act were not lost on Tennyson's generation is amply confirmed by Hunt's interpretation of "The Lady of Shalott." Yet the alternatives seemed to Tennyson no less unrealistic. He imagines Oenone watching her lovely forests disappear at the vindictive command of the gods, until her "green valley" and "green hill" were little more than desert, which she interprets as one more arbitrary instance of the tenuousness of the human claim to leafy paradise ("Oenone," 203–30); and, contrariwise, he sees Tithonus "at the quiet limit of the world" roaming disconsolately the "ever-silent spaces" of Aurora's eastern "gleaming halls of morn," an aging immortal captive in the marble palace of a goddess ("Tithonus," 7–10). Tennyson's need to believe in some kind of ideal abode – with its compulsive insistence that the ancient rift between human and divine was not irrevocable – led him in another poem of the same period, "The Palace of Art" (1832, 1842 much revised), to essay his most elaborate translation of Western civilization into a microcosm of the terrestrial paradise. Here, art becomes with ruthless logic the building block of paradise.

No poem of Tennyson's better qualifies as a Bible for the Pre-Raphaelites and the Aesthetes of the *fin de siècle* in its reduction of the organic to a moralistic aesthetic. It stands as a *media via* from the Romantic identification of paradise with a beloved locale, *spiritus loci*, at the beginning of the century to the aesthete's stand at the end of the century on an art that was above the changeful circumstances of nature and hence closest to the static perfection of a super reality. It occupies the midway point in a tradition that traces the progress of the paradisal pilgrim step by step from Blake for whom art is a *means* to Eden, and Golgonooza the city of art its earthly avatar; to Coleridge for whom art translates with as equal congeniality as nature his vision of the garden of Xanadu – its pleasure dome, encircling walls, ordered privacy, and pervasive incense;[7] to Whistler for whom harmonious arrangements of grey, silver, and gold were tidily superior in their abstract patterns of shape and color to nature's untended vagaries.

In a discussion of the evolution of paradise in the Western tradition from "primeval Oriental scene" to modern urban idyll, E. S. Shaffer describes the half-way place it had become by the early nineteenth century:[8]

In Gessner's poem [*The Death of Abel*], we find the ancient city-kingdom described at the point of its Biblical origin: the settlement built by Adam and Eve after their expulsion from Eden. We are shown the still lovely landscape of a holy mountain, reminiscent of Eden, still visited by spirits, yet new and bleak, a wholly human settlement, a raw stockade barely maintained against the wilderness, an altar visited as much in despair as in reverence. Adam and Eve echo their situation, wonderfully combining their original patriarchal dignity, simplicity and virtue with new labours, plaints, and pains. Gessner with great success and delicacy created a world half original paradise, half fallen nature.

Just this landscape, combining still-remembered paradise, wilderness, enclosed city, and cultivated court, is captured in "Kubla." City and country, rural yet populous, idyllic yet threatening, holy yet secular, sacred yet fallen, court and cot – it is tempting to see the stereotypes of the eighteenth century merging into those that will dominate the nineteenth. Just for this moment, in this exotic setting, they exist simultaneously, and express a permanent condition of man.

In the Biblical poems of the eighteenth century, this primeval Oriental scene recurs in a dazzling variety of forms. "Eden" was an immensely diversified scene, a mobile location, not merely of the Creation and the Fall, but of that characteristically eighteenth-century *topos*, the founding state of civilization in general, the centre of *Urmonotheismus*, archetypal monotheism. Typically, as in Gessner, the scene was paradise displaced, paradise already lost though still visible, paradise beset by the ambiguities of human culture. Only with the Fall could civilization begin and develop. Eden had taken on new significance for a century that liked to believe in the progress of civilization and yet profoundly knew its corruption.

"The Palace of Art" takes the gradual westernizing and urbanizing of a new paradise one step onward in its cultural metamorphosis from natural garden to civilized metropolis to decorative abstraction. For all its fervid projection of a symbolic structure of aesthetic order, as imagined in architectural terms, the poem also embraces moral and social orders. Not only does the Palace echo the melodious pleasure dome of Xanadu but it anticipates the dedicated community of Camelot. At a literal level of allusion, the four courts of the Palace are a loving recreation of Trinity College, Cambridge, an enclave of noble humans devoted to contemplation of the good, the true, and the beautiful. In one another's room within its enclosing courtyards the Apostles treated the poem with special esteem, discussing it, and expanding its lists of great names, as a codification of their thoughts and feelings. At a further remove from the public ways, the Palace ("this great mansion . . . So royal-rich and wide," 19–20) draws for its appurtenances on those great repositories of art and architectural glory the English country houses, "A haunt of ancient Peace" (88).[9] On a grander scale than the Lady of Shalott's selective weaving of reflections of the outside world, the speaker in "The Palace of Art" attempts to fix a total world in the permanent materials of her abode. On the walls of its "mimic heaven" is limned the whole "human tale" (146) since time began. Hints of an institutionalized paradise lurk uneasily just beneath the architectural thrust of the language. In the four courts, "East, West and South and North," the Soul has constructed a lasting Eden encloistered by rows of stone columns in the form of trees, "branched like mighty woods," and watered with "A flood of fountain-foam" issuing from the "golden gorge" of carved dragons (21–26). Thus are the "four currents" which once watered paradise symbolically transformed from natural springs rising unpredictably out of the earth into "four jets" whose flow can be thermostatically regulated (33).

Despite the effort to create in the palace a higher order than was to be found in the rural seat of the First Garden, the Soul's glory in her "God-like isolation" (197) is soon transmuted into "Deep dread and loathing of her solitude" (229). The palatial "perfect whole" (58) ultimately houses "dull stagnation" (245). "Shut up as in a crumbling tomb, girt round / With blackness as a solid wall" (273–74), the Soul "Lay there exilèd from eternal God" (263). That is the final irony. In creating a heaven out of durable stone and unchanging art the maker finds she has banished her soul to a "dreadful eternity" which turns out to be an architectural mockery of paradise, like Urizen's petrification of the unfathomable intellectual flames of Eternity in his similar effort to realize "a joy without pain . . . a solid without fluctuation" (*Book of Urizen*, 4:10–11; E,70), and like John Martin's imaginative attempt some twenty-five years later to visualize the plains of Hell.

The punishment for human presumption of divine power, since Adam and Eve – and Lucifer before them – has been loss of paradise. And the Soul's fate is no less. Like Lucifer, and first man and woman, she falls, "Struck through with pangs of Hell," the "abysmal deeps" of her personality bared to "sore despair" (220–24). Tennyson's piling on of symbolic references at this climactic point in the poem causes the Palace to suffer some architectural ambiguity. It acquires along with the precincts of Hell a few harrowing prophetic reminders of Babylon. The Soul begins to find written on her Palace walls the words, "Mene, mene" (227). All this is too much for her. Rather than risk destruction of her lovely Palace, as did Belshazzar that of Babylon, she elects to leave. Preferable in her eyes is to share the exile of Adam and Eve, sentenced to dwell henceforth eastward among the sons and daughters of man in "that dark world" (33) Tithonus glimpses nostalgically through partings of the clouds from his lonely security in the empty halls of Aurora. The Soul's voluntary decision to depart, however, is made with the reservation that she will eventually return, an intention more justifiable than Tithonus, or Adam and Eve, had the luxury of supposing. As she departs for a "cottage in the vale" (itself a version of the earthly paradise humbler than the heavenly palace to be sure but a stereotype of it nonetheless for the age), her last words are, "'Yet pull not down my palace towers,'"

> 'So lightly, beautifully built;
> Perchance I may return with others there
> When I have purged my guilt.'   (291–96)

The Soul speaks here for Tennyson probably as much as for herself. He was to return to the same essential setting twenty-five years later in the *Idylls of the King*, this time enlarged to a civic paradise nobler than a selfish retreat for one.

In "The Hesperides," published in 1832 but contemporaneous in composition with "Timbuctoo," Tennyson had glanced longingly at a mythological confirmation that the divine and the human sometimes conjoin. But his strange hesitancy when faced with the imaginative possession of the Hesperidean paradise was not promising. If in "The Lotos Eaters" he identifies paradise with opiate somnolence, even death, in "The Hesperides" he recoils from what turns out to be yet another self-imposed imprisonment: that of "Hesper, the dragon, and sisters three" (107) linked in "a golden chain" (106) about a golden apple hanging from a tree. The dominant assumption underlying these poems is that of "The Lady of Shalott" and "The Palace of Art." It is less a belief in man's inalienable right to sojourn in a pristine natural world than it is a conviction about the impermanence of human possession of it, here explored in terms of that most intangible and fragile of arts, music: that which keeps us tethered to this world yet cognizant of the other, and holds us enthralled with less than full possession of the fruit of paradise. For, contrary to the mythological sequence of events involving Hercules's successful invasion of the island, the poem's historical would-be intruder into this earthly paradise is Hanno the Carthaginian navigator, who is inexplicably denied the opportunity to land. He is allowed only the sensation as in a dream of hearing the Hesperidean song. As with Hanno – and the three daughters of Hesper – Tennyson sees humans as much lonely prisoners of the idea of earthly paradise as free agents in an ideal realm of their own creation. Captive Adams and Eves, we are doomed to sing bravely of "the apple holy and bright" (92) to the rattling accompaniment of our chains which link us to a primeval paradise, thus minimizing in blissful elegy the "golden chain" (107) that ever restricts us to the footage of one tree.

Ideally for Tennyson the perfect society was a social unit of one; but Eve without Adam, or Eden without a pair of lovers, is self-consuming. So the Lady of Shalott and the sole inhabitant of the Palace of Art discover to their unappeasable discontent, and so Ulysses's mariners and Hesper's daughters feel at subliminal levels below the beat of their pulses. Twenty-five years later, and ten years into his marriage which began at age forty-one, Tennyson began his most ambitious evaluation of a noble society of men and women committed to the promulgation of order and wisdom and good – of an earthly facsimile of paradise.

Written principally between 1859 and 1885 *Idylls of the King*[10] ends no less equivocally on a note of the sad impossibility of renewing even an analogue of paradise in the second half of the nineteenth century. John D. Rosenberg suspects that Tennyson was haunted by the passings "of a city, a civilization, of the earth itself."[11] "The old order changeth, yielding place to new" ("The Coming of Arthur," 508)[12] Arthur confidently informs his Knights at the beginning of his reign; but in Tennyson's mouth these words convey the pervasive Victorian lament for the passing of social stability and cultural value. Both cyclic and apocalyptic change conspire to destroy man's hubristic aspiration to a temperate and fixed station in life. Conceived out of an overwhelming sense of time and change, the *Idylls* at its heart presents an intrinsic denial of the terms – permanence and order – of Eden. The poem explores "the ambiguous results of man's quest for such values, and the disastrous effects of abandoning them."[13] The emotional longing was as strong as ever; but human nature militated against a return to the original innocence. Nor did industrial growth offer a panacea for man's fallen state. In his conception of Camelot, Tennyson draws on the myth of the city "as a sacred center, as *axis mundi* where heaven and earth intersect . . . supernatural in origin and supertemporal in duration."[14] But the myth fails to accord with reality. The city, and its technological ally the machine, are replicas of human aspirations and human deficiencies. An expression of man's faulty capabilities, the urban experience proved to be both providential and destructive.

At the outset of Arthur's reign, however, no black Ruskinian clouds spoiled "the golden days" ("Guinevere," 377). In late years, when the light kindled by Arthur had departed the land, Guinevere recalls the time of her bridal escort to Camelot, when "as yet no sin was dreamed." She

> Rode under groves that looked a paradise
> Of blossom, over sheets of hyacinth
> That seemed the heavens upbreaking through the earth.
>
> ("Guinevere," 385–88)

It was spring when Lancelot escorted her to "a city all on fire / With sun and cloth of gold" ("The Coming of Arthur," 478–79) to be married and crowned Queen. It was a moment of fusion of the natural, sacred, and human. The "fields of May" sparkled visible through the open door: the "altar blossomed white with May," and "The Sun of May descended" on the King and his "boundless purpose" ("The Coming of Arthur," 459–74). "Between the forest and the field" rose the "sacred mount of Camelot" ("The Holy Grail," 227),

> a city of shadowy palaces
> Which Merlin's hand . . . had . . . tipt with lessening peak
> And Pinnacle, and had made it spire to heaven.
>
> ("Gareth and Lynette," 188, 295–302)

On the low bricks and stones laid by ancient hands Merlin had raised walls flashing in the sun until they "moved so weirdly in the mist," like a city elevated by the magic enchanters for fairy kings and queens. To the music of harps the city was built, "therefore never built at all, / And therefore built for ever" ("Gareth and Lynette," 241, 273–74).

That Tennyson conceived of Camelot as an earthly paradise is suggested by his earliest outline about 1833 of an Arthurian poem. The physical setting draws on the tradition of classical and Biblical Edens. The "sacred Mount" rises

from the deeps with gardens and bowers and palaces, and at the top of the Mount was King Arthur's hall, and the Holy Minster with the Cross of gold. . . . The Mount was the most beautiful in the world, sometimes green and fresh in the beam of morning, sometimes all one splendour, folded in the golden mists of the West.[15]

There is an unearthly enchantment about the city. Preserved by Merlin's magic it owes its being, like the garden of Xanadu, to the constant voice of the muse, with this difference that it is a voice positing noble social purposes. Arthur's reign restores order to a land ravaged by brigandage. All who accept his leadership have vowed to push back the wilderness, to clear the woods of evil, and ever to uphold the right and the good. It is no wonder that Gareth's companions discover Camelot at first sight to be as unreal as Pilgrim finds the Heavenly City, now visible, now lost to mortal sight, shimmering in the "silver-misty morn" ("Gareth and Lynette," 186), not unlike John Martin's painting of the Heavenly Plains.

Even at the outset a note of disbelief is heard. He might herald the future, see

> the heavens fill with commerce, argosies of magic sails,
> Pilots of the purple twilight, dropping down with costly bales;
> ("Locksley Hall [1842]" 121–22)

but, like Coleridge, Tennyson had more faith finally in a perfect society created by poetic song than that produced by geography, commerce, and industry.

A Victorian sense of doom hangs over Arthur's perfect community, present as an underlying premonition in Tennyson's earliest, and latest, drafts of the poem, and explicit in his 1833 prose prospectus. Like the "ancestral voices prophesying war" and heralding the eventual destruction of Xanadu, all the while Arthur dwells "in glory apart, . . . the Saxons whom he had overthrown in twelve battles ravaged the land, and ever came nearer and nearer . . . and there ran a prophecy that the mountain and the city on some wild morning would topple into the abyss and be no more."[16] It is not accidental that Tennyson's first essay of the story, as a true expression of his deepest vision, is "Morte d'Arthur." "From the great deep" came Arthur, and "to the great deep" he returned at the end of his reign, his "fragile new experiment in civilization"[17] in ruins, and his mind "clouded with a doubt" ("The Passing of Arthur," 426) about the reality and the legitimacy of his sojourn on earth. Unwilling to accept the bleak instincts of his pulse, Tennyson deleted more than one early allusion to the intrinsic defect in Arthur's "vast design and purpose" ("Guinevere," 664) of founding a perfect community. In the prose summary of "Gareth and Lynette" Tennyson originally explained that Queen Bellicent's insistence upon Gareth entering Arthur's service disguised as a country churl was because she had heard "a noise that Queen Guinevere was false with Lancelot,"[18] and wished to ascertain its truth. In the final version of "Gareth and Lynette" Tennyson deleted this pessimistic foreshadowing of the moral deterioration of Camelot, explaining Queen Bellicent's stipulation instead as her way of exacting from Gareth a sign of humility as proof of his readiness to be one of Arthur's knights in the service of God and society.

As one of the last stories written, in 1870–71, "The Last Tournament" reflects Tennyson's post-1859 despair. Written almost in tandem with "Gareth and Lynette" (1871–72), and within the context, so to speak, of its glorious description of Camelot, "The Last Tournament" carries an ironic undertone of bitterness in its bleak outlook at the end of a noble experiment gone sour. The original beauty of the prelapsarian earth has turned sere. The glittering morning when Gareth first caught sight of Camelot has vanished with Arthur's dream of a community dedicated to civil and holy usefulness. Now a wet wind blows. The "Tournament of the Dead Innocence" is held in Autumn under a drear English sky, "yellowing leaf / And gloom and gleam, and shower and shorn plume" ("The Last Tournament," 136, 154–55). The "wan day" goes "down in wet and weariness" (214–15), and with it goes courtesy and glory and innocence. Not

Arthur, but guilty Sir Lancelot presides over the lists; and not Sir Lancelot, as in those early years of innocence now hidden in the mist of his guilty liaison with Guinevere, but venial Sir Tristram wins the coveted prize. Whereas the flowers were bursting into bloom when Gareth rode to enter Arthur's service, now the multiple colors of mountain bloom masquerade artificially in the glittering dresses of dame and damsel.

In *The Princess* (1847) Tennyson has the Prince praise love as a prelapsarian virtue still capable in the postlapsarian world of reversing the Fall.

> Then comes the statelier Eden back to men:
> Then reign the world's great bridals, chaste and calm:
> Then springs the crowning race of humankind. (VII, 277–79)

By the time he finished the *Idylls* Tennyson sang a more despondent tune. He saw the canker of disorder reaching back irrevocably to Eden. Vivien and Merlin's re-enactment of the primal scene in the "wild woods of Broceliande" ("Merlin and Vivien," 202), not to mention Lancelot's and Guinevere's in Camelot, nullifies the lingering faith he might have had in the likelihood of recapturing Edenic purity. It is for Tennyson, as for his generation, the twilight of the English belief in rural retreat as an all-purpose panacea. Vivien sporting in the wood and there bestializing Merlin figures as the latest recurrence of Eve/ Circe. In keeping with Victorian suspicion that the garden may now be not unlike the rest of tainted nature, Tennyson locates Lancelot's and Guinevere's lawless tryst (at least Balan's witness of it) in a garden crossed by beds of lilies and of roses. All nature is implicated in their guilt, both cultivated and natural, urban and pastoral. With skillfully deployed irony, Tennyson has Lancelot look with troubled eye on the "long white walk of lilies," "perfect-pure" emblem of "stainless maidenhood," as he is accosted by Guinevere, the loving source of his guilt. Troubled in even more complex degree by her passion, Guinevere perversely clutches to her heart the contrary emblem of the blood-red rose, determined in this morning tryst to chastize him and herself, alike unchaste, for their uncharitable thoughts toward each other and unfaithful action toward their liege ("Balin and Balan," 235–75). And the serpent is more than half-allegorically present, for in a later unhappier year than that of Balan's mischanced observations of them, green-clad Modred is caught by Lancelot spying on Guinevere in another garden and is plucked from the wall "and as the gardener's hand / Picks from the colewort a green caterpillar" is flung metamorphosed "as a worm upon the way" ("Guinevere," 31–35).

Rather than imaginatively possessing another happier civic time when a "fair city" ("The Passing of Arthur," 460) with its community of devoted and disciplined knights stood firmly as a bastion of accord and civilization – a reassurance to mankind that paradise is historically within its reach – Tennyson found himself instead rehearsing the end of things. He had envisioned a King "In whom High God has breathed a secret thing" that all Adamites can follow and emulate. The vision of Arthur as a man "not made since Adam . . . more perfect" was so fixed in Tennyson's mind that he mistakenly thought "perhaps he had not made the real humanity of the King sufficiently clear in his epilogue," and was moved in 1891 to insert the disclaimer that Arthur was "Ideal manhood closed in real man."[19] A. Dwight Culler has wittily characterized the *Idylls of the King* as Tennyson's *Decline and Fall of the Roman Empire*, distinctly written "with the somber, the saturnine spirit of Gibbon."[20] The latter half of this appraisal probably states too strongly Tennyson's conscious intentions; yet there is no denying that the *Idylls* essentially retells the story of the eternally recurring Fall of humankind. The history of the human race spirals down through time, endlessly repeating itself. Adam and Eve's disobedience re-echoes in Lancelot and Guinevere's mendacity. Like Merlin and Vivien, like Tristram and Isolt, they made "broken music" ("The Last Tournament," 258–59), with disruptive consequences to the harmony that had held together Arthur's city. The mystery of Arthur's birth, parentage, and death – "'From the great deep to the great deep he goes'" ("The Passing of Arthur," 445) – aligns him with the mythical once and forever God. He is a version of Christ come for a short sojourn to found his holy city on earth and with that "fair beginning of a time" ("Guinevere," 463) to lay the foundation for a lasting moral order on earth. And like Christ he cries at the end, "My God, thou hast forgotten me in my death" ("The Passing of Arthur," 27). But Arthur's sacrifice lacks the transcendent promise for all mankind of Christ's implicit in the typology of the *hortus conclusus*. The terrestrial peace of Camelot (it lasts twelve years) proves to be no more possible for flawed human nature to maintain indefinitely than was the original paradise.

As early as "Oenone" Tennyson had gloomily intuited this truth about the irrevocable rift between heaven and earth. That poem can be read as Tennyson's version of the temptation scenes in *Paradise Lost* and *Paradise Regained* – and as his farewell to the paradisal bower.[21] Within the same context of temptation and loss the poem reminds us that the future of Troy was equally insecure. With the traditional securities of both the earthly garden and the heavenly city seemingly suspect, Camelot is foredoomed to corruption, cynicism, destruction, and disappearance. Arthur is unable to hold the celestial center, or the civil, against the base self-interests of each of his followers; nor is the periphery of his realm safe against evil forces from the outside. At the end he walks in an empty city, his knights scattered about the countryside in pursuit of "wandering fires" ("The Holy Grail," 369). Even he finally flees his sacred Mount, preferring death in defence of his western frontiers to incarceration in a city become his living tomb. Camelot exists finally as an historical metaphor for a nineteenth-century industrial civilization suffering the fate of all terrestrial societies, and *Idylls of the King* as a noble instance of historical man's vain searching of myths for a corrective to his fate. In its nostalgic glance backward to a nobler time, and in its susceptibility to temptation, Camelot coincides with and parodies the transcendent paradise that was, and is perennially, lost.

In the early poems "The Two Voices" (1833; published 1842) and "Supposed

Confessions of a Second-rate Sensitive Mind" (1830), Tennyson already revealed a troubled awareness of his compulsion toward an unchanging self-contained universe. Unlike his progenitors, the Romantics, he could not find it in nature. In effect disinherited by that world, he laments with the speaker in "The Two Voices":

> 'That type of Perfect in his mind
> In Nature can he nowhere find.'
>
> (292–93)

There is thus poignancy in Tennyson's imagination instinctively resorting to nature imagery in an allusion to "The Palace of Art" and its builder–occupant in a dedicatory prologue. With saturnine scorn, not without its backlash of self-reflection, he comments on the Soul as "sinful,"

> possessed of many gifts,
> A spacious garden full of flowering weeds.

These lines resonate with negative paradisal implications when one reads them with the *hortus conclusus* as analogue in mind. There the fair garden of Mary's womb is fruitfully entered into by God. Here the Soul's remains barren. Tennyson makes somewhat the same wry point when at the outset of the *Idylls*, in "The Coming of Arthur," he describes Arthur's marriage to Guinevere as a May-time of sunny flowers (446–74); by the end of his reign Camelot is no less rank than the Palace of Art's garden, for Arthur the God King has neglected Guinevere to fulfill the "boundless purpose" of his civic ambition.

Both references can be read as containing covert laments for the lost garden. In the *Idylls of the King* the perfection and harmony of the prelapsarian world is created anew in the towers of Camelot – "the world [made] / Other" ("The Coming of Arthur," 471–72). It is a noble attempt to imagine a humanistic version of paradise; but Camelot turns out to be as much of a chimera as the promises of the Lotos Eaters. It will not stay fixed and visible to ordinary mortals any more than it did to the two churls who accompany Gareth, for Camelot is built of the same materials as are Xanadu and "the beautiful . . . palace . . . rampired [round with] walls of gold as transparent as glass" (9–19) of Browning's "Abt Vogler" (1864). The "pinnacled glory" (24) of each has for building blocks the evanescent notes of music, which allows "earth [to attain] to heaven" (32). Improvisations of their makers, who are "made perfect too" (40) in the process, they do not survive the inspired moment of "all triumphant art" (47). Coleridge awoke involuntarily (he tells us) from his reverie, tantalized by the fitful memory of its glory. Abt Vogler similarly, after an interlude of concocting "a perfect round" equivalent to heaven's perfect whole (72), sinks back to "the common chord again . . . the C Major of this life" (91, 96), to stand again "on alien ground" (93) surrounded by "the broken arcs" (72) of his aspirations.

The medieval poets and painters did well to keep the *hortus conclusus* walled off from the brutish natural world. Arthur's effort to unite the two becomes a rueful tale of failed Victorian aspirations. The nineteenth century rediscovered medieval wisdom the hard way, by trying to better it. Instead of reaching the all-encompassing center toward which he strived life-long, the Victorian pilgrim found himself girdled by the traps of his early compromises whenever he translated the boundless circles of the heavenly plains into the bounded arcs of earthly replicas. So Arthur is caught within the labyrinthine confines of his triangular relationship with Lancelot and Guinevere, which spirals in ever-widening references to similar relationships among his followers, none able to extricate himself except through destruction of self and kingdom.

12

Mid-Victorian London and the Angel in the House

THE SELF-CONGRATULATORY MOOD of 1851, amplified by the Great Exhibition, was heard like a shrill falsetto above the insistent registers of doubt and fear. If engineers and manufacturers were feeling omnipotent at mid-century, having weathered Malthus, inept poor laws, naive faith in human perfectibility, and the depression-ridden, hungry, and gloomy decades from the 1820s to the 1840s, some poets and intellectuals were voicing an elegaic mood. Nature loomed before their eyes as a complex, ambiguous, and monstrous hybrid, owing to its Romantic heritage its positive and spiritual values, and to its scientific legacy its neutral and materialistic energies. Gone was the unmediated perception of luminous lakes and hills. Visible instead was a world the sum of "the patient accumulation of fact." Under the weight of geologic history and scientific observation, the mysterious power dwelling in "the light of setting suns, / And the round ocean and the living air, / And the blue sky" ("Tintern Abbey," 97–99) was evolving into a force "red in tooth and claw" (*In Memoriam*, LVI, 15). Life had turned dangerous and gray, and was to subside in self-defense into domestic comfort, common-sensical enterprise, and social utility.[1]

Equally important as the changing intellectual assumptions about what constituted reality, with their consequent structures of thought and feeling, was the actual day-to-day experience of an environment once rural, now insistently urban. In two hundred years, from 1660 to 1860, England had evolved from an island with prospects of pastures and plowed fields to one choked with "the deformities of crowded life" (Wordsworth, *Prelude*, VIII, 465). The industrial cities of the Midlands and the North threatened to displace the "Green joys and cloudless skies" of an agrarian land that once for Clare were "Fancy [spread]ing Edens" ("Joys of Childhood," stanza 3). London seemed bent on spreading across the whole of the south of the island. In 1660 it already had a population of half a million, when Bristol the next largest had only 30,000. By 1800 it contained over one million. Raymond Williams points out that London's inexorable growth at each stage drew in part of the rest of the country, first as the center of agrarian capitalism, then of mercantile ventures, and finally of all the industries of trade and distribution, shipping, and marketing.[2] Its symbolic importance to the nation had similarly evolved from being a place alien to the rural rhythms of "Englands green & pleasant Land" (Blake, *Milton*, Preface, 1:16) to being the cynosure of millennial yearnings, heralded in Blake's words once again, now in context, as the re-establishment of the holy city of "Jerusalem, / In Englands green & pleasant Land." As early as the sixteenth century, London was established as the center of England's social and political life; in the eighteenth and nineteenth centuries it came increasingly to occupy a place central to the imagination of the country.

If the city was the sinful alternative to an innocent rural life, it was also the repository of civilization, the center of culture and order. It was Wordsworth's "vast Metropolis, / The Fountain of my Country's destiny / And of the destiny of Earth itself" (*Prelude*, VIII, 746–48). And it was King Arthur's celestial Camelot, with towers "Pinnacled dim in the intense inane" (Shelley, *Prometheus Unbound*, III, iii, 204). But the city was also an organism, as Arthur discovers. The sad truth is that Camelot too grows old, decays, and threatens to fall, a city aging "strange and rich, and dim," into a shambling assemblage of "crazy walls" and roofs that totter toward each other ("The Holy Grail," 340–47). In *Idylls of the King* the condition of Camelot is a metaphor for the inner moral decay of Arthur's community of men and women. Its decrepitude also describes what Tennyson coming up to London from Lincolnshire could see when he descended into older sections of the city, and it reflects the shock of recognition, and the weary disillusionment, when Victorians looked with disenchanted eyes at what they had wrought in their cities.

One hears in Tennyson's description of Camelot an ambivalent note, which echoes a similar tone of puzzlement and barely controlled fear toward the city felt by mid and late Victorians, a new kind of fear that was already being sounded by the second generation of Romantics. Shelley prefigures it in the closing lines of *Adonais* (1821). He begins literally enough with a reference to Rome as the burial place of Keats: "Or go to Rome, which is the sepulchre / O, not of him, but of our joy" (xlviii, 424–25). But then the mixed desire implicit in the lines, with their ambiguous reference simultaneously to a man and a place and with their compulsive outburst of longing, prompts his imagination to respond to the idea of a city that is at once a compendious ruin of civilization and an ever-present promise of eternity:

> Go thou to Rome, – at once the Paradise,
> The grave, the city, and the wilderness . . .   (xlix, 433–34)

Heard here is a strain different from Wordsworth's lament for Luke's falling into temptation in the city. The easy contrast between country and city is no longer available to Shelley. For him the city has become a complex tyranny of hope and despair, a terrifying reminder of the goal to which the highest order of civilization can aspire and of the discord into which such ventures in human concourse can fall.

Some forty years later Victorian Londoners were finding out that there was little solace to be had either from the new industrial underpinning to the ancient vision of the city on the hill, or, for that matter, to be had from the old dispensation of the garden, any longer, either as ideal exponent of nature or as providential sign of God's grace. Boffin's Bower with its dust mounds now commanded the imaginative skyline. The rapturous optimism of the Crystal Palace and its Great Exhibition had suffered the fate of King Arthur's glorious hopes. "The Last Tournament," written by Tennyson in 1870–71, reflects the change in mood. Blake had envisioned England as one vast millenarian scene of building, husbandry, and wine-making where a choir of flowers and birds (heard with the imagination) each day sings the song of spring (*Milton*, plate 31). Victorians were acquiring instead first-hand acquaintance with the squalor of the new industrial cities. The ideal of urban civilization collided as often as not with actual urban experience. Its oppressive uniformity, its stultifying "blank confusion" of "anarchy and din / . . . Monstrous in colour, motion, shape, sight, sound" (*Prelude*, VII, 695, 659–61), forced mid-Victorians back onto themselves. What kind of paradise is it, they asked, which recognizes no individuality? Which, in Wordsworth's words, restricts men to

> Living amid the same perpetual flow
> Of trivial objects, melted and reduced
> To one identity, by differences
> That have no law, no meaning, and no end.
>
> (*Prelude*, VII, 701–04)

By the 1860s there was an impressive body of literature decrying the urban shame, full of horror at the "deformities of crowded life" (*Prelude* [1805], VIII, 465), man had wrought in nineteenth-century cities. Engels had already been to Manchester, recording in *Condition of the Working Class in England in 1844* (1845) the excremental basis of life in the courts which constituted the back-streets of the working-class districts:

In one of these courts, just at the entrance where the covered passage ends there is a privy without a door. This privy is so dirty that the inhabitants of the court can only enter or leave the court if they are prepared to wade through puddles of stale urine and human excrement.[3]

Marx was soon to be at work in the British Museum constructing a metaphysical–political frame of reference, which would make historical sense out of this event in time. Using a paradisal frame of reference, Dickens defines the parameters of the Satanic view with Betty Higden's hallucination of the celestial city on the night of her death. Wandering upriver from London, ever fearful of being apprehended as a vagrant and ending her days in a workhouse, she breathes her last in sight of the textile mill in which Lizzie Hexam works:

There now arose in the darkness, a great building full of lighted windows. Smoke was issuing from a high chimney in the rear of it, and there was the sound of a water-wheel at the side. Between her and the building, lay a piece of water, in which the lighted windows were reflected, and on its nearest margin was a plantation of trees. "I humbly thank the Power and the Glory," said Betty Higden, holding up her withered hands, "that I have come to my journey's end!"   (*Our Mutual Friend* [1864–65], ch. 41)

So concludes one poor Londoner's earthly pilgrimage, her soul gladdened, after her long journey, at the sight of the only New Jerusalem she has ever known, the lights of a working factory.

When no work was available, London effectively functioned as a prison of the poor. Charles Kingsley has Alton Locke in manhood effectively recall the inner city of his boyhood:

And one day, I recollect it well, in the little dingy, foul, reeking, twelve-foot-square back yard, where huge smoky party-walls shut out every breath of air and almost all the light of heaven, I had climbed up between the water-butt and the angle of the wall for the purpose of fishing out of the dirty fluid which lay there, crusted with soot and alive with insects, to be renewed only three times in the seven days, some of the great larvae and kicking monsters which made up a large item in my list of wonders: all of a sudden the horror of the place came over me; those grim prison-walls above, with their canopy of lurid smoke; the dreary, sloppy, broken pavement; the horrible stench of the stagnant cesspools; the utter want of form, colour, life, in the whole place, crushed me down, without my being able to analyse my feelings as I can now . . .   (ch. 1)

At its worst, to the fearful eyes of Calvinists like the child Alton Locke and his mother, London easily corresponded to an anti-Jerusalem, a polluted fog-and-smoke bound Babylon Carlyle liked to call it.[4] Recalling his childhood phantasms, Alton Locke singles out London as "the City of Destruction" from which he was charged to flee:

I was Christian; the Wicket of the Way of Life I had strangely identified with the turnpike at Battersea-bridge end; and the rising ground of Mortlake and Wimbledon was the Land of Beulah – the Enchanted Mountains of the Shepherds.   (ch. 1)

No one more persistently after mid-century excoriated England – and London – as a lost, abandoned (in its several senses), and demoralized paradise than Ruskin. In 1859 in a lecture on "Modern Manufacture and Design" he paints an industrial landscape by way of describing the fate of a cottage and garden in the suburbs of a manufacturing town. The place has become a modern Golgotha:

blighted utterly into a field of ashes, not even a weed, taking root there; the roof torn into shapeless rents; the shutters hanging about the windows in rags of rotten wood; before its gate, the stream which had gladdened it now soaking slowly by, black as ebony and thick with curdling scum; the bank above it trodden into unctuous, sooty slime: far in front of it, between it and the old hills, the furnaces of the city foaming forth perpetual plague of sulphurous darkness; the volumes of their storm clouds coiling low over a waste of grassless fields.[5]

In essay after essay Ruskin tolls the organic and moral changes for the bad that the Industrial Revolution has brought to the land. The technological sublime becomes the incarnation of evil, the "glittering cylinders" and "fine ribbed rods" of the locomotive the writhing of satanic serpents. The machine as god, a grimy, air polluting deity, has replaced the old transcendent sky gods who once sat in ethereal splendor in the clear empyrean. The new god is of earth, polluted and dirty. Modern man has fallen once again from God's grace. Such is Ruskin's message in "The Storm Cloud of the Nineteenth Century."

The drab monotony of London's "charter'd" streets, which Arthur Clennam found so oppressive upon his return from years abroad, was soul destroying to those millions imprisoned for life within its sooty canyons. "Melancholy streets in a penitential garb of soot, steeped the souls of the people who were condemned to look at them out of windows, in dire despondency," Dickens writes in chapter 3 of *Little Dorrit* (1855–57), captioned "Home."

Nothing to see but streets, streets, streets. Nothing to breathe but streets, streets, streets. Nothing to change the brooding mind, or raise it up. Nothing for the spent toiler to do, but to compare the monotony of his seventh day with the monotony of his six days.

"What secular want," Dickens asks ironically, "could the million or so of human beings whose daily labour six days in the week, lay among these Arcadian objects . . . possibly have upon their seventh day?" What, indeed, but respite from the city in the form of a home, the Englishman's castle, and an angel at the hearth awaiting at end of the day "the spent toiler" and fugitive from the City!

The London of middle and late Dickens is reflected in his lapsarian eyes as a hideous reversal of Eden – soot-filled muddy streets, savagery, lawlessness, and grime, where once were antediluvian meadows, blue sky, and gentle innocence. Clearly a situation to flee from if possible. In *Bleak House* (1852–53) the sooty fog of London conjures a vision of the end to a world that is identical with its geological beginnings.

As much mud in the streets, as if the waters had but newly retired from the face of the earth, and it would not be wonderful to meet a Megalosaurus, forty feet long or so, waddling like an elephantine lizard up Holborn Hill. Smoke lowering down from chimney-pots, making a soft black drizzle, with flakes of soot in it as big as full-grown snow-flakes – gone into mourning, one might imagine, for the death of the sun . . .

(*Bleak House*, ch. 1)

Factory Commissions, Blue Books, and White Papers testify with dismal repetition to the horrifying living conditions of the poor, not in London alone, but in most manufacturing cities: Liverpool, Manchester, Leeds, Oldham, Ashton, and Bolton. Dickens's Jacob's Island and Tom-All-Alone's were symbols for much of England's urban habitation in the middle decades of the nineteenth century.

People lived in crowded density that awes even us struggling in the second half of the twentieth century with the Malthusian spectre come true. One wonders if the celebrated pictures of William Powell Frith – *The Derby Day* (1858, Tate Gallery) and *The Railway Station* (1862, Royal Holloway College, University of London) – which observe a multitudinous population and its multifarious activities, are not responses as much to Victorian congestion as to Victorian *horror vacui*. The urban poor were crammed into jerry-built row and block buildings – called warrens, in wry acknowledgement of the "tight packing and prolific breeding" that characterized them. Two and three large families often occupied a single room, six, seven, and eight children and adults sleeping in one bed. A single communal privy, overflowing with excrement, might serve forty multifamily dwellings. In the first fifty years of the century, the population of London doubled, with no appreciable increase in sanitary facilities or conveniences. Drinking water still came from a reach of the Thames into which two hundred sewers flowed.

> Fleet-ditch with disemboguing streams
> Rolls the large tribute of dead dogs to Thames   (II, 259–60),

Pope had written in *The Dunciad* (*c.* 1728). Since then the change had been quantitative. Now the pollutants were so thick that land birds could walk on the surface of the streams. Cholera and typhoid epidemics were commonplace to the age. In 1832, cholera killed 16,437 people in England and Wales; and in 1849, it killed 16,000 in London alone.[6]

Given the congestion in a city like London, homelessness was a *sine qua non* of Victorian existence. The novels of the age are full of vagrant wandering. Graphic portrayals of unsheltered ways of life are even more insistent. Indeed, so pervasive was the social phenomenon that an unfixed abode provided the age with part of its vocabulary and its structure of feeling. Illustrations for the popular press and for fiction, unmediated by moral conventions, concentrate on the pathetic tale of the homeless plight of a goodly percentage of London's citizenry. Both Gustave Doré (1832–83) and Sir Luke Fildes (1844–1927) present searing indictments of a society which tolerated an underworld of abandoned, discarded, and expendable humanity. In the late 1850s and early 1860s, the London *Illustrated Times* documented a dismal state of destitution, of men's casual wards where the homeless slept like animals in stalls on straw, and of park benches that provided all the domestic furniture many would ever know. In one acrid series the *Illustrated Times* depicted the absurd lengths to which the census takers of 1861 were willing to penetrate casual wards, park recesses, and the dark arches of bridges and embankments, all in the interests of getting an accurate census of London's population! Savagely implied is the absence of decent concern for one's fellow human being other than as an anonymous digit in a numerical compilation.

The closest the urban poor could get to a natural paradise once the birthright of all was by way of the Straw House, a cheap public house where for a few pence one could buy enough raw spirits to get drunk and where fresh straw was provided for those unable to walk home.[7] In Leeds, in the first half of the century, there were 451 public houses and 98 brothels to two churches. Thus people tried, with questionable results, to steal from a hostile environment a modicum of pleasure and a sop of material comfort that roughly accorded with the "remembered" pleasures of paradise.

In flight from the daily affairs of the industrial and mercantile hells, from the clangorous presence of the poor, and from the lofty monuments to folly of the technocrats and visionaries alike, the average Victorian turned to the sanctity of his hearth and home as a post-paradisal refuge. The perfectly ordered community founded on moral values remained an ideal, which the modern industrial society, despite its heterogeneous character, acted to reaffirm through the psychic relief of domestic security and of familial presence. From the vulnerable and fast disappearing paradises of natural groves, leafy bowers, lakes, and mountains once taken for granted Victorians fled into literary towers and palaces of private thought. Then, in final retreat, they crowded into the parlor, its impregnable respectability representing to them the ultimate sanctuary. How seriously the Victorian took this ideal is illustrated by the family portrait Lord and Lady Folkestone and their son Jacob chose to commemorate their domestic bliss and solidarity. They sit around a piano, the mother at the keyboard, the son with violin in hand, and the father turning the pages of the music, which is "Home, Sweet Home." Like a chatelaine wearing the proud badge of her household authority, Lady Folkestone is adorned with a heavy chain necklace that extends in a long loop down her side and to which is attached a purse. It is not inappropriate that the picture, painted by Edward Clifford about 1879, is entitled *Home, Sweet Home.*

Philippe Ariès argues in his monumental study of *Centuries of Childhood* that with the seventeenth century the European concept of the family began to include the Holy Family as a model.[8] Paintings depicted them as ordinary mother and housewife, paternal provider, and child of grace whose presence blesses all. The iconography of Mary, Joseph, and the two children John the Baptist and Jesus the "second Adam" implies a continuity of generations stretching back to the mythic first family of Adam and Eve, Cain and Abel. This sanctification of the household round of life was affirmed with rededicated fervor in the joys, pieties, and consecrated aftermaths of Victorian conjugal life.

Two mid-Victorian writers – Charles Dickens (1812–70) and Coventry Patmore (1823–96) – gave literary voice and symbolic significance to this domestication of the "everlastingly green garden . . . unregainable and far away" (*The Mystery of Edwin Drood* [1870], ch. 22). At a popular, and often conscious level, the transfiguration of Eden into a steamy east-end parlor, a cosy Hampstead cottage, or a fine Kensington house represented a resurgence of "remembrances . . . [and] tender encouragement" of the old religion "of the Household Gods,"[9] which Dickens sentimentalized, Ruskin and George Eliot historicized, Patmore mysticized, and Tennyson institutionalized. "All dipt / In Angel instincts, breathing paradise," the mother of the Prince in Tennyson's *The Princess* (1847) typified the ideal role of the Victorian woman. She was

> Interpreter between the Gods and men,
> Who looked all native to her place, and yet
> On tiptoe seemed to touch upon a sphere
> Too gross to tread, and all male minds perforce,
> Swayed to her from their orbits as they moved,
> And girdled her with music.   (VII, 301–08)

The wish of the Victorian was to have presiding over his blessed hearth (in Alexander Welsh's striking phrase) "a cheerful female eidolon"[10] known variously in the literature of the age as "the bride from heaven," the "little mother," the "angelic sister," "the Good Angel of the race" (*The Old Curiosity Shop* [1840–41], ch. 69), the "gentle Madonna" (Eliot's *Scenes of Clerical Life* [1857], ch. 2), "the Lady of Saving,"[11] the "dear home-Angel" (Meredith's *The Ordeal of Richard Feverel* [1859], ch. 47), "the ministering angel to domestic bliss" (*Edwin Drood* [1870], ch. 22), and "the good angel inviting to industry, sobriety, and peace" (Eliot's *Silas Marner* [1861], ch.3). Most often, she was familiarly enshrined (to cite the title of a poem by Leigh Hunt in 1834), *sui generis*, as "An Angel in the House."

Welsh has commented, with some surprise and scholarly hesitance, at the readiness of the male mid-Victorian to identify his salvation with the female sex.[12] Whatever the original impetus for it in a Protestant society conventionally rigid in its sexist orientation, the beleaguered male fostered a worship reaching epidemic proportions in mid-nineteenth-century social mores. The forces for good were eagerly concentrated in a woman – beloved wife, sister (Dickens's fictional favorite), or sister-in-law (Dickens's real-life favorite) – who went about her daily tasks with all the devotion and intercessory power of the Holy Madonna. To name our favorite childhood models of comforting females in Dickens alone – Lizzie Hexam, Little Dorrit, Little Nell, Florence Dombey, Esther Summerson, and Sissy Jupe – will suffice to recall the ministering type. All exhibit dependable fidelity to real and adopted father, grandfather, and husband alike. Thackeray alludes in *The History of Pendennis* (1848–50) to the uplifting presence in the early Victorian house of "women angelically pure and good, who dwell there" like nineteenth-century vestal virgins (ch. 50). Their presence transfigured the nineteenth-century leaseholder's brickbound domestic sanctuary into a new middle-class *hortus conclusus*, however confined by four walls and restricted by stuffy conventions, and scaled down from the eighteenth-century aristocrat's landscaped Eden, and from the walled great house and garden, the fortified earthly paradise, of earlier centuries.

More than one critic has rightly called our attention to the idealization of women and the religious crisis that obsessed the age.[13] Anxious to reaffirm the transcendental Christian myth Victorians modified it to accommodate reassuring moral and domestic virtues. The primordial failure of Adam and Eve is recast into the familial drama of historical man and woman; and each sex is given its typological burden to bear. In the perception of the family as a sacred unit, Eve – first woman and mother of us all – especially undergoes a redemptive transformation. If Arthur Hugh Clough's attempt to come to terms with the religious temper of his times in his tough-minded dramatic fragment *Adam and Eve* (1848–50, 1869) is an honest index of the prevalent attitude, Eve's is the voice of guilt, remorse, devotion, and humility; and Adam's that of optimism, perplexity, secularity, and resolution. In bidding farewell to his father after Abel's murder, Cain neatly epitomizes the respective roles of the sexes when he says, "You read the Earth, as does my mother Heaven" (*Adam and Eve*, xiii, 31). Given this context of sentiment, Dickens's *The Cricket on the Hearth* (1845), with the Peerybingles's kettle "hung about the chimney-corner as its own domestic

Heaven," asserted a paradisal reality that few early Victorians could resist – and which has become a sentimental index of the 1840s and 50s for us.[14]

The spiritualized women who figure in the literature and art may reflect an influential fashion of the time rather than faithfully mirror a deeply-rooted mode of feminine life. Most women may have continued to live their lives in the more earthly and practical ways they have always done. Nevertheless, whatever difficulty we have now in understanding their attenuated view of the female sex, the evidence points to the early Victorians fostering in themselves the belief that they felt lifted to the heights of self-improvement when they contemplated womanhood. Like a real-life anticipation of Coventry Patmore's poetic drama that redoubtable Christian warrior Charles Kingsley wrote in 1840 to Frances Grenfell, the woman who helped him recover his faith and who eventually married him: "I feel that in the tumult and grossness by which I am surrounded my mind is seldom, very seldom, in a tone capable of . . . coming pure and calm into your pure and calm presence. I feel that I am insulting you when I sit down reeking with the fumes of the world's frivolities and vices to talk to you . . . [who] are to me a middle point between earthly and ethereal morality. I begin to love good for your sake. At length I will be able to love it for God's sake."[15] Lionel Trilling as usual cuts through peripheral concerns to reach the essential fact when in his introduction to an edition of *Little Dorrit* he boldly calls her (and by symbolic extension all Victorian women) "the Beatrice of the *Comedy*, the Paraclete in female form."[16]

Dickens's girl-child angels, however, too often present us with a version of the Blessed Virgin more virginal out of Oedipal submission to an earthly father than filled with the grace of a Divine Father, and more sisterly and childless in her relationship to her husband than was Mary the earthly mother of Jesus. The most fully articulated religious codification of the mid-century passion for salvaging the impersonal cosmic grin in the "matrimonial smile" of a wife[17] is to be had in Patmore's *The Angel in the House*, in two parts, *The Betrothal* (1854) and *The Espousals* (1856); and its sequel, also in two parts, *Faithful for Ever* (1860) and *The Victories of Love* (1861–63), under which title it was generally known.

The poem presents two spousal songs. *The Angel in the House* narrates the courtship and wedding of Felix Vaughan and Honoria Churchill, mostly in the form of rhyming octosyllabic odes Patmore called Preludes. After six years away in foreign travel and study Felix returns home. On a visit to the deanery he discovers that the three daughters of the Dean have grown into young ladies. The beauty and reserve of Honoria the eldest charms him. His rhapsodies on her virtues, along with the traditional courting activities of picnic, dance, first kiss, and walks, take up the bulk of the two parts of the poem, which concludes with the wedding and a final eulogy of marriage and meditation on the "vestal grace" of the wife. *The Victories of Love* concentrates on the marriage of the Naval Officer Frederick Graham, a cousin and rejected suitor of Honoria, and Jane the daughter of his chaplain, in the form of letters considerably less lyrical than the poems of *The Angel in the House*. Mismatched, Frederick and Jane suffer through years of boredom and misery, each treating the other with devoted regard, but uncertain of how to satisfy the longing each is witness to. Their psychological distance from one another is subtly indicated by their disclosing their inmost thoughts and feelings always by letter to a third party. Children are born. Through the obligations and kindnesses of a dozen years of marriage they struggle toward mutual feelings of love. Frederick is finally ready to face his past, with its disappointment in love, and he and his wife visit the Vaughans. Intimacy between the two families develops. Jane dies, able at the end to communicate to her husband her deep sense of God's spirit working in both of them, and her approval of his marrying and loving another after she is gone. For the first time in the poem she addresses Frederick directly by letter. The poem ends with the next generation – children of the Vaughans and the Grahams – marrying and continuing the endless spousal song.

During the years he was working on the poem Patmore was harmoniously married to his first wife, Emily Augusta Andrews (m. 1847, d. 1862), and still an ardent Anglican communicant. It was not until 1864 that he converted to Catholicism and married his second wife, both events setting him on an intellectual course divergent from the main impulses of his contemporaries and of the nation. But in the forties and fifties he was at the intellectual center of things, the friend and confidante of Tennyson, Ruskin, Carlyle, and Browning, and an admired adviser of the slightly younger and newly formed Pre-Raphaelite Brotherhood of Rossetti, Millais, Woolner, and Hunt, who asked him to contribute a poem "The Seasons" to the first issue of their paper *The Germ* and who proudly listed him as one of the immortals in the Manifesto of Immortals which they drew up. These were the years, roughly a quarter of a century, when his popularity as a Victorian poet was at its height. *The Angel in the House* went through five editions in nine years, successfully rivaling the appeal of Tennyson's *Idylls of the King* (first installment, 1859) and *Enoch Arden* (1864). Between its publication in 1854 and Patmore's death in 1896 an estimated quarter of a million copies were purchased by Victorian readers eager to find in the symbolic action of this marital epic affirmation that they too could ritualistically partake of paradise by way of the sacramental commonplaces of courtship and marriage. Thus, it is fair to read the poem as a summary of Victorian attitudes and ideals at mid-century toward love, marriage, and "the gentle words, / Wife, Mother, Sister" ("Olympus," 1861–66).

Patmore broached the subject of sexual love with greater ease than most of his compatriots allowed themselves. What made this possible for him, and made his freedom with the subject acceptable to others more inhibited, was his association of it with the doctrinal sanctity of Christianity. According to Edmund Gosse, "Patmore loathed and rejected the scholastic theory that marriage is nothing but a *remedium amoris*, a compromise with frailty, a best way of getting out of a bad business."[18] Tennyson captures the view with witty succinctness when he has a fat country curate Edward Bull dogmatically dismiss romantic and sacramental views of love as contrary to divine edict: "'God made the woman for the man, /

And for the good and increase of the world'" ("Edwin Morris" [1839], 43–44). Against such a carnal evaluation of woman and of marriage Patmore raised "the spousal bond" to an "image of . . . Christ and Church" conjoined. From that perspective, marriage becomes the equivalent of human love for God; "and He dwells in us," Jane assures her husband, "If we each other love" ("Letter VII, From Jane to Frederick," *Victories*, II).

With evangelical fervor Patmore was bent on redressing what he considered to be an inexplicably neglected theme for poetry: married love – the paradisal joys of this "Primal Love" and the merits of a wife, round whose "happy footsteps blow / The authentic airs of Paradise" ("Honoria," Prelude i, "The Lover," *Angel*, I, III). At the end of *The Victories of Love* (II) he appended a "Wedding Sermon" which sums up in a succession of pithy aphorisms his complex philosophy of love.

> No giddiest hope, no wildest guess
> Of Love's most innocent loftiness
> Had dared to dream of its own worth,
> Till Heaven's bold sun-gleam lit the earth.
> Christ's marriage with the Church is more,
> My Children, than a metaphor.
> The heaven of heavens is symbol'd where
> The torch of Psyche flash'd despair.

Essentially, Patmore defines human love as an unlost part of paradise available to every man and woman. Such love, however, is not the romantic once-in-a-lifetime ecstasy Byron cynically allows the sons and daughters of Eve. It is an earned regard available to the mismatched as well as to those whose marriage seems to have been arranged in heaven. This view is set forth movingly by Jane Graham to her husband Frederick, who had wed her on the rebound from a rejected love. After years of "trials, duties, service, tears," they have won through to "the joy of body, mind, and heart" of a "love that grew a reckless growth." Secure in her hard-won love Jane can humbly insist with her questions,

> Are we not 'heirs,' as man and wife,
> 'Together of eternal life?'
> Was Paradise e'er meant to fade,
> To make which marriage first was made? . . .
> Shall the humble preference offend
> In heaven, which God did there commend?
> Are 'honourable and undefiled'
> The names of aught from heaven exiled?
> ("Letter VII, From Jane to Frederick," *Victories* II)

The answer to Jane's assertive questions lies in Patmore's belief, reassuring to mid-Victorians, that if as woman she shares with Eve the guilty loss of Eden, by her equal descent from Mary she ensures as wife to her husband their incontrovertible claim on paradise.

Throughout both parts of *The Angel in the House* and of *The Victories of Love* is heard an extended hosanna to this "household Madonna"[19] as the incarnate daughter of Eve and Mary – and by extension, of God. She is to be loved "in the name of God, / And for the ray she was of Him" ("Going to Church," Prelude i, "The Joyful Wisdom," *Angel*, I, x), for as bride each woman "wears within her eyes," like a many-splendored promise down through the generations of man, a constantly renewed "report of paradise" ("Letter xi, From Mrs. Graham," *Victories*, I). Better yet, each woman brings to her marriage "happy virtues," which in "dancing round the Tree of Life . . . make an Eden in her breast" ("The Comparison," *Angel*, I, v) and guarantee a similar one in her husband's. Sensing this gift, the despondent Frederick Graham feels momentarily, until Jane revives his stultified feelings, that in his loss of Honoria he has forfeited his birthright to the "great garden" ("Letter viii, From Frederick," *Victories*, I).

Despite their popularity Patmore's ideas about marital love were less socially activist and less pertinent to the feminist issues of the time than those of his poetic rival Tennyson. In his apparent championship of women Patmore hardly alludes to the feminist movement of the 1830s and 40s for legal and educational equality, as does Tennyson in *The Princess*.[20] This is not to say that Patmore did not address himself to the "female question" on occasion in his journalistic writings. Generally, though, he adopts a conventional, if sympathetic attitude toward the differences between the sexes. Women are affectionate, men have understanding. Each complements the other, and it is union of "unequals sweet" brought about by "equal love."[21] On the subject of social independence, he rather sharply (to our ears) declares that the "emancipated woman . . . would prove to men that she is as good as a man, by shewing them that she is as bad."[22] Worse, "emancipated women are too often tempted to measure their freedom by the degree of their emancipation from the Christian faith."[23] Indeed, for all the apparent tranquility of his own domestic life, Patmore's remarks about women's rights probably allied him on that subject with Tennyson's boorish curate Edward Bull as much as his often scandalous put-downs of contemporary clerics would have arraigned him against the Reverend Bull. It is not surprising that mid-Victorians found Patmore's version of domesticity attractive. Perhaps its popularity lay, in part, in his not challenging the mythology of male mental superiority. Patmore's woman, albeit for all seasons – loving wife, tender mother, resourceful keeper of the hearth, and sexual guide to the joys of paradise – achieves this universality through exercise of her feelings.

There was one topic of discussion in the early 1850s, at least in the circles Tennyson and Patmore frequented, which was apparently appealing to both poets. Tennyson closes *The Princess* by bringing a chastened Princess and a loving Prince together in professions of devotion. Acknowledging their differences because of gender the Prince conjectures that a reverent union of these "Distinct . . . individualities" will bring "the statelier Eden back to men." Fired by his own rhetoric he sees a paradisal millennium based on marriage.

> Then reign the world's great bridals, chaste and calm:
> Then springs the crowning race of humankind.   (VII, 275–79)

"Either sex alone / Is half itself," he generously assures the Princess,

> and in true marriage lies
> Nor equal, nor unequal. Each fulfills
> Defect in each, and always thought in thought,
> Purpose in purpose, will in will, they grow,
> The single pure and perfect animal,
> The two-cell's heart beating, with one full stroke,
> Life.   (VII, 283–90)

One encounters similar sentiments in *The Angel in the House*. Early in his courtship the love-graced Felix Vaughan muses on his supernal joy, conjecturing that

> Female and male God made the man;
>   His image is the whole, not half;
> And in our love we dimly scan
>   The love which is between Himself.
>
> ("Sarum Plain," Prelude iv,
> "The Prototype," *Angel*, I, VIII)

A. Dwight Culler would have Tennyson "probably . . . influenced by Plato's theory, as propounded by Aristophanes in the *Symposium*, that every individual is but half a soul and that by love we seek to find our counterpart. But he is more obviously influenced simply by the bisexual character of human reproduction."[24] Patmore's sources for the same set of precepts are more difficult to sort out, or identify satisfactorily for that matter, although one critic singles out the same section of the *Symposium* expounding on male and female constituents to account for Patmore's "idea of sexual duality as a basic principle in the universe."[25] Here, though, Swedenborg is advanced as another important influence. The fact is that Patmore's reading in philosophy, and especially in Catholic mystical literature, was idiosyncratically speculative, intense but narrow; and his vehemently individualistic personality suggests that much of his thought was intuitive. What is beyond question is the explicit Christian interpretation he gave it.

That such Edenic dogma, almost, was assumed in some religious circles to be part of a Christian couple's dowry – was implied, so to speak, in their marital vows – is conveyed in the quietly pious tone and language of William Howitt's narrative of his early life, which is included in Mary Howitt's autobiography begun in 1868 (when William probably wrote his account) and finished after her husband's death in 1879. William's description of his first meeting with his future wife reads like a prose redaction of Felix Vaughan's courtship of Honoria in *The Angel in the House*, particularly the "series of tea-parties, of walks in the very pleasant country round, and excursions to distant places of beauty and interest," and especially his sense that his marriage with this "best friend, truest companion" promised to be "an actual piece of idyllian life."[26]

At one level of statement, as the poet's great grandson Derek Patmore notes, *The Angel in the House* is "the poet's 'Epithalamium' to his wife, Emily."[27] The poem is also in a profound sense one Victorian's epithalamium celebrating in the marriage of man and woman the loftier sacramental union of the soul with God.

The Angel represents God's love, uniting in the bodies of man and woman the complementary halves of their mental and physical beings. The image has further analogues. It is the soul in the body, the saved human spirit in heaven, and finally the blessed and beloved being in whose person resides wife, mother, and earthly female companion. In Mary's spousal with "The Husband of the Heavens" Patmore derives the legitimacy of human physical love and the claim that all men through Christ are "Heirs of the Palace glad, / And inly clad / With the bridal robes of ardour virginal" ("Deliciae Sapientiae De Amore," *Unknown Eros*, II, ix). The same point is made with nervous poetic energy in "The Child's Purchase," which similarly praises Mary for reconciling in her female nature, in mystical simultaneity, virginity, love of God, married love, and motherhood.[28]

> Life's cradle and death's tomb!
> To lie within whose womb,
> There, with divine self-will infatuate,
> Love-captive to the thing He did create,
> Thy God did not abhor,
> No more
> Than Man, in Youth's high spousal-tide,
> Abhors at last to touch
> The strange lips of his long-procrastinating Bride;
> Nay, not the least imagined part as much!   (*Unknown Eros*, II, xvii)

Key concepts for Patmore's female oriented intuition of human salvation, as he set them forth in the 1870s and 80s, are a mystical notion of the "virginity of mind" and a theory of divine love in which all married humans participate. Both are prefigured in the "virgin spousals" of Adam and Eve, which is a presage of Mary's, "a heaven-caress'd and happier Eve" who would bring in "proud virgin joy the appropriate birth" of "The Son of God and Man" ("The Contract," *Unknown Eros*, II, ii). The direct link of Eve with Mary by way of their virgin marriage is made explicitly by Patmore in a note he wrote apropos of a projected poem on the subject:

The birth of our Lord was the natural result of the virgin marriage in its perfection, and Jesus would probably have been born of Eve had she and Adam persevered – for the Incarnation was necessary, and independent of the idea of Redemption, and there would have been no reason for four thousand years delay, but for the sin of Adam and Eve.[29]

In the "Wedding Sermon" concluding *The Victories of Love* Patmore had elliptically charged his contemporaries:

> Love's inmost nuptial sweetness see
> In the doctrine of virginity.
> ("The Wedding Sermon," v, *Victories*, II)

It is to this mystique of Eros, its virginal essence and redemptive promise, that he kept reverting in the second half of his life; and his mature reflections on its mysteries are most attractively conveyed in his collection of poems *The Unknown Eros* (1877–78) and in the collection of prose pensées *The Rod, the Root, and the Flower* (1895) published a year before his death.

Patmore also long contemplated a poem on "The Marriage of the Blessed Virgin," in which he hoped to set forth fully all he had touched upon in his previous poetry. The poem would have shown how Mary "is co-redemptrix with Christ. His visit converts the soul to acknowledge the truth and to obey it in intention, destroying the old Adam. Her visit converts the body, giving gentle disposition and affection, destroying the old Eve."[30] "Crowned with the glory and honour of bearing God in her womb," she is "the one woman . . . in whom the whole of womanhood had been more or less reconstituted and perfected."[31] The central mystery of the Incarnation was not for Patmore "a thing past, or a figure of speech," but a living assurance to each married couple of "their becoming the intimately and humanly beloved of a divine yet human Lover; and his local paradise and heaven of heavens."[32] This observation occurs in the section of *The Rod, the Root, and the Flower* headed "Knowledge and Science," which tries to hold past and future, temporal and eternal, in a readily accessible continuum. The dogma of the Incarnation clings fast to traditional knowledge; while the celebratory role of sexual love extrapolated from it extends this knowledge into innovative and naturalistic areas. Thus did Patmore involve the experience of the Virgin Mary in each person's marital realization of paradise. By Mary's "bliss pale" was "Wrought for our boon what Eve's did for our bale" ("The Child's Purchase," *Unknown Eros*, II, xvii).

The Mariolatry guiding Patmore's thought in the second half of his life lies outside the mainstream of militantly Protestant Victorian England. The readers of *The Angel in the House* and of *The Victories of Love* in the fifties and sixties would have rejected the divine metaphysics of *The Unknown Eros*, as the ordinary reader of the seventies and eighties did do. By then a new image of woman, more Eve-Magdalene than Mary, was the artistic ideal. Dickens had enshrined on the household hearth, in updated mid-Victorian versions of the Cinderella fairy tale, a series of long-suffering sexless child-women. Tennyson had portrayed his ladies of salvation, locked away in gardens of their own mind, as potential Marys, while suspecting them of being instead doomed Eves. The Pre-Raphaelites and their followers were to reverse this ambivalence, painting Eves while thinking Marys. Regardless, the sensual soul-beauty of the New Woman of the seventies and eighties was an avant-garde vision beyond the everyday dreams of the harassed small London lease-holder. She was the stuff of myths, the cynosure of the *fin de siècle*'s conjuration of itself, as the Angel in the House had been thirty years earlier when the average Englishman was eager to believe proudly that "'home / And private love did [n]e'er so smile / As in that ancient English isle!'" ("Letter XII, From Felix to Honoria," *Victories*, II). Ironically, the paradisal image of the sixties in any complete sense as conveyed by *The Angel in the House* was no less beyond the ordinary Londoner's resources than was that of the eighties. The drama of Patmore's poem had been played out against the backdrop of rural Wiltshire, whose round of activities was as far afield from the experience of a cockney as was that of Hardy's Wessex peasants. Still, they had read Dickens's avowals that the English home, and the angel at its hearth, insured the blessed continuity and daily security of every Englishman, and were ready to believe that such a lot was the next best thing to occupancy of Eden, or of Old Sarum or other down country village green. Contrariwise, anyone who wished could have a wife, and it did not take a great exercise of imagination to picture her, however strident of voice and care-worn in body, as a ministering angel when one returned to her at the end of a day in the clamorous city.

13

Pre-Raphaelite Tainted Gardens, Lost Ladies, and Intruders on the Green

IN 1849–50, in the youthful flush of Pre-Raphaelite enthusiasm for quattrocento religious art, Dante Gabriel Rossetti (1828–82) painted an up-dated mid-nineteenth-century version of the Annunciation in *Ecce Ancilla Domini!* (Tate Gallery). There are two things, for our purposes, to be noted about the picture: its ambivalent handling of Mary's spirituality and its bizarre displacement of the *hortus conclusus*. Mary seems to abide simultaneously in this world and in the next. Her figure is practically bodiless – conveniently protective of family honor and of the modesty and reputation of his sister Christina, who was his model – covered by a white nightgown whose folds reveal almost nothing of substance beneath, with the exception of a bent leg which is pulling her gown taut; contrariwise, her lank copper-colored hair is palpable, her eyes and lips sentient, her face a study in mixed reactions. Mary cringes against the wall away from the angelic afflatus, her downcast eyes taking in the Angel's proffered lily with apprehension even as they gaze inwardly with alarmed concentration on the timeless. As well she might. Still dishabille and slugabed, she has been caught by the Archangel in embarrassing spiritual unreadiness. Rossetti has ignored the medieval and Renaissance practice of including in scenes of the Annunciation a glimpse of the promised garden or celestial city on a hill usually visible in the background through an archway or open window, as in the *Annunciation* (1495, Hermitage, Leningrad) by Giovanni Battista Cima (1459–1517). That painting, and Bellini's *Annunciation* (*c.* 1490, Galleria del Accademia, Venice), could have provided the prototype of the angel and of the bedroom setting of Rossetti's picture. Where Rossetti innovates is in his curious concentration on the boudoir setting without reference to a paradisal or heavenly world, and on the young virgin's being taken by surprise in the embarrassing intimacy of her bed, as contrasted to Cima's placement of her kneeling on her *prie-dieu* with prayer book in hand. The result is that Rossetti's painting gives scant allusion emblematically to the divine promise of eventual human salvation, which is so significant a part of the Annunciation paradigm.

A similar ambivalence, half-earthly, half-ethereal, animates the Damozel and characterizes the heavenly meadows in both poem (1847) and painting (two versions, 1874, Tate Gallery: and 1875–78, with predella, Fogg Museum of Art, Harvard Univ.) of *The Blessed Damozel*. Despite the Dantesque idealism of the poem, the Blessed Damozel is no Beatrice. The Italian maiden's translation into

249

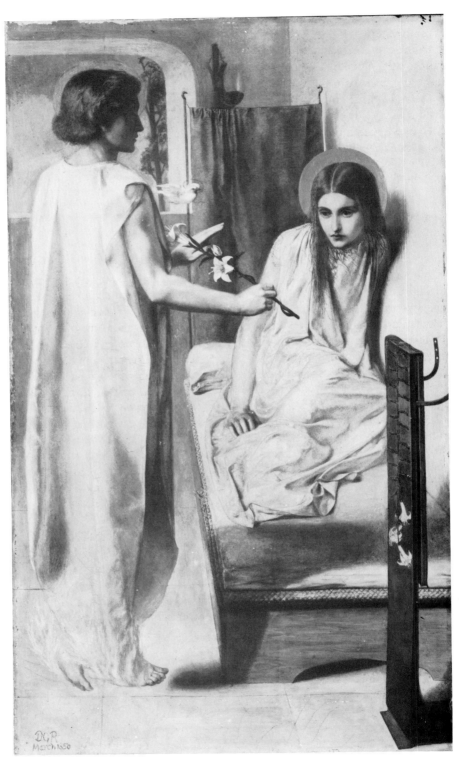

31   Rossetti, *Ecce Ancilla Domini!*

heaven belongs to the otherworldly desires of an earlier age. More like Keats's Madeline the Damozel longs to "melt" into blissful oneness with her still earthbound beloved. One exploratory study (*c.* 1873, Victoria and Albert Museum) for the painting, using Alexa Wilding as model, shows Rossetti striving for a beatific image and getting mostly pensive tenderness. The result, for all her chaste beauty, however, speaks a more sensual language in her full lips, heavy-lidded eyes, long thick neck, strongly delineated chin and nose, and flowing mass of hair than heaven normally hears. The preliminary sketch that Rossetti made in 1876 for the background (in the Fogg Art Museum, Harvard University) reflects the same contradictions. Designed to embellish the lines:

> Around her, lovers, newly met
> 'Mid deathless love's acclaims,
> Spoke evermore among themselves
> Their rapturous new names

it depicts a heavenly field of lovers standing waist deep in flowering shrubs. As befits the dual emphasis of the lines on the lovers newly reunited and on their love newly spiritualized, their embraces demonstrate equal portions of ardor and *agape.* An uncertainty of tone pervades poem, painting, and sketch, excess vying with restraint, not least in the modulation of the enclosed garden into a May-Day gathering of lovers. An alternative last line of the verses illustrated by the predella has the lovers rapturously recalling in "Their heart-remembered names" their previous flesh-bound lives. In effect, Rossetti appears to be fusing the spiritual message of divine love related in the *hortus conclusus* with the guilty tale of carnal love enacted in Eden. The unintended result is to put in question the symbolism linking the two gardens in a promised restoration of paradise. Rossetti's is an unsure parody of that restoration. He lacked the rectitude of mind for realizing unambiguously his visionary enthusiasms. As he advanced from generous-hearted youthfulness toward prematurely exhausted, bitter middle age, his darkening vision became ever more bifurcated between joyous celebration of the tangible and somber devotion to the intangible.

Long gone were the innocent days when Blake could cheerfully and indiscriminately equate "every Generated Body in its inward form" with "a garden of delight & a building of magnificence" (*M*, 26:31–32; E,122). The patina of both country and city had darkened since those blissful far-away years, and not just by the action of the soot-filled industrial atmosphere. Science had added eons to the youthful earth of Blake's day. The corrosion of religious rust had also taken its toll. Queen Victoria in her widowhood (Prince Albert died in 1861) reigned as the conscience of the age, setting an unreal moral tone for the rest of the century.

The original sin enacted in Eden was a truism never far from Victorian consciousness in these decades. Many of Holman Hunt's paintings unabashedly assert the moral theme of fallen man – *The Hireling Shepherd* (1851, City Art Galleries, Manchester) and *The Awakening Conscience* (1852, Trustees of Sir Colin and Lady Anderson). Others exhort the strayed sheep to return to the fold of the

Shepherd Jesus – *The Light of the World* (1853–56, City Art Galleries, Manchester) and *Our English Coasts* (commonly known as *Strayed Sheep*, 1852, Tate Gallery). When Rossetti contributed designs in 1857 to the Moxon edition of Tennyson's poems, he chose for one of his themes *The Vision of Sin*, and when Augustus Egg (1816–63) painted *Past and Present* (RA 1858, Tate Gallery), a tripartite sermon on the horrors of sexual infidelity, he included such easily recognized *topoi* of the wife's (and mother's) error as the abandoned core of a half-eaten apple on the table and a picture on the living room wall of Adam and Eve's banishment from Eden. The subject of the painting repelled and thrilled viewers. Critics dismissed it as "a piece of very commonplace vice,"[1] even as they salaciously recounted its carefully planted details of depravity. While its tale of "The Adulteress and her fate" (so the *Athenaeum* termed it in 1862) excited a fascinated horror when it was shown, no one had the courage to buy the painting and it was still on Egg's hands when he died.[2]

It was not entirely arbitrary on Rossetti's part then, that when he envisioned the ascendant Mary he found himself as often as not seeing the fallen Magdalene, or when he conceptualized the scene of the Annunciation he saw the Virgin in her room still abed instead of at her devotions. Nor was the enfeeblement of his idealizing powers to be blamed wholly on the encroaching darkness of paranoia and drug abuse.

Signposts of the confusing directions taken by the age include the upsurge of taste in the 1860s and 70s among the art patrons of the manufacturing classes for a more sensuous and erotic treatment of subject than the romantic medievalism pioneered in the early 1850s by the ascetic-minded Pre-Raphaelite Brotherhood[3] and Robert Buchanan's puritanical counter-attack on Rossetti, Swinburne, and

32   Rossetti, Preliminary sketch for background of *The Blessed Damozel*

Morris, as comprising "The Fleshly School of Poetry" (1871). Rossetti reacted to the conflicting signals of his milieu by finding it increasingly impossible to image spiritual beauty in the lineaments of a full-bodied woman without her fleshliness telling a contrary story. John Everett Millais similarly reflects the dichotomy of the time as early as the 1850s, honestly depicting Tennyson's heroine *Mariana* (1851, Lord Sherfield's Collection, Royal Academy) in the awkwardly twisted torso of a thick-hipped mature woman stretching with boredom and wasting sexuality; but turning the next year in *The Huguenot* (1852, Huntington Hartford Collection) to a technically slick rendering of innocent, almost angelic, star-crossed love. Nor were the Pre-Raphaelites in their portrayal of ideal love free from cultural stereotypes and market values. Arthur Hughes's efforts to capture "The Eden of Love's watered ways" tended to dwindle into scenes of "trysts and *tristess*, of sweet sadness rather than grief,"[4] as in *April Love* (1855–56, Tate Gallery). Rossetti's contempt for his patrons, and his inexhaustible need for money, led him to make repeated copies of the love "Whose speech Truth knows not from her thought, / Nor Love her body from her soul" ("Love-Lily" [1869], 23–24).

The religious dualism of the post-Darwinian period, with clerics struggling to salvage Christian dogma by separating it from the mundane sphere, and to save its ethics by sentimentally compartmentalizing daily life, exacted a daily price in self-confidence and in moral ambiguity for clinging to the dream of paradise. It is not surprising then that when Rossetti and the Pre-Raphaelite poets and painters associated with him in the second half of the nineteenth century, as well as some older poets like Matthew Arnold, tried to envision their world as partaking of the original perfection, they as often as not failed to catch the right tone. They vacillated between the worldly and the spiritual, caught in hapless ambivalence of mood; or, avoiding that, they either castigated an unsatisfactory earth or escaped to an unconvincing heaven. The garden image of paradise was never more "fallen" than in the last decades of the century. Its deterioration tended to take two forms. The Eden of enclosed garden offering joy, divine harmony, and promise of eternal life is perceived hallucinatorily as a prison, or alternatively as a place of graves, a Gomorrah of sterile plains and despondent nostalgia. Scenes of the Annunciation often lack a perspective of the garden (and its emblematic reminder of paradise), or, contrariwise, garden scenes with a virgin have no angel bringing his heavenly message. As for symbolic presentations of ideal beauty and pure love, they tend to translate ambiguously into depictions of the fleshly and the demonic. Eve preens as Lilith, the Virgin Mary lapses into Mary Magdalene, and Beata Beatrix blurs into Astarte Syriaca.

The ambivalence with which the Pre-Raphaelites painted versions of the enclosed garden speaks to a postlapsarian anxiety that they shared with their con-temporaries even though they were consciously bent on a Christian reaffirmation of the moral life. Perhaps because of his tangential relationship to the Pre-Raphaelite circle, and because his was a minor talent, as compared to the undeviating moralism of Holman Hunt and the complex gifts of John Everett

Millais, Charles Allston Collins's *Convent Thoughts* (1851, Ashmolean Museum, Oxford) reveals this anxiety in easily recognized, although finally unsorted, ambiguity of feeling.

The painting shows a nun standing beside a lily pond in a walled convent garden. She has been reading her devotional book, but her attention has been diverted to a passion flower held in her other hand. The picture is not without painterly panache, both in its elegant finish and in its formal composition. But the completeness of execution, as well as the completeness of the world depicted in the picture – the walled garden, the well-defined formal beds of flowers, the committed religious vocation – contains a contrary fragmented perception, which adheres, in the face of certitude of details and religious faith, to Collins's final disposition of his Christian subject.

The "convent thoughts" (the plural form is suggestive) are left unspecified. Does the picture offer a "sermon" on the spiritual gain – and heavenly paradise – won in a life devoted to emulation of the continuing passion drama that was Jesus's? Or is it questioning the unnatural sacrifice of human desires in the interests of a problematic future? The reviewer for *Punch*, when the painting was first exhibited, posed the same set of questions.

Whether by the passion-flower he [the painter] put into her hand, he meant to symbolize . . . the passion the young lady is in with herself, at having shut up a heart and life capable of love and charity, and good works, and wifely and motherly affections and duties, within that brick wall at her back – whether the flower regarded, and the book turned aside from, are meant to imply that the life of nature is a better study than the legend of a saint, and that, therefore, the nun makes a mistake when she shuts herself up in her cloister, we are not sufficiently acquainted with MR. COLLINS's ways of thinking to say.[5]

As Martin Meisel has sensibly remarked, "The poise of views and possibilities is the painting's delicate though perhaps slender achievement."[6] The nun is from one point of view very much a member of the restricted world of the garden. Like the staked flowers in their narrow beds she is a disciplined part of a severely controlled environment. At one remove from this basic composition, however, is the contrasting riotous luxuriance of the blossoms and leaves. In comparison to them the ironed folds of the nun's habit place her outside the realm of the natural world. The equipoise of these formal elements, especially the hesitant antithesis of confined natural fecundity to disciplined spiritual passion, addresses however unwittingly the mid-Victorians' postlapsarian anxieties, which were complicated by new uncertainties about nature. While the painting may leave the nun's "convent thoughts" problematical, it is less reticent in its worried confrontation with the more generalized question of man's Edenic future.

There are hints that Collins was not unaware, in his placement of the nun in a garden, of the tradition of the *hortus conclusus*. She has been meditating on the Blessed Virgin and on the passion of Christ, as is indicated by the two illuminated pages of her book still marked by her fingers and held open for us to see. But Collins's departures from common typological reference are as significant as his echoes of the sacred images. The visible pages of the devotional book ask us to

33 Charles Allston Collins, *Convent Thoughts*

keep in mind the full mystery of Jesus's earthly pilgrimage – from Annunciation to Crucifixion – with its promise of afterlife. Contrariwise, the nun contemplates the passion flower, seemingly oblivious to the greater narrative whole of which the flower symbolically partakes. She is momentarily distracted by its emblematic concentration on Jesus's death, and hence diverted from meditation on the sacred promise of the garden in which she stands, a promise concentrated in the horticultural recall of Eden and in the replacement of Eve's occupancy of it with the Virgin's. Our attention, unlike the nun's, is also directed to the lilies

34   Millais, *Mariana*

associated with the spiritual message of Jesus's birth. Meisel has noted that "The lilies and the severely gowned, almost bodiless, young woman recall Rossetti of the Annunciation [that is, Rossetti's painting *Ecce Ancilla Domini!*, 1850] (the shape and angle of the nun's head recalls the Virgin's, as does the framing by wimple and veil, hair and aureole). But it is Rossetti brought into the age beyond miracles, the age of the English garden."[7]

Unspecified by Meisel, because his attention was concentrated on an internal dialogue among the Pre-Raphaelites about the relationship of art to nature, is that Rossetti, no less than Collins, found that the old mysteries offered treacherous footing for a modern painter. The virgin of *Ecce Ancilla Domini!* is a frightened neurotic shrinking from the reality of the lilies in the angel's hands, a weak vessel for carrying the grace of knowledge that from her would issue a child who would salvage the fallen garden world. It is no wonder then that Collins, following Rossetti's faltering lead, should paint a garden more Country-House English than *hortus conclusus*, revealing a painter fraught with doubts about the specific symbolic significance from the past to be attached to it. Collins's garden enclosure contains a virgin forced to wrest from the emblems of death promise of a spiritual future. She is reduced to emulating the life of the Virgin without the divine presence of the angel and the security of his Annunciation (in the "English garden" the lilies grow naturally instead of being offered sacramentally by the angel), and without the human knowledge of conception, gestation, and birth – in short, of involvement in life – that was both Eve's and Mary's. The question the painting puts finally is whether the garden can continue to be read as a sacramental sign of God's traditional comforting assurance that man will reclaim its paradisal purlieus.

An answer of sorts is given by Millais's *Mariana* painted the same summer as Collins's. The subject is drawn from Tennyson's poem of the same title, and the picture was exhibited with the refrain lamenting her abandonment:

> She only said, 'My life is dreary,
>   He cometh not,' she said;
> She said, 'I am aweary, aweary,
>   I would that I were dead!' (9–12)

Mariana stands at her work table, where she has been embroidering leaves and staring in boredom at a scene of riotous garden wilderness through stained glass windows depicting the Virgin Mary and Gabriel of the Annunciation. Her external world contains all the sacred images of the *hortus conclusus*, but reduced either to rank disorder or to stylized art. They are ironic correlatives of an inner secularized world which has lost touch with its unmediated mythopoeic past. (A make shift table altar containing a triptych, candles, and censer is shunted into a dark corner of the room, religious objects reduced like the saints in the windows to decorative art.) More radically than Collins's nun, this daughter of Eve has abandoned the garden to its rank growth and withdrawn to her chamber. There, she is a virgin for whom the Annunciation will never come.

These two pictures display gardens in thematic contexts and with figural references, which consciously evoke the Christian drama. Yet they disquietingly resist our efforts to read them as unqualified affirmations of eventual re-entry (to use Cardinal Newman's language of faith in his sonnet "Hope") through "Eden's long-lost gate." It is not that Millais was unable to invent modern images to replace conventional religious iconography. He had demonstrated his facility in this regard in *Christ in the House of His Parents* (1849, Tate Gallery). Rather, it is that the garden was losing much of its mystical aura as it was being democratized into a mundane experience. The embarrassing poetic clamor of Thomas Edward Brown's assertion that "God walks" in his garden exhibits more a desperate verbal affirmation of a paradisal archetype no longer felt on the pulse than it does ardor for a religious mythology recalling the faith of the Middle Ages. The nineteenth century witnessed a series of refinements of gardening models, which brought gardening within reach of almost everyone, as contrasted to the landscaping of Kent and Brown in the previous century, which had been the plaything of aristocrats. Repton reintroduced flower beds around the house; exotic plants from around the world were successfully acclimated to English weather and soil. Italian floridity became popular again. In the second half of the century William Robinson systematized the "wild" garden, no doubt in part on the model of Darwinian nature. And Gertrude Jekyll worked a variation on the flowery cottage garden by devising the herbaceous border. Gardening flourished as an activity of the average English leaseholder as never before, even as painters and poets were questioning the paradigmatic import of gardens, or worse, trivializing its paradisal symbolism. The misdirected efforts of Albert Moore (1841–93) and Frederic, Lord Leighton (1830–96) to recapture some of its original mystery resulted more often than not in an artificial and incongruous, rather than otherworldly, air. Their scenes of females picking flowers like any ordinary English woman in her garden except for being garbed like a fifth-century B.C. Greek matron (as, for example, in Moore's *A Garden*, 1869, Tate Gallery), portray, finally, displaced women – Roman, Greek, romantic, make-believe, or whatever – out of their century, and out of their culture. The traditional symbolism of the *hortus conclusus* would have received, perhaps, its *coup de grâce* by the end of the century at the hands of Sir Richard Burton, if he had not died in 1890 before completing his perfervid exercise in steamy orientalism, a translation from the Arabic of *The Perfumed Garden*.

A sign of the garden's emblematical status is its assimilation into the convention of the mirror image in Pre-Raphaelite paintings with indoor settings. Rossetti's *Lady Lilith* and Hunt's *The Awakening Conscience* exploit this development skillfully. As suggested by the moral handling of their subjects, as well as by the oblique allusions of their titles, these pictures do not exclude their being read at one level as nineteenth-century commentaries on the enclosed garden. That it impinges on the hermetic world of the boudoir and love nest of *Lady Lilith* and *The Awakening Conscience* as a mirrored reflection signals that the earthly paradise is a lost part of these fallen ladies' knowledge. And by focusing our attention on the garden as a detail of secondary importance both Rossetti and Hunt indicate, elegiacally perhaps, that Victorians had wandered far afield from primal innocence in comparison to their grandparents who had imagined the earthly paradise to be still of easy and innocent access.

The narrative bent of the Victorians did not restrict itself to explicit treatments of the themes of Adam and Eve, the Annunciation, and the Nativity. Their literature, but especially their art, is full of recondite references to a vanished *hortus conclusus*, to an angel and dove who bring often as not word of a barren Annunciation. The bird being killed by a cat under the table in *The Awakening Conscience* is easily read as allegorical of the young woman whose soul has similarly been imprisoned and murdered by lust. But how else account for the doves in the lower-right hand corner of Hunt's *The Lady of Shalott*, yet another painting in which a lady glimpses her walled garden and the world outside it in the mirror on her wall? There is no reference to the birds in Tennyson's poem. It is an invention of the painter, whose obsessively moral movements of mind could not resist crowding his pictures with typology demanding the kind of interpretation I am suggesting. Given the religious subjects of the icons on the wall and the supernatural character of the Lady, the picture cries out to be read allegorically at a more profound level than called for when viewed simply as an illustration of the poetic text. The Lady is a Blessed Virgin *manquée*, her Angel of Annunciation an adulterous knight whose apparition concludes her vigil, and her existence, without the alleviating hope of divine love that Jesus's birth confirmed in another far different Annunciation.

For most intellectual mid-Victorians, who saw themselves as actors in a continuous historical drama, Eden had merged with the geological story of earth. Adam and Eve, once happy inhabitants of a divinely inspired garden, had lost their sacred immediacy, had become ordinary residents of earth participating in the same history as their progeny down to the present moment. There is a Burne-Jones illustration to William Morris's *A Dream of John Ball and a King's Lesson* (1892), which shows an animal-skin clad Eve seated on an outcropping of rock, her small children Cain and Abel clinging to her legs. All three watch a muscular Adam ineffectually trying to plow the flinty ground with a makeshift spear. That pathetic portrayal of the first family as beleaguered humans, struggling with puny tools to reclaim from the earth a marginal subsistence, gives voice to the nagging self-doubts that would not be stilled, and is witness to the dark underside of mid and late Victorian dreams. The illustration has its poetic counterpart in Rossetti's "Eden-Bower" (*c.* 1869), which recounts Lilith's malicious glee over Adam and Eve's future of backbreaking labor to get their daily bread:

> 'In the planted garden eastward in Eden,
>> (*Sing Eden Bower!*)
> Where the river goes forth to water the garden,
> The springs shall dry and the soil shall harden.'

Both picture and poem provide a counterpoint of loss to the self-congratulatory

35 Millais, *The Blind Girl*

reception accorded the Crystal Palace and Great Exhibition of 1851, with their arrogant parade of technology for subduing the earth.

Victorians' doubts about the sacramental significance not only of nature but also of their industrial civilization – specifically in the context of the world as garden – were extended to the optical phenomenon of the rainbow, which had enjoyed an equally precise Biblical ascription of covenantal promise. Scripturally the sign of God's second covenant with man and so used typologically for centuries, the rainbow appears increasingly in eighteenth- and nineteenth-century landscape paintings merely as a visual motif, as a natural event without allegorical reference to a sacramental universe. So Ford Madox Brown uses the rainbow in *Walton-on-the-Naze* (1860, City Museum and Art Gallery, Birmingham).

George P. Landow[8] has traced the complicated treatment of this traditional Christian symbol in Victorian paintings, showing the distinct accommodation painters, especially landscape painters, made between historical and predictive handling of religious themes. The story of Noah and the Flood could be painted as an explicit representation, complete with rainbow, of sacred history, as in Daniel Maclise's *Noah's Sacrifice* (1847, City Art Gallery, Leeds), with every expectation on the painter's part that the viewer would be conversant with the conventions. But if religious significance is extended to an ordinary landscape of people and natural scenery, as in Millais's *The Blind Girl* (1856, City Museum and Art Gallery, Birmingham) showing a blind girl seated with her back to a glorious double rainbow at which her companion and guide gazes entranced, the painter is forced to signal the special meaning with specific iconographical images, in this instance a butterfly, emblem of the soul, painted on the blind girl's shawl.

Landow's argument is beset by more than one solecism. He assumes that our puzzled disbelief before such pictures was shared by the Victorian viewers. And in a supporting argument intended to establish the aesthetic dimensions of his thesis, he disregards the widespread custom in Victorian England of displaying pictures with supporting epigraphs and other verbal texts. Turner had the habit of so introducing his paintings, as did Rossetti and other of the Pre-Raphaelites. Hence, the accompaniment of a landscape with scriptural text is not necessarily indicative of the painter's lack of confidence in his viewer's ability to read his picture correctly. With this said, one can yet note a faltering of control, and even an insincerity, fundamental to Millais's shaping of *The Blind Girl* that is uncharacteristic of his usual sure touch and suggests unsettled cultural assumptions, if not religious convictions. He was a matter-of-fact young man of awesome artistic skill who early defected from Pre-Raphaelite ideals of 1848–50 to follow admired Victorian goals of fame and fortune. Those gains, however, were at times accompanied by a distressing slide into slickness and sentimentality, counter weights to the sanctimony which the Victorian drive for success had often also to carry. Between the rainbow in the far distance and the two girls in the foreground is a pastoral scene which is no doubt meant to remind us pictorially of God's second covenant with man and of the original Edenic dispensation carried symbolically in the natural phenomenon of the rainbow. But what do we make of the ravens distributed about the pasture? The dove of the Annunciation and of the Ark has evolved into one of nature's scavengers. Besides this suggestive under-note of doubt, an insincerity adheres to the gratuitous poverty and social isolation of the girls (their dresses are old and rent), and to the uncertain scale of the birds superimposed on the field. As if this is not enough conceptual inconsistency for an important painting, there is its resistance to a precise thematic reading. One cannot discount the probability that many Victorians saw the contrast between blind girl and beautiful scene as simply an enactment of pathos, a response that undermines the propensity of the Victorian's trained eye to discover typologically in the details of the painting a conflicting message. Assuming the latter account of the picture, however problematic, can we determine without additional informa-tion that the girl's inability to see the rainbow is allegorical of her defective spiritual vision? Or that her sightlessness is emblematic of humankind's spiritual blindness? And how are we to read the deplorable accident of her blindness, and its accompanying social and economic deprivation, as part of a Divine plan of Christian Dispensation? Is the visual darkness of her mortal life to be attributed finally to Eve's original act of disobedience in the Garden; and her immortal accession to light secured by God's convenant with Noah, that harbinger of Christ and a second garden? That this picture, like Collins's *Convent Thoughts*, raises more questions than it answers is symptomatic of the profound uncertainty attending the once secure image of earthly paradise.

Ten years younger than Millais and Rossetti, Thomas Hardy (b. 1840) incorporates the paradisal pessimism of their generation with low-keyed irony in an analogy to the Nativity in that high Victorian tribute to a vanished pastoral life *Far From the Madding Crowd* (1874). Keeping lonely watch over his sheep on a night within four days of Christmas, Gabriel Oak encounters Bathsheba whose lantern's "artificial light" he had first mistaken "to be a star low down" (ch. 2). The insinuation of Yuletide allusions pointedly excludes from Gabriel's view of the starry night any acknowledgement of the auspicious event that had taken place nineteen hundred years earlier. Gabriel's unselfconscious participation in the ever recurrent paradisal scene is further established by an allusion to *Paradise Lost*: he peers at Bathsheba through an opening in a shed, seeing her in this first glimpse "in a bird's-eye view, as Milton's Satan first saw Paradise" (ch. 2). With the context of their meeting thus established, Gabriel and Bathsheba sub-sequently re-enact at a subliminal level of the narrative the ancient tale of loss. A bitter measure of the distancing of the alien ground on which they stand from the original divine event is underscored by Hardy's leaving them to suffer the old score anew without the alleviating knowledge, subsumed under the divine Dispensation of Jesus according to Romantic dogma, that Wessex is part of the original acreage of Eden.

The anti-catastrophe, uniformitarian, and evolutionary theories of Charles Lyell (*Principles of Geology*, 1830), Robert Chambers (*Vestiges of the Natural History of Creation*, 1844), and Herbert Spencer (*The Development Hypothesis*, 1852) helped bring a new ice age to England's island garden. As early as 1818 Mary Shelley's *Frankenstein* – that modern myth of the soaring ambition of scientific man and harbinger of the next century-and-a-half's fears about mankind's guilty complicity in the original aggrandisement of divine power – reveals in at least one of its multi-stranded narratives the desperate human search for remnants of one's divine heritage caused by a blasted earth. Robert Walton, the main narrator, clings pathetically to his hypothesis that beneath the frost and desolation of the North Pole he will find a "region of beauty and delight" (Letter 1). Walton's fantastic hopes are extreme. But their very extremity points to the dissonance inhabitants of nineteenth-century England experienced when they tried to read nature for signs of providence.⁹ As the century advanced, they discovered less and less solace, allegorical or otherwise, in literal gardens, which took the form increasingly of parks hemmed round by "the girdling city's hum" (Arnold, "Lines Written in Kensington Gardens," 1852) or of sooty patches of courtyard enveloped by houses,¹⁰ with Lewis Carroll inadvertently contributing for the times an irreverent gloss on the garden gloom in the title of his 1867 parody of Swinburne, "Atalanta in Camden-Town." Ruskin, equally glum, relegated earthly paradise to a lovely medieval past when there were no industrial cities, to when "Paradise [was] surrounded by a moat" ("Of Medieval Landscapes: – First, the Fields," *Modern Painters*, III, IV, xiv, in *Works*, eds. Cook and Wedderburn, V, 260.) And William Morris spells the end of faith for his generation in the paradisal garden enclosure, when he testifies in his long poem *The Earthly Paradise* (1868–70) to its being now more a "shadowy isle of bliss" built by "the poor singer of an empty day" ("Apology," 38, 42) than the solid patch of real estate Milton was still able to see in his mind's eye.

Prior to about 1835 Tennyson was able while under the spell of the Romantic poets to imagine "the world / Like one great garden" ("The Poet," 1830). He could not, however, hold on to that untroubled vision of paradise at all times. Disturbing discrepancies kept intruding. The huntress "Goddess of an English wood" looked uncomfortably like a boorish peasant girl when she held "the dappled partridge fleckt with blood" (Sonnet: "She took the dappled . . ." ?1830). Nor was his perception of mythology reassuring. The paradisal bower of Oenone and Paris is swept away in the aftermath of Paris's judgment ("Oenone," 1832). This Lincolnshire rector's son found it almost impossible to follow his Romantic preceptors and imagine that "woody hollows" were remnant "valleys of Paradise" (*Maud*, I, XXII, vii), given that his experience, now buttressed by science, showed them to harbor "a world of plunder and prey" (I, IV, iv). *In Memoriam* (1833–50) is an explicit expression of his despair over an indifferent nature, whose record is one of callous unconcern: " 'A thousand types are gone: / I care for nothing, all shall go' " (LVI). Gardens of the mind fared little better. The young Tennyson often sought imaginative relief there, but they could not hide from his eyes sight of "the iron hills" of earth (*In Memoriam*, LVI). Where once cedars grew to shelter "the thornless garden," now briar roses and anemic lilies waved as emblematic signs of nature's erotic violence and letting of blood.¹¹

Tennyson appropriately places in his most famous gardens of the mind doomed high-born maidens[12] – Mariana, the Lady of Shalott, Maud, Princess Ida – who strive with tragic lack of success to fashion an inner paradise to replace the "level waste, the rounding gray" ("Mariana," 44), of the desolate outer garden. Late in life, in "Locksley Hall Sixty Years After" (1886), Tennyson visualized a future when "Every grim ravine" will have become "a garden" (168). The extravagance of this prophecy is a commentary on what Tennyson thought of man's chances ever to recover the world of Eden. Ordinarily he saw the garden as a place where human disappointment is enacted over and over, a setting where men and women repeatedly experience bitter-sweet betrayal of hopes. More like Eve than the Blessed Virgin, his high-born maidens in their reduced expectations are inexorably doomed to surrender their hold on the garden and on life.[13]

Among poets at mid-century Matthew Arnold (1822–88) speaks out with most overt distress at his, and his generation's, being limited to seeing, not feeling, how beautiful is nature. Like Coleridge he can only entertain intellectually the idea that in "wedding Nature" man receives "in dower / A new Earth and new Heaven" ("Dejection," 68–89). Problematic for Coleridge at the time of the poem, in addition to the autobiographical allusions to his unhappy domestic life embedded in the original version ("Verse Letter to Sara Hutchinson"), was an aesthetic–metaphysical question of how he might re-activate his imaginative apprehension of the "one Life within us and abroad." For Arnold the problem was emotive and religious. Elegiac on the best of days, he indicates indirectly on the occasion of Wordsworth's death in 1850 his loss of feeling for the sustaining immediacy of nature. He must resort to Wordsworth's poetic voice (and at times Keats's) to aid his recall of when "the cool flowery lap of earth" cradled human hopes "that had long been dead" to the "freshness of the early world" ("Memorial Verses," 49, 55, 57). Two years later, in "Lines Written in Kensington Gardens," Arnold tries to fix the garden in a timeless world of childhood innocence, "Screened by deep boughs" (2) from "the huge world, which roars hard by" (21). Time is not so easily arrested, however. Night inevitably comes on, and Arnold must depart the city glade, condemned like all fallen men to wander far afield, exiled from a garden he can return to only in memory. And even that form of possession turns out to be "an infinitely distant land" (74), as Arnold confesses in "The Buried Life," another poem of the same year. Too deep to reach (where "none ever mines," 56) the terrain of innocence is effectively "guarded even from our own trespasses," insuring that "the garden is closed for good."[14] In "Stanzas from the Grande Chartreuse," written during the same years, he can only conclude, with the eschatological understanding one comes to expect of Dr. Arnold's son, that his expectations are more consistent with an abbey "close of graves" (174) than with the paradisal enclosure. The child who romped in Kensington Gardens has come fearfully of age in the shade of a burial ground.

Among painters at mid-century there is no more poignant parallel to Arnold's effort to elicit from the pallid succadaneum of Kensington Gardens the

transcendent experience of nature that was an earlier generation's than Samuel
Palmer's. In the spring of 1848 he moved his family from a crowded house in run-
down Marylebone to Victoria Road, Kensington. The hopes Palmer pinned on
the move are alluded to by his son and biographer: "Kensington Gardens formed
a better apology for the country than dank Regent's Park, and gave him some
opportunities (such as they were) of studying foliage and sylvan effects."¹⁵ But the
park's tame flower beds, scattered trees, and flat stretches of grass, not surprisingly, were unable to stir the sensibility which had been hibernating since
Palmer's departure from Shoreham twenty years earlier. Not until another
twenty or more years had elapsed, after his removal in 1862 to Furze Hill House,
near Red Hill Junction, Surrey, would his imagination miraculously reawaken to
Arcadian visions of Kentish coombes with such Milton and Virgil illustrations as
The Bellman, The Eastern Gate, The Lonely Tower, and *Opening the Fold* executed
in the 1870s and early 1880s, in the last years of his life.

No one at mid-century responded to the divine approbations – and contradictions – of life, death, and nature with more desperation, however, than Rossetti.
To Wordsworth the two voices of sea and mountain spoke of human freedom. To
Rossetti, in "The Sea-Limits" (1849), the sea and woods, "voices of twin
solitudes" (17), speak not just of human mutability, but of total dissolution. Here
is a sensibility radically different from the elegiac yet healing and redemptive
imagination (one thinks of John Stuart Mill and his heartfelt acknowledgement)
of Wordsworth. A sea shell gathered on the beach, remnant of a marine animal
that once was, sounds hollowly when Rossetti holds it to his ear. An "echo of the
whole sea's speech" (25), its "listless chime" (1) tells only of the "lapse of time"
(7). Mankind is like earth and sea, Rossetti concludes; man is what he appears to
be ("Not anything but what thou art," 27). The voice of the sea ("waters,
torrents, streams . . . roaring with one voice," *Prelude*, XIII, 58–59), which
Wordsworth read as

The perfect image of a mighty Mind,
Of one that feeds upon infinity,
That is exalted by an under-presence,
The sense of God, or whatso'er is dim
Or vast in its own being   (XIII, 69–73),

is the same voice which drives Rossetti to question the meaningful existence of
man.

One of the freshest rhapsodies on the spring-tide of nature written at mid-
century was George Meredith's (1828–1909) "Love in the Valley" (1851,
expanded and rewritten 1878). The speaker seems to take unqualified delight in
the "beauty that makes holy" ([1878], 175), an innocent country maiden, whom
he equates in Wordsworthian fashion to the beauties of nature. One reacts with
surprise to such a late Romantic feel for the natural world – until one notices the
extravagant rhetoric of the analogues, and the excessive ardor at first and then
reversal of sentiments of the speakers.¹⁶ In the 1851 version the pastoral
innocence of this world is flushed with erotic anticipation of consummated

passion: "Lo! the nest is ready, let me not languish longer! / Bring her to my arms on the first May night" (87–88). In the 1878 *Macmillan's Magazine* version (reprinted by Meredith in his third volume of poetry, 1883, where it is expanded from eleven to twenty-six stanzas) the lover shies away from experiencing the mutability ("heaven is my need," 202) that all earthly life suffers, which includes seeing one's "seraph love" (198) undergo through marriage and sexual possession ("Sweeter unpossessed," 44 and 109) metamorphosis into an earth-bound woman:

> Love that so desires would fain keep her changeless.   (47)

In *The Ordeal of Richard Feverel* (1859) Meredith satirizes Romantic pride in human perfection and in an unfallen Adamic world. Sir Austin Feverel denounces the " 'Apple-Disease with which Nature has striven since Adam.' " He educates his son Richard instead according to a System which assumes that " 'we have forfeited Paradise, but were yet grown there. Belonging, then, by birth to Paradise, our tendency should even be towards it: allowing no lower standard than its Perfection' " (ch. 1). The tragic end of such Romantic vainglory comes as inevitably as in a Greek drama, when Lucy the abandoned country-girl bride of Richard, having ingratiated herself into his father's house as an angelic madonna and become the "good Victorian wife," dies in the aftermath of her husband's silly duel, barring Richard, the product of the System, forever from the paradise he had known briefly during his life with her.[17]

Both Meredith's sonnet-like sequence *Modern Love* (1862) and Rossetti's *House of Life* sonnets mostly of the 1860s and 70s reverberate with echoes of an earthly garden tainted by perverse human nature. Sir Austin's "Apple-Disease" is accepted as the law of the land. Predominant is a bitter sense of loss, all that remains to remind each speaker that he fancied himself an inhabitant of Eden. The poems dwell obsessively on a married love once mistaken for the "fair garden" each had hoped through that love to win. "More brain, O Lord, more brain! or we shall mar / Utterly this fair garden we might win," Meredith cries out in frenzied criticism of women's sense (i.e., intellect) being "all mixed in" with their senses (i.e., emotions) until they are "Destroyed by subtleties" (XLVIII). Desolate with remorse over Elizabeth Siddal's suicide, Rossetti roams bereft of both place and person where once Adam had enjoyed the companionship of Eve. Like Jehovah's Eden, Love's paradise harbors treacherous fruit, whoste taste yields "death's sterility" (L), and the "apple-blossom's part" is "To breed the fruit that breeds the serpent's art" (LXXXIII). Everywhere Rossetti looks, he is reminded of what will never come again. Not Eve but her wicked predecessor Lilith of the enchanting golden hair reigns in a garden of roses and poppies (LXXVIII). Earth is a place of total temptation, all apple orchard ("The Orchard-Pit," 1869), and among its trees "High up above the hidden pit" stands an infernal redemptrix, a goddess of death and damnation.

The image of a woman standing against, or in, the fork of a tree with one hand holding forth an apple, arms outstretched like Christ on the cross, recurs in

Rossetti's work. It first appears in the Oxford Union design *Launcelot's Vision of the Sanc Grael* (1857), and reappears in an innocent form as late as 1880 in *The Day Dream* (Victoria and Albert Museum). A prose version of "The Orchard Pit" (1869) describes the apple held by the woman as having at its heart "a red stain like a woman's mouth" and as the speaker bites it he feels a kiss upon his lips. The conflation of Eve and Christ into a sexual temptress presages the negative turn that the typology of the garden was taking in the last third of the century.

These same decades hear similar refrains sung by William Morris (1843–96) and Algernon Charles Swinburne (1837–1909). In "A Garden by the Sea" (1867), Morris exhibits toward a desired perfect existence complex, and contradictory, attitudes more characteristic of Rossetti than of the ordinarily robust Morris. The garden-close he imagines, is a strangely barren place, foreign to life, joy, and beauty. Within it, no birds sing, no habitation stands, no bee feeds, and no ship visits. Its "apple-boughs are bare / Of fruit and blossom" (8–9). Yet, he would seek this place even if he had to enter it through "jaws of death" (28). Inexplicably, the narrator labels this garden of his heart's desire a "happy place" (29), although there is in the way of recommendation only his sentimentalized association of it with an "unforgotten face, / Once seen, once kissed, once reft from me" (30–31). The felt sense of loss, which at one remove from the poetic statement is metaphysical in the insinuation of the language, has been ambiguously trivialized into a chance encounter idealized out of all proportion to the transitory event.

Swinburne too laments the "forsaken garden." In a poem of the same name, written in 1876, he loads the human sense of loss with the additional psychological freight of childhood innocence known once and then vanished forever. Like Morris's garden this one is a "ghost" of its former glory. No life stirs in it. "Walled round with rocks" and "A girdle of brushwood and thorn," even "weeds that grew green from the graves of its roses / Now lie dead" (3–8). It is a "waste place" (19): "The seed-plots are dry" (26). No flower falls. No nightingale sings.

> Only the sun and the rain come hither
>   All year long.
> The sun burns sere and the rain dishevels
>   One gaunt bleak blossom of scentless breath.   (31–34)

Swinburne imagines how a hundred years ago the garden might have known the press of footsteps of a latter-day Adam and Eve. Cynically, however, he conjectures that their love died almost before their lips had pledged eternal fidelity, or, assuming they remained faithful to the end, they are no less "loveless now as the grass above them / Or the wave" (55–56). In a concluding vision of the roses and lovers all "at one now . . . Not known of the cliffs and the fields and the sea" (57–58), he conceives of the garden in the grip of changeless eternity, not unlike the original garden, but where as then all was life now all is death. And this stasis will continue to the end of time when the slow geological action of sea against crumbling cliff will have at last entropically dissipated terrace, meadow, fields, and rocks. One can hardly imagine paradise in a more ironic grip of the absolute, or its unchanging days in a more satanic parody of the eternal.

Nor does Swinburne glimpse this anti-garden only occasionally on dyspeptic days. He sounds the same note of gloomy permanence in "Hymn to Proserpine" (1862), which celebrates the goddess who alternatively promises fecund life as the daughter of Ceres and visits us with death as the wife of Pluto. In another poem his imagination is moved by underwater gardens where flowers simulate motion and life, swaying to "the slow passionate pulse" of sea currents ("Hesperia," 30). Such a garden, Pauline Fletcher concludes, "represents a return, not to Eden, but to the primordial flux."[18] Both poems also reassert the medieval and Renaissance association of gardens with mutability and death as naturally as with Eden and an Arcadian golden age.

No poem of Swinburne's seems more inevitable, nor more apt a Pre-Raphaelite translation of the garden of life into a vale of death, than "Ave Atque Vale" (1868), Swinburne's pastoral elegy for the demise in 1867 of Charles Baudelaire. In the tradition of Milton's "Lycidas" and Shelley's *Adonais*, the poem — appropriately, as a commemoration of the great urban poet of *Les Fleurs du Mal*, the "gardener of strange flowers" (68) – is a hymn to the ultimate "mystic and . . . mournful garden" (180).

Less than fifty years before, Shelley had given unqualified assent to nature's eternal cycle of "the revolving year" – "Fresh leaves and flowers deck the dead Seasons' bier; / The amorous birds now pair in every brake" (*Adonais*, XVIII) – his perspective able to accommodate the meaning of Keats's death within a frame of reference that simultaneously distinguished between death and life and envisioned them ultimately as portions of the same loveliness.

> He is made one with Nature: there is heard
> His voice in all her music, from the moan
> Of thunder, to the song of night's sweet bird;
> . . . bursting in its beauty and its might
> From trees and beasts and men into the Heaven's light.   (XLII-XLIII)

No such traditional Platonic–Christian consolation, with its long philosophical view, soothes Swinburne's lament. Mother earth has become Baudelaire's *Géante*, an anthropomorphic garden of "dead yew-leaves and a little dust" (50), under whose sleeping "great knees and feet . . . like a lover" (58–59), Baudelaire is now vouchsafed "gainless glimpse of Proserpine's veiled head" (83). In death as in life the joyous garden of promise of Shelley, of Milton, and of Adam and Eve is for Swinburne a mournful place, where the singing Baudelaire once

> all day through thine hands in barren braid
> Wove the sick flowers of secrecy and shade,
> Green buds of sorrow and sin, and remnants grey,
> Sweet-smelling, pale with poison, sanguine-hearted,
> Passions that sprang from sleep and thoughts that started,
>
>   (181–85)

and where, now a "silent soul" (188), he lies amidst the "lovely leaf-buds poisonous" (25) of his own making.

> Thin is the leaf, and chill the wintry smell,
> And chill the solemn earth, a fatal mother,
> With sadder than the Niobean womb,
> And in the hollow of her breasts a tomb. (190–93)

The negative connotation that the earthly paradise came to have for poets in the last third of the nineteenth century is the logical outgrowth of the eighteenth-century's extension of paradise to include the cosmic smile. There is no way to improve on that incautious affirmation. Even the sanguine Coventry Patmore, who ordinarily articulated a transcendental drama of love played in a Words-worthian setting of quiet country vicarages, as the fount of the spiritual life, found irresistible "the 'wilder'd garden of the dead" in the late idyll "Amelia" (1878). For unaccountable reasons, which we might interpret as in part a response to the time, Patmore has a middle-aged suitor woo his fair maiden in the local cemetery, "The darnell'd garden of unheedful death," where they sit and kiss "nigh the little mound" of his previous affianced's grave. Into this otherwise characteristic celebration of a sacred betrothal is intruded an almost modern conjunction of sexual urges with death instincts that could hardly be more unexpected, yet ingenuously insistent. Darwin had confirmed everyone's worst fears, inaugurat-ing the geological frown of the late 1850s and 60s and implicating paradise with guilt by association. For the previous 150 years an ahistorical Eden had enjoyed a continuing literal existence as identical with both the cultivated and the natural landscape of earth. Now the concept of paradise was fated to share with flora and fauna alike the newest redefinition of the world. Not just the evolution of single species but Eden itself was sucked into the slow geological spell of time – in which each organism had its moment of growth and then inevitably suffered its long period of defilement and deterioration.

Millais records the elegiac mood in *Autumn Leaves* (1856, City Art Galleries, Manchester). The preposterously high pile of fallen leaves in the foreground, three of the four girls on the threshold of womanhood, the tangled sward of brown bushes and trees in the middle distance, "the serious *whisper* of the twilight"[19] – all announce the iron grip of change (and decay) in which nature is held, and thus image the poignant despair, just barely skirting in this instance the ever-present temptation to sentimentality, with which Victorian poet and painter alike faced the "melancholy, long, withdrawing roar" of "The Sea of Faith" ("Dover Beach," 25, 21). As if to drive home his implicit religious theme, Millais places in the hand of the fourth girl, still a child, an apple from which she has taken several bites. With this youngest, most recent Eve, he reiterates the melancholy story of the loss of Eden, and reconfirms the old law of fallen human nature, now but-tressed by the new law of natural selection of species. Even Ford Madox Brown's *The Last of England* (1855, City Museum and Art Gallery, Birmingham), that treatment "of the great immigration movement, which attained its culmination point in 1852,"[20] when read within this frame of reference, becomes an allegorical record of the cataclysmic end of that "demi-paradise" England, the crowded boat containing the traumatized immigrant survivors of a second deluge staring from a modern ark with shocked unseeing eyes upon a watery leaden-gray world.

And that is the view which sticks like an irritating mote in the eyes of Swinburne and Morris, try as they might to blink it away with eye-watering visions of bygone or futuristic alternatives. Morris had his fling in *News from Nowhere* (1890) at a future that reversed the present to secure an endless spring tide of life. To the Victorian narrator, introduced abruptly into the new world of 2003, the morning appears as it must have to Adam and Eve, as must all pristine beginnings look. Standing on the bank of the Thames River at 5 a.m. near Hammersmith Bridge, he looks about himself in surprise: "The soap-works with their smoke-vomiting chimneys were gone; the engineer's works gone; the lead-works gone; and no sound of rivetting and hammering came down the west wind from Thorneycroft's" (ch. 2). And from Hammersmith to east of Bloomsbury he discovers everywhere wild spots, forest gardens, and "houses . . . scattered wide about meadows" where once was the "brick and mortar desert of London" (ch. 10). Trafalgar Square is an apricot orchard, the Houses of Parliament a storage place for manure, Kensington "a beautiful wood spreading out on either side" to Primrose Hill (ch. 5).

Morris wrote *News from Nowhere* as a reply to Edward Bellamy's *Looking Backward* (1887). He rejected that popular book's presentation of an utopia founded on the Benthamite-like regimentation of the populace into an industrial army devoted to creating material benefits for all. He wrote a friend that he "wouldn't care to live in such a Cockney paradise" and told his daughters that "if they brigaded *him* into a regiment of workers he would just lie on his back and kick."[21] Morris's own conception of a latter-day paradise, however, is curiously ambivalent. He wishes to reclaim a kind of fourteenth-century village Arcadia; but he is not ready to revert to a wholly natural, primitive existence that historically must have been Adam and Eve's. His picture of England's post-Edenic recapture of its bucolic past is at best a compromise. Out of the decaying houses of the cities and manufacturing centers streamed people, we are told, invading the country, until the "difference between town and country grew less and less" (ch. 10). Whereas England was once "a country of huge and foul workshops . . . surrounded by an ill-kept, poverty-stricken farm, pillaged by the masters of the workshops," it is now "a garden . . . with the necessary dwellings, sheds, and workshops scattered up and down the country, all trim and neat and pretty" (ch. 10). The population is spread evenly over the land. Visible everywhere are fields; but habitations are equally present in every direction one looks. Morris reclaims the rural England of Chaucer's day but transforms it into a metropolitan sprawl. He at once repudiates the city and retains it in dispersed form throughout the countryside, unable to make a clean break with the urban

36   Millais, *Autumn Leaves*

world he knows, or to embrace without qualification the leafy paradise he has been taught to value.

Morris reveals his disillusionment with the Edenic model in his rebellious rejection not only of the rusticity but also of the innocence of the unfallen bower. He introduces playful sex into paradise redeemed. His Victorian narrator enthuses over the frank sensual joys he discovers in the new bucolic England: "The spirit of the new days, of our days, was to be delight in the life of the world; intense and overweening love of the very skin and surface of the earth on which man dwells, such as a lover has in the fair flesh of the woman he loves" (ch. 18). An added irony here is that man is relieved from the dread edict of having to labor for his bread by the sweat of his brow, with free time to dally in flirtation and in development of his emotional life, by his resort to the forbidden evil of the machine. Following his master John Ruskin, Morris railed against the Victorian use of machines "for the production of measureless quantities of worthless make-shifts" (ch. 15). The inhabitants of England a hundred years later have not succumbed to this peculiar temptation of the machine; they have instead put machines to perform tedious tasks, "work which would be irksome to do by hand" (ch. 15), rather than to multiply meaningless merchandise. The distance Morris has traveled from the guilt of the Fall is nowhere more fully revealed than in his delight, set against the history of his personal industriousness, in a work-free technological world. But the equal hold on his imagination of the late-Victorian pessimism about the nature of the world and of man distinctly compromised his faith in the imminence of another Eden, however remodeled by the power and the devices of industrial invention and however repopulated with individuals in harmony with a naturalized–mechanized environment.[22]

Morris wanted to arrest change and decay while retaining progress and civilization. No land exists which can accommodate these contraries. Morris's England of 2003 is literally nowhere, a meaning ironically embedded in the title. To such desperate shifts had industrial civilization at the end of the nineteenth century pushed sensitive residents of England and of its cities in particular. Once a demi-paradise for its inhabitants, England had become in the eyes of its most vocal critics irreversibly anti-paradisal, however bright and strident their utopian vision. The factory town had transfigured its "flowery meads," "sunny glades," and "fair corn-fields" into a modern hell where sooty demons cluster in cold brick hovels and labor long hours daily.[23]

To find Edenic disillusion in London backyards in the second half of the nineteenth century is not surprising. Those who would preserve the garden idyll in its pinched precincts as a modern correlative of paradise were hard pressed to find convincing instances. The country life to which aristocrats for hundreds of years had fled for long week-ends and during recesses of Parliament – and whose redemptive value at that was roundly deflated by Byron in the English Cantos of *Don Juan* – was not available to the majority of Londoners. Nor was the narrow belt of garden suburbs surrounding the city, like Hampstead Heath spread out before the infatuated couple in Ford Madox Brown's *An English Autumn* (1852–54, City Art Gallery, Birmingham), within reach of more than a fortunate few from teeming London. The Little Dorrits could get only as far from Bow Church, up river towards Richmond and Kew Gardens or down river towards Greenwich, as their feet might carry them to and fro in a day. With the transformation of muddy eighteenth-century London into a smoky mercantilistic colossus, the iron age that Thomas Love Peacock had joked about at Shelley's (and all poets') expense seemed to have come to pass. Already by mid-century, Frederick Denison Maurice could agree without hesitation with his fellow Christian Charles Kingsley in a letter of 25 February 1851 that "Wordsworth's Prelude seems to me the dying utterance of the half century we have just passed through, the expression – the English expression at least – of all that self-building process in which . . . Byron, Goethe, Wordsworth, the Evangelicals . . . were all engaged."[24]

Not many Londoners were of Thomas Edward Brown's persuasion, in "A garden is a lovesome thing," that God still delighted in taking an evening constitutional in their garden. ("Not God! in gardens! when the eve is cool? / Nay but I have a sign: / 'Tis very sure God walks in mine.") More numerous were the Dickenses who watched, half horrified, half fascinated, as innumerable Staggs's Gardens were violently altered in the name of progress into sterile chaos by the manufactory of civilization. A caricature of forgotten pastoral ways, a verdant suburb gone stagnant, Staggs's Gardens is an ironic tribute to the mythic memory of an unfallen world and to the eventual source of its demise. "Some were of opinion" that its name derived "from a deceased capitalist, one Mr. Staggs, who had built it for his delectation. Others, who had a natural taste for the country, held that it dated from those rural times when the antlered herd, under the familiar denominations of Staggses, had resorted to its shady precincts." It was "a little row of houses, with little squalid patches of ground before them, fenced off with old doors, barrel staves, scraps of tarpaulin, and dead bushes; with bottomless tin kettles and exhausted iron fenders, thrust into the gaps." A suburban community in transition, basking unreflectively amidst its rubbish, it survives as one of Dickens's sardonic laments for the browning of the earth. The *genius loci* of God known as Eden has dwindled into an "unhallowed spot" standing squarely in the advance of the railroad. Afflicted with the same degree of impercipient confidence as their predecessors in Eden, however, its inhabitants regarded Staggs's Gardens "as a sacred grove not to be withered by railroads" and were confident "of its long outliving any such ridiculous inventions." Given such "uncommonly incredulous" complacency, the railway right-of-way was cheerfully ignored by Staggs's Gardeners.

There were frowzy fields, and cow houses, and dunghills, and dustheaps, and ditches, and gardens, and summer-houses, and carpet-beating grounds, at the very door of the Railway. Little tumuli of oyster shells in the oyster season, and of lobster shells in the lobster season, and of broken crockery and faded cabbage leaves in all seasons, encroached upon its high places. Posts, and rails, and old cautions to trespassers, and backs of mean houses, and patches of wretched vegetation, stared it out of countenance. Nothing was the better for it, or thought of being so. If the miserable waste ground lying near it could have laughed, it would have laughed it to scorn, like many of the miserable neighbours.

(Dombey and Son, I, 6)

We are unavoidably reminded here of the end product of "the mighty course of civilization and improvement" (I, 6). In its detritus carelessly offered to the forces of change, Staggs's Gardens is already half way to becoming yet another of the Golden Dustman's rubbish heaps. Faced with this form of urban transformation it is no wonder that mid and late Victorians looked on the garden with betrayed expectations, identifying it simultaneously with an ideal of perfection that was and with the reality of decay that is. The paradigm of eternity has undergone a considerable metamorphosis. Whereas bountiful growth was once a constant, now barren entropy prevails to the end of time.

14

Rossetti's Blessed Eve and Her Daughters

THE DISILLUSIONMENT AND DESPAIR expressed toward the Edenic garden enclosure in mid and late Victorian poetry has its counterpart in Pre-Raphaelite art's response to the woman in the garden.

For over 150 years feminine presence in the paradisal garden had been minimal. By definition, Mary occupied center stage in Renaissance conceptions of the *hortus conclusus*. Eighteenth-century gardenists, however, preferred staffing their grottoes and hermitages with hermits. Continuing this secularizing and genderizing practice, Wordsworth found mostly male beggars and vagrants, with some peasant girls and girl children, often hardly distinguishable from their natural habitat, in his mountains. Daemonic women sometimes haunted Coleridge's bower recesses and romantic chasms; but they are isolated instances over whom he seems to have had limited and uncertain control. Similarly, the women with whom Shelley fled imaginatively to island paradises were more wraiths and figments of transcendentalized fantasy than recognizable flesh and blood embodiments of Eve or Mary. Those whom Byron placed in erotic congress "after nature's fashion" (*Don Juan 2*, cxci) on island paradises come closest to Eve of the Fall: "Half naked, loving, natural" (*2*, cxciv) and a child, that peculiarly Byronic doomed girl-bride of the Napoleonic generations who was "not made in the real world to fill / A busy character in the dull scene" (*4*, xv). Closer to Byron and Coleridge in their sense of sin than to Shelley and Wordsworth, most Victorian writers had difficulty imagining an unsullied Eve in an ever-blossoming garden. Tennyson's innocent and guilty women alike were for the most part sequestered in castle towers and faery pinnacles, or wards of knights in forests, while Dickens's angelic keepers of the hearth found themselves still outside the garden, tireless denisons of airless sickrooms where they nursed tyrannical old men through the sickness of life and helped usher them into the darkness of an uncertain afterlife. Although some of Emily Brontë's and George Eliot's untamed women stalked Lilith-like through a half-wild Eden, the landscape associated with them forever threatened to unleash destruction anew on unwary men. Only Patmore's beloved angels in the house were offered a psychological and sexual–spiritual Eden of sorts, which in practice however turned out to be as much Catholic and virginal–mystical turn of mind as actual state of being.

However appropriate it was aesthetically for the Pre-Raphaelite Brotherhood, given its peculiar moralistic intensity of viewpoint, to try to revive the religious fervor and linear purity of *quattrocento* painting, of Giotto, Cimabue, and Memling – and no one would quarrel with that – it was also daring that the Brotherhood should try to resuscitate Eve, forlorn of the First Garden, whose hold on it through her avatar the Blessed Virgin Mary had become again tenuous as in the centuries that had intervened since her medieval apogee. Although the Pre-Raphaelite lady – and her lineal descendants – occasionally reappear in the garden, this moden Eve's presence there has an air of awkward uncertainty about it . Despite the effort to transfigure her anew as an embodiment of divine love, she remains, however disguised by the desire to worship her from afar, an object of profane love, her roles of sister-wife-mother relegating her more fittingly to be a bored prisoner of the boudoir.

The *hortus conclusus*, Blessed Virgin, Madonna and Child, and Holy Family do not figure much as subjects in nineteenth-century English art – perhaps because of the age's cold religiosity and doubts concerning Christianity. The tepid enthusiasm of the Church of England, and of the English populace, for anything smacking of Roman Catholicism and popery may also have had something to do with the neglect. The old subjects, however, continue to be marketed, in the more acceptable forms of transfigured innocence, prostitution, besieged virtue, and domestic fidelity. As regards the last named avatar, the Pre-Raphaelite lady should be viewed at least initially against the backdrop of Patmore's idyllic parsonage and its covey of female angels. If she did not emerge directly from his house, she was a familiar guest there, a step-sister so to speak – one who goes partly bad – of the mid-Victorian Angel in the House. The 1849–51 goals of the Pre-Raphaelite Brotherhood were not unsimilar to Patmore's. They shared the same religious turn of mind, the same idealistic belief in the role of art and poetry. And Rossetti particularly was to pursue, as did Patmore, the *ignis fatuus* of the soul in the fleshly contours of female beauty.

Rossetti was at his best as a painter of women. Four appear and reappear in his pictures: Elizabeth Siddal, Fanny Cornforth, Alexa Wilding, and Jane Burden Morris. Lizzie Siddal, the first of his loves, he met in 1850, set up housekeeping with in 1852, married in 1860, and buried in 1862. Misses Cornforth and Wilding were desultorily model, housekeeper, and mistress. Jane Burden was discovered by Rossetti's roving eye for female beauty at a theater in 1857 when she was seventeen. After her marriage to William Morris in 1859 she and Rossetti drifted into separate lives until Lizzie Siddal's death when he turned increasingly to her from the late 1860s onward for supportive love and artistic inspiration. In appearance Lizzie Siddal typified the Pre-Raphaelite ideal of the blessed damozel, Fanny Cornforth the temptations of the flesh, and Jane Morris the soul incarnate. Their composite nature – savior and seductress – is ultimately symbolized by the languorous physicality of Jane Morris, whose large eyes, full and shapely lips, flaring nostrils, long thick neck, and masses of wavy hair were to become the prototype of the Pre-Raphaelite woman for the rest of the century.

Giotto and Cimabue celebrate the mother of God, whose holy love through the

Grace of God insures the eventual return of man to paradise and completion of the cycle of paradise lost and regained. For Rossetti *caritas* kept shading into carnal love, posing *in potentia* an ever present danger to the soul of eternal damnation.

> She hath the apple in her hand for thee,
>   Yet almost in her heart would hold it back;
>   She muses, with her eyes upon the track
> Of that which in thy spirit they can see.
> Haply, "Behold, he is at peace," saith she;
>   "Alas! the apple for his lips, – the dart
>   That follows its brief sweetness to his heart, –
> The wandering of his feet perpetually!"
>
> ("Venus Verticordia" [1865], 1–8)

He kept seeing Eve as Venus, while wishing to see both as Mary, "Soul's Beauty," whom he painted as *Sibylla Palmifera* (1866–70, Lady Lever Art Gallery, Port Sunlight). Rossetti's imagination even while searching out instances of Lady Beauty and ideal love was repeatedly aroused by human susceptibility to sin – by the idea of Lancelot and Guinevere encountering each other at Arthur's grave (*Arthur's Tomb*, 1855–60, E. W. Huddart), by Paolo and Francesca stealing a kiss in a window niche and floating clasped together in Hell (*Paolo and Francesca da Rimini*, 1855, Tate Gallery), by the three Fates standing imperiously over a fallen woman (*The Maids of Elfen-Mere*, 1854, now lost), and by doomed lascivious Mary Magdalene going in her unnatural rouge and seductive finery to wash and kiss Jesus's feet (*Mary Magdalene at the Door of Simon the Pharisee*, 1858, Fitzwilliam Museum, Cambridge). The theme of the fallen woman confronting her virginal past obsessed him. He labored for years (unsuccessfully because of his rudimentary mastery of perspective) on the painting *Found* (1854–82, Samuel and Mary R. Bancroft Collection, Delaware Art Museum, Wilmington) which shows a country drover on the way to market with a calf, trying to raise his former sweetheart, now a prostitute in the city, from the pavement where she cringes in all her shameful finery against a wall, her eyes closed and head averted from his compassionate entreaty, crying "in her locked heart,—/ 'Leave me – I do not know you – go away'"[1]

As Bernini's *Santa Teresa in Estasi* (1651, Cornaro Chapel, S. Maria della Vittoria, Rome) dramatizes, and mystics from St. John of the Cross to St. Catherine of Siena have told us, the intensest experiences of God often take an erotic form, and in making the spiritual palpable render it indistinguishable from the sensations of the flesh. Nowhere in Rossetti's paintings is this truth more evident than in *Beata Beatrix* (c.1864, Tate Gallery), his *memento mori* of Lizzie Siddal who had died the previous year. She appears as Beatrice at the moment of rapturous transfiguration from earth to heaven. But as more than one observer has noted, her body is bent slightly forward, head raised and eyes closed, in concentration on a vision of "unheard melodies" with an ecstasy that appears as much sexual as religious.[2] Into her cupped hands a red bird is dropping a poppy, symbol of sleep and death, as a reminder of her turbulent drug-haunted years

37   Rossetti, *Beata Beatrix*

with Rossetti, and of how she had died from an overdose of laudanum. The dove
of Annunciation with its lily of purity has metamorphosed sinisterly to bring a
gloomy message of human frailty. A sundial calls our attention with less guilty
self-reflection to the same tale of temporality. In the background is an enclosed
garden, containing Dante and the female figure of Love, who clarify the otherwise
ambiguous identification of Beatrice with Mary, and of Dante's spiritualized
garden of love with the *hortus conclusus*. The fact that the girl is Lizzie Siddal, and

278

the picture is as much a remorseful commemoration of Rossetti's love for her as an evocation of Dante's apotheosis of Beatrice, darkens the ambiguity with its memories of a sexual desire that was self-destructive.

The history of Rossetti's struggle to introduce the nineteenth-century woman, modern Eve transfigured, into the timeless moment of Eden[3] again is one of shifting allegiances and uncertain directions. In the late 1840s and 1850s Dante's love for Beatrice appears over and over as a theme in Rossetti's drawings and paintings. "Paradisal Love . . . sublimed to heavenly mood" (10, 6) he nostalgically invokes it in 1870 in a poem "On the *Vita Nuova* of Dante." Despite his dedication to her memory, Beatrice is displaced in the mid 1850s in favor of Guinevere as the subject of his pictures, Dantean idealism yielding ground to Tennysonian reality. For the next two decades Rossetti vacillated between "Soul's Beauty" and "Body's Beauty." Although *Beata Beatrix* and *Sibylla Palmifera*, representative of "Soul's Beauty," as well as the portrait of the bride of God in *The Beloved* (1865–66, Tate Gallery), were painted in the 1860s, more characteristic of his state of mind at the time, perhaps, are such pictures of the "imperial trouble of beauty"[4] as *Fair Rosamund* (1861, National Museum of Wales, Cardiff), *Pandora* (1871, private collection), *Lucrezia Borgia* (1860–61, Tate Gallery), *Girl at a Lattice* (1862, Fitzwilliam Museum, Cambridge), *The Loving Cup* (1867, believed lost), *Monna Vanna* (1866, Tate Gallery), *Venus Verticordia* (1864–68, Russell-Cotes Art Gallery, Bournemouth), *Morning Music* (1864, Fitzwilliam Museum, Cambridge), and *Helen of Troy* (1863, Kunsthalle, Hamburg). These paintings reflect the *frisson* of Rossetti's vision, its post-paradisal pessimism.[5]

His emotional involvement with Jane Morris, starting up in the late 1860s and continuing through the 1870s, prompted Rossetti to attempt anew to capture "woman's budding day-dream spirit fann'd" ("The Day-dream"), this time in Jane's drooping earth-heavy figure; but an air of languor and theme of imprisonment keep intruding into the very posture and visage of his subject. The pictures are haunted by female *Sehnsucht* and sexual lassitude. The despairing note of barren, destructive love becomes obsessive. It tends to be of two kinds: coldly Narcissan in its all-consuming regard of self, or Lethean in its siren's call to embrace self-forgetfulness. Fanny Cornforth usually provided the model for the former, Jane Morris and Alexa Wilding the latter. Together the pictures comprise an astonishing, compelling tribute to the eternal duality of Eve–Mary, and one of the most honest explorations in mid-Victorian England of a typology that had lost certainty of meaning, that had strayed into a cul-de-sac which looked like the traditional enclosed garden but contained little of the psychological and emotional conviction of old.

The perfidious nature of Eve tends to be envisioned by Rossetti as the product of a worldly and sophisticated civilization. In *Lady Lilith* (1864, Samuel and Mary R. Bancroft Collection, Delaware Art Museum, Wilmington), subtitled by Rossetti "Body's Beauty" in contrast to the "Soul's Beauty" of *Sibylla Palmifera*, a woman of marmoreal and disdainful beauty sits in negligent dishabille in her boudoir, combing her long locks of hair with one hand and staring with single-minded intensity at her image in a mirror held by the other hand.

> And, subtly of herself contemplative,
> Draws men to watch the bright web she can weave,
> Till heart and body and life are in its hold.

So Rossetti described her with the lines from Sonnet LXXVIII of *The House of Life*. The subject of the painting is significant. According to Talmudic legend Adam's wife Eve was preceded by Lilith, a lovely woman governed by evil. Rossetti's Lilith is the pampered female focus, the *femme fatale*, of a self-indulgent society.

38   Rossetti, *Lady Lilith*

Scattered about her on the vanity table and on her lap, with telling iconographic effect, are "The rose, foxglove, and poppy," all establishing the artificial context of her being. In a mirror over her vanity table is reflected the natural greenery of a garden, its promise of eternal joy now contained in a lifeless reflection between frames. In *Monna Vanna* (1866, Tate Gallery) another latter-day Eve and erstwhile inhabitant of a contemporary Eden is portrayed as "the Venetian ideal of Female beauty." Elaborately clothed in a rich dress of white and gold,[6] heavily necklaced and bejeweled, she anticipates her fate with controlled eagerness, the eternal courtesan of the demi-monde. With more explicit iconography, Rossetti displays the listless *La Bella Mano* (1875, Samuel and Mary R. Bancroft Collection, Delaware Art Museum, Wilmington) at her toilet enclosed in a stifling environment of hot-house plants, ornate wash basin, and orbed mirror. She is a modern Venus, attended by androgynous loves, preparing to receive her lover. "A flower of Venus' own virginity, / Go shine among thy sisterly sweet band," Rossetti wrote in a sonnet on the painting; yet there is no joy in her demeanor. Hers is a vitality that is being wasted in the service of love in a crowded bedroom; and the claustrophobia of her spirit is emphasized by the composition's restriction of La Bella Mano to a corner of her room, with the bed and fireplace indicated, not without the suggestion of a leer, only by their reflection in the mirror on the wall.

Of those paintings which picture the Lethean promise of love *Astarte Syriaca* (1877, City Art Galleries, Manchester) is Rossetti's supreme tribute to the passion that passes understanding. Behind the figure of the Syrian Aphrodite two attendant hermaphroditic angels lift their heads heavenward, symbolic of her aspiration, which is counterpoised, however, and neutralized, by the carnal languor of her heavy shoulders and breasts, and modeled arms and limbs. She stares past the viewer into the depths of worlds beyond, her person suffused with the mystery of an ecstasy finally less religious than sexual, as the sonnet Rossetti wrote about Astarte makes clear:

> Her twofold girdle clasps the infinite boon
> Of bliss whereof the heaven and earth commune:
>   And from her neck's inclining flower-stem lean
>   Love-freighted lips and absolute eyes that wean
> The pulse of hearts to the spheres dominant tune.

As with Lady Lilith and Monna Vanna, communion with Astarte leads to endless forgetfulness more than life everlasting.

Lurking beneath the surface of the will to life lies the contrary temptation to succumb to inertia. Coleridge struck this note when he remarked in a letter to his brother George in 1798 on the bliss of repose induced by laudanum: "You, I believe, know how divine that repose is – what a spot of inchantment, a green spot of fountains, & flowers & trees, in the very heart of a waste of Sands!" (*CL*, I, 394). Not the least fascinating parts of this confession are its foreshadowings of "Kubla Khan" and its sidelong glances at the Hebraic–Miltonic topography and the Moslem reward system of paradise. At the same time it establishes Coleridge as prefigurative of the late Victorian sensibility, with his unexpected insistence

39   Rossetti, *Proserpine*

here on the symbiosis of death (laudanum, desert, unconsciousness) and life (oasis) in the infinite regress to reclamation of Eden. Already in 1798 Coleridge was not unconscious of the barren horrors lurking on the periphery of his opium paradise; and his perception reverberates through the next century. De Quincey, another explorer of these strange borderlands of the soul, probes in *The English Mail-Coach* (1848–54) the psychological implications of the human urge to mystic nirvana; while Tennyson gives archetypal expression to the idea of the opiate that is likewise anodyne in the languorous rhythms of "The Lotos Eaters" (1830–32). Like the subject of Tennyson's sexually guilty Queen Guinevere, the myth of Persephone, who combines in her person the twin halves of Eve–Mary, intrigued the Pre-Raphaelites, especially Rossetti, as also Swinburne and Burne-Jones. It answered an ambivalent attraction in their natures to both the chthonic and the divine.

In *Proserpine* (1874, Tate Gallery) Rossetti captures some of the attractive poignancy which clings to the bride of Pluto ever poised between mortal and immortal realms. Modeled by Jane Morris, the goddess stands gazing pensively downward, a thick mass of hair surrounding her head and neck like a halo. She faces the daylight world visible to her through a window that casts a square of brightness on the wall behind her, even as the encroaching gloom of the room envelopes her. Clutched in her hand is the partly eaten "drear / Dire fruit" of a pomegranate, which "tasted once," Rossetti tells us in accompanying verse, "must thrall" her to the nether world. Here, Persephone and Eve, the daughters of Zeus and Jehovah, merge indivisibly into the female archetype symbolizing human gain of knowledge at the cost of personal contentment.

A similar mood – and theme – is depicted in *La Pia de' Tolomei* (1868–80, Univ. of Kansas Museum of Art, Lawrence, Kansas), inspired by Dante's commiseration in *Purgatorio* (Canto V) with the suffering spirit of La Pia, who was confined by her husband to a fortress in the marshes of Marrema, where she died without receiving absolution. Rossetti poses her seated on the fortress terrace, a prisoner, her head bowed in melancholy meditation, her prayer books stuffed with papers and dismissed at her side, her averted eyes transfixed by a large sundial on the stone bench beside her. She is a Mary doomed to wait for an Annunciation that will never come, condemned to muse on after her orisons, while rooks fly free overhead, and her fingers clasp in barren gesture the "fair jewel" with which she "was ringed and wed" (Rossetti's translation of the pertinent lines from *Purgatorio* placed on the frame of the picture).

The theme of loss runs throughout Rossetti's *oeuvre*, from the early Dante drawings, and watercolors, with their emphasis on Dante's mourning of Beatrice's death,[7] to such late paintings as *Proserpine*, *La Pia de' Tolomei*, *La Donna della Finestra* (1879, Fogg Museum of Art, Harvard Univ.), *Mariana* (1870, Aberdeen Art Gallery and Regional Museum), and *Veronica Veronese* (1872, Samuel and Mary R. Bancroft Collection, Delaware Art Museum), with their suggestions of imprisonment, and death. Rossetti is continually drawn to the subject of abandoned, doomed, and betrayed women: of Cassandra, Ophelia,

Guinevere, Helen of Troy, Persephone, and La Pia, whose loss he tries to transfigure into transcendent gain. The recurrence in many of these paintings of a musical motif speaks ambivalently of the soul's escape into a heaven of the spirit, and yet also of its entrapment by earthly desires. Rossetti never can quite forget that female beauty "from the first" has been a "perilous principle in the world" luring men to repeat the primordial sin. The painting of *Proserpine* was originally intended as a subject of "Eve holding the apple," according to William Rossetti, and "was converted by afterthought into Proserpine holding the pomegranate."[8] In *A Sea Spell* (1877, Fogg Museum of Art, Harvard Univ.) the siren's "lute hangs shadowed in the apple-tree," as she sits listening to "the sweet-strung spell" of her music, "gulf-whispers" from the nether world designed to divert men from their appointed earthly tasks. "What creatures of the midmost main shall throng / In furrowed surf-clouds to the summoning rune," Rossetti asks in a poetic description of *A Sea Spell*,

> Till he, the fated mariner, hears her cry,
> And up her rock, bare-breasted, comes to die?

In *A Sea Spell*, *Veronica Veronese*, *The Blue Bower* (1865, Barber Institute of Fine Arts, Univ. of Birmingham) and *La Ghirlandata* (1873, Guildhall Art Gallery, London), the women are simultaneously imprisoned and imprisoning. The sea bird lured ashore by the siren's song in *A Sea Spell*, and shown amidst the branches of the apple tree and the leaves of a Venus Fly Trap, ironically counterpoints the canary at the open door of its cage above Veronica Veronese's head.

Rossetti's fixation is more often on the garden of Eden, and on the sexual temptation which lost it than on the hope of its eventual retrieval as held out by the Annunciation, the Blessed Virgin, and the *hortus conclusus*. The latter idea seldom enters thematically the pictorial frame. The *topos* of love, and of the beloved as spiritual saviour, figures with ambivalent frequency less as a vital force in the reclamation of Eden than as a continuing confirmation of its deprivation.

In one painting and poem Rossetti came consciously close to adumbrating the theme of paradise regained. That the painting captures unmediated a dream whose negative possibilities haunted the Victorian consciousness may account for the picture's bland absence of tension. It is as if with the relaxation of Rossetti's censors there occurred a comparable relaxation of resistance to the nightmarish conclusion to the dream. The result – artistic distancing of the event of loss – was psychologically satisfactory, if aesthetically disappointing. The picture is *The Bower Meadow* (1872, City Art Galleries, Manchester). Rossetti began it in 1850, its tentative title "the meeting of Dante and Beatrice in the garden of Eden." Quickly abandoned in an unfinished state, it was taken up twenty-two years later and transformed into a Renaissance pastoral that goes one step beyond the Dantesque theme to celebrate Eden as a female abode of perfection. Nevertheless, its static artificiality is without conviction. On a terrace overlooking a tree bordered meadow, two ladies dance to the stringed accompaniment of two other women. A dovecote ironically tells us that there is a *locus amoenus* which will never

40 Rossetti, *The Bower Meadow*

need the intercession of God and the promise of the *hortus conclusus*. The maidens gaze about them in trancelike expectancy, as if bewildered by their female heaven, incredulous about the purpose of a paradise without men. Theirs is a bower of Eves which will know neither the shattering loss of innocence nor the solemn ecstasy of the Annunciation. They are sleep-walkers in a garden reduced to a painter's exercise in rich reds, lush greens, and regal blues – the colors of the Virgin Marys lovingly painted in Italy from the fourteenth to sixteenth centuries.

The metaphysical despair residual in *The Bower Meadow* is given verbal expression in the Provençal-like love chaunt, "The Song of the Bower," which Rossetti wrote as an accompaniment to the picture. Here, "Fettered Love" becomes a metaphor for a paradisal bower, once the scene of joyous union, now permanently barred to human presence and human love. The lover laments that he can never recover the lost scene. "'Ah God, if again it might be!'" The bower of his beloved has become for him, however, a tainted garden. He imagines his heart flying there and finding everything, once familiar, now foreign:

> There it must droop like a shower-beaten flower,
> Red at the rent core and dark with the rain. (7, 36, 11–12)

If Rossetti's women are more often than not figures of salvation betrayed by their human natures, "so pure,—so fall'n!" ("Jenny," 207), spirits doomed repeatedly to enact profane roles, Burne-Jones's are blank-faced angels whose feet have never known the insubstantial meadows of heaven, heavy-footed nymphs who have always trod the barren plains of earth. Occasionally, demonic urges buried deep in the female breast are revealed in a figure like the Medusa-headed Vivien in *The Beguiling of Merlin* (1874, Lady Lever Art Gallery, Port Sunlight), whose heavy limbs and sexually charged air recall Burne-Jones's discipleship to Rossetti; or in the "manic winsomeness"[9] of the mermaid in *The Depths of the Sea* (1886, private collection), who is pulling her captive sailor into the ocean depths. More characteristically, however, Burne-Jones's women sleepwalk through a beautiful romantic dream of something that never was, and never will be. They descend a curving stair in entranced rhythm, a vestal procession of automatons (*The Golden Stairs*, 1880, Tate Gallery); or drowse interminably in awkward positions into which they appear to have fallen under the weight of gravity and heavy slumber (*The Sleeping Beauty* panel from the Briar Rose Series, 1873–90, Buscot Park, Faringdon); or stare Narcissus-like into a pool, both their images and persons so immobile that reflection and reality are interchangeable (*The Mirror of Venus*, 1898–99, Calouste Gulbenkian Fdtn, Lisbon); or dance as Graces so stately and slowly that their trailing dresses seem rooted to the earth (*The Mill*, 1870, Victoria and Albert Museum). They are untouched by experience, not so much idealized as unformed. This applies even to the lithe cameo-like nudes Burne-Jones sometimes painted, chastely viewed from the side or from behind, such as the girlish waif Psyche in *Pan and Psyche* (c.1872–74, Fogg Art Museum, Harvard University) and the unsullied Andromeda in the tempera *Perseus Slaying the Sea Serpent* (c.1875–77, City Art Gallery, Southampton), an unravished beauty as attractively drawn as those by Ingres, who also found the theme irresistible. Their normal condition is a quiesence hardly distinguishable from the more moribund state. Earthly sleepwalkers in some middle border between life and death, they may be less tainted, but no less lost, than Rossetti's. And as often as not they occupy a blasted landscape of barren plains and rock-ribbed mountains, or inhabit an airless claustrophobic space defined by swirls of heavy drapery, tangled trees, and rose briar bushes, or coiling serpents, the antithesis of Eve's fecund paradise.

The somnolent ladies of Burne-Jones are not unique expressions of his dream world. Artists drawn to the classical ideal of beauty, such as Albert Moore and Lord Leighton, testified in their uncritical portrayals of similar women to a prevalent female mystique. Their paintings *Dreamers* (1882, City Art Museum and Gallery, Birmingham) and *A Summer Night* (1890, Walker Art Gallery, Liverpool), and *Flaming June* (c.1895, Luis A. Ferré Foundation, Museo de Arte de Ponce, Puerto Rico) capture women in the same fallen roles as does Burne-Jones in *The Sleeping Beauty* panel. They lie under a divine spell of body, supine in spent contortions on couches of cushioned and draped disarray, their voluptuous vitality inert yet still visible beneath filmy robes. Withdrawn into sleep they present us with an image of marmoreal beauty lost in post-coital exhaustion. The ambiguity of their trance-like condition combines inextricably the states of Eve sinning with Mary transfigured.

The daughters of Eve found the second half of the nineteenth century not one of their better periods – unless they were one of Charles Dodgson's "legions" of little girls staring out from the safe margins of one of his photographs, arrested in a moment of young girlhood forever. Frederick Denison Maurice enunciated as early as 1842 the Christian view of the role of the woman as it was to govern the minds of the mid-Victorians. In *The Kingdom of Christ* he appealed to her as Christ's handmaiden to serve the church, as she "alone can do, without departing for a moment from [her] own true estate," as wife, as sister, and as mother. He envisioned "how the whole sex may be an order of Sisters of Charity; and how, in each particular neighbourhood, this order may be at work in lowliness and meekness, softening and healing the sorrows of the world."[10] Sequestered for the most part in stifling domiciles as inviolate goddesses, a few escaped to fight the battle of bloomers and suffrage, and earned masculine enmity for their derring-do. A few *femmes fatales* fluttered, gorgeously apparelled butterflies, at society parties and balls (sympathetically captured by Joseph Jacques Tissot [1836–1902] in picture after picture in the 1870s). And a favored few led Edenic lives in isolated country houses, playing at croquet, tennis, and archery, all popular from the 1850s onward (charmingly painted by William Powell Frith in *English Archers, 19th Century* [1872, Exeter Art Gallery, Devon]). But most passively endured – lovingly assigned the hearth and the sickroom by Dickens, and worshipped as semi-divine sexual partners by Patmore – fated to bear maculate children annually, the cluttered parlor their Eden and the sanctified bedroom their *hortus conclusus*. The sacred circle of mother and child reaches its apotheosis in Alma-Tadema's painting *The Earthly Paradise* (1891, formerly Allen Funt collection) of a wealthy Roman matron nuzzling her naked offspring on a couch as she prepares the child for its bath in one of those all marble rooms Alma-Tadema limned so well. Not least of the picture's accomplishments is its reduction of the sacred drama of the enclosed garden to a period genre piece in a Roman bagnio.

The year after the death of Queen Victoria, for fifty years the national symbol of selfless parturition, Thomas Cooper Gotch (1854–1931) sums up the canonization of the Victorian mother in his painting *Holy Motherhood* (RA 1902, Laing Art Gallery, Newcastle), which depicts her as a virginal Mary with a Christ child, after the Quattrocento compositions of Benozzo Gozzoli and Bellini. Fifty years before, in *The Last of England*, Ford Madox Brown had given perfect expression to the Victorian worship of the family by way of his indirect affirmation of the Holy Family. The brooding persons of an English immigrant husband and wife sit separated by the fantail railing of a ship from their disappearing homeland, and separated by an enveloping umbrella from their angry and frightened fellow ship's passengers. The family group presents a tight private circle of interior fortitude to the departure confusion of the others. The mother protectively clutches the hand, all that is visible, of her child shielded from the cold sea air by a maternal woolen cape. *The Last of England* overtly treats of the immigration problem that reached epidemic proportions during the middle decade of the century. It also covertly renders the Flight into Egypt of Mary and Joseph as a modern study of besieged family solidarity.

As if betrayal by the social ideal of motherhood, of being turned into ever pregnant Marys, were not enough dubious worship to bear, their Eve-like *Doppelgänger* came competitively back into fashion in the 1870s, 80s, and 90s as a golden-age nude, after being frowned upon as in bad taste in the early years of Queen Victoria's widowhood. Henrietta Rae (1859–1928) cast her in the contrite role of a nude *Psyche before the throne of Venus* (RA 1894, untraced). John William Waterhouse (1849–1917) portrayed her as a water nymph, her nakedness exposed below the surface of the pool, in *Hylas and the Nymphs* (1896, City Art Galleries, Manchester). And Sir Lawrence Alma-Tadema (1836–1912) plunged her sportingly into the *Thermae Antoninianae (Baths of Caracalla)* (RA 1899, Lord Londonderry). Even that careful chronicler of Victorian virtues, and sentiments, now knighted and respectable, John Millais, indulged in the thrill of the undraped female body in *The Knight Errant* (1870, Tate Gallery); while Frederic Leighton betrayed the prurience of that thrill with almost comical unselfconsciousness by populating *The Birth of Psyche* (1890, Tate Gallery) with gratuitous nudes.

A fashionable variation on the female nude as the distillation of classical beauty is the vogue in the last three decades of Victoria's reign for photographs of children as God brought them into the world, a taste for angelic innocence which Lewis Carroll shared with his age at least until July 1880 when he inexplicably abandoned his hobby after several years of accelerated picture taking of feminine purity in the buff. Lovingly conceived as the Fair Maiden of ancient myth – Henry James's ambiguously flattering title was "Heiress of All the Ages" – the daughters of Eve glowingly nude in the first flush of the world's dawn, and of Mary serenely maternal in contemplation of man's salvation on her lap, found themselves by the end of the century established, and bored, prisoners of the prudent nursery and the stuffy parlor and the steamy Turkish bath, all an unconscionable remove from the unfallen Adamic world.

The obsessive interests of the second half of the nineteenth century in the female found the licentious Mary Magdalene irresistible. She was painted by Rossetti (1877) and Frederick Sandys (1858–60), for example (both pictures now

41   Thomas Gotch Cooper, *Holy Motherhood*

in the Bancroft Collection of the Delaware Art Museum, Wilmington) as the embodiment, in startlingly different degrees, of sensual abandonment and spiritual atonement. Under the guise of moral reclamation, prostitution and illegitimacy paintings were popular. Even matter-of-fact and common-sensical Ford Madox Brown, ever responsive to turns of taste and changes in belief, was compelled to try his hand at this theme. The result is the unfinished *Take Your Son, Sir!* (c.1857, Tate Gallery). Like *The Last of England* pictorially powerful as social document and as quasi-religious statement, it exhibits the complex mid-Victorian attitude toward sex and salvation. It reveals the difficulty of maintaining the traditional surfaces of the Eve–Mary symbolism, as conventionally and optimistically defined, in the face of the contrary thrust of human nature and the unpredictable turns of society.

42 Ford Madox Brown, *The Last of England*

Brown portrays a defiant unwed mother facing us frontally and displaying her baby to the protesting seducer (glimpsed in a mirror behind her head) whose hands are extended in an ambiguous gesture, face forward and downward, that leaves in question whether they are outstretched to receive the baby, or to deny his paternity.[11] The convex mirror, hung against a wallpaper design of night skies, stars, and moons, encircles the woman's head like a halo. The baby has been lifted from her lap and thrust forward in her hands toward the viewer – and the skeptical father. Its hospital gown, or swaddling clothes, wrapped around the mother's arms, forms another halo and in its suggestion of shroud reminds us of the Christ child's earthly fate. Its left arm swings down from its side and its head lolls limply backward, until it resembles in configuration the recumbent Christ in the arms of Mary after his deposition from the cross. Here is a Madonna and Child for the times, complete even to the indirect inclusion of the father, a protesting doubting Joseph. The positioning of mother and child in the form of a Pietà subsumes in the tableau the other great religious subject of medieval and Renaissance painting, reminding us in the glorious promise of Jesus's birth of the outcome of his pastorate on earth, his future agony, and resurrection, and our eventual salvation and return to paradise. No more unambiguous statement in the second half of the nineteenth century could be made about the profanement of Christian iconography: Mary mother of God reduced to a fallen woman, the Christ child to an illegitimate baby. Brown's uncompromisingly bleak version of the Christian mystery either lampoons traditional Christian iconography, or contrariwise, questions sacred social taboos. In either case, the picture points up the conflict between standard ethical-religious and socio-psychological perceptions complicating mid-Victorian habits of mind.

John Dixon Hunt has chronicled the evolution of the Pre-Raphaelite woman in poem and picture from Rossetti to Alfons Maria Mucha, from *La Pia de' Tolomei* to the girl in the Job cigarette poster, at the end of the century.[12] William Morris, Arthur Symons, George Moore, Lionel Johnson, Ernest Dowson, and Oscar Wilde – all invoke her mysterious fascination, the duality of her innocence as the highest ideal of feminine beauty coupled with her seductiveness as the portal to evil. She is their "Impenitentia Ultima" according to Dowson, eternal living proof of their sense of man's fatal susceptibility to the female lure. She is the "donna della finestra,"[13] a spirit of heaven consumed by distinctly earthly passions, who holds out the promise of love – and plentitude – but ends imprisoning one's soul, destroying one's will, and relegating one's heart to a desert of feeling. Swinburne summarizes neatly the catastrophic implications of her attractiveness:

some woman, real or ideal, in whom the pride of life with its companion lusts is incarnate. In her lover's half-shut eyes, her fierce unchaste beauty is transfigured, her cruel sensual eyes have a meaning and a message; there are memories and secrets in the kisses of her lips. She is the darker Venus.[14]

Among English novelists, Thomas Hardy was most susceptible to the combination of her physical charms and her rebellious nature, portraying in Eustacia Vye (see ch. 7, "Queen of the Night," *The Return of the Native*, 1878) a sensitive appreciation of the tormented female spirit that lay imprisoned in the Pre-Raphaelite woman. Nor was Henry James immune to her ambiguous charms, describing Jane Morris at great length in his letters in an effort to distinguish the person from the image: "It's hard to say [whether] she's a grand synthesis of all the pre-Raphaelite pictures ever made – or they a 'keen analysis' of her – whether she's an original or a copy."[15] And in novel, story, and art criticism for thirty years, from 1875 to 1905, he pursued her spoor in the persona of Salome,[16] the *"macabre maiden of the Christian story"* (*Roderick Hudson*, 1907 New York Edition, ch. 9) now sadly reduced to *fin de siècle* decadence; and he darkened the fate of his undefiled American daughters of Eve, by condemning them to suffer the common lot of their English and European postlapsarian sisters.

Among non-English artists, the French painter Gustave Moreau (1826–97) eulogized the same fatal virgin as emblematic of a destructive female principle in *Salomé Dancing Before Herod* (1876, Armand Hammer Collection). The Austrian Gustave Klimt (1862–1918) made her an elegant Viennese society lady, and fated killer, in *Judith and Holofernes* (1901, Österreichische Gallerie, Vienna). And the Norwegian Edvard Munch transformed her into a vampire in *Madonna* (1894–95, Munch-Museet, Oslo), framed by an obscene halo of hair and by a circle of fetuses and spermatozoa.

Aesthetically one cannot fault John Dixon Hunt for finding this figure as conceived by the end of the century writers and artists to be the product of "artistic and emotional laziness": a compilation of derivative metaphors pointing back to Rossetti rather than outward to life.[17]

> O that languishing yawn!
>   O those eloquent eyes!
> . . .
> I was stung by a look, I was slain by a tear, by a tempest of sighs.
>
> (26–27, 30)

Thus Lewis Carroll parodied her vaporous mannerisms in "Atalanta in Camden-Town" in 1867, indicating that her hackneyed features had not escaped at least one early sharp-eyed observer.[18] Still, Carroll and Hunt are too hasty in dismissing her as without redeeming social value. The stock epithets of her *fin de siècle* beauty are no less bankrupt of poetic content than those similes likening his mistress's eyes to the sun, and her cheeks to roses, which Shakespeare laughed at in Sonnet 130. The sterile boudoir, no less than the "barren bower" with its canopy of "withered leaves," through which Pre-Raphaelite beauty and sixteenth-century nymph respectively wander, points to a myth still able to evoke once deeply felt, now no longer always poignant, promptings of the spirit. However indirect, however incomplete often the reference, and however worn the metaphors, at one level of typological response these laments are half-remembered keenings for the passing of paradise.

Practically everyone in the waning decades of the nineteenth century tried his hand at depicting Eve, or one of her recent more socially sophisticated daughters.

43   Ford Madox Brown, *'Take Your Son, Sir!'*

The near-pagan Edward Calvert includes her among his nude studies of dryads and classical models of elemental life (in the oil study *Eve*, c.1860s, British Museum) as a young nymph thigh-deep in flowers reaching up in rapt concentration to caress the blossoms of a tree, her nude innocence at one with the sylvan scene. John Roddam Spencer Stanhope (1829–1908), a follower of Burne-Jones, casts her in *Eve Tempted* (1877, City Art Galleries, Manchester) as a wistful nude vaguely receptive to temptation. Even so unsentimental a personality as Whistler felt compelled to subtitle his portrait of *Dorothy Seton* (c.1903, Birnie Philip Bequest, Glasgow) as "A Daughter of Eve." It is as if in bidding nostalgic farewell to a lovely myth, once passionately clasped, and still fondly recalled as the most precious of family traditions, they were fixing it forever in the cultural memory. Some such unexpressed subliminal feelings, enwrapped in the spiritual mystery of adolescence, seem to animate the portrait of the fifteen-year old Ellen Terry (1864), painted by George Frederic Watts (1817–1904) the year he married her. His explicit painting of *Eve Tempted* (1884, Tate Gallery) twenty years later probably better epitomizes the end of the century's fascination with the theme as a frivolous act. An unblushing nude, she leans forward to reach for an apple with her mouth, her coquettish demeanour more fit for an apple-bobbing contest than for the act that shook mankind out of its complacency for all time. However trivial the conception and however trite the vocabulary in which it is tricked out, the picture nevertheless measures the felt sense of postlapsarian loss which lingered below the surface jaundice of "the Beardsley period."[19]

Although more savage than almost anything to be found in *fin de siècle* England, Munch's art defines the ultimate perimeters of this felt sense of the passing of the earthly paradise ambiguously visible at murky levels of the Victorian psyche. In no pictures is this loss more pessimistically explored than in his cycle of paintings on *Love* (1895, Munch-Museet, Oslo) and in his repeated motif of *Metabolism* (1898, Munch-Museet, Oslo). In the latter, which depicts Adam and Eve separated by the tree of life now become the tree of knowledge, the tree's roots extended and carved into the wooden frame ultimately draw our attention away from the forlorn parents of mankind. The comforting solace of a religious apprehension of human experience has yielded to the secular despair of the evolutionary viewpoint. In the garden of Eden, the eternal abode, the tree of life is found rooted in death, in mortality and decay. With the laboriousness of Theodore Spencer re-interpreting the story of creation, Munch literally represents the biological truth that all life comes from the earth, and is consigned to it again in death. The picture *Madonna*, and even more explicitly the pictures he painted on the theme of the kiss (e.g., *Death and the Maiden*, 1893; and *Vampire*, 1893–94; both in Munch-Museet, Oslo), present the female devotion to this cycle as vampirish in her erotic exploitation, and then psychological abandonment, of man. To insure the continuation of biological life woman wantonly embraces death. The mystery of life continues to be celebrated; but the medieval identity of the eternal with the spiritual has been replaced by a modern materialistic version which continues to confirm life, but confirms it as an endless nightmare of erotic threat to the self. In the act of love all ultimately is lost: one's personality, one's independence of choice, even one's being, in the witless will to survival of the species.

Among English artists none portrayed the impersonal sexual threat of Eve with more verve than Aubrey Beardsley (1872–98). His malignant version of the good life might be characterized as the wish–hate image of a consumptive, sharply facetious young man doomed to die young, if his impishly perverse vision were not so accurately a ribald expression of nineties gloom and were it not echoed by so many of his contemporaries. Beardsley's drawings are the moving record of a generation's bleak loss of faith in the timeless future, a sense of loss given poignant utterance by Thomas Hardy in his secular ode on the end of the century:

> The tangled bine-stems scored the sky
> Like strings of broken lyres,
> And all mankind that haunted nigh
> Had sought their household fires.

> ("The Darkling Thrush," 5–8)

And it is that archetypal sense of the end, with its proneness to metaphysical self-pity, which the sardonic genius of Beardsley celebrates, in part, in the foppish elegance of *The Mysterious Rose Garden* (*The Yellow Book*, IV, January 1895) and of *Et in Arcadia Ego* (*The Savoy*, VIII, December 1896), and in the mordant wit of *The Kiss of Judas* (1893, *Pall Mall Magazine*).

Intended as one of a series of illustrations to the Bible, and originally entitled "The Annunciation" by Beardsley, *The Mysterious Rose Garden* turns that promissory scene of hope for man's future into a ribald tale of seduction. A hard-eyed nude girl listens attentively to a divine messenger whispering with exaggerated confidentiality into her ear. In contrast to her bare-forked meagerness of person he has adopted the artificial pose of one who has strayed into the garden from an extravagantly costumed court masque. With his Charles the Second wig and moustache, Mercury winged slippers, staff and lantern (the latter an ironic allusion to Holman Hunt's *The Light of the World*, as well as possibly to the parable of the wise and foolish virgins),[20] and lavish flower-printed robe with flame hem, he is more jaded courtier than angelic legate. Against the backdrop of a rose-trellis Mary's appointment with divine grace becomes a Restoration drama of sophisticated sin, a garden tryst between corrupt nobleman and soiled courtesan, from which no joyful or hopeful outcome is contemplated. Sir Kenneth Clark goes so far as to suggest that "the corrupter" of the "flat, virginal body" of the girl is the Arch Fiend himself,[21] making of the Annunciation another instance of the original scene of sin in the Garden of Eden. A blasphemous parody of the *hortus conclusus*, the picture announces that there is no Christ Savior, nor will be – only the prototype of betrayal, a woman succumbing to foolish blandishments.

The Kiss of Judas makes this point succinctly and sardonically. Here, the betrayal of Christ is redefined as the original – and continuing – betrayal of man.

44   George Frederick Watts, *Eve Tempted*

In a parodic reconciliation of *Lady Lilith* and *La Pia de' Tolomei* it depicts a woman slumped against a tree, her limp hand being kissed by a "repulsive goblin," by what Sir Kenneth Clark has defined, apropos of a similar figure in *Enter Herodias* (illustration from Oscar Wilde's *Salome*, 1894) as a "curious symbol of depravity . . . looking like a bad-tempered, elderly fetus."[22] She stares blindly at a flat landscape relieved by a grove of three trees and by a second trio of similarly situated bushes clinging in serpentine twists around tall stakes. Both trees and staked bushes are positioned like the crosses on Calvary, but without the visible Christ – hence iterating, and reiterating, the decay of the paradisal promise. Death without the hope of resurrection has entered the *hortus conclusus* and laid it waste. The garden inherently and irrevocably contains the presence of destruction, so Beardsley assures us in a sardonic interpretation of *Et in Arcadia Ego*, in which he depicts "an aging roué in frock coat and spats tiptoe[ing] toward the storied urn"[23] atop a tombstone on which are engraved the fatal words.

Beardsley's "lady friends"[24] run a wide range of historical and literary types; but they tend to share a similiar fate: they are ill-fated rebels, star-crossed lovers, sexual marionettes, unlucky courtesans, consumptives, or social pariahs – all sisters to Ernest Dowson's Cynara. Beatrice Cenci, La Dame aux Camélias, Madame Bovary, Joan of Arc, Manon Lescaut, Phèdre, Belinda (*The Rape of the Lock*), Francesca da Rimini, Mary Magdalene, Sappho, Messalina, Atalanta, Salome, Lysistrata, Helen, The Witch of Atlas, Hermaphroditus, Guinevere – the fascination of "the Fra Angelico of Satanism"[25] for the fallen daughters of Eve is unflagging. Sir Kenneth Clark avers that Beardsley "has no feelings of moral indignation."[26] Nor does he have many illusions about the nobility of man. He seems instinctively to see through sham and posture, as his graphic jibes – and gentle jokes at the expense of Wilde, Whistler, and Beerbohm – suggest. Thus, in comparison, Gustave Moreau's Salome (in the painting *Salomé Dancing Before Herod*, 1876) is a perversely virginal rather than sensual woman, at once childlike and fatal, whose unhealthy, restless search for a vague ideal destroys saints and sinners alike;[27] while Beardsley's Salome is a mean-visaged minx, an end-of-the-century Englishwoman play-acting in an age-old Eastern scandal, who after an unsavory youth will grow up into the not quite respectable aunt of the Shavian Englishwoman indomitably civilizing the world and in the process corrupting it. That Beardsley's eyes were unclouded by romantic illusion did not stop him from recording, with some of the naughtiness of the Cambridge undergraduate that he might have been, the twilight of the nineteenth century. The lost ladies of *The Yellow Book*, *The Savoy*, and Beardsley's omnipresent portfolio (he carried it with him wherever he went) offer a gallery of postlapsarian souls subsisting in *fin de siècle* disillusion. They invade formal gardens, their Gainsborough hats and elaborate coiffures taking a decorative place alongside frieze-like flowers, trees, and rose-lattices (cf. proposed title page for *Venus and Tannhäuser*, first published in *The Studio*, 1898; *The Slippers of Cinderella*, in *The Yellow Book*, II; and design for the title page of *The Yellow Book*, II, July 1894). They lean forward provocatively on the inky sward of a lakeside meadow listening to a faun read

45   Beardsley, *The Mysterious Rose Garden*

THE KISS OF
JVDAS

46   Beardsley, *The Kiss of Judas*

47   Beardsley, *Et in Arcadia Ego*

from a book (cf. proposed design cover for *The Yellow Book*, v). They dance with jaded languor (cf. *The Stomach Dance*, from *Salome*) or sit in sterile boudoirs amid paint pots and powder puffs (cf. *The Toilette of Salome*). So much for the garden Milton's Adam and Eve once tended as part-time day gardeners!

Beardsley's economy of line and control of hand and pen, as Stanley Weintraub notes,[28] "was inimitable" and his illustrations were expressive of a very special order of consciousness; yet they were the art of one still young enough (Beardsley died like Keats in his twenty-sixth year) that his consciousness partook for the most part of the fantasies of his society and reflected them back in his drawings. It is not surprising then that his contemporaries on the whole, even when they were scandalized by what they surmised to be his erotic turn of mind, found his images of evil descriptive of the landscape of their own minds. Nor was his choice of subject always his to make. It was dictated, in part, by the market, not only by what was presumed to be avant-garde, but also by what, it was hoped, would be bought and read by a respectable public hungry for a taste of the indecent. His lost ladies are more a construct for the end-of-the-century eschatological mind than the angry critics who forced his removal from *The Yellow Book* in 1895 were ready to recognize.

For all its assumed lasciviousness the Beardsley picture fundamentally denies the biological life. Its flat, volume-less world is a logical – and aesthetic – extension to the stylization of Burne-Jones, which Beardsley paid the compliment of imitating in his *Le Morte d'Arthur* illustrations (1893–94) before moving on to the liberating influence of Whistler. Its fields of black and white are drained of pulsating blood. Rounded modeling of figure is eschewed in favor of linearity and pleasing arrangements in undefined space of mass and line. Beardsley's ladies are truly lost. Despite the nervous Beardsley line animating them, even their erotic posturing is lacking in sexual joy, or for that matter, in desire. They are moving toward pure design, a process which banishes them irrevocably, as daughters of Eve, from the natural garden while installing them, like Yeats's bird "Of hammered gold and gold enamelling" ("Sailing to Byzantium," 28), in an unchanging garden where the trees and flowers frame the grounds with decorative borders of artificial leaves and tendrils. No longer possible is the Romantic expectation that the order of nature harbors in its earthly parameters and in its cosmic design a paradigm of paradise, or that it fits a similar order of mind. For the generation of Beardsley – of Ernest Dowson, Lionel Johnson, Arthur Symons – nature continued, for want of any new possibility, to be the repository of the secret of life; but they read its sibylline leaves as livid gatherings from stygian wastes, not as astrophel bouquets from Edenic plains. James Thomson's *The City of Dreadful Night* (1880) was their Genesis:

> And now at last authentic word I bring,
> Witnessed by every dead and living thing;
>   Good tidings of great joy for you, for all:
> There is no God; no fiend with names divine
> Made us and tortures us; if we must pine,

It is to satiate no Being's gall.

. . .

This little life is all we must endure,
The grave's most holy peace is ever sure,
  We fall asleep and never awake again;
Nothing is of us but the mouldering flesh,
Whose elements dissolve and merge afresh
  In earth, air, water, plants, and other men.

. . .

I find no hint throughout the Universe
Of good or ill, of blessing or of curse;
  I find alone Necessity Supreme;
With infinite Mystery, abysmal, dark,
Unlighted ever by the faintest spark
  For us the flitting shadows of a dream.[29]
              (XIV, 37–42 (722–27), 49–54 (734–39), 73–78 (758–63)

One of Beardsley's early influences was the American expatriate Whistler, whose resolute rejection of mimetic realism, fascination with the flattened dimensions of Japanese prints, and reduction of natural forms to ornate designs in the Peacock Room reinforced Beardsley's instinctive sorting of biomorphic forms into abstract patterns of black and white masses. Beardsley marshalled the "Whistlerian economy"[30] of these configurations in support of his thematic statement with seeming effortlessness, particularly in *The Yellow Book* drawings and in the illustrations to Oscar Wilde's *Salome* (1894).

La Dame aux Camélias (from *The Yellow Book*, III) delineates a formally gowned courtesan of the haut-monde standing pensively before her mirror, ready to depart for an evening's entertainment or just returned from it. Against a solid black floor and alternating wall panels of camelias her white silhouette is exaggerated by her bulky coat with high collar and enormous sleeves, which all but obscure her tiny head. A vanity table on which stand two tall lit candles with a barely visible mirror between – all white – complete the scene. La Dame aux Camélias is a *fin de siècle* Aphrodite, all virginal white, in silent communion with her image before the altar of her self-worship. The black world of the room balanced against the white apparel and accoutrements of love of La Dame aux Camélias condenses an ironically profane commentary into an abstract design that says it all with irreducible economy of means.

In this drawing the dearly won perceptions of Rossetti are pushed to their extreme with effortless wit and prankish high spirits beyond his apprehension. Eve the temptress, and Mary Magdalene the seductress, however refined and historical the context of their appearance, are presented as visible, eternal manifestations of the flawed human spirit. A corrupt sophistication taints them. The boudoir has replaced the original garden as the place of human iniquity. Hard-edged forms of abstract art have thrust out its vegetative life. In that powerful, but sadistic and sanguinary, drawing *The Climax* (from *Salome*), the garden in which Salome lifts aloft the severed head of Jokanaan is reduced to claustrophobic circles of black and white. Salome kneels within a cloud of white,

48   Beardsley, *La Dame aux Camélias*

49 Beardsley, *The Climax*

on the enveloping marge of an inky pool of blood over which she holds the dripping head, and out of which thrusts an erect pudendal lily and a drooping phallic stem. Behind her the swaths of cloud break into black flower bubbles bordered in white. Salome and La Dame aux Camélias both enact the same continued crime against the self. Whether Old Testamentary voluptuary, Restoration courtesan, or *fin de siècle* lady, the actress in this never-ending melodrama is always the same woman. She belongs to the ages, now fixed in a timeless moment of abstraction. Thus has art triumphed over the idea of Eden in these drawings, has transplanted the fallen flora and fauna of Eden inside an abstract orangerie of its own construction.

15

Whistler's Peacock Room: a Curvilinear *Locus Spiritus* for the Times

IN 1876–77 when James McNeill Whistler (1834–1903) decorated the dining room of the Liverpool shipowner Frederick R. Leyland in a harmony of blue and gold, the place of Eden in the English imagination was effectively reduced to a dining room 14×33×20 feet. Equally significant, the Peacock Room, as it came to be known, retrieved paradise from the natural world, its biomorphic forms translated into curvilinear lines. Milestones along the way to the nineteenth century's retreat indoors include Morris's and Swinburne's rejection of earthly gardens, Rossetti's placement of his madonnas in boudoirs, and Whistler's delight with the restricted spaces of interior corners as backdrops to his portrait studies. Apotheosis is reached with the Peacock Room. There, shuttered from the out-of-doors, the mystery of the eternal and perfect is given full embodiment by an aesthete in the decorative terms of an artist's perception of the good, the true, and the beautiful, whose worship will win for mankind a new more lasting kind of paradise.

Although no interior decoration or artifact more completely realizes the end-of-the-century conception of perfection, the Peacock Room owes its occurrence to the ruthless dreams of an English merchant prince and to the audacious intolerance of a prophet-artist. In 1876, Leyland engaged the architect Norman Shaw to remodel and redecorate his London home at No. 49, Prince's Gate, Kensington. Shaw entrusted the remodeling of the dining room to a young assistant, the architect Henry Jeckyll. Active in introducing oriental domestic decoration into England during the craze for Chinoiserie and Japonaiserie in the 1860s and 70s, Jeckyll designed a room to hold Leyland's collection of blue-and-white porcelain and Whistler's painting *Rose and Silver: La Princesse du Pays de la Porcelaine* (1864, Freer Gallery of Art, Washington, D.C.). On the walls he attached gilded Spanish leather brought to England more than 300 years before by Catherine of Aragon, on which was painted her device, the open pomegranate, and a series of small, red flowers. Against the walls he arrayed walnut shelving, carved to simulate embossed leather and gilded in the Japanese manner. He constructed full-length shutters over the three windows, adorned the panel ceiling with eight pendant gas light fixtures, hung *La Princesse* above a fireplace at one end of the room, and placed a rug with a red border on the floor.

Whistler was also on the scene – he had been painting portraits of the Leyland

50 Whistler, *La Princesse du Pays de la Porcelaine*

family for some years, and he was currently enriching the panels of the house staircase with pale pink and white floral patterns in the Japanese style. He found the red in Jeckyll's color scheme uncomplimentary to the delicate rose and silver of his painting, and protested to Leyland. The subsequent chronology of events is unclear: when Whistler hit upon the Peacock scheme of decoration? what Leyland arranged with Whistler before leaving for his home in Liverpool? Less uncertain is that Whistler toiled from approximately August–September 1876 to February 1877 to decorate the room, glorying in the ideal setting he was creating for his picture, and that Leyland was dismayed when he returned to London in the early part of 1877 by what Whistler had wrought.

"Pictures have been painted often enough with consideration of the room in which they were to hang," Whistler is reported to have said: "in this case I have painted a room to harmonize with my picture."[1] What then had he done to the room to anger Leyland? Primarily he had covered the ceiling and walls (and that meant the historically valuable leather for which Leyland had paid £1,000), with gold leaf and turquoise-blue paint. The window shutters he had decorated with golden peacocks who reach from floor to ceiling, and throughout the rest of the room, on the wainscot, above the Dado, and on the ceiling, he painted clouds of peacock feathers, and stylized half circles adapted from the "eyes" on the peacock's breast and tail feathers as subsidiary decorative features. The consequences of Whistler's drastic redecoration was to render unsuitable Leyland's plan to display his collection of blue-and-white porcelain on the shelves.

But Whistler had not yet finished with the room. In response to the insulting offer of a tradesman's £1,000 for his labors, instead of the 2,000 guineas he demanded, Whistler added on the wall opposite that on which hung *La Princesse* two golden peacocks, known as the rich and poor peacocks, one bird with its feathers covered by gold coins and its claws clutching silver shillings, the other looking on with aloof disdain.

Despite the "peacocks in paradise" and the Japonaiserie lady, the room communicates a unity that is essentially abstract. It prefigures the curvilinear motifs of Art Nouveau just beginning to be popular. The slender shelving and posts cover the walls in complicated symmetrical arrangements around the doors, windows, and fireplace, rising and falling in cascades of horizontal and vertical lines from floor to ceiling. Five-sided polygonal panels on the ceiling, terminating in lighting pendants offer a faintly gothic but no less abstract variation, to the patterning of the walls. A border of half squares and half polygons completes the ceiling. The only natural forms in the room belong to the peacocks painted on the window shutters, and to the portrait of Miss Christine Spartali, daughter of the Greek Consul General in London, who had posed as *La Princesse*, but the peacock tails are exaggerated into golden swirls of curvilinear design, while Miss Spartali, gowned in kimono and holding a fan, is transformed into a graceful "S" curve placed against a Japanese screen. On the left window shutters a bird lifts its tail feathers in billows to the ceiling, on the right window shutters another similarly displays its beauty. The center shutters consolidate and reverse this pattern: two birds stand proudly, heads to the ceiling, their train of feathers plunging in a shower of blue and gold to the floor. All is stylized – and artificial – the natural world of biomorphic beings transferred by art into circles, half-circles, and polygonal designs in blue and gold.

The abstract decor of the Peacock Room, of course, owed something to Jeckyll's inspiration as well as to Whistler's. The interior design of Jeckyll already exhibited a pronounced oriental slant, undoubtedly inspired in part by Leyland's intention of using the room for the display of his blue porcelain and of his Whistler painting. More than Jeckyll or Whistler would have willingly admitted, theirs was an unwitting collaboration, reflecting the zeal with which the 1860s and 70s were responding to the flattened tones and foreshortened configurations of Japanese and Chinese art.

Almost from the start Whistler's art[2] reveals a tendency to reduce the transiency of reality and its natural forms to unchanging patterns of color and design. He put this aim succinctly when asked in the course of his celebrated lawsuit in November 1878 against Ruskin to explain the "almost abstract space[s]"[3] of his Nocturnes.

"I have perhaps meant . . . to indicate an artistic interest alone in the work, divesting the picture from any outside sort of interest which might have been otherwise attached to it. It is an arrangement of line, form and colour first, and I make use of any incident of it which shall bring about a symmetrical result. Among my works are some night pieces; and I have chosen the word Nocturne because it generalises and simplifies the whole set of them."[4]

One of his earliest successful paintings, *At the Piano* (1858, Taft Museum, Cincinnati, Ohio), stylishly balances a girl in white frock against a woman in black seated at a piano; their heads, on a level with each other, are spatially bounded by two pictures hanging on the wall behind them, whose frames also parallel the lines of the piano. The picture is an elegant exercise in the massing of black and white, and in the counter-balancing of perpendicular (woman and girl, two piano legs, and two sides of the picture frames) and horizontal (piano top and bottom level of the picture frames) lines. Whistler was to repeat this artful massing of color and line with even subtler arrangements of tonality in his justly famous paintings *Arrangement in Grey and Black, No. 1: Portrait of the Painter's Mother* (RA 1872, Louvre, Paris) and *Arrangement in Grey and Black, No. 2: Portrait of Thomas Carlyle* (1872, City Art Gallery, Glasgow) – where the effect, as one biographer has observed, is "of a flat silhouette . . . cunningly placed" against "flat-painted scenery,"[5] all reminiscent of the studied reality of the theater.

A different exercise in decorative panache is *Symphony in White, No. 1: The White Girl* (1862, National Gallery of Art, Washington, D.C.), the first of his celebrated symphonies in white painted a few years after *At the Piano*. It is an exhilarating *tour de force* of abstract patterning of white against white: Joanna Heffernan, Whistler's model and mistress, stands in a floor-length white dress on a white bear skin rug before white satin drapery. Her copper red hair at the top of

51 and 52 Whistler, The Peacock Room

the picture and a blue patterned carpet at the bottom anchor the elongated figure, which appears tipped toward us because of the foreshortened perspective, extended train of the dress, and shallow space produced by the white on white. Whistler has accented this exercise in white with the bravura pinpointing of a lily held by Jo against her dress in the exact center of the canvas.

The auburn hair, graceful swan neck, full lips, pensive demeanor, and touching air of innocence of the Pre-Raphaelite beauty are all there, linking her in sisterhood with the Sainted Courtesans of the day, all brightly modern and all damned. With one difference! Whistler's reduction of the White Girl, wistful air and all, to an artfully contrived pattern of unvarying white tones removes her from the haunted temporality of the doomed garden. Like Keats's Arcadians on the frieze of the Grecian urn, she will never suffer the heat of midday or the chill of evening. She has escaped "the fever, and the fret" (Keats, "Ode to a Nightingale," 23) of days that ever dissolve into tomorrows, to take up abode in the shallow corner of a pastel colored room.

Two years later, in *Symphony in White, No. 2: The Little White Girl* (1864, Tate Gallery), using Jo again as model, Whistler caught once more the fragile spirituality of the Pre-Raphaelite beauty. The effect, however, is quite different from a Rossetti painting, particularly in its skillful economy of space, which resolutely restricts the eternal world even further than the abstracted planes of *The White Girl*, to the dimensionlessness, almost, of a private thought made representational. Jo, a winsome girl in shining white dress, is positioned at a mantel and mirror, in which is duplicated her image, a tired shadowy face "flattened" to the plane of the glass along with several pictures hanging on the wall behind her. Both girl and image appear almost to be jostling each other in the same space further crowded by porcelain vase, floral spray, and Japanese fan. She is an Eve contemplative of her eventual fallen subservience to time even as she is translated into a timeless artifact like those in whose midst she has momentarily strayed. She is at once inviolate, a cosmos complete unto herself like "The rose at heart, that heaves / With love of her own leaves and lips that pair" (Swinburne's poem "Before the Mirror," 27–28, which was inspired by the painting), and vulnerable to the "grief or joy" that is the human "dower" (41).

Whistler could go no further in representation of the inviolate self-sufficiency within the convention of the arbitrarily contained field of figurative easel painting. The next logical step was to give up the figure in favor of an abstract form. In *Harmony in Green and Rose: The Music Room* (1860, Freer Gallery of Art, Washington, D.C.), he had squeezed his figures into a corner of the room, relying with what seemed odd perversity on a mirror to convey a sense of the rest of the room and particularly of the ostensible subject of the picture, the lady at the piano. *The Little White Girl* reduced this space to the still point of a woman's inner concentration, with her careworn visage in the mirror establishing the larger spatial dimensions of her world and thus rendering visible her invisible inner life. In effect, the girl gazes on her disembodied self. The painting is a brilliant adaptation of a traditional subject to new spiritual–aesthetic aims. Whistler sought the same identification of inner and outer life, of dynamic human and timeless artifact, without the use of a mirror in *Purple and Rose: The Lange Leizen of the Six Marks* (1864, John G. Johnson Collection, Philadelphia Museum of Art) – but with far less success. There were still the unexplored possibilities of the three-dimensional, which he had approached, to date, only in the limited experiments in sparse furnishings and decorations of his private quarters. As if in answer to his needs, the Peacock Room offered itself. It is no wonder Whistler seized on the opportunity with manic avidity.

The history of humankind can be described by its architectural landmarks, all seen in one form or another as outgrowths of the tree and branch of Adam and Eve's abode in Eden. The post and lintel inspired by their rustic environment was most memorably adapted by the Greeks into stunning marble-columned temples.[6] One version of the story of man's infatuation with paradise then takes the form of a continuing tension between natural and man-made shelters, with the two maintaining an uneasy alliance through most centuries. The medieval period saw a limited, religiously inspired compass of the garden in ascendancy, which reaches its apogee in the late eighteenth century as nature in the grove, along the wayside, and on the mountain top. In the nineteenth century the pendulum swung back to enshrine artfully engineered walls and stylistically eclectic rooms as more reliable links with antique glory than uncertain cataclysmic nature. By the end of the century simple faith in the efficacy of the garden was sorely tried; with distrust of gardens echoing and re-echoing through the poems of Swinburne and Morris. Parallel developments in garden design at the end of the century, reflecting the post-Darwinian suspicion of nature, include the herbaceous border of Gertrude Jekyll (1843–1932) with its controlled unruliness and the "wild garden" of William Robinson (1839–1935) with its frank acknowledgement that nature originates in and inexorably reverts to wilderness. It is in the context of such historical developments that Whistler's creation of the Peacock Room should be viewed. As a key part of the noble structure of a large town house, and as a decorative embodiment of domestic space according to unchanging principles abstracted from the laws of nature, it epitomizes the mind set of the late Victorians.

From the 1860s on not just Whistler but the art world generally seemed to be reaching out for a *je ne sais quoi* that would neutralize the ravages of time, and counteract the age's intense sense of biological instability. William Morris transliterated the flora and fauna of the garden paradise into stylized foliations when he began designing wallpapers in 1862. Only thus could he sustain the fiction of its continuing viability. It is probably no accident that vegetative forms, with their religio-gothic and other-world associations, predominated in his designs. Among the first group issued in 1864 were the "Fruit," "Trellis," and the popular "Daisies" patterns. In his early book of illustrations Aubrey Beardsley similarly translated nature into decorative designs that fixed the vital shapes of fruit, vegetable, and flower in unchanging configuration. The cover

53 Whistler, *The White Girl*

54   Whistler, *The Little White Girl*

design for *Le Morte d'Arthur* transforms the petal, pistil, stem, and leaf of two lily-like flowers into a sinuous pattern of waving lines, heraldic in feeling, faintly anthropomorphic and martial in suggestiveness, and unmistakably artful in symmetry. The same artifice, pleasing proportion, and plenitude of form describes the designs for the cover of *Discords*, the title page of *Salome*, and border pages of *Salome* and *Le Morte d'Arthur*. Elsewhere, one finds the worship of *aesthetique* in the rhythmic repetition of furled sails and masts, like so many mysterious totems, in the Thames paintings of Whistler, such as *Battersea Reach*, (*c*.1863, Corcoran Gallery of Art, Washington, D.C.) and *Variations in Pink and Grey: Chelsea* (*c*.1871, Freer Gallery of Art, Washington, D.C.), as much as in the famous blurring of outlines, shapes and identities, and the watery reductions of color to misty greys, blues, silvers, and greens in the Nocturnes. It lay behind the serious comparison of painting to music in the response of the French critic Paul Mantz to *The White Girl*, which he called a "Symphonie du Blanc," when he reviewed the show at the Salon des Refusés. (Ten years later in his essay on Giorgione Pater was to give quasi-philosophical validity to this notion of the intrinsic abstract nature of beauty when he wrote that "All Art constantly aspires toward the condition of music.") It is assimilated into the ballet-like rhythm of outstretched arms of Perseus and the three sisters in Burne-Jones's painting *Perseus and the Graiae* (1892, Stuttgart Staatsgalerie), and into the folds of drapery clothing the nude females of Burne-Jones, Albert Moore (1841–93), Frederic, Lord Leighton, Sir Edward Poynter (1836–1919), and George Frederic Watts (1817–1904). It pervaded Whistler's starkly linear, pastel colored rooms, with their untypical cold and abstract spaces,[7] at Lindsey Row in Chelsea and at the White House on Tite Street. And it crops up in Whistler's legendary *bon mots* too often not to have served him as a perspective on the world. "Your tie is in G Major, and I am painting this symphony in E Minor," he might tell a hapless visitor; "now I will have to start it again." Or he would dismiss an unwelcome suitor for a portrait with the words, "You are nobody . . . just a conglomeration of bad colours."[8] The taste for an abstract version of reality characterized the waning decades of the nineteenth century. Whistler's butterfly signature – with its recall of Japanese art, its abstract rendering of an initial and an insect into an enigmatic icon, and its devilish forked tail occasionally raised in threatening sting – which he began to use in the 1870s, becomes an emblem of the ideology of a period that was to end in the sinuosities of *The Yellow Book* and Art Nouveau of the 1890s.

Out of his tribute to Baudelaire and to *Fleurs du Mal* Swinburne fashioned a supreme statement in "Ave Atque Vale" (1876–78) of Pre-Raphaelite despair with the old garden in its previous traditional guises. As *locus amoenus* it had become a place of "half-faded fiery blossoms, pale with heat / And full of bitter summer" (8–9); as *hortus conclusus* it confirmed that "the end and the beginning / Are one thing to thee, who art past the end" (45–46), but the emphasis, in bitter reversal of the Christian comfort of the familiar phrases, is now in the funnel of time forever closed in death rather than opening into life everlasting.

It is Tennyson, however, the grand old bellwether of Victorian sensibility, who captures with its own consecrated language the century's slow disenchantment with the garden as symbol of untainted, unending organic life. In "Merlin and The Gleam" (1889) Tennyson prefigures the *fin de siècle* acceptance of the abstract and the inorganic as the norm and model of perfection. The poem is a summation of his poetic aspirations and accomplishments. After a lifetime of debate with himself over the social arena in which the artist should play out his role, he comes down unequivocally on the side of the imagination and its artifices. Merlin the archetypal artist-magician is uttering his last testament, so to speak. It is the story of his lifelong dedication to following The Gleam, a lesson he had learned from his predecessor "Mighty the Wizard"(11) and which he in turn is passing on to a "young Mariner." The gist of his advice is to trust in the necromancy of the imagination, in its ability to absorb the fluctuations of nature and inconstancies of society into the magic stillness of art. Everything this side of the horizon, or beyond it ("Not of the sunlight, / Not of the moonlight," 120–21), whether a wilderness of "desolate hollows," caverns, and "wraiths of the mountain" (42–43), or the pastoral ways of "Silent river, / Silvery willow, / Pasture and plowland" (52–54), or stately city and palace, all vanishes into the black hole of time. Only the persistence of The Gleam rescues life from nonentity. Thus Tennyson reflected in his old age with the freshness of his youth the spirit of the times.

Whistler is the artist in whom it is most interesting to watch the turning of the age away from the fateful biological determinism of the garden to enter a man-made enclosure approximating the unchanging perfect world of abstract art. His lawsuit against Ruskin in 1878 pits a headstrong proselytizer for the *avant-garde* against the arbiter of an attenuated moral aesthetic. Although the popular temper (and the spirit of the law) were in sympathy with the past as represented by Ruskin, Whistler spoke for the future. For the moment, however, Ruskin's view carried the day. The trial turned the British public against Whistler. They stopped buying his pictures. He filed for bankruptcy, and then fled England for fourteen months. A retrospective at the Goupil Gallery in 1892 vindicated his perspective on art, regaining for him the public recognition he had lost at the time of Ruskin's attack. His reductive world of variations, arrangements, harmonies, and symphonies was honored as an ideal version of reality.

One need only compare Whistler's 1880 etchings of Venice with the paintings of that city some fifty years earlier by Turner to sense the new attitudes which were distancing the paradisal paradigm both from the sterile garden enclosure and from the equally suspect urban panacea. Whistler saw not the stirring sunrises and sunsets that enflamed Turner's imagination but the deterioration of a once glorious organism. Everywhere he looked walls were crumbling, buildings flaking away, and gardens going to weed. When the enclosed garden is casually glimpsed as an untended urban courtyard given over to dusty underbrush and leafless trees contained by a decaying brick wall (see the 1886 etching *Garden* [Los

Angeles County Art Museum]), or when the Bay of Baiae is depicted with
obtrusive train tracks and belching smoke stacks violating its primal serenity by
dragging it out of the pastoral into a clanking steam age (see the lithograph *The
New Baiae* [1913, Los Angeles County Art Museum] by Joseph Pennell [1860–
1926] the confidante and biographer of Whistler), one knows that the nostalgic
recall of paradise as a garden is in trouble.

In his "Ten O'Clock Lecture" Whistler articulates the anti-nature aperçu with
force and clarity. Delivered at the old St. James's Hall, Piccadilly, 20 February
1885, to a fashionable audience who had previously dined well and who had even
had time to linger over their port and cigars before coming to the lecture in a
receptive frame of mind (hence the unorthodox hour of 10:00 p.m.), the lecture
denounced the heresies of referring artistic judgment to the yardsticks of social
improvement, of usefulness, of moral virtue, and of sublime nature. Like an Old
Testament *iconoclastes* in evening dress and monocle – he jocosely alludes to
appearing before his audience "in the character of The Preacher" (p. 135) –
Whistler cheerfully, somewhat mischievously, preaches a modern creed that sets
the artist above the prophet, and the artifact above nature. In his climactic
remarks he singles out the latter heresy – "the slovenly suggestion of Nature"
(p. 140) as norm – to inveigh against with all the invective and eloquence at his
command.

That Nature is always right, is an assertion, artistically, as untrue as it is one whose truth is
universally taken for granted. Nature is very rarely right, to such an extent even, that it
might almost be said that Nature is usually wrong: that is to say, the condition of things that
shall bring about the perfection of harmony worthy a picture is rare, and not common at all.

Whistler acknowledges that such "a doctrine" may sound even to the intelligent
as "almost blasphemous." Belief in the rightness of nature is a pervasive part of
our education until the words "have, in our ear, the ring of religion." Still, as
Whistler points out with the ingenuousness of the child looking at the emperor's
new clothes, "seldom does Nature succeed in producing a picture" (p. 143).

Nature contains the elements, in colour and form, of all pictures, as the keyboard contains
the notes of all music.
But the artist is born to pick, and choose, and group with science, these elements, that
the result may be beautiful – as the musician gathers his notes, and forms his chords, until
he bring forth from chaos glorious harmony.
To say to the painter, that Nature is to be taken as she is, is to say to the player, that he
may sit on the piano. . . .
How little this is understood, and how dutifully the casual in Nature is accepted as
sublime, may be gathered from the unlimited admiration daily produced by a very foolish
sunset.
(pp. 142–44)

In the choice selection of "brilliant tones and delicate tints" of nature the artist
draws "suggestions of future harmonies." His goal is to reduce the chaotic
superfluity of nature to its underlying sparse design. Not by "purposeless
copying, without thought, each blade of grass," but by observing the essential

abstract line "in the long curve of the narrow leaf, corrected by the straight tall stem," the artist learns "how grace is wedded to dignity, how strength embraces sweetness, that elegance shall be the result" (p. 145).[9]

No instance of Whistler's art illustrates the lessons of the "Ten O'Clock Lecture" more consummately than the Peacock Room. In its combination of natural forms and geometric lines it epitomizes Whistler's effort – and the aesthetic movement's in the declining decades of the nineteenth century – to translate mundane, uncooperative reality into a timeless order. As such it is an elegant wayside stop on the nineteenth-century pilgrim's route by way of an architectural environment to an Eden once identified with the primal garden.

Whistler told Lord Redesdale that he was "doing the most beautiful thing that ever has been done, you know—the most beautiful room!" – a room in which "Art and Joy go together."[10] Art Nouveau in decor, and utilitarian in purpose, it manages to emanate a medieval, and faintly oriental, atmosphere that is at the same time distinctly devotional in feel. Whistler's painting, *La Princesse*, hangs like an altar piece above the mantel of the fireplace. A portrait of Miss Christine Spartali in Japanese kimono, it is a Pre-Raphaelite icon of a modish, but virginal, daughter of Eve–Mary.

In a real sense, then, the room is consecrated to the worship of art. And the dark blue walls absorb the lamplight to produce a soft glow of artificial light appropriate to such sacred ends. Since the famous peacocks are painted on the window shutters, Whistler presumably intended the room to remain closed off from the profane outside world. Only thus could his renderings of nature into decorative abstractions be ever present and visible to the diners, and the harsh northern light and sooty London air kept from the room. A transmutation of the messy, intrusive world of appearances is similarly realized in the Thames River Nocturnes with their high, closed-in horizons, and with the river become a gray spume between foreground and background, a gleam of silver-green bordered by dense darkness, as in *Variations in Pink and Grey: Chelsea* (c.1873, Freer Gallery, Washington, D.C.).

For all his dandyism, his witty put-down of bourgeois solemnity, and his espousal of irresponsible Bohemian life, Whistler approached art almost as a religion, as his ardent remarks at the Ruskin trial made clear even to those who previously had doubts of his seriousness. In his rented lodgings he had striven to demonstrate art's capacity to "build a Heaven in Hell's despair," to translate an ordinary room into a shrine to art, an uncongested space defined by light and color rather than by stuffed furniture, heavy drapes, and knicknacks. How much such rooms held for him a transcendent significance is problematical. Regardless, the Peacock Room gave conscious reality, with no expenses barred – not an inconsiderable factor for an artist who was chronically impecunious – to a recurrent human dream.

In this chapel of art, with its "paradise of peacocks" (so one London newspaper termed it)[11] and its icon consecrated to a Japonaiserie maiden from the land of

Porcelain, all was fixed and certain. The slender vertical posts of the shelves, the hexagonal moldings on the ceiling with its "border" of half hexagonals and half squares, and the balanced arrangement of shelves lent to the room a sanctified air of the completely realized form. One half-expected to smell incense, as when viewing a painting of Gustave Moreau. All life, all animal and human forms represented here, have slipped the leash of the inexorable processes of mortality. Like Yeats's Byzantine bird of "hammered gold" Whistler's princess and peacocks occupy a late Victorian holy of holies: a timeless atelier of the artist's imagination.

It is no wonder Whistler reacted angrily and obdurately when Leyland treated him like a tradesman calling at the back door with his bill for work done instead of like a high priest who had introduced into a mundane house an artful version, though no less holy for that, of the paradisal enclosure. Leyland came in time wryly to appreciate the sanctuary that had been foisted upon him. He was as human as Whistler, and no more immune finally to the appeal of a world messy and biological being made serene and whole and perfect.

The Peacock Room, and the townhouse of which it was the cynosure, was a modern urban avatar of the *hortus conclusus* – possibly the final, most refined instance in the nineteenth century of the enclosed sanctuary. A paradise now domesticized and become more metaphor than myth, it was a *locus spiritus* where man and woman might still contrive to know the primal joy and mystery of God's gift of life. In this respect, it is fitting that the place was used as a dining room, where the communion of breaking bread, so to speak, could be enacted daily, in homage to the unchanging beauty of art as a necessary condition of civilized intercourse.

What was on Whistler's part ostensibly an aesthetic act was also in its final effect a social and quasi-religious gesture, which Whistler would have been hard put to deny had he been confronted with that conjecture. No irony qualified the concentration of his imagination, or diluted the dedication of his artistry and of his energies to completion of the room. His well-known penchant for that state of mind was reserved for Leyland's role in its use. The Peacock Room announces that the industrial mogul was no longer in command of his Eden, as was the laird of the eighteenth century. Leyland could proudly entertain guests and routinely take his repast there, as he did for years; but he could not avert his eyes perpetually from the "virgin" in rose and silver or from the peacock decorations every time he lifted his head from his plate. With each meal he was forced to commune with an inspired vision of the eternal and infinite. In the teeth of his prosaic and pragmatic instincts a normal everyday activity had been elevated, whether he willed it or not, through the prophetic medium of art to the high ritual of a divine event – one which carries implicit in it the promise of eventual return to paradise.

The identification of art with the everlasting seems to have been an idea right for the time. It touched more than one *fin de siècle* heart with ardor. Théophile

Gautier's poem "L'Art" – imitated by Austen Dobson with appropriate artifice in unyielding elliptical syntax – speaks for the generations of Whistler and Beardsley, of Rossetti and Pater, of aspirations to find in the aesthetic a way to the divine.

> All passes. Art alone
>   Enduring stays to us;
> The Bust outlasts the throne, —
>   The Coin, Tiberius;
>
> Even the gods must go;
>   Only the lofty Rhyme
> Not countless years o'erthrow, –
>   Not long array of time.   ("Ars Victrix," 29–36)

The curious assimilation in the late nineteenth century of life into enduring monuments of artifice, allied to the perennial delight of the English in envisioning England as a demi-paradise, receives its ultimate memorial shape from Havelock Ellis, writing in 1890, when he fantasizes a future England, no longer the center of industry, as "a museum of antiquities and as a Holy Land for the whole English-speaking race."[12]

In fighting to free themselves from the spell of the Romantic "cosmic grin," many nineteenth-century writers and artists yielded to the alternative security of imagined constructs. Thus did the enclosed center reach new apotheosis in Whistler's Peacock Room – an abstract orangerie as fitting for the late nineteenth century as were for their time the eighteenth-century hot-house tempiettos and pantheons in which real oranges were grown.

Afterthoughts

IN THIS LONG PILGRIMAGE to – and through – the earthly gardens, south downs, and lake country fells of eighteenth-century England, and its urban purlieus, parlors, and boudoirs of the nineteenth century – to and through what were taken by their inhabitants for paradisal precincts – the true agent and guide has been the human imagination. The landscape gardens of Cobham, Hoare, and Johnes are as much tributes to their earthly imaginations as exempla of their spiritual longing. Nor do these shaped natural Edens owe any less to their imaginations than the curvilinear designs and environments of Beardsley and Whistler owe to theirs. Between their respective gardens and boudoir-dining rooms the eighteenth and nineteenth-century avatars of Blake's Los engineered urban facsimiles of Jerusalem, these technological paradises coalescing in the glass and iron greenhouse palace of the gardener–engineer Paxton. All are humanly imagined variants of the old enclosed paradise. And all are witnesses to Wordsworth's uncanny attribution of two centuries of recreated Edens to the figuration of the imagination, "the moving soul / Of our long labour" that leads us to "Infinity and God." Thus, he apotheosized the imagination as he neared the end of *The Prelude* ([1805], XIII, 171–72, 184).

That the story of English attempts in the eighteenth and nineteenth centuries to recreate paradise is, at the same time, the story of the imagination's ascendancy over what has traditionally been the province of religious thought is not surprising. Since the seventeenth century, at least, one silent assumption, and working hypothesis, has been that the earthly paradise is concocted out of the elements, and bound to the fortunes, of mundane earth and its aspiring inhabitants. The religious thinkers of Coleridge's day, and the generations of worried theologians who followed him into the second half of the nineteenth century, contentiously re-examined questions of justification, natural theology, evidences of God, the concept of evil and the reality of sin, the role of the sacraments, and the fact of the historical Jesus; but the nature of Eden – lost or regained – rarely entered into their doctrinal polemics. Even Milton's recreation of Eden is heavily indebted to his generation's daydreams about the good life, rural retirement, estate planning, and gardening. In short, latter-day restorations of earthly paradise follow blueprints everywhere answering to the self-help dogmas of profane imaginations.

When they internalized paradise, translating it into a landscape of the mind, the Romantics were, as well, following an earlier Christian tradition of finding a paradise within the self preparatory to reclaiming it at the end of time. This enabling act of the imagination, however, even when urged toward the transcendental by Blake, Coleridge, and Wordsworth also was working to naturalize the original divine context of paradise. The turn of the Victorians outward to a secular world for the relocation of Eden reflects at once the decline of belief in an historical Fall and the rise in acceptance of aesthetic authentications of the Christian dispensation. The Peacock Room of Whistler encapsulates both movements of mind in its imaginative internalizing and concrete actualizing of an Edenic space.

The historical mind thus translates into ever new imaginative terms the apprehension, and realization, of the earthly paradise. As symbol and as actuality it continually renews, and tautens, human hopes with the tension of the alternating redirection of its sacred nature. Both modes of translating the paradigm into fact to repossess Eden have left their mark the past three hundred years on English literature and art, and on the way the English have literally seen themselves as a nation occupying a specific spot on earth.

Nor, in the twentieth century, has this dual approach to paradise slackened or changed direction. Regardless of the recurrent failure to give permanent form to an earthly paradise – or perhaps because of it, since the pattern of possession, loss, and retrieval, with the accompanying sensations of deprivation and gain, seems to be an intrinsic part of the trope – humans never seem to tire of anticipating paradise anew. The belief that one can construct an Eden in this world, whether by planting a landscape garden, erecting a park square or entire garden city, dreaming a greenhouse world of art, teases the minds of twentieth-century intellectuals as much as it excited the imaginations of Georgians and Victorians. All too familiar are our century's experiments with political routes to the promised land. Other cultural and economic attempts recur of subtler but no less materialistic forms to regain a "golden age." Some historians, for example, detect as yet another phase in the nostalgic evocation of the rural round as the true "English way of life," a movement working counterproductively between the wars and in post-World War II England to reverse the Industrial Revolution of the previous century. It is vehemently secular, anti-Gothic (which had been co-opted by and accommodated to industrial and middle-class commercial uses), and historically conscious. The venerable, and worn, and modestly English are enthroned as the rule. "Merrie England" is again lauded as a "fair green garden" but with hardly a lingering recall of its descent from the Edenic prototype. The village values admired are not unlike those preserved in Bewick, Constable, and Palmer's art, only less religiously inspired, the premium on tranquility now more social and cultural in impetus. Martin J. Wiener[1] has traced the impact of this backward look to explain England's economic decline in our century as the result of its glorification of pre-industrial cultural patterns which honor village life. In the process he also documents how much this revivification of the rural idyll is the creation of early twentieth-century wealthy, professional, and elite upper-class historians rejecting industrial capitalism, and redefining what it means to be English.

No less compulsive is the symbolic attachment of the age-old millenarian itch to ordinary human practices. One instance of far-reaching reverberations is the self-gratifying identification, available to all classes, of paradise with love, and love with successful sex. As an early spokesman for our Dionysiac celebration of love, D. H. Lawrence challenges the dogma of restraint and ancient lesson of wariness enunciated in the Bible and present usually in even the bucolic fête celebrating swain and nymph. In *Women in Love*, for example, Gerald and Gudrun re-enact Adam and Eve's perplexity, this time discovering a hallowed blessing in an ancient sin.

She looked up, and in the darkness saw his face above her, his shapely, male face. There seemed a faint, white light emitted from him, a white aura, as if he were a visitor from the unseen. She reached up, like Eve reaching to the apples on the tree of knowledge, and she kissed him, though her passion was a transcendent fear of the thing he was, touching his face with her infinitely delicate, encroaching, wondering fingers. Her fingers went over the mould of his face, over his features. How perfect and foreign he was – ah, how dangerous. Her soul thrilled with complete knowledge. This was the glistening, forbidden apple, this face of a man. She kissed him, putting her fingers over his face, his eyes, his nostrils, over his brows and his ears, to his neck, to know him, to gather him in by touch . . . til she had him all in her hands, til she had strained him into her knowledge. Ah, if she could have the precious *knowledge* of him, she would be filled, and nothing could deprive her of this. For he was so unsure, so risky in the common world of day.   (ch. 24)

As the delicate italicizing of "knowledge" and the *double entendre* of the rest of the sentence, especially the play of meanings on the verb "filled," suggests, the key to Gudrun's full happy possession of the world is sexual experience. Lawrence would have us believe that her love offers a version of Edenic wholeness, a modern transcendence of primal knowledge, worriedly wrestled with by Rossetti when he tried to update Dante's Beatrice in the Pre-Raphaelite woman, arrogantly codified by Herbert Marcuse and Norman O. Brown when they translated *eros* and *agape* into the new religious languages of Marxism and Freudianism, and temporarily apotheosized by Hugh Hefner when he airbrushed the centerfold Playgirl of the Month into a Blessed Virgin.

Thus is the eternal primal pattern ever repeated anew, and the earthly paradise re-imagined (and re-instituted) in the changing image of time.

Notes

Preface

1 Suzanne Fields, "Man's First Journey: Out of an American Eden," *Los Angeles Times Book Review*, February 1, 1981, pp. 1, 6. The book reviewed is Jeffrey Goodman's *American Genesis* (New York: Summit Books, Simon and Schuster, 1981).

2 Fredric Jameson, "Towards Dialectical Criticism," *Marxism and Form, Twentieth-Century Dialectical Theories of Literature* (Princeton: Princeton Univ. Press, 1971), pp. 309–12 (in order of quotation, 312, 312, 309, 311).

3 For a consideration of this approach see E. S. Shaffer's survey of *"Kubla Khan" and The Fall of Jerusalem: The Mythological School in Biblical Criticism and Secular Literature 1770–1880* (Cambridge: Cambridge Univ. Press, 1975).

4 Cf. Maren-Sofie Røstvig's survey of *The Happy Man: Studies in the Metamorphosis of a Classical Ideal*, 2 vols. (Oslo: Oslo Univ. Press, 1954, 1958). I have organized chapters 13 and 14 around the transformations of the enclosed garden and of the Eve–Mary figure.

5 Representative analyses are Renato Poggioli's *The Oaten Flute: Essays on Pastoral Poetry and the Pastoral Ideal* (Cambridge: Harvard Univ. Press, 1975); Thomas G. Rosenmeyer, *The Green Cabinet: Theocritus and the European Pastoral Lyric* (Berkeley: Univ. of California Press, 1969); Richard Feingold's *Nature and Society: Later Eighteenth-Century Uses of the Pastoral and Georgic* (New Brunswick, N.J.: Rutgers Univ. Press, 1978); and Kenneth Clark's *Landscape Painting* (New York: Charles Scribner's, 1950). One might think the pastoral to be a "ready-made" of metaphors for the Edenic situation, since its paean to a golden age from the Latin poets on implies a lament for the fallen human condition. This is not the case. Whatever efforts were made in the eighteenth century to enlist the imaginative construct of the pastoral, with its post-Theocritean resonances of a golden age, in the interests of the corollary Christian *mythos* of paradise, they were doomed to fail. The interest of Virgil's Fourth Eclogue in a future Golden Age notwithstanding, the pastoral looks to existent Arcadian pleasances of earth for its inspiration, backward to a Golden Age which will never come again, and everywhere acknowledges the unremitting presence of death. Christian eschatology contrariwise looks to heaven for redemption, forward to Judgment Day and re-admittance into paradise, and everywhere affirms the after-life of the soul. Under these terms, the pastoral lends itself to rationalized versions of the earthly paradise. And the eighteenth-century English pastoral drew on Virgil's *Eclogues* and *Georgics* to formulate secularized visions of England as an enlightened center of a country-city, farm-factory continuum; but such pastorals proved to be more the vehicle of an imperial ideal linking politics and society than a vision uniting humanity and divinity. They were, in addition, no more able (Feingold shows, as also does Raymond Williams in his seminal *The Country and the City* [1973]) to adjust the classical pastoral's structure of values to the stresses of the changes that capitalist production and consumption were bringing to

rural life in the seventeenth and eighteenth centuries than they were to absorb the special expectations of the Eden myth. Besides undiscriminating invocations of eclogue and georgic to praise the virtues of English rural labor and mercantile expansion, such as John Dyer's *The Fleece* (1757), two less direct enlistments of the pastoral mode on behalf of the Edenic life are Blake's *Songs of Innocence and of Experience* which veer off into political, social, and religious protest, and into psychological systemizing; and Clare's eclogues which betray him into fulminations against enclosure.

6 For example, the controversy between Vulcanists and Neptunists, and the controversy that raged around Thomas Burnet's identification of paradise with the whole of antediluvian earth and his adjudication of scientific and scriptural explanations of the natural world, in *The Sacred Theory of the Earth* (1684; Latin version *Telluris Theoria Sacra*, 1681).

7 The imminent expectation of the New Jerusalem usually enlists the lunatic fringe of society whose adherents are often identified with political dissent, or worse, and as often as not end in jail. Hence, though curious and of interest in themselves, the value of millenarists as an index to the eschatological beliefs of their time is restricted. A case in point is the unfortunate Richard Brothers (1757–1824) whose prophecies about the end of empire won him an eleven year commitment as a lunatic in Dr. Samuel Foart Simmons's asylum in Islington rather than eternal sojourn in the Promised Land. See Morton D. Paley, "William Blake, the Prince of the Hebrews, and the Woman Clothed with the Sun," *William Blake: Essays in Honour of Sir Geoffrey Keynes*, eds. Morton D. Paley and Michael Phillips (Oxford: At the Clarendon Press, 1973), pp. 260–93. For a history of millenarianism see Norman Cohn, *The Pursuit of the Millennium* (London: Temple Smith, rev. ed. 1970).

8 Clark, *Landscape Painting*, pp. 71–80.

9 Northrop Frye, "Expanding Eyes," *Critical Inquiry*, II (1975), 211.

10 Jack J. Boies, *The Lost Domain: Avatars of the Earthly Paradise in Western Literature* (New York: Univ. Press of America, 1983). Boies cuts distantly and obliquely across the terrain under my scrutiny. He concentrates on medieval and Renaissance examples, on British fairy tales and fantasies, on American distortions of the trope, and on Kafka's *The Castle* and on Alain-Fournier's *Le Grand Meaulnes* (1929; trans. as both *The Lost Domain* and *The Wanderer*). His methodological frame of reference, equally distant from mine, is primarily the psychological phenomenon of the mind's sense of loss.

Introduction. The Continuing Mystique of Paradise

1 For example, A. Bartlett Giamatti, *The Earthly Paradise and the Renaissance Epic* (Princeton: Princeton Univ. Press, 1966); Stanley Stewart, *The Enclosed Garden: The Tradition and the Image in Seventeenth-Century Poetry* (Madison: Univ. of Wisconsin Press, 1966); Joseph E. Duncan, *Milton's Earthly Paradise: A Historical Study of Eden* (Minneapolis: Univ. of Minnesota Press, 1972); and R. W. Chapman, "The Literature of Landscape Gardening," *Johnsonian and Other Essays and Reviews* (Oxford: At the Clarendon Press, 1953), pp. 57–70.

2 *MP*, LXXI (1974), 440.

3 Cf. Carole Fabricant, "The Garden as City: Swift's Landscape of Alienation," *ELH*, XLII (1975), 531–55.

4 Mircea Eliade, *Myths, Dreams, and Mysteries: The Encounter Between Contemporary Faiths and Archaic Realities* (1957), trans. Philip Mairet (New York: Harper & Row, 1967, 1975), p. 66. A representative list of studies that convey the involvement of the period with paradise directly and indirectly would include Dorothy Stroud, *Capability Brown* (London: Country Life, 1950; rev. ed. 1957); Maren-Sofie Røstvig, *The Happy*

Man: Studies in the Metamorphoses of a Classical Ideal, 2 vols (Oslo: Oslo Univ. Press, 1954, 1958); Kenneth Woodbridge, "Henry Hoare's Paradise," *The Art Bulletin*, XLVII (1965), 83–116; John H. Armstrong, *The Paradise Myth* (London: Oxford Univ. Press, 1969); Edward Malins, *English Landscaping and Literature, 1660–1840* (New York: Oxford Univ. Press, 1966); Maynard Mack, *The Garden and the City: Retirement and Politics in the Later Poetry of Pope 1731–1743* (Toronto: Univ. of Toronto Press, 1969), esp. pp. 3–40; John Barrell, *The Idea of Landscape and the Sense of Place 1730–1840* (Cambridge: Cambridge Univ. Press, 1972); and Jeffry B. Spencer, *Heroic Nature, Ideal Landscape in English Poetry from Marvell to Thomson* (Evanston, Illinois: Northwestern Univ. Press, 1973).

5 Maynard Mack, "On Reading Pope," *CE*, VII (1946), p. 272.
6 Rosalie L. Colie, *"My Ecchoing Song": Andrew Marvell's Poetry of Criticism* (Princeton: Princeton Univ. Press, 1970), p. 185.
7 Sir Thomas Browne, *The Garden of Cyrus*, in *The Works*, ed. Geoffrey Keynes, 4 vols. (Chicago: Univ. of Chicago Press, new ed. 1964), IV, 226.
8 John Dixon Hunt charts this change in "Gardens of a New Model," *The Figure in the Landscape* (Baltimore: The Johns Hopkins Univ. Press, 1976), pp. 25–36.
9 Cf. especially Mircea Eliade, *Le Mythe de l'éternel retour: archetypes et répétition* (Paris: Librairie Gallimard, 1949), trans. Willard R. Trask as *The Myth of the Eternal Return* (New York: Pantheon Books, 1954), reprinted as *Cosmos and History: The Myth of the Eternal Return* (New York: Harper Torchbooks, 1959).

1. "Gardening Lords"

1 Selections of "The Country Seat" from a manuscript of 1731 in the Clerk Papers in the Scottish Record Office are printed by John Dixon Hunt and Peter Willis in *The Genius of the Place: The English Landscape Garden 1620–1820* (New York: Harper & Row, 1975), pp. 197–203. For a history of the writing of the poem, and a summary of its contents, see Stuart Piggott, "Sir John Clerk and 'The Country Seat,'" *The Country Seat: Studies in the History of the British Country House Presented to Sir John Summerson*, eds. Howard Colvin and John Harris (London: Allen Lane for The Penguin Press, 1970), pp. 110–16.
2 Douglas Chambers, "The Tomb in the Landscape: John Evelyn's Garden at Albury," *Journal of Garden History*, I (1981), 46.
3 Stephen Switzer, *Ichnographia Rustica: or, the Nobleman, Gentleman, and Gardener's Recreation*, 3 vols. (London, 1718), I, 98–99; Vol. I was published originally, with differences, in 1715 as *The Nobleman, Gentleman, and Gardener's Recreation*.
4 Cf. *The Correspondence of Alexander Pope*, ed. George Sherburn, 5 vols. (Oxford: At the Clarendon Press, 1956), IV, 459.
5 Joseph Spence, *Observations, Anecdotes, and Characters of Books and Men Collected from Conversation*, ed. James M. Osborn, 2 vols. (Oxford: At the Clarendon Press, 1966), I, 425; hereafter cited as Spence.
6 William Shenstone, "Unconnected Thoughts on Gardening," collected in *The Works in Verse and Prose of William Shenstone, Esq.*, ed. Robert Dodsley, 2 vols. (London: R. Dodsley, 1768; 3rd ed.), II, 111n. Handy facsimile reprints of William Mason's revised 1783 edition of *The English Garden* have been issued with commentary and notes by William Burgh (Farnborough, Hants.: Gregg International Publishers, 1971) and by John Dixon Hunt, The English Landscape Garden Series, No. 17 (New York: Garland Publishing, Inc., 1982).
7 The phrase is Derek Clifford's, in *A History of Garden Design* (New York: Praeger, 1963), pp. 144–45. Cf. Ronald Paulson, "Hogarth and the English Garden: Visual and

Verbal Structures," in *Encounters: Essays on Literature and the Visual Arts*, ed. John Dixon Hunt (New York: W. W. Norton & Co., 1971), pp. 82–95.

8 For a socio-literary study of John Kyrle (1637–1724), the real Man of Ross and Pope's poetic use of him, see Howard Erskine-Hill, *The Social Milieu of Alexander Pope: Lives, Example and the Poetic Response* (New Haven: Yale Univ. Press, 1975), pp. 15–41, 304–09. Throughout, quotations of Pope's verse come from *The Twickenham Edition of the Poems of Alexander Pope*, general ed. John Butt, 6 vols. (London: Methuen & Co., Ltd., 1951, 2nd. ed. 1961).

9 *Elizabeth Montagu, The Queen of the Blue-Stockings: Her Correspondence from 1720–1761*, ed. Emily J. Climenson, 2 vols. (London: John Murray, 1906), II, 16.

10 *Ibid.*, I, 189.

11 *The Correspondence of Alexander Pope*, III, 217 and II, 176. Cf. also II, 13–14, for a letter to Lord Bathurst in which Pope employs the trope of the Fall in jocular chastisement of Bathurst's habit of forging ahead in his development of Oakly Wood and Cirencester Park without referring every step to Pope for approval. See also Morris R. Brownell, *Alexander Pope & the Arts of Georgian England* (Oxford: At the Clarendon Press, 1978), pp. 189–90 and 217.

12 Edward Stephens, "On Lord Bathurst's Park and Wood," *Miscellaneous Poems* (Cirencester, 1747), pp. 51–56.

13 Eva M. Neumeyer, "The Landscape Garden as a Symbol in Rousseau, Goethe and Flaubert," *JHI*, VIII (1947), 189; and Harry F. Clark, "Eighteenth Century Elysiums: The Rôle of 'Association' in the Landscape Movement," *Journal of the Warburg and Courtauld Institutes*, VI (1943), 168.

14 Scottish Record Office, Edinburgh, GD/18/2111, ff. 3, 5; quoted by William Spink, "Sir John Clerk of Penicuik: Landowner as Designer," *Furor Hortensis: Essays on the History of the English Landscape Garden in Memory of H. F. Clark*, ed. Peter Willis. (Edinburgh: Elysium Press, 1974), p. 32. For references to Clerk's visits to English country seats, and to the "great improvements in Gardening" (p. 125), see *Memoirs of the Life of Sir John Clerk of Penicuik, Baronet: Baron of the Exchequer Extracted by Himself from His Own Journals 1676–1755*, ed. John M. Gray (Edinburgh: Printed at Edinburgh Univ. Press by T. and A. Constable for Scottish Historical Society, 1892), Vol. XIII of Publications of the Scottish Historical Society.

15 Joseph Warton, *Essay on the Genius and Writings of Mr. Pope*, 2 vols. (London, 1756), II, 179–80.

16 *Letters of Anna Seward*, ed. A. Constable, 6 vols. (Edinburgh: A. Constable, 1811), IV, 10.

17 Horace Walpole, *The History of the Modern Taste in Gardening* (1771), in *Horace Walpole: Gardenist*, ed. Isabel Chase (Princeton Univ. Press for Univ. of Cincinnati, 1943), pp. 14–15, 3, and 17. George Mason in another history of modern gardening, *Essay on Design in Gardening* (1768), forthrightly asserts that Milton's "model of Eden remains unimpeachabl[y]" the inspiration for the current style (pp. 22–23). For additional allusions by Walpole and by others such as John Aiken to Milton's Garden of Eden as the prototype of modern gardening, see Chase, pp. 172–75 and 174n.

18 See Anthony Ashley Cooper, third Earl of Shaftesbury, *The Moralists* (1709–10); Alexander Pope, *Essay on Criticism* (1711), and "To Richard Boyle, Earl of Burlington" (1731); and Joseph Addison, *The Spectator*, nos. 411–21, on "The Pleasures of the Imagination" (1712), and *The Guardian* (1713). Roland Mushat Frye, *Milton's Imagery and the Visual Arts: Iconographic Tradition in the Epic Poems* (Princeton: Princeton Univ. Press, 1978), rehearses the innumerable sources that went into the conception of Milton's Garden of Eden, not least being the gardens he visited in Italy; see especially Chap. 13 "Landscape Art and Milton's Garden of Eden," pp. 218–34, where he makes the point, apropos of the Boboli Gardens laid out around the Pitti Palace in Florence

between 1550 and 1600, that informal, naturalistic planting was often as prominent as regular, ordered design in these gardens.

Charles H. Hinnant, "A Philosophical Origin of the English Landscape Garden," *Bulletin of Research in the Humanities*, LXXXIII (1980), 292–306, suggests that practitioners of the new landscape garden could still accept with philosophical consistency the New Science of the seventeenth century, which is usually cited in justification of the formal garden. They accommodated the seemingly conflicting assumptions by falling back on a version of the Platonic dichotomy. The trick was to distinguish between the geometry *known* to underlie the inorganic structure of the universe and the irregularities of nature *observed* in its organic appearances.

19 Shaftesbury, *The Moralists, in Characteristics of Men, Manners, Opinions, Times*, 3 vols. (Farnborough, Hants.: Gregg International Publishers Ltd., 1968; facsimile of 1714, 2nd rev. ed.), II, 406, 427.

According to Ronald L. Bogue, "The Meaning of 'Grace' in Pope's Aesthetic," *PMLA*, XCIV (1979), 434–48, by the early eighteenth century two views of Nature prevailed: (1) the traditional idea of a "perfect, orderly system of harmony and ideal beauty" called into being at the beginning of time, and the "imperfect, sublunary estate of flux and jarring multiplicity which is our wretched legacy from Adam," but which Art "through the imitation of ideal Nature . . . improves upon actuality, restoring us, as it were, to Eden" (Martin C. Battestin, *The Providence of Wit* [Oxford: At the Clarendon Press, 1974], p. 50); and (2) "the supposition that the creation is representative not of disorder but of order," and "both the heavens and the earth testify not to the sin of Adam but to the wisdom of God" (Michael Macklem, *The Anatomy of the World: Relations between Natural and Moral Law from Donne to Pope* [Minneapolis: Univ. of Minnesota Press, 1958], p. 19). In the latter view the artist (the gardener) "improves, not Nature, but our perception of it, by reducing Nature to a scale more easily comprehended by human beings" (Bogue, 445). Bogue argues for Pope's adherence to the second. Obviously, I believe that Shaftesbury expounded the first, and that it was still commonly adhered to by eighteenth-century gardenists.

20 Shaftesbury, *The Moralists*, II, 374, 394.

21 Christopher Hussey, *English Gardens and Landscapes 1700–1750* (London: Country Life, 1967), p. 147. For a succinct summary of the early influences and literature on the new gardening, see ch. 3, "Sources of the Landscape Garden."

22 From a letter of Henry Hoare to his nephew, Richard Hoare, January 1755; quoted by Kenneth Woodbridge, "Henry Hoare's Paradise," *The Art Bulletin*, XLVII (1965), 83.

23 Martin Price, *To the Palace of Wisdom: Studies in Order and Energy from Dryden to Blake* (Garden City, N.Y.: Doubleday & Co., 1964), p. 376.

24 Reputedly by the Earl of Carlisle's daughter Lady Irwin, *Castle Howard* (c.1733) is reprinted, in part, by Hunt and Willis in *The Genius of the Place*, pp. 228–32.

25 Hussey, *English Gardens and Landscapes 1700–1750*, caption to plate 168.

26 Cf. Thomas Whately, *Observations on Modern Gardening* (London: T. Payne, 1770, facsimile rpt., Garland Publishing Inc., 1982), pp. 167–69.

27 From a letter by MacClary, quoted in Kenneth Woodbridge, "William Kent's Gardening: The Rousham Letters," *Apollo*, C (October 1974), 289.

28 See Kenneth Woodbridge, "Henry Hoare's Paradise," *The Art Bulletin*, XLVII (1965), 97–99; "The Sacred Landscape: Painters and the Lake-garden of Stourhead," *Apollo*, LXXXVIII (September 1968); and *Landscapes and Antiquity: Aspects of English Culture at Stourhead 1718–1838* (Oxford: At the Clarendon Press, 1970), pp. 31–37.

29 For a succinct statement of this commonplace of the age, cf. Morse Peckham, *Beyond the Tragic Vision: The Quest for Identity in the Nineteenth Century* (New York: G. Braziller, 1962), p. 50. Contrasting the Hebraic vision of paradise attainable in historical time to the Platonic–Christian promise of heaven in the other world outside of

time, Peckham remarks that "because the Hebrews were originally a wandering desert tribe . . . Their drive was away from the inimical desert and toward a land flowing with milk and honey, as Palestine was when they first came to it" (p. 50). To put this pattern of experience and *mythos* into an eighteenth-century aesthetic context, one can say that the great Whig lords, tiring of *le jardin français*, turned away from a notion of the world as a perfect mathematical/geometric formulation (equivalent to the Platonic–Christian version of reality) to the Hebraic view of the world as a patchwork of fruitful gardens, which was eventually by the end of the century to emerge as an organized metaphor for the world.

30 Maggie Keswick, *The Chinese Garden: History, Art, and Architecture* (London: Academy Editions, 1978), p. 24. For a comparison of English and Chinese gardens, to which I am indebted for my remarks, see especially pp. 9–24.

31 Cf. Kenneth Clark, *Landscape Painting* (New York: Charles Scribner's Sons, 1950), ch. 4, "Ideal Landscape," pp. 54–73.

32 For a bibliography of eighteenth-century gardening books, see Mrs. Evelyn Cecil (Alicia Margaret [Tyssen-Amherst] Cecil Rockley, Baroness), *A History of Gardening in England* (London, 1896; 3rd and enl. ed., New York: E. P. Dutton, 1910). There is also a reprint of the 2nd edition (Detroit: Singing Tree Press, 1969).

33 Switzer, *Ichnographia Rustica*, I, iii–v.

34 Rudolf Wittkower, *Palladio and Palladianism* (New York: George Braziller, 1974), p. 187, is referring in general to the great English landscape gardens of the 1730s, 40s, and 50s. The contemporary witness is Mrs. Elizabeth Montagu, *Her Correspondence from 1720–1761*, ed. Climenson, I, 189.

35 Gilbert West, *Stowe, The Gardens of the Right Honourable Richard Viscount Cobham* (London, 1732), p. 1.

36 *Elizabeth Montagu . . . Her Correspondence from 1720–1761*, ed. Climenson, I, 189–90.

37 John Dixon Hunt, *The Figure in the Landscape: Poetry, Painting, and Gardening during the Eighteenth Century* (Baltimore: The John Hopkins Univ. Press, 1976), p. 186.

38 William Gilpin, *A Dialogue upon the Gardens of the Right Honourable the Lord Viscount Cobham, at Stow in Buckinghamshire* (1748), ed. John Dixon Hunt (Los Angeles: William Andrews Clark Memorial Library, Univ. of California, 1976), The Augustan Reprint Society, no. 176, pp. 26, 24, and 60.

39 For a brief review of the evolution of the gardens at Stowe, see George Clarke, "The Gardens of Stowe," *Apollo*, XCVII (June 1973), 558–65. Clarke cautions scholars to use with care the guide book plans of Stowe printed after 1738. Although the sequence of changes they chronicle is basically accurate, their precise dating of alterations is suspect.

40 Hussey, *English Gardens and Landscapes 1700–1750*, pp. 100–01.

41 See Woodbridge, "William Kent as Landscape-Gardener: A Re-Appraisal," and "William Kent's Gardening: The Rousham Letters," *Apollo*, C (August 1974), 126–37, and C (October 1974), 282–91; and Hussey, *English Gardens and Landscapes 1700–1750*, pp. 147–53, and plate 202, which reproduces Kent's plan for the Rousham garden, "drawn probably by Bridgeman, 1737–38." For Stowe, see George Clarke, "The Gardens of Stowe," and "Grecian Taste and Gothic Virtue: Lord Cobham's Gardening Programme and its Iconography," both in *Apollo*, XCVII (June 1973), 558–65, and 566–71; and Hussey, *English Gardens and Landscapes 1700–1750*, pp. 89–113.

42 J. Henrietta Pye, *Short Account of the Principal Seats and Gardens in and about Richmond and Kew* (London, 1760), p. 53; also published as *A Short View of the Principal Seats and Gardens at and about Twickenham* (London, 1767); and, with revisions, as *A Peep into the Principal Seats and Gardens at and about Twickenham* (London, 1775), p. 52.

43 Quoted by Hussey, *English Gardens and Landscapes 1700–1750*, pp. 95–96, from Egmont Mss., St. James Palace.

44 See Peter Willis, "Jacques Rigaud's Drawings of Stowe in the Metropolitan Museum of Art," *Eighteenth-Century Studies*, IV (1972), 85–98. Willis accepts George Virtue's implication that Rigaud completed the ink and wash sketches by 1736 and Virtue's record that Bernard Baron (1696–1762) probably engraved only five of the sixteen plates of Stowe (fifteen views and a plan). Willis conveniently reproduces drawings 1–8. For additional discussion of the drawings, see Willis, *Charles Bridgeman and the English Landscape Garden* (London: A. Zwemmer Ltd., 1977), pp. 113–20. Willis also reproduces here fourteen of the drawings (no. 6 is missing from Rigaud's originals) in large finely rendered reproductions (see plates 129–42), the Baron engraving of no. 6, plus two details from other of Baron's engravings from the drawings (plates 143–45), as well as many other contemporary layout plans of the gardens.

45 Reprinted by John Dixon Hunt and Peter Willis in *The Genius of the Place: The English Landscape Garden 1620–1820*, plate 7, p. 7.

46 John Scott, *"Amwell"* (1776; although written in part by 1761), *The Poetical Works of John Scott Esq.* (London: J. Buckland, 1782), p. 61. Horace Walpole writes his friend George Montagu on 7 July 1770 a funny story of a "small Vauxhall" entertainment held on a cold damp night at the grotto in the Elysian Fields of Stowe – "none of us young enough for a pastoral" forced to descend fifty stone stairs in the dark, everyone "hobbling down, by the balustrades, wrapped up in cloaks and great-coats for fear of catching cold" – when he was forced to call on all the Roman discipline he could muster. He includes a poem he wrote on the occasion for the Princess Amelia, all about Venus complaining at the neglect of her altars since a new nymph has appeared, and then apologizes: "So many heathen temples around, had made me talk as a Roman poet would have done" (*Horace Walpole's Correspondence*, eds. W. S. Lewis and Ralph S. Brown, Jr. [New Haven: Yale Univ. Press, 1941], X, 314–16).

47 A. Bartlett Giamatti, *The Earthly Paradise and the Renaissance Epic* (Princeton: Princeton Univ. Press, 1966), p. 357.

48 Writing to his elder daughter Susanna 23 October 1762, Henry Hoare confided his picturesque hopes for this view: "you allways wishd I would build at the passage into the orchard & the scheme of carrying the water up and loosing out of sight towards the parish. This Bridge is now about. It is simple & plain. I took it from Palladios Bridge at Vicenza, 5 arches, & when you stand at The Pantheon the Water will be seen thro the Arches & it will look as if the River came down thro the Village & that this was the Village Bridge for publick use; the View of the Bridge, Village & Church altogether will be a Charmg Gasp[ar]d picture at the end of that Water." Quoted in Kenneth Woodbridge, *The Stourhead Landscape* (The National Trust, 1974), p. 12; also quoted in Woodbridge, "Henry Hoare's Paradise," *The Art Bulletin*, XLVII (1965), 109.

My discussion of Stourhead is based on a pleasurable Sunday stroll around the lake and on the complete record of the garden's history to be found in Christopher Hussey, "The Gardens at Stourhead," *Country Life*, LXXXIII (1938), 608–14, 638–42; and *English Gardens and Landscapes 1700–1750*, pp. 158–64; and in Kenneth Woodbridge, "Henry Hoare's Paradise," *The Art Bulletin*, XLVII (1965), 83–116; *Landscape and Antiquity: Aspects of English Culture at Stourhead 1718 to 1838* (Oxford: at the Clarendon Press, 1970); and *The Stourhead Landscape*.

49 James Sambrook, rev. of Jeffry B. Spencer's *Heroic Nature, Ideal Landscape in English Poetry from Marvell to Thomson*, in *JEGP*, LXXIII (1974), 246.

50 Quoted by Woodbridge, "Henry Hoare's Paradise," pp. 112–13.

51 Bampfylde, *Panoramic sketches of the lake at Stourhead* (c.1770, British Museum); Piper, *Drawings of Stourhead* (1779, Royal Academy of Fine Arts, Stockholm); and Nicholson, *Views at Stourhead* (1813–14, British Museum). Woodbridge conveniently reproduces a selection of them in *The Stourhead Landscape*.

52 Robert Rosenblum, "The Dawn of British Romantic Painting, 1760–1780," *The*

Varied Pattern: Studies in the 18th Century, eds. Peter Hughes and David Williams, Publications of the McMaster Univ. Association for 18th-Century Studies, Vol. 1 (Toronto: A. M. Hakkert, Ltd., 1971), pp. 194–95. Rosenblum includes a reproduction of Webber's *Poedooa*.

53 The phrase comes from Emblem xlvii ("The Hermit," p. 137) of Francis Tolson's amalgam of verse, emblem, and religio-scholastic commentary on nature, the Fall, and man's arduously pious reclamation of Eden, in *Hermathenae, or Moral Emblems and Ethnick Tales* (?1740):

>Within this lonely melancholy Cell
>Shou'd no vain Thoughts, no Pride, nor Envy dwell;
>The Soul within herself serene, shou'd here
>Like Nature's Golden Infancy appear,
>Religious, unambitious, and sincere.

54 Hussey, *English Gardens and Landscapes 1700–1750*, p. 161. Woodbridge, *The Stourhead Landscape*, pp. 16, 23–31, itemizes the trees planted, and the dates of planting, from the time of Colt Hoare to 1969.

55 *The Correspondence of Alexander Pope*, ed. Sherburn, II, 14–15.

56 Hussey, *English Gardens and Landscapes 1700–1750*, p. 149.

57 The mixed forest is celebrated in the description of Alcinous's orchard in *The Odyssey* (Bk. VII) and in the epic catalogue in Ovid's *Metamorphoses* (Bk. X).

58 Woodbridge, "Henry Hoare's Paradise," *The Art Bulletin*, XLVII (1965), 83; and *Landscape and Antiquity*, p. 1. In an agreement dated 9 January 1724 for installation of a water pump, for example, the epithet for the area occurs, "from Withy bed pond to Ye top of Parradice Coppice."

59 Richard Payne Knight, *The Landscape* (1794); quoted from the selection in John Dixon Hunt and Peter Willis, *The Genius of the Place: The English Landscape Garden 1620–1820*, p. 344.

60 For the changing attitude in the eighteenth century towards mountains and natural scenery, see Marjorie Nicolson's *Mountain Gloom and Mountain Glory: The Development of the Aesthetics of the Infinite* (Ithaca, N.Y.: Cornell Univ. Press, 1959). I have not alluded to another whole area of garden-making on a lavish and public scale at Kew, Richmond, and Kensington Gardens, and to the psuedo-Orientalism championed by Sir William Chambers, because they do not, in general, seem to have been inspired by dreams of creating an Eden. Although many of the private landscape gardens of the day were also open to the public, they differ from Kew Gardens, etc., in that the constant planting and redesigning there reflect royal ambitions, botanical research, and civic responsibility more than personal paradisal propensities.

61 I am generally indebted in this chapter to Diana Uhlman, *Croft Castle* (The National Trust, 1975); and, above all, to Elisabeth Inglis-Jones, *Peacocks in Paradise* (Shoreham-by-Sea, Sussex: Service Publications Ltd., for Galloway and Morgan Ltd., The University Booksellers, Aberystwyth, 1950; rpt. 1960 and 1971), which is cited in the text as *P Paradise*. Other useful references to Hafod include a memoir of Johnes in the *Gentleman's Magazine*, LXXXVI, pt. 1 (1816), 563–64; B. H. Malkin, *The Scenery, Antiquities, and Biography of South Wales* (1804); and Sir James Edward Smith, *A Tour to Hafod in Cardiganshire, the Seat of Thomas Johnes, Esq. M.P.* (1810), which contains fifteen aquatint scenes of the gardens and house by John Constantine Stadler after drawings by John "Warwick" Smith (1749–1831).

62 *The Royal Pavilion at Brighton*, official catalogue of the Pavilion, with text by David Higginbottom (London, n.d.).

63 It is possible that Coleridge saw Hafod in 1794 on his walking tour through Wales with his friend John Hucks. See Hucks's *A Pedestrian Tour through North Wales* (1795), eds. Alun R. Jones and William Tydeman (Cardiff: Univ. of Wales Press, 1979); and

Geoffrey Grigson, "Kubla Khan in Wales," in *Places of the Mind* (London: Routledge & Kegan Paul, 1949), pp. 8–15, who argues for the house and grounds having possibly contributed to Coleridge's vision of Xanadu.

64 George Cumberland, *An Attempt to Describe Hafod* (London, 1796), pp. v and 4–5.

65 *Ibid.*, p. 40. The allusions are to *Paradise Lost*, IV, 134–43. Throughout, I have quoted the 1674 2nd edition of the poem, ed. Merrit Y. Hughes (New York: The Odyssey Press, Inc., 1935).

66 A reliable biography of *The Ladies of Llangollen: A Study in Romantic Friendship*, by Elizabeth Mavor, is readily available in Penguin Books (1973). The appellation "Little Paradise" appears in the auctioneer's catalogue when Plas Newydd was put up for sale in 1832 six months after the death of the surviving lady, Sarah Ponsonby.

67 *Jerusalem*, 41 [46]: 3–4 (Erdman, 186). See Morton D. Paley, "Thomas Johnes, 'Ancient Guardian of Wales,'" *Blake News Letter*, II (1968–69), 65–67; and Ruthven Todd, "The Identity of 'Hereford' in *Jerusalem*, with Observations on Welsh Matters," *Blake Studies*, VI (1975), 139–51.

68 *Gentleman's Magazine*, LXXXVI, pt. 1 (1816), 564.

69 John Summerson, *John Nash: Architect to King George IV* (London: George Allen & Unwin, 1935), p. 59.

70 I am indebted in these observations to a spirited and suggestive conversation with Sir George Lowthian Trevelyan one evening during the Attingham Summer School session of 1977.

71 Cf. George Sherburn, "Rasselas Returns – to What?" *PQ*, XXXVIII (1959), 383–84.

72 Gilpin, *A Dialogue Upon the Gardens . . . at Stow* (Los Angeles: William Andrews Clark Memorial Library, Univ. of California, Los Angeles, 1976), The Augustan Reprint Society, no. 176, p. 10.

73 Quoted in Kenneth Woodbridge, *Landscape and Antiquity*, p. 30.

74 Hussey, *English Gardens and Landscapes 1700–1750*, p. 100.

75 See George Clarke, "Moral Gardening, The History of Stowe – XI," *The Stoic*, XXIV (July 1970), 118–19; and "Grecian Taste and Gothic Virtue: Lord Cobham's Gardening Program and Its Iconography," *Apollo*, XCVII (June 1973), 566–71; and Kenneth Woodbridge, "The Sacred Landscape," 210–11; and *Landscape and Antiquity*, p. 35.

76 See *Collected Works of Oliver Goldsmith*, ed. Arthur Friedman, 5 vols. (Oxford: At the Clarendon Press, 1966), Vol. IV for "The Deserted Village." For an excellent discussion of the early eighteenth-century landscape garden and its didactic associative designs on the visitor vs. the late eighteenth-century Brownian landscape and its latitude for free association, see the pioneering study of this subject by Harry F. Clark, "Eighteenth-Century Elysiums," *Journal of the Warburg and Courtauld Institutes*, VI (1943), 165–89; and John Dixon Hunt, *The Figure in the Landscape* (Baltimore: The Johns Hopkins Press, 1976). For a summary of the characteristics of the Brown landscape, see Dorothy Stroud, *Capability Brown* (London: Country Life, 1950).

77 The dedication of Brown to his calling is proverbial. Still, he remains a shadowy inexplicable legend, for all the plenitude of contemporary references to his imperious landscaping. Dorothy Stroud's fine biography is able only to hint at what moved this low-born Scotsman above and beyond pecuniary gain to criss-cross the land, replanting and resloping England into a replica of the original cosmic diagram. When he stalked the fields and terraces of his aristocratic clients, who knows what ordinary human yearnings led Brown to ignore the intricate artifice of garden beds, pavements, and geometrical overlays of nature to follow his instinctive perception of a pristine world which had yielded itself to the elements long before art had debased it? The life of this common Scotsman, the plain gardener raised to symbolic significance, coughing and sneezing his way through dusty fields as he unconsciously follows the divine spoor of an irretrievable past, is nothing less than heroic, fitting complement to the noble

landscapes he designed. Traveling with missionary-like zeal from one country estate to the next, he was often on the road half the year, laying out grounds, surveying work done, and supplementing previous improvements. Through it all he stoically disregarded symptoms of massive respiratory allergy for the meadows he relied upon as paradigmatic natural forms.

78 So Blake remembers them as part fact and part mythicized landscape of the mind. The quoted phrases come from *Jerusalem*, 77:5 (Erdman, 231); and *Milton*, 1:4 (Erdman, 95). John Dixon Hunt makes no allowance for this possibility in his effort to establish a dichotomy from the 1780s onwards between landscape gardens, which "became the conventional idea of beauty," and "the sublimity of mountains," into whose horrific precincts poets were straying, leaving the gardens behind them. See Hunt, *The Figure in the Landscape*, p. 191.

79 Mavis Batey has gathered considerable evidence in support of the identification of Nuneham Courtenay with Auburn, including grounds for linking Lord Chancellor Harcourt with Goldsmith's "man of wealth and pride" (275). See her "Oliver Goldsmith: An Indictment of Landscape Gardening," *Furor Hortensis: Essays on the History of the English Landscape Garden in Memory of H. F. Clark*, ed. Peter Willis (Edinburgh: Elysium Press Ltd., 1974), pp. 57–71; and "Nuneham Courtenay: An Oxfordshire Eighteenth-Century Deserted Village," *Oxoniensa*, XXXIII (1968), 108–24.

80 For a summary of the conflicting critical interpretations of the poem's rhetorical strategies (specifically Ricardo Quintana's, Richard Eversole's, Leo F. Storm's, R. J. Jaarsma's, and Robert H. Hopkins's), along with the development of a new interpretation, see Roger Lonsdale, "'A Garden, and a Grave': The Poetry of Oliver Goldsmith," *The Author in his Work: Essays on a Problem in Criticism*, ed. Louis L. Martz and Aubrey Williams (New Haven: Yale Univ. Press, 1978), pp. 3–30.

81 Some anthropologists and linguists have argued that a binary organization of experience – for example, the structuring of language and the ordering of space on the analogy of up–down, front–back, night–day, left–right – is at least as intrinsic to human perception as is that of ritual repetition. Cf. Roman Jakobson and Morris Halle, *Fundamentals of Language* (The Hague: Mouton, 1956), pp. 44–49; Talcott Parsons and Robert F. Bales, *Family Socialization and Interaction Process* (Glencoe, Ill.: Free Press, 1955); and Claude Lévi-Strauss, *The Raw and the Cooked* (New York: Harper & Row, 1969).

82 *The Rise and Progress of the Present Taste in Planting Parks, Pleasure Grounds, Gardens, Etc.* (1767); quoted from the selection printed by Hunt and Willis, in *The Genius of the Place*, pp. 299–300.

2. Blake and the Unending Dialectic of Earth and Eden

1 Alistair M. Duckworth, *The Improvement of the Estate: A Study of Jane Austen's Novels* (Baltimore: The Johns Hopkins Press, 1971), pp. 36–80.

2 Charles Cotton, "The Wonders of the Peake," *The Genuine Works of Charles Cotton, Esq.* (London: R. Bonwicke, 1715), p. 296.

3 Cf. Duckworth, *The Improvement of the Estate*.

4 All references to Blake's writings are taken from David V. Erdman's edition, *The Poetry and Prose of William Blake* (Garden City, N.Y.: Doubleday & Co., 1970), with poem title, plate and page numbers given in parentheses after the quotation. The plate numbers used in reference to the illustrations follow the numbering system in David V. Erdman, *The Illuminated Blake* (Garden City, N.Y.: Doubleday [Anchor Press], 1974). Abbreviations used are *J* for *Jerusalem*, *M* for *Milton*, *MHH* for *The Marriage of Heaven*

and Hell; *FZ* for *The Four Zoas*, and E for Erdman's edition of the *Poetry and Prose*.

5 The fullest discussion of this point is Morton D. Paley's *Energy and Imagination: A Study of the Development of Blake's Thought* (Oxford: At the Clarendon Press, 1970). A summary of the positions of Blakean critics on the issue, with a dissenting corrective, is given by Dennis M. Welch, "In the Throes of Eros: Blake's Early Career," *Mosaic*, XI (1978), 101–13.

6 See, for example, W. J. T. Mitchell, *Blake's Composite Art: A Study of the Illuminated Poetry* (Princeton: Princeton Univ. Press, 1978), pp. 176–85; and Karl Kroeber, "Delivering *Jerusalem*," *Blake's Sublime Allegory: Essays on The Four Zoas, Milton, Jerusalem*, eds. Stuart Curran and Joseph Anthony Wittreich, Jr. (Madison: Univ. of Wisconsin Press, 1973), pp. 347–67.

7 For discussions of the expansive center, see E. J. Rose, "The Symbolism of the Opened Center and Poetic Theory in Blake's *Jerusalem*," *Studies in English Literature*, V (1965), 587–606. I am also indebted to Dennis M. Welch, "Center, Circumference, and Vegetation Symbolism in the Writings of William Blake," *Studies in Philology*, LXXV (1978), 223–42.

8 John Locke, *An Essay Concerning Human Understanding* (1690), ed. Alexander Campbell Frazer (New York: Dover Publications, 1959), I, 252–56, 258–92. Cf. Welch, "Center, Circumference, and Vegetation Symbolism in the Writings of William Blake," pp. 226–28.

9 Locke, *Essay Concerning Human Understanding*, I, 401; Welch, "Center, Circumference, and Vegetation Symbolism in the Writings of William Blake," p. 236.

10 Hazard Adams, *Blake and Yeats: The Contrary Vision* (Ithaca, N.Y.: Cornell Univ. Press, 1955), p. 36.

11 On the Polypus cf. *The Book of Los* (4:56–70, 5:1–2; E,92) and *The Book of Urizen* (11:1–6; E,74–75, and Plate 17); also Paul Miner, "The Polyp as Symbol in the Poetry of William Blake," *Texas Studies in Language and Literature*, II (1960), 198–205.

12 Erdman, *The Illuminated Blake*, p. 304.

13 There are two prints. The original line engraving has a gross moth and worm at Albion's feet. Joseph Anthony Wittreich, Jr., *Angel of Apocalypse: Blake's Idea of Milton* (Madison: Univ. of Wisconsin Press, 1975), argues that this engraving shows "Albion in the posture of error" (p. 65). Mitchell, *Blake's Composite Art*, pp. 54–55, while voicing doubt on that possibility, agrees that the color print, especially, in which the moth and worm are deleted, "may be seen as the moment of birth and liberation, or as the moment of death [i.e., the death of death], Albion sacrificing himself like Samson by destroying himself along with the oppressive structures he opposes."

14 Mitchell, *Blake's Composite Art*, p. 80.

15 *Ibid.*, p. 201.

16 Erdman, *The Illuminated Blake*, p. 258; Susan Fox, *Poetic Form in Blake's Milton* (Princeton: Princeton Univ. Press, 1976), pp. 229–30. Cf. Wittreich, *Angel of Apocalypse*, pp. 27–34, who further complicates the identifications. The man on the rock with his emanation could be Milton in his regenerated prophetic life.

17 Fox, *Poetic Form in Blake's Milton*, pp. 190–91.

18 *Ibid.*

19 *Ibid.* Apropos of Fox's allusion to the lark as being "no angel," cf. "The Lark is Los's Messenger" (*M*, 35:63; E, 135): to "Mortal's eyes & those of the Ulro Heavens" it appears to be a bird, but "to Immortals, the Lark is a mighty Angel" (*M*, 36:11–12; E, 135).

20 Erdman, *The Illuminated Blake*, p. 267.

21 S. Foster Damon, *A Blake Dictionary: The Ideas and Symbols of William Blake* (Providence, Rhode Island: Brown Univ. Press, 1965; rpt. New York: E. P. Dutton, 1971), p. 114.

22 Fox, *Poetic Form in Blake's Milton*, p. 195; cf. also pp. 195–99. Fox goes so far as to observe that "Damon's distinction between Eden and eternity does not . . . resolve the incongruity" (p. 196). Could this be because Fox humanly errs in unconsciously reasoning from the *idée fixe* that Eden is other than in this world – a Urizenic dogma that clings to the mind-set of this fine Blakean critic and demonstrates what mental resistance Blake was up against?

23 In the prose preamble "To the Public" (*J*, 3;E, 143), Blake deleted words expressive of his belief in the public's charitableness. Erdman has recovered some of these, of which [Dear] in the term of address is one. See his "The Suppressed and Altered Passages in Blake's *Jerusalem*," *Studies in Bibliography*, XVII (1964), 1–54.

24 Mitchell, *Blake's Composite Art*, p. 181.

25 *Ibid.*, p. 171.

26 A third figure in the center facing the reader with hammer and compass-like tongs is identified by Erdman (*The Illuminated Blake*, p. 379) as Los, with the male figure on the left as "the spectre of Urthona" and the female on the right as "the poet's emanation, Enitharmon." Mitchell argues more persuasively for identifying the center giant as "the perfected Urthona flanked by his temporal and spatial emissaries" Los and Enitharmon (*Blake's Composite Art*, p. 181).

27 See Blake's letters to Thomas Butts of 6 July 1803 and 10 May 1801; and to John Flaxman of 21 September 1800, *The Letters of William Blake*, ed. Geoffrey Keynes (Cambridge, Mass.: Harvard Univ. Press, 1968), pp. 69, 50, and 41.

3. Coleridge and the Enchantments of Earthly Paradise

1 I am paraphrasing John Vernon's fine definition of the garden as it figures in man's mythic and cultural structuring of reality, in *The Garden and the Map: Schizophrenia in Twentieth-Century Literature and Culture* (Urbana: Univ. of Illinois Press, 1973), especially pp. xii–xv and 5–6.

2 Maren-Sofie Røstvig, *The Happy Man: Studies in the Metamorphoses of a Classical Ideal* (Oslo: Akademisk Forlag; Oxford: Basil Blackwell, 1954, 1958), II, 287–88.

3 *Collected Letters of Samuel Taylor Coleridge*, ed. Earl Leslie Griggs, 6 vols. (Oxford: At the Clarendon Press, 1956–71), I, 349; henceforth referred to as *CL*. References to the *Biographia Literaria* (*BL*) are to James Engell and W. Jackson Bate's two-volume edition in *The Collected Works of Samuel Taylor Coleridge*, eds. Kathleen Coburn and Bart Winer (Princeton Univ. Press, 1983), which is commonly alluded to as the *Collected Coleridge* (*CC*). Citation of poems is to *The Poems of Samuel Taylor Coleridge*, ed. Ernest Hartley Coleridge (London: Oxford Univ. Press, 1912).

   In his use of the striking phrase "*all things* counterfeit infinity!" Coleridge probably did not intend quite the negative sense with which I have used it here; but I doubt that Coleridge was insensitive to the full range of meanings residual in *counterfeit* even as he wrote it, especially since the phrase came from Ralph Cudworth's *True Intellectual System of the Universe* (1678). See W. Schrickx, "Coleridge and the Cambridge Platonists," *REL*, VI (1966), 80–82.

4 For illuminating expositions of Coleridge's philosophy of nature, to which I am everywhere indebted, see M. H. Abrams's two detailed and near-exhaustive articles on "Coleridge and the Romantic Vision of the World," *Coleridge's Variety: Bicentenary Studies*, ed. John Beer (London: Macmillan, 1974), pp. 101–33; and "Coleridge's 'A Light in Sound': Science, Metascience, and Poetic Imagination," *Proceedings of the American Philosophical Society*, CVI (1972), 458–76; Owen Barfield's *What Coleridge Thought* (Middletown, Conn.: Wesleyan Univ. Press, 1971); Richard Haven's *Patterns of Consciousness: An Essay on Coleridge* (Amherst: Univ. of Massachusetts Press, 1969);

and Craig W. Miller's "Coleridge's Concept of Nature," *JHI*, xxv (1964), 77–96.

5 *The Notebooks of Samuel Taylor Coleridge*, ed. Kathleen Coburn, vols. I and II (New York: Pantheon Books, 1957, 1961), vol. III (Princeton: Princeton Univ. Press, 1973); henceforth referred to as *CN*.

6 As noted by Abrams, "Coleridge's 'A Light in Sound,'" pp. 461–62 and n, the "one Life" passage inserted as errata in the 1817 *Sibylline Leaves* was sent to the printer on paper that makes almost certain its composition between spring 1816 and spring 1817.

7 *Ibid.*, pp. 458–76.

8 Coleridge's ponderings on the nature of reality, as he veers away from *Naturphilosophie*, are extended and tortuous, but intellectually consistent, in 1817–19. See especially *CN*, III, 4418–56; August–November 1818; and letters to James Gillman, Ludwig Tieck, Lord Liverpool, and C. A. Tulk from November 1816 to January 1818, *CL*, IV, 688–809.

By the mid-1820s he had evolved a sophisticated cosmology based on transcendental triune logic and Christian trinitarianism that is an amalgam of Boehme, Kant, Newton, Steffens, and Schelling among others. See Coleridge's entry of the mid-1820s in Notebook 23, *ff.* 28–32v. For an exposition of Coleridge's dynamic concept of nature, with its construction of the world out of Genesis and general physics, Kantian powers and gravitational forces, polar and triadic logic, as perceived sympathetically by an historian of science, see Trevore H. Levere's *Poetry Realized in Nature: Samuel Taylor Coleridge and Early Nineteenth-Century Science* (Cambridge Univ. Press, 1981), especially pp. 127–34, 156–58.

Since I am making no special claims for the intellectual status of Coleridge's ideas of paradise, I see no need to raise the question of his use of others' writings. His purview of paradise consists both of the enclosed garden and the cosmic extension of that enchanted plot of ground. There is little question that his response to the millennialism of his age partakes of the centuries-long development of a tradition, to which he brings his peculiar personal needs and unique penchant for clear-headed hard thought.

9 Edwin Arthur Burtt, *The Metaphysical Foundations of Modern Physical Science* (New York: Harcourt, Brace, 1925), pp. 137, 153.

10 Abrams, "Coleridge and the Romantic Vision of the World," p. 122.

11 *The Statesman's Manual*, ed. R. J. White, in *The Collected Works of Samuel Taylor Coleridge* (Princeton: Princeton Univ. Press, 1972), VI, 72.

12 *Ibid.*, pp. 72–73.

13 Cf. Michael G. Cooke, "The Manipulation of Space in Coleridge's Poetry," *New Perspectives on Coleridge and Wordsworth*, ed. Geoffrey Hartman (New York: Columbia Univ. Press, 1972), p. 176.

14 For an analysis of the complex verbalization of "Limbo," and allied poems "Ne Plus Ultra" and "On Donne's First Poem," and their subsequent complicated history of publication, see *CN*, III, 4073n.

15 Notebook 23 *ff.* 31v–32; quoted by Kathleen Coburn, *The Self Conscious Imagination: A Study of the Coleridge Notebooks in Celebration of the Bicentenary of His Birth 21 October 1772* (London: Oxford Univ. Press, 1974), pp. 31–32.

16 Røstvig, II, 287–88.

17 A. Bartlett Giamatti, *The Earthly Paradise and the Renaissance Epic* (Princeton: Princeton Univ. Press, 1966), p. 126.

18 I am familiar with the many critical arguments demonstrating the unity of the poem on the basis of a narrow interpretation of the grammatical reference of this or that word, thus limiting the range of Coleridge's recantation. And when I read some of them I wish to believe the persuasive arguments; but when one places Coleridge's hesitancies in "The Eolian Harp" in the context of the other poems where like compunctions occur, one cannot ignore what is a recurrent pattern of thought. Within such a context the

reading of "The Eolian Harp" with grammatical fastidiousness and push-pin pedantry appears wrong-headed when the poem is otherwise calling for a reading that embraces its whole statement. See, for example, William H. Scheuerle, "A Reexamination of Coleridge's 'The Eolian Harp,'" *SEL*, xv (1975), 591–99; and Ronald C. Wendling, "Coleridge and the Consistency of 'The Eolian Harp'" *SIR*, viii (1968), 26–42. For other opinions see Humphry House, *Coleridge: The Clark Lectures 1951–52* (London: Hart-Davis, 1952) and Albert Gérard, *English Romantic Poetry* (Berkeley: Univ. of California Press, 1968).

19 Cf. Max F. Schulz, "Coleridge, Milton and Lost Paradise," *N&Q*, vi (1959), 143–44; William H. Marshall, "The Structure of Coleridge's 'Reflections on Having Left a Place of Retirement,'" *N&Q*, vi (1959), 319–21; and Albert Gérard, "Clevedon Revisited: Further Reflections on Coleridge's 'Reflections on Having Left a Place of Retirement,'" *N&Q*, vii (1960), 101–02.

David Aers, Jonathan Cook, and David Punter, *Romanticism and Ideology: Studies in English Writing 1765–1830* (London: Routledge & Kegan Paul, 1981), pp. 82–102, minimize the import of the Christian context of Coleridge's poetry, by arguing that Coleridge habitually withdraws from real social issues into solipsistic reverie, providential pattern, and idealistic Christian generalities and apologetics. Characteristic, according to their socialistic poetics, are the rhetorical evasions, for example, in the resolution of the speaker at the end of "Reflections" to "join head, heart, and hand" in the "bloodless fight / Of Science, Freedom, and the Truth in Christ" (60–62). Aside from the obscure nature of the opponents, the speaker seems here to be joining his disjointed self together (so Aers, Cook, and Punter ironically remark) more than allying himself with the "unnumbered brethren" who are ostensibly his fellow sufferers.

20 Anthony John Harding, *Coleridge and the Idea of Love: Aspects of Relationship in Coleridge's Thought and Writing* (Cambridge: Cambridge Univ. Press, 1974), p. 260. Harding is paraphrasing from John Passmore's *The Perfectibility of Man* (London: Duckworth, 1970), p. 145.

21 Røstvig, *The Happy Man*, ii, 291–92.

22 Stanley Stewart, *The Enclosed Garden: The Tradition and the Image in Seventeenth-Century Poetry* (Madison: Univ. of Wisconsin Press, 1966).

23 Conveniently reproduced by Christopher Hussey in *English Gardens and Landscapes 1700–1750* (London: Country Life, 1967), plate 2; and by John Dixon Hunt and Peter Willis in *The Genius of the Place: The English Landscape Garden 1620–1820* (New York: Harper & Row, 1975), plate 51.

24 John H. Armstrong, *The Paradise Myth* (London: Oxford Univ. Press, 1969), p. 102.

25 *Ibid.*

26 Charles I. Patterson, Jr., "The Daemonic in *Kubla Khan*: Toward an Interpretation," *PMLA*, lxxxix (1974), 1042 n. Humphry House, *Coleridge*, p. 120, observes that the opening stanza presents a "conjunction of pleasure and sacredness." John B. Beer, *Coleridge the Visionary* (London: Chatto & Windus, 1959) and Carl Woodring, "Coleridge and the Khan," *EIC*, ix (1959), 361–68, insist on the disjunction, Beer characterizing Xanadu as the contrived postlapsarian Eden of an oriental poet–king, and Woodring as the attempt of a profane potentate to appropriate the unencompassable sacred for his pleasure.

27 For a summary of these sources and parallels, see my chapter in *The English Romantic Poets*, ed. Frank Jordan (New York: MLA, 1972), pp. 135–208.

28 E. S. Shaffer, *'Kubla Khan' and The Fall of Jerusalem: The Mythological School in Biblical Criticism and Secular Literature 1770–1880* (Cambridge: Cambridge Univ. Press, 1975), p. 108. For the full discussion, see pp. 96–190.

29 *Archetypal Patterns in Poetry: Psychological Studies of Imagination* (London: Oxford Univ. Press, 1934; rpt. New York, 1958), p. 143.

30 Alethea Hayter, *Opium and the Romantic Imagination* (London: Faber & Faber, 1968).

31 Elisabeth Schneider's insistent arguments notwithstanding, it is probable that "Kubla Khan" was written before Coleridge met Sara Hutchinson at the end of October 1799, although interestingly Schneider does link Sara in Coleridge's mind on other and subsequent grounds to the Abyssinian maid; cf. *Coleridge, Opium and 'Kubla Khan'* (Chicago: Univ. of Chicago Press, 1953), pp. 233–36. For an extended discussion of the place of the Abyssinian maid in Coleridge's emotional, as well as imaginative, life, see Geoffrey Yarlott, *Coleridge and the Abyssinian Maid* (London: Methuen, 1967), especially pp. 152–53 and 310–312; and for a perceptive discussion of Coleridge's spiritualization of love, see Harding, *Coleridge and the Idea of Love*, especially pp. 79–124.

32 Bodkin, *Archetypal Patterns in Poetry*, p. 146.

33 Cf. Norman Fruman, *Coleridge, The Damaged Archangel* (New York: Braziller, 1971), pp. 402–26.

34 The date of the manuscript, conjectured to be as early as 1797, remains uncertain. See Alice D. Snyder, "The Manuscript of 'Kubla Khan,'" *TLS*, 2 August 1934, p. 541; and follow-up by E. H. W. Meyerstein, *TLS*, 12 January and 9 February 1951, pp. 21, 85; Schneider, *Coleridge, Opium and 'Kubla Khan,'* pp. 153–237; and J. Skelton, "The Autograph Manuscript of *Kubla Khan* and an Interpretation," *REL*, VII (1966), 32–42. For summaries of the arguments on dating of the poem, see Schulz, "Coleridge," *The English Romantic Poets*, ed. Jordan, pp. 158–59.

35 See H. W. Piper, "The Two Paradises in *Kubla Khan*," *RES*, XXVII (1976), 148; and "Mount Abora," *NQ*, XX (1973), 286–89.

36 Bodkin, *Archetypal Patterns in Poetry*, p. 110.

37 R. J. White, *The Statesman's Manual*, in *Collected Works of Samuel Taylor Coleridge*, VI, xxix.

38 For an analysis of the polarity of truth and reorigination in Coleridge's aesthetics, see Joel Weinsheimer, "Coleridge on Synonymity and the Reorigination of Truth," *Papers on Language and Literature*, XIV (1978), 269–83.

39 A useful summary of this episode in Coleridge's life is given by Suzanne R. Hoover, "Coleridge, Humphry Davy, and Some Experiments with a Consciousness-Altering Drug," *Bulletin of Research in the Humanities*, LXXXI (1978), 9–27.

40 *Ibid.*, p. 25.

41 William James, *The Varieties of Religious Experience* (New York, 1902), pp. 388–89; quoted by Hoover, p. 26.

42 Mary Robinson, "Mrs. Robinson to the Poet Coleridge" (dated "Oct. 1800"), *Memoirs of the late Mrs. Robinson, written by Herself. With some posthumous pieces*, 4 vols. (London: R. Phillips, 1801), IV, 145–49.

4. Wordsworth and the *Axis Mundi* of Grasmere

1 *Home at Grasmere*, 2. All citations, unless otherwise indicated, are to MS.B Reading Text (1800–06), of *Home at Grasmere*, ed. Beth Darlington (Ithaca: Cornell Univ. Press, 1977); both the poem and this edition are henceforth referred to as *HatG*. Other texts used throughout are *The Prelude, 1798–1799*, ed. Stephen Parrish (Ithaca: Cornell Univ. Press, 1977); and *The Prelude*, eds. Ernest De Selincourt and Helen Darbishire (Oxford: At the Clarendon Press, 2nd rev. ed., 1959). Unless otherwise indicated references are to the *1805 Prelude*.

The dating of composition of *Home At Grasmere* between 1800 and 1806 has generated much conjecture and controversy, beginning with John A. Finch, "On the Dating of *Home at Grasmere*," *Bicentenary Wordsworth Studies in Memory of John Finch*, ed. Jonathan Wordsworth (Ithaca: Cornell Univ. Press, 1970), pp. 14–28; and including reasonable appraisals of information bearing on the topic, with descriptions of the manuscripts, by Mark L. Reed, *Wordsworth: The Chronology of the Middle Years 1800–1815* (Cambridge: Harvard Univ. Press, 1975), pp. 16–17, 57–58, and Appendix VI; and by Beth Darlington in her Cornell edition of the poem; to the latest review of evidence for its dating, by Jonathan Wordsworth, "On Man, On Nature, and On Human Life," *RES*, n.s. XXXI (1980), 17–29.

2 Coleridge left two lengthy (to Wordsworth surely daunting) descriptions of what *The Recluse* was supposed to contain: (1) in a letter to Wordsworth of 30 May 1815, *Collected Letters of Samuel Taylor Coleridge*, ed. Earl Leslie Griggs, 6 vols. (Oxford: At the Clarendon Press, 1956–71), IV, 574–75; and (2) in a reminiscence of 21 July 1832 recorded in *Specimens of the Table Talk of the Late Samuel Taylor Coleridge*, ed. Henry Nelson Coleridge (London: John Murray, 1835), II, 70–71. Too long to quote in full, some idea can be had of the Coleridgean tenor of "the Plan" as he remembered it by two or three all-encompassing Coleridgean sentences:

I supposed you first to have meditated the faculties of Man in the abstract, in their correspondence with his Sphere of action, and first, in the Feeling, Touch, and Taste, then in the Eye, & last in the Ear, to have laid a solid and immoveable foundation for the Edifice by removing the sandy Sophisms of Locke, and the Mechanic Dogmatists, and demonstrating that the Senses were living growths and developments of the Mind & Spirit . . . Next, I understand that you would take the Human Race in the concrete . . . Fallen men contemplated in the different ages of the World, and in the different states – Savage – Barbarous – Civilized – the lonely Cot, or Borderer's Wigwam – the Village – the Manufacturing Town – Sea-port – City – Universities – and not disguising the sore evils, under which the whole Creation groans, to point out however a manifest Scheme of Redemption from this Slavery, of Reconciliation from this Enmity with Nature . . . and to conclude by a grand didactic swell on the necessary identity of a true Philosophy with true Religion, agreeing in the results and differing only as the analytic and synthetic process . . . in short, the necessity of a general revolution in the modes of developing & disciplining the human mind by the substitution of Life, and Intelligence.   (*CL*, IV, 574–75)

3 M. H. Abrams, "English Romanticism: The Spirit of the Age," *Romanticism Reconsidered*, ed. Northrop Frye (New York: Columbia Univ. Press, 1963), pp. 26–72, authoritatively surveys the age's literary expression of revolutionary fervor; and George Dekker, *Coleridge and the Literature of Sensibility* (New York: Barnes & Noble, 1978), pp. 124–76, neatly reviews the fading belief in the eighteenth century in a mystical world harmony with its basic components of joy, the *prima musica* of the divine *Logos* and the original act of creation, and the *musica mundana* of earthly voices.

4 Wordsworth was not alone in succumbing to the supra-mundane aura of the place. Thomas Gray, for example, viewing it in 1769, calls it a "little unsuspected paradise" where "all is peace, rusticity, & happy poverty in its neatest most becoming attire," *Correspondence of Thomas Gray*, ed. Paget Toynbee and Leonard Whibley, 3 vols. (Oxford: Clarendon Press, 1935), III, 1099. It is a sentiment perhaps that Wordsworth found easier to share with the 1770s and 80s than with the 1800s and 1810s.

On the vexed question of *Home at Grasmere*'s optimism and joyousness versus its swerve into anxiety and self-doubt, see Kenneth R. Johnston, "The Idiom of Vision," *New Perspectives on Coleridge and Wordsworth*, ed. Geoffrey Hartman (New York: Columbia Univ. Press, 1972), p. 32, who postulates that Wordsworth's repetitions and redundancies, double negatives, faint oxymorons, tautologies, regressive tendencies, circularities of argument, and absence of predication (Johnston is alluding to "A Night-Piece" but has in mind Wordsworth's poetic practice generally as well) represent an heroic effort at verbal control of the apocalyptic thrust of his verse. Three years later, in "'Home at Grasmere': Reclusive Song," *SIR*, XIV (1975), 1–28, Johnston darkens his judgment, concluding on the same evidence that *Home at Grasmere* reveals a "feeling of loss . . . literally at its center" (p. 7). Karl Kroeber, "'Home at Grasmere': Ecological Holiness," *PMLA*, LXXXIX (1974), 132–41, contrariwise, accepts the poem's "triumphant declaratives" and its reticent denials alike as part of a conscious poetic strategy anticipating contemporary attitudes towards nature. There is more meeting of minds about Wordsworth's faltering, in "The Tuft of Primroses," when in 1808 he tried again to transfigure Grasmere into a central symbol of home and paradise. See James A. Butler, "Wordsworth's Tuft of Primroses: 'An Unrelenting Doom,'" *SIR*, XIV (1975), 237–48; and Kenneth R. Johnston, "Wordsworth's Lost Beginning: *The Recluse* in 1808," *ELH*, XLIII (1976), 316–41.

5 *Collected Letters*, II, 1013. See also *The Notebooks of Samuel Taylor Coleridge*, ed. Kathleen Coburn, 3 vols. to date (Princeton: Princeton Univ. Press, 1957, 1961, 1973), I, 1546.

6 Jonathan Wordsworth, "On Man, On Nature, and On Human Life," *RES*, n.s. XXXI (1980), 17–29, advances persuasive textual and textural evidence that "the spousal verse," published separately as a Prospectus to *The Excursion* (1814), was originally intended to introduce *Home at Grasmere*.

7 Wordsworth pillaged lines from "The Tuft of Primroses" for *The Excursion*, III, 367–405, and for the 1850 *Prelude*, VI, 420–71; and from *Home at Grasmere* for *The Excursion*, VI, 1079–1191. A run-down of other sackings is given in *HatG*, pp. 22–25.

Citations to "The Tuft of Primroses" are to *The Poetical Works of William Wordsworth*, ed. Ernest De Selincourt and Helen Darbishire, 5 vols. (Oxford: Clarendon Press, 1949; rev. 1952), V, 348–362; henceforth referred to as *PW*.

8 So Wordsworth tags Grasmere in fugitive lines written probably in 1800 (*PW*, V, 347).

9 See also *HatG*, 821, 876–77, 887, 901, 903.

10 Letter of 7 February 1805, in *The Letters of William and Dorothy Wordsworth: The Early Years, 1787–1805*, ed. Ernest De Selincourt, rev. Chester L. Shaver (Oxford: Clarendon Press, 1967), p. 534. Cf. Dorothy's letter of 23 July 1806 to Catherine Clarkson referring to the dwelling as "Mr. Crump's monster of a house," *Letters . . . The Middle Years, Part I, 1806–1811*, ed. Ernest De Selincourt, rev. Mary Moorman (Oxford: Clarendon Press, 1969), p. 61.

11 Cf. Muriel J. Mellown, "The Development of Imagery in 'Home at Grasmere,'" *TWC*, V (1974), 23–27, who accepts uncritically that Wordsworth's boyhood dream of paradisal sylphs and angels is "replaced by an inner state of mind which allows him to perceive . . . the 'Perfect Contentment, Unity entire' of the valley as it really is" (p. 26). Frederick Garber, in "The Landscape of Desire," *The Autonomy of the Self from Richardson to Huysmans* (Princeton: Princeton Univ. Press, 1982), pp. 184–202, also forcefully plumps for the poetic movement culminating in Wordsworth's affirmation of "The unassailable center of self" (p. 195) and "the self's harmony with itself" (p. 196). Garber is led to this hypothesis unerringly along a thesis-guided route which situates Grasmere at a distance from the one world – real and ideal – haled by the "spousal verse." In this geo-metaphysical transfer the Vale becomes a "temporary Paradise," or provisional stopover, on the road to the next world – "a figure for the final one" (p. 189).

In an acute general observation, which is nevertheless equally off-center as regards the paradisal anomalies of *Home at Grasmere* and "The Tuft of Primroses," George Dekker, *Coleridge and the Literature of Sensibility*, pp. 103–04, remarks that Thomson's *Castle of Indolence* (1748), though not offering exactly a Bower of Bliss, enticed poets for the remainder of the eighteenth century, including the generation of Coleridge and Wordsworth, into the bone-yard of a false paradise. The bower retreat of private poetic feelings was always more attractive to the Coleridge of "The Eolian Harp," however, than to Wordsworth, who was bent on universalizing his personal psychological shocks into human–national–cosmic reverberations.

Jonathan Wordsworth, *William Wordsworth: The Borders of Vision* (Oxford: Clarendon Press, 1982), Chapter 4 "Visions of Paradise: Spring 1800," pp. 98–148, is closest in point of view to me as regards the discrepancies inherent in Wordsworth's conferring on Grasmere and its inhabitants the prefigurative value of "all the Vales of earth and all mankind" (*HatG*, 256), although I find too schematic his division of *Home at Grasmere* into "Paradise Regained" (lines 1–667) and "The Serpent in Eden" (lines 667–1048). Most in accord with my sketch of the "social-to-personal movement" of Wordsworth's *Recluse-Prelude* composition in the years 1797–1814, and the ultimate "movement toward institutional forms of mental discipline" of Wordsworth's poetry, is Kenneth R. Johnston's magisterially summary article "Wordsworth and *The Recluse*: The University of Imagination," *PMLA*, XCVII (1982), 60–82. Johnston has collected all his articles, plus much more, in *Wordsworth and The Recluse* (New Haven: Yale Univ. Press, 1984), tracing the fragmented fate of *The Recluse* through the permutations of *Home at Grasmere*, *The Prelude*, and *The Excursion*.

12 All citations, unless otherwise indicated, are to the 1805 *Prelude*.

13 John A. Finch's persuasive argument for this date has been generally accepted as a description of how, in an untypical Wordsworthian way, the Glad Preamble came into being. See "Wordsworth's Two-Handed Engine," in *Bicentenary Wordsworth Studies*, ed. Jonathan Wordsworth, pp. 1–13. Cf. also Jonathan Wordsworth, *William Wordsworth: The Borders of Vision*, p. 101, who treats the sequence of events now as fact.

14 I am indebted to Linda Palumbo's ground-breaking dissertation-in-progress on the late self-chastizing voice of Wordsworth (University of Southern California) for the genesis of my remarks on these three *Ecclesiastical Sonnets*.

15 A rejected variant of these lines, for example, has earth only "partially embellish'd as becomes / The fix'd abiding place of fallen mankind" (MS. A, the text on which De Selincourt based his edition of the 1805 *Prelude*; see *The Prelude*, ed. Ernest De Selincourt and Helen Darbishire, dual page edition, 1805 and 1850 (Oxford, rev. ed. 1959), *apparatus criticus*, p. 77.

16 *HatG*, p. 221, *apparatus criticus*, MS. R. These lines are thought to be earlier than those of MS. B.

17 "Composed When a Probability Existed of Our Being Obliged to Quit Rydal Mount as a Residence" (1826), *PW*, IV, 385 (l. 161).

5. Byron's and Shelley's Hesperian Islands

1 The Horatian antecedents of *Don Juan* are discussed at some length by George Ridenour, *The Style of "Don Juan"* (New Haven: Yale Univ. Press, 1960), chap. 1; and Jerome J. McGann, *Don Juan in Context* (Chicago: Univ. of Chicago Press, 1976), chap. 5. I have quoted *Don Juan* from the *Variorum Edition*, eds. Truman Guy Steffan and Willis W. Pratt, 4 vols. (Austin: Univ. of Texas Press, 1957); *Childe Harold's Pilgrimage* from *Lord Byron: The Complete Poetical Works*, ed. Jerome J. McGann, Vol. II (Oxford: At the Clarendon Press, 1980); and Byron's other poems from *The Works of Lord Byron: Poetry*, ed. E. H. Coleridge, 7 vols. (London: J. Murray, rev. ed. 1903–22). I have abbreviated in-text references as follows: *DJ* for *Don Juan*, and *Childe* for *Childe Harold's Pilgrimage*.

2 Two critics, in particular, have written perceptively about the pervasive importance – the organizing and thematic significance – in Byron's poetry of the "personal myth" of a paradise glimpsed and lost, which he generalized into a fate each individual, each

community of people, and each civilization is doomed to repeat. See Ridenour, *The Style of "Don Juan," passim*; and Robert F. Gleckner, *Byron and the Ruins of Paradise* (Baltimore: The Johns Hopkins Univ. Press, 1967). The range of Byron's actual and metaphoric association of paradise with terrestrial objects, persons, and places is vividly illustrated by the entry under paradise in the index of both books.

See also Frederick L. Beaty, "Byron's Concept of Ideal Love," *Keats–Shelley Journal*, XII (1963), 37–54; M. K. Joseph, *Byron the Poet* (London: V. Gallancz, 1964); and E. D. Hirsch, Jr., "Byron and the Terrestrial Paradise," *From Sensibility to Romanticism: Essays Presented to Frederick A. Pottle*, eds. Frederick W. Hilles and Harold Bloom (New York: Oxford Univ. Press, 1965), pp. 467–86.

3 Gleckner, *Byron and the Ruins of Paradise*, p. xviii.

4 *Ibid.*, p. xviii.

5 Cf. Gleckner, *Byron and the Ruins of Paradise*, pp. 99–100; Ridenour, *The Style of "Don Juan,"* p. 45; and McGann, *Don Juan in Context*, pp. 142–52.

6 *Byron: Complete Poetical Works*, ed. McGann, II, 46.

7 Charles E. Robinson, *Shelley and Byron: The Snake and Eagle Wreathed in Fight* (Baltimore: The Johns Hopkins Press, 1976), pp. 237–40, offers a quirky perspective on this reading, which leaves Byron's final position ambiguous. Robinson hypothesizes that Byron gracefully muted his skepticism as a memorial tribute to his friend Shelley's idealistic contention that there must be "Other flowering isles . . . / In the sea of life and agony" ("Lines written among the Euganean Hills," 335–36).

8 See E. H. Coleridge, *Works*, V, 581–82; and Leslie Marchand, *Byron's Poetry: A Critical Introduction* (Boston: Houghton Mifflin, 1965), pp. 72–73. News of the mutual slaughter of Fletcher Christian and his fellow Polynesian colonists on Pitcairn Island reached England in 1810, accounts of visits to the island appearing in the *Quarterly Review* (February 1810) and (July 1815).

9 *A Journal of a Voyage to the South Seas, in His Majesty's Ship, The Endeavour . . . from the Papers of the late Sydney Parkinson* (1773), Australeana Facsimile Eds. No. A 34 (Adelaide: Libraries Board of S. Australia, 1972), p. 15.

10 *Byron's Letters and Journals*, ed. Leslie Marchand, 12 vols. (London: John Murray, 1973–82), X, 90. Marchand, *Byron's Poetry*, p. 74, flatly asserts that Byron resolved "the ambivalence of sympathies apparent in the beginning of the tale." The "happy ending of the idyll of Torquil and his Noble Savage bride," Marchand believes, is an unique instance among Byron's poems of "an ideal world unspoiled by the cynical intrusions of the critical intelligence."

11 Robert D. Hume, "*The Island* and the Evaluation of Byron's 'Tales,'" *Romantic and Victorian: Studies in Memory of William H. Marshall*, eds. W. Paul Elledge and Richard L. Hoffman (Rutherford: Fairleigh Dickenson Univ. Press, 1971), pp. 158–80.

12 Judith Chernaik, *The Lyrics of Shelley* (Cleveland: Case Western Reserve Univ. Press, 1972), p. 19. For quotations from Shelley's poetry I have relied principally on *Shelley's Poetry and Prose*, eds. Donald H. Reiman and Sharon B. Powers (New York: W. W. Norton, 1977).

13 *The Letters of Percy Bysshe Shelley*, ed. Frederick L. Jones, 2 vols. (Oxford: At the Clarendon Press, 1964), II, 339.

14 Chernaik, *The Lyrics of Shelley*, p. 69.

15 For representative attempts to come to terms with the poem's contradictoriness, cf. Earl R. Wasserman, *The Subtler Language: Critical Readings of Neoclassic and Romantic Poems* (Baltimore: The Johns Hopkins Press, 1959), pp. 251–84; Priscilla P. St. George, "The Styles of Good and Evil in 'The Sensitive Plant,'" *JEGP*, LXIV (1965), 479–88; Seymour Reiter, *A Study of Shelley's Poetry* (Albuquerque: Univ. of New Mexico Press, 1967), pp. 236–40; Donald H. Reiman, *Percy Bysshe Shelley* (New York:

Twayne Publisher, 1969), pp. 110–13; and Richard S. Caldwell, "'The Sensitive Plant' as Original Fantasy," *Studies in Romanticism*, xv (1976), 221–52.

16 Reiman, *Shelley's Poetry and Prose*, p. 219n.
17 Chernaik, *The Lyrics of Shelley*, p. 125.
18 "Detached Thoughts," No. 55, *Byron's Letters and Journals*, ed. Marchand, IX, 31.

6. Bewick's, Constable's, and Palmer's *Locus Paradisus*

1 *Samuel Palmer's Sketch-book 1824*, ed. Martin Butlin, facsimile reproduction by the Blake Trust (London: Trianon Press, 1962), p. 82.
2 Thomas Bewick, *A Memoir of Thomas Bewick Written by Himself* (1862), ed. Iain Bain (London: Oxford Univ. Press, 1975), p. 75; henceforth referred to as *Memoir*. Useful to an understanding of Bewick's art, thought, and world are Montague Weekley's biography *Thomas Bewick* (London: Oxford Univ. Press, 1953) and S. Roscoe's *Thomas Bewick: A Bibliography Raisonné* (London: Oxford Univ. Press, 1953), a survey of editions of Bewick's major books – *General History of Quadrupeds*, *History of British Birds*, and *Fables of Aesop* – issued in his lifetime. For further studies, editions, and catalogues raisonnés, consult Iain Bain's select bibliography, *Memoir*, pp. xl–xli.
3 Reproductions of these vignettes can be found respectively in *Memoir*, pp. xxxii, 35, 162, 163, 130; Weekley, *Thomas Bewick*, pp. 124, 125, 157, 164.
4 I am indebted to Anne Mellor, *English Romantic Irony* (Cambridge: Harvard Univ. Press, 1980), for calling my attention to this vignette, which she considers to be "an excellent visual example of romantic irony." See also Henri Zerner's review of Bewick's *Memoir* in *The New York Review of Books*, 30 September 1976, pp. 27–29. A convenient collection of Bewick's tailpieces has been published by Iain Bain, *Vignettes* (London: The Scolar Press, 1978).
5 Humphry Repton, *Fragments on the Theory and Practice of Landscape Gardening* (London, 1816), reprinted in *The Landscape Gardening and Landscape Architecture of the Late Humphry Repton*, ed. J. C. Loudon (London, 1840; reprinted Gregg International Publishing Ltd., 1969), pp. 467–68.
6 I have in mind, here, the agrarian community occupying a perilous middle ground between the two encroaching forces of the city and wilderness, such as Leo Marx has eloquently analyzed in *The Machine in the Garden* (New York: Oxford Univ. Press, 1964). See also Raymond Williams, *The Country and the City* (New York: Oxford Univ. Press, 1973), pp. 16–17, who debunks the tendency of poetry to idealize the original "contact with the working year and with the real social conditions of country life" of Virgil.
7 I am aware that the 1802 painting "has long been recognized as the source from which Constable composed his large oil painting 'Dedham Vale,' exhibited at the Royal Academy in 1828" (Graham Reynolds, *Victoria and Albert Museum Catalogue of the Constable Collection* [London: Her Majesty's Stationery Office, 1960], p. 44) and now in the National Gallery of Scotland. That the two pictures are instances of the same composition does not necessarily negate my interpretation that they represent different seasons of the year. One does not have to observe many of Constable's successive studies or oil sketches preliminary to the full-scale painting, as with *The Leaping Horse*, to recognize his habit of restlessly altering details and at times perspective, composition, and time of year in a trial-and-error effort to arrive at the best statement of his subject.
8 See Williams, *The Country and the City*, pp. 9–19. John Barrell, *The Dark Side of the Landscape: The Rural Poor in English Painting, 1730–1840* (Cambridge: Cambridge

Univ. Press, 1980), indicts Constable for his painterly reticence in depicting rural labor and laborers – for the discrepancy between his observance of the pastoral tradition and his non-observation of contemporary agricultural working conditions and social inequities. For arguments against Barrell's hypothesis, cf. Ronald Paulson's *Literary Landscape: Turner and Constable* (New Haven: Yale Univ. Press, 1982), which offers a psycho-analytic deconstructionist explanation of Constable's concentration on an unpeopled sunny meadow in the distance occluded by a tangled and obscuring foreground.

9 Karl Kroeber, "'Tintern Abbey' and *The Cornfield*: Serendipity as a Method of Intermedia Criticism," *JAAC*, XXXI (1972), 70–71. This essay and others of Kroeber on the subject are conveniently reprinted in revised and extended form in his book *Romantic Landscape Vision: Constable and Wordsworth* (Madison: Univ. of Wisconsin Press, 1975), where the citation just made appears on p. 33.

10 C. R. Leslie, *Memoirs of the Life of John Constable*, ed. Jonathan Mayne (London: Phaidon Press, 1951), p. 273.

11 R. B. Beckett, *John Constable's Correspondence* (Ipswich: W. S. Cowell, 1962–68), VI, 77.

12 Leslie Parris, with Ian Fleming-Williams and Conal Shields, *Constable Paintings, Watercolours & Drawings* (London: Tate Gallery, 1976), p. 10, catalogue for the Tate Gallery exhibition commemorating the bicentenary of Constable's birth.

13 Kroeber, *Romantic Landscape Vision*, p. 31.

14 Graham Reynolds, *Constable: The Natural Painter* (London: Cory, Adams & Mackay, 1965), p. 19.

15 Kroeber, *Romantic Landscape Vision*, p. 112.

16 Meyer H. Abrams, *Natural Supernaturalism: Tradition and Revolution in Romantic Literature* (New York: W. W. Norton, 1971).

17 Parris, *Constable Paintings, Watercolours & Drawings*, p. 10. I am indebted also to Parris for several of the instances of change that follow this observation.

18 From a letter of 21 December 1828 to John Linnell, in *The Letters of Samuel Palmer*, ed. Raymond Lister, 2 vols. (Oxford: Clarendon Press, 1974), I, 48, 50.

19 *Samuel Palmer's Sketch-book 1824*, ed. Martin Butlin, pp. 81–82.

20 Other "Ancients" intermittently associated with Palmer's Shoreham years were Henry Walter, Arthur and Frederick Tatham (sons of the architect Charles Heathcote Tatham, the latter of whom was executor, and destroyer, of many of Blake's remains), Welby Sherman, and Palmer's cousin the stockbroker John Giles. See Laurence Binyon, *The Followers of William Blake* (New York: Benjamin Blom, 1968).

21 The quotation comes from one of Palmer's pocket-notebooks of 1822–24 cited by A. H. Palmer, *The Life and Letters of Samuel Palmer* (London: Seeley & Co., 1892), reissued with an essay by Raymond Lister (London: Eric & Joan Stevens, 1972), p. 15. See also Raymond Lister, "'The Ancients' and the Classics," *SIR*, XV (1976), 395–404.

22 Eliza Finch, *Memorials of the late Francis Oliver Finch* (London, 1865), pp. 349–50.

23 Geoffrey Grigson, *Samuel Palmer: The Visionary Years* (London: Kegan Paul, 1947), p. 33. Grigson also gives a descriptive catalogue of Palmer's paintings, watercolors, drawings, and engravings, pp. 155–95, which I have relied on for locating and dating of specific works.

24 A. H. Palmer, *Life and Letters of Samuel Palmer*, pp. 12–13.

25 From a gargantuan letter to George Richmond of September 1828, *Letters of Samuel Palmer*, ed. Raymond Lister, I, 34–35.

26 *Samuel Palmer's Sketch-book 1824*, ed. Martin Butlin, "Twilight Time," pp. 74–75; "The Shepherd's Home," p. 127.

27 *Letters of Samuel Palmer*, ed. Raymond Lister, I, 50.

28 *Ibid.*, I, 49. The quotation is from William Wordsworth's sonnet "From the Italian of Michael Angelo," *Miscellaneous Sonnets*, XXIV.

29 For a discussion of the books Palmer read at Shoreham, see Grigson, *Samuel Palmer: The Visionary Years*, pp. 53–59.

30 Grigson, *ibid.*, p. 178, apropos of *The Magic Apple Tree*. James Sellars, *Samuel Palmer* (New York: St. Martin's Press, 1974), argues that Palmer's paintings and drawings of the Shoreham period are charged with allusions to "procreation and fecundity" (p. 57), and gives a restrained psycho-analytical explanation for these sexual resonances.

31 *Letters of Samuel Palmer*, ed. Raymond Lister, I, 47.

32 The most nervously sexual of such views is a drawing of *Culbone, Somerset* (1832/33, formerly Melbourne Art Gallery). Here the "smooth belly of the land above dips sharply over a shadowy pubic mound textured and patterned with trees and shrubs while, on either side spring the thighs of the valley" (Sellars, *Samuel Palmer*, p. 87).

33 Lister, "'The Ancients' and the Classics," *SIR*, XV (1976), 403.

34 See William Feaver, *The Art of John Martin* (Oxford: Clarendon Press, 1975), pp. 72–87; and Thomas Balston, *John Martin* (London: Camelot, 1947).

35 Cf. George H. Ford, "Felicitous Space: The Cottage Controversy," *Nature and the Victorian Imagination*, eds. U. C. Knoepflmacher and G. B. Tennyson (Berkeley: Univ. of California Press, 1977), pp. 29–48; and J. Hillis Miller, "'Wessex Heights': The Persistence of the Past in Hardy's Poetry," *Critical Quarterly*, X (1968), 339–59.

7. Crabbe's and Clare's Enclosured Vales

1 Raymond Williams, *The Country and the City* (New York: Oxford Univ. Press, 1973), p. 68; see also pp. 69–95.

2 Anya Taylor, *Magic and English Romanticism* (Athens: Univ. of Georgia Press, 1979).

3 Terence Bareham, *George Crabbe* (New York: Barnes & Noble, 1977). I have taken my quotations of Crabbe's poetry from *The Poetical Works of George Crabbe*, eds. A. J. Carlyle and R. M. Carlyle (London: Oxford Univ. Press, 1914); and *Poems by George Crabbe*, ed. Adolphus Ward, 3 vols. (Cambridge: Cambridge Univ. Press, 1905–07). Another indispensable edition is *The Poetical Works of the Rev. George Crabbe: with his Letters and Journals, and his Life, by his Son*, also George, 8 vols. (London: John Murray, 1834). For criticism of the poetry, see Lilian F. Haddakin, *The Poetry of Crabbe* (London: Chatto and Windus, 1954); Oliver F. Sigworth, *Nature's Sternest Painter: Five Essays on the Poetry of George Crabbe* (Tucson: Univ. of Arizona Press, 1965); and Peter New, *George Crabbe's Poetry* (New York: St. Martin's Press, 1976).

4 Robert L. Chamberlain, *George Crabbe* (New York: Twayne Publishers, 1965), p. 24. "Infancy" is reprinted in *George Crabbe: Tales, 1812 and Other Selected Poems*, ed. Howard Mills (Cambridge: Cambridge Univ. Press, 1967).

5 John Barrell, *The Idea of Landscape and the Sense of Place 1730–1840* (Cambridge: Cambridge Univ. Press, 1972), p. 184. I am generally indebted to this stimulating original book for my observations about enclosure, spatiality, and Clare. The literature on the enclosure of English farmland is extensive. For some recent examinations of it within a literary frame of reference see Williams, *The Country and the City*, pp. 96–107; and Alice Chandler, *A Dream of Order: The Medieval Ideal in Nineteenth-Century English Literature* (Lincoln: Univ. of Nebraska Press, 1970).

6 *The Prose of John Clare*, eds. J. W. and Anne Tibble (London: Routledge & Kegan Paul, 1951), p. 13. The Tibbles have also served Clare well with the standard biography, *John Clare: A Life* (London: Joseph, 1932; rev. ed., 1972); *The Letters of John Clare* (London: Routledge & Kegan Paul, 1951); and *The Poems of John Clare*,

2 vols. (London: J. M. Dent, 1935). Also useful are Eric Robinson's and Geoffrey Summerfield's editions of *Selected Poems and Prose of John Clare* (London: Oxford Univ. Press, 1966, 1967), and *The Later Poems of John Clare* (Manchester: Manchester Univ. Press, 1964).

7 Barrell, *The Idea of Landscape and the Sense of Place 1730–1840*, p. 106, conjectures that the major work took place between 1813 and 1816.

8 *Selected Poems and Prose of John Clare*, ed. Eric Robinson and Geoffrey Summerfield (London: Oxford Univ. Press, 1967), pp. xvi–xvii.

9 Barrell, *The Idea of Landscape*, pp. 113–14.

10 *Ibid.*, p. 175. For an extended examination of the 1820 poems, and argument that they reveal Clare's having viewed "Nature as Eden, innocent and eternal" (p. 64), and pre-enclosure Helpston as embodying this paradise, with its "enslavement and destruction" through enclosure as equivalent to the loss of Eden, see Janet M. Todd, *In Adam's Garden: A Study of John Clare's Pre-Asylum Poetry* (Gainesville: Univ. of Florida Press, 1973), especially pp. 53–80.

11 *The Prose of John Clare*, eds. J. W. and Anne Tibble, pp. 17–18 and 24.

12 Williams, *The Country and the City*, pp. 9–12.

13 William Cobbett, *Rural Rides*, ed. James Paul Cobbett (London: A. Cobbett, 1853), pp. 586 and 254; cf. also *ibid.*, pp. 583, 591, and 595–602; and *The Autobiography of William Cobbett*, ed. William Reitzel (London: Faber, 1947), pp. 15–16. Besides Williams, *The Country and the City*, passim, Chandler, *A Dream of Order: The Medieval Ideal in Nineteenth-Century English Literature*, sensibly discusses, with many facts, "the idealization of the past" which "held the English mind for at least a quarter of a century 1820's to 1840's" (p. 115).

14 Barrell, *The Idea of Landscape*, p. 157. Timothy Brownlow, "A Molehill for Parnassus: John Clare and Prospect Poetry," *Univ. of Toronto Quarterly*, XLVIII (1978), 23–40, while retaining the sense of "circling" activity central to Clare's poems, describes Clare's poetic effort at "comprehensiveness, a circular all-at-onceness" as the consequence of a "kaleidoscopic" vision which strives for "a kind of fluid crystallization of images" (pp. 32, 25). For variant analyses of the structure of Clare's poetry, see Thomas R. Frosch, "The Descriptive Style of John Clare," *Studies in Romanticism*, X (1971), 137–49; and L. J. Swingle, "Stalking the Essential John Clare: Clare in Relation to His Romantic Contemporaries," *Studies in Romanticism*, XIV (1975), 273–84.

15 Barrell, *The Idea of Landscape*, pp. 162–63.

16 Cf. Richard Feingold, *Nature and Society: Late Eighteenth-Century Uses of the Pastoral and Georgic* (New Brunswick: Rutgers Univ. Press, 1978).

17 Williams, *The Country and the City*, pp. 138–39.

18 Christopher Johnstone, *John Martin* (New York: St. Martin's Press, 1974), p. 111.

8. From Natural Landscape to Controlled Environment

1 Herbert L. Sussman, *Victorians and the Machine: The Literary Response to Technology* (Cambridge: Harvard Univ. Press, 1968), in an analysis of seven writers – Carlyle, Dickens, Ruskin, Morris, Butler, Wells, and Kipling – discusses how Victorians often additionally confused mechanistic thought with mechanization, and the machine as philosophical symbol with it as tangible influence.

One final note of indebtedness; I may have gotten the phrase "technological sublime" from Sussman. I cannot remember if I read his book when it was first published. Suffice it to acknowledge here that when I read (reread?) it three or four years after having written section B of this chapter in which the concept figures extensively, I had a distinct sense of *déjà vu* and found (refound?) there the phrase.

2 Claude-Nicolas Ledoux, *L'architecture considérée sous la rapport de l'art, des moeurs et de la législation*, 2 vols. (Paris: De l'imprimerie de H. L. Perronneau, Chez l'auteur, 1804; rpt. 1961), I, 1.

3 [James Stuart], *Critical Observations on the Buildings and Improvements of London* (1771), reprinted by The Augustan Reprint Society, No. 189–90, ed. Dianne Sigler Ames (Los Angeles: William Andrews Clark Memorial Library, Univ. of California, Los Angeles, 1978), p. 10.

4 The vivid verbs are John Summerson's characterization of a part of what was happening to *The London Building World of the Eighteen-Sixties* (London: Thames and Hudson, 1973), 5th Walter Neurath Memorial Lectures, pp. 7–8. In the discussion that follows I have also found especially helpful Summerson's *Georgian London* (London: Pleiades, 1945, rev. ed. 1978), and his *John Nash: Architect to King George IV* (London: G. Allen & Unwin, 2nd ed. 1949, rpt. 1965); Walter L. Creese's essay "Imagination in the Suburb," *Nature and the Victorian Imagination*, eds. U. C. Knoepflmacher and G. B. Tennyson (Berkeley: Univ. of California Press, 1977), pp. 49–67, and his *The Search for Environment* (New Haven: Yale Univ. Press, 1966); *The Victorian City*, eds. H. J. Dyos and Michael Wolff, 2 vols. (London: Routledge & Kegan Paul, 1973); Myron F. Brightfield, *Victorian England in Its Novels: 1840–1870* (Los Angeles: Univ. of California Press, 1968); and John Gloag, *Victorian Comfort* (London: A. and C. Black, 1961).

5 [Stuart], *Critical Observations*, pp. 9–15, 20.

6 See Summerson, *Georgian London*, pp. 269–87.

7 J. C. Loudon, *The Suburban Gardener, and Villa Companion* (London, 1838; facs. rpt. Garland Publishing, Inc., 1982), p. 8. The facsimile reprint is part of The English Landscape Garden series, No. 29, ed. John Dixon Hunt.

8 Creese, "Imagination in the Suburb," *Nature and the Victorian Imagination*, pp. 50–52.

9 Catherine Gore, *Cecil: or, The Adventures of a Coxcomb*, 3 vols. (London: Richard Bentley, 1841), I, 285.

10 Edward Akroyd, *On Improved Dwellings for the Working Classes* (London, 1862), p. 8; quoted from Creese, "Imagination in the Suburb," *Nature and the Victorian Imagination*, p. 57.

11 John Summerson, "John Wood and the English Town-Planning Tradition," *Heavenly Mansions and Other Essays on Architecture* (1949; New York: W. W. Norton & Co., 1963), pp. 87–110.

12 Summerson, *Georgian London*, pp. 181–85.

13 A ready and near inexhaustible source of information on the subject is Warwick Wroth's compilation of histories of *The London Pleasure Gardens of the Eighteenth Century* (1896), newly reissued by A. H. Saxon (Hamden, Conn.: Archon Books, 1979).

14 In the same letter, Lydia describes Vauxhall, as well, which she and her party, in a whirlwind tour of London nightspots, visited after Ranelagh. See Tobias Smollett, *The Adventures of Humphry Clinker*, ed. Lewis M. Knapp (London: Oxford Univ. Press, 1966), pp. 92–94. For other contemporary descriptions of the gardens at Spaniards Inn, Ranelagh, and Vauxhall, see Wroth, *The London Pleasure Gardens of the Eighteenth Century*, pp. 184–85, 199–218, and 286–326.

15 *Ibid.*, in order of quotation pp. 273, 11, 132, 134, and 159.

16 He now lies in the crypt of St. Michael's Church, in The Grove, Highgate.

17 Cf. Sir Edwin Chadwick, *Practice of Internment in Towns* (1839). Cemeteries were established in Kensal Green (1833), Norwood (1838), Highgate (1839), Abney Park, Nunhead, and Brompton (1840), and twenty-four miles out of London near Woking on 2100 acres purchased in 1855 by the London Necropolis Company for a massive burial ground estimated to last five or six centuries, which has matured according to one

commentator until "more than one hundred years after its foundation the cemetery has all the evergreen luxuriance of a landscape by J. C. Loudon" (J. Mordaunt Crook, "Sydney Smirke: The Architecture of Compromise," *Seven Victorian Architects*, ed. Jane Fawcett [London: Thames and Hudson, 1976], p. 63).

18 *Ibid.*, p. 60.

19 Thomas Bewick, *A Memoir of Thomas Bewick Written by Himself*, ed. Iain Bain (New York: Oxford Univ. Press, 1975), p. 104.

20 Melville Carr Selway has compiled a convenient collection of these prints in *The Regency Road; the Coaching Prints of James Pollard*, with introduction by James Laver (London: Faber & Faber, 1957), pp. 15–30; along with a short memoir of Pollard, pp. 31–37.

21 *Ibid.*, pp. 21, 55, and 86.

22 For a history of this "commercial expansion" see Paul Mantoux, *The Industrial Revolution in the Eighteenth Century* (London, 1928; rev. ed., New York: Harper Torchbook, 1962), especially pp. 105–35; and L. T. C. Rolt, *Thomas Telford* (Harmondsworth, Middlesex: Penguin Books, 1958, 1979). For contemporary accounts see John Aikin, *A Description of the Country from Thirty to Forty Miles Round Manchester* (London, 1795); Arthur Young, *A Six Months Tour Through the North of England*, 4 vols. (London, 1770), II, 196–241; and Samuel Smiles, *Lives of the Engineers* (1862), 2 vols., intro. L. T. C. Rolt (Newton Abbot, Devonshire: David and Charles Reprints, Redwood Press, 1968).

23 Mantoux, *The Industrial Revolution in the Eighteenth Century*, p. 129.

24 John Scott, "Amwell" (1776, although written in part by 1761), *The Poetical Works of John Scott Esq.* (London: J. Buckland, 1782), pp. 66–67.

25 The co-organizer of the 1982 bicentenary exhibition of Cotman, and editor of the catalogue, Miklos Rajnai, *John Sell Cotman 1782–1842* (Ithaca: Cornell Univ. Press, 1982), p. 87, casts doubt on the identification of the aqueduct as Chirk.

26 Still the best source guide for artists and pictures of the period is F. D. Klingender's *Art and the Industrial Revolution* (1947), rev. and ed. Arthur Elton (London: Evelyn, Adams and Mackay Ltd., 1968).

27 So the agricultural journalist Arthur Young describes Coalbrookdale Gorge in 1776, in "A Tour to Shropshire," in *Tours in England and Wales by Arthur Young*, London School of Economics and Political Science Series of Reprints, No. 14, selected from Young's contributions, beginning in 1792, to the *Annals of Agriculture* (London: Univ. of London, 1932), p. 152. The "Tour of Shropshire," from which the remarks about Coalbrookdale are taken, occurred in the summer of 1776. Neil Cossons, *Ironbridge: Landscape of Industry* (London: Cassell, 1977), contains a fine pictorial survey past and present of bridge and town. See also Asa Briggs, *Iron Bridge to Crystal Palace: Impact and Images of the Industrial Revolution* (London: Thames & Hudson, 1979).

28 See Michael Overman, *Sir Marc Brunel and the Tunnel* (London: Macdonald, 1971); John Pudney, *Brunel and His World* (London: Thames & Hudson, 1974); and *The Works of Isambard Kingdom Brunel: An Engineering Appreciation*, ed. Sir Alfred Pugsley (London: Institution of Civil Engineers, 1976).

29 Young, *Tours in England and Wales*, p. 152.

30 Raymond Williams, *The Country and the City* (New York: Oxford Univ. Press, 1973), especially pp. 78–86.

31 See Christopher Wood, *Victorian Panorama: Paintings of Victorian Life* (London: Faber, 1976), pp. 207–15.

32 See, e.g., letter of 13 September 1839 to John Aitken Carlyle; the relevant passage is quoted by J. A. Froude, *Thomas Carlyle, A History of his Life in London, 1834–1881* (1884), ed. John Clubbe (Columbus: Ohio State Univ. Press, 1979), p. 384. For the quotation from *Sartor Resartus*, see the Centenary Edition of *The Works of Thomas*

Carlyle, ed. H. D. Traill, 30 vols. (London: Chapman & Hall, 1896–99), I, 133.
33 Jack Lindsay, *J. M. W. Turner: His Life and Work* (New York: Harper & Row, 1966), p. 187.

9. Paxton's Hyde Park Crystal Palace

1 "History of the Great Exhibition," *The Art-Journal Illustrated Catalogue. The Industry of All Nations, 1851* (London, 1851), available in an unabridged republication, ed. John Gloag (New York: Dover Publications, Inc., 1970), p. xxi. Another indispensable contemporary account of the Great Exhibition is the *Official Descriptive and Illustrated Catalogue*, issued by authority of the Royal Commission that directed the Exhibition (London, 1851), 3 vols. See also *Great Exhibition of the Works of Industry of All Nations, 1851: Reports by the Juries . . .*, 4 vols. (London, 1852); *Lectures on the Results of the Great Exhibition of 1851* (London, 1852); and *The Great Exhibition of 1851 A Commemorative Album*, compiled by C. H. Gibbs-Smith for the Victoria and Albert Museum (London: H. M. Stationery Office, 1950). Among recent books Asa Briggs, *Iron Bridge to Crystal Palace: Impact and Images of the Industrial Revolution* (London: Thames & Hudson, 1979), places the Crystal Palace within the developing history of Western technology; and Patrick Beaver, *The Crystal Palace: 1851–1936, A Portrait of Victorian Enterprise* (London: Hugh Evelyn Ltd., 1970), gives a comprehensive story of the Hyde Park Crystal Palace, and of its reconstruction at Sydenham, with a generous number of drawings and photographs.
   The citation of Philip James Bailey is to *The Age; A Colloquial Satire* (Boston: Ticknor and Fields, 1858), pp. 27–28.
2 Beaver, *The Crystal Palace*, p. 40.
3 *Ibid.*
4 *Ibid.*, pp. 40–42.
5 Quoted by Asa Briggs, "The Crystal Palace and the Men of 1851," in *Victorian People: A Reassessment of Persons and Themes 1851–1867* (Chicago: The Univ. of Chicago Press, 1954, rev. ed., 1972), p. 37.
6 Charles Kingsley, "The Fount of Science," preached at St. Margaret's Church, Westminster, 4 May 1851, published in *Sermons on National Subjects* (London, 1852), I, 140–73. In the quotation from *Yeast* that follows, I have used the edition of 1851 (London: John W. Parker), pp. 95–96.
7 *The Stones of Venice*, I, in *The Complete Works of John Ruskin*, eds. E. T. Cook and Alexander Wedderburn (London: G. Allen, 1903–12), IX, 456; cf. also "The Opening of the Crystal Palace [Sydenham] Considered in Some of its Relations to the Prospects of Art" (1854): "in the centre of the nineteenth century, we suppose ourselves to have invented a new style of architecture, when we have magnified a conservatory! . . . [and we congratulate ourselves] because fourteen acres of ground have been covered with glass," *Works*, XII, 419, 421.
8 Beaver, *The Crystal Palace*, p. 28.
9 Robert Hunt, "The Science of the Exhibition," *Art-Journal Catalogue*, p. I*.
10 "History of the Great Exhibition," *Art-Journal Catalogue*, p. xiii.
11 More than a hundred years would pass before another structure encapsulated the aspirations of an age so succinctly and appositely. Then it would be the Vehicle Assembly Building – the largest structure in the world – of the National Aeronautics and Space Administration (NASA) at Cape Kennedy, which has been called by Norman Mailer a "giant cathedral of a machine," likened by him to the "great churches of a religious age," and characterized as the "antechamber of a new Creation" (*Of a Fire on the Moon* [Boston: Little, Brown and Co., 1970], p. 55).

12 "History of the Great Exhibition," *Art-Journal Catalogue*, p. xxv.

13 *Ibid.*

14 For illustrations of some of these and other equally outlandish items exhibited, see the *Art-Journal Catalogue*, for example, pp. 33, 74, 287, 150, 52, 222–23, 245, 251. See also Nikolas Pevsner, *High Victorian Design; A Study of the Exhibits of 1851* (London: Architectural Press, 1951), p. 87; and Briggs, *Victorian People*, p. 39.

15 William Morris, "Lectures on Art and Industry": "Art and the Beauty of the Earth. A Lecture Delivered at Burslem Town Hall on October 13, 1881"; and "Some Hints on Pattern-Designing. A Lecture Delivered at the Working Men's College, London, on December 10, 1881," in *The Collected Works of William Morris*, with introduction by May Morris (London: Longmans, Green and Co., 1910–15), XXII, 169, 182; cf. John Dixon Hunt, *The Pre-Raphaelite Imagination, 1848–1900* (London: Routledge & Kegan Paul, 1968), p. 64.

16 John Ruskin, "The Opening of the Crystal Palace [Sydenham] Considered in Some of Its Relations to the Prospects of Art," *Works*, XII, 420.

17 Jerome Beaty, "All Victoria's Horses and All Victoria's Men", *NLH*, I (1969–70), 271–92, characterizes the Victorian period, 1830–70, as one of "Change, fragmentation . . . and relativism not only of truths but of reality itself" (291). Consequently, "The 'medley' or 'miscellany' is perhaps the most dramatic and diagrammatic of the modes that inform the Victorian period-frame" (291).

10. Turner's Fabled Atlantis: London, Venice, and Carthage as Paradisal Cityscape

1 John Gage, *Colour in Turner: Poetry and Truth* (New York: Praeger, 1969), p. 96.

2 See especially Byron's poems "Ode on Venice" (1818), *Childe Harold's Pilgrimage*, Canto 4 (1817–18), and *Beppo* (1817); and Robert F. Gleckner, *Byron and the Ruins of Paradise* (Baltimore: The Johns Hopkins Press, 1967), pp. 306, 310, 316, and *passim*.

3 Letter to Thomas Moore of 17 November 1816, *Byron's Letters and Journals*, ed. Leslie A. Marchand, 12 vols. (Cambridge, Mass.: Harvard Univ. Press, 1973–82), V, 129.

4 John Ruskin, *The Stones of Venice*, I, in *The Complete Works of John Ruskin*, eds. E. T. Cook and Alexander Wedderburn (London: G. Allen, 1903–12), IX, 17. For Ruskin's analysis of, and extended meditation on, the Fig-tree and Vine Angles see *Works*, X, 358–439.

5 Andrew Griffin, "The Interior Garden and John Stuart Mill," *Nature and the Victorian Imagination*, eds. U. C. Knoepflmacher and G. B. Tennyson (Berkeley: Univ. of California Press, 1977), p. 173.

6 *Samuel Palmer's Sketch-book 1824*, ed. Martin Butlin, facsimile reproduction for the Blake Trust (London: Trianon Press, 1962), pp. 81–82.

7 Jack Lindsay, *J. M. W. Turner: His Life and Work* (New York: Harper & Row, 1966), p. 144.

8 Jack Lindsay, *The Sunset Ship: The Poems of J. M. W. Turner* (Lowestoft, Suffolk: Scorpion Press, 1966), p. 58; henceforth cited in the text as *Turner Poems*.

9 See R. F. Storch, "Abstract Idealism in English Romantic Poetry and Painting," *Images of Romanticism: Verbal and Visual Affinities*, eds. Karl Kroeber and William Walling (New Haven: Yale Univ. Press, 1978), pp. 198–203.

10 This is the count given in the Probate Court's catalogue of September 1856. In June 1861 the count stood at 105 finished pictures and 219 unfinished (changed by the end of the year to 257); see A. J. Finberg, *The Life of J. M. W. Turner, RA* (Oxford: At the Clarendon Press, 2nd ed., 1961), p. 445. For an up to date accounting see Martin Butlin and Evelyn Joll, *The Paintings of J. M. W. Turner*, 2 vols., Text and Plates (New Haven: Yale Univ. Press, 1977), I, xviii.

11 For an example of how these conflicting strands of experience enter into one of Turner's paintings, see Karl Kroeber's interpretation of *Dido Building Carthage*, in "Experience as History: Shelley's Venice, Turner's Carthage," *ELH*, XLI (1974), 321–39. See also John Gage, *Turner: Rain, Steam and Speed* (New York: Viking Press, 1972).

12 Like Turner, who had himself lashed to a mainsail on a trip up the coast of England to watch a snowstorm at sea, resulting in the painting *Snow Storm: Steam Boat off a Harbour's Mouth*, Vernet had himself tied to a mast to observe a storm at sea, on a trip to Italy in 1732. Apropos of a seascape by Ruysdael, Turner wrote: "A brown picture which pervades thro' the water so as to check the idea of it being liquid. . . . The chief light is upon the surge in the foreground – but too much is made to suffer – so that it is artificial – and shows the brown in a more glaring point of view and *this* inattention of the forms which waves make upon a lee shore embanked." From A. J. Finberg, *Inventory of the Drawings of the Turner Bequest* (London: H. M. Stationery Office, 1909), I, 182. See also T. S. R. Boase, "Shipwrecks in English Romantic Painting," *Journal of the Warburg and Courtauld Institutes*, XXII (1959), 332–46.

13 I am indebted for this observation, and some of the examples that follow it, to A. Dwight Culler, *The Poetry of Tennyson* (New Haven: Yale Univ. Press, 1977), pp. 21–22.

14 Lindsay, *Turner: His Life and Work*, p. 98.

15 In the spring of 1799 William Beckford bought two Claudes, *The Sacrifice to Apollo* and *The Landing of Aeneas*, installing them in his house in Grosvenor Square, where Turner viewed them on more than one occasion, remarking to Farington, as recorded in the latter's diary, on 8 May, that *The Sacrifice* left him "both pleased & unhappy" because "it seemed to be beyond the power of imitation." See Joseph Farington, *The Farington Diary*, ed. James Greig, 8 vols. (London: Hutchinson & Co., 3rd ed., 1923–28), I, 270.

16 Gage, *Colour in Turner: Poetry and Truth* (New York: Praeger, 1969), p. 139.

17 John Ruskin, "Notes on the Turner Gallery at Marlborough House," *Pre-Raphaelitism Lectures on Architecture and Painting: etc., by John Ruskin*, ed. Laurence Binyon (London: J. M. Dent, 1906), p. 373.

18 Lindsay, *Turner*, pp. 144–45. I have quoted from *The Pleasures of Imagination* (London: R. Dodsley, 1754).

19 *Ibid.*, p. 145, see also pp. 253–54. The quotation inside the parentheses is from p. 132. Those interested in the influence of James Thomson's *The Seasons* on Turner's treatment of landscape should consult Lindsay's comprehensive biography. I have cited the final 1746 version of *The Seasons*, in *The Complete Poetical Works of James Thomson*, ed. J. Logie Robertson (London: Oxford Univ. Press, 1908). The fullest gathering of Turner's poetic sibylline leaves from his notebooks and sketchbooks, with the most complete discussion of his poetry, is Jack Lindsay's edition and essay in *The Sunset Ship: The Poems of J. M. W. Turner* (Lowestoft, Suffolk: Scorpion Press, 1966).

20 *Ibid.*, p. 144.

21 John Rothenstein and Martin Butlin, *Turner* (New York: George Braziller, 1964), p. 74.

22 William Hazlitt, "On Imitation," from *The Round Table*, in The Centenary Edition of *The Complete Works of William Hazlitt*, ed. P. P. Howe (London: J. M. Dent, 1930), IV, 76n.

23 Robert Melville, "Pictures of Nothing," *New Statesman*, LXVIII (27 November 1964), 847.

24 Lindsay, *Turner*, p. 203.

25 See Jerrold Ziff, "Turner and Poussin," *The Burlington Magazine*, CV (1963), 315–21; and his "'Backgrounds, Introduction of Architecture and Landscape': a Lecture by

J. M. W. Turner," *Journal of the Warburg and Courtauld Institute*, XXVI (1963), 144. Turner gave this lecture on perspective at the Royal Academy on 1 February 1811, although it had been written originally as early as the winter of 1809–10.

26 See Ziff, "Turner and Poussin," *The Burlington Magazine*, CV (1963), 316.

27 Finberg, *Life of Turner*, p. 25. For a summary of Turner's activities the preceding several years as a topographical and architectural artist, see Finberg, *ibid.*, pp. 18–26. For the catalogue raisonné of Turner's oils, see Butlin and Joll, *The Paintings of J. M. W. Turner*, 2 vols. Text and Plates.

28 See Robert Moore, "The Art of Piranesi: Looking Backward into the Future," *Changing Taste in Eighteenth-Century Art and Literature: Papers Read at a Clark Library Seminar April 17, 1971* (Los Angeles: William Andrews Clark Memorial Library, University of California, 1972), pp. 3–40.

29 John Ruskin, "The Two Boyhoods," *Modern Painters*, V, in *Works*, eds. Cook and Wedderburn, VII, 376–77.

30 See Lindsay, *Turner*, pp. 72–73, 89–97, 146, for the theory that Turner's preoccupation with the theme of betrayal of love under the compulsion to follow a higher duty, and with the theme of paradise won and lost, has to do with the tragic circumstances of his family situation; a beloved father and an abusive schizophrenic mother, which left Turner permanently suspicious of marital bonds and which led him to explore again and again in his paintings the subject of Aeneas and Dido and of Apollo and Sibyl.

31 Kroeber, "Experience as History: Shelley's Venice, Turner's Carthage," *ELH*, XLI (1974), 329n, cites a comparison of England to Carthage made by Thomas Love Peacock in a letter to E. T. Hookham of 28 November 1818, *The Works of Thomas Love Peacock*, eds. H. F. B. Brett-Smith and C. E. Jones (London: Constable & Co., 1924–34; rpt. New York: AMS Press, 1967), VIII, 162; and Lynn R. Matteson, "The Poetics and Politics of Alpine Passage: Turner's *Snowstorm: Hannibal and His Army Crossing the Alps*," *The Art Bulletin*, LXII (1980), 393–96, explores the allusions to France and Napoleon and to early English history in *Hannibal and His Army Crossing the Alps*, and notes in passing that "Benjamin Robert Haydon also was inclined to identify Rome with France and England with Carthage (*The Diaries of Benjamin Robert Haydon*, ed. W. B. Pope, Cambridge, Mass., 1963, I, 3)." That England might suffer the fate of past imperial city-states was a prefigurative fear shared by more than one Englishman during the nineteenth century, see Ruskin's similar comparison of Victorian England to ancient Tyre and Renaissance Venice, in *The Stones of Venice*, I, in *Works*, eds. Cook and Wedderburn, IX, 17–18.

32 But see Ronald Paulson, "Turner's Graffiti: The Sun and Its Glosses," *Images of Romanticism: Verbal and Visual Affinities*, eds. Karl Kroeber and William Walling (New Haven: Yale Univ. Press, 1978), pp. 167–88, who follows John Gage's thesis in *Turner: Rain, Steam and Speed* (1972) and in *Colour in Turner* (1969) to argue that out of pure form – painting as pigment on canvas, as color and texture – Turner is trying in his use of the sun, among other things, "to reconstitute the iconography of history painting in the genre of landscape" (p. 167).

33 See Robert R. Wark, *Ten British Pictures 1740–1840* (San Marino: Huntington Library, 1971), pp. 124–26.

34 Rothenstein and Butlin, *Turner*, p. 52; Moore, "The Art of Piranesi," *Changing Taste in Eighteenth-Century Art and Literature*, p. 20.

35 The lines, based on some from Thomas Gray's "The Bard," are reprinted in Finberg, *Life of Turner*, p. 507; in Lindsay, *The Sunset Ship*, p. 87; and in Butlin and Joll, *The Paintings of J. M. W. Turner*, I, 227–28. See also Lawrence Gowing, *Turner: Imagination and Reality* (New York: Museum of Modern Art, distributed by Doubleday, 1966), p. 51, who cites Ruskin with approval in thinking that "Turner's deepest subject was

death," with the sea the "'dreadful and tumultuous home of Death!'" (the latter being an apostrophe Turner leveled at the power of the ocean).

36 Butlin and Joll, *The Paintings of J. M. W. Turner*, I, 230–31, point out that Ruskin noted the "partly imaginary" elements in the architectural details and landscape, "there being no church of San Benedetto visible in this view looking west along the Canal della Giudecca towards Fusina . . . and yet, without one single accurate detail, the picture is the likest thing to what it is meant for – the looking out of the Giudecca landwards, at sunset – of all that I have ever seen."

37 For a contrary emphasis on the solidity of the Turnerian reflection, its "transcendent radiance" as real and more glorious than the object it mirrors, see James A. W. Heffernan, "Reflections on Reflections in English Romantic Poetry and Painting," *Bucknell Review*, XXIV (1978), 15–37. We agree on the ultimate idealism of the Turnerian vision but disagree about its "optimism."

11. Tennyson's Celestial Camelot

1 "St. Paul's" ([1808]; 9, 26, 25), *The Poetical Works of William Wordsworth*, eds. Ernest De Selincourt and Helen Darbishire, 5 vols. (Oxford: Oxford Univ. Press, 1940–49), IV, 374–75.

2 Max Byrd, *London Transformed: Images of the City in the Eighteenth Century* (New Haven: Yale Univ. Press, 1978), pp. 175–77.

3 Clyde de L. Ryals, *From the Great Deep: Essays on "Idylls of the King"* (Athens: Ohio Univ. Press, 1967), adumbrates the dilemma thus: "the tower [that is, the isolated artist's vision] and the city [the public perspective] remain in opposition to each other"; in a radical way, the artist cannot through his art bind others to his will, and contrariwise, any expression of truth of his "is compromised by the perception of others" (p. 53). Unless otherwise noted, all citations are to *The Poems of Tennyson*, ed. Christopher Ricks (London: Longmans, Green and Co. Ltd., 1969).

4 For a discussion of these iconographical conventions in reference to the *hortus conclusus*, see Stanley Stewart, *The Enclosed Garden: The Tradition and the Image in Seventeenth-Century Poetry* (Madison: Univ. of Wisconsin Press, 1966), pp. 45–59.

5 Ryals, *From the Great Deep*, p. 102. The quotation from Schopenhauer, cited by Ryals on pp. 99–100, is taken from William Wallace, *Life of Schopenhauer* (London, n.d.), p. 97. Henry Kozicki, *Tennyson and Clio: History in the Major Poems* (Baltimore: The Johns Hopkins Press, 1979), pp. 13–31, presents evidence that the early Tennyson accepted the "influential ideas of Vico" (21) about the periodicity of history. According to that cyclical explanation of human events cultural growth and decline represents the collective action of a society effected by the heroic service of individuals and symbolizing the divine spirit of mankind. This possibility bears on Tennyson's fascination with the *agon* of King Arthur and of Camelot. In the early 1830s Tennyson still believed that history could be affected positively by such individuals. With the 1850s and 60s, as Kozicki demonstrates, Tennyson came to see only progressive anarchy in the social organism, concomitant with loss of the ascetic will to create and maintain the ideal.

5a Although he has other psycho-analytical and deconstructive axes to grind, Ronald Paulson, *Literary Landscape: Turner and Constable* (New Haven: Yale Univ. Press, 1982), explores the implications of the sun vortexes of Turner in ways that underscore my remarks here. Worth noting, since Paulson implies otherwise, is that the Turnerian vortex is not consistently lucid or single-mindedly referential. As befits his living well into the Victorian years, it appears ordinarily in scenes of implied, or actual, cataclysmic change in nature or violence among humans. In many views of cities, rivers, and hills (see, for example, *Richmond Hill*, 1819; *The Bay of Baiae*, 1823; and *View of Orvieto*, 1828, 1837, all Tate Gallery) light is diffused evenly throughout the picture without show of the sun's vortex.

6 Jerome H. Buckley, *The Triumph of Time: A Study of the Victorian Concepts of Time, History, Progress, and Decadence* (Cambridge, Mass.: Harvard Univ. Press, 1966), p. 74. Among the "forces of decadence that undermine the city-state," Buckley lists "the failure of idealism, the substitution of self-interest for civic virtue, the decay of manners, the surrender of reason to sensuality," the questioning of the authority of the King, the bad example of the Queen, and the lust after unearned spiritual satisfaction. Buckley argues, however, that "Though the settings of the separate Idylls reflect the cycle of the seasons, the implication of the poem as a whole is not that decadence must supplant cultural vigor as inevitably as autumn and winter follow summer. The fate of Camelot is not predestined; it depends on the will of the citizenry, the free decision to respond or not to the changing challenge of the time." The epilogue to the poem, he adds, makes this moral explicit in its application to Victorian England (p. 75).

7 So argues Geoffrey Yarlott, *Coleridge and the Abyssinian Maid* (London: Methuen, 1967), p. 151.

8 E. S. Shaffer, *"Kubla Khan" and The Fall of Jerusalem: The Mythological School in Biblical Criticism and Secular Literature 1770–1880* (Cambridge: Cambridge Univ. Press, 1975), pp. 108–09.

9 See A. Dwight Culler, *The Poetry of Tennyson* (New Haven: Yale Univ. Press, 1977), pp. 72–74.

10 "Morte d'Arthur" (1833–34), published 1842, is an exception.

11 John D. Rosenberg, *The Fall of Camelot; a Study of Tennyson's "Idylls of the King"* (Cambridge, Mass.: Harvard Univ. Press, 1973), p. 14; for development of this idea, see pp. 14–16. Cf. Ryals, *From the Great Deep: Essays on "Idylls of the King"*: "With its lesson that the world is irredeemable, the *Idylls of the King* seems to reflect much of the pessimism of nineteenth-century philosophy" (p. 94).

12 All citations are to *A Variorum Edition of Tennyson's "Idylls of the King,"* ed. John Pfordresher (New York: Columbia Univ. Press, 1973).

13 Rosenberg, *The Fall of Camelot*, pp. 24–25.

14 *Ibid.*, p. 49.

15 Printed by Hallam Tennyson in *Alfred, Lord Tennyson: A Memoir by His Son*, 2 vols. (1897). I have used the one-volume edition issued by Macmillan in 1905 (II, 122).

16 *Ibid.*, II, 122–23.

17 Rosenberg, *The Fall of Camelot*, p. 112.

18 Pfordresher, *Variorum Edition of Idylls*, p. 127.

19 The citations in this paragraph, so far, are to Hallam Tennyson's *Memoir*, II, 129–30.

20 Culler, *The Poetry of Tennyson*, p. 221.

21 *Ibid.*, p. 79.

12. Mid-Victorian London and the Angel in the House

1 Cf. Humphry House, "Man and Nature: Some Artists' Views," in *All in Due Time* (London: Hart-Davis, 1955), p. 141.

2 Raymond Williams, *The Country and the City* (New York: Oxford Univ. Press, 1973), p. 146. Williams distinguishes sharply between the city of London and the industrial cities of the North (see pp. 146–47) – those rookeries of boredom, like Coketown, with "several large streets all very like one another, and many small streets still more like one another, inhabited by people equally like one another, who all went in and out at the same hours, with the same sound upon the same pavements, to do the same work, and

to whom every day was the same as yesterday and tomorrow, and every year the counterpart of the last and the next" (Dickens, *Hard Times* [1854], I, 5). Still, in any consideration of the city as paradise, the kind of city is less important than the generic concept. The industrial cities of the North owed their existence usually to a single industry, while London "could not easily be described in a rhetorical gesture of repressive uniformity" (p. 153). Throughout I am quoting from the New Oxford Illustrated Dickens.

3 Friedrich Engels, "The Great Towns" (ch. 3), *The Condition of the Working Class in England*, eds. W. O. Henderson and W. H. Chaloner (Oxford: Blackwell, 1958), p. 58. For an analysis of the excremental and sexual strata in Engels's study, see Steven Marcus, *Engels, Manchester, and the Working Class* (New York: Random House, 1974). The passage from Engels is cited with variants by Marcus on pp. 183–84.

4 Cf., for example, the letter to John A. Carlyle of 17 June 1834, *The Collected Letters of Thomas and Jane Welsh Carlyle*, eds. Charles Richard Sanders, Kenneth J. Fielding, et. al., 9 vols. to date (Durham, N. C.: Duke Univ. Press, 1970–81), VII, 214. The Kingsley citations are to *Alton Locke*, 2 vols. (London: Chapman and Hall, 1850), I, 14–15.

5 "Modern Manufacture and Design" (a lecture delivered at Bradford, 1 March 1859), *The Two Paths* (1859), in *The Complete Works of John Ruskin*, eds. E. T. Cook and Alexander Wedderburn (London: George Allen, 1905), XVI, 339.

6 For much of the information in this paragraph I am indebted to Richard D. Altick, *Victorian People and Ideas* (New York: W. W. Norton, 1973), particularly pp. 43–45. Cf. also for descriptions of working conditions J. L. and Barbara Hammond, *The Town Laborer*, preface by Asa Briggs (Garden City, N. Y.: Anchor Books, 1968).

7 Paul Mantoux, *The Industrial Revolution in the Eighteenth Century*, preface by T. S. Ashton (New York: Harper and Row, 1961).

8 See especially Philippe Ariès, *Centuries of Childhood: A Social History of Family Life*, trans. Robert Baldick (New York: Alfred A. Knopf, 1962), pp. 356–64 (III, i).

9 Charles Dickens, "What Christmas Is As We Grow Older" (1851), *Christmas Stories*, intro. by Margaret Lane (London: New Oxford Illustrated, 1956), p. 25.

10 Alexander Welsh, *The City of Dickens* (Oxford: At the Clarendon Press, 1971), p. 150. To show that there was another seamier side to the feminine question, Martha Vicinus has compiled two collections of essays presenting views of the conditions and assumptions governing the lives of women in nineteenth-century England contrary to the mythology that "The Perfect Victorian Lady" was the happy stereotype of an angel: *Suffer and Be Still: Women in the Victorian Age* (Bloomington: Indiana Univ. Press, 1973) and *A Widening Sphere: Changing Roles of Victorian Women* (Bloomington: Indiana Univ. Press, 1977).

11 John Ruskin, "Ad Valorem" (ch. 4), *Unto This Last* (1860), *Complete Works*, eds. Cook and Wedderburn, XVII, 85.

12 Welsh, *The City of Dickens*, pp. 150 and 177, but also *passim*, especially pp. 141–228.

13 Besides Welsh, *The City of Dickens*, particularly the final section on "The Bride from Heaven," where the assumption everywhere influences his thematic exploration of how the theme of death affects the structure of the Victorian novel, see Walter Houghton, *The Victorian Frame of Mind* (New Haven: Yale Univ. Press, 1957), pp. 389–93; and Humphry House, "The Mood of Doubt," *All in Due Time* (London: Hart-Davis, 1955), pp. 94–100.

14 Charles Dickens, *Christmas Books*, intro. Eleanor Farjean (London: Oxford Univ. Press, 1954), p. 161. The Clough quotation comes from *The Poems of Arthur Hugh Clough*, ed. F. L. Mulhauser (Oxford: At the Clarendon Press, 2nd ed., 1974), p. 184.
    For convenient recent studies of the early nineteenth-century vogue for hearth and cottage, cf. George H. Ford, "Felicitous Space: The Cottage Controversy," pp. 29–48; and Robert L. Patten, "'A Surprising Transformation': Dickens and the Hearth,"

pp. 153–70; in *Nature and the Victorian Imagination*, eds. U. C. Knoepflmacher and G. B. Tennyson (Berkeley: Univ. of California Press, 1977).

15 Quoted by Susan Chitty, *The Beast and the Monk: A Life of Charles Kingsley* (London: Hodder and Stoughton, 1974), p. 58, from a collection of unpublished letters to Fanny Kingsley, letter no. 3, November 1840.

16 Reprinted in Lionel Trilling, *The Opposing Self* (New York: Viking Press, 1955), p. 65.

17 "The Country Ball," Prelude i, *Angel in the House*, II, III, *The Poems of Coventry Patmore*, ed. Frederick Page (London: Oxford Univ. Press, 1949). In addition to those cited below, books essential to understanding Patmore include Basil Champneys's *Memoirs and Correspondence of Coventry Patmore*, 2 vols. (London: George Bell & Sons, 1900); Osbert Burdett, *The Idea of Coventry Patmore* (London: Oxford Univ. Press, 1921); Frederick Page, *Patmore: A Study in Poetry* (London: Oxford Univ. Press, 1933); and J. C. Reid, *The Mind and Art of Coventry Patmore* (London: Routledge & Kegan Paul, 1957).

18 Edmund Gosse, *Coventry Patmore* (New York: Charles Scribner's Sons, 1905), p. 85.

19 *Ibid.*, p. 185.

20 John Killham, *Tennyson and "The Princess": Reflections of an Age* (London: Athlone Press, 1958), especially pp. 86–141, presents a fine review of the feminist controversy in England prior to *The Princess*.

21 Patmore, "Thoughts on Knowledge, Opinion and Inequality," *Fortnightly Review* (August 1887), XLVIII, 259–66.

22 Patmore, "The Social Position of Woman," *North British Review*, XIV (February 1851), 527–28.

23 *Ibid.*, p. 526. For Patmore's seeming desire to "keep woman in her place," and the discussion it has entailed, see Virginia Crawford, "Coventry Patmore," *The Fortnightly Review*, LXXV (February 1901), 304–11; Reid, *The Mind and Art of Coventry Patmore*, pp. 130–47; and Burdett, *The Idea of Coventry Patmore, passim*; who defend throughout and at great length Patmore's conception of woman; and Carol Christ, "Victorian Masculinity and the Angel in the House," in *A Widening Sphere: Changing Roles of Victorian Women*, ed. Martha Vicinus (Bloomington: Indiana Univ. Press, 1979), pp. 146–62.

24 A. Dwight Culler, *The Poetry of Tennyson* (New Haven: Yale Univ. Press, 1977), p. 142.

25 Reid, *The Mind and Art of Coventry Patmore*, p. 41.

26 *Mary Howitt: An Autobiography*, ed. Margaret Howitt, 2 vols. (Boston: Houghton, Mifflin & Co., 1889), I, 149.

27 Derek Patmore, *The Life and Times of Coventry Patmore* (London: Constable and Co., 1949), p. 85. For a discussion of the symbolism of the Angel see also Page, *Patmore: A Study in Poetry*, pp. 100–101.

28 Reid, *The Mind and Art of Coventry Patmore*, p. 146.

29 Quoted by Page, *Patmore: A Study in Poetry*, p. 133.

30 One of the unpublished aphorisms of Patmore printed as "Aphorisms and Extracts" by Champneys, *Memoirs and Correspondence of Coventry Patmore*, II, 66. Cf. also Page, *Patmore: A Study in Poetry*, pp. 129–46, who reviews Patmore's intentions in "The Marriage of the Blessed Virgin."

31 Patmore, "Dieu et Ma Dame," *Religio Poetae* (London: George Bell and Sons, 1893), p. 213.

32 Patmore, *The Rod, the Root, and the Flower*, ed. Derek Patmore (London: The Grey Walls Press, 1950), p. 69.

13. Pre-Raphaelite Tainted Gardens, Lost Ladies, and Intruders on the Green

1 John Ruskin in a letter of 20 July 1858 to Mrs. John Simon. See John Lewis Bradley, "An Unpublished Ruskin Letter," *The Burlington Magazine*, C (1958), 25–26.

That typological symbolism charged and deepened the pictures of the Pre-Raphaelites has been defended and analyzed in several recent studies: Herbert Sussman's *Fact into Figure: Typology in Carlyle, Ruskin, and the Pre-Raphaelite Brotherhood* (Columbus: Ohio State Univ. Press, 1979); and George P. Landow's two books *William Holman Hunt and Typological Symbolism* (New Haven: Yale Univ. Press for the Paul Mellon Centre for Studies in British Art, 1979) and *Victorian Types, Victorian Shadows: Biblical Typology in Victorian Literature, Art, and Thought* (Boston: Routledge & Kegan Paul, 1980).

2 Rosemary Treble, Catalogue of the 1978 show at the Royal Academy of Arts of *Great Victorian Pictures* (London: Arts Council of Great Britain, 1978), p. 33.

3 John Nicoll, *Dante Gabriel Rossetti* (New York: Macmillan, 1975), pp. 143–44. James Sambrook has conveniently gathered key statements from 1850 to 1975 in *Pre-Ralphaelitism: A Collection of Critical Essays* (Chicago: Univ. of Chicago Press, 1974).

4 Timothy Hilton, *The Pre-Raphaelites* (New York: Praeger, 1974), p. 113,

5 *Punch* (January–June 1851), p. 219. The discussion that follows is indebted to Martin Meizel's article " 'Half Sick of Shadows': The Aesthetic Dialogue in PreRaphaelite Painting," *Nature and the Victorian Imagination*, eds. U. C. Knoepflmacher and G. B. Tennyson (Los Angeles: Univ. of California, 1977), pp. 309–40.

6 *Ibid.*, p. 329.

7 *Ibid.*, p. 328.

8 George P. Landow, "The Rainbow: A Problematic Image," *Nature and the Victorian Imagination*, eds. Knoepflmacher and Tennyson, pp. 341–69; rpt. Landow, *Images of Crisis: Literary Iconology, 1750 to the Present* (London: Routledge & Kegan Paul, 1982).

9 For the most recent attempt to consider *Frankenstein* in the light cast on it by Milton's version of how paradise was lost – specifically as "a fictionalized rendition of the meaning of *Paradise Lost* to women" – which also unintentionally underscores the gloomy prognosis the Romantics and their Victorian heirs granted humankind's chances for paradise regained, see Sandra M. Gilbert and Susan Gubar, *The Madwoman in the Attic: The Woman Writer and the Nineteenth-Century Literary Imagination* (New Haven: Yale Univ. Press, 1979), pp. 221–47.

10 Cf. Andrew Griffin, "The Interior Garden and John Stuart Mill," *Nature and the Victorian Imagination*, pp. 171–86.

11 Cf. E. D. H. Johnson, "The Lily and the Rose: Symbolic Meaning in Tennyson's *Maud*," *PMLA*, LXIV (1949), 1222–27.

12 See Lionel Stevenson, "The 'High-Born Maiden' Symbol in Tennyson," *Critical Essays on the Poetry of Tennyson*, ed. John Killham (London: Routledge & Kegan Paul, 1960), pp. 126–36.

13 Cf. Pauline Fletcher, "Romantic and Anti-Romantic Gardens in Tennyson and Swinburne," *SIR*, XVIII (1979), 81–97, who has much in passing to say about the paradisal reverberations of meaning embedded in Tennyson's deployment of the garden, but whose main argument, following Raymond Williams, has to do with an allied symbolic pattern of social–antisocial references. Her final conclusion is that "neither poet sees the garden as a very comfortable or safe place" (p. 97); rpt. *Gardens and Grim Ravines: The Language of Landscape in Victorian Poetry* (Princeton: Princeton Univ. Press, 1983), in which Fletcher extends her study of the private–public ramifications of man's relationship to nature as a political act to include Arnold, Browning, Rossetti, Morris, and Hardy.

14 Griffin, "The Interior Garden and John Stuart Mill," *Nature and the Victorian*

Imagination, p. 175. These are Griffin's words, although the context of his remarks involves a discussion of Arnold's anxieties over the "buried life" of his affections, "past thirty, and three parts iced over" (*The Letters of Matthew Arnold to Arthur Hugh Clough*, ed. Howard Foster Lowry [London: Oxford Univ. Press, 1932], p. 128). Here and elsewhere I have quoted from *The Poems of Matthew Arnold*, eds. Kenneth and Miriam Allott (London: Longmans, 2nd ed., 1979).

15   A. H. Palmer, *The Life and Letters of Samuel Palmer* (London: Seeley & Co. 1892), reissued with an essay by Raymond Lister (London: Eric and Joan Stevens, 1972), p. 87.

16   See *The Poems of George Meredith*, ed. Phyllis B. Bartlett, 2 vols. (New Haven: Yale Univ. Press, 1978), which prints both versions. Many critics have dealt with the ambivalence in the poem. Two who address the specific problem of the mutable vs. the eternal are John Von B. Rodenbeck, "The Classicism of Meredith's 'Love in the Valley,'" *Victorian Poetry*, 11 (1973), 27–37; and Barbara Fass Leavy, "The Romanticism of Meredith's 'Love in the Valley,'" *SIR*, XVIII (1979), 99–114.

17   Leavy, *SIR*, XVIII (1979), 103. The quotations about "Apple-Disease" come from the original version of *The Ordeal of Richard Feveril*. Meredith in later editions condensed the first four chapters into one and in the process deleted these sentiments. A handy compilation of Meredith's revisions is given in *Bibliography and Various Readings: George Meredith* (New York: Haskell House Publishers, 1973). Cf. *The Works of George Meredith*, Memorial Edition, 27 vols. (London: Constable & Co., 1909–11).

18   Fletcher, "Romantic and Anti-Romantic Gardens in Tennyson and Swinburne," *SIR*, XVIII (1979), 96. I have quoted throughout from the Bonchurch Edition of *The Complete Works of Algernon Charles Swinburne*, eds. Sir Edmund Gosse and Thomas Wise, 20 vols. (London: William Heinemann, 1925–27).

19   Andrew Lang, quoted in Percy Bate, *The English Pre-Raphaelite Painters and Their Successors* (London: G. Bell, 1899), pp. 35–36.
     The four girls were all under thirteen. The two centered behind the pile of leaves were the sisters of Millais' wife; the other two were local girls of Perthshire, where Millais was living when he painted the scene (see Julian Treuherz, *Pre-Raphaelite Paintings from the Manchester City Art Gallery* (London: Lund Humphries, 1980), p. 49.

20   Hilton, *The Pre-Raphaelites*, p. 152. Cf. also Christopher Wood, *Victorian Panorama: Paintings of Victorian Life* (London: Faber, 1976), pp. 220–27.

21   *The Collected Works of William Morris*, ed. May Morris (London: Longmans, Green and Co., 1910–15), XVI, xxviii.

22   An excellent evaluation of Morris's attitude toward the machine is made by Herbert L. Sussman, *Victorians and the Machine: The Literary Response to Technology* (Cambridge: Harvard Univ. Press, 1968), pp. 104–34.

23   The paradisal references to England come from John Scott's poem "Amwell" (1761, 1776), *The Poetical Works of John Scott Esq.* (London: J. Buckland, 1782), p. 74. The extremity of England's metamorphosis from Edenic to industrial landscape is portrayed by novelists from the 1840s onward: cf. Dickens's *The Old Curiosity Shop* (chs. 43–45) and *Hard Times* (I, 5, 11; II, I); Mrs. Gaskell's *Mary Barton* (ch. 6); and Disraeli's *Coningsby* (IV, 2). That this view is as much a state of mind as a valid description of reality, since much of pastoral England still existed as Herbert L. Sussman demonstrates in *Victorians and the Machine*, see especially his chapter on Dickens, pp. 41–75.

24   *The Life of Frederick Denison Maurice Chiefly Told in His Own Letters*, ed. Frederick Maurice (London: Macmillan, 1884), II, 59.

14. Rossetti's Blessed Eve and Her Daughters

1 Final lines of the sonnet Rossetti wrote to accompany the painting. For "a critical reference guide to the whole subject of Pre-Raphaelitism" (p. vii), including Rossetti's poems and paintings, see William E. Fredeman, *Pre-Raphaelitism: A Biblio-critical Study* (Cambridge, Mass.: Harvard Univ. Press, 1965); and for a catalogue raisonné of Rossetti's art, see Virginia Surtees, *The Paintings and Drawings of Dante Gabriel Rossetti (1828–1882)*, 2 vols., Text and Plates (Oxford: At the Clarendon Press, 1971). In dating and provenance of the pictures, as well as in quotations from poems associated with the paintings, I have followed Surtees, although in the latter regard I have also collated the verse, where appropriate, with *The House of Life: A Sonnet-Sequence*, ed. Paul Franklin Baum (Cambridge: Harvard Univ. Press, 1928) and with Baum's edition of Rossetti's *Poems, Ballads and Sonnets* (New York: Doubleday, Doran & Co., 1937), which follows the 1881 publication by Rossetti of *Poems* and *Ballads and Sonnets*.

2 Timothy Hilton, *The Pre-Raphaelites* (New York: Praeger Publishers, 1974), p. 181. Jerome J. McGann, "Rossetti's Significant Details," *Victorian Poetry*, VII (1969), 41–54, argues for Rossetti's lovers rejecting the distinction between soul and body in favor of "divinized human love: sensational in effect and sublime in value" (p. 53), as they seek to be "one" spiritually "in the sense that they are one on earth" (p. 50). Contrariwise, Wendell Stacy Johnson, "D. G. Rossetti as Painter and Poet," *Victorian Poetry*, III (1965), 9–18, contends that Rossetti longs "for some supernatural reality which the poet and painter can represent by his visions of unearthly maidens. His inability to merge form and reality completely, to merge the heavenly ideal with the earthly flesh, can be both a cause of incoherence in his poetry and – in certain poetic moments, as in some early pictures – a source of tension that is formally controlled" (p. 11n). The most exhaustive study of Rossetti's vacillating treatment of earthly human love as the route to salvation and heavenly bliss is David Sonstroem's *Rossetti and the Fair Lady* (Middletown, Conn.: Wesleyan Univ. Press, 1970). Sonstroem distinguishes among Rossetti's fantasies of fair ladies: (1) the Blessed Damozel, or Heavenly Madonna, (2) the *femme fatale*, (3) the fallen fair lady, or sinful woman, and (4) the fair lady victimized by a man.

3 The phrase is John Dixon Hunt's in "A Moment's Monument: Reflections on Pre-Raphaelite Vision in Poetry and Painting," *Pre-Raphaelitism: A Collection of Critical Essays*, ed. James Sambrook (Chicago: Univ. of Chicago Press, 1974), pp. 243–64.

4 Algernon Swinburne, *Essays and Studies* (London: Chatto and Windus, 1875).

5 Sonstroem, *Rossetti and the Fair Lady*, p. 4, summarizes Rossetti's changing view of the Fair Lady thus: "the Madonna predominates at first; in 1853 and for a while thereafter, the sinful woman; about 1860, the victimized woman; in the mid-1860's, the femme fatale; and later, something of a combination of Madonna and femme fatale."

6 Rossetti to John Mitchell in a letter of 27 September 1866, *Letters of Dante Gabriel Rossetti*, eds. Oswald Doughty and John Robert Wahl (Oxford: At the Clarendon Press, 1965), II, 606.

7 Some of the Dante pictures, e.g., *The Salutation of Beatrice* (1859), celebrate the contrary vision of Dante's "sight of the higher love which will lead him to Paradise" (George P. Landow, "'Life touching lips with immortality': Rossetti's Typological Structures," *Studies in Romanticism*, XVII [1978], 253); but as part of the corpus of Rossetti's treatment of this subject, it carries implicitly the poignant recognition that the loss of Beatrice is the price Dante paid for her aid in gazing on Heaven.

8 William M. Rossetti, *Dante Gabriel Rossetti as Designer and Writer* (London: Cassell and Co., 1889), p. 80; Surtees, *Paintings and Drawings of Dante Gabriel Rossetti*, I, 131n.

9 Hilton, *The Pre-Raphaelites*, p. 201. The duality of the Burne-Jones women – simultaneously "saving angel" and "bewitching enchantress" – aside from reflecting

the general tendency in the second half of the nineteenth century to portray women ambiguously as nourishing and destructive, virginal and seductive, has its source according to Joseph Kestner, "Edward Burne-Jones and Nineteenth-Century Fear of Women," *Biography*, VII (1984), 95–122, in Burne-Jones's sexual fears, leading him to sublimate their sexual allure in androgynous figures.

10 Frederick Denison Maurice, *The Kingdom of Christ or Hints to a Quaker Respecting the Principles, Constitution, and Ordinances of the Catholic Church*, ed. Alec R. Vidler (London: SCM Press, 1958), II, 338. For a recent study of Victorian women as the age enshrined them on "the three panels of the mythical triptych of the woman" (p. xix): wife-mother, debased single working woman, and impure damned woman, see Françoise Basch, *Relative Creatures: Victorian Women in Society and the Novel* (New York: Schocken Books, 1974).

11 For a review of the differing interpretations advanced for *Take Your Son, Sir!* see the catalogue of the exhibition of *The Pre-Raphaelites* (London: Tate Gallery/Penguin Books, 1984), pp. 149–51.

12 John Dixon Hunt, *The Pre-Raphaelite Imagination, 1848–1900* (London: Routledge & Kegan Paul, 1968).

13 *Ibid.*, pp. 78, 80. See also Patrick Bade, *Femme Fatale: Images of Evil and Fascinating Women* (New York: Mayflower Books, 1979).

14 Algernon Swinburne, *Notes on Poems and Reviews* (1866), in *The Complete Works of Algernon Charles Swinburne*, eds. Sir Edmund Gosse, C. B. and Thomas James Wise (London: William Heinemann, 1926), VI, 361.

15 *Henry James Letters*, ed. Leon Edel, 4 vols. (Cambridge: Harvard Univ. Press, 1974–84), I, 93.

16 Adeline R. Tintner, "Henry James's *Salomé* and the Arts of the *Fin de Siècle*," *The Markham Review*, V (1975), 5–10.

17 Hunt, *The Pre-Raphaelite Imagination*, p. 196.

18 *The Complete Illustrated Works of Lewis Carroll*, ed. Edward Guiliano (New York: Avenel Books, Crown Publishers, Inc., 1982), pp. 293–95. Cf. Jeffrey Stern, "Lewis Carroll the Pre-Raphaelite: 'Fainting in Coils,'" *Lewis Carroll Observed*, ed. Edward Guiliano (New York: Clarkson N. Potter, Inc., 1976), pp. 161–80, who argues that because Carroll shared Arthur Hughes's "melancholic bittersweetness," and Rossetti's obsession with the female figure as an *anima* image, he "was a Pre-Raphaelite" (p. 179).

19 Max Beerbohm, *The Works of Max Beerbohm* (1895), quoted by Stanley Weintraub, *Aubrey Beardsley: Imp of the Perverse* (University Park, Penna., 1976), p. xiii.

20 D. J. Gordon, "Aubrey Beardsley at the V. & A.," *Encounter*, XXVII (October 1966), 13. For provenance and reproductions of Beardsley drawings, see *The Collected Drawings of Aubrey Beardsley*, ed. Bruce S. Harris (New York: Crown Publishers, Inc., 1967); *The Early Work of Aubrey Beardsley*, text by H. C. Marillier (London: John Lane, The Bodley Head, Ltd., 1899, rev. 2nd ed., 1911, rpt. DaCapo Press, 1967); and *The Later Work of Aubrey Beardsley*, text by H. C. Marillier (London: John Lane, The Bodley Head, Ltd., 1900, rev. 2nd ed., 1911, rpt. DaCapo Press, 1967).

21 Sir Kenneth Clark, "The Genius of Aubrey Beardsley," *New York Review of Books*, 9 December 1976, p. 47.

22 *Ibid.*, p. 43.

23 *Ibid.*, p. 47.

24 Thus E. Nesbit in a satirical skit *A Pomander of Verse* (1895); quoted by Weintraub, *Aubrey Beardsley*, p. 113.

25 Roger Fry so prophesied that Beardsley would be known in time (Weintraub, *Aubrey Beardsley*, p. 261).

26 Clark, "The Genius of Aubrey Beardsley," p. 45.

27 Tintner, "Henry James's *Salomé* and the Arts of the *Fin de Siècle*," *The Markham*

Review, v (1975), 6; and Hugo Daffner, *Salome* (Munich: H. Schmidt, 1912). Tintner gives a succinct survey of the images of Salome in the last quarter of the nineteenth century.

28 Weintraub, *Aubrey Beardsley*, p. 265.

29 *Poems and Some Letters of James Thomson*, ed. Anne Riddler (Carbondale: Southern Illinois Univ. Press, 1963).

30 Clark, "The Genius of Aubrey Beardsley," p. 42.

15. Whistler's Peacock Room: a Curvilinear *Locus Spiritus* for the Times

1 *The Whistler Peacock Room* (Washington, D.C.: Freer Gallery of Art, 1972), pp. 9–10.

2 In addition to the indispensable, but ultimately irritating, tributes to Whistler by his "Boswellian" fellow Americans Joseph and Elizabeth Robbins Pennell, *The Life of James McNeill Whistler*, 2 vols. (Philadelphia: J. B. Lippincott, 1908; 6th rev. ed. in one vol., 1919); and *The Whistler Journal* (Philadelphia: J. B. Lippincott, 1921); still useful older studies include James Laver, *Whistler* (New York: Cosmopolitan Book Corp., 1930); Arthur Jerome Eddy, *Recollections and Impressions of James A. McNeill Whistler* (Philadelphia: J. B. Lippincott, 1904); and, more recently, Denys Sutton, *Nocturne: The Art of James McNeill Whistler* (London: Country Life Ltd., 1963); and Stanley Weintraub, *Whistler: A Biography* (New York: Weybright and Talley, 1974). There is a catalogue raisonné, by Andrew McLaren Young, Margaret MacDonald, Robin Spencer, with the assistance of Hamish Miles, of *The Paintings of James McNeill Whistler*, 2 vols., Text and Plates (New Haven: Yale Univ. Press, published for The Paul Mellon Centre for Studies in British Art, 1980).

3 Sutton, *Nocturne: The Art of James McNeill Whistler*, p. 140.

4 Testimony of the Ruskin vs. Whistler trial is recorded by the Pennells in *The Life of James McNeill Whistler*, I, 229–44 and by Whistler in *The Gentle Art of Making Enemies* (New York: John W. Lovell, 1890), pp. 1–19.

5 Laver, *Whistler*, pp. 140–41.

6 See John Summerson, *The Classical Language of Architecture* (Cambridge, Mass.: M.I.T. Press, 1966).

7 Horace Gregory, *The World of James McNeill Whistler* (New York: Thomas Nelson & Sons, 1959), p. 124.

8 Hesketh Pearson, *The Man Whistler* (London: Methuen and Co., 1952), p. 53.

9 "Ten O'Clock Lecture," *The Gentle Art of Making Enemies* (New York: John W. Lovell, 1890), pp. 135–59.

10 Whistler's remark about the Peacock Room comes from the Pennells, *Life of James McNeill Whistler*, I, 206; *The Whistler Journal*, p. 108; that about "Art and Joy", from his "Ten O'Clock Lecture," *The Gentle Art of Making Enemies*, p. 153.

11 Weintraub, *Whistler*, p. 179.

12 Havelock Ellis, *The New Spirit* (Boston: Houghton, Mifflin, 4th ed., 1926), p. 24.

Afterthoughts

1 Martin J. Wiener, *English Culture and the Decline of the Industrial Spirit, 1850–1980* (Cambridge: Cambridge Univ. Press, 1981).

Index

362